Environmental Politics

Environmental Politics

Domestic and Global Dimensions

FIFTH EDITION

JACQUELINE VAUGHN
Northern Arizona University

THOMSON

WADSWORTH

Australia • Brazil • Canada • Mexico • Singapore • Spain
United Kingdom • United States

Environmental Politics:
Domestic and Global Dimensions, **Fifth Edition**
Jacqueline Vaughn

Executive Editor: David Tatom
Assistant Editor: Anne Gittinger
Editorial Assistant: Eva Dickerson
Technology Project Manager: Michelle Vardeman
Marketing Manager: Janise Fry
Marketing Assistant: Theresa Jessen
Marketing Communications Manager:
  Nathaniel Bergson-Michelson
Project Manager, Editorial Production:
  Kimberly Adams
Creative Director: Rob Hugel
Executive Art Director: Maria Epes

Print Buyer: Barbara Britton
Permissions Editor: Bob Kauser
Production Service: International Typesetting
  and Composition
Copy Editor: Chris Thillen
Cover Designer: Sue Hart
Cover Image: Greg Vaughn/Getty Images
Cover Printer: Phoenix Color Corp
Compositor: International Typesetting
  and Composition
Printer: Courier Corporation/Westford

Thomson Higher Education
10 Davis Drive
Belmont, CA 94002-3098
USA

For more information about our products, contact us at:
Thomson Learning Academic Resource Center
1-800-423-0563
For permission to use material from this text or product, submit a request online at
http://www.thomsonrights.com.
Any additional questions about permissions can be submittted by e-mail to
thomsonrights@thomson.com

Printed in the United States of America
1 2 3 4 5 6 7 09 08 07 06

Library of Congress Control Number: 2005933699

ISBN 0-495-00799-4

For Riva and Bob Frederick

Contents

List of Tables

List of Figures

Preface

Each edition of *Environmental Politics* represents my own personal journey of environmental awareness, and this fifth edition is no exception. In 2004, I had the opportunity to travel widely as part of my sabbatical research, and the threads of what I found and experienced have been interwoven into this book.

A visit to Costa Rica exposed me to some of the environmental issues facing Central America, including the pressures and economic benefits of ecotourism. On a road trip through the Rocky Mountain West, my first views of the Tetons were marred by the sounds of private jets landing at the Jackson Hole, Wyoming, airport. On that same trip, the conservation philanthropy of John D. and Laurance Rockefeller impressed me as I drove the parkway between two of America's most impressive national parks. In Yellowstone, the remnants of the massive wildfires of 1988 contrasted with the herds of bison grazing quietly on the meadowlands as tourists received warnings about how fast the animals can run. In Ireland, I watched volunteers attempt to remove nonnative, invasive rhododendrons—the same plants I saw being carefully tended in Portland's municipal green spaces when I attended a conference there. In Arkansas, I looked on in horror as a rural resident dumped rancid cooking oil off his dock into a lake where he would later attempt to fish for crappie.

In my own Arizona, I watched local groups clash over a local ordinance that would limit "big-box development," and coughed from smoke from prescribed burns that I knew were designed to reduce the fuel load in local forests to prevent wildfires in the future. I listened to the contentious debate over U.S. Forest Service proposals to expand a ski area considered a sacred site by 13 Native American tribes. Driving down to Phoenix, the litter along the interstate blew past new housing developments inching up the slopes of rocky outcrops.

Since the last edition was published in 2004, my perspectives on environmental politics have been colored by the presidential campaign and election. I kept waiting for President Bush or Senator Kerry to speak to the issues that are the subject of this book, but for the most part, I heard very little. The political rhetoric focused on Iraq and terrorism, the price of prescription drugs and the potential of stem cell research, the budget deficit, and each candidate's military record, and I knew that the environment was not on the public's agenda of hot-button issues.

Earth Day observances are smaller, the protests over international trade less violent, and national polls rank the environment near the bottom of the list of problems Americans report they are most concerned about. Still, I have an abiding optimism that people do care about the environmental health of the planet, whether politicians talk much about it or not. I see that concern in my students, for whom I write each edition of this book, and their belief that they can make a difference in finding ways to protect the Earth and its resources.

As in previous editions, the process model is used as a paradigm for exploring environmental politics and policy. I have found that in my classes, it is a useful model for understanding the interaction among institutions, such as the president and Congress, administrative agencies, courts, and state and local governments. The process model also provides a way to explain the role of nongovernmental organizations both in the United States and abroad as essential stakeholders, as well as the role of the media and public opinion in a world that is increasingly electronically connected. Ultimately, the process model allows us to understand how politics affects policy making and progress toward solving environmental problems. Thanks to the suggestions of reviewers and students, there is now a greater emphasis on relating the policy process to the outcomes of decision making.

Although the organization of the book remains basically unchanged, many sections have been completely updated to reflect upon the most recent political events worldwide. Perhaps the most notable example is the expanded coverage of the environmental policies of the administration of George W. Bush and the 2004 presidential campaign. Each of the "Another View, Another Voice" segments has been revised to provide a personal glimpse of an individual or organization that has made an impact on a particular policy issue. Many of these individuals are not well known to most readers. Others, like 2004 Nobel Peace Prize winner Wangari Maathai, are profiled because of recent achievements and honors. Discussions of international perspectives on issues are identified in new segments titled "Thinking Globally."

As before, the book does not attempt to provide in-depth coverage of every issue, but it does provide an overview that goes beyond the "headline news" approach. Sections at the end of each chapter that suggest books for further reading represent the newest books that have become available since 2003, so that readers will become aware of the resources that have become available since the fourth edition was published. Similarly, the appendices include an updated list of major U.S. environmental legislation and international environmental agreements, new video resources have been added, and the environmental politics timeline on the inside cover is also expanded.

To place environmental politics in context, the introduction provides an overview of the policy process using a cross-cultural perspective by comparing the first national parks in the United States and the Republic of Ireland. The historical context of Chapter 1 explores the philosophical and political beginnings of environmental concern, up through and including the second term of

President George W. Bush. Chapter 2 identifies the key stakeholders who influence policy, followed by an expanded analysis of the role of political institutions in Chapter 3. Chapters 4 through 11 are devoted to specific environmental problems, with the addition of issues that have arisen in the last three years. Although many of the problems associated with environmental protection are overlapping and interrelated, these chapters update the reader on the most critical issues and analyze the progress that has been made. New to Chapter 2 is coverage of the 20th anniversary of the American Green Movement and Native American environmental activism, and Chapter 4 now includes an explanation of the controversy over roadless areas and rock-climbing sites on public lands. Some issues that have reappeared on the political agenda, like the controversy over nuclear waste storage at Yucca Mountain in Nevada outlined in Chapter 5, are contrasted with coverage of enduring ones like air quality regulations in Chapter 8. Chapter 9 includes a discussion of wildlife issues, such as the battle to protect buffalo and wild horses in the West, and the World Wildlife Fund's "alarming state of the world" report. Updates in Chapter 10's coverage of the global commons include policy implementation since the Kyoto Protocol went into force, and the activities of the U.S. Ocean Commission. Population and sustainability issues, found in Chapter 12, are expanded to cover migration and urbanization.

Each edition's final chapter on emerging trends in environmental politics and policy builds upon new developments or ones that have been reframed in light of current controversies and events. Many of these issues have not yet been examined fully enough for book-length treatments, but they provide a glimpse of problems that may soon join the more familiar items on the environmental agenda, such as outdoor accessibility for people with disabilities and electronic waste. The environmental impacts of natural disasters, from the Kuwaiti oil fires to Hurricane Katrina, have developed into an expanding area of research and policymaking, also new to this edition.

A portion of the royalties from this book, as well as from the third and fourth editions, has been donated to the Jack and Ruby Vaughn Graduate Internship Scholarship Fund at Northern Arizona University, named in honor of my parents. The scholarship is awarded to a graduate student pursuing an internship in public service, and although the size of the award is small, the opportunities it can provide are endless. Your support, comments, and suggestions from the past four editions, along with this one, are greatly appreciated and integral to its success.

About the Author

Jacqueline Vaughn is Professor of Political Science at Northern Arizona University, where she specializes in public policy and administration. Professor Vaughn holds a Ph.D. in political science from the University of California, Berkeley, where she also attended the Graduate School of Public Policy. She taught previously at the University of Redlands and at Southern Oregon University. Professor Vaughn has a broad spectrum of nonacademic experience in both the public and private sectors. Her environmental background stems from her work with the South Coast Air Quality Management District in southern California, and with Southern California Edison, where she served as a policy analyst. Professor Vaughn's previously published books include *The Play of Power; Green Backlash: The History and Politics of Environmental Opposition in the United States Disabled Rights: American Disability Policy and the Fight for Equality; Environmental Activism: A Reference Handbook;* and *Healthy Forests: Reframing the Environmental Debate* (coauthored with Hanna Cortner).

Acknowledgments

The most helpful reviewers are those who use this book in their classes, whether faculty or students. I am always appreciative of their candid comments, both formal and informal. I like to think that with each edition of *Environmental Politics,* I am a little closer to providing an objective and timely resource. For the fifth edition, I am indebted to the scholars who provided manuscript reviews from previous editions to guide me in this revision, as well as the most current reviewers: I have benefited from the editorial assistance of Anne Gittinger and the support of David Tatom at Wadsworth Publishing. I tried hard not to exploit the talents of my graduate assistants at Northern Arizona University, Stephanie Barnett, who provided research assistance and moral support throughout the project and Courtney Kleinert, who helped me conquer the production process. Becky Schwartz, Taylor McKinnon, and the staff of the Grand Canyon Trust kindly assisted me in accessing several of the photographs on the facing pages and Tom Till graciously allowed me to use several of his photographs. Lastly, this edition marks the passing of a dear friend and political science colleague, Earl Shaw. He passed suddenly and left my world without his support for my writing and research, and without a presidential scholar with whom I could watch *The West Wing*.

Introduction

I want especially to have the young people to come to Muckross to trail
these mountains and to enjoy nature in all its aspects.
—ARTHUR VINCENT, DONOR, KILLARNEY NATIONAL PARK[1]

In December 1932, Arthur Rose Vincent and his wealthy American parents-in-law, Mr. and Mrs. William Bowers Bourn II, made a gift to the Republic of Ireland in memory of Vincent's late wife—the land now known as Killarney National Park. The gesture came 60 years after U.S. President Ulysses S. Grant signed a law on March 1, 1872, declaring that Yellowstone National Park would forever "be set apart as a public park or pleasuring ground for the benefit and enjoyment of the people." Ireland's Killarney and America's Yellowstone national parks have much in common. They are an expression of the desire to protect and preserve scenic areas for aesthetic, ecological, and recreational reasons. Both are considered the "jewels" of a developing system of government-managed landscapes that draw millions of visitors each year. But they developed along totally different policy pathways.

The prominent but not lesser known Bourn family of San Francisco had amassed a fortune on the backs of California Gold Rush miners as store owners, later investing in western mines and buying up utility companies and creating a water monopoly.[2] In 1910, William Bowers Bourn II rented an Irish fishing and hunting lodge, the Muckross House and Estate, owned by members of the Guinness family. Shortly thereafter, he purchased the property as a wedding present for his only child, Maud, who had married Arthur Rose Vincent, a judge in the British Colonial Service. Maud died in 1929, and Vincent and their two children continued to live at the 10,700-acre estate for three more years. The family had found that they were unable to pay for the upkeep of the breathtakingly beautiful grounds, although they had tried to operate it as a working farm open to the public.

The Old Faithful Inn in Yellowstone National Park was built by the Northern Pacific Railroad to bring East Coast tourists to the frontier West.

HANNA J. CORTNER

Some contend that Vincent admired the model of the American national park system and gave the land so the Irish government could start a system of its own; others believe he simply wanted to unload the costly management of a family treasure he had inherited. Under the 1932 Bourn Vincent Memorial Park Bill, the Irish Parliament (Dail Eireann) required the Commissioners of Public Works to "maintain and manage the Park as a National Park for the purpose of the recreation and enjoyment of the public."[3]

Yellowstone's treasures, in contrast, had been "discovered" when John Colter accidentally stumbled into the area that the native Minnetaree tribe called *Mi tsi a da zi,* which means "Rock Yellow River." Yellowstone was not even a part of the United States until Napoleon agreed to sell the land in 1803 as part of the Louisiana Purchase. Colter's stories of geysers, abundant game and wildlife, and strange accounts of the region were considered fabrications by some, and there were few major expeditions to the area until after the Civil War. The idea of making the land into a national preserve may partially be credited to Nathaniel Langford, a member of the 1870 Washburn Expedition whose work was financed by the Northern Pacific Railroad. The railroad's financiers had a government contract to build a line from St. Paul, Minnesota, to Puget Sound, and company officials urged Ferdinand Hayden, the official in charge of the U.S. Geological Survey of the Territories, to lead another extensive expedition and to lobby Congress for a national park. Congress was also influenced by the landscape artist Thomas Moran and photographer William Henry Jackson; the Senate bought Moran's huge canvas, *The Grand Canyon of the Yellowstone.* Not coincidentally, the Northern Pacific's railroad tracks would be built within 50 miles of the proposed park, and the company later built the Old Faithful Inn and other accommodations. Approximately 500 tourists visited Yellowstone during its first decade; several were taken hostage by members of the Nez Perce tribe who were running from the military.[4]

On December 18, 1871, Kansas Sen. Samuel Clarke Pomeroy and William Clagett, the congressional delegate from the Montana Territory, introduced proposals to make Yellowstone a national park. There was minimal debate; California's Sen. Cole said that legislation protecting the area was superfluous because the area had no industrial value whatsoever, with its only possible value being pleasure seeking. Sen. Walter Turnbull of Illinois responded that federal protection was necessary because "some person may go there and plant himself right across the only path that leads to the wonders, and charge every man that passes along between the gorges of these mountains a fee of a dollar or five dollars." The measures passed in the Senate on January 30, 1872, without a roll-call vote and in the House on February 27 on a vote of 115 to 65, with 65 not voting. President Ulysses S. Grant signed the bill making Yellowstone a National Park on March 1, 1872.[5]

Thus both Killarney and Yellowstone became national parks, protected by the government for the enjoyment of future generations; but these decisions did not happen in a vacuum. In each example, there were separate focusing events; different political processes, stakeholders, and policy entrepreneurs; and other forces that make up what we call public policy making.

To understand how and why events like these happen, it is first important to develop an overview of the policy-making process and the people who have a stake in policy outcomes. One way of doing so is through Anthony Downs's 1972 model, called the "issue-attention cycle." According to Downs, the public's interest in an issue, such as the preservation of natural resources, goes through a cycle of ebb and flow—a process that is continuous, but not always predictable. Initially, a condition must be recognized as a problem; subsequent steps to solve that problem make up the policy process.[6] Public policies are those developed by the arms of government, like the Department of Agriculture or the Nuclear Regulatory Commission. Downs's model helps explain why some issues find their way to the policy agenda and others do not.

John W. Kingdon presents a similar concept by starting with the question, "How does an idea's time come? What makes people in and around government attend, at any given time, to some subjects and not to others?"[7] He notes that little is known about the predecisional process when agendas change from one time to another, how a series of alternatives is narrowed down from a large set of choices to a very few, and how subjects drift onto the agenda and then drift off. "The patterns of public policy, after all, are determined not only by such final decisions as votes in legislatures, or initiatives and vetoes by presidents, but also by the fact that some subjects and proposals emerge in the first place and others are never seriously considered."[8]

There are many approaches to policy study, including political systems theory,[9] group theory,[10] elite theory,[11] institutionalism,[12] and rational choice theory.[13] Other political scientists, such as James Anderson, have built upon the ideas of earlier theorists to conceptualize policy making as a sequential model of stages that represent distinct periods of time, political institutions, and actors in (official policy makers) and outside (unofficial policy makers) of government. Some participants in making policy serve as gatekeepers, acting as checkpoints where a determination is made about what problems the government ought to consider.[14]

All of these models are useful in understanding how environmental policy is influenced by politics. This book relies upon an amalgamation of previous theorists' work as a way of illustrating what many consider to be the processes of solving problems, using stages as a metaphor for what takes place.

1. *Problem identification and agenda setting:* In this stage, policy issues are brought to the attention of government officials in a variety of ways. Conditions become problems when there is sufficient belief that something ought to be done about them; not all conditions become problems, however. Some problems are uncovered by the media; others, like wildfires, become prominent through crisis or another type of focusing event. In some cases, there is a gradual accumulation of knowledge by scientists or issue specialists; once a critical mass of information is collected, reports are issued and press conferences held, as has happened with global warming. There may be a technological breakthrough that leads to a call for change, such as the development of hybrid fueled cars. Sometimes, organized groups may demonstrate or lobby officials to focus attention on the problem, which is how

Greenpeace activists gained support for the protection of marine mammals. Celebrities like Leonardo di Caprio or Ted Danson may use their status to bring a problem to the government's attention. Some problems may exist without being recognized except by a few isolated individuals or groups, who clamor to have their voices heard. Other problems are so immediate or visible that there is an immediate call for resolution. Once identified, problems are said to be part of the policy agenda, a list of subjects or problems to which people inside and outside of government pay serious attention at any given time.

Agenda setting is also affected by processes such as election results and changes in the partisan balance in the White House or Congress; economic ups and downs in inflation, stock market performance, or consumer confidence, swings in public opinion and the national mood. The agenda is subjected to forces like the motivations of individuals seeking to bring about change, trade-offs among political actors, and persuasion. But overall, the process is a dynamic one that is in a constant state of change.

2. *Policy formulation:* After a problem is identified as worthy of government attention, policy makers must develop proposed courses of action to solve it. Policy formulation may involve a variety of actors, which will be covered in more detail in Chapter 3. Some policies come directly from the president, such as President George W. Bush's Healthy Forest Initiative. Other policies, such as the opening of roadless areas on public lands, are developed by federal agencies or cabinet-level departments, such as the U.S. Forest Service, a topic that is explored in Chapter 4. Congress and state legislatures are often the source of policy initiatives, including Oregon's landmark "bottle bill," which established cash refunds for recycled products, and California's vanguard air pollution regulations. Interest groups, the subject of Chapter 2, often place pressure on legislators or provide their expertise on matters that are scientifically or technically complex. The control of greenhouse gases, for example, has been made more difficult due to issues of scientific uncertainty and the application of the precautionary principle, discussed in Chapter 10.

3. *Policy adoption:* The acceptance of a particular policy is a highly politicized stage, often involving legislation or rule making, that legitimizes the policy. This is usually referred to as the authorization phase of policy making, and it often occurs outside the public's direct view. Hearings on competing proposals, meetings among stakeholders, and the publication of new standards of regulation may be conducted with minimal public participation or media attention. The process of making a choice among competing alternatives (such as different energy bills in the Congress) has been studied extensively by political scientists, who often refer to this area as the decision sciences.

Although important policy outcomes may be the result of informal, intuitive judgments, three theories of decision making are generally used when trying to explain policy adoptions. The rational-comprehensive theory is used to explain the procedures for maximizing the attainment of specific goals. These goals are intended to solve problems that can be clearly identified and defined. It is the process of problem definition that makes this approach quite difficult.

Incrementalism, in contrast, involves making relatively limited changes—fine tuning—rather than major alterations in policy. Incrementalism is built on the premise that there is no single "right" answer to problem solving, but rather a limited number of potential choices. This type of decision making tends to be conservative and is unlikely to lead to innovative solutions.

Multiple advocacy calls for the use of a "broker" who brings together a wide range of (often conflicting) alternatives and opinions. Leaders listen to the various arguments and ideas as they are presented, ideally with a neutral perspective. Although this format allows for greater participation by numerous actors, not all actors are equal in their resources, powers, or level of information about the nature of a problem.

4. *Policy implementation:* To put an agreed-on policy into effect, this fourth stage involves conflict and struggle as the administrative machinery of government begins to turn. Affected groups must now turn their attention from the legislative arena to the bureaucracy, and in some cases the judicial branch, to get the policy to work. Usually implementation is conducted through a complex administrative process, which may force agencies to make decisions based on very broad, ambiguous legislative intent, as was the case with the 1990 Clean Air Act. Implementation may become politicized and may force agencies to compete against one another for government resources and attention. The interest groups that were instrumental in getting the policy problem identified and placed on the policy agenda may become enmeshed in the implementation process, making further demands on the bureaucracy. Contending interests, such as those seeking protection for a specific endangered animal, will push their own agendas forward, often at the expense of the initial policy they sought to have adopted.

5. *Policy evaluation:* An ongoing process, this stage involves various determinations as to whether the policy is effective. This appraisal may be based on studies of program operations, systematic evaluation, or personal judgment; but whatever the method, the evaluation may start the policy-making process all over again. Public policies are usually evaluated by the agencies that administer them, by the Government Accountability Office (GAO),[15] or occasionally at the president's request. Policy evaluation takes a number of forms. Researchers may use cost-benefit analysis to determine whether the amount of money being spent on a project is matched by the value obtained. They may conduct an evaluation midway through the implementation process so that changes can be made or errors corrected. However, policy evaluation also takes many other forms. Elected officials may make a determination about how well a policy is doing based on comments they receive not only from their constituents but also from organized groups attempting to lobby their support or responding on the basis of partisan concerns.

However, the elements of this model of policy making are not separate, distinct events: Policy making is an organic, even messy, process of defining and redefining problems; formulating and implementing policies and then reformulating them; and moving off and back on the policy agenda. Throughout each of the chapters that follow, these policy terms will be used to show how various problems, from waste management and biodiversity to water pollution and energy, go through the various stages of the policy process. Although not every scholar of environmental policy agrees with the precise terminology used here, it is a way of helping explain what happens.

In the Yellowstone National Park example, the idea of protecting a scenic area came from a variety of sources: explorers who brought back unbelievable tales of bubbling pools of mud and abundant wildlife. The media publicized the stories and sent out reporters of their own to confirm or deny the information they were receiving. Early miners and railroad executives put their own spin on the region's resources and potential for development; some agency officials cashed in on their relationships with those outside the government to protect the idea of a national park. In the end, it was congressional enthusiasm and presidential leadership that brought the wilderness under federal management and protection.

In contrast, Killarney National Park was developed out of a combination of altruism and financial necessity, with little of the political wrangling that characterized the debate over Yellowstone. Although the Irish mountains and lakes could certainly be said to be as deserving of protection for future generations as the geysers of Yellowstone, the process of designation followed a totally different policy pathway.

Understanding the policy process allows us to consider the various points where public participation is allowed or encouraged. It helps to explain why some problems seem to be ignored while others have a mercurial rise to prominence. Knowledge of the political aspects of policy making points toward determining which actors play the most important role, and in which arena. For those seeking changes in environmental policy, this book provides a guide for activists as well as those seeking to understand what has already happened.

NOTES

1. Killarney National Park, "History of the Park," at www.homepage.tinet.ie/~knp, accessed July 11, 2004.

2. See Ferol Egan, *Last Bonanza Kings: The Bourns of San Francisco* (Reno: University of Nevada Press, 1998). See also Muckross Research Library, "The Bourn Vincents," at www.muckross-house.ie, accessed February 27, 2005.

3. See Bill Quirke, ed. *Killarney National Park: A Place to Treasure* (Cork, Ireland: Collins Press, 2001).

4. There is a wealth of literature on the early history of Yellowstone both before and after it became a national park. See, for example, Hiram Martin Chittenden, *The Yellowstone National Park* (Norman, OK: University of Oklahoma Press, 1964); Nathaniel Pitt Langford, *The Discovery of Yellowstone National Park* (Lincoln, NE: University of Nebraska Press, 1972); Aubrey L. Haines, *Yellowstone National Park: Its Exploration and Establishment* (Washington, DC: U.S. Department of Interior, 1974); Chris J. Magoc, *Yellowstone: The Creation and Selling of an American Landscape, 1870–1903* (Albuquerque, NM: University of New Mexico Press,

1999); David Rains Wallace, *Yellowstone: A Natural and Human History* (Washington, DC: U.S. Department of Interior, 2001); and Paul Schullery and Lew Whittlesey, *Myth and History in the Creation of Yellowstone National Park* (Lincoln, NE: University of Nebraska Press, 2003). A different perspective on Yellowstone's history, originally written as a college thesis, is provided by James S. Macdonald Jr., "The Founding of Yellowstone into Law and into Fact," at www.yellowstone-online.com/paper, accessed February 7, 2005.

5. The text of the language is from the Forty-Second Congress, Second Sess. Ch. 21–24, March 1, 1872, "An Act to set apart a certain Tract of Land lying near the Head-waters of the Yellowstone River as a public Park."

6. Anthony Downs, "Up and Down with Ecology—The 'Issue-Attention Cycle,'" *The Public Interest*, 28 (Summer 1972): 38–50.

7. John W. Kingdon, *Agendas, Alternatives, and Public Policies*, 2nd ed. (New York: Longman, 2003), 1.

8. Ibid., 2.

9. See David Easton, *A Systems Analysis of Political Life* (New York: John Wiley, 1965); and Harold Lasswell, *Politics: Who Gets What, When, How* (Cleveland, OH: Meridian Books, 1958).

10. See Earl Latham, *The Group Basis of Politics* (New York: Octagon Books, 1965), and a more contemporary discussion of the roles of groups in Frank R. Baumgartner and Beth L. Leech, *Basic Interests: The Importance of Groups in Politics and Political Science* (Princeton, NJ: Princeton University Press, 1998).

11. See Thomas R. Dye and L. Harmon Zeigler, *The Irony of Democracy*, millennial ed. (Ft. Worth, TX: Harcourt Brace, 2000).

12. Institutionalism is defined as the study of the more formal and legal aspects of government decisions. It is assumed that the structure, rules, and procedures of institutions (such as Congress or state legislatures) will affect policy making.

13. See Anthony Downs, *An Economic Theory of Democracy* (New York: Harper and Row, 1957).

14. James E. Anderson, *Public Policymaking: An Introduction*, 4th ed. (Boston: Houghton Mifflin, 2000).

15. The Government Accountability Office was called the General Accounting Office until 2004.

1

A Historical Framework for Environmental Protection

> . . . the greatest good, for the greatest number, for the longest run.
> —GIFFORD PINCHOT, U.S. FOREST SERVICE (1905)[1]

On July 1, 2005, the United States Forest Service (USFS) celebrated its centennial year, recognizing 100 years "as an agency with a unique mission: to sustain healthy, diverse, and productive forests and grasslands for present and future generations."[2] Among the events was the Forest Service Centennial Congress, held in Washington, DC, and convening leaders of Congress, representatives of environmental agencies, academicians and researchers, media leaders, representatives from state and local governments, and Forest Service officials. The 2005 observance also recognized the 1905 Forest Congress, which was held in Washington, DC, and had this goal:

> To establish a broader understanding of the forest in its relation to the great industries depending upon it; to advance the conservative use of forest resources for both the present and future need of these industries; to stimulate and unite all efforts to perpetuate the forest as a permanent resource of the nation.[3]

◁

Loggers in the Pacific Northwest worked in teams to fell mature timber, ca. 1936, in this archival photograph from the Forest History Society.

FOREST HISTORY SOCIETY, DURHAM, NC

In the period between these two events, U.S. forests—and the policies adopted to regulate their use—changed considerably. From the beginning, trees were considered a "crop" that could be grown, harvested, and replanted year after year. Just after the turn of the century, President Theodore Roosevelt proclaimed his support for the protection of millions of acres of forests protected by presidents Benjamin Harrison and Grover Cleveland under the 1891 Forest Reserve Act. He sought advice from his friend, Gifford Pinchot, chief forester of the U.S. Department of Agriculture's Division of Forestry. Pinchot, the self-proclaimed first American-born professional forester in the United States, was not only European-trained in the newly emerging profession of forestry but also a savvy politician and media strategist.

Pinchot, who directed much of the president's conservation agenda, convinced Roosevelt that responsibility for managing the reserves should be transferred from the General Land Office to the Division of Forestry. He lined up the necessary congressional votes, and once passage of the legislation for the transfer was secured, built up the agency's workforce from 60 to 500. Summer hires of forestry students, who made $25 per day, further expanded the Forest Service's bureaucratic clout in Washington.[4]

Now 30,000 Forest Service employees manage 191 million acres of land in 155 national forests and 20 grasslands. The agency conducts research on scientific and technical issues, cooperates with state and local agencies, nongovernmental environmental organizations, private landowners, and timber industry groups. On a global level, the USFS is liaison with the Agency for International Development, U.S. Department of State, and the Environmental Protection Agency in dealing with international forest management.[5] As part of the centennial, the agency proclaimed a New Century of Service "to provide leadership for a national commemoration of the 100th anniversary of the Forest Service in 2005; support the agency's natural resource goals in the 21st century through public service and collaboration; and promote the Forest Service's value of working collaboratively with internal and external partners and customers."[6]

Although the Forest Service centennial marks a milestone in American conservation history, concern about the environment dates back to the nation's infancy and has since been a recurrent theme. From time to time, other issues—the economy, national security, or an energy crisis—push the environment down on the public policy agenda. It may even languish toward the bottom as other issues are perceived to be more pressing or more important.

The governmental agenda is also affected by environmental disasters and crises that made headlines. Some, like the 100,000-ton oil spill caused by the sinking of the supertanker *Torrey Canyon* off the coast of England in 1967, have been upstaged by more recent events such as the 1999 spill that killed more than 50,000 seabirds along the coast of France. The radiation leak at the Soviet Union's Chernobyl plant in April 1986 has become synonymous with contemporary concerns about nuclear power that are reflected in congressional debates over a nuclear waste site at Yucca Mountain, Nevada. The December 26, 2004, tsunami that devastated Southeast

Asia made other environmental problems pale in comparison to the death and destruction experienced by millions of people. These types of focusing events, as they are called by policy scholars, are crises that "come along and simply bowl over everything standing in the way of prominence on the agenda."[7]

The development of an environmental policy agenda can be viewed in two ways. First, it is a history of ideas, a philosophical framework about our relationship to nature and the world. This history is punctuated with names ranging from Thomas Malthus and Charles Darwin to Karl Marx and Francis Bacon, to modern commentators Barry Commoner, Garrett Hardin, Rod Nash, Paul Ehrlich, and David Suzuki. Second, it is a factual history, made up of events, individuals, and conditions. This chapter focuses on factual history to identify six distinct periods in the development of policies to protect the environment. It also summarizes the ways in which public opinion and attitudes about the environment have framed the environmental debate and resulting policy.

GERMINATION OF AN IDEA: FROM THE COLONIAL PERIOD TO 1900

Even before the American states were united, there was an awareness of the need to limit the use of the new land's natural resources. As early as 1626, members of the Plymouth Colony passed ordinances regulating the cutting and sale of timber on colony lands. Other colonial leaders recognized the importance of preserving the region's resources, prohibiting the intentional setting of forest fires, and placing limits on deer hunting. In 1681, William Penn, proprietor of Pennsylvania, decreed that for every five acres of land cleared, one must be left as virgin forest. In 1691, Massachusetts Bay leaders began to set aside "forest reservations"—large stands of pines valued for their use as ships' masts. Forest preservation became an entrenched principle of colonial land management as early as the 17th century.[8]

During the 18th century, the nation was consumed with the building of a new government, but individual states made efforts to preserve the resources within their boundaries. Massachusetts in 1710 began to protect coastal waterfowl and in 1718 banned the hunting of deer for four years. Other states, such as Connecticut (1739) and New York (1772), also passed laws to protect game.[9] Political leaders at the beginning of the 19th century expressed interest in studying soil erosion; both Washington and Jefferson wrote of their concerns about the lands at their estates. The opening of the Erie Canal in 1825 brought pine forests within the reach of eastern markets and forced states to confront the issue of timber poaching—one of the first environmental crimes.[10]

By mid-century, the public began to be interested in preserving natural resources. George Perkins Marsh's 1864 book, *Man and Nature,* captured attention with its call for the protection of songbirds and the use of plantings to prevent soil erosion.[11] In 1866, German scientist and philosopher Ernst Haeckel coined the term *ecology,* and the subject became a thriving research discipline.[12] Still, there was no philosophy of protection that dominated either American or European thought. Studies of the popular literature of the 1870s led some historians to conclude that the environmental movement came alive with the advent of sportsmen's magazines. In October 1871, *The American Sportsman,* a monthly newspaper, marked a turning point in environmental history when it became the first publication to interrelate the subjects of hunting, fishing, natural history, and conservation. Two years later, *Forest and Stream* advocated the protection of watersheds, scientific management of forests, uniform game laws, and abatement of water pollution.[13] Diminishing supplies of fish in the Connecticut River resulted in development of the fish culture industry and the formation in 1870 of the American Fisheries Society, the first biological society to research a diminishing natural resource. A year later, the U.S. Fish Commission was created, the first federal agency responsible for the conservation of a specific natural resource.[14]

Adventure and exploration enhanced the public's interest in the environment throughout the 19th century. Lewis and Clark's transcontinental explorations beginning in 1804, and John Wesley Powell's journey down the Colorado River in 1869, increased Americans' awareness of the undiscovered beauty of the frontier.[15]

Tremendous urban population growth between 1870 and the turn of the century led to new environmental problems, including contamination of drinking-water sources and dumping of garbage and sewage. The problems were most evident in the cities of the Northeast and Midwest, where the population increases were the most rapid. Although New York remained the nation's largest city, nearly tripling its population over the 30-year period, Chicago had the biggest percentage increase—nearly sixfold. Similarly, Philadelphia, St. Louis, and Boston nearly doubled the sizes of their populations. Although industrial development did not reach the West Coast's cities as quickly, San Francisco, which served as the major shipping port, doubled its population between 1870 and 1890. The biggest increase was in Los Angeles, which grew to over 20 times its size from 1870 to 1900. American cities became centers of industry; and industry, with its accompanying population growth, meant pollution. By 1880, New York had 287 foundries and machine shops and 125 steam engines, bone mills, refineries, and tanneries. By the turn of the century, Pittsburgh had hundreds of iron and steel plants. Chicago's stockyards, railroads, and port traffic filled the city with odors and thick, black smoke.[16]

Pollution problems caused by rapid industrial growth resulted in numerous calls for reform, and women became key leaders in cleaning up the urban environment. Upper-class women with extended periods of leisure time, believing that "the housekeeping of a great city is women's work," formed civic organizations dedicated to monitoring pollution and finding solutions to garbage and sanitation problems. The first of these groups, the Ladies' Health Protective Association, was founded in 1884 with the goal of keeping New York City's streets free of garbage. The Civic Club of Philadelphia, formed in 1894, began by placing trash receptacles at key intersections. Other groups were organized in Boston (the Women's Municipal League) and St. Louis (the Women's Organization for Smoke Abatement).[17]

The nation's environmental awareness was enhanced by the actions of specific individuals. George Catlin first proposed the idea of a national park in

1832.[18] Henry David Thoreau spoke poetically in 1858 of his return to a natural world.[19] George E. Waring built the first separate sewer system in Lenox, Massachusetts, in 1876 and was a pioneer in the study of sanitary engineering. Waring, known as "the apostle of cleanliness," crusaded about the impact of garbage on public health and was responsible for the beginnings of contemporary solid waste science.[20] Later, after the turn of the century, progressive reformers like Dr. A. Wilberforce Williams brought advice on hygiene and sanitation to the urban black community.[21]

The concept of preserving natural areas came from a variety of sources. In 1870, a group of explorers recommended that a portion of the upper Yellowstone River region be set aside to protect its geothermal features, wildlife, forests, and unique scenery. The result, the establishment of Yellowstone National Park in 1872, was the beginning of a pattern of preserving large undisturbed ecosystems. The public endorsed the idea, and Congress responded by creating Sequoia, Kings Canyon, and Yosemite National Parks in 1890, followed by Mount Rainier National Park in 1899. Interest in trees and forests was an important element of preservationism, symbolized by the proclamation of the first Arbor Day on April 10, 1872. The event was the culmination of the work of J. Sterling Morton, editor of Nebraska's first newspaper, and Robert W. Furia, a prominent nursery owner who later became governor. The two men convinced the Nebraska state legislature to commemorate the day with tree plantings to make Nebraska "mentally and morally the best agricultural state in the Union." More than 1 million trees were planted the first year, and Nebraska became known as the "Tree Planter's State" in 1895. With the Forest Reserve Act of 1891, the U.S. Congress set aside forest lands for preservation for the first time. Several years later, President Grover Cleveland ordered lands to be protected because few states were willing to protect their forests from logging.

The founding of the Sierra Club by John Muir in 1892 marked the beginning of interest in a more broad-based environmental organization.[22] Although the early organizations have been called "pitifully weak" in membership and finances, these early groups had a strong sense of determination. Most groups debated the scientific management of resources rather than organizing to protect them. But the idea of preserving land and natural resources was germinating within American society.[23]

PROGRESSIVE REFORMS AND CONSERVATIONISM: 1900–1945

Despite these whispers of ideas and early efforts, most environmental historians place the beginning of an actual "movement" at the turn of the 20th century, when conservationism became a key element of the Progressive era. The term *conservation* sprang from efforts by pioneers such as Frederick H. Newell, George Maxwell, and Francis G. Newlands to construct reservoirs to conserve spring floodwaters for later use during the dry season. The concept behind conservation was "planned and efficient progress."[24]

In the United States, the infant environmental movement split into two camps: preservationists and conservationists. Under the leadership of Pinchot, the conservationists believed that sustainable exploitation of resources was possible. The preservationists, led by John Muir, sought to preserve wilderness areas from all but recreational and educational use. Generally, the conservationists' position won, at least at the national level.

Before the turn of the century, there had been little federal consideration of conservation. The zenith can be traced to May 13–15, 1908, when 1,000 national leaders met to attend the White House Conference on Resource Management, coordinated by Pinchot. This meeting was one of the first official agenda-setting actions in environmental policy making.[25] At the end of the conference, the leaders asked the president to create a National Conservation Commission to develop an inventory of all natural resources. Roosevelt did so, appointing Pinchot as its chairman. By mid-1909, forty-one states had created similar organizations.[26] Pinchot organized the Conservation Congresses, which convened to discuss the familiar subjects of forest, soil, and water problems and management and eventually expanded to include issues such as public control of railroads, regulation of speculation and gambling in foodstuffs, coordination of governmental agencies, and creation of better rural schools.[27] The congresses provided an opportunity for debate among federal, state, and local conservation leaders but were heavily politicized. Bitterness and internal struggles brought an end to the annual events in 1917. Of prime importance to many conservation leaders was the "public land question." The possibilities of unlimited economic growth in the West caused President Theodore Roosevelt to appoint a Public Lands Commission in 1903. While many hoped the commission would promote orderly growth, there was also concern that the old practice of disposing of nonagricultural lands to private owners would give way to public ownership and management.[28] During the presidencies of Theodore Roosevelt, William Howard Taft, and Woodrow Wilson, Congress created new national forests, passed laws to protect historic sites and migratory birds, and enacted the National Park Service in 1916.

The Progressive era is noted also for the birth of conservation organizations such as the National Audubon Society, in 1905; the National Parks Association, in 1919; and the Izaak Walton League, in 1922. Pinchot organized the National Conservation Association in 1909, with the group's primary interests being limited to water power and mineral leasing, reflecting an extension of Roosevelt's policy. The group disbanded in the 1920s. Progressive era reforms were focused on efficiency, striving to make better use of natural resources. The reformers were not radicals in the traditional political sense, so progressive conservation posed only a modest threat to the existing distribution of power in the United States.[29]

As use of the term *conservation* broadened, it gradually lost its initial meaning. Roosevelt began referring to the conservation of human health, and the National Conservation Congress devoted its entire 1912 session to "the conservation of human life." While conservationists focused attention on the sustainability of natural resource use, progressives in urban areas began working for new laws and regulations to reduce pollution and protect public health. Cities were the first to regulate air pollution; the first clean air laws were enacted in the late 1800s. Public health advocates and activists such as Alice Hamilton and Jane Addams provided the impetus for state and local regulatory programs to improve water quality, provide for sanitation and waste removal, and reduce workers' exposure to toxic chemicals.[30]

During the 1930s, the environmental movement again became a battle between conservation and preservation. As a result, environmental leaders redoubled their efforts to preserve scenic areas. In 1935, Aldo Leopold founded the Wilderness Society to protect public lands, and the National Wildlife Federation (1936) served as the first of the conservation education organizations, sponsoring National Wildlife Week in schools beginning in 1938. Conservation organizations were closely allied with the four major engineering societies: the American Society of Civil Engineers, the American Society of Mechanical Engineers, the American Institute of Electrical Engineers, and the American Institute of Mining Engineers, all of which spearheaded the drive for efficiency. The Great Depression brought the federal government into new areas of responsibility, including environmental policy. Federal conservation interest intensified with the growth of agencies with specific resource responsibilities, beginning with the Tennessee Valley Authority in 1933, the Soil Conservation Service in 1935, and the Civilian Conservation Corps, which from 1933 to 1942 gave productive work to 2 million unemployed young men. By the time the United States entered into World War II, conservation and resource management were firmly entrenched as part of the federal government's environmental mission.

RECREATION AND THE AGE OF ECOLOGY: POST-WORLD WAR II TO 1969

After World War II, Americans' interest in the environment shifted to a new direction. Concern about the efficient scientific management of resources was replaced with a desire to use the land for recreational purposes. Over 30 million Americans toured the national parks in 1950. The parks were, in the words of one observer, "in danger of being loved to death," because roads and services were still at prewar levels.[31] National Park Service (NPS) Director Conrad Wirth presented Congress with a "wish list" of park needs that came to be known as Mission '66—a 10-year improvement program that would coincide with the 50th anniversary of the NPS. That plan served as the blueprint for massive growth in national parks as well as recreational areas during the next 20 years.[32] Habitat protection became the focus of groups like the Defenders of Wildlife, founded in 1947 to preserve, enhance, and protect the diversity of wildlife and its habitats. In 1951, The Nature Conservancy began to acquire, either through purchase, gift, or exchange, ecologically significant tracts of land, many of which are habitats for endangered species.

The 1960s brought a battle between those who supported industrial growth and those who worried about the effects of pollution caused by growth. It was a decade when an author's prose or a single event could rouse the public's indignation. The 1960s marked the beginning of legislative initiatives that would be fine-tuned over the next 30 years and of tremendous growth in environmental organizations.

Two authors brought public attention to environmental problems during this decade. Rachel Carson, in her book *Silent Spring*,[33] and Paul Ehrlich, in *The*

Population Bomb,[34] warned the world of the dangers of pesticides and the population explosion, respectively. Several authors served up "doom-and-gloom" predictions of the problems facing the planet, and there was a spirit of pessimism regarding the environmental situation. In January and February 1969, two oil spills 5.5 miles off the coast of Santa Barbara, California, hit a public nerve like never before. Only eight days into his administration, President Richard Nixon was faced with an environmental crisis for which he was totally unprepared. The media captured the essence of the spills with images of birds soaked in gooey, black oil and pristine, white beaches soiled with globs of oil that washed up with each tide.[35]

Legislatively, the 1960s heralded a period of intense activity (see Appendix A). In a carryover of issues from the postwar period, parks and wilderness remained high on the public's and legislature's agendas. By 1960, the number of national park visitors had grown to 72 million, and Congress responded by creating the Land and Water Conservation Fund to add new wilderness areas and national parks. Congress also expanded recreational areas with the passage of the National Wilderness Act in 1964 and the Wild and Scenic Rivers and National Trails Acts in 1968. President Lyndon Johnson, as part of his environmental policy, which he called "the new conservation," sought congressional support for urban parks to bring the land closer to the people.[36] Johnson's wife, Lady Bird, spearheaded the drive to improve the nation's roadways through her highway beautification program and sought, and found, congressional support for the 1965 passage of the Highway Beautification Act.[37]

Although there were several legislative precursors during the 1940s and 1950s, many hallmark pieces of pollution legislation were enacted during the 1960s, with the signing of the first Clean Air Act in 1963 (amended as the Air Quality Act in 1967) and the Water Quality Act in 1965. The Endangered Species Preservation Act (1966) marked a return to the federal interest in animal and plant habitat that had begun earlier in the century. The National Environmental Policy Act (NEPA), signed by President Nixon in 1970, served as the foundation for policy initiatives that were to follow throughout the next 20 years.

Political leadership on environmental issues during the 1960s focused on several individuals, and environmental organizations began to grow. Senator Edmund Muskie of Maine was among the most visible, but he turned out to be the target of considerable criticism, especially when he became a leading contender for the Democratic presidential nomination. A 1969 report by Ralph Nader's consumer organization gave Muskie credit for his early stewardship in the air pollution battle but accused the senator of subsequently losing interest.[38] Other leaders, such as Senator Henry Jackson of Washington (who chaired the Senate Interior and Insular Affairs Committee and was largely responsible for shepherding NEPA through Congress) and Representative John Dingell of Michigan, were primarily involved in the legislative arena. Not only did the number of environmental groups expand during the 1960s, but existing ones experienced tremendous growth. New organizations like the African Wildlife Foundation (1961), the World Wildlife Fund (1961), the Environmental Defense Fund (1967), and the Council on Economic Priorities (1969) broadened the spectrum of group concerns. Meanwhile, the Sierra Club's membership grew tenfold from 1952 to 1969, and the Wilderness Society expanded from 12,000 members in 1960 to 54,000 in 1970.[39]

One of the most compelling themes to emerge from the decade of the 1960s was that the federal government must take a more pervasive role in solving what was beginning to be called "the environmental crisis." The limited partnership between the federal government and the states was insufficient to solve what was already being spoken of in global terms.

EARTH DAYS AND DEREGULATION: 1970–1992

In August 1969, Wisconsin Senator Gaylord Nelson was on his way to Berkeley when he read an article in *Ramparts* magazine about the anti–Vietnam War teach-ins that were sweeping the country. Nelson, one of the few members of Congress who had shown an interest in environmental issues, thought a similar approach might work to raise public awareness about the environment. In September, he proposed his idea during a speech in Seattle. Later that fall he incorporated a nonprofit, nonpartisan organization, Environmental Teach-In, and pledged $15,000 of his own funds to get it started.[40] In December 1969, Nelson asked former Stanford student body president Denis Hayes to serve as national coordinator for what was to become Earth Day on April 22, 1970. Hayes, who postponed plans to enter Harvard Law School, worked with a $190,000 budget, purchasing a full-page ad in the *New York Times* to announce the teach-in. Not everyone was supportive. President Nixon, who had presented a 37-point environmental message to Congress a few months earlier, refused to issue a proclamation in support of Earth Day. Instead, the White House issued proclamations for National Archery Week and National Boating Week.[41]

Certainly 1970 marked a watershed year for new environmental organizations, with the founding of the Center for Science in the Public Interest, Citizens for a Better Environment, Environmental Action, Friends of the Earth, the League of Conservation Voters, Natural Resources Defense Council, and Save the Bay. Greenpeace and Public Citizen were formed the following year. This period marks the beginning of a turnaround in leverage, as business and industry mobilized to slow the pace of environmental legislation (see Chapter 2). Environmental organizations were no longer able to monopolize the policy debate to serve their own interests. The range of environmental issues had become so extensive that organized environmental groups were unable to act effectively in all areas. Even more important, many issues had become matters not for public debate and legislative action, but for administrative choice, an area in which politics was dominated by technical issues that placed a premium on the financial resources necessary to command expertise. This gave considerable political advantage to administrators and private corporate institutions, which employed far more technical personnel than did environmental organizations.

The American public's attitude about the environment has never been very stable, and the decade of the 1970s is a perfect example. When George Gallup asked respondents in his national survey to identify the most important problem facing the nation in November 1967, the environment did not even make the list; nor did it appear when the question was asked in three surveys in 1968 or another survey in 1969. The Vietnam War and the economy overshadowed other concerns of Americans during that period. Not until May 1970 (after Earth Day) did the topic appear as an issue, when it ranked second and was mentioned by 53 percent of those responding. By June 1970, the subject had dropped off the list, replaced in the number one spot by the campus unrest caused by the Vietnam War. Pollution and ecology returned to the list in March 1971 (ranked sixth, with only 7 percent of respondents naming these as the most important problem); by June 1971, these two topics ranked 10th. Environmental issues reemerged as a topic of concern in August and October 1972, and in March 1973, when the subject ranked sixth. But in May 1973, although pollution was ranked as the fifth most important problem facing the nation, it began to be overshadowed by another problem—the energy crisis, which ranked 13th. In January 1974, Gallup found that the public considered the energy crisis to be its most important problem, being selected by 46 percent of the public. By July, that ranking dropped to number four, mentioned by 4 percent of those surveyed—a figure that stayed relatively constant throughout the rest of the decade.

President Nixon, whose position on environmental protection often reflected public opinion, used the signing of the National Environmental Policy Act (NEPA) in 1970 to declare the next 10 years as "the environmental decade" and instructed his staff to rush the issue of new legislative proposals. NEPA became one of the nation's most important environmental statutes by requiring an extensive analysis of the environmental impact of proposed projects and the development of ways to minimize negative impacts. With his creation of the Environmental Protection Agency (EPA) by executive order in 1970, Nixon moved ahead in the race with Congress to take advantage of the public's mood.

In the meantime, Congress too was firmly on the environmental protection bandwagon, enacting more than 20 major pieces of legislation, many of which were refinements of earlier bills. Other laws, such as the Marine Mammal Protection Act (1972), the Federal Environmental Pesticides Control Act (1972), the Resource Conservation and Recovery Act (1976), and the Toxic Substances Control Act (1976), brought the federal government into new areas of environmental protection.

As had been the case in the 1960s, unexpected events periodically refocused attention on the environment.[42] The 1973 Arab oil embargo pushed energy to the top of the policy agenda, although a succession of presidents had sought to make the United States "energy independent." President Jimmy Carter pushed through most of his energy conservation program while turning down the White House thermostat and wearing a sweater indoors. Nuclear power, which was being touted as a cleaner, more reliable alternative to foreign oil, suffered a major setback in 1979 when cooling water at the Three Mile Island nuclear power plant near Harrisburg, Pennsylvania, dipped below safe levels and triggered a meltdown. Although no radioactive fuel escaped and no one was injured, the accident cast a shadow of doubt over the entire nuclear energy program.

During the summer of 1978, media coverage of incidents near the Love Canal in Niagara Falls, New York, reawakened American concerns over toxic waste. The abandoned canal had been used as a dumping ground for waste during the 1940s by the Hooker Chemicals and Plastics Corporation, which filled in the site and sold it to the Niagara Falls Board of Education for $1. A school was then built near the site, which was located in the midst of a residential area. When local health officials found higher than normal rates of birth defects, miscarriages, and other medical problems among Love Canal residents, President Carter ordered the federal government to purchase the 240 homes nearest the site; the government eventually spent more than $30 million in relocation costs.[43]

Similar incidents occurred in 1979 in West Point, Kentucky, where 17,000 drums of leaking chemicals were discovered, and in 1983 in Times Beach, Missouri, where high levels of dioxin were thought to have contaminated the entire town. The Hudson River was found to be contaminated by more than a million pounds of polychlorinated biphenyls (PCBs), and well water in the West was contaminated with cancer-causing trichloroethylene (TCE). The impact of publicity surrounding Love Canal and similar disclosures can be seen in public opinion polls. In July 1978, Resources for the Future (RFF) surveyed Americans' attitudes at a time when the inflation rate topped 10 percent and an endangered fish, the tiny snail darter, had stopped progress on the Tellico Dam. The RFF survey found that environmental public support continued to hold firm, with the number of people who felt "we are spending too little on environmental protection" increasing despite widespread economic problems.[44]

Just as the 1969 Santa Barbara oil spill had galvanized public opinion, the December 3, 1984, leak of deadly methyl isocyanate gas at a Union Carbide plant in Bhopal, India, reawakened interest in environmental disasters. The leak, which killed more than 2,000 people and injured 200,000, was brought closer to home when it was revealed that an identical Union Carbide plant was located in Institute, West Virginia. The public and governmental outcry resulted in a shutdown of the plant for several months for inspections and safety checks. These events also caused a shifting of legislative gears as interest changed to toxic and hazardous waste and the health impacts of pollution. With congressional enactment of the Resource Conservation and Recovery Act and the Toxic Substances Control Act in the 1970s, the foundation was laid for the Comprehensive Environmental Response, Compensation, and Liability Act ("Superfund") in 1980 (reauthorized in 1986) and the Hazardous and Solid Waste Amendments in 1984. Concerns about health found their way into the Safe Drinking Water Act Amendments of 1986 (an expansion of the 1974 law) and the Federal Insecticide, Fungicide, and Rodenticide Act Amendments of 1988.

But the 1980s brought an increase in the pessimistic attitudes Americans had toward the efforts that had been made in the previous decade. A Cambridge Reports survey from 1983 to 1989 found that respondents believed that the overall quality of the environment was worse than it had been five years before, with a sharp increase in pessimism beginning in 1987.[45] When the question of "most important problem" was asked again during the 1980s by a Gallup poll, energy often made the list of most important problems, although the environment did not. A separate Gallup survey conducted in September 1989 found that 66 percent of the respondents said they were "extremely concerned" about the pollution of sea life and beaches from the dumping of garbage, medical wastes, and chemicals into the ocean, with the same percentage also expressing extreme concern about the pollution of freshwater rivers, lakes, and other sources of drinking water. Fifty percent of those surveyed said they were extremely concerned about air pollution, and 41 percent expressed concern over the disposal of household garbage and trash.[46]

The 1980s environmental policy agenda was molded most by the administration of President Ronald Reagan, whose main concern was to reduce the amount of governmental regulation (see Chapter 3). Reagan's budget cuts and personnel decisions and a weakening of the previous decade's legislative efforts had a profound effect on policy for the next 10 years. Despite those changes, public concern over environmental degradation had risen substantially in this period, commanding support from large majorities. What was less clear at the end of the 1980s was the strength of the public's commitment to environmental protection.[47]

After declaring himself "the environmental president" after his 1988 campaign, George Bush was faced not only with the Reagan legacy of environmental slash and burn but also with a host of newly discovered environmental problems and crises, many of which had a global focus. Two major pieces of legislation enacted during the Bush administration were the Clean Air Act Amendments of 1990 and the 1992 Energy Policy Act, both of which represented a break in the legislative gridlock that had characterized Congress under Republican administrations. Environmental organizations, many of which experienced a decline in membership growth after the initial burst of activity in the early 1970s, received a booster shot with Earth Day 1990. The Gallup organization classified about 20 percent of the American public as hard-core environmentalists—those who call themselves strong environmentalists and feel that major disruptions are coming if we do not take drastic environmental actions, even at the cost of economic growth.[48]

Perhaps the most important development of this period was the globalization of environmental protection. The 1992 Earth Summit refocused the need for environmental issues to be viewed globally, rather than locally. It also provided dramatic evidence of the need for international cooperation to solve the larger issues of global warming, transboundary pollution, and biodiversity and raised the critical question of whether the industrialized world is willing to pay for environmental protection in developing countries. It also spotlighted the north-south split (the split between nations of the Northern and Southern Hemispheres) between industrialized and developing nations—a controversy that would re-emerge over the next two decades. In 1992, the Gallup International Institute's Health of the Planet survey showed that concern about the environment was not limited to wealthy industrialized nations of the Northern Hemisphere. In half of the 22 nations surveyed, environmental problems were rated as one of the three most serious problems, and only small percentages of people in any nation dismissed environmental issues as not serious. The survey found that air and water pollution were perceived as the most serious environmental problems affecting nations, with the loss of natural resources mentioned most often by residents of other nations.[49] The Bush administration's global focus was on trade, however, rather than on the environment. The president all but ignored the 1992 Earth Summit, opening the door, some hoped, for a candidate who would bring an end to the Reagan/Bush policies.

GLOBAL AWARENESS AND GRIDLOCK:
1993–2000

The inauguration of President Bill Clinton and Vice President Al Gore in 1993 marked yet another turning point in environmental politics. The vice president was widely known as an aggressive advocate of environmental regulation and author of a best-selling call to environmental arms, titled *Earth in the Balance*.[50] The president gave Gore responsibility for developing the administration's environmental policies, pleasing environmental group leaders who believed Clinton was going to follow through on his campaign pledges. Although the environment never surfaced as a key issue in the 1992 presidential campaign, Clinton administration officials immediately called for peaceful coexistence between environmentalists and business as the administration prepared its legislative agenda. Early in 1993, the Clinton administration proposed sweeping changes in public lands policies, including raising grazing fees and imposing hard-rock mining royalties and below-cost timber sales in national forests, as part of a budget bill aimed at reducing the federal deficit. The proposals were immediately attacked by members of Congress from western states, many of whom were Democrats or represented states where Clinton had won in 1992; as a result, the president quickly retreated and shifted his attention to other policy initiatives.

In October 1993, the administration's initiative to add grazing-fee hikes and new environmental safeguards for grazing lands to the Interior Department appropriations bill failed when the Senate was unsuccessful in ending a filibuster of the bill by Republicans and western Democrats. The proposals were eventually dropped from the bill, but not until western Senators blasted the administration as launching a war on the West. However, while the Senate resisted changes, the media gave increasingly favorable attention to Secretary Bruce Babbitt's efforts to get westerners to pay fair prices for using public lands and to increase environmental protection. Babbitt's agenda of reorienting the Bureau of Reclamation away from dam building and toward water conservation, amending the Endangered Species Act to increase habitat preservation, and updating mining and logging policies raised tremendous opposition among some in the West while encouraging many others who believed such changes to be long overdue. Babbitt argued that public lands policy should be guided by the idea of "dominant public use," requiring the preservation of ecosystems, rather than "multiple use," in which logging, mining, and ranching interests dominate. Babbitt argued that dominant public use requires policy makers to look at the needs for biodiversity, watershed protection, and landscape, as well as the opportunities for extractive industries, and to set priorities accordingly.[51] However, by the time Congress adjourned in 1994, the only conservationist legislation that had been enacted created two new national parks in California, Death Valley and Joshua Tree, and a third protected area, the Mojave Desert.

In 1994, Republican candidates in a number of western states were successful in running against Babbitt and Clinton's western lands reforms. The Republicans effectively integrated attacks on Democrats for launching a war on the West with antitax, anti-Washington, and antiregulation rhetoric.

The election in 1994 of a Republican Congress shifted the attention to the economic costs and regulatory burdens of environmental protection. There was a growing belief that environmental politics had been guided by popular opinion rather than by science. Critics pointed to sweeping governmental regulations enacted during the Reagan and Bush administrations to reduce concentrations of toxic compounds in water, air, and land even when there was little scientific evidence of risk to humans. Congress, responding to highly publicized concerns about the dangers of asbestos, radon, and toxic waste dumps, quickly wrote legislation that has resulted in costing the government and business an estimated $140 billion a year. Even William Reilly, the EPA administrator under Bush, has said that action in the past was "based on responding to the nightly news. What we have had in the United States is environmental agenda-setting by episodic panic."[52]

When the American economy was relatively healthy, few bothered to question the cost-benefit ratio for such expenditures. But with resources growing increasingly scarce and with the federal government placing a new emphasis on domestic problems like crime, drugs, health care, and the urban infrastructure, this questioning of environmental priorities seemed long overdue. The 1994 House Republican Contract with America, written by Newt Gingrich and other Republican House leaders, outlined a set of national issues for House Republican candidates to run on and, after the Republicans won, played a major role in shaping the policy agenda. Among other things, the contract promised to "roll back government regulations and create jobs."[53] Frank Lutz, the Republican pollster who worked with Gingrich in creating the Contract with America, told his clients that "Americans believe Washington has gone too far in regulating and they want to turn the clock and paperwork back." Party strategist William Kristol suggested that Republicans immediately identify regulatory "excesses," and he organized a meeting entitled, "What to Kill First: Agencies to Dismantle, Programs to Eliminate, and Regulations to Stop." William Niskanen, head of the Cato Institute, called on Congress to "rein in what I call the 'Nanny State.' Stop telling states where to set speed limits. . . . Stop telling businesses about whether and when employees and customers may smoke."[54] Heritage Foundation analysts published "real life 'horror' stories of individuals who have lost their property or had their business harmed because of overzealous government regulators" and offered the following agenda for reforming regulation: force environmental agencies to base their evaluations of proposed regulations on sound scientific criteria; place a ceiling on the estimated total cost of all regulations promulgated by the agency; force regulators to account for the costs of their proposals, whenever possible; insist that regulators rely on markets rather than red tape; and enact legislation specifying exactly when the federal government must compensate property owners for regulatory takings.[55]

The Contract with America did not mention the environment directly, but it included numerous provisions aimed at reducing regulation and promoting economic development rather than preservation. These provisions included requirements that Congress fund the regulatory mandates imposed on states and that agencies perform cost-benefit analyses before issuing regulations, reduce paperwork requirements, compensate landowners for costs resulting from regulation, and formulate a regulatory budget of compliance costs being imposed on business. Republicans in Congress sought to reduce environmental regulation by cutting EPA and Interior Department budgets, attaching riders to appropriations bills that reduced specific protections, and introducing major rewrites of the leading environmental laws.

Another View, Another Voice

Republicans for Environmental Protection America

The assertion that "We're Republicans, too, but we're embarrassed to admit it," may have been the clarion call for conservation-minded Republican reformers who created their own environmental organization in 1995. Sometimes called "Green Elephants," Republicans for Environmental Protection (REP) America's estimated 2,500 members have opposed Bush administration policies and nominees as "the environmental conscience of the GOP."

The Albuquerque, New Mexico–based organization notes that the Republican Party was once a leader on environmental issues, based on the legacy of Theodore Roosevelt and other presidents like Calvin Coolidge, Dwight Eisenhower, and Richard Nixon. "Conservation is fundamentally conservative. Republican Party values of fiscal prudence, reducing waste, love of country, and responsibility to future generations mesh neatly with environmental goals," says one of the group's founders.

The foremost goal of REP America is to make the environment a two-party issue. From a contemporary historical perspective, the Democratic Party has benefited most from environmentalists' support, with little competition for votes from Republicans. Attempts to "green up" the GOP are one part of the strategy as a way of making both parties focus more on environmental protection and ensure progress on key legislative issues. They cite senators Lincoln Chafee (R-RI) and Peter Fitzgerald (R-IL) and members of Congress like Sherwood Boehlert (R-NY), Connecticut's Christopher Shays, and Wayne Gilchrest (R-MD) as exemplars of those working to continue the party's conservation legacy.

Although its political action committee, REP PAC, has few monetary resources to contribute to the campaigns of Republicans who advocate stronger pollution control laws and energy policies, REP America has adopted the strategy of increasing its clout by joining with other groups like the American Council for Renewable Energy, the Alaska Wilderness Coalition, and the Natural Resource Council of America. They have also piggybacked on blocs of other conservation voters through gun clubs, shooting-range owners, hunters, and fishing enthusiasts.

Recognizing that the group cannot move from the margins of the political arena without significant changes, the organization developed a four-year plan that would build capacity in 2005–2008. Like many similar groups, REP America seeks to establish a presence in Washington, D.C. by hiring a government affairs director, opening an office, and conducting regular planning meetings with members of Congress. Another high priority is the convening of conferences, briefings, and issue reports for distribution to the public, other conservation groups, and the media. Because its membership is nationwide but small, REP America also plans to launch a high-level membership campaign and to increase outreach.

ConservAmerica, the group's sister organization, is designed to build a conservative constituency for environmental protection, but as a nonpartisan, nonprofit organization with charitable tax status. It produces a booklet, *Conservation Is Conservative!* and is responsible for policy and research.

REP America did not endorse either President Bush or his opponent, John Kerry, in the 2004 presidential race. The group's communication director noted, "There's just no leadership from D.C., and aggressive national leadership must come from the Oval Office."

Instead, it hopes to build a war chest to support conservation-minded Republican congressional candidates in 2006, and in 2008, to participate in the Republican Party's convention and development of its platform.

———

SOURCES:
Margo Horner, "Green Elephants," *The Planet,* Winter 2003, at www.planet.wwu.edu/winter03, accessed December 30, 2004.
Martha Marks, "Greening the Elephant," *Grist Magazine,* May 13, 2003, at www.gristmagazine.com, accessed July 31, 2004.
Martha Marks, "The Green Old Party," *Sierra,* July–August 2004, at www.sierraclub.org/sierra/200407, accessed July 31, 2004.
Paul Rauber, "Green Elephants," *Sierra,* March–April 2003, at www.sierraclub.org/sierra/200303, accessed December 30, 2004.
REP America at www.repamerica.org
Geordie Romer, "'Green Elephants' Abandon Bush," *High Country News 36,* no. 20 (October 25, 2004).

However, Republican efforts to reduce environmental regulation were short-lived. To begin with, environmental groups challenged the new Republican agenda in the spring of 1995. The largest environmental organizations proposed an Environmental Bill of Rights, to be signed by Americans throughout the nation and presented to Congress and the White House.[56] President Clinton began vetoing appropriations bills with provisions aimed at reducing environmental protection and saw his popularity climb. That encouraged more vetoes and more challenges to the Republican agenda, and by 1996, the Republicans had abandoned their attacks on environmental laws and programs. Clinton skillfully positioned himself between the Republican radicals and popular environmental programs during the 1996 presidential campaign, and his reelection was, in part, the result of his willingness to challenge the congressional Republicans' deregulatory agenda. Bruce Babbitt had become one of the most popular members of the Clinton administration, and he led the criticism of the Republican Congress, which contributed greatly to the president's political rehabilitation in 1996. He was most effective at drawing attention to the Republican Congress's environmental agenda, particularly when he charged that some Republicans were seeking to sell off the national parks. Babbitt's shift from public lands issues in the West to national environmental issues defused criticism of him from inside the administration and in the environmental community.[57] Congress and the White House came together to pass new pesticide and safe drinking-water laws in the summer of 1996, which were widely heralded as examples of the potential of bipartisan environmentalism. But the demands for more environmental protection and less burdensome regulation are not easily satisfied, a factor that characterized environmental politics in Clinton's second term.

President Clinton began his second term on the heels of a Harris public opinion poll that showed (despite Republican claims to the contrary) that Americans continued to favor strong environmental policies and did not support reducing the powers of the EPA. Researchers found that over half those surveyed believed that the EPA is needed now more than when it was founded.[58] The study confirmed the findings of another Harris Poll conducted just a few months earlier that found 60 percent of the public opposed to the Republicans' efforts at environmental deregulation, which indeed had failed miserably during Clinton's first term. By 1998, the Harris Poll "feel good index," which measures how people feel about their lives, noted substantial increases in the number of respondents who felt good about the quality of the air, water, and environment where they live and work.[59]

Against this backdrop, many assumed that the president would capitalize on rising public support for environmental protection by proposing new initiatives or the reform of older laws like the Endangered Species Act and Superfund. But Clinton's administration became so engrossed in dealing with scandal and impeachment proceedings that the last four years of his term as president are marked by few notable environmental achievements. The business of retaining the presidency in times that were tumultuous both nationally and globally left Clinton neither time nor congressional support for proposals that environmental groups had long hoped would be passed. Despite his 1993 pledge, Clinton and Vice President Al Gore were more often seen at largely symbolic photo opportunities with the press than at bill-signing ceremonies in the White House.

Clinton and Gore observed Earth Day in April 1998 by traveling to Harper's Ferry, West Virginia, to help volunteers maintain America's longest footpath, the 2,157-mile-long Appalachian Trail. The president used the occasion to urge Congress to "end its attacks on the environment and help build on America's conservation legacy."[60] Later that year they went to the New River in North Carolina to formally designate 14 American Heritage Rivers.

While the president used the Council on Environmental Quality to trumpet an accelerated cleanup of toxic waste sites and a reduction of paperwork at the EPA,[61] several other initiatives hit a dead end. For example, the administration's efforts at issuing more stringent air quality standards were struck down by a federal court in 1999. The EPA had tried to issue new regulations for particulate matter and ozone, but the court ruled that the standards had not been based on public health concerns and thus constituted an unconstitutional delegation of power to the agency by Congress.[62] Attempts to strengthen right-to-know laws about toxic chemical releases were overshadowed by research that showed existing laws to be ineffective. In mid-1999, a study by the Environmental Working Group showed that almost 4 of every 10 factories tracked by the EPA over a two-year period were guilty of significant violations of air quality regulations. The study noted that although major violations were punishable by fines that could have ranged into the millions of dollars, government officials had disregarded guidelines for setting the amounts, and in some cases, offending firms paid no penalty at all. The report blamed the EPA for poor oversight and state regulators for enforcement failures.[63] A 1999 EPA study also found that, rather than meeting the administration's goals of a reduction in toxic chemical releases, the amount of toxic chemicals released into the environment by industrial plants had actually increased. The report attributed the increase to factories sending their metal wastes to landfills instead of to recycling centers, thus ending years of steady decline in toxic chemicals entering the environment.[64] But the president did herald the fact that the administration had established a Brownfields National Partnership, which brought together the resources of more than a dozen federal agencies to help thousands of communities clean up abandoned pieces of land that had been contaminated by previous industrial use. Moreover, in October 1999, Clinton used his weekly radio address to announce that, effective January 1, 2000, new rules would significantly lower the amount of 27 dangerous chemicals, including dioxin, that companies could use before reporting discharges to the public.

Clinton could point to some victories in the area of natural resource protection. For example, the federal government agreed to acquire mining property near Yellowstone National Park and to decontaminate the site from the effects of earlier mining activities. Among the more noteworthy preservation accomplishments was the acquisition of the largest privately owned stand of ancient redwoods in the Headwaters Forest in northern California—a deal negotiated among the landowner, the federal government, and the state. The president also sought funds to continue the restoration of the South Florida ecosystem and to purchase 50,000 additional acres of land on the northern edge of Everglades National Park—issues important to the region's politically powerful leaders.

On a global level, the administration called on a reluctant Congress for more bilateral and multilateral environmental assistance to address issues such as biodiversity and to fund contributions to the United Nations' environmental agencies. In the area of global climate change, the United States participated in negotiations calling for cuts in greenhouse gas emissions, which became formalized as the Kyoto Protocol in December 1997; but by the end of the decade, there was little sign that the projected reductions would be realized. Although the United States signed the treaty in 1998, Clinton could not persuade Congress to ratify the agreement or to begin implementing the necessary reductions in greenhouse gas emissions.

Clinton's "commonsense environmental reforms," such as helping American business compete more effectively in the global market through environmental technology, were not new, and they lacked the luster of even the Bush administration's environmental efforts. The president had, for the most part, piggybacked on proposals that preceded his administration, thus disappointing environmental leaders who had supported the Clinton-Gore ticket as a potential for reawakening the nation's environmental conscience. Those hopes became lost in issues that, by the end of 1999, had pushed the environment almost to the bottom of the political agenda: sexual scandals, impeachment, conflict in the Balkans, and violence in the workplace and the schools.

Most observers have commented that, although there was some disappointment that the Clinton-Gore ticket failed to live up to its advance billing as proactive on environmental protection, the administration was able to stop the Republican-controlled Congress from dismantling controversial laws like the Endangered Species Act or cutting agency budgets, as had been feared. Clinton abolished the controversial Council on Competitiveness and was widely praised for his appointees. The Clinton administration was able to build on the groundwork laid by congressional leaders and environmental organizations. His goal, Clinton said, was to block attempts to roll back safeguards for the nation's food, water, and air: "I want an America in the year 2000 where no child should have to live near a toxic waste dump, where no parent should have to worry about the safety of a child's glass of water, and no neighborhood should be put in harm's way by pollution from a nearby factory."[65]

In the 2000 presidential race neither candidate Al Gore nor George W. Bush paid much attention to the environment as an issue. Gore received endorsements from environmental groups like the Sierra Club and the League of Conservation Voters, but seemed to abandon his once ambitious environmental agenda. Just months before the election, a Gallup Poll survey found that 29 percent of the respondents considered the candidates' position on the issue of the environment extremely important, ranking it ninth overall behind issues such as education, the economy, health care, and Social Security. According to the poll,

> The environment's mid-range importance in terms of the presidential race this year is similar to the relatively low "seriousness" rating Americans give it in relation to other problems facing the country. Only a slim majority of Americans believed that environmental problems are an extremely or very serious problem—putting it fifth on the list of seven problems tested.[66]

ROLLBACK: 2001–

Just prior to leaving office in January 2001, Clinton decided to wield his power as president, using the 1906 American Antiquities Act, to make last-minute designations of national monuments—actions that some believe salvaged his environmental record. While the move pleased environmental leaders, it added more responsibilities to an already financially strapped National Park Service. The actions also infuriated members of Congress, who felt the designations had been made without appropriate consultation with political leaders or the public. They responded by opening the 2001 session with a series of bills designed to repeal the president's actions.

After the bitter presidential race, it was clear that George W. Bush did not assume office with a policy mandate, especially an environmental one. His appointments set the tone for his actions, with critics noting that many of the key positions were given to corporate interests, especially those in the oil industry. His appointee for secretary of energy, Spencer Abraham, was a longtime opponent of increasing fuel efficiency standards. Gale Norton, named secretary of the interior, was a supporter of opening up oil drilling in the Alaska National Wildlife Refuge, and she had served under controversial Reagan appointee James Watt. Ann Veneman, secretary of agriculture, had served on the board of directors for the first company to bring genetically engineered food to consumers.

Bush and Congress may have been trying to gauge public opinion about environmental problems in the new millennium as the president developed his own environmental agenda. If that were the case, they would have found that Americans were anxious, but moderate in their views. In a Gallup Poll survey in March 2001, almost half of those surveyed viewed the current state of environmental conditions in the United States as "good" or "excellent," with 42 percent saying they worry "a great deal" about the quality of the environment. Combining the two ratings, only a quarter of Americans are "highly concerned" about the environment. Yet when asked what steps are necessary to address the Earth's environmental problems, 27 percent report that "immediate and drastic" action is needed.[67]

The nation's economic situation clearly affected other poll results, which showed that 57 percent say protection of the environment should be given priority over economic growth—down from 67 percent in 2000. About a third favored giving priority to economic growth, "even if the environment suffers to some extent," an all-time high for the measure. When asked what they thought was the most important problem facing the country, respondents ranked the environment 16th on the list, and only 2 percent of respondents named it as the primary issue.[68]

During his first term, Bush made clear that his environmental agenda would be different from that of his predecessor. On his first day in office, Bush ordered a 60-day moratorium on all Clinton regulations and executive orders that had not yet gone into effect, including the controversial monument designations. He retracted his campaign pledge and support for regulating carbon dioxide emissions at power plants and announced that the United States would not adhere to the limits on emissions that were part of the Kyoto Protocol. Shortly after the announcement, he went a step further by saying that the United States would withdraw from the treaty altogether. The abrupt change angered environmental groups and the rest of the world's leaders, who met in Johannesburg in 2002 in an attempt to finalize global climate change policies. Bush refused to attend, sending secretary of state Colin Powell instead. But the president was on solid ground in terms of public opinion. Surveys showed that most Americans believe the effects of global warming are already occurring or likely to occur in their lifetime. But barely one third of those questioned predicted that global warming will pose a serious threat to their way of life. When asked about the environmental issue they worry about most, respondents ranked global warming 12th out of the 13 issues tested—just barely ahead of acid rain.[69]

The Bush administration has been compared to that of Ronald Reagan, especially in relation to oversight of the regulatory process. The president has called for stricter cost-benefit analyses and more rigorous risk assessment studies prior to the approval of any new environmental regulations. Critics believe this opens up the process to industry interests, which have a greater influence on policy making than ever before. Vice President Dick Cheney quickly filled the role of the president's surrogate on energy policy (discussed in Chapter 6), which, along with energy-related air quality issues, were at the forefront of political maneuvering.

Most noticeably, however, Bush made clear his intention to do whatever he could to roll back the Clinton administration's environmental efforts, along with 30 years of legislation to protect natural resources. On May 20, 2002, the Council on Environmental Quality (CEQ) established the National Environmental Policy Act (NEPA) Task Force, charged with reviewing current practices and procedures. While the charge to the group sounded harmless at first, environmental organizations quickly realized that the administration planned to water down if not altogether repeal the law. The director of the task force denied reports the group was out to gut NEPA, saying, "We're out there to try to make it better. In common parlance, we want to cut the fat if there's fat out there and we want to beef up the beef."[70] An April 2002 memorandum from the Chair of the CEQ stated that the task force would "focus on modernizing the NEPA process," citing the terrorist attacks of September 11, 2002 as one reason for the analysis of the law.[71] Another target of the administration was the Northwest Forest Plan, which was adopted in 1993 after the Forest Summit in Portland, Oregon, to set aside millions of acres of federal forests to protect endangered wildlife, but still allowed the logging of nearly 1 billion board feet of timber annually. An April 2002 U.S. Forest Service internal memo entitled "Fixes to the Northwest Forest Plan" telegraphed the administration's plans to increase timber production on lands previously off–limits to harvesting. The president has the authority to make changes to the Forest Plan without Congressional approval.[72] The administration followed through on its pledge to streamline NEPA, and by October 2002, the House of Representatives had already held hearings and was in the process of amending proposals to repeal portions of the law.

One of the president's major legislative achievements during his first term was passage of the Healthy Forests Restoration Act, which he signed in December 2003. The law and its accompanying regulatory framework (discussed in Chapter 4) began to serve as a template for similar strategies on issues from grazing to mining. He revived efforts to permit oil exploration and drilling in the Arctic National Wildlife Refuge and continued to support efforts to open a long–term nuclear waste site in Nevada.

Results from public opinion polls during Bush's first term reinforced his choice of positions on key environmental issues. The Gallup/CNN/*USA Today* polls conducted between April 2001 and January 2005 showed that the president's approval ratings for how he was handling the environment went from 46 to 53 percent; the ABC News/*Washington Post* surveys from March 2001 to January 2005 ranged from a low approval rating of 41 percent in June 2001 to a high of 54 percent in January 2002. A more extensive PSRA/*Newsweek* poll found that the percentage of those who approved the president's handling of the environment remained consistently higher than the percentage of those who disapproved of his performance between April 2001 and January 2004.[73]

Any hopes that environmental advocates might have had that the 2004 presidential campaign might put the spotlight on problems like pollution and sustainability were quickly deflected and, for the most part, the environment was a nonissue. Democratic presidential nominee John Kerry received the League of Conservation Voters endorsement for his "unparalleled record on environmental issues," along with the support of 48 Nobel Prize–winning scientists. But the issues of terrorism, the continuing war in Iraq, and accusations over Kerry's Vietnam War record allowed Bush to sidestep any serious consideration of issues his opponent tried to raise. Bush defeated Kerry by more than 3 million popular votes and 34 electoral college votes.

At the start of Bush's second term, his environmental approval ratings began to drop. PSRA/*Newsweek* reported that 45 percent of those surveyed in March 2005 said they disapproved of the way in which the president was handling the environment, and 41 percent approved. That dip in rankings corresponds to the March 2005 poll by Harris Interactive, which found an even larger gap, with 36 percent approving and 47 percent disapproving. The numbers do not appear to be tied to any particular environmental issue or problem, but they do correlate to the public's growing disapproval of the Iraq war and backlash against a proposed revision of Social Security regulations.[74]

Overall, the Bush administration appears to have solidified its environmental agenda from both a partisan and strategic perspective. Republican members of Congress have been tutored in how to stay "on message" and how to neutralize opposition. Those who might potentially flee from the fold have been brought back by framing environmental problems as being caused by bureaucratic red tape and unnecessary regulatory hurdles, so that they need not appear to be anti-environmental. One confidential memo advised members to "use the three words Americans are looking for in an environmental policy: 'safer,' 'cleaner,' and 'healthier'" and to "emphasize common sense." Despite numerous environmental report cards from advocacy groups that criticized the Bush administration's approach to environmental policy, the president's focus on foreign policy allowed numerous regulatory actions and legislative initiatives to proceed almost without focused opposition. The administration had found a successful strategy for pushing its environmental agenda without making it seem like it was on the policy agenda at all.

NOTES

1. This phrase is often attributed to Pinchot, although the context varies. According to historian Char Miller, "the 'greatest good' concept is imbedded in the 1905 letter to Pinchot from James Wilson, secretary of agriculture, in which the mission of the new Forest Service is outlined, a letter that Pinchot ghostwrote." See Char Miller, *Gifford Pinchot and the Making of Modern Environmentalism* (Washington, DC: Shearwater Books, 2004), 406–407.

2. USDA Forest Service, "Join Us in Caring for Our Natural Legacy," at www.fs.fed.us/centennial, accessed May 1, 2005.

3. Gerald W. Williams, "Centennial Congress History," February 4, 2004, at www.natlforests.org/centennial/history, accessed May 1, 2005.

4. There is an extensive literature chronicling the development of forest history in the United States, from the early policies to the Forest Service itself. See, for example, Paul Hirt, *A Conspiracy of Optimism: The Management of the National Forest Since World War Two* (Lincoln: University of Nebraska Press, 1994); M. Nelson McGeary, *Gifford Pinchot: Forester-Politician* (Princeton: Princeton University Press, 1960); Char Miller, ed., *American Forests: Nature, Culture, and Politics* (Lawrence: University Press of Kansas, 1997); Harold T. Pinkett, *Gifford Pinchot: Private and Public Forester* (Urbana: University of Illinois Press, 1970); Harold K. Steen, *The U.S. Forest Service* (Seattle: University of Washington Press, 1970); and Michael Williams, *Americans and Their Forests: A Historical Geography* (New York: Cambridge University Press, 1989). Pinchot himself was a prolific author, as seen in his books, *A Primer of* Forestry (Washington, DC: U.S. Government Printing Office, 1899); *Breaking New Ground* (New York: Harcourt Brace, 1947); *Fishing Talk* (Harrisburg, PA: Stackpole Books, 1993); *The Fight for Conservation* (New York: Doubleday, 1910); and *The Use of the National Forests* (Washington, DC: U.S. Department of Agriculture, 1907).

5. USDA Forest Service, "About Us: Meet the Forest Service," at www.fs.fed.us/aboutus/meetfs, accessed April 4, 2005.

6. USDA Forest Service, "New Century of Service: Fact Sheet," at www.fs.fed.us/newcentury/fact_sheet, accessed May 1, 2005.

7. John W. Kingdon, *Agendas, Alternatives, and Public Policies,* 2nd ed. (New York: Longman, 2003), 96.

8. For more on the development of environmental awareness, see Roderick Nash, in *American Environmentalism,* 3rd ed. (New York: McGraw-Hill, 1990); *The American Conservation Movement* (St. Charles, MO: Forum, 1974); *Wilderness and the American Mind* (New Haven: Yale University Press, 1982); and *The Rights of Nature: A History of Environmental Ethics* (Madison: University of Wisconsin Press, 1988).

9. Nash, *American Environmentalism,* xi.

10. David Cushan Coyle, *Conservation* (New Brunswick, NJ: Rutgers University Press, 1957), 8–9, 21.

11. George Perkins Marsh, *Man and Nature; or Physical Geography as Modified by Human Action* (New York: Scribner, 1864). See also David Lowenthal, *George Perkins Marsh: Versatile Vermonter* (New York: Columbia University Press, 1958).

12. Donald Worster, *American Environmentalism: The Formative Period, 1860–1915* (New York: Wiley, 1973), 3.

13. Among the historians who have researched the sportsmen's movement is John E. Reiger; see *American Sportsmen and the Origins of Conservation* (Norman: University of Oklahoma Press, 1986).

14. Ibid., 53.

15. The biographical materials on these early pioneers provide an excellent background on the formation of the early conservation movement. See, for example, George T. Morgan Jr., *William B. Greeley, A Practical Forester* (St. Paul, MN: Forest History Society, 1961); and Wallace Stegner, *Beyond the Hundredth Meridian: John Wesley Powell and the Second Coming of the West* (Boston: Houghton Mifflin, 1954).

16. Another major contributor to the field of American environmental history is Joseph Petulla; see *Environmental Protection in the United States* (San Francisco: San Francisco Study Center, 1987).

17. Suellen Hoy, "Municipal Housekeeping: The Role of Women in Improving Urban Sanitation Practices," in *Pollution and Reform in American Cities 1870–1930,* ed. Martin Melosi (Austin: University of Texas Press, 1980), 173–198.

18. See Harold McCracken, *George Catlin and the Old Frontier* (New York: Dial, 1959), for a biographical perspective on one of the frontier environmentalists.

19. There are two ways to gauge Thoreau's impact on the development of the environmental movement, especially his sojourn at Walden Pond. One is to read his own words, such as *The Annotated Walden* (New York: Potter, 1970) and *Consciousness in Concord* (Boston: Houghton Mifflin, 1958). Many biographers have attempted to characterize this complex individual; see Milton Meltzer and Walter Harding, *A Thoreau Profile* (New York: Crowell, 1962); Sherman Paul, *The Shores of America: Thoreau's Inward Exploration* (Urbana: University of Illinois Press, 1959); and Robert Richardson, *Henry Thoreau: A Life of the Mind* (Berkeley: University of California Press, 1986).

20. The urban sanitation issue became one of the cornerstones of urban environmentalism. See George Rosen, *A History of Public Health* (New York: MD Publications, 1958).

21. See Suellen Hoy, *Chasing Dirt: The American Pursuit of Cleanliness* (New York: Oxford University Press, 1995), 117–120.

22. Few comprehensive studies of the early organizations exist, except for those produced by the groups themselves. See, for example, Michael Cohen, *The History of the Sierra Club 1892–1970* (San Francisco: Sierra Club, 1988).

23. For more information on this early period, see Henry Clepper, *Origins of American Conservation* (New York: Ronald Press, 1966); and Peter Wild, *Pioneer Conservationists of Western America* (Missoula, MT: Mountain Press, 1979).

24. Samuel P. Hays, *Conservation and the Gospel of Efficiency* (Cambridge: Harvard University Press, 1959), 5.

25. To see how Pinchot's view contrasted with Muir's, see Muir's books, *Our National Parks* (Boston: Houghton Mifflin, 1901), and *The Yosemite* (New York: Century, 1912). One of the most widely researched environmental pioneers, Muir has been the subject of dozens of biographers, including Michael P. Cohen, *The Pathless Way: John Muir and the American Wilderness* (Madison: University of Wisconsin Press, 1984); Stephen Fox, *John Muir and His Legacy* (Boston: Little, Brown, 1981); Frederick Turner, *Rediscovering America: John Muir in His Time and Ours* (New York: Viking, 1985); and Linnie M. Wolfe, *Son of the Wilderness: The Life of John Muir* (New York: Knopf, 1945).

26. Hays, *Conservation and the Gospel of Efficiency,* 132.

27. The activities of the Conservation Congresses are outlined by Grant McConnell in "The Conservation Movement—Past and Present," *Western Political Quarterly, 7,* no. 3 (September 1954): 463–478.

28. Hays, *Conservation and the Gospel of Efficiency,* 69.

29. Many historians and analysts of the Progressive period have downgraded its importance to contemporary environmentalism. See Geoffrey Wandesforde-Smith, "Moral Outrage and the Progress of Environmental Policy: What Do We Tell the Next Generation about How to Care for the Earth?" in *Environmental Policy in the 1990s,* ed. Norman J. Vig and Michael E. Kraft (Washington, DC: Congressional Quarterly Press, 1990), 334–335.

30. For a discussion of the evolution of public health and environmental protection, see Robert Gottlieb, *Forcing the Spring: The Transformation of the American Environmental Movement* (Washington, DC: Island Press, 2005).

31. For a summary of the development of the parks and wilderness areas, see Dyan Zaslowsky and the Wilderness Society, *These American Lands* (New York: Henry Holt, 1986).

32. There is a wealth of historical information on the National Park Service and its programs, including the following books: William C. Everhart, *The National Park Service* (New York: Praeger, 1972); Ronald A. Foresta, *America's National Parks and Their Keepers* (Washington, DC: Resources for the Future, 1984); Alfred Runte, *National Parks: The American Experience* (Lincoln: University of Nebraska Press, 1982); David J. Simon, ed., *Our Common Lands* (Washington, DC: Island Press, 1988); and *Investing in Park Futures: A Blueprint for Tomorrow* (Washington, DC: National Parks Conservation Association, 1988).

33. Rachel Carson, *Silent Spring* (Greenwich, CT: Fawcett, 1962). For biographical material on the woman who is largely credited with reviving the contemporary environmental movement, see Paul Brooks, *The House of Life: Rachel Carson at Work* (Boston: Houghton Mifflin, 1972); Carol Gartner, *Rachel Carson* (New York: Ungar, 1983); H. Patricia Hynes, *The Recurring Silent Spring* (New York: Pergamon Press, 1989); and Philip Sterling, *Sea and Earth: The Life of Rachel Carson* (New York: Crowell, 1970).

34. Paul Ehrlich, *The Population Bomb* (New York: Ballantine, 1968).

35. For an account of this event, see Carol Steinhart and John Steinhart, *Blowout: A Case Study of the Santa Barbara Oil Spill* (Belmont, CA: Wadsworth, 1972). An extensive bibliography on the spill was compiled by Kay Walstead, *Oil Pollution in the Santa Barbara Channel* (Santa Barbara: University of California, Santa Barbara Library, 1972).

36. Zaslowsky, *These American Lands,* 37.

37. See Lewis L. Gould, *Lady Bird Johnson and the Environment* (Lawrence: University of Kansas Press, 1988). See also Cormac O'Brien, *The Secret Lives of the First Ladies* (Austin, TX: Eakin Press, 2005).

38. John C. Esposito, *Vanishing Air* (New York: Grossman, 1970), 292.

39. Samuel P. Hays, "From Conservation to Environment," *Environmental Review, 6* (Fall 1982): 37.

40. Jack Lewis, "The Spirit of the First Earth Day," *EPA Journal, 16,* no. 1 (January–February 1990): 9–10.

41. See John C. Whitaker, *Striking a Balance: Environment and Natural Resources Policy in the Nixon-Ford Years* (Washington, DC: American Enterprise Institute, 1976), 6.

42. Samuel P. Hays, *Beauty, Health and Permanence: Environmental Politics in the U.S., 1955–1985* (Cambridge: Cambridge University Press, 1987), 61.

43. See Lois Gibbs, *Love Canal* (Albany: State University of New York Press, 1983); and Adeline Gordon Levine, *Love Canal: Science, Politics and People* (Lexington, MA: Heath, 1982).

44. Robert Cameron Mitchell, "The Public Speaks Again: A New Environmental Survey," *Resources, 60* (September–October 1978): 2.

45. David Rapp, "Special Report," *Congressional Quarterly,* January 20, 1990, 138.

46. "Household Waste Threatening Environment; Recycling Helps Ease Disposal Problem," *Gallup Report 280,* January 1990, 30–34.

47. See Riley E. Dunlap, "Public Opinion in the 1980s: Clear Consensus, Ambiguous Commitment," *Environment, 33,* no. 8 (October 1991): 9–15, 32–37.

48. George Gallup Jr. and Frank Newport, "Americans Strongly in Tune with the Purpose of Earth Day 1990," *Gallup Poll Monthly,* April 1990, 6.

49. The increasingly global nature of perceptions about the nature of environmental problems is illustrated by a series of public opinion polls conducted in 1992. See the press release "Environment Given Priority over Economic Growth in Both Rich and Poor Nations" (Washington, DC, George H. Gallup International Institute, May 4, 1992). See also Riley E. Dunlap, George H. Gallup Jr., and Alec M. Gallup, *The Health of the Planet Survey* (Washington, DC: George H. Gallup International Institute, May 1992).

50. Albert Gore, *Earth in the Balance* (Boston: Houghton Mifflin, 1992).

51. Margaret Kriz, "Quick Draw," *National Journal,* November 13, 1993, 2711–2716, quote on 2713.

52. Keith Schneider, "New View Calls Environmental Policy Misguided," *New York Times,* March 21, 1993, 1.

53. See Ed Gillespie and Rob Shellhas, eds., *Contract with America* (New York: Times Books, 1994): 125–141. For a discussion of the history and evolution of the Contract with America, see Elizabeth Drew, *Showdown: The Struggle between the Gingrich Congress and the Clinton White House* (New York: Simon and Schuster, 1996), 28–34.

54. Quoted in Cindy Skryzycki, "Hill Republicans Promise a Regulatory Revolution," *Washington Post,* January 4, 1995, A1.

55. Craig E. Richardson and Geoff C. Ziebart, *Red Tape in America: Stories from the Front Lines* (Washington, DC: Heritage Foundation, 1995), v.

56. B. J. Bergman, "Standing Up for the Planet," *Sierra* (March–April 1995): 79–80.

57. Tom Kenworthy, "In Smooth Water Now," *Washington Post National Weekly Edition,* December 11–17, 1995.

58. Harris Poll: Americans Want Conservation Laws," *Columbia University Record, 21,* no. 13 (January 19, 1996): 29.

59. Humphrey Taylor, "Nation's 'Feel Good Index' Rises Sharply," *The Harris Poll #26,* June 3, 1998.

60. White House news release, "President Clinton: Saving America's Natural Treasures," April 22, 1998.

61. White House. "Protecting the Environment: President Clinton and Vice President Gore," at www.whitehouse.gov/CEQ, accessed March 18, 2000.

62. *American Trucking Association v. U.S. Environmental Protection Agency,* 175 F3d 1027 (D.C. Cir., 1999).

63. Traci Watson, "Study: 4 of 10 Factories Violated Clean Air Act," *USA Today,* May 20, 1999, 3A.

64. "Toxic Chemical Release Rises," *Arizona Republic,* May 23, 1999, A28.

65. Protecting the Environment: President Clinton and Vice President Gore.

66. Joseph Carroll, "Environment Not Highest-Priority Issue This Election Year," *Gallup Poll Monthly,* No. 420 (September 2000), 15–16.

67. Riley E. Dunlap and Lydia Saad, "Only One in Four Americans Are Anxious About the Environment," *Gallup Poll Monthly,* No. 427 (April 2001), 6.

68. Ibid.

69. Frank Newport and Lydia Saad, "Americans Consider Global Warming Real, but Not Alarming," *Gallup Poll Monthly,* No. 427 (April 2001), 2–3.

70. Matthew Daly, "Bush Administration Takes Up Review of Landmark Environmental Law," *San Francisco Chronicle,* August 29, 2002, at www.sfgate.com, accessed August 30, 2002.

71. Memorandum, Council on Environmental Quality, "NEPA Task Force," April 10, 2002, at http://ceq.eh.doe.gov, accessed September 1, 2002

72. See "Internal Forest Service Memo Suggests Changes to Northwest Forest Plan," *The Forestry Source, 7,* no. 8 (August 2002), 1; Tom Detzel, "Bush Team Looks at Forest Plan Facelift," *The Oregonian,* August 26, 2002, at www.oregonlive.com/environment/oregonian, accessed September 1, 2002; Matthew Koehler, "Mark Rey Wants to Take Our Forests Away," *Forest Advocate,* Summer 2002, 1.

73. American Enterprise Institute, *Polls on the Environment,* at www.aei.org/docLib 11, accessed May 16, 2005

74. Ibid.

FURTHER READING

Harvey Blatt. *America's Environmental Report Card: Are We Making the Grade?* Cambridge, MA: MIT Press, 2005.

Dave Foreman. *Rewilding North America: A Vision of Conservation in the 21st Century.* Covelo, CA: Island Press, 2005.

Mark H. Lytle. *Gentle Subversive: Rachel Carson and the Rise of the Environmental Movement.* New York: Oxford University Press, 2005.

Char Miller. *Gifford Pinchot and the Making of Modern Environmentalism.* Covelo, CA: Island Press, 2004.

Priscilla Coit Murphy. *What a Book Can Do: The Publication and Reception of Silent Spring.* Amherst: University of Massachusetts Press, 2005.

Jouni Paavola and Ian Lowe. *Environmental Values in a Globalizing World*. Philadelphia: Taylor and Francis, 2005.

John F. Richards. *The Unending Frontier: An Environmental History of the Early Modern World*. Berkeley: University of California Press, 2006.

David B. Woolner and Henry L. Henderson, eds. *FDR and the Environment*. New York: Palgrave Macmillan, 2005.

2

Participants in the Environmental Debate

"We have become convinced that modern environmentalism, with all its unexamined assumptions, outdated concepts and exhausted strategies, must die so that something new can live."
—MICHAEL SHELLENBERGER AND TED NORDHAUS, "THE DEATH OF ENVIRONMENTALISM"[1]

Michael Shellenberger and Ted Nordhaus distributed an essay at the October 2004 meeting of the Environmental Grantmakers Association that angered and outraged environmental activists, provided fodder for conservative commentators, and led to heated debate among scholars, bloggers, and policy makers. "The Death of Environmentalism" was based on the authors' criticisms of single-issue movements, like environmentalism, that turn themselves into a special interest by defining problems narrowly and offering technical policy solutions instead of an inspiring vision.

In researching their essay, Shellenberger and Nordhaus interviewed two dozen of the nation's environmental leaders, most of whom are not household names. They are, however, the driving forces behind major organizations and stakeholders in the environmental debate. In the essay, the authors recommend that the environmental movement's leaders "take a step back to rethink everything. We will never be able to turn things around as long as we understand our failures as essentially tactical, and make proposals that are essentially technical."[2]

Shellenberger and Nordhaus use global warming as an example of a policy that has been a defeat for

Older women are key participants in protests, such as this blockade against Oregon's Biscuit timber sale.

LESLEY ADAMS

37

environmental groups because of a "failure to craft inspiring and powerful proposals" and the focus on the Kyoto Protocol as the only solution mechanism. "The size of this defeat can't be overstated. In exiting the Clinton years with no law to reduce carbon emissions—even by a minuscule amount—the environmental community has no more power or influence than it had when Kyoto was initiated." Similarly, they argue, environmentalists failed to gain support for changes in fuel efficiency standards because of an orientation they call "literal-sclerosis"—the belief that social change happens only when people speak a literal "truth to power."[3]

The essay concludes with a series of prescriptions.

> If environmentalists hope to become more than a special interest we must start framing our proposals around core American values and start seeing our own values as central to what motivates and guides our politics. Doing so is crucial if we are to build the political momentum—a sustaining movement—to pass and implement the legislation that will achieve action on global warming and other social issues.[4]

Another View, Another Voice

Michael Shellenberger and Ted Nordhaus
The authors of the controversial essay, "The Death of Environmentalism," deny accusations that they made exaggerations and generalizations for the sake of debate, although they admit it was written to be provocative and to get the attention of those who fund environmental advocacy. Their main goal, they say, was to "begin a discussion and a dialogue, not to suggest that we had all the answers."

Both men, who consider themselves "strategists," could be classified as policy entrepreneurs, with records of environmental activism that they have parlayed into a variety of companies and initiatives. Shellenberger, a graduate of the University of California, Santa Cruz, has been active in causes ranging from protection of the Headwaters Forest, a campaign to put Martin Luther King Jr.'s image on the $20 bill, the plight of Nike's factory workers, Wal-Mart's environmental and business practices, and a campaign to defeat the increased incarceration of children in adult jails and prisons. He cofounded California's largest public interest communications firm and the Apollo Alliance, a coalition of labor, environment, business, and civil rights leaders seeking to create new energy jobs and free the United States from its dependence on foreign oil. Shellenberger is the head of several organizations whose goal is to build a progressive political majority, including the Breakthrough Institute and a political consulting firm, Lumina Strategies. He cofounded a group, Defend Majority Rule, that opposed the recall election of California's governor, and in March 2004 he was a campaign strategist for the Humboldt County (California) District Attorney who faced a recall election funded by the timber industry.

Nordhaus is a partner in several of Shellenberger's projects and vice president of an opinion research firm. Graduating from the University of California, Berkeley, with a degree in history, he began his activist career in politics as a campaign director with the Public Interest Research Groups in California. He moved on to positions with organizations focused on water policy and as a strategist for the group, Next Generation, working with clients such as Environmental Defense, the California Futures Network, and Clean Water Action. Like his coauthor, Nordhaus has spread himself over a wide range of organizations such as the Headwaters Sanctuary Group and the Living Forest Project. In his current position, he specializes in land-use and transportation issues, interpreting survey research and moderating focus groups.

   What remains to be seen is the long-term impact, if any, of the two young men's attempts to shake up the environmental community and the grantmakers who fund advocacy groups. Shellenberger notes, "This paper is about coming to terms with change. Our message is that it's time to acknowledge both an end and a new beginning and not fear it."

SOURCES:
Apollo Alliance, at www.apolloalliance.org, accessed January 16, 2005
Ron Arnold, "The 'Death of Environmentalism' Controversy: Obituary? Or Sales Pitch?" at www.cdfe.org, accessed January 17, 2005.
Breakthrough Institute, at www.thebreakthrough.org, accessed January 16, 2005
Amanda Griscom Little, "An Interview with Authors of the Controversial Essay 'The Death of Environmentalism,'" Grist Magazine, January 13, 2005, at www.grist.org, accessed January 16, 2005.

Responses to the essay varied from support to stinging criticism, and from various political perspectives. Adam Werbach, who was elected president of the Sierra Club at age 23, spoke before San Francisco's Commonwealth Club in December 2004 on the topic, "Is Environmentalism Dead? A Speech on Where the Movement Can and Should Go From Here," echoing the Shellenberger and Nordhaus perspective.[5]

Werbach, who has coauthored articles with Shellenberger, said his assessment of the demise of the environmental movement rests on the premise that support for environmental protection has always been shallow, and not a major priority for Americans. He says the leadership must "create a new language, a new set of strategic initiatives, a new set of institutions, and a new metric for evaluating our success" that leads to becoming progressive Americans. Citing the defeat of John Kerry as an example, Werbach argues that the presidential election had been lost years before 2004 because environmentalists "are now in a minority position, with a minority party as our advocate." He outlines a series of recommendations ranging from taking over the Democratic Party and firing the movement's lobbyists and policy makers to dismantling environmental programs in foundations.[6]

Others who had been interviewed were not as kind. Carl Pope, executive director of the Sierra Club, called the essay "shoddy in its analysis" and "counterproductive." Phil Clapp, president of the National Environmental Trust, admitted that a reassessment of strategy was part of a healthy debate, but criticized Shellenberger and Nordhaus for engaging "in an enormous amount of rhetoric and diatribe." The executive director of the Natural Resources Defense Council, Frances Beinecke, defended current efforts that he believes do not reflect a dead movement but agrees that more energy needs to be focused on framing problems as human issues.[7] Conservatives were critical as well. Ron Arnold, a wise use advocate who heads the Center for the Defense of Free Enterprise, called Shellenberger and Nordhaus "issue entrepreneurs" and described the essay as "supercilious self-importance dressed up as simpering sincerity."[8]

Grassroots activists have a different perspective about the movement's future. Nearly three years after Oregon's Biscuit Fire charred 308,000 acres in the Siskiyou National Forest, protestors were still attempting to stop salvage logging to allow the forest to recover naturally. Two thirds of the 19,000 acres slated for logging are in late-successional reserves in one of the most diverse conifer forests in the world. Forty percent of the proposed timber sale is in federally designated roadless areas; 90 percent is within the watershed of the wild and scenic Illinois River.[9]

Small local groups, including the Siskiyou Project, Kalmiopsis Earth First! and the Cascadia Wildlands Project, held a series of protests in March 2005. One man chained himself to a pipe buried in the road leading to one timber sale. Joan Norman, who sat on a bridge in her walker to delay logging trucks, was one of the dozens of local residents who were arrested. "No," she told reporters, "I am not afraid. I am 72 years old. I would rather go out in a blaze, defending the world I love."[10] Meanwhile, larger national organizations such as Native Forest Network and Earthjustice fought the U.S. Forest Service's plans in the courts to determine whether the Biscuit project violates federal laws and policies.

Ironically, the burned timber is quickly decaying and losing its commercial value to the point where the Forest Service is lowering its predictions of potential revenues and scrambling to find bidders to do fuel reduction and restoration. Trees in some areas need to be taken out by helicopter; this task increases the cost of logging considerably. One of the area's largest mills showed no interest in bidding due to the low value of the burned trees. Agency staffers are concerned that the Forest Service will actually lose money; within less than two years after the fire, $5.8 million was spent on preparing environmental documents, early restoration, and timber prep work.[11]

Did the grassroots activists "win" in the battle over salvaging the Biscuit Fire timber? Will companies continue to fight efforts by environmental organizations to reduce if not eliminate logging in old-growth forests? Will the Bush administration circumvent the National Environmental Policy Act through rulemaking and planning processes that reduce public participation?

It has been argued that the key question is not whether environmentalism is dead, but whether the movement itself can continue to function using "old" strategies like civil disobedience, lobbying, and litigation. To examine the roles of participants in environmental policy making, this chapter begins with a look at the theoretical framework exemplified by Harold Lasswell, who sought to explain the science of politics as "who gets what, when, and how."[12]

The chapter continues with a discussion of how the concept of group theory can be used to explain how unofficial participants in the policy-making process influence environmental policy, deciphering the actions of the primary actors and stakeholders in the debate over the environment and natural resources. Adherents to this approach believe that political decisions are the result of the struggles among competing interests with access to the political process. Key to understanding group theory is the assumption that some groups will have more political access than others because of superior financial resources, leadership, organization, or public support for their cause.[13] Although this book does not attempt to delve into the theoretical debate over applying the pluralist tradition of American politics to other countries to explain their environmental politics, it does describe the role of international stakeholders in the environmental debate. The chapter begins with an overview of the major mainstream U.S. environmental organizations, followed by a discussion of the environmental justice movement, radical environmentalism, and the development of an environmental opposition. This is followed by an analysis of the role of the media in shaping public opinion and the environmental debate. In "Thinking Globally," the chapter then shifts to a discussion of international actors, ranging from nongovernmental organizations to the Green Party movement and to the international organizations that attempt to protect the environment on a global scale. The chapter touches briefly on these participants' strategies, successes, and failures and summarizes their participation in the policy-making process.

U.S. ENVIRONMENTAL ORGANIZATIONS

In the 100 years since the founding of the first American environmental associations, there has been a gradual evolution of the movement. Seven of the 10 most powerful groups (known collectively as the "Group of Ten") were founded before 1960. Most have influential local or regional chapters and have expanded their interests from land and wildlife issues to broader, "second-generation" issues, which are not necessarily site- or species-specific.[14] Membership in environmental organizations has ebbed and flowed over the past three decades, often in response to the government's environmental initiatives or electoral change. With the flurry of environmental legislation enacted in the late 1960s and early 1970s, membership in these organizations grew enormously. When energy replaced the environment as a key issue during the Carter administration, the groups' direct mail campaigns generally yielded just enough members to replace those who failed to renew. But two of Reagan's appointees, Secretary of the Interior James Watt and Environmental Protection Agency Administrator Anne Burford, were perceived as a threat to the movement. This resulted in a surge in membership as environmental organizations warned potential members of what might happen if they did not have the funds to closely monitor Reagan administration policies. The Wilderness Society's membership grew by 144 percent between 1980 and 1983, with the Sierra Club increasing by 90 percent and the Defenders of Wildlife and Friends of the Earth by 40 percent each. Another surge took place at the turn of the decade, when the national environmental lobby's U.S. membership exceeded 3 million and attention was focused on Earth Day 1990. But by the early 1990s, even though the environment appeared to be a core value for most Americans, membership decreased again, with many of the groups reducing staffing, closing field offices, and narrowing their program focus to just a few key issues.

Despite the loss of members among the largest organizations, small grassroots groups appeared to be gaining in strength, with their concentration on local or regional issues. For the most part, membership in these groups has grown over the last decade, especially for the groups focused on litigation as a strategy for forcing compliance with environmental protection statutes and regulations, as seen in Table 2.1.

Mainstream organizations have as a common strategy an emphasis on lobbying, although their specific focus often varies. The Sierra Club, the Wilderness Society, and the National Parks Conservation Association, for example, have tended to emphasize the preservation of public lands for future generations. Groups such as the National Wildlife Federation and Izaak Walton League, with a large percentage of sports enthusiasts and hunters within their constituencies, are more involved with habitat preservation for wildlife. Friends of the Earth and other small groups are involved in a broad range of issues, from factory farms and energy policy, to protection of the Potomac River, and public health.

TABLE 2.1 **Membership of "Group of Ten" Environmental Organizations, 1995–2005**

Group	Year Founded	Membership 1995	Membership 2005
Sierra Club	1892	570,000	700,000
National Audubon Society	1905	570,000	550,000
National Parks Conservation Association	1919	450,000	300,000
Wilderness Society	1935	310,000	250,000
National Wildlife Federation	1936	1.8 million	4 million
Nature Conservancy	1951	825,000	1 million
World Wildlife Fund*	1961	1.2 million	4 million
Environmental Defense	1967	300,000	400,000
Greenpeace*	1969	1.6 million	2.5 million
Natural Resources Defense Council	1970	185,000	1 million

*Figures for World Wildlife Fund and Greenpeace membership are worldwide.

SOURCE: Individual organization websites and brochures

When the Environmental Defense Fund (now called Environmental Defense) was founded in 1967, a new breed of organization joined these mainstream groups. Environmental Defense—and later, the Natural Resources Defense Council (NRDC)—made environmental litigation an art form, moving group strategy from the legislative to the judicial arena. These groups have benefited from the citizen suit provisions in virtually every federal environmental statute since the 1970 Clean Air Act. The provisions allow "any person" to sue private parties for noncompliance with the law; and to sue not only for injunctive relief, but for civil penalties. This allows those who sue to recover the cost of attorneys' fees and "mitigation fees" in lieu of, or in addition to, civil fines. The question about when and whether to enter the court system is a controversial one. During the debate over the Healthy Forests Restoration Act in 2002–2003, environmental groups were demonized for filing lawsuits.[15]

Other mainstream groups, although smaller in size and resources, conduct research or grassroots campaigns. Two of the most prominent are the Environmental Working Group (EWG) and the League of Conservation Voters (LCV). One of the newer watchdog organizations, EWG was founded in 1993 and is considered one of the most effective lobbying organizations in Washington. It was the first to raise questions concerning the health risks of a substance used to make Teflon, and it has released reports on how environmentally sensitive areas in Utah were being leased to oil and gas companies. The LCV, founded in 1970, has two goals: to help elect pro-environment candidates and to monitor congressional performance. It is not the group's members that give it clout, but its annual report, the National Environmental Scorecard, which ranks the voting records of each member of Congress on environmental legislation.

Some environmental organizations are characterized by their emphasis on a single issue. These groups rarely shift from their area of concern to another issue, although some overlap is developing. Clean Water Action, founded in 1971, conducts research and lobbies on issues related to drinking water and groundwater resources. Recognizing the interrelatedness of pollution, Clean Water Action also became involved in the passage of the 1986 Superfund legislation and the 1990 Clean Air Act Amendments. The Clean Air Network is an umbrella organization that brings together national and grassroots groups to promote implementation of the Clean Air Act and oppose efforts by industry to weaken its provisions. The Defenders of Wildlife work, as their group's name implies, to protect wildlife habitats through education and advocacy programs. Founded in 1947, the group is now working to strengthen the Endangered Species Act and develop funding for wildlife refuges.

Among the more recently created environmental organizations are those, often with a purely regional base of operation, seeking to preserve individual species. Many of these groups were organized in the 1980s after the initial burst of momentum in the environmental movement had passed. Although these groups limit their activities to individual species, they often form coalitions to preserve natural habitats and wildlife ranges. Their membership is typically smaller (10,000–40,000) and may include researchers dedicated to scientific study of the species. Typical of such groups are Bat Conservation International, founded in 1982, and the Mountain Lion Preservation Foundation, founded in 1986. Both of these organizations emphasize education as well as research and habitat studies. The Mountain Lion Preservation Foundation, for example, has developed an aggressive media campaign in California to educate the public on the habitat needs of this animal, as well as lobbying for a permanent state ban on the hunting of the mountain lion (also known as the cougar, puma, or panther).

Property-oriented groups, such as The Nature Conservancy and Ducks Unlimited, represent examples of long-standing organizations that focus their efforts on management and preservation. Both groups mentioned here have invested private funds for purchasing lands that are then reserved for wildlife habitats. One of the older environmental groups, Ducks Unlimited, with chapters throughout the United States, was founded in 1937 by hunters seeking to preserve wetland habitats. The Nature Conservancy, founded in 1951, has privately purchased land for habitat protection throughout the United States as well as global ecological preserves that are home to endangered species. The organization is also known for developing creative solutions to land acquisition.

Another subgroup is comprised of organizations that originated or are based in the United States, have members throughout the world, and have broadened their interests to more global concerns. The largest international environmental organization, Greenpeace, was founded in 1969 as the Don't Make A Wave Committee by a small group of Sierra Club members and peace activists. In 1971, a crew of 11 activists leased a fishing vessel, the *Phyllis Cormack,* to bear witness and protest nuclear weapons testing in the Aleutian Islands, although the boat never reached its destination. But the activity focused worldwide attention on the issue of nuclear testing, and shortly afterward, the group took the name Greenpeace.

Its initial effort was the Save the Whales campaign, which was later expanded to include other sea animals such as the Steller sea lion and dolphins. Since then, Greenpeace has extended its concerns to six major efforts that parallel the expansion of environmental policy: saving ancient forests, stopping global warming, exposing toxic pollutants, protecting the oceans, eliminating the threat of genetic engineering, and ending the nuclear age. Headquartered in Amsterdam, Greenpeace now has 40 offices worldwide and maintains consultative status to the United Nations.[16]

Greenpeace activities have often bordered on violence, as was the case in 1989 when a Greenpeace ship protested a Trident missile test and was rammed by a U.S. Navy vessel. The group is known, too, for its ability to use the media to its advantage, as demonstrated when its activists are pictured in small boats placing themselves between whales and whaling ships. In 2002, the organization was roundly criticized for posting a color map on the Internet that showed how a terrorist attack on a New Jersey bleach plant would release chlorine vapors that could drift into New York. In the wake of the terrorist attack on the World Trade Center in 2001, the action was labeled as bordering on treason. The owner of the bleach facility said it was like painting a gigantic bull's-eye on the plant's roof, even though the Environmental Protection Agency (EPA) had already made detailed information about U.S. chemical plants widely available to the public as part of a Clinton administration policy.

Environmental organizations have periodically attempted to put aside their individual interests and have formed coalitions in an attempt to advance their collective interests. Coalitions are especially important to groups engaged in long-term policy struggles, such as public land management, air and water pollution, and global climate change. In 1946, the Natural Resources Council of America was formed to bring together conservation organizations to serve as an information-sharing body and sponsor policy briefings and surveys of public opinion on issues such as energy needs and conservation. Coalitions have also been formed to lobby specific pieces of legislation, such as the National Clean Air Coalition, which came together during debate over the 1977 and 1990 Clean Air Act Amendments.

THE ENVIRONMENTAL JUSTICE MOVEMENT

From the early 1960s through the 1980s, the majority of mainstream environmental organizations focused on issues related to natural resource management and preservation, along with efforts to control air and water pollution. Their leadership (and support) came primarily from middle- and upper-middle-class whites, and surveys found that members of environmental groups were considerably better educated, more likely to have white-collar jobs, and more likely to have high incomes in comparison to the larger population.

At the same time, the civil rights movement had become a fixture in American politics, with a focus on bringing jobs and social justice to poor communities and improving the economic conditions of minorities and people of color. Often community leaders made trade-offs between bringing jobs and industry into neighborhoods faced with high unemployment and the cost of exposing workers and their families to industrial pollution and toxic hazards, a condition political scientist Robert Bullard refers to as "job blackmail."[17] Bullard notes that, eventually, there was a convergence of environmentalism and the civil rights movement that called for a balancing of economic development, social justice, and environmental protection. In cities like Los Angeles, African American and Latino groups formed in the mid-1980s to fight the siting of municipal and hazardous waste incinerators in poor, largely minority neighborhoods. Native American groups have organized against landfills on their reservations, which are not subject to federal or state environmental laws, and farmworkers in California's Central Valley protested the hazardous waste landfill and a proposed incinerator in one tiny community.[18]

These community struggles developed a political focus from two hallmark events. In 1987, the United Church of Christ Commission for Racial Justice published a controversial study, *Toxic Wastes and Race in the United States: A National Report on the Racial and Socio-Economic Characteristics of Communities with Hazardous Waste Sites,* which concluded that the poor and members of racial minority groups were being treated inequitably in the siting of such facilities.[19] The report was followed in October 1991 by the First National People of Color Environmental Leadership Summit in Washington, D.C. The meeting produced a set of Principles of Environmental Justice that called upon people of color to secure their economic and social liberation, which had been denied them as a result of the "poisoning of our communities and land and the genocide of our peoples." In calling for environmental justice, the summit's leaders demanded the right to participate as equal partners in environmental decision making, free from any form of discrimination or bias. But it also placed a responsibility on individuals to make personal and consumer choices in their life styles that minimized the use of natural resources and produced as little waste as possible.

Subsequently, national civil rights leaders criticized environmental organizations and political decision makers for "environmental racism"—a term used to describe the fact that "whether by conscious design or institutional neglect, communities of color in urban ghettos, in rural 'poverty pockets,' or on economically impoverished Native American reservations face some of the worst environmental devastation in the nation."[20]

Responses to these charges varied. Civil rights organizations like the National Association for the Advancement of Colored People and the American Civil Liberties Union have begun working side by side with mainstream environmental organizations such as the Natural Resources Defense Council. Larger environmental groups, such as the Sierra Club and the Wilderness Society, have attempted to diversify their governing boards and staff, with a corresponding "trickling down" to state governments that, in turn, have begun to enact some form of environmental justice laws.[21]

At the federal level, the EPA responded with the creation of the Environmental Equity Workgroup in 1990 to assess the evidence that minority and low-income communities bear a higher environmental risk burden than does the general population, and how EPA might deal with any disparities. EPA created an internal Office of Environmental Justice in 1992, and a year later, the National Environmental Justice Advisory Council (NEJAC) was established to provide stakeholder input and to serve as a forum for discussion. The council's charter was renewed in 2003. In 1994 President Bill Clinton issued an executive order that instructed federal agencies to integrate environmental justice into their ongoing missions, and EPA administrator Carol Browner announced that she would make environmental equity a part of her agency's decision-making processes. After the Clinton administration left office, the issue of environmental justice appeared to have stagnated within the executive branch. Although EPA Administrator Christine Whitman recommitted the agency to "integrating environmental justice into all agency programs,"[22] NEJAC meetings have been infrequent and considered to be more symbolic than substantive.

There is, however, a discordant note among those who believe that the environmental justice movement is facing challenges it cannot overcome. Brookings Institution scholar Christopher H. Foreman Jr. has argued that many goals of the environmental justice movement—such as community empowerment, social justice, and public health—are difficult for federal officials to address using the environment as a policy "hook." He also believes that such advocacy directs community attention away from the problems that pose the greatest risks and "may therefore have the ironic effect of undermining public health in precisely those communities it endeavors to help." He cautions that there are significant political hurdles to be overcome as well, such as a lack of congressional support and the infeasibility of attempting to ban new siting in and near low-income communities and communities of color. Many leaders concur with Foreman's conclusion that what is really at stake, not only in the environmental justice movement but also in the environmental movement itself, is what he calls "an abiding hunger for livable communities."[23]

There is also a global element to environmental racism, whether the issue be toxic waste dumping in poorer, usually nonwhite countries (see Chapter 5), exploitation of resources by multinational corporations, or "eco-catastrophes." The term refers to events like toxic gas releases or oil spills that result in severe environmental damage. In the Niger delta region of Africa, for example, grass-roots groups like Environment Rights Action and the Niger Delta Human and Environmental Rescue Organization have documented incidents where oil lines have burst or punctured, spilling crude oil. The spills, often in remote areas, are sometimes not discovered immediately, and land, water, and fish and wildlife are degraded or die. One researcher notes:

> Foreign oil companies doing business in Africa are typically immune from paying for their mistakes. They engage in practices that are not tolerated in their home countries and they get away with atrocities.... This has led some to question whether companies operating abroad should be held to the same standard that their countries of origin demand.[24]

RADICAL ENVIRONMENTALISM

On May 18, 2005, the U.S. Senate Committee on Environment and Public Works heard testimony from witnesses about the threat posed by animal rights extremists and eco-terrorists in the United States. John Lewis, Deputy Assistant Director of the Federal Bureau of Investigation (FBI), told committee members:

> One of today's most serious domestic terrorism threats comes from special interest extremist movements such as the Animal Liberation Front (ALF), the Earth Liberation Front (ELF), and Stop Huntingdon Animal Cruelty campaign. Adherents to these movements aim to resolve specific issues by using criminal "direct action" against individuals or companies believed to be abusing or exploiting animals or the environment.[25]

At a time when most Americans were thinking of terrorism in the form of suicide bombers, commercial airlines, and roadside bombs in Iraq, the FBI signaled it was "working to detect, disrupt, and dismantle the animal rights and environmental extremist movements that are involved in criminal activity."[26] Were the committee's, or the agency's concerns, justified? Do radical environmental organizations have an impact on policy, and if so, how?

The most well-known radical group is Earth First! which took its name in 1979 "in response to a lethargic, compromising, and increasingly corporate environmental community." Activists are not described as members of an organization, but as part of a movement who share "a belief in biocentrism, that life of the Earth comes first, and a practice of putting our beliefs into action." Its website asks, "Are you tired of namby-pamby environmental groups? Are you tired of overpaid corporate environmentalists who suck up to bureaucrats and industry? Have you become disempowered by the reductionist approach of environmental professionals and scientists?"[27]

Initially associated with civil disobedience and later with environmental sabotage against the timber industry, Earth First! has broadened its agenda to include genetically modified organisms, drilling in the Arctic National Wildlife Reserve, over-the-counter emergency contraception, and Iraq war profits. Direct actions alleged to have been conducted by Earth Firsters! include two arson attacks against sport utility vehicles at a Chevrolet dealer's lot in Eugene, Oregon. An anonymous communiqué claimed "Gas-guzzling SUVs are at the forefront of this vile, imperialistic culture's caravan toward self-destruction. We can no longer allow the rich to parade around in their armored existence, leaving a wasteland behind in their tire tracks." Other actions that are sometimes attributed to groups similar to Earth First! include directing a sabotage attack at the Pure-Seed Testing Company, which grows grass seed; the Anarchist Golfing Association claimed credit for $500,000 in damage. Other facilities have eliminated the word *research* from their signs because company officials worried they would be accused of conducting genetic engineering research.[28]

Earth Liberation Front (ELF), another of the major groups designated as eco-terrorists, has claimed responsibility for a series of actions ranging from spraying red paint on the Mexican consulate in Boston in 1997 to protest the treatment of peasants in Chiapas, Mexico, to setting fires at U.S. Department of Agriculture buildings in Olympia, Washington, and the "freeing" of 310 animals from a Wisconsin fur farm in collaboration with the Animal Liberation Front. In October 1998, ELF claimed credit for a series of seven fires at the ski operation on Vail Mountain, Colorado, to protest the expansion of the ski resort in an area proposed for the reintroduction of the North American lynx. ELF surfaced again in January 1999 when the group said it was responsible for a fire that destroyed the corporate headquarters of U.S. Forest Industries in Medford, Oregon. This time, the ELF sent a fax that stated: "To celebrate the holidays, we decided on a bonfire. . . . This action is a payback and it is a warning, to all others responsible we do not sleep and we wont [sic] quit."[29]

The FBI believes that there has been an escalation in violent rhetoric and tactics, and an increase in the frequency and size of attacks. Lewis testified:

> Harassing phone calls and vandalism now co-exist with improvised explosive devices and threats to employees. ELF's target list has expanded to include sports utility dealerships and new home developers. We believe these trends will persist, particularly within the environmental movement, as extremists continue to combat what they perceive as "urban sprawl."[30]

While the FBI's figures include 1,200 criminal incidents by animal and radical environmental rights activists between January 1990 and June 2004, it is not always clear whether the activities are accurately credited to these individuals or organizations. In December 2004, Maryland officials focused on eco-terrorists after 26 new homes in a subdivision were burned near an environmentally sensitive wetlands area.[31] Federal authorities eventually charged five men, including a member of a volunteer fire department, for the arson. Prosecutors said that the crime was aimed at black families moving into the neighborhood, although it was not charged as a hate crime. In March 2005 a teenager who went on a shooting rampage at a Minnesota high school was believed to have connections to a neo-Nazi website run by the Libertarian National Socialist Green Party that was alleged to promote environmental extremism and eco-terrorism.[32]

The radical beliefs and tactics of groups like ALF, ELF, and Earth First! are an important part of the environmental debate. Radical organizations shun traditional structure and administrative rules, preferring militant action—termed "monkeywrenching" and "ecotage"—to the traditional political strategies used by mainstream environmental organizations. Study results regarding the motivations of environmental radicals vary. One researcher says these activists are driven by a combination of spiritual conviction, science, and politics, including a deeply held belief that the earth is sacred.[33]

Are the tactics of radical environmentalists effective in changing policy? Generally, their actions are shunned by both environmental organizations and groups associated with the environmental opposition. Some actions may, in fact, be counterproductive. Mink ranchers say that when saboteurs release the animals from their cages into the wild, they simply hasten their deaths. At the University of Washington's Center for Urban Horticulture, a fire allegedly set by environmental radicals damaged the work of researchers seeking to save endangered plants and efforts to find trees that could be used instead of logging old-growth stands.[34] But the mainstream groups also use the radicals as a foil, realizing that the posturing and activities of such groups cause their own agendas to be perceived as much more reasonable and acceptable in contrast.

ENVIRONMENTAL OPPOSITION
IN THE UNITED STATES

The Progressive era ideals of the conservation movement had almost universal support throughout the early 20th century, although the early groups were still dominated by business organizations, which were much more influential in the political arena. As the goals of the movement began to expand from conservation to environmentalism in the late 1960s and early 1970s, so, too, did the potential impact on business and industry, which had never really felt threatened before. The development of an organized environmental opposition involved three interests—farmers and ranchers, organized labor, and industry—and has recently coalesced into three grassroots opposition movements—wise use, property rights, and county supremacy. The initial concern of farmers and ranchers was the tremendous influx of city dwellers who sought the tranquility of rural life after World War II. "Recreationists," as they were called, brought tourist dollars to rural economies badly in need of them; but they also brought with them litter, congestion, and noise. Urban visitors seldom paid much attention to property lines, and major battles developed over public access along the California coastline and through inland wetlands. Farmers who were used to controlling predators on their private property were suddenly facing raptor protection programs and angry wildlife enthusiasts who sought preservation of wolves and coyotes. Agricultural land use also came under fire, as environmental groups sought to legislate farm practices relating to pesticide use, soils, and irrigation. As development, including oil pipelines and utility transmission lines, began to intrude onto rural areas, farmers felt even more threatened.[35]

The two issues that have most galvanized farmers have been proposals to restrict the use of agricultural pesticides and herbicides and agricultural use of water. In the case of pesticide use, rural interests have formed a coalition with chemical companies and their associations, bringing together such disparate groups as the American Farm Bureau Federation and the National Agricultural Chemical Association, along with the National Association of State Departments of Agriculture; the Association of American Plant Food, Pesticide and Feed Control Officers; the National Association of County Agents; and the Christmas Tree Growers Association. But the land-use issue has become even more controversial because of the Sagebrush Rebellion and the development of the grassroots environmental opposition movements discussed later in this chapter.

Organized Labor

Some environmental issues have had an impact on workers, who have often been forced to take sides in the policy debate. On the one hand, organized labor has traditionally supported attempts to make a safer workplace and working conditions. Most labor unions have also supported programs that involve occupational health issues, such as exposure to airborne particulates and toxic chemicals. The United Steelworkers of America, for example, has long supported clean air legislation to alleviate an environmental problem caused, to some extent, by the steel industry.[36] Farmworkers in California have been active participants in federal pesticide legislation, and cotton dust exposure led the Amalgamated Clothing and Textile Workers Union to lobby the Occupational Safety and Health Administration to develop rules to protect workers in textile mills.

Labor has often opposed pollution control efforts (and more recently, implementation of the Endangered Species Act) that affect job security. The United Auto Workers union has consistently supported environmental regulations, except when they affect the auto industry. The fear of losing jobs due to environmental regulations has permeated many regions of the United States, often when the real reason for job loss is technological change and innovation. Environmentalists working within the energy industry unions have repeatedly argued that energy conservation has no negative impact on jobs and is, in fact, beneficial to workers.

Industry Interests

Industry interests have traditionally opposed environmental rules, for two reasons: The cost of complying with regulations threatens a company's ability to make money, and there is little incentive for voluntary compliance. Sometimes, industry opposition results from disagreement over the goals or means used to protect the environment. Yet industry leaders recognize that they (and their employees and their families) breathe the same polluted air and face the same toxic contamination as the rest of America. Industry's role has been described as "marked not by agreement on values but by tactics of containment, by a working philosophy of maximum feasible resistance and minimum feasible retreat."[37]

Businesses were initially slow to recognize the potential impact of the environmental movement on their operations, characterizing the activities of most groups as no more than a fad. But officials within the pulp and paper industry began, in the late 1950s, to understand how desires for more recreation land would likely mean a call for reduction in logging activities and expansion of wilderness area designations. Eventually, other industry leaders became alarmed at the rapid pace of environmental legislation, which accelerated during the late 1960s and into the 1970s. They countered by forming trade associations and nonprofit research groups or think tanks to further their aims, pouring millions of dollars into education and public relations. The American Forest Institute, for example, was specifically created to justify the need for increased, rather than reduced, timber production. The oil industry has been especially hard hit as the environmental movement gained more clout. Companies have been ordered by the courts to pay for special cleanups or fines and have faced lengthy and costly litigation due to compliance suits brought by environmental groups.

Today, industries affected by environmental regulations rely on a fourfold approach in their opposition to environmental groups:

1. There is a continuation of the public relations campaigns that began in the early 1960s to paint industry with an environmentally green brush. Chevron Oil, for example, ran advertisements in national publications promoting its "People Do" projects to protect the habitat of endangered species to counter the public backlash that results after every oil spill.

2. Industry has taken a more proactive role in crafting legislation and seeking allies, rather than simply reacting to initiatives proposed by environmental groups. The chemical industry, which for years was accused of intransigence, decided in the late 1980s to move toward a pollution prevention approach as a way to improve the marketability of its products. They were active in the debate over the 1990 Clean Air Act Amendments, and politicians gave the industry's lobbyists credit for drafting its own legislation rather than just opposing what was on the table. During the administration of George W. Bush, lobbyists for the energy industry were accused of being too aggressive in the policy-making process, virtually handing over their demands to the president (see Chapter 6).

3. Virtually every sector of the economy relies on a stable of federal and state lobbyists to review legislation that could potentially affect its operations. Although federal law prohibits them from contributing directly to candidates, corporations can form political action committees (PACs) that funnel campaign contributions directly to legislators as a way of enhancing their access to the political system. Companies and trade associations also employ their own scientists, economists, and policy experts to refute the claims made by

environmental groups and usually have more financial resources to devote to this strategy than do grassroots groups.

4. Once programs reach the implementation stage, most industry interests regroup to press their case through the administrative maze. Because many implementation decisions are made by low-level administrators, or in a less public arena than Congress, industry has been much more successful in molding programs at this phase of the policy process. EPA rule development has frequently been hampered by companies arguing that information about products and processes constitutes trade secrets or is proprietary. Industry lawyers have also launched a flurry of lawsuits aimed at regulations and enforcement actions.

Still, it is important to note that industry interests are not monolithic. There is sufficient competition within the economy to provide competition in certain sectors. The stereotype of "big business" speaking with a single voice is more mythology than reality. While it may be in some companies' interest to share information or form coalitions, there is at least an equal amount of distrust over who will have the most to gain (or lose) from legislators and regulators.[38]

Grassroots Opposition

In 1988, a different type of environmental opposition surfaced as an outgrowth of a meeting of 250 groups at the Multiple Use Strategy Conference, sponsored by the Center for Defense of Free Enterprise. One of the group's leaders, Ron Arnold, applied the phrase "wise use" (originally used by conservationist Gifford Pinchot) in describing 25 goals to reform the country's environmental policies, including opening up national parks and wilderness areas to mineral exploration, expanding visitor facilities in the parks, and restricting application of the Endangered Species Act.[39] Now, grassroots opposition is focused on three issues led by large umbrella organizations: wise use, property rights, and the county supremacy movement. The umbrella groups serve as a clearinghouse for information and share a deep anti-government sentiment and opposition to efforts by government and environmental groups to further regulate the use of public and private lands and natural resources. Although some of the opposition efforts are supported by private interests, ranging from the Mountain States Legal Foundation to agricultural groups, and oil, timber, and mining companies, there is a strong grassroots component of individuals who perceive the government to be intruding into their lives by telling them what they can do with their private property or how lands and resources within the public domain ought to be used. It is difficult to estimate the membership of these groups; many individuals are members simply because they belong to another group that has supported one or more of the umbrella groups' tenets. The 4 million members of the American Farm Bureau Federation (AFBF), for example, are counted as members of the wise use movement simply because the AFBF has endorsed some wise use policies.

The Sagebrush Rebellion began in the 1970s as an effort by wealthy ranchers and others to gain control of public lands in the West. The movement had proponents in government in the 1980s, particularly Interior Secretary James

Watt. The movement was reinvigorated in the early 1990s as the wise use and county supremacy movements garnered attention. Although there are similarities between the wise use movement and the Sagebrush Rebellion of the late 1970s and early 1980s, one difference between the two is that the current efforts are marked by steps to broaden the base of support beyond purely western issues. Like other political movements, the groups employ a wide variety of strategies and tactics to push their agenda forward. The Blue Ribbon Coalition, which represents motorized recreational interests, tracks legislation and alerts its members to contact their congressional representatives when a bill affects their interests. Some of the more militant opposition groups, like the Sahara Club, boast of vandalizing property or disrupting environmental group activities. In addition to cattle ranchers resisting higher grazing fees, the grassroots efforts tap into gulf shrimpers opposing the use of turtle-excluding devices, Alaskans seeking to expand oil drilling, and private property owners from eastern states battling the National Park Service over boundary disputes. The three movements are well organized, tapping into an electronic network that keeps even the most isolated adherents in touch with one another.[40]

From a political standpoint, the grassroots opposition has had moderate success legislatively. During President Clinton's first term, it stalled proposed grazing fee increases and was able to get congressional approval for a brief moratorium on listings under the Endangered Species Act. Organizations like the Mountain States Legal Foundation and the Individual Rights Foundation have led the legal fight against federal lands. Between 1991 and 1995, fifty-nine western counties passed ordinances that claimed authority to supersede federal environmental and land-use laws and regulations, and 34 counties in Nevada, California, Idaho, New Mexico, and Oregon passed ordinances challenging federal control of local lands.[41] The resolutions declared that federal land in the county actually belonged to the state and that the county alone has the authority to manage it. Although the resolutions are not technically law, local officials were enforcing them as though they were. The Justice Department challenged the ordinances as illegal and sought an injunction to ban their enforcement.

The courts have dealt a serious blow to county supremacy groups by striking down ordinances that would have given counties the right to determine how public lands within their boundaries would be used. Most individuals involved in the property rights movement are mired in a legal system that takes years to resolve issues, thus reducing their ability to accomplish goals. The grassroots movements have as much success as they do because they have been led by policy entrepreneurs, charismatic individuals who have capitalized on the public's distrust of the government's natural resource policies, as well as mistrust of the federal government in general, and turned that distrust into self-perpetuating organizations. Although they have often been at odds with most environmental organizations, some opposition group leaders appear to be seeking common ground and compromise as a more effective way of influencing environmental policy during an era when the vast majority of Americans still adhere to a protectionist ethic. But the wise use movement's adherents are highly motivated; moreover, they are well organized through a network of web pages, e-mail, and grassroots chapters and continue to press their concerns forcefully.

THE ROLE OF THE MEDIA

The media play two important roles in bringing environmental problems to the attention of both the public and policymakers. One, they report events and conditions that are considered to be "newsworthy" and in doing so, may help to convert a problem to an item on the policy agenda. For example, most Americans are probably familiar with the 1989 Exxon *Valdez* oil spill in Alaska because of the massive amount of publicity surrounding the event. In the aftermath of the *Valdez* spill, policy makers rushed to create new disaster protocols for marine cleanups, safety regulations were reviewed, groups formed to help save birds and marine mammals, and engineers and oil company officials discussed the design of oil tankers.

But there was little media coverage of the 2005 oil cleanup operations at the site of the *Selendang Ayu* wreck on Unalaska Island, considered the worst Alaska oil spill in the last 25 years. The incident, in which a Malaysian freighter broke in two in December 2004, received only minor attention from the press. Nor was there much attention paid to a complaint by the Hawaii State Department of Health against Chevron Hawaii Refinery, Inc. in 2005. The agency assessed a fine of $107,000 against the company for failing to obtain a permit for storage of hazardous waste. Chevron operates a refinery on Oahu that processes crude oil from Alaska that is transported in tankers with the same potential for a massive spill. Why would media coverage of one incident influence policy, while the two events just described would not?

Part of the reason stems from what political scientists Roger Cobb and Charles Elder call the governmental agenda and the systemic agenda.[42] They define the governmental agenda as those problems to which political leaders decide to give their more serious attention. Not all problems identified by the media will make their way to the governmental agenda, especially if there is little public knowledge of the issue. This is the situation with the events that took place in Alaska and Hawaii in 2005. The systemic agenda, in contrast, includes those issues which are perceived by members of the political community as being worthy of public attention and are part of the jurisdiction of governmental authority. The systemic agenda is primarily made up of discussion items; often, there are few distinct or specific answers to a perceived problem. While the environment is most commonly thought to be a problem dealt with on all levels of government, the media often focus on issues that are more localized or regional.

This represents the second major role of the media's coverage of the environment. If an issue or problem is not yet widely recognized by the public, the media can make it more salient, that is, worthy of attention. The most common way in which the media perform this function is through long-term, comprehensive coverage, including follow-up stories and features. In this sense, the discretion the media have is not so much to tell people or leaders what to think, as what to think about.[43] International media coverage of the *Valdez* has continued for more than two decades, with follow-up stories on the trial of the ship's captain, the costs of cleanup, and the anniversary of the tanker spill.

Sometimes, the media affect the agenda-setting process by choosing which stories to cover and which to ignore, a process that leads to what researchers Peter

Bachrach and Morton Baratz have called nondecision making.[44] The suppression of discussion may not always be deliberate, but it may also be enough to keep a problem from agenda status. In 1989, for instance, a steam tube ruptured in the McGuire nuclear facility outside Charlotte, North Carolina, and the plant's operators quickly shut down the reactor. Local television crews arrived within minutes, followed by national media and preparations for a community evacuation. Network newscasters reported "a terrifying nuclear 'accident'" even though the event was over in less than an hour and no radiation was released either inside or outside of the plant. The widely publicized incident was the subject of months of public hearings, and local and national environmental organizations demanded that the nuclear facility be closed. In contrast, a petroleum refinery in Pasadena, Texas, exploded that same year. Over 300 workers were injured, and 23 were killed. Although the nightly news carried helicopter footage of the fiery blaze, the story subsequently vanished from the media.[45] The difference is reflective of the media's (and public's) perceptions about energy and fears about anything nuclear.

However, the media have brought a number of environmental problems to the governmental agenda that might never have been considered serious problems without highly visual coverage. Sensitivity toward the plight of endangered species is a result of extensive coverage of whales, dolphins, and other marine mammals, especially when there are highly charged images of overfishing. When the media do not have direct access to these images, they often rely on videos or photographs provided by interest groups, which are more than willing to share graphic illustrations of clear-cut forests, uranium mine tailings, or plumes of smoky pollutants rising from industrial smokestacks. Media coverage thus becomes important in shaping public opinion, which in turn, may shape how decision makers choose to respond to perceived problems.

The media cover the environment because it is politically attractive to do so. Without media coverage of environmental problems, for instance, most Americans would undoubtedly continue to believe that pollution and other issues were no longer serious and, thus, not worthy of government action. It is also likely that they would fail to connect the environmental problems of one nation with global issues, such as the United States' emission of greenhouse gases and global climate change. But the short life span of any media coverage, from a 15-second sound bite to a photo opportunity with the president when legislation is signed, moves any environmental issue on and off the policy agenda. Even the enduring problems like sustainability and resource depletion are given limited coverage when other events, such as the treatment of prisoners in Iraqi prisons or celebrity trials, seem to capture more of the public's attention.

Another type of media presence is found in electronic cyberspace—a phenomenon that has changed the policy process considerably due to three factors:

1. It gives the public access to the identification of global problems and the discussion of issues that previously might have gone unnoticed. In addition, the Internet has made access to news easier and more immediate, regardless of a person's geographic location or income level. Anyone with access to a

computer can read major international newspapers, watch simultaneous coverage of events anyone in the world, or read e-books online.

2. A positive consequence of the growing reliance on the Internet is that it serves as an important resource and research tool for activists and leaders in developing countries. Prior to the late 1990s, many nations were unable to access, let alone store, published collections of journals in paper form. The economic impact of journal subscriptions, as well as storage space, was beyond the reach of most universities and libraries. Even smaller microfiche versions were difficult to work with and required equipment that often was unavailable. Now scholarly information, especially technical journals, is available online.

3. Organizations now rely heavily upon the Internet to instantaneously transmit information and to mobilize their members, solicit contributions, and provide a sense of cohesiveness that would be impossible through traditional group meetings and periodic publications. Groups can influence the policy process by informing members when Congress is about to vote on legislation or when an appointee is going through the process of confirmation. Little-known problems can be made more visible when they are posted on a website, no matter how geographically distant they might be from the person reading them. Links to other organizations and information further expand the reach of a group with limited resources.

As the world's communications networks expand, the media and cyberspace become additional tools for participants in the environmental debate. Whether the focus is group mobilization, information transfer, outreach, or the shaping of public opinion, the process is sometimes subtle and difficult to ascertain. But it is also clear that without the media, most environmental problems would never find their way to the policy agenda.[46]

Thinking Globally

Concern about the environment is universal. Although this chapter has thus far focused on development of the environmental movement and opposition groups in the United States, the environmental debate involves a number of international actors. Some global activism parallels what was taking place in the United States during the 19th century, beginning with the founding of the Commons, Open Spaces and Footpaths Preservation Society in Britain in 1865. There appears to be a trend in industrial nations that ties the development of environmental awareness to business cycles; in Britain, for example, support for environmental protection has been strongest toward the end of periods of sustained economic expansion. With greater economic prosperity, people shift their interest from immediate material needs to the nonmaterial aspects of their lives. As a result, economic advances in the late 1960s and early 1970s led to a tremendous growth spurt in the membership of existing nature groups and the formation of new groups, paralleling activity in the United States during that same period.

Nongovernmental organizations (NGOs) now play a key role in environmental policy making in both industrialized and developing countries. The term is used to describe all organizations that are neither governmental nor for-profit, and it may include groups ranging from rural people's leagues and tribal unions to private relief associations, irrigation user groups, and local development associations. NGOs can be classified as grassroots organizations (membership oriented, often in developing nations), service NGOs (supporting the development of grassroots groups), or policy specific (environment, human rights, family planning). One characteristic many of the groups have in common is that they are often parochial—concerned almost exclusively about environmental issues in their region. A typical example is the group Dasohli Gram Swarajya Mandal, which began a logging public awareness campaign in India in 1964 that led to the Chipko Andalan movement. Chipko, which means "to cling to," literally is composed of India's tree huggers, Himalayan Indians who launched protests over logging. Indian environmentalists developed political clout over the issue of proposed dams and hydroelectric projects, but have often limited their activism to specific projects. These groups not only help shape policy but also play a major role in generating demands within individual countries for governments to comply with and implement the global agreements they have signed.

NGOs are growing in both number and influence, particularly in developing nations. Unlike their counterparts in Northern Hemisphere countries, NGOs in the south perform somewhat different functions. They often fill a vacuum left by ineffective or nonexistent government programs or extend the reach of resource-poor national governments. They may also forge links with NGOs whose issues are decidedly non-environmental, such as the networking that is beginning to occur between human rights and economic development NGOs. Last, NGOs in developing countries may serve as an independent voice for public participation, either in opposition to a government program or by placing pressures on government to create new programs. (See Table 5.2.)

Studies of NGOs indicate that they are evolving in three directions: the southern NGOs are seeking greater autonomy from those in the north; NGOs are forming international networks and coalitions to keep abreast of issues; and they are performing new roles in legal defense and policy research. The first trend appears to be the most critical as Southern Hemisphere NGOs seek to distance themselves from their dependence on their northern partners. Long dependent for financial support on their northern donors, these groups now seek the transfer of the technical expertise they need to gain independence. They hope to set their own environmental protection agendas rather than have the terms of their activities dictated by outside sources that they perceive to be less familiar with local problems. Technological advances such as facsimile machines and computer-linked networks have allowed groups to coordinate their efforts on a global scale, and they have steadily increased their presence in the diplomatic world as well. NGOs held a parallel conference at the 1972, 1992, and 2002 United Nations environmental meetings, and several organizations were accredited by the United Nations to participate in the preparatory meetings leading up to the summits. Although these trends indicate that NGOs are growing in numbers as well as importance, their influence on global environmental protection is still limited by a lack of stable funding sources and political sophistication.

Only a handful of organizations have begun to address the global issues of concern to many of the mainstream organizations in the United States, such as global warming and stratospheric ozone depletion. Friends of the Earth International, for example, has affiliates throughout the world, as does Greenpeace. NGOs are especially important in regions where environmental concern has only recently begun to emerge, as evidenced by the founding of a Russian affiliate of Greenpeace. Without the support of an international organization and its resources, environmental activists in the republics of the former Soviet Union would have little voice for their efforts to draw international attention to decades of environmental degradation.

Cultural differences are the major factor behind the variations in how environmental interests become structured or operate. In democratic nations, the pluralist system legitimizes interest group membership. But acceptable tactics in one nation may be considered unacceptable or even criminal in others.

In nondemocratic countries such as the People's Republic of China, the government crackdown on Western influences has made it difficult even for NGOs such as the World

TABLE 2.2 **Major International Environmental and/or Developmental Nongovernmental Organizations (NGOs)**

A Rocha International

Amazon Watch

Amigos de la Tierra

Bureau of International Recycling

Center for International Climate and Environmental Research

Consejo Iberico para la Defense de la Naturaleza

Corporate Watch

Cousteau Society

Earth Action

Earth Charter Initiative

Earth Council

Earthscan

Earth Watch Institute

EUROPARC Federation

Friends of the Earth

Global Witness

Green Cross International

Greenpeace International

International Council of Environmental Law

International Rivers Network

International Wildlife Coalition

Inuit Circumpolar Conference

Islamic Academy of Sciences

Nature Conservancy

Physicians for Social Responsibility

Public Services International

Rainforest Action Network

Rainforest Alliance

Taiga Rescue Network

World Business Council for Sustainable Development

World Commission on Dams

World Conservation Union

World Rainforest Network

World Resources Institute

World Water Council

World Wide Fund for Nature

Wildlife Fund to have much of an impact, leaving little room for environmental groups, domestic or foreign. International pressure and the government's expanded involvement in international trade and politics have led to substantial advances in China's environmental policies; and small groups, such as Friends of Nature, have been successful at lobbying against clear-cutting of old-growth forests.[47]

The most cohesive and powerful environmental movements are found in western Europe, where public opinion polls have shown that support for the environment is especially strong and continues to grow. Still, the environmental movement in Europe is best characterized as diverse, with each group developing its own structure, strategy, and style. Coalition building is a common strategy, with umbrella groups monitoring proposed legislation and lobbying. Group activism has historically been focused on the issues of nuclear power and nuclear weapons, leading to massive public protests in 1995 when the French government resumed weapons testing in the South Pacific. Great Britain is well known for direct action, a phenomenon that changed environmental activism completely in the 1990s. While some analysts characterize the increasing militancy and radicalism as simply a pendulum swing, others feel it represents a new spirit and ethos.

> Not content to try to influence politicians or institutions, protesters have seen direct action as disruption seeking to delay environmentally damaging projects and to escalate their costs. At many sites of direct action there was an avowed goal of actually stopping particular projects going ahead by getting in the way, damaging equipment and creating physical obstacles like tunnels, as well as building a groundswell of opinion to make the project politically untenable.[48]

> Protesters have stopped road-building projects—especially in pastoral or scenic areas, incinerator and waste facilities—and research on genetically modified foods.

GREEN POLITICAL PARTIES

On a global level, Green political parties, identified in Table 2.3, vary considerably in strength and impact on their respective political systems, in membership, and in the percentage of the electorate they represent. The term *green party* is sometimes used generically, and many groups represent a broader social movement or consist of activists focused on a single issue. In the United States, the first national green party organization formed at a 1984 meeting of 62 activists on the campus of Macalester College in Minnesota. Known as the Green Committees of Correspondence after the grassroots efforts of rebels during the War of Independence, the group defined "greenness" as interweaving "ecological wisdom, decentralization of economic and political power wherever practical, personal and social responsibility, global security, and community self-determination within the context of respect for diversity of heritage and religion. It advocates non–violent action, cooperative world order, and self reliance."[49]

The definition that developed from the 1984 meeting was later developed as the Ten Key Values: Ecological Wisdom, Grassroots Democracy, Decentralization, Community-Based Economics, Feminism, Respect for Diversity, Personal and Global Responsibility, and Future Focus/Sustainability. The goal was to develop grassroots organizations throughout the United States; but the process was slow and there was dissension among group members, who questioned whether their activities were primarily symbolic or whether a Green political party was realistic.

TABLE 2.3 Major Green Parties, by Regional Federation (2005)

Federation of Green Parties of Africa

Benin	Les Verts du Benin
Burkina Faso	Rassemblement des Ecologistes du Berkino Faso
Cameroon	Defense de l'Environnement Camerounais
Guinea	Parti des Ecologistes Guineens
Guinea-Bissau	Liga Guineense de Proteccao Ecologica
Ivory Coast	Parti pour la Protection de l'Environnement
Kenya	Mazingira Green Party
Mali	Parti Ecologiste du Mali
Mauritius	Movement Republicain
Morrocco	Les Verts
Niger	Rassemblement pour un Sahel Vert
Nigeria	Green Party of Nigeria
Senegal	Les Verts
Somalia	Somalia Green Party
South Africa	Green Party of South Africa

Federation of Green Parties of Asia-Pacific

Australia	Australian Greens
Japan	Rainbow and Greens
Mongolia	Mongolian Green Party
New Caledonia	Les Verts Pacifique
New Zealand	Green Party of Aotearoa
Papua New Guinea	Greens Party
South Korea	Noksaek Pyounghwa Dangg
Taiwan	Green Party of Taiwan

Federation of the Green Parties of the Americas

Brazil	Partido Verde do Brasil
Canada	Green Party of Canada
Chile	Partido Ecologista
Colombia	Partido Verde Oxigeno
Dominican Republic	Partido Ecologista Dominicano
Mexico	Partido Ecologista Verde de Mexico
Nicaragua	Partido Verde Ecologista de Nicaragua
Peru	Partido Ecologista Alternative Verde del Peru
United States	Green Party of the United States
Uruguay	Partido del Sol

(Continued)

TABLE 2.3 Major Green Parties, by Regional Federation (2005) *(Continued)*

European Federation of Green Parties	
Austria	Die Grunen
Belgium	Groen!
Bulgaria	Bulgarian Green Party
Cyprus	Cyprus Green Party
Czech Republic	Strana Zelenych
Denmark	De Gronne
Estonia	Eesti Rohelised
Finland	Vihrea Liitto
France	Les Verts
Georgia	Georgia Greens
Germany	Die Grunen
Greece	Ecologoi-Prasinoi
Hungary	Zold Demokratak
Ireland	Comhaontas Glas
Italy	Federazione dei Verdi
Latvia	Latvijas Zala Partija
Luxembourg	Dei Greng
Malta	Alternattiva Demokratika
Netherlands	De Groenen
Norway	Miljopartiet de Gronne
Portugal	Os Verdes
Romania	Federatia Ecologista din Romania
Russia	The Interregional Green Party
Slovakia	Strana Zelenych na Slovensku
Spain	Confederacion de Los Verdes
Sweden	Miljopartiet de Grona
Switzerland	Grune
Ukraine	Partija Zelenych Ukrajiny
United Kingdom	Green Party of England and Wales

SOURCE: Global Greens, at www.globalgreens.info, accessed January 2, 2005.

By 1990, there was sufficient support for the formation of state-level parties, initially in California and Alaska. In 1996 the National Association of State Green Parties was created as a more conventional structure for nominating candidates under the Green Party USA. Most Green Party victories were at the local level, especially on city councils in California during the 1990s. In 2000, consumer activist Ralph Nader was nominated as the party's presidential candidate, along with running mate Winona LaDuke. Although the Green Party candidates did not win any electoral votes, they picked up about 2.8 million popular votes nationwide, enraging Democrats who believed defections from voters in Florida and New Hampshire cost Al Gore Jr. the election. In Florida, Nader collected more than 97,000 votes; George W. Bush narrowly won the state by 537 votes.

In 2004, Nader ran for president under the banner of the Reform Party USA; but his name ended up on the ballot in only 34 states, compared to 44 in 2000. He had few resources except for student volunteers, and liberals feared he might once again serve as a campaign spoiler. Instead, the Green Party nominated two relative unknowns, David Cobb and Pat LaMarche. Overall, 430 Green candidates ran in 356 races, in 41 states, for 74 types of offices, with 63 victories. By year's end, there were 212 elected Green Party members in 27 states, 75 of them in California.[50]

International green parties are often more difficult to track, because they frequently change their names or form new alliances with other groups to bolster their political clout. In Hungary, for example, "greens" were initially called "blues" in reference to the Blue Danube Circle (those opposed to the building of the Nagymaros Dam); and in Poland, the largest environmental organization was not a party per se, but the Polish Ecology Club.

The first green party was the United Tasmania Group, which contested the local elections in the Tasmanian region of Australia in 1972. Although the party was unsuccessful in the 10 elections it contested before its dissolution in 1976, it was instrumental in placing the environment at the top of the Australian political agenda. The major wave of green party activity has been in Europe, primarily because the structure of European political systems allows political parties, even small ones, a role in policy making. During the 1970s, one of the first green parties to form was in Germany, where a loose coalition of groups, the Bund Burgerinitiativen Umweltschutz (BBU), organized massive demonstrations opposing nuclear energy but exercised little political power. Over the past two decades, the German greens have formed several electoral alliances, becoming what many believe is the most powerful environmental force in Europe. Their increasing role in national politics has come despite the death of one of their most influential leaders, Petra Kelly, in 1992.

The achievements of the German Greens have not been matched elsewhere, however. Initially, green parties' successes seemed to be limited to getting their members elected at the local and regional levels. In countries such as Sweden, where legislative seats are allotted based on a threshold level of representation, green parties have struggled to attract the necessary numbers of voters or often have been shut out of the process entirely. Even in those countries with proportional representation, most green parties have had little support, in large part because they modeled their strategy on the atypical German model. The "fading of the greens," as the phenomenon has been called, is not an indication of the public's lack of environmental interest or its saliency as a political issue. One observer has argued that in one sense the national green parties simply outlived their usefulness once the major political parties adopted the greens' issues as their own.[51] In addition, many environmental activists, sensing that structural barriers limited their ability to attain status as a potent political entity, shifted their energies toward affecting legislation and policy through NGOs.

During the 1990s, efforts focused on building coalitions of international green groups, developing a Global Green Network (GGN) and issuing joint statements on French nuclear testing in the South Pacific (1996) and the Kyoto climate change agreement (1997). In 2001, eight hundred representatives from 72 countries met in Canberra, Australia, to adopt a Global Green Charter; Green Federations represent regional attempts at organizing individual countries' parties.[52]

INTERNATIONAL GOVERNMENTAL ORGANIZATIONS

The concept of protecting the global environment through some form of international regime or institution did not occur until well into the 20th century.[53] The United Nations (UN) Charter of 1945, for instance, included no mention of the environment in its mission. Although 40 or more international environmental agreements were signed prior to World War II, most international governance was conducted through regional commissions. In 1909, for example, the United States and Canada formed the International Joint Commission to deal with transboundary issues between their shared 3,000-mile border; the United States and Mexico signed a similar treaty in 1906.

Since then, international governmental organizations (IGOs) have become important participants in the global effort to protect the environment. The United Nations has increasingly served as a diplomatic platform for negotiation of international agreements. In 1949, the UN held its first environmental conference on the Conservation and Utilization of Resources. Five years later, it sponsored the Conference on Conservation of Living Resources of the Sea, which resulted in the International Convention for the Prevention of Pollution of the Sea by Oil.

The UN entered a second phase of international environmental protection on January 17, 1972, when its General Assembly passed a Resolution on Development and Environment that criticized highly developed nations for improper planning and inadequate coordination of industrial activities that had led to serious environmental problems worldwide. In language highly critical of the United States, the UN General Assembly called upon the industrialized nations to provide additional technological assistance and financing, starting a decades-long debate over who should bear the cost of environmental cleanup in developing nations.

Today, environmental IGOs have begun to bring together the often competing issues of environmental protection and economic development. They can be structurally divided into two types: (a) organizations and programs developed under the auspices of the UN and (b) IGOs made up of states or national government bodies. The primary UN body charged with natural resource protection is the UN Environment Programme (UNEP), which was conceptualized at the 1972 Stockholm Conference on the Human Environment. UNEP was established in 1973 and is facilitated by a secretariat in Nairobi—a significant siting, as it is the only major global UN agency headquartered in a developing country. It is directed by a 58-member Governing Council, made up of representatives elected by the UN General Assembly and based on geographic region. The mission of the agency is set forth in 10-year-long work plans known as the Montevideo Programmes. Each work plan sets out the tasks and goals the UNEP expects to achieve; the 1992–2002 work plan identifies 18 areas for global environmental action.

UNEP has been widely criticized for becoming too bureaucratic and unwieldy and for problems with its financial management. It is primarily funded through voluntary contributions from member nations, and throughout the 1990s it faced a financial crisis that many observers believed could not be overcome. A subsequent compromise reorganization created a smaller advisory body that is charged with reviewing UNEP's administrative structure and making recommendations for change. Most recently, the organization has focused on outreach efforts to promote global observances related to children and the environment, planting trees, and cleanup efforts.

In the last decade of the 20th century, the issues of environment and development became even more closely intertwined. The Commission on Sustainable Development (CSD), established in 1993 as a body within the UN Economic and Social Council, has the primary responsibility for implementing the recommendations that were produced from the 1992 United Nations Conference on Environment and Development in Rio de Janeiro. The recommendations, known as Agenda 21,[54] encourage national and subnational governments to integrate environmental and economic concerns; but the CSD has no legal authority and has only the power to make recommendations. Another major IGO, the UN Development Programme (UNDP), is more active on the issues of development and trade.

Most funding for global efforts to protect the environment comes from the Global Environmental Facility (GEF), which was originally established in 1991 as a pilot project under the organizational umbrella of the World Bank. GEF has now become the largest multilateral source of funding for grants to individual countries for environmental projects. It, too, has been criticized because it focuses its funding priorities on only four areas: climate change, the conservation of biological diversity, the protection of international waters, and ozone depletion. Most of GEF's grants have been made to developing countries based on recommendations by its own scientific panel of experts. In contrast, the handful of IGOs that affect natural resource policy are made up of states or national government bodies. The most visible is the European Union Environment Agency, which serves as a regional IGO.

International governmental organizations are critical to global environmental protection, for a number of reasons. They allow problems like water or air pollution to be approached from an integrated perspective, rather than unilaterally. By standardizing policies such as acid deposition emissions, they recognize the importance of transboundary issues. They provide a forum for the diplomatic negotiation of issues, such as whaling, and serve as a clearinghouse for information and scientific research. The drawback of IGOs is that they have limited powers and virtually no enforcement capabilities. When a nation fails to abide by an international regime, such as the Convention on International Trade in Endangered

Species of Wild Fauna and Flora, there is little an IGO can do except attempt to apply the force of public opinion to the rogue state. However, forums like the UN are critical because without them, there would be no singular body or mechanism for disputes to be aired or problems to be addressed. Efforts to reform IGOs and make them stronger have failed to date, largely due to a lack of financial support and a fear by some developed nations that they might force industrialized countries to turn over valuable technology to poorer nations. A more likely future for IGOs is the continuing development of regional bodies and agreements, such as those that have been created as a result of the North American Free Trade Agreement and the General Agreement on Tariffs and Trade.

In addition, other major UN-based IGOs, like the Food and Agriculture Organization (FAO), United Nations Children's Fund (UNICEF), and the UN Population Fund (UNFPA), are assuming a more active role in environmental and development issues. Each of these IGOs is now interacting with UNEP and UNDP to coordinate global environmental initiatives.[55] (See Table 2.4.)

T A B L E 2.4   Major International Environmental and/or Developmental Intergovernmental Organizations (IGOs)

Commission for Environmental Cooperation (CEC)

Commission on Sustainable Development (CSD)

European Union Environment Agency (EUEA)

Food and Agriculture Organization (FAO)

Global Environmental Facility (GEF)

Intergovernmental Panel on Climate Change (IPCC)

International Atomic Energy Agency (IAEA)

International Council for the Exploration of the Sea (ICES)

International Fund for Agricultural Development (IFAD)

International Labour Organization (ILO)

International Maritime Organization (IMO)

International Monetary Fund (IMF)

International Oil Pollution Compensation Fund (IOPCF)

United Nations Children's Fund (UNICEF)

United Nations Development Programme (UNDP)

United Nations Education, Scientific, and Cultural Organization (UNESCO)

United Nations Environment Programme (UNEP)

United Nations Industrial Development Organization (UNIDO)

United Nations Population Fund (UNFPA)

World Bank

World Food Programme (WFP)

World Health Organization (WHO)

World Meteorological Organization (WMO)

TRANSNATIONAL ADVOCACY NETWORKS

Another type of participation in global environmental policy making is through what Margaret Keck and Kethryn Sikkink refer to as transnational advocacy networks, or TANs. They serve a key role by waging campaigns in which the members of a diffuse, principled network develop explicit, visible ties and mutually recognized roles in support of a common goal, or against a common target. Despite the cultural diversity found within TANs, there is agreement on focused and planned efforts.[56]

TANs might be made up of NGOs, local social movements, foundations, the media, churches, trade unions, consumer organizations, parts of IGOs, and parts of government bodies. They share values, exchange information, and form a dense web of formal and informal connections. Personnel may circulate within and among networks, as may funding. TANs emerged as part of the growth of IGOs committed to social change. Those devoted to environmental issues have grown dramatically, with other major increases found in groups dealing with human rights and women's rights. Issues surrounding tribal populations and indigenous peoples are often the catalysts for TAN development. Using the media, networks publicized the tremendous amount of environmental degradation left behind by the Soviet military in eastern Europe. Networks have also focused on the logging of tropical forests in Indonesia and boreal forests in arctic areas. Only the concerted campaigns of the members, combined with a consistent message, have made these environmental issues of global importance, rather than just local.

NOTES

1. Michael Shellenberger and Ted Nordhaus, "The Death of Environmentalism," at www.grist.org, accessed January 16, 2005.

2. Ibid.

3. Ibid.

4. Ibid.

5. Adam Werbach, "Is Environmentalism Dead?" at www.grist.org, accessed January 16, 2005.

6. Ibid.

7. Amanda Griscom Little, "Green Leaders Say Rumors of Environmentalism's Death Are Greatly Exaggerated," *Grist Magazine,* January 13, 2005, at www.grist.org, accessed January 16, 2005.

8. Ron Arnold, "The 'Death of Environmentalism' Controversy: Obituary? Or Sales Pitch?" at www.cdfe.org, accessed January 17, 2005.

9. Kathie Durbin, "Unsalvageable," *High Country News 37,* no. 9 (May 16, 2005), 8–13, 19.

10. Native Forest Network, "Logging of Old-Growth Ancient Forest Reserves Begins in Siskiyous," at www.nativeforest.org/biscuit, accessed April 4, 2005. Norman was killed in an automobile collision July 23, 2005.

11. Durbin, "Unsalvageable."

12. Harold D. Lasswell, *Politics: Who Gets What, When, How.* (New York: P. Smith, 1936).

13. For the classical tenets of group theory, see David Truman, *The Governmental Process* (New York: Knopf, 1951), and Earl Latham, *The Group Basis of Politics* (New York: Octagon Books, 1965).

14. Riley E. Dunlap and Angela G. Mertig, "The Evolution of the U.S. Environmental Movement from 1970 to 1990: An Overview," in *American Environmentalism: The U.S.*

Environmental Movement, 1970–1990, ed. Riley E. Dunlap and Angela G. Mertig (Washington, DC: Taylor & Francis, 1992), 4.

15. See Michael S. Greve, "Private Enforcement, Private Rewards: How Environmental Suits Became an Entitlement Program," in *Environmental Politics: Public Costs, Private Rewards,* ed. Michael S. Greve and Fred L. Smith Jr. (New York: Praeger, 1992), 105–109.

16. Greenpeace, "About Us," at www.greenpeaceusa.org/aboutus/, accessed February 20, 2005.

17. Robert D. Bullard. *Dumping in Dixie: Race, Class, and Environmental Quality,* 3rd ed. (Boulder, CO: Westview, 2000), 10.

18. See, for example, Allan Schnaiberg, *The Environment: From Surplus to Scarcity* (New York: Oxford University Press, 1980); Bunyan Bryant and Paul Mohai, eds., *Race and Incidence of Environmental Hazards* (Boulder, CO: Westview Press, 1992); Richard Hofrichter, ed., *Toxic Struggles: The Theory and Practice of Environmental Justice* (Philadelphia: New Society, 1993); Bunyan Bryant, ed., *Environmental Justice: Issues, Policies, and Solutions* (Covelo, CA: Island Press, 1995); and David E. Camacho, ed., *Environmental Injustices, Political Struggles: Race, Class, and the Environment* (Durham, NC: Duke University Press, 1998).

19. United Church of Christ Commission for Racial Justice, *Proceedings: The First National People of Color Environmental Leadership Summit* (New York: United Church of Christ Commission for Racial Justice, 1993), xiii–xiv.

20. Robert D. Bullard, ed., *Confronting Environmental Racism: Voices from the Grassroots* (Boston: South End Press, 1993), 17.

21. Robert D. Bullard, "The Environmental Justice Movement Comes of Age," *Amicus Journal, 16,* no. 1 (Spring 1994): 32–37.

22. U.S. Environmental Protection Agency, "National Environmental Justice Advisory Council Overview," at www.epa.gov/compliance/environmentaljustice, accessed May 23, 2005; and U.S. Environmental Protection Agency, "Environmental Justice: Frequently Asked Questions," at www.epa.gov/compliance/resources/faqs, accessed May 23, 2005.

23. Christopher H. Foreman Jr., *The Promise and Peril of Environmental Justice* (Washington, DC: Brookings Institution, 1998), 3, 133.

24. Segun Gbadegesin, "Multinational Corporations, Developed Nations, and Environmental Racism: Toxic Waste, Exploration, and Eco-Catastrophe," in *Faces of Environmental Racism: Confronting Issues of Global Justice,* ed. Laura Westra and Bill E. Lawson (Lanham, MD: Rowman & Littlefield, 2001).

25. Statement of John Lewis, U.S. Senate Committee on Environment and Public Works, May 18, 2005, at http://epw.senate.gov/hearing_statements, accessed May 23, 2005.

26. Ibid.

27. Earth First! "About Earth First!" at www.earthfirst.org/about, accessed May 23, 2005.

28. Eco-Saboteurs Adding to Their List of Targets," *Arizona Republic,* July 1, 2001, A6.

29. For various perspectives on the Vail incident and ELF, see Daniel Glick, *Powder Burn: Arson, Money, and Mystery on Vail Mountain* (New York: Public Affairs, 2001); Alex Markels, "Backfire," *Mother Jones,* March–April 1999, 60–64, 78–79; Steven K. Paulson, "Environmental Activists Criticized," *Yahoo! News,* October 23, 1998; Jan Faust, "Earth Liberation Who?" ABC News.com, October 22, 1998; Robert Weller, "Group Claims It Caused Fires," ABC News.com, October 22, 1998; and Michelle Nijhuis, "ELF Strikes Again," *High Country News,* February 1, 1999, 3.

30. Statement of John Lewis.

31. Felicity Barringer, "Arsonists Tried to Burn More Homes, Maryland Officials Say," *New York Times,* December 9, 2004, at www.nytimes.com, accessed May 23, 2005; and Tom Pelton, "Ecoterror–A Clearer Threat," *Baltimore Sun,* December 12, 2004, at www.baltimoresun.com/news, accessed May 23, 2005.

32. Marc Morano, "Eco-Extremism Being Ignored in School Shooting Case, Critic Alleges," *Cybercast News Service,* March 23, 2005, at www.cnsnews.com, accessed May 23, 2005.

33. See Robert Hunter, *Warriors of the Rainbow: A Chronicle of the Greenpeace Movement* (New York: Holt, Rinehart and Winston, 1979); Paul Watson, *Sea Shepherd* (New York: Norton, 1982); Rick Scarce, *Eco-Warriors: Understanding the Radical Environmental Movement* (Chicago: Noble Press, 1990); and Dave Foreman, *Confessions of an Eco-Warrior* (New York: Harmony Books, 1991).

34. Scott Sunde and Paul Shukovsky, "Elusive Radicals Escalate Attacks in Nature's Name," *Seattle Post-Intelligencer,* June 18, 2001, at www.seattlepi.com, accessed August 7, 2001.

35. Samuel P. Hays, *Beauty, Health and Permanence: Environmental Politics in the United States 1955–1985* (Cambridge: Cambridge University Press, 1987), 295.

36. See United Steelworkers of America, *Poison in Our Air* (Washington, DC: United Steelworkers of America, 1969).

37. Hays, *Beauty, Health and Permanence,* 308.

38. Perspectives on the role of industry in environmental policy making vary widely. See, for example, Neil Gunningham, Robert A. Kagan, and Dorothy Thornton. *Shades of Green: Business, Regulation, and Environment* (Stanford: Stanford University Press, 2003); Hugh S. Gorman, *Redefining Efficiency: Pollution Concerns, Regulatory Mechanisms, and Technological Change in the U.S.* (Akron, OH: University of Akron Press, 2001); and Jack Doyle, *Taken for a Ride: Detroit's Big Three and the Politics of Pollution* (New York: Four Walls Eight Windows, 2000).

39. Alan M. Gottlieb, ed., *The Wise Use Agenda* (Bellevue, WA: Free Enterprise Press, 1989).

40. For different views of the grassroots movements, see Ron Arnold, *Ecology Wars: Environmentalism As If People Mattered* (Bellevue, WA: Free Enterprise Press, 1987); David Helvarg, *The War against the Greens: The "Wise Use" Movement, the New Right, and Anti-Environmental Violence* (San Francisco: Sierra Club Books, 1994); John Echeverria and Raymond Booth Eby, eds., *Let the People Judge: Wise Use and the Private Property Rights Movement* (Washington, DC: Island Press, 1995); Philip D. Brick and R. McGreggor Cawley, eds., *A Wolf in the Garden: The Lands Rights Movement and the New Environmental Debate* (Lanham, MD: Rowman & Littlefield, 1996); and Paul R. Ehrlich and Anne H. Ehrlich, *The Betrayal of Science and Reason* (Washington, DC: Island Press, 1996).

41. Keith Schneider, "A County's Bid for U.S. Land Draws Lawsuit," *New York Times,* March 9, 1995, A1.

42. Roger W. Cobb and Charles D. Elder, *Participation in American Politics: The Dynamics of Agenda-Building,* 2nd ed. (Baltimore: Johns Hopkins University Press, 1983).

43. James Anderson, *Public Policymaking,* 4th ed. (Boston: Houghton Mifflin, 2000), 100.

44. Peter Bachrach and Morton Baratz, *Power and Poverty* (New York: Oxford University Press, 1970), 44.

45. Gregg Easterbrook, *A Moment on the Earth: The Coming Age of Environmental Optimism* (New York: Viking, 1995), 493.

46. On the role of the media, see, for example, Anthony J. Eksterowicz and Robert N. Roberts, eds., *Public Journalism and Political Knowledge* (New York: Rowman & Littlefield, 2000), P 2–36.

47. See Lester Ross, "The Politics of Environmental Policy in the People's Republic of China," in *Ecological Policy and Politics in Developing Countries,* ed. Uday Desai (Albany: State University of New York Press, 1998, 47–64; and John Leicester, "A 'Green' Movement Takes Root in China," *San Francisco Examiner,* November 29, 1998, A22.

48. See Benjamin Seel, Matthew Paterson, and Brian Doherty, eds., *Direct Action in British Environmentalism* (London: Routledge, 2000); Derek Wall, *Earth First! and the Origin of the Anti-Roads Movement* (London: Routledge, 1999); and Russell J. Dalton, *The Green Rainbow: Environmental Groups in Western Europe* (New Haven, CT: Yale University Press, 1994).

49. "Twentieth Anniversary of the American Green Movement," at www.greenparty.org, accessed November 10, 2004.

50. Jonathan Finer and Spencer S. Hua. "Repeat Role as Spoiler Is Unlikely," *Washington Post,* November 3, 2004, at www.washingtonpost.com, accessed November 10, 2004; Green Party USA. "Green Party Election Highlights," at www.gp.org/2004election, accessed November 10, 2004.

51. Anna Bramwell, *The Fading of the Greens: The Decline of Environmental Politics in the West* (New Haven: Yale University Press, 1994).

52. John Rensenbrink, "A Brief History of the Global Green Network," at www.globalgreens.info, accessed November 10, 2004.

53. Marvin S. Soroos, "Global Institutions and the Environment: An Evolutionary Perspective," in *The Global Environment,* ed. Norman J. Vig and Regina S. Axelrod (Washington, DC: Congressional Quarterly Press, 1999), 27–51.

54. United Nations, *Agenda 21: Report of the United Nations: Conference on Environment and Development* (New York: United Nations, 1992).

55. For an overview of IGOs and their role in environmental protection, see Oran Young, *International Governance: Protecting the Environment in a Stateless Society* (Ithaca, NY: Cornell University Press, 1994); Lamont C. Hempel, *Environmental Governance: The Global Challenge* (Washington, DC: Island Press, 1996); and Ronnie D. Lipschutz with Judith Mayer, *Global Civil Society and Global Environmental Governance: The Politics of Nature from Place to Planet* (Albany: State University of New York Press, 1996).

56. Margaret E. Keck and Kathryn Sikkink. *Activists Beyond Borders: Advocacy Networks in International Politics* (Ithaca, NY: Cornell University Press, 1998). See also Pamela S. Chasek, ed., *The Global Environment in the Twenty-First Century: Prospects for International Cooperation* (New York: United Nations University Press, 2000).

FURTHER READING

Melissa Checker. *Toxic Doughnut: Environmental Racism, Community Activism and Social Justice.* Philadelphia: Routledge, 2005.

Timothy Doyle. *Environmental Movements in Majority and Minority Worlds: A Global Perspective.* Piscataway, NJ: Rutgers University Press, 2005.

Taj I. Hamad, Frederick A. Swarts, and Anne Ranniste Smart. *Culture of Responsibility and the Role of NGOs.* Washington, DC: World Association of Non-Governmental Organizations, 2003.

Norichika Kanie and Peter M. Haas. *Emerging Forces in Environmental Governance.* New York: United Nations University Press, 2004.

Steve Lerner. *Diamond: A Struggle for Environmental Justice in Louisiana's Chemical Corridor.* Cambridge, MA: MIT Press, 2005.

Jenny Pickerill. *Cyberprotest: Environmental Protest On-Line.* Manchester, UK: Manchester University Press, 2003.

Tom Turner. *Justice on Earth: Earthjustice and the People It Has Served.* White River Junction, VT: Chelsea Green, 2003.

Gerald R. Visgilio and Diana M. Whitelaw, eds. *Our Backyard: A Quest for Environmental Justice.* Lanham, MD: Rowman & Littlefield, 2003.

Rex Weyler. *Greenpeace: How a Group of Ecologists, Journalists, and Visionaries Changed the World.* New York: Rodale Books, 2005.

3

The Political Process

"The EPA is no longer a public health agency. It's become a country club for America's polluters."
—FORMER EPA CHIEF PROSECUTOR ERIC SCHAEFFER[1]

The Environmental Protection Agency (EPA) is considered by many to be the most visible yet controversial of the federal government's environmental agencies. Created by executive order in 1970, the EPA has responsibility for implementing most of the nation's pollution control statutes. As this chapter illustrates, the agency's history has frequently paralleled the ups and downs of the nation's environmental movement and partisan politics during its often turbulent history.

Although the EPA is not an official part of the president's cabinet, the agency's administrator is among the most watched appointees within the administration. From 2001 to 2005, President George W. Bush made three appointments to the position, reflecting his attempts to reconcile his policy views with the agency's mission and leadership.

His first appointee, Christine Todd Whitman, a former governor of New Jersey, was called an unlikely choice for the position. "From the outset it was clear she knew relatively little about environmental policy and would have preferred a more high profile post," noted one observer, who called her two-year term "relatively unremarkable."[2]

The Capitol builiding in Washington, DC is the focus of two stages in the policymaking process—policy formulation and adoption—as Congress identifies and frames environmental problems.

TOM TILL

Whitman appeared to have difficulty adhering to the administration's views, especially on global warming, and some criticized her for insensitivity toward the concerns of state and local governments. Others felt that the agency's internal battles reflected fundamental differences over agency direction and Whitman's attempt to distance herself from lobbyists. She resigned in May 2003 and was replaced by another governor, Utah's Mike Leavitt, in November 2003.[3] Leavitt, in contrast, was considered an antiregulatory advocate who won praise from oil, gas, and off-road vehicle interests while being attacked by environmental groups. His low-key, soft-spoken style seemed to fit well with the Bush administration's desire to keep environmental issues out of the news.[4]

Leavitt fit the administration's leadership needs at the EPA for a year before Bush appointed him Secretary of Health and Human Services just after the 2004 election, replacing former Wisconsin governor Tommy Thompson. The vacancy at EPA left the agency in limbo for several months, with some observers speculating that Bush preferred that EPA be run from the White House. In January 2005, Stephen L. Johnson became acting administrator; he had previously served as acting deputy administrator and worked at EPA for 24 years. President Bush nominated Johnson as administrator in March 2005.

A career scientist with degrees in biology and pathology, Johnson worked his way up through the agency hierarchy, primarily in senior-level positions dealing with toxic substances and hazardous waste. He received the Presidential Rank Award—the highest award that can be given to a civilian federal employee—from Bush in 2001. He became the first EPA administrator to rise from the agency's professional ranks. Johnson's nomination won praise from the major power producers of the Electric Reliability Coordinating Council, who called him "a capable leader . . . a respected, seasoned professional."[5] Some environmental organizations approved, with a representative of the Environmental Working Group noting Johnson is "a spectacularly good appointment . . . known for his intellectual rigor, knowledge of environmental issues, and his fairness."[6]

The leadership shuffle illustrates how political appointments can be an effective tool in policy development and implementation. Leaders of the Natural Resources Defense Council noted that "Our experience with [Johnson's] predecessors, however, proved that it's not the man who matters in this job, so much as the mission set by the White House," and Sierra Club Executive Director Carl Pope hoped that Johnson would "rise above the White House's expectations that he will be a figurehead."[7] Johnson himself may have underscored that perception; when he was nominated by Bush, Johnson pledged that he would continue to advance the administration's environmental agenda while maintaining the nation's economic competitiveness.

Chapters 1 and 2 provided an overview of the political context in which environmental policy is made, outlining the historical development of environmental consciousness and awareness and identifying the key stakeholders who participate in the environmental debate. Policy scholars characterize those activities and actors as the first and second stages of the policy-making process: problem identification and agenda setting, followed by policy formulation. This chapter continues with an explanation of the third stage, policy adoption, and then moves to the fourth stage, policy implementation. The discussion begins with an analysis of two government institutions that are often referred to as the "official policy makers": the president and Congress.

PRESIDENTIAL LEADERSHIP

Most scholars consider the president to be one of the key stakeholders in setting the policy agenda and in directing the discussion of potential options in formulating policy. Historically, however, the president has had a limited role in environmental politics, with much of the power delegated to the executive branch agencies.[8] Not until Richard Nixon's tenure began in 1969 did the environment become a presidential priority, and even then, Nixon was reluctant to act. After years of study and staff negotiations, Nixon agreed to a federal reorganization plan calling for an independent pollution control agency that later became the EPA, discussed later in this chapter.

The agency opened its doors under the stewardship of William Ruckelshaus, a graduate of Harvard Law School and former Indiana assistant attorney general. Although he had virtually no background in environmental issues, Ruckelshaus had the support of Nixon's attorney general, John Mitchell, and was confirmed after only two days of hearings. On the day of his selection as administrator, Ruckelshaus was briefed by Nixon, who gave him the impression that he considered the environmental problem "faddish."[9] Ruckelshaus came to the EPA with three priorities: to create a well-defined enforcement image for the agency, to carry out the provisions of the newly amended Clean Air Act, and to gain control over the costs of regulatory decision making.[10] In setting up the agency, Ruckelshaus decided each regional organization within the EPA should mirror the full agency's structure, with staff capabilities in every program area and delegation of responsibility to regional offices, creating an organizational structure that gave the agency a rare capability to make decisions, move programs ahead, and motivate people to produce high volumes of work.[11] Inside the EPA, morale was high, in large part due to the accessibility of Ruckelshaus to his staff. Outside, he became a forceful spokesperson for the public interest and was well respected by both sides in the environmental debate. Early on, Ruckelshaus concentrated on air and water pollution, assigning three quarters of his staff to that task. As a result, there was an improvement in noncompliance with air quality standards in most cities, and the agency effected a change from aesthetic concerns about the recreational uses of water to health concerns.[12]

Nixon's efforts to give credibility to the Department of the Interior were not nearly as successful. It appears that the creation of the EPA relegated the Department of the Interior to backseat status as far as environmental issues were concerned. A succession of secretaries came and went (see Table 3.1) while the

TABLE 3.1 Department of Interior and EPA Leadership, 1970–2005

President	Secretary of the Interior	EPA Administrator
Nixon	Rogers Morton (1971–74)	William Ruckelshaus (1970–73)
Ford	Rogers Morton (1974–75)	Russell Train (1973–77)
	Stanley Hathaway (1975)	
	Thomas Kleppe (1975–77)	
Carter	Cecil Andrus (1977–81)	Douglas Costle (1977–81)
Reagan	James Watt (1981–83)	Anne (Gorsuch) Burford (1981–83)
	William Clark (1983–85)	William Ruckelshaus (1983–85)
	Donald Hodel (1985–89)	Lee Thomas (1985–89)
Bush	Manuel Lujan Jr. (1989–92)	William Reilly (1989–92)
Clinton	Bruce Babbitt (1993–2001)	Carol Browner (1993–2001)
Bush (G.W.)	Gale Norton (2001–)	Christine Whitman (2001– 03)
		Mike Leavitt (2003–04)
		Steve Johnson (2005–)

EPA administrators garnered publicity and notoriety. Despite these efforts, there is some doubt as to how much Nixon really cared about the environment as an issue. Some staff members believed the Nixon reorganization experts were neither proponents nor opponents of environmental reform; their specialty was management and organization. They focused on the environment because that was the area in which political pressures were creating a demand for action.

Typical is the case of Walter Hickel, whom Nixon chose in late 1968 as the new interior secretary, setting off a storm of protest. Hickel, who had grown up in Kansas and lived on a tenant farm during the Depression, was a Golden Gloves boxer who loved to fight. As governor of Alaska, he was accused of being a pawn of the U.S. Chamber of Commerce and of the oil industry. After four days of defensive hearings, his nomination was confirmed. Hickel's bold style was his undoing; he offended the president in a rambling letter about Nixon's policies (eventually leaked to the press) after the Kent State shootings. The gaffe came at a time when the president's staff was considering the reorganization proposal that would have elevated Hickel to head the new Department of Natural Resources. He was fired Thanksgiving Day, 1970.[13]

In 1971, Nixon chose Earl Butz as his secretary of agriculture; Butz was an academician who had taught and served as an administrator at Purdue University and had worked in the U.S. Department of Agriculture (USDA) for three years. But as would become the case with subsequent presidents, leadership of the Forest Service would be less controversial and more stable. Edward Cliff, who had been named Chief in 1962, served for 10 years before Nixon named his replacement, John McGuire, who would serve Nixon, Ford and Carter.

To Nixon's credit, it should be noted that it was under his administration that the United States first began to take a more global approach to environmental protection. Ruckelshaus was successful in convincing Nixon of the important role the United States could play at the <u>UN Conference on the Human Environment in June 1972 in Stockholm</u>. Although the United States was not totally in agreement with the priorities of the United Nations Environment Programme, which grew out of the Stockholm conference, <u>Nixon persuaded Congress to pay the largest share (36 percent) of the new secretariat's budget.</u>[14]

When <u>Gerald Ford</u> took over as president upon Nixon's resignation, he made <u>few changes in the way environmental policy was being conducted.</u> Russell Train remained head of the EPA under Ford and served in that position until Ford was defeated by Jimmy Carter in 1976. Carter kept most of Nixon's other environmental appointees, including Interior Secretary Rogers Morton and Agriculture Secretary Robert Berglund. For the most part, the crush of environmental programs that marked the Nixon years slowed considerably under Ford, for three reasons. One, <u>the energy shortage created by the 1973 Arab oil embargo pushed pollution off the legislative agenda for several years</u> (see Chapter 6). A second factor was a <u>growing concern that the cost to industry to comply with EPA standards was slowing the economy</u> at a time when expansion was needed. Last, the environ<u>mental momentum of the early 1970s faded by 1976</u>, and Ford did little to refuel it. Congressional initiatives expanded the EPA's authority with the <u>Safe Drinking Water Act of 1974</u>, the <u>Toxic Substances Control Act of 1976</u>, and the <u>Resource Conservation and Recovery Act (RCRA) of 1976</u> (legislation discussed in later chapters), but Ford's unsuccessful presidential campaign made him an observer, rather than a participant, in the policy-making process. The environmental slate for Gerald Ford is a clean, albeit empty, one.

In 1976, groups such as the League of Conservation Voters gave presidential candidate Jimmy Carter high grades for his environmental record as governor of Georgia, although his campaign focused more on other issues, such as human rights and the economy. <u>President Carter openly courted environmental groups during his single-term administration, and he counted on their support to carry him through to reelection in 1980</u>, when he lost to Ronald Reagan. He received high marks from environmental groups that believed he would emphasize environmental issues in his administration, but he initially offended one of the environmental movement's heroes, Maine Senator Edmund Muskie. Carter began by choosing <u>Douglas Costle to head the EPA over the objections of Muskie</u>. Costle, a Seattle native, attended Harvard and the University of Chicago Law School and had worked at the Office of Management and Budget under Nixon. His main environmental credential was a stint as Commissioner for Environmental Affairs in Connecticut, but he had a strong financial management background from working at the Congressional Budget Office.

 <u>Under Costle, the EPA became the first federal agency to adopt Carter's plan of zero-based budgeting.</u> Costle's main aim in taking over the agency was <u>"to convince the public that EPA was first and foremost a public health agency, not a guardian of birds and bunnies."</u>[15] Taking Costle's lead, Congress responded by passing the <u>Superfund authorization in late 1980, establishing a $1.6 billion emergency fund to clean up toxic contaminants spilled or dumped into the environment.</u> The result was a major shift in the agency's regulatory focus from conventional pollutants to toxics. This allowed the agency room to grow, and

justified a 25 percent budget increase at a time when the president was preaching strict austerity.

Carter had a number of environmental achievements during his term, including passage in 1980 of the landmark Alaska National Interest Lands Conservation Act, or Alaska Land Bill, which brought millions of acres of pristine wilderness under federal protection. As part of his attempt to gain group support, Carter convinced Congress to consider a windfall profits tax on oil to fund solar research and pushed stronger energy conservation measures. But the inability of Congress to develop a comprehensive energy policy under his administration has led most observers to conclude that Carter was not an especially effective leader in environmental policy or in protecting the environment.

The eight years of Ronald Reagan's administration mark a stormy chapter in environmental politics. Critics believe that he almost single-handedly destroyed the progress that had been made in the area of pollution control. Supporters point to his legislative achievements and say the picture was not so bleak after all; but critics argue that those successes came as a result of congressional initiative, not from Reagan. During his stints as governor of California and then as president, Reagan was heavily influenced by pro-business interests like Colorado brewer Joseph Coors, who urged him to take a more conservative approach to environmental regulation. Coors and his allies were represented in Reagan's inner circle by Nevada Senator Paul Laxalt, and they focused their attention on the appointment of a conservative secretary of the interior who would show prudent respect for development interests, especially in the West.[16]

Their candidate was James Watt, a Wyoming native who had served as a legislative aide to Senator Milward Simpson. He had served as a member of the Nixon transition team in 1968 to help Walter Hickel through his confirmation hearings as secretary of the interior and was then appointed deputy secretary for water and power. In 1977, he founded the Mountain States Legal Foundation, a conservative anti-environmental regulation law firm, and was later connected to the leadership of the Sagebrush Rebellion (see Chapter 2). Although some of Reagan's advisors preferred Clifford P. Hansen, former governor and senator from Wyoming, for the Department of the Interior slot, Watt's rhetorical style and ability to bring in dollars as a conservative fund-raiser for Reagan gave him a decided edge. He was a spokesperson for the New Right, among those who believed Reagan was drifting too close to the political center.[17]

Watt divided people into two categories—liberals and Americans—and called the Audubon Society "a chanting mob."[18] He perceived environmentalists as "dangerous and subversive,"[19] suggesting they sought to weaken America and to undermine freedom. He called them extremists and likened them to Nazis. More telling, however, was the comparison of Watt to his predecessor, Cecil Andrus, who had said, "I am part of the environmental movement and I intend to make the Interior Department responsive to the movement's needs."[20] Watt discovered he had great independence in molding the agency to conform to his policy interests. Among his first directives, he ordered a moratorium on any further National Park acquisitions and announced his intention to open up federal lands to mining and logging. He proposed to permit leasing of 1.3 million acres off the California coast for offshore oil and gas exploration and auctioned off 1.1 billion tons of coal in the Powder River Basin of Montana and Wyoming, actions that infuriated environmentalists. By summer 1981, Watt had made enough enemies that the Sierra Club, National Wildlife Federation, and Audubon Society gathered more than 1 million signatures seeking Watt's ouster. Together, 10 organizations urged President Reagan to fire Watt, issuing a stinging indictment that purported to show how he had subverted environmental policy.

His supporters, however, point out that under Watt, the federal government spent more than $1 billion to restore and improve the existing national parks, and 1.8 million acres were added to the nation's wilderness system. Watt's vision was to develop America's energy resources and to remove what many perceived as excessive regulation of business, efforts at which he was successful.[21] But by late 1982, Watt was under heavy criticism for his actions, although he was blunt enough to say out loud what many in the Reagan administration were thinking. Reagan called Watt's record "darn good"[22] but urged him to reconcile with environmental groups, to whom he had stopped speaking just six weeks into his job. They continued to criticize him for refusing to touch more than $1 billion in the Land and Water Conservation Fund, which had been set aside for national park acquisition, and for spending only about half of the amount of funds for land acquisition appropriated by Congress.[23]

Watt's bluntness turned out to haunt him after he banned the musical group, the Beach Boys, from performing a concert on the Capitol Mall, embarrassing the president and the first lady (a great admirer of the musicians), who rescheduled the event. Then, in a speech before Chamber of Commerce lobbyists, Watt recalled that an Interior Department coal advisory panel comprised "a black, a woman, two Jews and a cripple," a remark widely criticized in the press. Eventually this made Watt a major liability to Reagan, who then asked for his resignation. Shortly thereafter, Reagan appointed William Clark, a man whose term was as undistinguished as Watt's had been tumultuous, to head the Department of Interior. Clark served less than a year and a half and was replaced by Donald Hodel, another moderate.

Reagan's appointment of Anne (Gorsuch) Burford as administrator of the Environmental Protection Agency proved to be even more of an embarrassment than Watt. Burford, a former member of the Colorado legislature, became one of the youngest of Reagan's appointees despite her lack of administrative experience. She began her term as administrator by reorganizing the agency, abolishing divisions only to reestablish them later. The EPA's highly politicized staff members demoralized careerists, and the agency was constantly under siege both from environmental groups (who believed Burford's appointment signaled Reagan's support for industry interests) and from members of Congress. More telling, perhaps, was the loss of a fifth of the EPA's personnel and the major cuts in the agency's budget that began in 1980.[24]

Under Burford, the Office of Enforcement was dismantled, and personnel within the agency found their positions downgraded. Environmental professionals were often passed over for promotion by political appointees, and neither of the two original associate administrators served more than 100 days.[25] The Reagan administration became embroiled in further controversy when several top EPA administrators, including the agency's general counsel, were investigated or accused of conflict of interest, perjury, giving sweetheart deals to polluters who had influential political ties, and other misdeeds. By the end of Reagan's third year in office, more than 20 senior EPA employees had been removed from office and several key agency officials had resigned under pressure.[26]

The biggest fall was Burford's. In fall 1982, John Dingell, chairman of the House Committee on Energy and Commerce, initiated an investigation of alleged abuses in Superfund enforcement and sought EPA documents as part of the case. Dingell subpoenaed Burford to appear in court to provide the committee with the documents; but based on Justice Department advice, she declined to do so, citing the doctrine of executive privilege. In December 1982, the House voted to declare her in contempt of Congress. Eventually a compromise was struck that allowed the committee to examine nearly all the documents they sought, and the contempt citation was dropped.

The contempt charge was coupled with charges of EPA mismanagement of cleanup operations after discovery of the toxic chemical dioxin in roadways at Times Beach, Missouri. The project had been handled by EPA Assistant Administrator for Hazardous Waste, Rita Lavelle, who was eventually fired by Reagan. Lavelle was the only EPA official to face criminal charges, and she was convicted of perjury and obstructing a congressional investigation. She was sentenced to six months in prison and fined $10,000. The incident cast further doubt on Burford's ability to manage the agency, and she resigned March 9, 1983. At a press conference two days later, Reagan said he believed that it was he, not Burford, who was the real target of Congress's action. He said that he never would have asked for her resignation.[27] Congress did not let up even after Burford resigned. At the end of August 1984, a House Energy and Commerce Oversight Committee concluded that from 1981 to 1983, "top level officials of the EPA violated their public trust by disregarding the public health and environment, manipulating the Superfund program for political purposes, engaging in unethical conduct, and participating in other abuses."[28]

To return the agency to some semblance of credibility, Reagan called upon the EPA's first administrator, William Ruckelshaus, who returned to coordinate salvage operations. Ruckelshaus restored morale to the middle-level EPA staff, reversed the adversarial posture of the EPA toward Congress and the media, and brought in new and experienced administrators to replace political appointees.[29] During his second stint as administrator, Ruckelshaus revised the standards for the lead content in gasoline and declared an emergency ban on ethylene dibromide (EDB), a pesticide widely used in grain and food production. Ruckelshaus served until after Reagan's reelection, when the president appointed his third EPA administrator, Lee Thomas.

Thomas, a South Carolina native, became the first nonlawyer to head the agency. He had previously worked in the Federal Emergency Management Administration and headed the Times Beach Task Force that led to Rita Lavelle's firing. When Lavelle left, Thomas took over her position as coordinator of hazardous waste, Superfund, and RCRA programs. Seen as a career EPA employee, he redefined the agency's mission. On the one hand, he focused attention on localized concerns such as medical waste and the garbage crisis that was threatening urban areas. At the same time, he brought attention to global concerns like the weakening of the ozone layer and chlorofluorocarbons (CFCs).

Thomas made sure that the EPA became an active participant in international forums and returned the environment to the policy agenda.[30] Another major achievement was the full restoration of the EPA's reputation for strong enforcement, especially after the agency reached a 1985 agreement with Westinghouse Corporation to spend $100 million to clean up toxic waste at its Indiana facilities. This was followed in 1986 by an agreement with Aerojet General to clean up a toxic dump near Sacramento (estimated to cost the company $82 million) and in 1988 by a $1 billion cleanup agreement with Shell Oil and the U.S. Army at the Rocky Mountain arsenal near Denver.

Keeping to the tradition of naming farmers to head the Department of Agriculture, Reagan appointed John Block, a West Point graduate, farmer, and former Illinois secretary of agriculture. Block was followed by Richard Lyng, owner of a family seed and bean firm who had served under Reagan in California. The Forest Service, unlike the other agencies, had one chief during the Reagan administration—Max Peterson, who served until George H. W. Bush named Dale Robertson as his successor.

Many environmentalists believed George H. W. Bush's campaign promise to be "the environmental president" when he appointed William Reilly to head the EPA in 1989. Reilly, who had previously served as head of the U.S. branch of the World Wildlife Fund, was the first environmental professional to serve as administrator. He had also established a reputation as a moderate while serving with the Washington, D.C.–based Conservation Foundation. The Sierra Club took a wait-and-see attitude, declaring that Reilly was "clearly tagged to be the administration's good guy in a very tough job."[31] Reilly's agenda was different from those of the Reagan appointees. In several early speeches and articles, he reiterated the need for pollution prevention as "a fundamental part of all our activities, all our initiatives, and all our economic growth," making it the theme of EPA's Earth Day celebrations in April 1990.[32] He also pointed to science and risk assessment "to help the Agency put together a much more coherent agenda than has characterized the past 20 years."[33] Reilly and Bush were jointly praised for having broken the legislative gridlock that characterized clean air legislation since the amendments had last been revised in 1977 (see Chapter 8).

Some observers believe, however, that Reilly's efforts were often derailed by members of the White House staff, especially by then Chief of Staff John Sununu, who ridiculed EPA pronouncements on global warming and wetlands preservation, and by budget director Richard Darman, who once called Reilly "a global rock star."[34] Sununu was criticized by environmentalists, who believe he blocked serious international negotiations on global warming. Reilly was caught up in White House politics again in June 1992 when a memo to President Bush on negotiations at the Earth Summit was leaked to the press; some insiders believe that Vice President Dan Quayle's office was responsible.

Bush's other appointees were given mixed reviews, from Michael Deland, head of the Council on Environmental Quality (CEQ) and an ardent environmentalist, to James Watkins, Bush's secretary of energy, who won praise for his commitment to alternative energy and energy conservation policy, although critics of the administration felt that his views had not been translated into substantive policy change. The appointment of Manuel Lujan Jr., a former congressional representative from New Mexico, as secretary of interior was criticized by environmental groups that believed he favored the logging and mining interests of the West. Lujan's critics became even more alarmed when he agreed in October 1991 to convene the so-called Endangered Species "God Squad" to review the denial of timber permits on Bureau of Land Management (BLM) property because they threatened the habitat of the northern spotted owl, a species that had been declared threatened the previous year. But the secretary's supporters argued that he was taking a more reasonable approach to the Endangered Species Act and simply invoking a mechanism provided for under law. Equally controversial was the president's wetlands policy. By redefining what constitutes a wetland, the administration had exempted thousands of acres of land from federal protection—a move that pleased the business community and angered environmentalists, who took the matter to court.

Did Bush live up to his claims as "the environmental president?" In his 1991 message on environmental quality, Bush pointed to adoption of an international agreement on CFCs, enactment of the Oil Pollution Act of 1990, enactment of an environmentally progressive farm bill, and his commitment to environmental stewardship. He noted that in 1990, the EPA's enforcement staff had a record of felony indictments that was 33 percent higher than that for 1989. His America the Beautiful tree-planting initiative sought to add 1 billion new trees annually over the next 10 years.[35] In December 1990, he established the President's Commission on Environmental Quality to build public/private partnerships to achieve concrete results in the area of pollution prevention, conservation, education, and international cooperation. Critics counter that under Vice President Dan Quayle, the Council on Competitiveness thwarted congressional intent by preventing agencies from issuing regulations required by environmental laws. House Subcommittee on Health and the Environment Chairman Henry Waxman accused the council of "helping polluters block the EPA's efforts" through its regulatory review process.[36] Proving that almost everything he did offended someone, Bush was criticized by both environmentalists and conservatives.

Voters had a clear choice on environmental issues in the 1992 presidential election. While Bush proposed giving greater consideration to protecting jobs in enforcing the Endangered Species Act, Bill Clinton ran on an environmentalist's dream platform. His vice presidential running mate, Tennessee senator Al Gore, had solid ties to Congress and was an outspoken advocate for the environment. A key provision of the Clinton campaign was a promise to limit U.S. carbon dioxide emissions to 1990 levels by the year 2000 to halt global warming—an issue that Bush was soundly criticized for failing to support at the Earth Summit. Clinton also pledged to create recycling and energy conservation incentives, to set national water pollution runoff standards, and to support a 40-miles-per-gallon fuel standard. In direct contrast to Bush, Clinton promised to restore to the UN Population Fund monies that had previously been cut off and to oppose drilling in the Arctic National Wildlife Refuge. These viewpoints, along with his appointments to executive branch agencies, gave environmentalists room for hope and a sense of renewed executive branch leadership.

Clinton faced a unique situation during his first term. During his first two years as president he worked with a Democratic Congress, while the sea-change congressional elections of 1994 made a historic transfer of power of both houses to the Republicans, effectively bottling up the few legislative initiatives the administration tried to make. Even during the first two years, Clinton's environmental successes were minimal. Clinton's White House staff initially set the tone by eliminating the Council on Competitiveness, which both Bush and Reagan had used to sidestep EPA regulations, and by proposing to replace the CEQ with a new White House environmental policy office. The CEQ was a statutory agency of Congress, not subject to presidential fiat, and therefore could not be abolished. But it was merged in 1994 with the new Office of Environmental Policy, headed by Gore protégée Kathleen McGinty. The president also appointed a Council on Sustainable Development—made up of business leaders, representatives from environmental groups, and government officials—that issued a 1996 report calling for a change from conflict to collaboration to maximize environmental protection. Less than a month into his administration, Clinton also endorsed a Senate bill to create the Department of the Environment, elevating the EPA to cabinet-level status. Similar legislation had been introduced in Congress before but never gained sufficient support, especially when the Republicans took control of Congress. Clinton's Office of Environmental Justice, established in 1994 by executive order, was the first effort by any administration to deal with the issue.

Clinton's initial appointees also gave his supporters hope that the president could bring organizational change to key agencies. Former Mississippi congressman Mike Espey became the first African American to serve as secretary of agriculture, having developed a reputation for his strong stance on consumer protection and hunger in his home state. He served only two years and was replaced in 1995 by Daniel Glickman, another former member of Congress from Kansas who had served on the House Agriculture Committee. Unlike previous presidents who relied upon career Forest Service insiders who had served as chiefs of the agency for 10 years, Clinton had two chiefs during his administration—Jack Ward Thomas and Mike Dombeck.

Clinton's first term was marked by the signing of only two environmental measures of any significance—the 1994 California Desert Protection Act and bipartisan-supported revisions in safe drinking-water amendments in 1996. In both cases, the groundwork for passage had been laid by Congress, and both measures reflect legislative momentum rather than presidential leadership. The majority of the nation's most important domestic environmental problems—grazing fees on public lands, designations of wetlands, storage of hazardous and nuclear waste, reauthorization of Superfund legislation—remained trapped in the legislative gridlock of a divided government. Environmentalists criticized the administration for switching sides and accepting a logging compromise in 1995 that opened old-growth forests to salvage timber cuts, and for compromising with automakers on implementation of the 1990 Clean Air Act Amendments. Industry groups were just as upset with the White House. There were some small preservationist victories, such as policies to reintroduce wolves into Yellowstone National Park and continuation of protection for the Arctic National Wildlife Refuge and the Tongass National Forest in Alaska. The 1997 Interior Department appropriations bill avoided the controversies that plagued the 1996 bill and actually increased overall spending for the department because of emergency funds for fighting Western fires.[37] However, the first Clinton term was hard on the EPA, resulting in staff cutbacks for research by one third and a shift toward external rather than in-house research. One report on the agency found that the agency's ability to produce sound environmental studies had been diminished and that the "quality of science produced in the EPA has plummeted into a state of crisis."[38]

In the area of global environmental politics, Clinton had promised to accelerate and expand U.S. involvement in international preservation efforts, expecting support from Gore and a new legion of activist Democratic members to implement a wide-ranging but unfocused plan. The president failed to establish a timetable to meet proposals to reduce emissions of greenhouse gases, but Clinton can be credited with his prompt signing of the biodiversity treaty that had been adopted at the Earth Summit in 1992. Clinton followed up by establishing a National Biological Service to survey American species—a program that immediately became the target of Republican budget slashers. Clinton also followed up on a campaign promise to restore support for international family planning programs and the Global Environmental Facility, a fund to help developing countries meet their global environmental obligations under international treaties, but these programs also were slashed by the new Republican majority in Congress. Clinton promised early in his first term that the United States would take the lead in addressing global climate change, and he proposed an energy tax in 1993 as part of his deficit reduction plan, but he abandoned both of those efforts in the face of strong opposition from the Republican-controlled Congress. These policy failures undermined the U.S. leadership in global environmental diplomacy that had seemed so certain when the Clinton-Gore ticket was first elected. By 1996, the administration had given modest support to legally binding limits on greenhouse gases, to be set sometime after the year 2005, but had failed to rally support to ratify the biodiversity convention.[39]

Clinton's administration will be remembered as one in which the president was successful in blocking Republicans who not only sought a major regulatory overhaul for laws covering issues such as wetlands, mining reform, and the Endangered Species Act but also tried to use the budget process to reduce environmental regulations and agency activities.[40] But environmental policy did not become a priority of the administration until blocking congressional environmental protection rollbacks became politically potent. Despite his efforts to reinvent government and make regulation more efficient, Clinton met with resistance virtually every time he sought collaborative agreements on environmental problems.[41] During his second term he had largely abandoned global environmental concerns, while his promises to protect Social Security, education, and health care from Republicans became core issues. As one political scientist, Martin Nie, has noted, "Clinton found himself to be not 'the candidate of change' in regard to the environment, but the defender of the environmental status quo."[42]

Under George W. Bush, the president used his powers to set an entirely different environmental agenda than Clinton had created. As outlined in Chapter 1, Bush relied on the president's powers to appoint executive branch officials who shared his views, especially those related to energy policy, forests and logging, and global climate change. Because most of the appointees did not require Senate confirmation, Bush filled his administration with allies who had industry and corporate experience. The new appointees were ready to carry out a two-pronged environmental agenda: reverse or delay Clinton-era programs and initiatives; and move forward with new initiatives that would, at a minimum, stall the environmental momentum of the previous eight years.

Immediately after Bush took office, Andrew Card, the president's chief of staff, announced that the administration would be reviewing the Clinton initiatives by issuing an order calling for a 60-day implementation moratorium. Some environmental leaders saw the move as a way for the president to begin rolling back the progress made under Clinton. Bush also attacked the Clinton administration's agenda by using the power of the purse and his control over the appropriations process. The first draft budget called for a 4 percent reduction in the EPA's funding, and similar cuts were proposed for other federal agencies with environmental policy responsibilities.[43]

During the 2000 presidential campaign, Bush talked about his support for the reduction of carbon dioxide emissions, and EPA administrator Whitman told a gathering of environmental ministers that the administration would support an internationally coordinated response to climate change (see Chapter 10). Bush then told Republican leaders that his campaign statements on the subject had been a "mistake" and that a cabinet-level review had found his prior position was incompatible with domestic energy production goals. He charged that the Kyoto Protocol, which had been supported by Clinton, was "fatally flawed" because it would lead to economic harm to the United States without establishing mandatory carbon-emission targets for developing countries.[44]

One of the Clinton administration's successes was a directive to the EPA to strengthen provisions of the Safe Drinking Water Act by developing a revised standard for arsenic, which occurs naturally in some water but is also a by-product of mining and wood processing. The original threshold standard had been established in 1942, but National Academy of Science (NAS) researchers subsequently found links to lung and bladder cancer in a 2001 study requested by Whitman. In a twist of political fate, the NAS report confirming the danger of arsenic-laced drinking water was released on September 10, 2001—the day before the terrorist attacks on New York's World Trade Center and the Pentagon. What might have been an important EPA policy announcement was eclipsed by coverage of the attacks; Whitman quietly announced a reduction in the arsenic standard a month later.

Bush earned what the Sierra Club called "at least three dozen environmental black marks" in his first year of office. Among the actions cited by the group were Bush's attempt to weaken efficiency standards for central air conditioners, a proposal to cut energy-efficiency research and development by 27 percent, a proposal to increase the BLM budget for oil drilling and exploration by $15 million and decrease its budget for conservation by the same amount, and a move to weaken Clinton's roadless initiative for national forests.[45]

The second prong of the Bush environmental agenda called for the president to introduce his own programs, most of which favored industry interests over natural resource protections. This included proposals to allow oil exploration in the Arctic National Wildlife Refuge and in the Rocky Mountains, a Healthy Forests Initiative and proposed legislation to repeal appeals procedures under the National Environmental Policy Act (NEPA) just as the 2002 wildfire season was ending, and an announcement that the federal government would pay $235 million to buy mineral rights near the Florida Everglades. Bush introduced his Clear Skies Initiative and changes in New Source Review regulations of emissions from diesel-fueled engines (see Chapter 8).

Following the example set by his father, Bush angered environmental organizations and foreign leaders when he decided not to attend the UN Earth Summit in Johannesburg, South Africa, in September 2002. The president stayed at his ranch in Crawford, Texas, further isolating the United States from the global environmental debate and making firm his decision not to capitulate on his controversial global warming policy.

The Natural Resources Defense Council (NRDC), in its report on the Bush administration's first-term environmental record, said that "administration agencies made more than 150 actions that weakened our environmental laws. Over the course of the first term, this administration led the most thorough and destructive campaign against America's environmental safeguards in the past 40 years."[46]

Even before the November 2004 presidential election, George W. Bush telegraphed that he planned to make substantial changes to his cabinet and key advisors, including several associated with environmental issues. During his cabinet shuffle, 9 of the 15 members resigned, two more than under Clinton or Reagan, both of whom served two terms. One scholar noted, "He's looking for more responsiveness in his cabinet. It looks like they want people who will be able to sell his policies on Capitol Hill rather than policy experts."[47]

Agriculture Secretary Ann Veneman, along with several other top political appointees in the department, announced they would step down from their positions two weeks after the election. Veneman had been criticized for a hands-off role by farmers and fiscal conservatives. In September 2002 she was diagnosed with breast cancer, and even though she recovered fully, the nation's first female agriculture secretary announced her resignation in a one-page letter saying she wanted to try something new. Less than three weeks later, the president announced his nomination of Mike Johanns, two-term governor of Nebraska, to replace Veneman. Johanns, who grew up on a dairy farm in Iowa, acknowledged his interests in rural economic development and his close relationship with the agriculture community. He seemed to have less interest in grazing and other key environmental policies administered by the department.[48]

The position of secretary of agriculture was being watched closely by industry groups like the National Cattlemen's Beef Association, as was the head of the Department of Energy (DOE). DOE Secretary Spencer Abraham stepped down and was replaced by Sam Bodman, who had previously served in the administration as deputy secretary of commerce and deputy secretary of the Treasury. The position of secretary was important, but lobbyists were also closely watching the Bush administration's appointments several levels down. A spokesman for the National Mining Association noted that lobbying for appointments was important because of competition among the various types of energy companies. "We have an interest, obviously, in the fossil fuels assistant secretary there because obviously that is a position which should be an articulate and forceful advocate for clean-coal utilization."[49]   *clean coal?*

CONGRESSIONAL POLICY MAKING

"When Congress passes a statute, it reflects the outcome of an agenda setting process that typically may include many months, if not years, about discussion of an issue."[50] This terse statement sums up one of the key roles of Congress in formulating and adopting environmental policy. Congress must initially identify and frame a problem, a process that Rochefort and Cobb refer to as ownership: the way in which a legislator characterizes a problem, identifies the causes and potential solutions, then determines which institutional structures, such as committees and subcommittees, will address the issue.[50] Unless a problem is identified by a person (or institution) with the authority to do something about it, it never *Incon-* reaches the policy agenda. In addition, the problem must be given sufficient *viaint* attention (such as by a major newspaper, or the issuance of a public report) to push *truth* it ahead of the dozens of other problems Congress must consider.

The committee system in Congress becomes the mechanism for most policy making. Committees and their myriad subcommittees may hold public hearings, issue reports, or consider budget requests on how to deal with the problem. For example, violent protests and eco-terrorism escalated in the 1990s, causing millions of dollars of damage to public and private property. In June 1998, the House Committee on the Judiciary, Subcommittee on Crime, held hearings on what it called "Acts of Ecoterrorism." The focus was on radical groups that "generate nothing but terror."[51] Three years later, the House Resources Subcommittee on Forests and Forest Health held a public hearing reflecting their interests. This time, the emphasis was on the threats to government employees, especially those working for natural resource agencies like the U.S. Forest Service. The "problem" was the same in both cases, but two different subcommittees approached it and framed it from different perspectives.

The House and Senate leaders also play primary roles in environmental policy as they set the agenda for their chambers and determine what issues will be given priority, based largely on the way an issue is defined. The use of symbols and rhetoric, congressional committee jurisdictions, the nature of the participants, and many other factors explain how environmental policies are defined, shaped, and implemented.

The most striking thing about environmental policy making in Congress is its fragmentation. James Anderson refers to this issue in his discussion of majority building in Congress as a part of the policy adoption phase of policy making.[52] The authorizing committees have primary responsibility for writing environmental laws. In the House, the Resources Committee is the primary focus of bills dealing with public lands and natural resources. The Commerce Committee has broad jurisdiction over energy, environmental regulation, and health. The Transportation and Infrastructure Committee has responsibility for water projects.

Several other committees regularly get involved in environmental issues: Agriculture, Government Reform and Oversight, International Relations, Science, and Small Business. Then there are committees that have a say in how much money is raised from special environmental taxes (the Ways and Means Committee), how much is spent on environmental programs in general (the Budget Committee), and how funds are distributed to specific agencies and programs (the Appropriations Committee). Each committee is further divided into subcommittees that create additional overlaps. The Senate is almost as fragmented for environmental policy, with a similar set of budget-related committees (the tax committee is Finance rather than Ways and Means). The Energy and Natural Resources and the Environment and Public Works committees are the major players, but the Agriculture, Commerce, Foreign Relations, Governmental Affairs, and Small Business committees are also regular participants in major environmental initiatives.

House leaders have taken a particular interest in environmental regulation, vowing to reduce its cost and intrusiveness. The House Government Reform and Oversight and Senate Governmental Affairs, as well as the other committees, have given particular scrutiny in oversight hearings and investigations of the U.S. Forest Service and the EPA. The chairs of committees play enormously important roles in deciding what bills are moved through the process and what committee resources are aimed at what issues.

When the 109th Congress convened on January 4, 2005, for instance, congressional committees and subcommittees reflected the changes brought by the 2004 elections. Committee structures, leadership, budgets, and staffs are allocated based on a ratio of Republicans to Democrats that gave the Republicans a 55–45 majority in the Senate and a majority in the House of Representatives. Sen. Larry Stevens (R-AK) took over the reins of the Commerce Committee, which has jurisdiction for issues such as oceans and global warming, from Sen. John McCain (R-AZ), who became chair of the Senate Indian Affairs Committee. McCain, who had previously sponsored legislation to control global warming, said he would focus on the impacts of climate change on native communities in the arctic region. The powerful Environment and Public Works Committee, chaired by Sen. Don Imhofe (R-OK), almost immediately set the agenda by holding two hearings on the president's Clear Skies legislation. Democratic opposition to the proposal came from an Independent, Sen. Jim Jeffords (I-VT), who countered by reintroducing his "4 Pollutant" bill that would mandate stronger controls on air pollution.

In the House, Rep. Richard Pombo (R-CA), the Resources Committee chair who had developed a reputation for being hostile toward environmental protection legislation, stripped all five subcommittees of any formal jurisdiction outline. He told committee members that jurisdictional delineations from past congresses would guide his consideration of where to refer bills. He also announced he would retain jurisdiction at the full committee level for issues such as endangered species and Native American affairs that would traditionally have gone to subcommittees for review.[53]

Although Congress has primary responsibility for policy formulation and adoption, the nature of the institution has hampered that role. Congress's inability to develop an overall national environmental policy has been termed "environmental gridlock,"[54] referring to the contrast between the institution's rapid pace and initiative during the 1960s and 1970s in comparison with the body's current inability to move forward with a legislative agenda. There are a number of reasons explaining current congressional inaction:

1. The fragmentation of the committee system decentralizes both power and the decision-making process. Environmental issues do not "belong" to any one committee within Congress. Eleven of the Senate's standing committees and 14 of those in the House claim some environmental jurisdiction. Depending on the title of a particular piece of legislation and the subject matter, there is a great deal of latitude in deciding which committee(s) should have jurisdiction. For example, a bill dealing with global warming could be heard by the Senate's Agriculture, Appropriations, Commerce, Science and Transportation, Energy and Natural Resources, or Environment and Public Works committees, because each claims some degree of jurisdiction over that subject. Similarly, in the House, the same bill might be heard by either the Agriculture, Appropriations, Foreign Affairs, or Committee on Technology and Competitiveness committees. When environmental issues are "hot," a certain rivalry exists that causes competition among committees as to which one will have the greatest chance of influencing the bill's content.

2. The pressures of an increasing number of "green" groups and industry interests have made it more difficult to build a congressional consensus. The same committee fragmentation that characterizes the modern Congress also gives interest groups more access to the legislative process. If a group feels one committee is less accommodating to its interests, it may seek a more favorable venue before another committee or subcommittee. At any one point in the legislative process, dozens of groups may be vying for members' attention; and environmental groups have lost the power advantage they once enjoyed in the agenda-setting phase of the policy process.

    In forest-related issues, for instance, Rep. Pombo has been a strong advocate for timber industry interests, pushing the Healthy Forests Restoration Act through the House. Sen. Peter Bingaman (D-NM) served as a conduit for concerns raised about the bill by groups such as The Wilderness Society and Forest Trust. Lobbyists identify and seek out those members of Congress who support their positions, and avoid those they recognize as blocking their progress as legislation is considered.

3. Members of Congress often lack the time and expertise needed to produce sophisticated legislation. One criticism of Congress is that it is "an assembly of scientific amateurs enacting programs of great technical complexity to ameliorate scientifically complicated environmental ills most legislators but dimly understand."[55] Nowhere is this incapacitation better viewed than in the congressional hearings on the 1990 Clean Air Act Amendments. Many of the more technical aspects of the legislation, such as those applicable only to utility oil-fired boilers, were so obtuse that several members left it to their staff to dicker with industry lobbyists over the feasibility of proposed controls. Similarly, when debate on highly sophisticated bills dealing with stratospheric

ozone depletion becomes a battle of one expert's research against another, many members of Congress are at a loss about whom to believe. The result is often legislation that is watered down or intentionally vague. The hectic pace of lawmaking also has an impact on congressional policy making. Staff members taking notes on the 1990 Clean Air Act Amendments hurriedly jotted down proposed amendments, the authors of which were often unsure of exactly where they would fit in the mammoth bill. Lobbyists, watching the markup process, found that their notes from committee sessions often differed from those of staff; and it was not unusual to see the two groups huddling over pages of redlined, handwritten legislation.

4. Localized reelection concerns override a "national" view of environmental policy making. It is difficult for a member of Congress from southern Oregon to convince a colleague from an urban district in New York of the relative importance of a bill barring timber exports to Japan. As reelection pressures mount (especially in the House, where the fever strikes every two years), bargaining becomes an essential style of policy making. Members with little personal interest in an issue often could care less about the legislative outcome, and only by bargaining for something of value to their own district do they have a reason to become involved. Votes on pork-barrel projects such as dams and parklands, for example, are often based on the "you scratch my back, I'll scratch yours" principle, with no thought given to consistency or even to the regional impact of the decision. Local concerns determine which authorizations get funded and which do not; and legislators in positions of seniority, especially members of the powerful budget committees, are particularly adept at bringing projects and facilities "back home."

5. The domination of the Republican Party in Congress (and from 2001 to 2008 in the White House) has seriously challenged the existing structure of environmental policy making. Republican leaders have sought to rewrite major laws, reduce the resources of the EPA and other agencies, and reshape the regulatory process so that agencies are much less likely to intrude on industrial and commercial activities. Although the extreme, antiregulatory agenda has been blocked by moderate Republicans, the party often fails to take into account widespread public support for environmental, health, and safety regulation.

As a result, the most recent congressional sessions are noteworthy for their lack of partisan environmental legislation, especially in comparison to prior years. The Republicans can claim some victories, such as the 1995 closure of the Office of Technology Assessment (OTA). Congress had established OTA in 1972 to provide its committees with neutral analyses of scientific and technical issues but defunded the $22 million program as part of an antiregulatory sweep in the 104th Congress. That same year, Congress voted to close the U.S. Bureau of Mines, which was created in 1910 in response to concerns about health and safety conditions in the nation's mines. Although Congress terminated all of the bureau's programs, many of its functions were simply transferred to the U.S. Geological Survey, the Department of Energy, and the Bureau of Land Management.

Even though the Republican Party gained control of both Congress and the White House in 2001, rollbacks of major environmental laws like Superfund and the Endangered Species Act have been largely untouched by legislators. Controversial cabinet appointments such as those for Gale Norton, John Ashcroft, and Spencer Abraham drew opposition from environmental groups, as did nominations for many agency officials, but almost all the Bush appointees survived confirmation. The Senate considered several major energy proposals, but the events of September 11, 2001, and the congressional elections of 2002 moved the environment even further down the policy agenda. The administration's Clear Skies Initiative was blocked in the Senate in 2005, and President Bush was stymied in his efforts to gain sufficient support from Congress for major changes in NEPA and other major environmental statutes.

Another View, Another Voice

Senator Harry Reid

When South Dakota senator Tom Daschle lost a contentious election on November 2, 2004, the Democratic Party found itself in search of a new minority leader. Their choice was Harry Reid from Searchlight, Nevada—a sharp contrast to the more well-known, telegenic Daschle but a veteran legislator whose style is less confrontational. After the election, Reid told a reporter, "I'm not too sure that we need a show horse at this stage. I think maybe a workhorse may be what the country needs." The *Las Vegas Sun* said Reid had gone "from underdog to the Senate's top dog."

Reid's ascension to the party's highest senate leadership position might come as a surprise based on his modest upbringing. Searchlight, Nevada, is a small community built upon a legacy of hard-rock mining. Reid's father Harry had an eighth-grade education and later in life committed suicide; his mother Inez never completed high school. Because Searchlight did not have its own high school, Reid boarded during the week to attend one in Henderson. Two years after graduation he married his wife, Landra, and through the generosity of Henderson business leaders, graduated from Utah State University in 1961. He received a law degree from George Washington University in 1964, working nights as a U.S. Capitol police officer.

Returning to Henderson, he was elected to the Nevada state legislature in 1968 at age 28, focusing on the state's first air pollution legislation. Two years later, he became Nevada's youngest lieutenant governor, and in 1974 lost a race for the U.S. Senate against republican Paul Laxalt by 624 votes. In 1977, Reid was appointed chair of the state Gaming Commission, developing a reputation for cleaning up the industry's practices. His political career resumed in 1982 when he was elected to the U.S. House of Representatives, where he served two terms before his election to the Senate in 1986.

Reid's voting record puts him in the mainstream of the Democratic Party on most issues, and he won praise as "a consistent friend and champion" from League of Conservation Voters president Deb Callahan. He has voted against Republican proposals to drill for oil in the Arctic National Wildlife Refuge, and supported efforts to protect Nevada's Lake Tahoe, Lake Mead, and Red Rock Canyon. The Harry Reid Center for Environmental Studies at the University of Nevada, Las Vegas focuses on issues in line with the senator's interests in nuclear science and technology, waste management, and forest health.

As minority leader, the soft-spoken Reid has an opportunity to serve as a consensus builder on environmental issues in a Senate dominated 55 to 45 by Republicans. He is considered a legislative technician; and one colleague said, "He's probably the best reader of human beings I've ever met." Environmental groups and other western politicians also believe Reid will bring issues to the table that are of interest to the region: water scarcity, land management policies, urban sprawl, and his vocal opposition to the building of a nuclear waste facility at Yucca Mountain, Nevada.

Journalist Jon Christensen sees Reid's role in a larger context. "More important for the nation, Reid will also be able to shape the legislative agenda behind the scenes. If he can shape the Democratic agenda, he might succeed in moving the party toward the center and toward the West." Others believe Reid is also likely to live up to the slogan he used when he first ran for Congress: "Harry Reid—independent like Nevada."

SOURCES:
Charles Babington. "Democratic Senate Whip Reid Moves Up," *Washington Post,* November 16, 2004, at www.washingtonpost.com, accessed December 28, 2004.
Charles Babington. "Reid Swims in Party's Mainstream," *Seattle Times,* December 19, 2004, at www.seattletimes.nwsource.com, accessed December 28, 2004.
Jon Christensen. "Go West, Democrats, in the Path of Harry Reid," *High Country News,* December 20, 2004, 21.
Billy House and Mary Jo Pitzl. "Tom Dem Real Westerner," *Arizona Republic,* November 21, 2004, A1.
"Harry Reid" at http://reid.senate.gov/biography, accessed December 28, 2004.

THE EXECUTIVE BRANCH AGENCIES

Despite the prolonged public interest in conservation and environmental protection outlined in Chapter 1, the federal government's involvement is actually relatively recent. During the first 100 years after the nation's founding, both the president and Congress were much more deeply involved with foreign affairs, paying little attention to internal domestic problems until the growth of the country literally demanded it. The creation of a federal environmental policy was sporadic and unfocused, with responsibility for the environment scattered among a host of agencies.[56] Today, environmental policy is largely in the hands of unelected but often partisan officials in the Department of Interior, the Department of Agriculture's Forest Service and the Fish and Wildlife Service, and the EPA. These agencies have jurisdiction over the implementation of most of the nation's environmental policies.

Under its first secretary, Thomas Ewing, the Department of Interior was given domestic housekeeping responsibilities different from those of today's cabinet-level department. Initially, the department controlled the General Land Office, Office of Indian Affairs, Pension Office, and Patent Office as well as supervising the Commissioner of Public Buildings, Board of Inspectors, the Warden of the District of Columbia Penitentiary, the census, mines, and accounts of marshals of the U.S. courts. Gradually, a shift occurred as the agency's responsibilities were transferred to other agencies within the executive branch. Eventually, the need to manage newly discovered public resources, especially land and mineral rights, led to the development of several agencies that later came under the Department of the Interior's umbrella, as seen in Table 3.2. The secretary of interior is nominated by the president and confirmed by the Senate, as are the agency directors.

Another agency within the department of interior, the U.S. Fish and Wildlife Service, has a convoluted past, starting in 1871 with the creation of the U.S. Commission on Fish and Fisheries—charged with studying and recommending solutions to the decline in food fishes—in the Department of Commerce, and in

T A B L E 3.2 **Agencies of the U.S. Department of the Interior**

Agency	Established
Bureau of Indian Affairs	1824*
Bureau of Land Management	1946†
Bureau of Reclamation	1902
Minerals Management Service	1982
National Park Service	1916
Office of Surface Mining Reclamation and Enforcement	1977
U.S. Geological Survey	1879
U.S. Fish and Wildlife Service	1940‡

*Originally in War Department; transferred to Interior in 1849.

†Combined the responsibilities of the General Land Office, created in 1812, and the Grazing Service, established in 1934.

‡Combined the responsibilities of the Bureau of Fisheries, established in 1871, and the Bureau of Biological Survey, created in 1885.

1885, with the creation of the Division of Economic Ornithology and Mammalogy in the Department of Agriculture. It was renamed the Bureau of Biological Survey and given jurisdiction over the interstate shipment of wildlife and importation of species. In 1903, within the first Federal Bird Reservation established by President Theodore Roosevelt, the Biological Survey took over management of what later became the national wildlife refuge system. Under Chief Jay Norwood "Ding" Darling, the Survey took on a more ambitious agenda, and in 1934, the bureau began acquiring wetlands and wildlife habitat throughout the United States. The Bureau of Fisheries and the Biological Survey were moved to the Department of Interior in 1939, and a year later, were combined to create the Fish and Wildlife Service. The agency created two new bureaus in 1956: the Bureau of Commercial Fisheries and the Bureau of Sport Fisheries and Wildlife. In 1970, the Bureau of Commercial Fisheries was transferred to the Department of Commerce and renamed the National Marine Fisheries Service.

In 30 years, the agency had been split between two cabinet-level agencies (Agriculture and Commerce), expanded its jurisdiction beyond fish and birds to wildlife habitat and wetlands, and created new divisions in response to congressional legislation like the Endangered Species Act and the Federal Aid in Sportfish Restoration Act. Today, the Washington office of the agency is divided into seven directorates:

1. Wildlife and Sportfish Restoration Programs
2. National Wildlife Refuge System
3. Migratory Birds
4. Fisheries and Habitat Conservation
5. Endangered Species
6. International Affairs
7. Law Enforcement[57]

TABLE 3.3 Department of Agriculture and U.S. Forest Service Leadership, 1962–2005

President	Secretary of Agriculture	Chief, U.S. Forest Service
Nixon	Earl Butz (1971–1974)	Edward Cliff (1962–1972)
		John McGuire (1972–1974)
Ford	Earl Butz (1974–1976)	John McGuire (1974–1976)
Carter	John Knebel (1976–1977)	John McGuire (1976–1979)
	Robert Bergland (1977–1981)	
Reagan	John Block (1981–1986)	R. Max Peterson (1979–1987)
	Richard Lyng (1986–1989)	Dale Robertson (1987–1988)
Bush	Clayton Yeutter (1989–1991)	Dale Robertson (1988–1993)
	Edward Madigan (1991–1992)	
Clinton	Michael Espy (1993–1994)	Jack W. Thomas (1993–1996)
	Daniel Glickman (1995–2001)	Mike Dombeck (1997–2001)
Bush (G.W.)	Ann Veneman (2001–2005)	Dale Bosworth (2001–)
	Mike Johanns (2005–)	

The U.S. Forest Service, which is now part of the Department of Agriculture, was originally called the Division of Forestry when it was established in 1876 under the leadership of Forestry Agent Franklin Hough. When Gifford Pinchot became chief of the division in 1898, he asked to have his title changed from "Chief" to "Forester," noting that there were many chiefs in Washington, D.C. but only one forester. That title remained in effect when the Division of Forestry was changed to the Bureau of Forestry in 1901 and then to the Forest Service in 1905. The "Forester" title remained in effect until 1935, when the title "Chief" was readopted under Ferdinand Silcox. See Table 3.3.

It was not by accident that the Forest Service was placed under the jurisdiction of the Department of Agriculture while most of the land and natural resources agencies were part of the Department of Interior. At the time, trees were considered a crop—a commodity just like cotton or soybeans. The Forest Service is also charged with providing a sustained yield of other natural resources, such as water, forage, and wildlife, while maintaining its mission, "Caring for the Land and Serving People." The 155 national forests and 20 national grasslands comprise 191 million acres (77.3 hectares) of land—an area equivalent in size to the state of Texas—in 44 states, Puerto Rico, and the Virgin Islands.

The agency's 33,000 employees work in four levels of national forest offices:

- Ranger districts. Most of the on-the-ground activities take place in the more than 600 ranger districts, ranging in size from 50,000 acres (20,000 hectares) to more than 1 million acres (400,000 hectares). The staff level at each district office may include from 10 to 100 people, with responsibilities for trail construction and maintenance, operation of campgrounds, management of vegetation and wildlife habitat, and public outreach and education.

T A B L E 3.4   EPA Regional Office Responsibility, by State and Territories

Region 1	Connecticut, Maine, Massachusetts, New Hampshire, Rhode Island, Vermont
Region 2	New Jersey, New York, Puerto Rico, U.S. Virgin Islands
Region 3	Delaware, Maryland, Pennsylvania, Virginia, West Virginia, District of Columbia
Region 4	Alabama, Florida, Georgia, Kentucky, Mississippi, North Carolina, South Carolina, Tennessee
Region 5	Illinois, Indiana, Michigan, Minnesota, Ohio, Wisconsin
Region 6	Arkansas, Louisiana, New Mexico, Oklahoma, Texas
Region 7	Iowa, Kansas, Missouri, Nebraska
Region 8	Colorado, Montana, North Dakota, South Dakota, Utah, Wyoming
Region 9	Arizona, California, Hawaii, Nevada, Guam, American Samoa
Region 10	Alaska, Idaho, Oregon, Washington

SOURCE: U.S. Environmental Protection Agency, "Regions" at www.epa.gov/epahome/locate2 accessed September 8, 2005.

- National forests. Each national forest comprises several ranger districts and is managed by a forest supervisor, who coordinates the activities among the districts, allocates the budget, and provides technical support.

- Regions. There are nine regions with the Forest Service, numbered 1 through 10 (Region 7 has been eliminated). Regions represent broad geographical areas that usually include several states and are managed by a regional forester. The regional offices coordinate activities within national forests, allocate budgets, and provide guidance in the development of forest planning.

- National office. The Washington Office, as it is called, provides broad direction and policy for the agency. The person in charge is the chief, who reports to the under secretary for natural resources and environment in the Department of Agriculture.[58]

The EPA, in contrast, is an independent agency in the executive branch; it is headed by an administrator, a deputy administrator, and nine assistant administrators, all nominated by the president and confirmed by the Senate. The agency divides the country into 10 geographic regions, with field offices that monitor and support environmental policies in their area, as seen in Table 3.4. The EPA has responsibility for administering a broad spectrum of environmental laws. In one sense, it is a regulatory agency, issuing permits, setting and monitoring standards, and enforcing federal laws; but it also gives grants to states to build waste water treatment and other facilities.

The president also receives policy advice on environmental matters from the Council on Environmental Quality (CEQ), created as part of the 1970 National Environmental Policy Act (NEPA). Members of CEQ recommend policy to the president and to some degree evaluate environmental protection programs within the executive branch and environmental impact statements prepared by federal agencies. The CEQ has no regulatory authority; its recommendations are purely advisory. The CEQ staff and budget were reduced under both Reagan and Bush,

T A B L E 3.5 **Other Federal Agencies and Commissions with Environmental Policy Jurisdiction**

Department	Agency or Commission
Commerce	National Bureau of Standards
	National Oceanic and Atmospheric Administration
Defense	Army Corps of Engineers
Energy	Federal Energy Regulatory Commission
	Office of Conservation and Renewable Energy
Health and Human Services	Food and Drug Administration
	National Institute for Occupational Safety and Health
Labor	Mine Safety and Health Administration
Transportation	Federal Aviation Administration
	Federal Highway Administration
	Materials Transportation Bureau
	National Transportation Safety Board
Commissions and/or Regulatory Agencies	
Consumer Product Safety Commission	
Federal Maritime Commission	
Federal Trade Commission	
Nuclear Regulatory Commission	

and the agency's primary task became the preparation of an annual report on the environment. Although the EPA, Department of Agriculture, and Interior Department are responsible for most policy implementation, they share jurisdiction with several other federal agencies, as seen in Table 3.5.

Sometimes an agency may have powers and an interest level comparable to that of a cabinet-level department or the EPA, as is the case with the Nuclear Regulatory Commission, which is currently engaged in relicensing nuclear power plants and supervising their operation. Other agencies, such as the Federal Aviation Administration (FAA), may not have environmental concerns as their primary mission but may be affected by regulations or legislation implemented by other agencies. Thus, the FAA was consulted in 1990 when air quality officials within the EPA began to consider legislation that would govern the amount of particulates released in aircraft exhaust emissions.

RULEMAKING

Administrative agencies are constantly engaged in the process of rulemaking—interpreting congressional intent and translating ideas into specific procedures, or rules. Congress enacted the Administrative Procedure Act of 1946 (APA) to establish standard procedures that agencies would use because they are the source of rules. The APA's definition is: "A rule means the whole of part of a statement of general or particular applicability and future event designed to implement, interpret, or prescribe law or policy."[59] The compilation of the rules made by the Executive Branch is found in the *Code of Federal Regulations,* or CFR, which is divided into 50 subject areas, called titles and chapters. Environmental rules can be found in several of the titles, because some issues overlap distinct topics. Title 10, for instance, deals with rules involving energy; Title 18 covers the conservation of power and water resources. Other titles that involve environmental policies include Mineral Resources (Title 30), Navigation and Navigable Waters (Title 33), Parks, Forests, and Public Property (Title 36), Protection of the Environment (Title 40), Public Lands (Title 43), and Wildlife and Fisheries (Title 50).

When Congress passes a new statute and it is signed by the president, the rulemaking process begins in earnest once authorization to proceed with rule-making is given. The process of drafting a rule usually involves lawyers working for the affected agency, along with technical staff who are familiar with the intricacies of the subject and its impact on those who will be affected by the new rule. Other stakeholders may include the president, members of Congress, consultants to affected parties, researchers, and groups and individuals supporting or opposing rule development.

Congressional legislation is often vague, indicating a general intention rather than a specific goal or description of how what it seeks to do will be accomplished. Usually, the draft rule undergoes a comprehensive external review; if the subject of the rule overlaps agencies, the process may be done concurrently, or one agency may take the lead in collecting relevant information, consulting with experts, and making sure the rule meets any legal requirements. The notice of proposed rulemaking appears in the *Federal Register* and indicates which title of the CFR would be affected, an overview of what the proposed rule would do, and information about how the public can participate in the process. This often involves hearings on the issue and provides the opportunity for groups and individuals to contribute written comments. Meanwhile, an agency may be conducting research studies, performing cost-benefit analyses, and determining the environmental impact if the rule is implemented.

Legislation that states Congress's intention to increase salvage timber that can be harvested after a major wildfire, for instance, must be compared to the existing rules in the CFR, and a proposed draft rule developed. Congress might signal what it wants the U.S. Forest Service to do—make more salvage timber available—without specifying how much salvage timber should be logged, in what regions of the country, or how quickly it expects the process to be implemented. Environmental organizations are likely to be monitoring the *Federal Register* to see what the agency plans to propose, or representatives might be asked to participate informally in the drafting of a rule. The timber industry is doing the same thing, and both sides are preparing comments and various forms of evidence for submission to the agency, which then considers the comments and may issue a revised rule based on public input. An interest with extensive resources, such as the pulp and paper industry, often conducts its own studies and analysis of the impact of a rule. Smaller organizations or individuals may not be able to participate fully in rulemaking if they are unable to provide an agency with similar studies refuting industry claims. Still, groups can mobilize their membership to participate during the written comment period or to appear at public hearings.

Sometimes an agency will schedule a hearing at a location outside Washington, D.C. so that those most affected by the proposed rule will have an opportunity to participate. A rule on salvage timber harvesting might be heard in a logging community in Oregon, for example. But the agency managing the rule is also subject to political pressures, so hearings may be held at a time and place more convenient to trade associations in Washington. Individuals may not be able to participate because they cannot afford the time and money to travel to the capital, and their voices may thus be muted. This is one reason so many environmental organizations have established a presence in Washington, D.C.—it allows them to monitor and participate in the various stages of rule making.

Once a final rule has been approved and published in the *Federal Register,* it must still undergo scrutiny by the Office of Management and Budget and by Congress. If major revisions are needed, the process may start over; and in some cases, a rule is abandoned. Rules that survive the process undergo formal congressional scrutiny, and a Notice of Final Rulemaking is published in the *Federal Register*. If a rule makes it through the entire process, it then becomes part of the CFR. There will still be work for agencies to do—interpreting the rule in its final form, making technical corrections once the rule is implemented, and preparing for litigation.[60]

COURTS AND ENVIRONMENTAL POLITICS

The courts have two primary functions in the making of environmental policy: to exercise their authority for judicial review and to interpret statutes through cases brought to them. In doing so, they use the Constitution to determine the legality of actions of the executive and legislative branches and define the meanings of laws that frequently are open to differing interpretations. Often courts have the authority to determine who has access to the judicial process and may play an activist role in policy making through their decisions. Courts can choose whether to hear a case, based on the concept of ripeness—whether there are concrete issues to be adjudicated, rather than hypothetical disputes. They may also determine what remedy is most appropriate, such as forcing statutory compliance or ordering the payment of punitive monetary damages to deter future violations.[61]

Before the passage of the major environmental laws of the 1970s, most courts' involvement in environmental issues was limited to the adjudication of disputes between polluting industries and citizens affected by pollution under the common law of nuisance. The result in most cases was a cease and desist order and, perhaps, a fine. The new generation of environmental laws opened up a variety of opportunities for private parties, usually environmental groups, to use the courts to compel agencies to take actions mandated by statutes or to sue polluters when government officials failed to enforce the law. Administrative requirements for environmental assessments of projects funded or carried out by federal agencies under NEPA spawned hundreds of administrative appeals and lawsuits challenging agency actions. Studies of NEPA litigation show that the willingness of the courts to review agency decisions, especially in the early 1970s, resulted from various factors including public support for the environment, a tendency toward strict enforcement of statutory procedural requirements, and most important, timing. When NEPA was enacted, the courts were generally tightening their review of agency decision making and increasingly taking a "hard look" at agency actions.[62]

Several important environmental decisions came about during this period of judicial activism. Interpreting congressional intent in the opening words of the 1970 Clean Air Act, the U.S. Supreme Court upheld a district court order that instructed the EPA to prevent the "significant deterioration" of air quality in regions that had already met federal standards. A 1973 decision by the District of Columbia Circuit Court forced the EPA to prepare plans to reduce ozone and carbon monoxide (key components of smog) for cities using transportation control measures. The legal concept of "standing"—the right of an individual or group to bring an issue before a court—was greatly expanded as well. The constitutional basis for standing is found in Article III, which gives courts the authority to decide "cases and controversies," and has historically been interpreted to mean that an individual had the right to bring a suit only when there was a clear showing that the person had been harmed, in terms of either personal injury or loss of property. Thus, most suits against polluting industries could be brought only by citizens actually affected by the pollution. Environmental groups found it difficult to qualify as litigants in most suits because many courts did not consider environmental harm to be personal in nature, so litigation was infrequent. Gradually, however, the courts began allowing members of environmental groups to sue on behalf of the public interest, thereby increasing the number of lawsuits against industries, and later against agencies, that failed to comply with environmental laws and regulations.[63]

It has been argued, however, that U.S. Supreme Court justices may defer to administrative decisions when cases brought before them are exceptionally technical. In analyzing cases involving environmental issues brought before the Court between 1972 and 1991—the heyday of environmental legislation—Robert Percival found that about one third of the cases were decided unanimously, with another third generating only one or two dissents. As environmental problems and laws become more complex, it appears that the courts have taken a less active role in intervening in established policies.[64]

As the issue of regulatory takings became more controversial, the courts became more important as they addressed the issue on Fifth Amendment grounds. Two U.S. Supreme Court decisions moved the courts closer to a policy-making role in land-use decisions. In a 2001 case, *Palazzolo v. Rhode Island,* the Court considered whether a property owner was entitled to challenge an environmental regulation that was in place when the land was acquired.[65] The case involved an owner who sought to fill 11 tidal wetland areas to build a private beach club. The state denied his request for a permit, refusing to give the owner an exemption because the activity did not serve a compelling public interest that benefits the public as a whole. Other courts had ruled that similar regulations form part of the title to the property, precluding the owner from raising a takings challenge against the rule.

In a second case in April 2002, the U.S. Supreme Court upheld the constitutionality of a nearly three-year-long moratorium on development around Lake Tahoe and local governments' regulation of land use. Several hundred owners of land in the area purchased property prior to 1980 changes in a compact established between California and Nevada. Under the compact administered by the Lake Tahoe Regional Planning Agency, development in environmentally sensitive areas was halted. The landowners argued that even though the action did not take away their future right to develop, it was a temporary taking during the moratorium period. They sought compensation for their losses. The justices ruled against the landowners in a 6–3 decision, affirming the right of local governments to utilize various techniques of land-use control, even if the control affects the value of private property.[66]

There is much evidence to conclude that the courts are the political arenas of choice for resolving all types of environmental disputes, although this is not necessarily a new development. On the one hand, the courts have been used to ensure enforcement of environmental regulations. The Natural Resources Defense Council, for example, successfully filed suit against the Department of Energy in 1984 to compel the agency to comply with environmental laws at its nuclear weapons facilities. In 2001, a coalition of environmental groups took similar action against the U.S. Fish and Wildlife Service, claiming the agency had failed to protect the spotted owl and the Pacific fisher under the provisions of the Endangered Species Act (ESA).

Over the last five years, environmental organizations have monitored the use of the courts carefully, arguing that there has been a systematic violation of laws and that judges have ruled consistently against the president's policies and strategies. The Defenders of Wildlife Accountability Project, undertaken in conjunction with the University of Vermont's Law School, analyzed all reported cases in which the Bush administration presented legal arguments regarding an existing environmental law, regulation, or policy before federal judges or magistrates between January 21, 2001, and October 31, 2003. The project released three reports dealing with NEPA, National Forests, and the ESA, noting that since taking office in 2001, the Bush administration worked systematically to undermine environmental law and weaken environmental protection.[67]

In one 2002 case involving the ESA, the judge admonished the executive branch, "What gives the Federal Government the right unilaterally to decide what agreements it will comply with and what it won't comply with? Indeed, this is not an agreement. It's a court order. . . The Federal Government is not above the law."[68]

On the other hand, it is usually to industry's advantage to litigate environmental regulations because the process has the net effect of stalling the implementation of new rules, as has frequently been the case with the 1990 Clean Air Act regulations. Industry can demur during the policy formation and adoption stage, thereby avoiding the bad press that comes from intrusive lobbying, in hopes of moving the courts closer to their position. Led by the American Trucking Associations, Inc., the U.S. Chamber of Commerce, the National Association of

Manufacturers, and three states (Michigan, Ohio, and West Virginia) industry groups challenged the 1997 EPA standards for ozone and particulate matter. They argued that the setting of the standards was both arbitrary and unconstitutional because that power belonged to Congress, not an executive branch agency. In its February 2001 decision, the U.S. Supreme Court ruled in favor of the EPA; the case was remanded to the U.S. Court of Appeals, which supported the more stringent air quality health standards in 2002. The importance of the case lies in the fact that it took five years for the legal fight to be decided.[69]

Similarly, federal agencies can rely upon the judicial arena to force compliance. In *Michigan v. EPA*, the U.S. Court of Appeals ruled in favor of the agency's attempts to enforce requirements that 22 state implementation plans be revised to show efforts to reduce nitrogen dioxide emissions in order to mitigate nonattainment of ozone standards in downwind states, an issue discussed further in Chapter 8. Northeastern states had previously complained to the EPA that they were unable to meet National Ambient Air Quality Standards due to the interstate transport of pollutants.[70]

Judicial challenges to agency actions have come to dominate the process of issuing regulations, and virtually every major agency decision is highly scrutinized. Regulatory officials must anticipate a lawsuit anytime they take an action of any consequence. It is difficult to assess the benefits that have come from more careful agency action when contrasted to the disadvantages of a regulatory process that is slow, expensive, and cumbersome. But some researchers believe that rulemaking increases public participation and agency accountability, despite the complexity of the process.[71]

STATE AND LOCAL POLICY MAKING

In what is called "a landmark decision," the Montana Supreme Court ruled in 2000 that the state constitution guarantees the state's citizens a "fundamental right" to a clean and healthful environment. The impact of the law is substantial: No state law can legally survive if it threatens citizens' environmental rights unless the state can establish a "compelling state interest" for overriding environmental concerns. The decision stems from a lawsuit challenging amendments to Montana's state water quality laws whereby the discharge of arsenic-laden groundwater from a proposed gold mine was exempted from state water quality standards.[72]

Montana's action may also indicate a backlash by citizens who feel it is time for state governments to take a less passive role in environmental protection. For most of the past 30 years, the federal government has been given low marks in its efforts to deal with the most serious environmental problems: water and air pollution, the handling of municipal and hazardous wastes, the protection of endangered species and habitats, and the management of public land resources, from wilderness areas to forests, grazing areas, minerals, and energy. The prevailing pattern has been fragmentation, and efforts to integrate federal, state, and local policy makers have been inconsistent and often unsuccessful.[73]

Beginning in the 1950s, states developed resource management agencies, most often to deal with forests or mining activities on state lands. However, the overall state interest in environmental problems like pollution was minimal. The local government contribution came from concerns about public health and air pollution, a function that local health departments gradually conceded to government scientists. In contrast, jurisdiction over water pollution was taken away from health officials and made a separate agency in most cities.[74]

Federal mandates, which began to proliferate in the late 1960s and 1970s, forced states to create environmental agencies on a single-media basis, such as state air quality boards or water commissions. It was clear, however, that the federal government expected the states to be the implementing agencies, while the federal agencies provided funds for planning, monitoring, management, and technical studies.[75]

Gradually, three patterns of state initiative emerged. Some states, such as New York and Washington, created "superagencies" or "little EPAs" for purposes of administrative efficiency. In some cases, this was done for political acceptability, rather than to integrate an entire program of environmental management.[76] Minnesota, for example, created its Pollution Control Agency (PCA) in 1967 and shifted responsibility for water pollution control to it, and out of the state health department, giving the PCA air and solid waste authority as well. Most of these consolidated programs include a citizen board, which often comes under criticism because of a perception that its members lack sufficient technical expertise. A second pattern was to create a totally new environmental agency focusing on pollution control. Illinois, for example, created a powerful, full-time, five-member Pollution Control Board with a full research staff, the Institute for Environmental Quality. In states like California where environmental issues are highly politicized, the single-media approach still reigns. The California Environmental Protection Agency was created in 1991 by executive order of the governor. Although the cabinet-level agency is ostensibly charged with coordinating the deployment of state resources, it maintains six boards, departments, and offices for air quality, pesticide regulation, toxic substances control, waste management, environmental health, and water resources. The heads of each agency are frequently selected not so much for their technical background as for their partisanship, and as a result, leadership changes hands with the election of a new governor and party.

As the technical competence of state government grows, so too has an "environmental presence" that some business and industry interests find unacceptable. They sometimes turn to the federal government for regulatory relief and federal preemption of state authority.[77] The New Federalism, which actually began with the State and Local Fiscal Assistance Act of 1972, is exemplified by the Reagan administration's philosophy of "getting government off the backs of the people."[78] Reagan's belief in a reduction in the scope of federal activity, privatization, and the devolution of policy and fiscal responsibility to the states resulted in an EPA unwilling to serve as policy initiator or congressional advocate. To fill that void, state officials began to band together to lobby collectively. In the area of air quality, for example, eight states formed the group Northeast States for Coordinated Air Use Management (NESCAUM) to actively lobby for reauthorization of the Clean Air Act in 1987 when the EPA was no longer its congressional policy advocate. The group prepared legislative proposals, technical support, and documentation for its position, termed "a complete role reversal, with states serving as policy initiators."[79]

During the 1980s, states were characterized as somewhat passive in their environmental leadership, with implementation of the 1986 Superfund amendments often cited as an example. One study found very low levels of compliance with the law, with some states in complete ignorance of the requirements of the statute.[80] However, other researchers have concluded that there is an "unevenness" in compliance with environmental regulations for a number of reasons, and that states are now taking a much more active role than they did during the 1980s and early 1990s. Among the reasons used to explain why some states approach environmental protection more comprehensively than others is the "severity argument"—that those states with the most concentrated population growth and urbanization (and therefore the most severe pollution problems) take the most active role in dealing with them. This may also be tied to states where the environmental movement has been strong and has pressured local officials to enact environmental regulations more stringent than those of the federal or state government, as is the case in several western states.

The "wealth argument" states that there is a direct relationship between the state's resource base and its commitment to environmental protection. States with budget surpluses or other resources may use those funds directly for environmental mandates, as compared to states where monies are extremely limited and where environmental problems compete with issues like education, crime control, and health care. The "partisanship argument" is that states with a Democratic-leaning legislature are more likely to work toward environmental protection than are those that are Republican controlled.[81]

One reason for the change in state-level response appears to be the expansion of state bureaucracies and the enhanced taxing powers they enjoy. Those bureaucracies have become more professionalized and stimulated as state political parties have become more competitive, which forces state officials to respond to their constituencies. Termed a resurgent "statehouse democracy," these forces are coupled with an increase in unfunded mandates from the federal governments which force, or even allow, states to develop their own answers to solving environmental problems.[82]

California, which has been at the forefront of state-level environmental initiatives, has moved forward on policies ranging from integrating its waste management programs to establishing air quality standards that go beyond EPA rules. It has been proactive in developing new programs as well. For instance, in August 2004, Gov. Arnold Schwartzenegger unveiled a new plan to encourage installation of solar panel systems on 1 million new and existing homes by 2017. "The proposal is about smart, innovative and environmentally friendly technologies that will help improve the state's ability to meet peak electricity demand while cutting energy costs for homeowners for years to come," the governor said.[83]

Despite efforts at developing cooperative arrangements between what the federal government wants states to do and what states are willing or able to do, there is still a need for strong federal oversight and funding. Without the presence of the federal government, states' willingness to implement environmental programs does vary dramatically. When policy cues involve highly detailed, domain-specific knowledge, vertical or "picket fence" federalism may develop vertical working relationships. Coercive controls, in contrast, appear to be the least effective approach for federal officials attempting to secure compliance.[84]

There have also been a few cases of backlash against state environmental agencies and the way they implement federal laws and policies. In 2005, the director of Arizona's Department of Environmental Quality (ADEQ) was targeted by business leaders who presented him with a 10-item list of policy concerns. The list alleged that the agency ignored industry concerns, acted outside the bounds of its rules, or leaned too heavily on industry. They also complained that the "stakeholder" process that previously defined relations between the agency and those it regulates is no longer a two-way street.[85]

In response, the Arizona legislature threatened to gut ADEQ's budget, and then to terminate the agency entirely. The action was reversed after reconsideration; but the lawmakers sought to continue the agency's operations for only two years, instead of the usual 10 provided for in state sunset legislation. If the state did terminate its congressionally delegated authority or allow the agency's funding to lapse, the EPA's Region 9 office in San Francisco would assume responsibility for implementation and enforcement for environmental protection. The state would also lose not only the $15.5 million in grants from the EPA, but the permit fees paid by industry, which would also go to the agency. The EPA's regional administrator visited Phoenix in at an attempt to determine the duties the agency would assume if necessary.[86]

Congressional delegation of power for environmental policy implementation might represent one way for states to control activities within their own boundaries, but the responsibility did not necessarily equate to sufficient funding, especially for enforcement of federal laws and standards. Mississippi, like other states experiencing fiscal crisis, threatened deep reductions in the 2006 budget for its environmental agencies following a round of slashing cuts the previous year. Unlike the situation in Arizona, however, the Mississippi legislature's actions were partisan, rather than focused on problems within its environmental agency. Battles between Democrats, who previously controlled the state's politics, and Republicans, were serious enough that the state legislature failed to approve a new budget during its three-month regular session. One newspaper chided lawmakers for having "time to meet celebrities like B. B. King and Faith Hill; criticize the offer of $50 million for education funding…and name a state reptile" but adjourning before agreement on funding could be reached. "It's time to get over the growing pains and come to the table like adults."[87]

NOTES

1. Quoted in Robert F. Kennedy Jr., *Crimes Against Nature: How George W. Bush and His Corporate Pals Are Plundering the Country and Hijacking Our Democracy* (New York: HarperCollins, 2004), 34.

2. Jonathan H. Adler, "Post-Whitman EPA," *National Review,* June 2, 2003, at www. nationalreview.com, accessed November 28, 2003.

3. For details on Whitman's career at EPA and her decision to leave the agency, see Christine Todd Whitman, *It's My Party Too: The Battle for the Heart of the GOP and the Future of America* (New York: Penguin Press, 2005).

4. "A Get-Along Voice at the EPA," *New York Times,* August 13, 2003, at www.nytimes.com, accessed August 13, 2003.

5. Brad Knickerbocker, "Bush's EPA Pick Comes with Outsider Insight," *Christian Science Monitor,* March 7, 2005, at www.csmonitor.com, accessed March 8, 2005.

6. Ibid.

7. Natural Resources Defense Council, "Will White House Allow New EPA Chief to Protect Environment and Public Health?" News release, March 4, 2005, at www.nrdc.org/media/pressreleases, accessed March 11, 2005; Sierra Club, "Sierra Club Reaction to Nomination of Stephen L. Johnson for Administrator of the Environmental Protection Agency," News release, March 4, 2005, at www.sierraclub.org/pressroom/releases, accessed March 11, 2005.

8. For an overview of the presidential role, see Dennis L. Soden, ed., *The Environmental Presidency* (Albany, NY: State University of New York Press, 1999).

9. Alfred A. Marcus, *Promise and Performance: Choosing and Implementing an Environmental Policy* (Westport, CT: Greenwood Press, 1980), 87.

10. Ibid., 85.

11. John Quarles, *Cleaning Up America: An Insider's View of the EPA* (Boston: Houghton Mifflin, 1976), 34.

12. Steven A. Cohen, "EPA: A Qualified Success," in Sheldon Kamieniecki et al., *Controversies in Environmental Policy* (Albany: State University of New York Press, 1986).

13. Quarles, *Cleaning Up America,* 17–19.

14. John McCormick, *Reclaiming Paradise: The Global Environmental Movement* (Bloomington: Indiana University Press, 1989), 110. See also Karen M. Hult and Charles E. Walcott, *Empowering the White House: Governance Under Nixon, Ford, and Carter* (Lawrence: University Press of Kansas, 2003).

15. Marc K. Landy, Marc C. Roberts, and Stephen R. Thomas, *The Environmental Protection Agency: Asking the Wrong Questions,* expanded ed. (New York: Oxford University Press, 1994), 41.

16. Lou Cannon, *President Reagan: The Role of a Lifetime* (New York: Simon and Schuster, 1991), 530–531.

17. C. Brant Short, *Ronald Reagan and the Public Lands* (College Station: Texas A&M University Press, 1989), 57.

18. Cannon, *President Reagan,* 531.

19. Jonathan Lash, Katherine Gillman, and David Sheridan, *A Season of Spoils: The Reagan Administration's Attack on the Environment* (New York: Pantheon Books, 1984), 231.

20. Ron Arnold, *At the Eye of the Storm: James Watt and the Environmentalists* (Chicago: Regency Gateway, 1982), 94.

21. Ibid., 93.

22. Cannon, *President Reagan,* 532.

23. Lash, Gillman, and Sheridan, *Season of Spoils,* 287–297.

24. Needless to say, Burford's account of the personnel loss and her subsequent fall from grace is somewhat different. She attributes the changes to natural attrition within the agency. See Anne Burford with John Greenya, *Are You Tough Enough?* (New York: McGraw-Hill, 1986).

25. See Richard E. Cohen, "The Gorsuch Affair," *National Journal,* January 8, 1983, 80.

26. Haynes Johnson, *Sleepwalking through History: America in the Reagan Years* (New York: Norton, 1991), 170.

27. *Public Papers of the President of the United States: Ronald Reagan, 1983* (Washington, DC: U.S. Government Printing Office, 1984), 388–389.

28. Johnson, *Sleepwalking,* 171.

29. Landy, Roberts, and Thomas, *The Environmental Protection Agency,* 252.

30. Ibid., 256.

31. Tom Turner, "Changing the Guards," *Mother Earth News,* May–June 1989, 56.

32. William K. Reilly, "Pollution Prevention: An Environmental Goal for the '90s" *EPA Journal, 16,* no. 1 (January–February 1990): 5.

33. "A Vision for EPA's Future," *EPA Journal, 16,* no. 6 (September–October 1990): 5.

34. "William Reilly's Green Precision Weapons," *The Economist,* March 30, 1991, 28.

35. Executive Office of the President, Council on Environmental Quality, *The 21st Annual Report of the Council on Environmental Quality* (Washington, DC: U.S. Government Printing Office, 1991).

36. "Quailing over Clean Air," *Environment, 33,* no. 6 (July–August 1991): 24.

37. Allan Freedman, "After Interior's Smooth Ride, Some Issues Left Behind," *Congressional Quarterly Weekly Report,* October 5, 1996, 2858.

38. Gary Lee, "Agency Takes a Hit from One of Its Own," *Washington Post,* June 27, 1997, A27.

39. Robert L. Paarlberg, "A Domestic Dispute: Clinton, Congress, and Environmental Policy," *Environment,* October 1996, 16–28.

40. See Colin Campbell and Bert A. Rockman, eds., *The Clinton Presidency: First Appraisals* (Chatham, NJ: Chatham House Publishers, 1996).

41. One notable exception was the administration's acceptance of the Safe Harbor program, initiated by the Environmental Defense Fund and the National Cattlemen's Beef Association. Under a safe harbor agreement, a landowner commits to restoring or enhancing habitats for endangered species and the government pledges not to "punish" the landowner by placing any new restrictions on the land if their actions result in the natural introduction of endangered species.

42. Martin Nie, "It's the Environment, Stupid! Clinton and the Environment," *Presidential Studies Quarterly, 27,* no. 1 (Winter 1997): 39–51.

43. Maurie J. Cohen, "George W. Bush and the Environmental Protection Agency: A Midterm Appraisal," *Society and Natural Resources, 17* (2004): 69–88.

44. Ibid., 72.

45. "Dozens of Doozies: Keeping Tabs on George W. Bush," *Sierra, 86,* no. 4 (July–August 2001): 21.

46. Natural Resources Defense Council, *Rewriting the Rules: The Bush Administration's First Term Environmental Record,* Executive Summary at www.nrdc.org/legislation/rolbacks/execsum, accessed February 20, 2005.

47. "Ins and Outs: Bush Cabinet Shuffle," *CBS News,* December 3, 2004, at http://www.cbsanews.com/stories/2004/12/03, accessed December 31, 2004.

48. Michael Doyle, "Veneman Ends Role as First Female USDA Chief," November 15, 2004, at www.knoxstudio.com, accessed December 13, 2004; Dan Looker, "Bush Announces Veneman Resignation as Ag Secretary," November 15, 2004, at www.agriculture.com, accessed December 13, 2004; and "Remarks by the President and Secretary of Agriculture Nominee Governor Mike Johanns," at www.lincolnjournalstar.com, accessed December 13, 2004.

49. "Lobbyists Keep a Close Eye on Bush Cabinet Nominees," *Washington Times,* December 31, 2004, at www.washingtontimes.com, accessed December 31, 2004.

50. David A. Rochefort and Roger Cobb. *The Politics of Problem Definition: Shaping the Policy Agenda* (Lawrence: University Press of Kansas, 1994).

51. *Acts of Ecoterrorism by Radical Environmental Organizations*, Hearing, Subcommittee on Crime of the Committee on the Judiciary, 105th Cong., 2nd sess., June 9, 1998.

52. James Anderson, *Public Policymaking,* 4th ed. (Boston: Houghton Mifflin, 2000), 152–155.

53. Leslie Ann Duncan, "Pombo to Decide Resources Jurisdiction on Case-By-Case Basis," *Congressional Green Sheets,* February 3, 2005.

54. Michael E. Kraft, "Environmental Gridlock: Searching for Consensus in Congress," in *Environmental Policy in the 1990s*, ed. Norman J. Vig and Michael E. Kraft (Washington, DC: Congressional Quarterly Press, 1990), 103–124.

55. Walter A. Rosenbaum, *Environmental Politics and Policy*, 2nd ed. (Washington, DC: Congressional Quarterly Press, 1991), 83.

56. U.S. Fish and Wildlife Service, "Washington Office: Table of Organization" at http://offices.fws.gov/orgcht, accessed April 10, 2005

57. For the historical background of the nation's earliest attempts at environmental protection, see U.S. Department of Interior, *Creation of the Department of the Interior* (Washington, DC: Author, 1976); Donald C. Swain, "Conservation in the 1920s," in *American Environmentalism*, 3rd ed., ed. Roderick Nash (New York: McGraw-Hill, 1990), 117–125.

58. USDA Forest Service, "About Us," at www.fs.fed.us/aboutus, accessed April 4, 2005.

59. 5 U.S.C. 551 (4).

60. See Cornelius M. Kerwin, *Rulemaking: How Government Agencies Write Law and Make Policy,* 2nd ed. (Washington, DC: CQ Press, 1999).

61. For more on the role of the courts, see Rosemary O'Leary, "Environmental Policy in the Courts," in Norman J. Vig and Michael E. Kraft, *Environmental Policy: New Directions for the Twenty-First Century* (Washington, DC: CQ Press, 2003): 151–173; and Richard J. Lazarus, "Restoring What's Environmental About Environmental Law in the Supreme Court," *UCLA Law Review, 47,* no. 3 (February 2000): 703–812.

62. Frederick R. Anderson, *NEPA and the Courts* (Baltimore, MD: Johns Hopkins University Press, 1973), 17. For more on NEPA, see Matt Lindstrom and Zachary Smith, *The National Environmental Policy Act: Judicial Misconstruction, Legislative Indifference, and Executive Neglect* (College Station: Texas A&M University Press, 2001.

63. The case that is generally regarded as opening the door to environmental group litigation is *Scenic Hudson Preservation Conference v. Federal Power Commission,* 453 F. 2d 463 (2nd Cir. 1971). The local conservation group challenged the application of New York Edison Company to build a power plant on Storm King Mountain in the Hudson River valley and was granted standing by the Second Circuit Court under the Federal Power Act, which directs the Federal Power Commission to consider the impact of proposed projects.

64. See Robert V. Percival, "Environmental Law in the Courts: Highlights From the Marshall Papers," *Environmental Law Reporter, 23,* no. 10 (October 1993): 10606; and Richard E. Levy and Robert L. Glicksman, "Judicial Activism and Restraint in the Supreme Court's Environmental Law Decisions," *Vanderbilt Law Review, 42* (March 1989): 343–431.

65. 121 S.Ct. 2448 (2001).

66. *Tahoe-Sierra Preservation Council, Inc. v. Tahoe Regional Planning Agency* 122 S.Ct. 1465 (2002). For commentary on the two cases, see John R. Nolan, "When Environmental Regulations Go 'Too Far,'" *New York Law Journal, 227* (June 19, 2002): 5; and Peter R. Paden and Laurence A. Horvath, "Takings in 'Tahoe': U.S. Supreme Court Veers to the Center," *New York Law Journal, 227* (July 1, 2002): 9.

67. See Defenders of Wildlife, *Weakening the National Environmental Policy Act: How the Bush Administration Uses the Judicial System to Weaken Environmental Protections; Undercutting National Forests Protections: How the Bush Administration Uses the Judicial System to Weaken Environmental Laws;* and *Sabotaging the Endangered Species Act: How the Bush Administration Uses the Judicial System to Undermine Wildlife Protections* at www.defenders.org/publications, accessed April 8, 2005.

68. *Save the Manatee Club v. Ballard*, Unpubl'd, July 9, 2002. (D. DC No. 00–76).

69. See *Whitman v. American Trucking Associations, Inc.* 121 S.Ct. 903 (2001).

70. 213 F.3d 663 (DC Cir. 2000). For a commentary on the ruling, see Nathan J. Brodeur, "Michigan v. U.S. Environmental Protection Agency," *Ecology Law Quarterly, 28*, no. 2 (2001): 275–296.

71. See, for example, Robert D. Behn, *Rethinking Democratic Accountability* (Washington, DC: Brookings Institution Press, 2001); Nancy C. Roberts, "Keeping Public Officials Accountable Through Dialogue: Resolving the Accountability Paradox," *Public Administration Review, 62*, no. 6 (2002): 658–669; and Nancy Manring, "From Postdecisional Appeals to Predecisional Objections: Democratic Accountability in National Forest Planning," *Journal of Forestry, 102*, no. 2 (2004): 43–47.

72. "Citizens Have Right to Clean Environment, Montana Court Says," *International Wildlife, 30*, no. 3 (May–June 2000), 9.

73. Barry G. Rabe, *Fragmentation and Integration in State Environmental Management* (Washington, DC: The Conservation Foundation, 1986), 17.

74. J. Clarence Davies, *The Politics of Pollution* (New York: Pegasus, 1970).

75. See Samuel P. Hays, *Beauty, Health, and Permanence: Environmental Politics in the United States, 1955–1985* (Cambridge: Cambridge University Press, 1987), 441.

76. Rabe, *Fragmentation*, 31.

77. Hays, *Beauty, Health, and Permanence*, 433.

78. For an explanation of the emerging trends of state innovation, see Barry G. Rabe, "Power to the States: The Promise and Pitfalls of Decentralization," in *Environmental Policy: New Directions for the Twenty-First Century*, 5th ed., ed. Norman J. Vig and Michael E. Kraft (Washington, DC: Congressional Quarterly Press, 2003), 33–56. See also John D. Donahue, *Disunited States: What's at Stake as Washington Fades and the States Take the Lead* (New York: Basic Books, 1997); Evan J. Ringquist, *Environmental Protection at the State Level: Politics and Progress in Controlling Pollution* (Armonk, NY: Sharpe, 1993); and William R. Lowery, *The Dimensions of Federalism: State Governments and Pollution Control Policies* (Durham: Duke University Press, 1992).

79. Edward Laverty, "Legacy of the 1980s in State Environmental Administration," in *Regulatory Federalism, Natural Resources, and Environmental Management*, ed. Michael S. Hamilton (Washington, DC: American Society for Public Administration, 1990), 68–70.

80. Susan J. Buck and Edward M. Hathaway, "Designating State Natural Resource Trustees under the Superfund Amendments," in *Regulatory Federalism, Natural Resources, and Environmental Management*, ed. Michael S. Hamilton (Washington, DC: American Society for Public Administration, 1990), 83–94.

81. James P. Lester, "A New Federalism?" in *Environmental Policy in the 1990s*, ed. Norman J. Vig and Michael E. Kraft (Washington, DC: Congressional Quarterly Press, 1990), 59–79.

82. Rabe, "Power to the States," 34–35.

83. "Governor Schwartzenegger Calls for One Million Solar Energy Systems in California Homes," News release, August 20, 2004, at www.governor.ca.gov/state, accessed April 10, 2005.

84. Denise Scheberle, *Federalism and Environmental Policy: Trust and the Politics of Implementation* (Washington, DC: Georgetown University Press, 1997), 12–16.

85. Mary Jo Pitzl, "ADEQ Chief, Businesses at Odds," *Arizona Republic,* April 10, 2005, B1.

86. Mary Jo Pitzl, "EPA Could Step in for State," *Arizona Republic,* April 8, 2005, B1.

87. "Wide Partisan Divide Hurting Mississippi," *Natchez Democrat,* April 7, 2005 at www. natchezdemocrat.com/articles accessed April 10, 2005.

FURTHER READING

Robert S. Devine. *Bush Versus the Environment.* New York: Anchor Books, 2004.

Douglas T. Kendall, ed. *Redefining Federalism: Listening to the States in Shaping Federalism.* Washington, DC: Environmental Law Institute, 2005.

Robert F. Kennedy. *Crimes Against Nature: How George W. Bush and His Corporate Pals Are Plundering the Country and Hijacking Our Democracy.* New York: HarperCollins, 2004.

Richard J. Lazarus. *The Making of Environmental Law.* Chicago: University of Chicago Press, 2005.

Randall Lutter and Jason E. Shogren, eds. *Painting the White House Green: Rationalizing Environmental Policy Inside the Executive Office of the President.* Washington, DC: Resources for the Future Press, 2004.

Robert McMahon. *The Environmental Protection Agency: Structuring Motivation in a Green Bureaucracy, the Conflict Between Regulatory Style and Cultural Identity.* East Sussex, UK: Sussex Academic Press, 2005.

John R. Noon. *New Ground: The Advent of Local Environmental Law.* Washington, DC: Environmental Law Institute, 2005.

Carl Pope and Paul Rauber. *Strategic Ignorance: Why the Bush Administration is Recklessly Destroying a Century of Environmental Progress.* San Francisco: Sierra Club Books, 2004.

Richard W. Waterman, Amelia A. Rouse, and Robert L. Wright. *Bureaucrats, Politics, and the Environment.* Pittsburgh, PA: University of Pittsburgh Press, 2004.

Christine Todd Whitman. *It's My Party Too: The Battle for the Heart of the GOP and the Future of America.* New York: Penguin Press, 2005.

4

The Public Lands Debate

> Devils Tower is a natural wonder and an object of historic and great
> scientific interest [and] warning is hereby given to all unauthorized persons
> not to appropriate, injure, or destroy any feature of the natural tower.
> —PRESIDENT THEODORE ROOSEVELT, 1906[1]

More than 20 Plains Indian tribes have cultural and spiritual ties to Wyoming's Devil's Tower, including the Arapahoe, Cheyenne, Crow, Kiowa, Lakota, and Shoshone people. Common threads of oral history and tradition among the tribes tell of an individual, or group of women or men, or sometimes children, being frightened by a bear. In most of the stories, the bear chases someone up a tree or giant rock, and that person offers prayers to the spirits asking for protection. Native people call the place Bear's Lodge; they use the site as a place of worship, ceremony, vision quests, and sacrifice, usually during the month of June.[2] Most nonnative people are familiar with the location because of the film, *Close Encounters of the Third Kind.*

The region was first identified by exploration parties looking for gold around 1875; geologists believed the rock was created as molten lava boiled up from under the earth's surface. Because it was thought to be of volcanic origin, some called it "the Devil's handiwork." In 1906, President Theodore Roosevelt used the Antiquities Act to designate Devil's Tower as the country's first national monument, and it eventually came under the management of the National Park Service (NPS).

> *National Parks are in danger of being "loved to death" by crowds of visitors such as these watching the eruption of Old Faithful in Yellowstone.*
>
> HANNA J. CORTNER

Rock climbers view the 867-foot rock structure as something to be conquered. Between 1970 and 1980, an estimated 6,000 people attempted the ascent each year, creating over 200 named routes. Climbing gear, pitons, ropes, garbage, and human waste are left behind, creating a huge management challenge for the NPS. In 1994, the park superintendent held a focus group to address the issues raised by various stakeholder groups, including tribal representatives who sought to put the monument off-limits so they could worship in peace. A year later, a compromise was reached that included a voluntary ban on climbing during June each year and enhanced public outreach efforts to explain the site's cultural and spiritual significance. Although there has been an estimated 75–80 percent compliance rate with the Final Climbing Management Plan, an estimated 200–300 climbers still make guided trips each June.[3]

Devil's Tower illustrates the ongoing debate over federal policy protecting Native American archaeological and cultural sites, most of which are on public land. In 1978, Congress enacted the American Indian Religious Freedom Act, designed to protect Indian sacred sites and traditional forms of worship.[4] Additional protections came with the Native American Graves and Repatriation Act of 1990, the National Historical Preservation Act Amendments of 1992, and a 1996 executive order by President Bill Clinton that agencies ensure access, and maintain the physical integrity of, sites considered sacred to local and indigenous tribes.[5]

In 1998, the voluntary climbing ban was challenged by the Bear Lodge Multiple Use Association and several local guides, represented by the Mountain States Legal Foundation, a conservative wise use legal organization. They sued Interior Secretary Bruce Babbitt, arguing that the NPS plan violated the First Amendment by "indoctrinating children into the religious beliefs of Native Americans, and the signs asking visitors to voluntarily stay on trails represented a coerced observance of indigenous religions."[6] The guides argued that their businesses had been negatively affected by the June climbing ban and that climbers were being coerced into refraining from climbing. Dozens of organizations and scholars filed as amici in the case, including the Medicine Wheel Coalition on Sacred Sites of North America, the National Congress of American Indians, the National Jewish Commission on Law and Public Affairs, and individual tribes.

The court ruled against the plaintiffs on the issue of standing to sue, which requires that those bringing suit have a factual showing of perceptible harm and that the alleged personal injury is likely to be redressed by the requested relief. The courts had previously ruled that "a litigant may invoke only its own constitutional rights and may not assert rights of others not before the courts."[7]

The NPS went a step further in 2005, proposing that Devil's Tower be made a National Historic Landmark to recognize its cultural and historical significance, but changing the name to Bear Lodge. The monument, however, would retain its original name. Local residents opposed the designation, and Rep. Barbara Cubin (R–WY) introduced legislation to prevent the change. But renaming sites has precedent throughout the United States. North Dakota's Devil's Lake is now called Spirit Lake, and Arizona Gov. Janet Napolitano renamed Squaw Peak as Piestewa Peak in honor of the first Native American soldier killed in Iraq.[8]

The name and use issues cited here exemplify the types of problems facing the nation's land-use management agencies today. Several continuing debates will be explored in this chapter, including the perspectives of the stakeholders involved with each issue. The chapter also summarizes governmental regulation of private lands, a highly litigious issue based on constitutional interpretation and America's belief in property rights.

THE PUBLIC LANDS

Today, the total area of the United States is 2.3 billion acres. When the United States was in its infancy, "public lands" referred to the area between the Appalachian Mountains and the Mississippi River that were held by seven of the original 13 colonies—the land claim states. In 1780, New York agreed to surrender its claim to the unsettled territory in order to persuade Maryland to sign the Articles of Confederation, deeding it to the federal government and creating the first land considered part of the "public domain." By 1802, the public domain consisted of over 1.8 billion acres.

The government, however, was not interested in being in the land business. Soldiers who served in the Revolutionary War were given land instead of monetary compensation; other parcels were sold to raise revenue for the new nation. Millions of acres were sold to private owners under the Ordinance of 1785, which allowed the sale of parcels of land to the highest bidder at a minimum price of $1 per acre, with a 640-acre minimum. In 1812, the General Land Office took over the administration of the land disposal process, and Congress aided the effort through passage of the Armed Occupation Law of 1842, which gave 160 acres of land in exchange for fighting the Indians in Florida. Couples willing to settle in "Oregon Country" could receive 640 acres. From 1812 until 1946, the General Land Office sold or gave away over 1 billion acres of public land, including 132 million acres granted to railroads.[9]

The federal government slowed its marketing approach to public land in 1872 when it established Yellowstone National Park. This shift in both attitude and policy—from selling land to preserving it—was mainly the result of the Progressive era and the pleas of Thoreau and Emerson for government intervention to protect natural areas. Under growing pressure from the conservation movement, Congress began to tighten up the government's somewhat cavalier attitude toward land in the public domain. With passage of the 1891 Forest Reserve Act (repealed in 1907), the federal government began to set aside forest land to protect future timber supplies. The American Antiquities Act of 1906 gave the president authority to withdraw federal lands from settlement and development if they had national or historic interest, and the 1920 Mineral Leasing Act authorized leases, rather than outright sales, of public lands for extraction of oil, gas, coal, and other minerals.

Today, the federal government holds responsibility for managing over 650 million acres of public lands. The Bureau of Land Management (BLM) manages nearly half the public domain (261 million surface acres), of which over 88 million acres are in Alaska. Most of the rest of the BLM lands are in 11 western states, and the following six states each have more than 100,000 acres: Alabama, Arkansas, Louisiana, Minnesota, South Dakota, and Wisconsin. The U.S. Forest Service (USFS) is responsible for another 192 million acres, 141 million of them in the West. Other public domain lands are the responsibility of the U.S. Fish and Wildlife Service (93 million) and the National Park Service (83 million); the remainder is administered by other federal agencies like the Department of Defense.

Each agency has its own clientele, some of which overlap, and its own agenda regarding how it implements federal law. The conflicts created by shared jurisdiction are epitomized by the term *multiple use,* which refers to those federal lands that have been designated for a variety of purposes, ranging from grazing to recreation. By its very name, a multiple-use designation means that groups compete for the permitted right to use the land. A second component of the multiple-use policy is *sustained yield,* which means that no more forage or timber may be harvested than can be produced.

Several legislative efforts demonstrate the government's continued commitment to the multiple-use concept. Congress enacted the Multiple Use Sustained Yield Act (MUSYA) of 1960 and, four years later, the Classification and Multiple Use Act. These two pieces of legislation recognized that land held within the public domain might be used for activities other than logging and grazing, although the laws were minimally successful in changing patterns of use that had existed for decades. When the Federal Land Policy and Management Act was enacted in 1976, it reiterated the government's position on multiple use. The legislation required full public participation in land management decisions and specified that all public lands under federal management were to continue under federal ownership unless their sale was in the national interest. Critics of multiple use, however, call the policy a charade, arguing that it is a smokescreen used by the federal government to justify the exploitation of public lands and resources by favored commodity interests.[10]

"THE BEST IDEA AMERICA EVER HAD":
THE NATIONAL PARKS

In the policy process, one of the most difficult tasks is finding a way to stimulate government to take action; equally perplexing is the question of why some problems are acted upon while others are not. Policy scholars believe that, oftentimes, government does not take action until the public considers a situation troubling or it causes discontent. If the public thinks that a condition is normal, inevitable, or its own responsibility, then nothing is likely to happen because that condition is not perceived as a problem. Conditions do not become public problems until they are defined as such, articulated by someone, and then brought to the attention of government.

Such is the case for America's national park system. Early naturalists and explorers of the West sought some form of preservation for the scenic wonders they discovered in the latter half of the 19th century. Led by John Muir, pre-servationists believed that only by setting aside areas of wilderness where no commercial or industrial activity was permitted could their value be preserved forever. But historians note that although there is a mythological aura to the telling of the national park story, reality actually has its roots in the efforts of the Northern Pacific Railroad Company to monopolize tourist traffic into the area that is now Yellowstone. Company officials, like other railroad entrepreneurs, wanted to prevent private land claims and limit competition for tourism, while establishing trade corridors for themselves. Tourism emerged in the 19th century "as an economic land use attractive to business investment. The success of such investment depended in part on the preservation of scenery through prevention of haphazard tourism development and other invasive commercial uses such as mining and lumbering."[11]

When President Woodrow Wilson signed the National Park Service Act in 1916, he brought 36 national parks under a single federal agency, in what was termed by former British ambassador to the United States, James Bryce, as "the best idea America ever had." The concept of a national park has now been copied by more than 120 other nations worldwide. But the popularity of the idea has also led to a tremendous amount of fragmentation. Congress has enacted legislation that creates myriad numbers and types of designations, most of which are under NPS authority but some of which have been managed with other federal agencies. This fragmentation is illustrated in Table 4.1.

Fragmentation in management and administration is complicated by the varying sizes of sites within the NPS system, from the largest area, Wrangell–St. Elias National Park and Preserve in Alaska (13.2 million acres) to the smallest unit, the Thaddeus Kosciuszko National Memorial in Pennsylvania (0.02 acre). The agency is attempting to channel increasingly limited funds to more and more properties, creating a deferred maintenance backlog of between $4.1 billion and $6.8 billion. The National Parks Conservation Association estimates that on average, national parks operate with only two thirds of the needed funding, creating a system-wide shortfall in excess of $600 million annually.[12]

Examples include the visitor center at the USS *Arizona* Memorial in Hawaii, which is sinking and may cost as much as $20 million to repair—a cost that exceeds the entire annual budget for the seven national park sites in the state; Yellowstone, where 150 miles of roads have not been repaired in years; and Washington's Mount Rainier National Park, where half of the $100 million backlog is attributed to road repair.[13]

Because legislative bodies are asked to deal with thousands of policy problems each year, only a small fraction of them will receive serious consideration. Because of limitations on their time and resources, policy makers will choose to

TABLE 4.1 Designation of National Park System Units

NPS Unit	Description	Examples
National park	Large places with a variety of attributes, including historic assets	Bryce Canyon (UT), Grand Canyon (AZ)
National monument	Places on government lands designated by the president with historic or scientific interest	Fort Pulaski (GA), Statue of Liberty (NY)
National preserve	Areas with characteristics of the national parks, but where Congress has permitted hunting, trapping, and oil and/or gas exploration and extraction	Big Cypress (FL), Tallgrass Prairie (KS)
National historic site	A single historical feature associated with its subject	Ford's Theater (DC), Vanderbilt Mansion (NY)
National historical park	Historic parks that extend beyond single properties or buildings	Chaco Culture (NM), San Antonio Missions (TX)
National memorial	A site commemorative of a historic person or episode	Lincoln Boyhood (IN), National World War II Memorial (DC)
National battlefield	Parklands including sites, parks, and military parks	Manassas (VA)
National recreation area	Sites focused on water-based recreation or near major population areas	Chattahoochee River (GA), Whiskeytown (CA)
National seashore	Sites on the U.S. coast	Cape Cod (MA), Cape Hatteras (NC)
National lakeshore	Lakeshore sites that are all located on the Great Lakes	Sleeping Bear Dunes (MI), Apostle Islands (WI)
National River	Includes major waterways, recreation areas along rivers, and wild and scenic rivers	Mississippi River (MS), Bluestone (WV)
National Parkway	Roadways intended for scenic motoring and the parkland paralleling the roadway	Blue Ridge (SC), Natchez Trace
National Scenic Trail	Lengthy, multistate linear parklands authorized under the National Trails System Act of 1968	Appalachian, Potomac Heritage
Other Designations (examples)	The White House	
	Poplar Grove (national cemetery)	
	City of Rocks National Reserve	
	Ebey's Landing (national historic reserve)	

SOURCE: National Park Service at www.nps.gov/legacy/nomenclature accessed June 16, 2005.

act on only a few problems, which then constitute the policy agenda. When there is substantial disagreement over the best solution to a problem, as is the case with the national parks, policy makers may choose not to put the item on the agenda, deciding instead to deal with other priorities or issues for which the choices are clearer.

Funding decisions may be based on many different factors, such as the political clout of an individual legislator, pressures from affected stakeholders, media coverage of a problem in a particular park unit, or the recommendations of the NPS itself. Nonprofit organizations that lend financial support to the national park may make recommendations on what projects should be prioritized, but park staff may not always agree. In some cases, where public funding is unavailable, private groups may choose to work in conjunction with the NPS to complete a project. In Yosemite National Park, for instance, there was virtual agreement that major improvements were needed at the base of Yosemite Falls. Exhaust from diesel tourist buses, a lack of parking space for cars, degraded landscape, insufficient signage, and accessibility were obvious problems. Over the year, visitors had created their own trails, destroying vital habitat and watershed areas in an effort to get closer to the falls or to take photographs.

The nonprofit Yosemite Fund successfully raised over $13.5 million from 14,500 contributors over an eight-year campaign to create a 52-acre visitor area. The largest public-private partnership in the park's history, the project is one of about 150 funded by the organization since it was created in 1988, contributing over $20 million to research, infrastructure repair, restoration, and interpretive outreach.[14] Without support groups, most national parks would be struggling even more than they are now.

Although there is little dispute that the country's existing national park units are in trouble and need vast amounts of additional resources, Congress has been pressured by various types of stakeholders to continue adding more and more lands and historical sites as protected areas. For instance, perceiving a "problem," members of Congress responded to interest groups' lobbying by enacting the 1994 California Desert Protection Act, which created more than 7.5 million acres of federally protected land in the California desert. This was the largest land withdrawal since the Alaska National Interest Lands Conservation Act of 1980 (ANILCA) and the largest wilderness law in any of the lower 48 states. The act included the creation of three national parks, totaling nearly 4 million acres: Joshua Tree, Death Valley, and East Mojave. The first two parks had been managed as wilderness areas by the NPS for more than a decade.[15]

Individual members of Congress can also seek to have areas included in the NPS system, as was the case with Sen. Paul S. Sarbanes (D-MD), who introduced a bill to redesignate the 6,000-acre Catoctin Mountain Park in Frederick County, Maryland. His measure, introduced in 2003 and again in 2005, sought to change the designation to a National Recreation Area. The site is best known as the home of the presidential retreat at Camp David, but it is also confused with Cunningham Falls State Park, which is not part of the NPS, and a privately owned wildlife preserve and zoo. The Sarbanes bill noted that the original 1933 designation—the Catoctin Recreation Demonstration Area—was transferred to the NPS by executive order in 1936, followed by a transfer of 5,000 acres to the State of Maryland for the state park; in 1954, the Demonstration Area was renamed as Catoctin Mountain Park. The changes, Sarbanes believes, have "long been a source of confusion for visitors to the area."[16]

Another View, Another Voice

Laurance S. Rockefeller
His interests were in aviation, electronics, high-temperature physics, nuclear power, data processing, optics, and lasers. He was a pioneer in the field of venture capital, helped develop one of the world's foremost cancer research and care facilities, and served as chairman of a resort management company. But it is said that Laurance Rockefeller's summers on Mt. Desert Island in Maine, visits to Yellowstone, and hours spent with leading national conservationists greatly influenced his life of philanthropy and environmentalism.

Born in 1910 in New York, Laurance was one of six children in the noted family of John D. Rockefeller Jr. He received a bachelor's degree in philosophy from Princeton University and spent two years at Harvard Law School. He began working in the family business in 1935, and in 1939 was appointed to the Palisades Interstate Park Commission (PIPC), the beginning of his public service to the conservation movement.

After World War II, Rockefeller joined the throngs of Americans who sought enjoyment of the outdoors and wilderness areas. During the 1950s, he served as an advisor to President Dwight D. Eisenhower, who appointed him chairman of the Outdoor Recreation Resources Review Commission; he later advised Presidents Kennedy, Johnson (who awarded him the Presidential Medal of Freedom in 1969), Nixon, and Ford. He established the American Conservation Association in 1958 as a philanthropic conservation service agency, and was active in the New York Zoological Society, the American Committee for International Wildlife Preservation, Resources for the Future, and the National Recreation and Park Foundation.

Preservation of natural and scenic areas was at the core of Laurance Rockefeller's environmental agenda, mentored by his family friend, Horace Albright, superintendent of Yellowstone National Park. In 1929, Albright had taken the family through the 30-mile long mountain corridor of Jackson Hole, Wyoming—a trip that would help to create Laurance's vision for the preservation of natural areas for the next 75 years. As part of his work with PIPC, Rockefeller brought new land acquisitions into the park system, including some he purchased and donated. In 1956, Rockefeller turned over 5,000 acres on the island of St. John, U.S. Virgin Islands, to help create Virgin Islands National Park. Even before the environmental movement began to coalesce, Laurance and his brother, New York Governor Nelson A. Rockefeller, gained public approval for a $100 million bond project to acquire recreational land for parks that set a precedent for other states. As chair of the Hudson River Valley Commission, he helped develop a plan to preserve the valley corridor in the mid-1960s, and he chaired and coordinated the 1965 White House Conference on Natural Beauty.

The entire Rockefeller family felt a special bond to the scenic lands near Jackson Hole and the Grand Tetons, and in 1940, they established Jackson Hole Preserve, Inc., as a nonprofit conservation and education organization. Nearly 34,000 acres in the Jackson Hole valley were purchased from ranchers and other landowners, and in 1949, Laurance made a gift of the land to the federal government to be included in Grand Teton National Park. In 1953 he also set up a wildlife preserve in the park, where the public could observe elk, moose, buffalo, and other animals year-round. For 20 years, he had a close relationship with Grand Teton National Park Superintendent Jack Neckles; and in 2000, to further expand Grand Teton National Park as a model for open-space land stewardship, he pledged to contribute a 1,100-acre parcel that made up the family's ranch.

Laurance Rockefeller's environmental philanthropy stems from not only having the resources of a family oil fortune to contribute but also belonging to a family dedicated for three generations to conservation and the tradition of giving back. Once called "America's leading conservationist" by the First Lady, Lady Bird Johnson, Laurance Rockefeller died July 11, 2004, leaving a legacy of outstanding efforts on behalf of the environment.

SOURCES:
Adam Bernstein. "Laurance Rockefeller Dies at 94," *Washington Post* (July 12, 2004), B-4.
"Laurance S. Rockefeller," at http://archive.rockefeller.edu/bio/laurance, accessed July 12, 2004.
Robin W. Winks. *Laurance S. Rockefeller: Catalyst for Conservation*. Washington, DC: Island Press, 1997.

U.S. FOREST POLICY

About one third, or approximately 730 million acres, of U.S. land area is forested; two thirds of that (about 480 million acres) is considered timberland, capable of growing commercial crops of trees. The federal government owns about 20 percent of those lands; 7 percent is owned by state and local governments, 1 percent by Native American nations, 58 percent by private nonindustrial owners, and 14 percent by the forest industry. American timber management is complex and involves concerns about jobs, economic diversity, endangered species and their habitats, and global warming. At opposite ends in the policy debate are timber companies and environmental groups, with federal agencies caught squarely in the middle.

Federal stewardship of the nation's forest resources can be traced back to 1873, when the American Association for the Advancement of Science petitioned Congress to enact legislation to protect and properly manage U.S. forests. Despite the creation of a special bureau in 1876, timber management practices were rife with scandal and exploitation. In the late 1890s and early 1900s, the Cornell School of Forestry engaged in intensive logging, called clear-cutting, in the Adirondacks, where virtually every tree was cut down and removed. The forest products industry was criticized for its cut-and-run practices of stripping timber, abandoning the land, and quickly moving on to other areas where trees were plentiful. The result was soil degradation, flooding, and the loss of wildlife habitat.

Forest policy was truncated by a division of responsibility between the commodity-oriented Division of Forestry (in the Department of Agriculture) and the General Land Office (in the Department of the Interior). In 1901, the Division of Forestry changed its name, becoming the Bureau of Forestry; four years later, it became the Forest Service. From 1910 to 1928, the agency concerned itself primarily with fire prevention and control, and Congress had little power over forests on private lands.[17]

It was not until the Forest Service gradually began increasing the harvest of national forest land after World War II that the agency became the target of environmental interests. The need for timber that resulted from postwar economic growth conflicted with public demand for recreational use of the nation's forests. Congress perceived the Forest Service as a commodity and income-producing agency, and timber harvests increased from 3.5 to 8.3 billion board feet during the decade of the 1950s.[18] In addition to competing public pressures, the development of a comprehensive federal forest policy was thwarted by the lack of congressional direction other than broad mandates. As a result, the Forest Service operated under the dual traditions of planning—utilitarian and protective—that were the legacy of its first chief, Gifford Pinchot, who believed that wise use and preservation of forest resources were compatible goals. The resulting policy—multiple use—meant that the national forests were to serve competing interests: ranchers seeking land for grazing their livestock, recreational visitors seeking to spend their leisure time outdoors, and miners hoping to make their fortunes on as yet undiscovered lodes.

Policy was also affected by the postwar increase in leisure time, when Americans began driving to national forests in an increasing number of automobiles over newly improved highways. Over a 70-year period from 1924 to 1994, with an exception during the 1980s, recreational visits to national forests exceeded those of the national parks. The concept of multiple use began pitting recreationists and those desiring a wilderness experience against other users, such as livestock owners, timber companies, and mining interests. The passage of MUSYA in 1960 gave the Forest Service discretion over how best to manage the national forests by balancing the interests of competing stakeholders. Congress followed with another major statute, the Wilderness Act, in 1964, designating more than 9 million acres of public land as the National Wilderness Preservation System, which has grown to over 100 million acres as a result of the Alaska National Interest Lands Conservation Act.

The transformation of forest policy in the 1970s has been said to have five fundamental components: the emergence of the organized environmental movement; the enactment of new laws like the Forest and Rangeland Renewable Resources Planning Act (RPA) of 1974 and the National Forest Management Act (NFMA) of 1976; the expansion of congressional control over policy through specific statutory provisions; increased judicial scrutiny of administrative actions; and increased public participation through formal procedural avenues; creating what one scholar has called a pluralist forest regime. Critics argued that the Forest Service was out of step with the emerging ethic of environmentalism, and the agency became perceived as an enemy of the people. Congressional leaders began to recognize the growing criticism over the federal government's lack of long-term planning, and the increasing polarization of forestry issues between the timber industry and environmental groups. Both the RPA and its amendments (the NFMA) provided the Forest Service with some direction, requiring inventories of forest resources and an assessment of the costs and benefits of meeting the nation's forest resource needs.[19]

Although the legislation satisfied some critics, forest policy was far from complete, and the agency came under fire from its own employees, who alleged the Forest Service had been captured by timber interests and was inconsistent in its implementation of the law. In 1988, former staffer Jeff DeBonis founded a group called the Association of Forest Service Employees for Environmental Ethics (AFSEEE) as a way of encouraging its members to speak out against agency policies and abuses.[20] The organization began as an in-house protest against the Forest Service policy of clear-cutting—the logging of all trees within a given stand.

The practice, in addition to being aesthetically unpleasing, often leads to erosion, and has been widely criticized by environmental groups. DeBonis's organization marked one of the first times government employees had rallied against a particular cause, although some observers felt his actions were not constructive, given the Forest Service's history of institutional loyalty.[21] But DeBonis and his group believed the agency had forgotten its mission of serving the public and had become totally politicized.[22]

Current forest policy evolved from battles between environmental groups and timber companies during the 1980s, when the Reagan and Bush administrations supported massive logging in the Pacific Northwest. At one point, more than 5 million board feet of timber were being cut per year in Washington and Oregon.[23] The most heavily logged areas were also home to several endangered or threatened species, including the northern spotted owl. In 1991, a federal judge ordered a ban on logging until a species recovery plan for the bird was adopted. The controversy continued for two more years until 1993, when the Clinton administration brought the parties together in an attempt to work out a compromise. The result was the Northwest Forest Plan, an ecosystem management proposal that covered 24 million acres of forest in three states. Under the proposal, up to 1.1 million board feet of timber could be harvested, allowing some mills to continue operation. The program has now entered into the policy implementation stage. The Forest Ecosystem Management Assessment Team, a group of more than 100 scientists, has been given responsibility for coordinating the plan. Their efforts are complicated because over the last century, logging has been conducted in a haphazard manner that has created a patchwork of heavily logged and reforested areas throughout the region. Full implementation means tying these patches of land together while balancing timber harvests and ecosystem protection.[24]

Many environmental organization leaders believe the plan has been a failure, charging that old-growth forests far from urban political constituencies have been heavily logged. There is also criticism that at least initially, the program did not adequately protect key watersheds, approximately 8 million acres of which are within the boundaries covered by the plan. Supporters, however, argue that the new timber regulations immediately reduced logging 80 to 85 percent below levels of the 1980s—a change few ever imagined would be possible.

FORESTS AND FIRES

Today's forest policies are shaped by natural forces as well as political ones, namely, wildfires. Table 4.2 shows the prevalence of wildfire in changing the natural landscape of the United States.

In 1910, fires burned an area about the size of Connecticut, including about 8 million board feet of timber. The fires were economically devastating; 86 lives and entire towns were lost, mostly in the West. The newly created Forest Service took on the added responsibility of becoming a firefighting agency, with an objective of spotting and extinguishing every fire before 10 a.m. the next day. Through its

TABLE 4.2 Historically Significant U.S. Wildland Fires, 1825–2005

Date	Name	Location	Significance
1825	Miramichi and Maine Fire	New Brunswick/Maine	3 million acres burned
1871	Peshtigo	Wisconsin Michigan	3.78 million acres burned; 1,500 deaths
1881	Michigan	Michigan	1 million acres burned; 169 deaths
1902	Yacoult	Washington/Oregon	1 million acres burned; 38 deaths
1910	Great Idaho	Idaho/Montana	3 million acres burned; 85 deaths
1933	Tillamook	Oregon	311,000 acres burned. Same area burned again in 1939.
1987	Siege of '87	California	640,000 acres burned
1988	Yellowstone	Montana/Idaho	1.5 million acres burned
1991	Oakland Hills	California	1,500 acres burned; 25 deaths, 2,900 structures destroyed
1997	Inowak	Alaska	610,000 acres burned
1999	Dunn Glen Complex	Nevada	288,000 acres burned
2000	Cerro Grande	New Mexico	48,000 acres burned; originally a prescribed fire
2002	Rodeo/Chedeski	Arizona	500,000 acres burned
	Biscuit	Oregon	500,000 acres burned

SOURCE: Adapted from National Interagency Fire Center Data, www.nifc.gov/stats

Smokey Bear public relations campaign, children were taught that "Only YOU can prevent forest fires."[25]

But the unintended consequence of fire suppression policy was the creation of millions of acres of forests choked with vegetation and small trees with little commercial value. Fires, which had previously been a natural force in thinning forests, were no longer fulfilling that role in the ecosystem; as a result, the dry timber was more fire-prone than ever. Some researchers began warning of the need for ecological restoration, including the use of prescribed burns and some logging, as a way of bringing the forests back to a natural state before suppression was introduced.

Prescribed fire—the deliberate application of fire to wildlands to achieve specific resource management objectives such as reducing fuel hazards and increasing specific responses from fire-dependent plant species—is just one tool in ecological restoration. William Jordan refers to the concept as the old "notion of helping land recover from the effects of human use" that dates back to biblical times. Jordan, who founded the Society for Ecological Restoration, believes that creating ecosystems for aesthetic purposes is grounded in traditions of landscape design, the pioneering work of Edith Roberts of Vassar College in the 1920s, and landmark work at the University of Wisconsin–Madison Arboretum. He sees restoration as "perhaps one way to resolve the contradiction between community and wilderness—not by keeping them apart but by revealing the wildness at the heart of both."[26]

In 1968 the National Park Service changed its attitude toward fires by adopting a policy to allow "prescribed natural fires"—lightning-caused fires would not be suppressed under certain conditions when officials could control the burning. By the mid-1970s "fire management" replaced "fire control," due in part to concerns over increasing costs of firefighting. But in 1985, the United States experienced the most severe wildland fire losses of the century up to that point; more than 83,000 fires burned about 3 million acres, destroying or damaging more than 1,400 structures and killing 44 people.

The use of prescribed burns and the government's evolving fire policies began to change in summer 1988, when people around the world watched in horror as Yellowstone National Park went up in flames. Yellowstone's beauty and resources symbolized what natural parks were all about: tall trees, big mammals, scenic vistas, and open spaces. The fire consumed nearly 1.6 million acres in Montana, Wyoming and Idaho, as Americans wondered why the federal government did not aggressively pursue the flames in the national park. What began as wonder turned into a public outcry that "indicated public intolerance for widespread use of burning as a tool in areas of high economic and scenic value."[27]

The federal government responded with the Federal Wildland Fire Management Policy and Program Review—an attempt to ensure that policies are uniform and programs are cooperative and cohesive. The policy created an "umbrella" that joined together the Departments of the Interior and Agriculture, together with tribal governments, states, and other jurisdictions with responsibility for the protection and management of natural resources on lands they administer. However, federal officials admit that these efforts must include education efforts to expose the public to accurate information on the environmental, social, and economic benefits that result when prescribed fire is used.[28]

Whatever those benefits might be, the public was unconvinced about the role of prescribed burns in May 2000 when a National Park Service fire got out of control near the town of Los Alamos, New Mexico. The fire started in the Bandelier National Monument and quickly spread to the wildland-urban interface (WUI), a term used to describe the area between natural areas like forests and human development. Other fires later that year burned in interface areas, putting pressure on Congress and the president to take immediate action. The resulting National Fire Plan gave priority to reducing the hazardous fuels that had built up in the WUI, placing an emphasis on community-based approaches and land stewardship contracts. In 2002, the issue gained the attention of the Western Governors' Association (WGA), whose members took the lead in developing a 10-Year Implementation Plan to commit local, state, federal, and nongovernmental organizations to address wildland forest fire and forest health issues.

In 2002—the nation's second worst fire season—7.1 million acres burned and 21 firefighters were killed. Three states—Arizona, Colorado, and Oregon—had their largest-ever wildfires, including the devastating Rodeo-Chedeski Fires in

Arizona and the Biscuit Fire in Oregon, each of which burned over 500,000 acres. The 2000 and 2002 fire seasons raised public awareness about the magnitude of the fire problem, deteriorating forests, and the need for fuels reduction to restore forests and protect communities, and opened the policy window for the Bush administration to reshape forest policy.

President Bush stood in the ashes of a fire on Squire Peak in southern Oregon in August 2002, challenging critics of his new Healthy Forests Initiative to "come and stand where I stand. We need to understand if you let kindling build up and there's a lightning strike, you're going to get yourself a big fire."[29] The Healthy Forests Initiative was a blueprint to step up efforts to prevent the damage caused by catastrophic wildfires by expediting procedures for foresting thinning and restoration projects. The president charged that current forest policy "is misguided policy. It doesn't work."[30]

Within hours of the announcement, environmental groups were already criticizing the proposal. The Natural Resources Defense Council called it "a smokescreen that misses the target" and "exploits the fear of fires in order to gut environmental protections and boost commercial logging."[31] The Wilderness Society's initial analysis registered concern over the portion of the proposal that would curtail or eliminate administrative appeals and lawsuits challenging fuels treatments and restoration projects.[32] When the president flew to Portland later in the day for a Republican fund-raising event, he was met by several hundred protestors who were angry about the administration's forest policies.

Not surprisingly, timber companies and forestry officials praised the president's announcement. A spokesperson for the American Forest and Paper Association acknowledged that reducing fire danger will cost money and not always produce timber for mills. "This isn't about economics, it's about forest health. You have to value it against what would be lost if you do nothing."[33] The National Association of State Foresters said the initiative was consistent with the goals and objectives of the National Fire Plan, noting, "There is an urgent need for broad-based fuels reduction efforts to prevent another fire season as severe as the one we are experiencing now."[34]

Political supporters of the initiative, such as Idaho Governor Dick Kempthorne, said the president's plan "is just the remedy Idaho and other western states need to reduce the threat of wildfire and protect communities."[35] Governor Bill Owens of Colorado praised the proposals, as did Montana governor Judy Martz, who called for change in the process by which Forest Service projects were developed.[36]

Using both the legislative and regulatory arenas as access points for policy change, the administration delivered a four-part legislative proposal to Congress to "streamline unnecessary red tape that prevents timely and effective implementation of wildfire prevention and forest health projects on public lands." Two of the four proposals called for expediting the reduction of hazardous fuels; a third would repeal the congressional mandate for appeals of Forest Service projects, and the fourth would "establish common sense rules for courts when deciding on challenges to fuels reduction projects."[37]

Members of Congress responded immediately, with bills designed to implement the Healthy Forests Initiative introduced into both houses. But the pressures of the 2002 elections and the inability to gain consensus for a bipartisan law killed the measures, which were introduced again in the 108th Congress. This time, with the Senate under Republican control and a series of agency reports backing up the need for forest and fire reform, a compromise measure looked promising. Once again, a focusing event made the difference between policy success and failure. A series of wildfires throughout southern California burned hundreds of thousands of acres just as the Senate was deliberating on the Healthy Forests Restoration Act (HFRA); in less than two months, President Bush signed the bill just as Congress went into its holiday recess. Supplementary regulations to implement the legislative provisions continued into 2004 and 2005.[38]

Passage of the HFRA has had a number of spillover effects—a chain of events establishing a principle that guides future policy decisions—that have also changed forest and fire policy. On December 22, 2004, the U.S. Forest Service announced a final rule that drastically altered the implementation of the National Forest Management Act (NFMA). The 1976 law was enacted to control what some considered as out-of-control clear-cut logging on the national forests, and since 1982, Reagan administration regulations have guided the development of forest planning. Although there has been significant criticism of the NFMA, groups like Forest Service Employees for Environmental Ethics have called the rules "moderately effective," noting that annual logging levels on national forests have dropped from 12 billion board feet to about 3 billion board feet.[39]

The new regulations, first proposed in 2002 and effective in January 2005, made broad changes to forest planning procedures, deleting requirements of previous rules to maintain viable populations of plant and animal species and removing detailed procedural requirements concerning species protection. The focus, according to the Forest Service, would make planning more timely, cost effective, and adaptive.[40] Critics argued that the new Bush administration rules eliminated the environmental "muscle" of predecessor regulations; they not only eliminated limits on clear-cutting and protections for water quality, recreation, or scenery but also ended public disclosure of the effects a forest plan would have on the environment under NEPA.[41]

Moreover, the strategies used by the Bush administration in gaining support for the Healthy Forests Initiative began to be used in shaping other legislation and rules, from grazing regulations to energy and mining. While most environmental organizations were focused on their opposition to the president's forest initiatives, numerous other rules and regulations were being considered, making it difficult for both supporters and critics to keep up with the barrage of *Federal Register* notices, public hearings, and comment periods.

> Several environmental organizations complained that as soon as they finished submitting comments on one rule or Environmental Impact Statement, they were already behind on several others due at almost the same time. The administration, on the other hand, had the advantage of relying upon different members of Congress and agency officials to shepherd legislation through dozens of hearings that were often held simultaneously or in different regions of the country.[42]

Thus the perceived rollback in forest policy during the Bush administration was accompanied by a secondary impact—the successful development of political strategies that could also be used in other policy debates.

WILDERNESS AND ROADLESS AREAS

The development of U.S. wilderness policy is often reduced to the somewhat simplistic battle between the perspectives of Gifford Pinchot and John Muir. In his biography of Pinchot, Char Miller argues that too much has been made of the role of John Muir in protecting American wilderness, as the de facto leader of the preservationist movement, and too little credit given to Pinchot. As the main publicist for what historians call "utilitarian conservationism," Pinchot is sometimes condemned for his failure to embrace the aesthetic conservationists who advocated the maintenance of wilderness *as* wilderness. Miller believes that Pinchot had an "ability to maintain what might seem to be contradictory impulses—the desire to live simultaneously within and on nature, to exult in its splendors while exploiting its resources."[43]

The preservation of wilderness outlined in Chapter 1 is found in a number of statutory provisions, beginning with the designation of wilderness areas in 1924 under the leadership of Forest Service officials Aldo Leopold and Bob Marshall. The agency began conducting roadless area reviews in 1929 to determine which landscapes should be preserved for back-country recreation and to protect entire ecosystems. After World War II, however, concerns were raised as to how many acres were coming under the protection of wilderness designation, reducing the amount of land available for timber. The forest industry requires an extensive road network in order to both cut and transport logs, with much of the cost subsidized by the Forest Service.

In 1971, the Forest Service conducted a Roadless Area Review and Evaluation (RARE) to determine which wilderness areas within the National Forests might have the potential for road building. Environmental organizations feared that the agency's actions were a preliminary step toward reducing the acreage designated as wilderness, and successfully sued to force the Forest Service to conduct an Environmental Impact Statement to identify the impact of any form of development. A second evaluation, RARE II, recommended that 36 million acres of National Forests be opened for logging, grazing, and other resource extraction; but another lawsuit halted any new development within the inventoried roadless areas.

In 1999, the Clinton administration sought to have 58 million acres of unroaded National Forests designated as off-limits to future development, raising questions about whether the agency could afford to build more roads in wilderness areas when it already had an estimated $8 billion maintenance backlog for the 380,000-mile road system it manages. Although 38 states and Puerto Rico have inventoried roadless areas within the National Forest system, 97 percent are contained within 12 western states.

As part of the rulemaking process, the Forest Service held 23 public hearings and received over 1.1 million public comments on what would become the 2001

Roadless Area Conservation Rule. It established blanket, nationwide prohibitions limiting timber harvest and road construction or reconstruction within inventoried roadless areas on national forests and grasslands. But the rule's effective date was extended by the incoming Bush administration, and when finally implemented in May 2001, the secretary of agriculture announced that amendments to the roadless rule were likely. Later that year, the Forest Service published an Advance Notice of Proposed Rulemaking, requesting public comment on the long-term protection and management of roadless areas.

Meanwhile a series of lawsuits were filed in federal courts beginning in May 2001, and in April 2003, a court of appeals ruling actually made the rule effective for the first time. The U.S. Department of Agriculture (USDA) announced it would implement the roadless rule, but would propose an amendment to identify how governors might seek relief from the prohibitions of the rule for limited exceptional circumstances in their state. A lawsuit with the state of Alaska was settled in June 2003 to temporarily exempt the Tongass National Forest from the road prohibitions. Then in July 2003, the U.S. District Court issued a permanent injunction setting aside the roadless rule, finding that it violated the Wilderness Act and NEPA.[44]

In July 2004, while the district court's actions were being appealed, the USDA published a new proposed rule to replace the 2001 version, allowing governors 18 months to petition for adjustments to management requirements for roadless areas. Public reaction was so extensive that the comment period was extended twice, for a total of 122 days. Finally, on May 5, 2005, the final rule was announced, along with plans for a national advisory committee to assist the USDA in its implementation. Agriculture Secretary Mike Johanns noted:

> Our actions today advance President Bush's commitment to cooperatively conserve inventoried roadless areas within our national forests. USDA is committed to working closely with the nation's governors to meet the needs of our local communities while protecting and restoring the health and natural health of our national forests.[45]

Petitions will now be evaluated, and if accepted by the secretary of agriculture, the Forest Service will initiate state-specific rulemaking that will be subject to NEPA.

Although environmental groups argued that the new rule potentially opens up millions of acres to possible development, others noted that the process sets a precedent for increased state control over public lands management. "[It] is also an excellent example of how the executive branch can use rulemaking to its political advantage. It provides the executive significant powers to judge the acceptability of state petitions, while also giving it a potential way out of making politically risky decisions."[46]

While the Western Governors Association had been working with its members in preparation for the final rule, initial reactions to the new petitioning process varied. Utah Governor Jon Huntsman Jr. said he doubted there would be any major alterations in the status of the state's 4 million acres of roadless area, beyond addressing issues related to wildfires. He said that he had no plans to submit a petition, intending to let the Forest Service take the lead on the issue through its forest management plan revision process. California Governor Arnold Schwartzenegger said he had already made plans with the agency to preserve the state's roadless areas, and Montana Governor Brian Schweitzer complained about the estimated $9 million necessary to analyze the state's roadless areas before submitting a petition. "The Forest Service has been trying to resolve this issue for upwards of 30 years with little or no success," he said in a letter to President Bush. "Now your administration, without the benefit of public hearings, has issued a final rule that asks the states to shoulder this burden both administratively and financially."[47]

But a final rule does not mean the end to the controversy. The 2001 rule remains in legal limbo, because the Ninth Circuit Court of Appeals upheld it on substantial and procedural grounds, while an unfavorable Wyoming District Court decision has been appealed to the Tenth Circuit. "It is quite possible, then, that two western Courts of Appeals will uphold the original roadless rule promulgated under Clinton. Or, we may have another circuit split and wait for the Supreme Court to sort things out."[48]

GRAZING RIGHTS

Cattle became a fixture in the American West long before there were regulations over grazing and public lands. In 1519, Hernando Cortez took the offspring of cattle originally brought to the New World by Columbus to ranches in Mexico. Sometimes roaming wild, the cattle crossed the borders of what would later become Florida, Texas, and California; others were shipped from Europe to New England. By the late 19th century, the cattle industry had begun to develop as farms and homesteads were carved out and railroad lines enabled ranchers to get their livestock to market.

Range rules were nonexistent in the emerging nation. Livestock owners strung barbed wire across lands, disregarding public and private land boundaries, and grazing wars broke out between cattlemen and sheepherders over scarce water supplies. By the 1870s, federal rangelands were greatly overgrazed; in 1887 a severe winter, coupled with malnutrition, killed millions of stressed livestock, bankrupting cattle companies that were involved in speculative grazing practices that damaged the lands. Concerns began to grow that grazing interests, along with timber and mining, had monopolized the frontier.[49]

In 1934, Congressional passage of the Taylor Grazing Act established a federal Division of Grazing to work with the General Land Office to establish grazing districts, set fees, and grant permits for use. The two agencies later merged to become the BLM.

Grazing is permitted within national forests, on many national wildlife refuges, and within some national parks. The BLM and the Forest Service administer about 22,000 grazing permits and leases. Fees are calculated on the basis of an animal unit month (AUM)—the amount of forage required to feed a cow and her calf, a horse, or five goats or sheep for a month. Access to federal lands is fixed to base property ownership, so that those who own the greatest amount of property get priority for federal grazing privileges. The livestock industry leases an estimated 160 million acres of public lands, mostly in 12 western states.

The issue of grazing on public lands is complex and polarized, fraught with symbolism, cultural traditions, economics, and environmental concerns. The livestock industry's perspective is best explained through the Colorado-based National Cattlemen's Beef Association (NCBA), which is among the most powerful stakeholders in the debate over public lands grazing. Originally formed as the National Cattlemen's Association, the group focused on deflated grain prices, agricultural legislation like the 1985 Farm Bill, the meatpacking industry, and the declining market share for beef. Gradually, industry leaders realized that by forming a coalition representing the various sectors of the beef market, they would have considerably more political clout. Several groups merged in the mid-1990s—including the Beef Industry Council of the National Livestock and Meat Board, the Beef Promotion and Research Board, the American National CattleWomen, and the U.S. Meat Export Federation—becoming the NCBA.

Today, the U.S. beef industry is worth an estimated $175 billion, operating 800,000 individual farms and ranches raising 95 million cattle. Although the United States has less than 10 percent of the world's cattle inventory, it produces nearly 25 percent of the world's beef supply, with 1.4 million jobs attributed to the industry. Beef and beef variety mix exports are worth nearly $4 billion, or about 9 percent of U.S. domestic beef production.[50]

Ranchers rely on grazing subsidies as a way of providing their industry with a stable source of forage for their livestock. They also believe that public subsidies keep the cost of meat at a reasonable level for consumers and help to sustain the economic base for the rural West. The NCBA notes that more than 90 percent of the land utilized for grazing throughout the United States is too high, too rough, too wet, or too dry to be used for crops. Using lands for grazing, especially those within the public domain, becomes an important element of local and regional economic vitality. In addition, the NCBA argues, removing the right to graze on public lands would force many livestock producers to reduce their herd numbers, selling their ranch land for conversion to residential development. Livestock ranching becomes, in one sense, a way of maintaining open space and preserving the landscape.[51]

Environmental groups have focused on three primary issues in their attempts to limit or ban livestock grazing on public lands: the subsidizing of the ranching industry, environmental degradation, and the domination of the livestock industry over BLM policy. When the Taylor Act went into effect in 1936, the fee was five cents per AUM, although the Forest Service and the BLM have often differed in the rates they charged. Congress enacted the 1978 Public Rangelands Improvement Act to require a uniform grazing fee, which reached a high of $2.36 per AUM in 1980. The AUM formula continued under a presidential Executive Order issued in 1986, which stipulates that the grazing fee cannot fall below $1.35 per AUM. The annually adjusted fee is computed by using a 1966 base value of $1.23 for livestock grazing on public lands in 16 western states. The figure is then adjusted according to current lease rates for grazing livestock on private lands, beef cattle prices, and the cost of livestock production.

Environmental organizations want the federal government to bring the charges more in line with what it costs to graze animals in the private market, rather than subsidizing ranchers. The direct and indirect cost to taxpayers has been estimated at $130 to $500 million annually, exceeding the estimated revenue from grazing fees (less than $15 million annually).[52] Because of a significant increase in livestock prices in 2004, the 2005 rate was raised from $1.43 to $1.79 per AUM. The Forest Service applies different grazing fees to national grasslands and to lands under its management in the eastern and midwestern states and parts of Texas. In 2005, the national grassland fee was raised from $1.52 to $1.90 per AUM.[53]

In addition to the financial subsidies provided by the federal grazing program, critics point to the ecological damage caused by livestock. Overgrazing is claimed to have led to erosion and stream sedimentation in riparian habitats and to have devastated populations of game birds, songbirds, and fish. In one study, the General Accounting Office (GAO) found that more U.S. plant species are wiped out or endangered by livestock grazing than by any other single factor. Livestock are also major consumers of one of the West's most precious resources—water, which is needed to irrigate hay and other crops. Some groups note that grazing is a major source of nonpoint water pollution. Grazing also forces out populations of wildlife that cannot compete for forage and water.[54]

Environmental advocacy groups have repeatedly criticized the BLM for allowing the cattle industry to dominate the grazing policy debate; one GAO report found that "the BLM is not managing the permittees, rather, permittees are managing the BLM." Occasionally, environmental groups have been successful in forcing the federal government to analyze the impact of grazing, as was the case in 1974 when the Natural Resources Defense Council won a landmark suit that forced the BLM to develop 144 environmental impact statements on grazing. But in response, ranchers fought back in a Rocky Mountain West movement during the late 1970s; environmentalists called it "The Great Terrain Robbery," but it is better known as "The Sagebrush Rebellion."

During the late 1970s, several western groups were formed by conservatives and ranchers dissatisfied with BLM policies. The movement had three objectives: to convince state legislators to pass resolutions demanding that BLM and Forest Service lands be transferred from the federal government to individual states, to create a financial war chest for legal challenges in the federal courts, and to develop a broad public education campaign to get western voters to support the movement. The rebellion was portrayed as a "states' rights" issue, although it became obvious that what the organizers really wanted was to eliminate the federal government from having any say in how ranchers used the land. The Sagebrush Rebellion was the first organized and politically viable challenge to the environmental movement since the early 1950s. One observer, however, believes that although there was a rebellion for a time, only one side showed up to fight.[55]

Contemporary grazing policies have been shaped by Presidents Clinton and Bush, especially under the stewardship of Clinton's Interior Secretary Bruce Babbitt. The former Arizona governor found himself in a position to reform grazing policy; and in 1990, 1991, and 1992, the House passed grazing fee increases (as high as $8.70 per AUM). But despite successes in the House, the bills died in the Senate or were stripped from the bills in the conference committees.[56] The Clinton administration then entered the grazing lands reform debate through the budget process, proposing to raise the grazing fee from $1.92 to $5.00 per AUM as part of its fiscal stimulation package. Western senators quickly opposed the administration's initiative, and the president just as quickly retreated, dropping his demands for public land reform and reduction of subsidies.

The failure of congressional reform prompted a series of 20 meetings throughout the West, convened by Secretary Babbitt and others. The meetings culminated in a March 1994 Department of the Interior proposal to raise the grazing fee, broaden public participation in rangeland management, and require environmental improvements on rangelands. The proposal, called Rangeland Reform '94, went into effect in August 1995. Rangeland Reform '94 created Resource Advisory Councils (RACs)—comprised of ranchers, conservationists, and other stakeholders to help create grazing policy—authorized permit holders to not use land for up to 10 years for conservation purposes and to graze fewer animals than permitted without losing leases, allowed federal officials to consider a permittee's past performance when determining future permits, required grazing land improvements to be owned by the federal government, raised fees to approximately $3.68 per AUM and subsequent fees to be negotiated, and required changes in grazing practices to ensure recovery and protection of endangered species and protect rangelands. Efforts by opponents in Congress to enact legislation to overturn Rangeland Reform '94 were unsuccessful.

Wise use advocates had achieved few of their policy goals during Clinton's second term. However, they had successfully placed their concerns on the policy agenda, and federal agencies, environmentalists, and members of Congress were all scrambling to anticipate their attacks on public lands policy and their defense of the traditional West. But when George W. Bush assumed office, grazing issues appeared to have been pushed further down the agenda, failing to capture the interests of ranchers or environmental groups, who moved on to other issues. A few Bush appointees raised eyebrows and voices, such as William G. Meyers, solicitor for the Department of the Interior, who had formerly worked as a lobbyist for the National Cattlemen's Beef Association and sued unsuccessfully to overturn the Clinton grazing reform regulations. Grazing interests simmered while many environmental organizations moved on to other initiatives introduced by the Bush administration.

In December 2003, the BLM proposed new grazing regulations the administration said would improve the agency's working relationships with public land ranchers, conserve rangeland resources, and address legal issues while enhancing administrative efficiency. Six public hearings were held in early 2004; 18,000 public comments were received, and the final rule was announced in June 2005. The new rule gives shared title to future permanent range improvements, such as fences, wells, or pipelines, if they are constructed under a Cooperative Range Improvement Agreement, a provision stemming from the Rangeland Reform '94 regulations. The rule also requires the phasing in of grazing-use decreases or increases of more than 10 percent over a five-year period to allow sufficient time for ranchers to make gradual adjustments in their operations. Existing restrictions that limit temporary nonuse of a grazing permit to three years would be removed, and the BLM would have up to 24 months (rather than the start of the next grazing season) for the agency to analyze and formulate an appropriate course of action in cases where grazing practices are at issue and need to be corrected. BLM would no longer be able to issue conservation use permits (purchased primarily by conservation groups to rest the land rather than using it for grazing.)[57]

Environmental advocacy groups made clear their opposition to the new rules, which went into effect in July 2005. "We are disgusted but not surprised by this administration's consistent concern for private economic interests at the expense of public awareness and involvement," said a spokesperson for the Center for Biological Diversity. "These new regulations allow the fox to guard the henhouse, and interested parties are left without recourse as soils, water, vegetation and imperiled species suffer from the economic exploitation of our public lands."[58]

Critics also assailed provisions in the new rule that would redefine the phrase "interested public" in a way that they believe limits the participation of new residents in an area and removes public involvement from biological assessments and evaluations for wildlife. "The Bush administration is making it clear that they want to take the 'public' out of public lands," the Forest Guardians noted. Others said, "The new regs are an unethical political scam from Interior Department appointees in Washington, D.C. BLM is trying to reverse years of progress on rangeland restoration to serve a handful of cowmen at great cost to the public interest."[59]

The grazing rule came under fire just days after it was announced when two former BLM employees revealed that the environmental impact statement they prepared had been altered by the Bush administration. A biologist and hydrologist who had contributed to the environmental impact statement (EIS) said their conclusions that the proposed rules might adversely affect water quality and wildlife, including endangered species, were excised and replaced with language justifying less stringent regulations. The original draft of the EIS warned that the new rules would have a significant adverse impact on wildlife, but that phrase was removed, and the revised version concluded that the grazing regulations would be beneficial to animals. "This is a whitewash, they took all of our science and reversed it 180 degrees," said the biologist, who retired before the rule was finalized. The agency's hydrologist, who also retired before the rule was published, said, "Everything in the report that was purported to be negative was watered down. Instead of saying, in the long-term, this will create problems, it now says, in the long-term, grazing is the best thing since sliced bread."[60]

The BLM's manager for rangeland resources said the report was written by a number of specialists from different offices within the BLM. When it was finished in November 2003, the agency believed it "needed a lot of work. We disagreed with the impact analysis that was originally put forward. There were definitely changes made in the area of impact analysis. We adjusted it."[61]

There is little doubt that like other Bush administration initiatives, the new grazing rules will affect public lands ranching, although BLM officials denied that the new provisions were a rollback of the Rangeland Reform '94 provisions that established the 24 citizen-based RACs across the West. "The rule will continue to require the Bureau to consult with the interested public in all key matters. Clearly, there is no 'locking out' of the interested public from the BLM's grazing decision-making process."[62]

Besides fee increases, several solutions have been proposed to deal with the grazing issue. Some environmental groups have lobbied for a complete prohibition against grazing on federal lands. Others believe that agencies like the BLM simply need more funds to repair overgrazing damage and to monitor land use. A third option, proposed by the Sierra Club, would be to allow grazing on those lands that have not been abused, but to ban the practice on those that are already in unsatisfactory condition. That option is viewed as an acknowledgment that conservationists' achievements are not keeping up with chronic abuse of public lands.

Some of the advocates for a more collaborative approach to grazing turned to a new policy option: the grazing buyout. The National Public Lands Grazing Campaign (NPLGC) has proposed a voluntary buyout of grazing permits in both the 108th and 109th Congresses. Under this proposal, which has been endorsed by more than 200 conservation groups, public lands permittees would be paid about four times the average market value to yield their grazing permits, averaging about $175 per AUM. Voluntary retirement, supporters argue, would allow struggling ranchers to get out of public lands grazing without serious economic consequences.[63]

Opponents to the grazing buyout, such as the Public Lands Council, have joined with the NCBA, noting the buyout is not feasible and is based on unsound public and fiscal policy. They estimate that the proposal, if approved, could cost American taxpayers over $3.2 billion. They also cite two federal court decisions ruling that federal grazing permits could not be held for conservation purposes. From a philosophical perspective, the grazing buyout would violate federal statutes such as the Multiple Use and Sustained Yield Act, National Forest Management Act, and the Federal Land Policy Management Act mandating that all federal lands must be managed under the concept of multiple use.[64]

The NPLGC has responded to the opposition to a nationwide buyout proposal with a plan that would create site-specific voluntary buyout programs in Arizona and central Idaho. "Buying out public lands livestock grazing is ecologically imperative, economically rational, fiscally prudent and socially just," said the campaign's director. "Public lands grazing is a part of the rural American West that is being left behind by the modern global economy and I believe we are a rich country that should not leave anyone behind. Permit buyout is a way to recapitalize a part of the American rural West that is in decline."[65]

MINING LAW AND PUBLIC LANDS

Decades before land-use issues were on the public's environmental agenda, the discovery of gold in California in 1849 and the subsequent gold rush became the foundation for the nation's mining policies. When California was admitted as a state a year later, the area, which was under control of the military, still had no federal regulation of land use, although officially, miners were considered trespassers on public lands. The overriding theme was one of economic liberalism. From 1848 to 1866, the military appears to have ignored mining activities, even though the miners themselves realized that some regulations were necessary to fill the legal vacuum.[66]

Responding to miners' efforts to strengthen property-rights claims yet cause minimal disruption to mining activities, Congress enacted one general mining law in 1866, followed by amendments in 1870 that allowed a person or group to patent up to 160 acres and to purchase the claims for $2.50 an acre. Congress recodified the provisions of the 1866 and 1870 laws with the 1872 Mining Law, later signed by President Ulysses S. Grant. The purpose of the law was simple—to encourage the expansion and settlement of the West. At the time, miners, who were confident of the fortunes that they could make in the largely unexplored western lands, used pickaxes, shovels, and pans to look for mineral treasures. There was little consideration for the environmental impacts of mining—a problem that developed in the 20th century as the industry used more highly mechanized equipment and dumped mining waste into rivers and streams.

The 1872 law allows an individual who finds a valuable mineral resource on public lands to obtain a mining claim for the deposit. The individual acquires a possessory interest in the claim, making it a form of transferable property, and thus granting the right to extract, process, and market whatever minerals are found. The holder of the claim may also obtain title to the land on which the claim is located at a nominal cost. The result is that the federal government has only minimal authority to control mining. Subsequent laws have fine-tuned the 1872 act, but the government has generally taken a hands-off attitude when it comes to the mining industry, as seen by the paucity of legislation that has been enacted (see Table 4.3).

In August 1996, the issue resurfaced on the political agenda when Crowne Butte Mines, a subsidiary of a Canadian company, applied to purchase 27 acres of public land near Yellowstone National Park. On the lands was a closed mine that had been used sporadically since the late 1800s. The company would have purchased the land, and the minerals beneath it, for only $135 under the terms of the

TABLE 4.3 Major U.S. Mining Laws

Year	Law	Provisions
1872	Mining Act	Authorizes and governs prospecting and mining for hard-rock minerals on public lands
1920	Mineral Leasing Act	Authorizes and governs leasing of public lands for development of deposits of coal, oil, gas, sulfur, phosphate, potassium, and sodium
1947	Materials Act	Regulates mineral material disposal
1947	Mineral Leasing Act	Authorizes and governs mineral leasing on acquired lands
1955	Common Varieties Act	Regulates minimal material disposal
1973	Mineral Leasing Act	Amends 1947 law to govern oil and gas leasing on federal lands
1977	Surface Mining Control and Reclamation Act	Regulates coal mining to prevent contaminants from entering groundwater

1872 law. The property is now estimated to contain $650 million in gold, silver, and copper reserves—revenues on which the company would have paid no royalties whatsoever. Environmental organizations like the National Resources Defense Council (NRDC) were also concerned that the cyanide-based chemical extraction process and use of heavy machinery would cause irreparable damage to the Yellowstone ecosystem.

Instead, the Clinton administration negotiated an agreement to purchase the site in exchange for the surrender of Crowne Butte's mining rights, payment of a cleanup fee of over $22 million, and a land swap giving the company federal land worth $65 million. Despite the publicity surrounding the agreement, Congress still refuses to enact legislation that would provide fair compensation to the taxpayer for the value of minerals extracted from public lands, establish long-term monitoring of all mine sites, and set standards for regulating water quality, with special provisions for environmentally sensitive areas.[67]

In January 2001, the Interior Department finalized a regulation that gave the BLM the power to veto proposed mining operations that would do "significant irreparable harm" to public lands. Environmental groups tasted victory, but two months later, Bush administration Interior Secretary Gale Norton suspended the rule; and in October 2001, she officially rescinded the BLM's authority. The administration also reversed prior policies that protected tribal lands from mining and approved permits for mining in wilderness areas, ending the string of environmental group success stories and returning power to the mining industry.[68]

Just months later, Norton said she supported making mining companies pay royalties for mining on federal land as part of revisions to the 1872 law. Members of Congress, like Rep. Christopher Shays of Connecticut, called the statute a "taxpayer ripoff" that provides insufficient environmental protection. More than 557,000 mines have been deserted since the 1800s, costing taxpayers more than $30 billion in cleanup costs, according to one estimate. Companies like Phelps Dodge, the world's second largest copper producer, have moved operations to Latin America because of federal regulations; officials for Newmont, the world's largest gold producer, have said they would consider the controversial royalty issue.

These examples illustrate how difficult it can sometimes be to get a problem placed on the policy agenda. Although there is almost total agreement on the need for the General Mining Law to be amended and for appropriate environmental safeguards to be placed on public lands, efforts to do so have been unsuccessful for over a century. Mining policy has not captured the interest of the general public, and a strong lobbying effort by extractive resource industries has put pressure on Congress to leave the law alone. Environmental organizations have focused on other issues while powerful western lobbyists have kept the law intact.[69]

PRIVATE PROPERTY AND PUBLIC LANDS

One of the most controversial land-use issues of the past 20 years, regulatory takings, has galvanized private property owners through the United States. These people feel the government has unfairly appropriated their land without paying them for its value.

The bases for their position are the Fifth Amendment to the Constitution, which states that private property may not be taken for public use without just compensation, and a 1922 U.S. Supreme Court case that affirmed the concept of a regulatory "taking."[70] For years the courts have attempted to interpret the meaning of the amendment, especially in cases where privately owned land was needed for public use, such as the construction of a new freeway. Local governments routinely have condemned houses in the freeway path and paid the owners damages, usually the fair market value of the homes.

In 1985, University of Chicago law professor Richard Epstein published a controversial book that placed the concept of takings in a regulatory context.[71] Epstein argued that all forms of government regulations are subject to scrutiny under the takings clause, leading advocates of private property rights to demand that the government pay those affected for the loss of the right to use their land, regardless of the reason. These people were joined in their efforts by conservative organizations like the Cato Institute and the Federalist Society, who used the takings and property-rights issue to bolster their attempts to reduce government intervention. Since Epstein's book was published, the concept of takings has been applied to a broad range of environmental legislation, from wilderness and wetlands designations to the protection of endangered species.

Under the Endangered Species Act, for example, the federal government has the power to prevent landowners from altering their property in any way that threatens a species or its habitat. From a legal perspective, the reasoning is that the protection of a species (the common good or public interest) must be weighed against the interest of an individual property owner. Proponents of property rights counter that view by arguing that the government should be prevented from imposing on individual landowners the cost of providing public goods. They cite regulations, such as those restricting development that would adversely affect wetlands, as examples in which individuals are unfairly being asked to give up the use of their land without being compensated for their loss. Other cases have involved the expansion of national park boundaries and wilderness designations or instances where a private property owner's land is appropriated for a wildlife refuge or recreational area. To press their demands upon the political system, individuals with property grievances have joined grassroots organizations like the American Land Rights Association, Defenders of Property Rights, and Stewards of the Range. The groups have attempted to gain media attention for their cause and have sought remedies in both the judicial and legislative arenas.[72]

The Supreme Court has not provided clear guidelines for determining when a taking has occurred and when compensation is due. There is little question that, when the government actually takes possession of land, fair compensation must be awarded the previous owner; the problem comes when government regulation places some limit on how property owners can use their land. The Court's decisions send mixed signals concerning the difference between a compensable taking and a regulation with which property owners must comply. In some cases, if the government requires a physical intrusion, the Court has required compensation. The Court assesses the economic impact of a regulation in determining whether it crosses the line to become a taking. But the justices have been unable to decide on enduring principles. They have devised some criteria for assessing government actions, but the weight given each factor varies from case to case. Many decisions appear to be the result of a judgment about whether the Court concludes that a regulation serves an important public purpose and is valid or whether it is unjustifiably meddling in the affairs of landowners and is a taking.[73] Property-rights activists have also pursued their cause in the U.S. Court of Federal Claims, which hears claims against the U.S. Treasury involving $10,000 or more.

In the legislative arena, activists have sought to gain protection for private property in both state legislatures and in Congress. One type of proposal, called "look before you leap," requires governments to assess the takings implications of laws, regulations, and other governmental actions. The bills seek to deter governments from taking actions that would require compensation to property owners, thus saving the government money. However, because there is no widely accepted definition of what constitutes a taking, the standards to be used are unsettled. A second type of legislative proposal (introduced in state legislatures and as a part of the Republican Contract with America) would trigger compensation when a property's value is diminished by a specific percentage because of government regulation. Supporters have also sought a "takings impact analysis" similar to that called for under the National Environmental Policy Act. The concept, which was advanced in an executive order during the administration of President Ronald Reagan, calls for an evaluation of whether a government regulation would deprive a property owner of the use of the land. But the proposals have been criticized by environmental groups, which warned that such legislation would slow down the wheels of government regulation and would bankrupt the government.[74]

When takings proposals have been placed before the voters in state referendums, they have largely failed. Opposition to such measures is due mainly to their projected costs and the likelihood that they will result in higher taxes. Opponents fear that takings regulations will become a "nightmare of dueling appraisers and dueling lawyers" who will argue over every analysis and every assessment, becoming an expensive new entitlement program that would have a chilling effect on environmental regulation.[75] Environmental organizations have somewhat belatedly realized the potential impact of the property rights movement as it relates to public land use. Their lethargy may have been because much of the debate was being carried out in the courts, where the judicial wheels move slowly and the justices seldom make sweeping new judicial interpretations. But highly publicized cases, a flurry of state initiatives, and the changeover to a Republican-controlled Congress have mobilized environmental groups to monitor state and federal legislation more closely. So far, they appear to have been successful in confining property-rights issues to the judicial arena where policy making is more likely to be incremental and limited.

TRENDS IN LAND USE AND MANAGEMENT

Given these examples of current land-use controversies, what does this tell us about trends in how America's land use policies have developed? First, attitudes about the management of public lands have evolved slowly in the United States, from a policy of divestiture and conservation to one of preservation. Those attitudes reflect the changing public consciousness about the environment, which has had its peaks and valleys throughout U.S. history. When citizens are concerned about land use, they demand to be involved and participate fully. When they are apathetic, decisions get made without them.

Second, land-use policies are tempered by politics. Frustrated by their attempts to influence presidential policy making, environmental groups have often turned to Congress or the president in hopes of exploiting regional and partisan rivalries. Many of the legislative mandates given to the agencies responsible for land management are vague and often contradictory, and Congress has seldom seemed eager to be more explicit in its direction. This is due partly to congressional sidestepping of many of the more controversial conflicts in resource use. Should deserts be opened up to all-terrain vehicles or left in a pristine condition where no one can enjoy them? Should the national parks be made more accessible so that they can accommodate more visitors, or should traffic be limited to prevent destroying the parks' scenic beauty through overuse? Should governmental regulatory agencies tell private property owners how their land can be used? The answers to those questions depend largely on which member of Congress, in what region of the country, is answering them.

Third, the future of public lands appears to have a price tag attached. Although there is a general sense that Americans want to preserve wilderness areas, scenic wonders, and some historic sites, they become less willing to do so when the decisions directly affect their pocketbooks. They may be willing to pay slightly higher fees to use state or national parks, but they rebel when the choice is between preservation of a single species and putting food on their family's table. As a result, land-use policies are more likely to take into account the economic rather than scientific impact of decisions.

Fourth, decisions about land-use policies are often made in the cloistered setting of administrative hearing rooms, and the hearings are poorly attended by those affected by the decision-making process and only marginally publicized. The language of resource management is esoteric, and the science often unsubstantiated. Thus the debate over the future of public lands has historically been dominated by resource users, such as timber and mining companies. More recently, however, environmental groups have "learned the language" of land and forest management, often hiring former industry experts. Still, most Americans know little about what is happening to the millions of acres still under federal control, and only well-organized groups that closely monitor regulatory actions (most of them based in the West) are in a position to speak for the public interest.

Last, it appears that stakeholders are realizing that no progress can be made as long as they stick to highly adversarial positions. Strategies of coordination and collaboration are becoming the rule rather than the exception, whether they are being used to develop community fire plans or private land trusts.[76] Although these initiatives and mechanisms cannot resolve all land-use conflicts, they represent a change in direction from refusing to come to the table, to at least taking a look at what is on the menu.

NOTES

1. Presidential Proclamation No. 458, 34 Stat. 3236 (September 24, 1906).

2. For accounts of the regional legends, see Wendy Rex-Atzet, "Narratives of Place and Power," in *Imagining the Big Open: Nature, Identity and Play in the New West,* Elaine Bapis, Thomas J. Harvey, and Liza Nichols, eds. (Salt Lake City: University of Utah Press, 2003), 259–264.

3. National Park Service, Devil's Tower General Management Plan, at www.nps.gov/deto/gmp, accessed April 3, 2005.

4. 42 U.S.C. Section 1996.

5. The Native American Graves and Repatriation Act is at 25 U.S.C. Section 3001; the National Historical Preservation Act Amendments of 1992 are at 16 U.S.C. Section 470; Executive Order 13007, 61 Fed. Reg. 26771 (1996).

6. *Bear Lodge Multiple Use Association et al. v. Bruce Babbitt et al.* U.S. Court of Appeals, Tenth Cir. 98-8021 (1998).

7. The prior rulings on standing to sue include *Lujan v. Defenders of Wildlife,* 504 U.S. 555 (1992), *United States v. Students Challenging Regulatory Agency Procedures,* 412 U.S. 669 (1973), and *National Council for Improved Health v. Shalala,* 122 F.3d. 878 (10th Cir. 1997).

8. Anne C. Mulkern, "Heritage at Center of Fight Over Devil's Tower's Name," *Arizona Republic,* April 3, 2005, A14.

9. Michael P. Dombeck, Christopher A. Wood, and Jack E. Williams; *From Conquest to Conservation: Our Public Lands Legacy.* (Washington, DC: Island Press, 2003), 9–13.

10. Denzel and Nancy Ferguson, *Sacred Cows at the Public Trough* (Bend, OR: Maverick Publications, 1983), 171–172.

11. Richard West Sellars, *Preserving Nature in the National Parks: A History* (New Haven, CT: Yale University Press, 1997), 9–10.

12. National Parks Conservation Association, "The Burgeoning Backlog," at www.npca.org, accessed June 16, 2005.

13. Ibid.

14. The Yosemite Fund, at www.yosemitefund.org, accessed June 16, 2005.

15. The California Desert Protection Act of 1994, P.L. 103-433.

16. Sen. Paul Sarbanes, "Sarbanes Renews Effort to Re-Designate Catoctin Mountain Park," News release, April 28, 2005, at http://sarbanes.senate.gov, accessed June 16, 2005. The measure, S. 777, was introduced as the Catoctin Mountain National Recreation Area Designation Act.

17. For a general overview of U.S. forest policy, see Frederick W. Cubbage, Jay O'Laughlin, and Charles S. Bullock III, *Forest Resource Policy* (New York: Wiley, 1993); Christopher McGrory Klyza, *Who Controls Public Lands? Mining, Forestry, and Grazing Policies, 1970–1990* (Chapel Hill: University of North Carolina Press, 1996), 67–107; Elizabeth May, *At The Cutting Edge* (San Francisco: Sierra Club Books, 1998).

18. See Marion Clawson. *The Federal Lands Since 1956: Recent Trends in Use and Management* (Baltimore: Johns Hopkins University Press, 1967); and Paul Culhane, *Public Lands Policies* (Baltimore: Johns Hopkins University Press, 1981).

19. George Hoberg, "The Emerging Triumph of Ecosystem Management: The Transformation of Federal Forest Policy," in *Western Public Land and Environmental Politics,* 2nd ed., Charles Davis, ed. (Boulder, CO: Westview Press, 2001), 55–85.

20. See, for example, Paul Schneider, "When a Whistle Blows in the Forest," *Audubon,* 7 (July 1990): 42–49; Jim Stiak, "Memos to the Chief," *Sierra, 75,* no. 4 (July–August 1990): 26–29.

21. For perspectives on the U.S. Forest Service and its employees, see the classic work by Herbert Kaufman, *The Forest Ranger: A Study in Administrative Behavior* (Baltimore: Johns Hopkins University Press, 1960); Harold K. Steen, *The U.S. Forest Service: A History* (Seattle: University of Washington Press, 1976); Robert D. Baker, Robert S. Maxwell, Victor H. Treat, and Henry C. Dethloff, *Timeless Heritage: A History of the Forest Service in the Southwest* (College Station, TX: Intaglio Press, 1988); David A. Clary, *Timber and the Forest Service* (Lawrence: University Press of Kansas, 1986). Some recent commentaries can be found in Roger A. Sedjo, ed., *A Vision for the U.S. Forest Service: Goals for Its Next Century* (Washington, DC: Resources for Future Press, 2000); William Dietrich, *The Final Forest: The Battle for the Last Great Trees of the Pacific Northwest* (New York: Penguin Books, 1992): 161–168.

22. See William Dietrich, *The Final Forest: The Battle for the Last Great Trees of the Pacific Northwest* (New York: Penguin Books, 1992): 161–168.

23. Ibid.

24. Chris Carrel, "A Patchwork Peace Unravels," *High Country News,* November 23, 1998, 1.

25. The foremost authority on the role of fire is Stephen J. Pyne, whose research explores the role of fire in culture, details about specific fires such as the one in 1910, and the history of wildland fire. See, for example, Stephen J. Pyne, *Fire in America: A Cultural History of Wildland and Rural Fire* (Seattle: University of Washington Press, 1982); Pyne, *Fire: A Brief History* (Seattle: University of Washington Press, 2001; Pyne, *Tending Fire: Coping with America's Wildland Fires* (Washington, DC: Island Press, 2004). See also Stephen F. Arno, *Flames in Our Forest: Disaster or Renewal?* (Washington, DC: Island Press, 2002).

26. William R. Jordan III, "Restoration, Community, and Wilderness," in Paul H. Gobster and R. Bruce Hull, eds., *Restoring Nature: Perspective from the Social Sciences and Humanities* (Washington, DC: Island Press, 2000), 23–36. See also Eric Katz, *Nature As Subject: Human Obligation and Natural Community* (Lanham, MD: Rowman & Littlefield, 1997); Katz, "The Problem of Ecological Restoration," *Environmental Ethics, 18* (1994): 222–224; Katz, "The Call of the Wild: The Struggle Against Domination and the Technological Fix of Nature," *Environmental Ethics, 14* (1992): 265–273; Andrew Light and Eric Higgs, "The Politics of Ecological Restoration," *Environmental Ethics, 18* (1996): 227–247; Andrew Light and Eric Katz, *Environmental Pragmatism* (New York: Routledge, 1996).

27. Thomas G. Alexander, "Struggle in an Endangered Empire: The Search for Total Ecosystem Management in the Forests of Southern Utah, 1976–1999," in *Forests Under Fire,* eds. Christopher J. Huggard and Arthur R. Gomez, 234. For more on the controversy, see Tom Kenworthy, "Burn Now or Burn Later," *Washington Post National Weekly Edition,* September 9–15, 1996, A22.

28. *Federal Wildland Fire Policy: Executive Summary,* at www.fs.fed.us/land, accessed March 18, 2000.

29. "Bush Sparks Protest with Planned National Forest Logging for Fire Prevention," August 24, 2002, at www.cbc.ca, accessed August 24, 2002.

30. "President Announces Healthy Forests Initiative," Remarks by the President on Forest Health and Preservation, August 22, 2002, Central Point, Oregon, at www.whitehouse.gov/news, accessed August 23, 2002.

31. Natural Resources Defense Council, "Bush's Forest Proposal a 'Smokescreen,' Says NRDC," News release, August 22, 2002, at www.nrdc.org/media, accessed August 24, 2002.

32. The Wilderness Society, "Analysis: Bush Administration's 'Healthy Forests Initiative,'" Fact sheet, August 22, 2002, at www.wildernesssociety.org/newsroom, accessed August 23, 2002.

33. Jeff Barnard, "Forest Plan Faces Obstacles," *The Missoulian,* August 26, 2002, at www.missoulian.com, accessed August 26, 2002.

34.· National Association of State Foresters, "NASF Commends Presidential Forest Health Initiative," News release, August 23, 2002, at www.stateforesters.org/news, accessed August 26, 2002.

35. Office of the Governor of the State of Idaho, "Kempthorne: President's Fire Plan Just What Idaho and the West Needs," News release, August 22, 2002, at www.state.id.us/gov, accessed August 24, 2002.

36. Jennifer McKee, "Martz: Ban Logging Appeals," *Billings Gazette,* August 22, 2002, at www.billingsgazette.com, accessed August 26, 2002.

37. "USDA and DOI Deliver Legislation to Implement President's Healthy Forests Initiative," News release, September 5, 2002, at www.doi.gov/news, accessed September 7, 2002.

38. The parallel strategy of introducing the Healthy Forest proposals in Congress and the bureaucracy are outlined in Jacqueline Vaughn and Hanna J. Cortner, *George W. Bush's Healthy Forests: Reframing the Environmental Debate* (Boulder: University Press of Colorado, 2005).

39. Andy Stahl, "Ashes to Ashes, Dust to Dust," *Forest Magazine,* Spring 2005, 5.

40. USDA Forest Service, "Forest Service Publishes Planning Rules for Better Management of National Forests and Grasslands," News release, December 22, 2004, at www.fs.fed.us/news/2004/releases, accessed December 23, 2004.

41. Stahl, "Ashes to Ashes."

42. Vaughn and Cortner, *George W. Bush's Healthy Forests,* 223.

43. Char Miller, *Gifford Pinchot and the Making of Modern Environmentalism* (Washington, DC: Island Press, 2001), 5.

44. U.S. Department of Agriculture, "Roadless Area Conservation: Background Paper," at www.roadless.fs.fed.us/xdocuments.shtml, accessed May 6, 2005.

45. U.S. Department of Agriculture, "USDA Forest Service Acts to Conserve Roadless Areas in National Forests," News release, May 5, 2005, at www.usda.gov, accessed May 6, 2005.

46. Martin Nie, "A Rule to Sue By," *Headwaters News,* at www.headwatersnews.org, accessed October 5, 2004.

47. Joe Baird, "Utah Roadless Areas in Danger?" *Salt Lake Tribune,* June 12, 2005, at www.sltrib.com, accessed June 19, 2005.

48. Nie, "A Rule to Sue By."

49. Dombeck, Wood, and Williams, *From Conquest to Conservation,* 17. For a comprehensive history of grazing policies, see George A. Gonzalez, "Ideas and State Capacity, or Business Dominance? A Historical Analysis of Grazing on the Public Grasslands," *Studies in American Political Development, 15,* no. 2 (Fall 2001): 234–244. See also Wesley Calef, *Private Grazing and Public Lands* (Chicago: University of Chicago Press, 1960); Phillip O. Foss, *Politics and Grass* (Seattle: University of Washington Press, 1960); Gary D. Libecap, *Locking Up the Range* (Cambridge, MA: Ballinger, 1981).

50. National Cattlemen's Beef Association, "Beef Industry at a Glance," at www.beefusa.org, accessed June 17, 2005.

51. Colorado Cattlemen's Association, "Ending All Grazing on Public Lands Can Hurt Everyone," News release, November 12, 2003, at http://cca.beef.org, accessed June 17, 2005.

52. National Public Lands Grazing Campaign, "Conservationists Mail Letter to 22,000 Federal Grazing Permittees," at www.publiclandsranching.org, accessed June 17, 2005.

53. USDA Forest Service, "2005 Federal Grazing Fee Announced," News release, February 7, 2005, at www.fs.fed.us/news/2005/releases, accessed February 21, 2005.

54. See William E. Riebsame, "Ending the Range Wars?" *Environment, 38,* no. 4 (May 1996): 4–9, 27–29; J. M. Feller, "What Is Wrong with the BLM's Management of Livestock Grazing on the Public Lands?" *Idaho Law Review, 30,* no. 3 (1993–1994): 555–602.

55. William L. Graf, *Wilderness Protection and the Sagebrush Rebellions* (Savage, MD: Rowman & Littlefield, 1990), 229.

56. 104th Congress, H.R. 643.

57. Bureau of Land Management, "Questions and Answers Regarding the BLM's New Grazing Regulations," at www.blm.gov, accessed June 17, 2005.

58. Center for Biological Diversity, "U.S. Bureau of Land Management's New Regulations Undercut Public Participation and Threaten Wildlife and Water With Hand-Outs to the Livestock Industry," News release, June 16, 2005, at www.biologicaldiversity.org, accessed June 17, 2005.

59. Ibid.

60. Julie Cart, "U.S. Altered Study, Scientists Say," *Arizona Republic,* June 19, 2005, A10.

61. Ibid.

62. Bureau of Land Management, "Questions and Answers."

63. National Public Lands Grazing Campaign, "Sierra Club, Greater Yellowstone Coalition Back Grazing Buyout Bills," News release, April 5, 2004, at www.ems.org/nws, accessed June 17, 2005.

64. National Cattlemen's Beef Association, "NCBA News," April 23, 2002, at www.beefusa.org, accessed June 17, 2005.

65. National Public Lands Grazing Campaign, "Conservationists Mail Letter."

66. Klyza, *Who Controls Public Lands?* 28–29.

67. In 1970, Congress enacted the Mining and Minerals Policy Act (consisting of three short paragraphs); but rather than reform practices, it simply provided that the secretary of the interior prepare a report on the domestic mining industry. The statute provided explicit support for domestic mineral production and has been termed "little more than a rhetorical device intended to placate the mining industry." See R. McGreggor Cawley, *Federal Land, Western Anger: The Sagebrush Rebellion and Environmental Politics* (Lawrence: University Press of Kansas, 1993), 57; John D. Leshy, *The Mining Law: A Study in Perpetual Motion* (Washington, DC: Resources for the Future Press, 1987).

68. Wilderness Society, *Bush Strikes Out on the Environment: A State of the Environment Report* (Washington, DC: Author, January 24, 2002) 7–8.

69. See Joshua Footer and J. T. VonLunen, "A Legacy of Conflict: Mining and Wilderness," in *Contested Landscape: The Politics of Wilderness in Utah and the West,* Doug Goodman and Daniel McCool, eds. (Salt Lake City: University of Utah Press, 1999), 117–136.

70. *Pennsylvania Coal Co. v. Mahon,* 260 U.S. 393 (1922).

71. Richard Epstein, *Takings: Private Property and the Power of Eminent Domain* (Cambridge, MA: Harvard University Press, 1985).

72. For a discussion of the strategies used by property-rights groups, see Bruce Yandle, ed., *Land Rights: The 1990s' Property Rights Rebellion* (Lanham, MD: Rowman & Littlefield, 1995); John D. Echeverria and Raymond Booth Eby, eds., *Let the People Judge: Wise Use and the Private Property Rights Movement* (Washington, DC: Island Press, 1995); David Helvarg, *The War against the Greens: The "Wise Use" Movement, the New Right, and Anti-Environmental Violence* (San Francisco: Sierra Club Books, 1994); and Jacqueline Vaughn Switzer, *Green Backlash: The History and Politics of Environmental Opposition in the U.S.* (Boulder, CO: Lynne Rienner, 1997).

73. See Karol J. Ceplo, "Land Rights Conflicts in the Regulation of Wetlands," in *Land Rights: The 1990s Property Rights Rebellion,* Bruce Yandle, ed. (Lanham, MD: Rowman & Littlefield, 1995), 106.

74. See Patricia Byrnes, "Are We Being Taken by Takings?" *Wilderness, 58,* no. 208 (Spring 1995): 4–5; Neal R. Peirce, "Takings—the Comings and Goings," *National Journal, 28* (January 6, 1996): 37.

75. See Barbara Moulton, "Takings Legislation: Protection of Property Rights or Threat to the Public Interest?" *Environment, 37,* no. 2 (March 1995): 44–45; Nancie G. Marzulla, *Property Rights: Understanding Government Takings and Environmental Regulations* (Rockville, MD: Government Institutions, 1997); George Skouras, *Takings Law and the Supreme Court: Judicial Oversight of the Regulatory State's Acquisition, Use, and Control of Private Property* (New York: P. Lang, 1998).

76. Heidi J. Albers, Amy W. Ando, and Daniel Kaffine, "Land Trusts in the United States: Analyzing Abundance," *Resources* (Spring 2004), 9–13; Richard Brewer, *Conservancy: The Land Trust Movement in America* (Dartmouth, NH: University Press of New England, 2003); Sally K. Fairfax and Darla Guenzler, *Conservation Trusts* (Lawrence: University Press of Kansas, 2001).

FURTHER READING

Terry L. Anderson. *The Not So Wild, Wild West: Property Rights on the Frontier.* Palo Alto, CA: Stanford University Press, 2004.

Michael P. Dombeck, Christopher A. Wood, and Jack E. Williams. *From Conquest to Conservation: Our Public Lands Legacy.* Covelo, CA: Island Press, 2003.

Ross W. Gorte. *National Forests: Current Issues and Perspectives.* New York: Nova Science Publishers, 2003.

Richard A. Grusin. *Culture, Technology, and the Creation of America's National Parks.* Cambridge, UK: Cambridge University Press, 2004.

Derrick Jensen and George Draffan. *Strangely Like War: The Global Assault on Forests.* White River Junction, VT: Chelsea Green, 2003.

Robert B. Keiter. *Keeping Faith with Nature: Ecosystems, Democracy, and America's Public Lands.* New Haven, CT: Yale University Press, 2003.

Paul Larmer, ed. *Give and Take: How the Clinton Administration's Public Lands Offensive Transformed the American West.* Paonia, CO: High Country News Books, 2003.

Stephen J. Pyne. *Tending Fire: Coping with America's Wildland Fires.* Covelo, CA: Island Press, 2005.

Alaric Sample and Anthony Cheng. *Forest Conservation Policy: A Reference Handbook.* Santa Barbara, CA: ABC-CLIO, 2004.

5

Waste and Toxics

ChevronTexaco employees work hard to ensure that our operations around the world are managed in a safe and environmentally sound manner. We believe the allegations made in this lawsuit are without merit, and the company intends to vigorously defend itself.

—STATEMENT OF CHEVRONTEXACO ON CURRENT ISSUES IN ECUADOR[1]

In 1964, Texaco Petroleum Company, a subsidiary of Texaco, accepted an invitation from the government of Ecuador to design and build the infrastructure for an emerging oil industry in the country's Oriente region of the northern Amazon rain forest. Petroecuador, the state-run oil company, served as the majority partner with a 62.5 percent interest, with Texaco serving as the minority partner in the operation, which included building an oil pipeline from the Andes Mountains to the Pacific coast. Texaco ended its participation in the project in 1990.

In 1993 the first of four lawsuits was filed in the United States against Texaco on behalf of indigenous tribal members who alleged that the company had dumped millions of gallons of highly toxic waste water into small ponds and nearby streams. The toxins in the water leached into the ground; some toxic water was alleged to have been burned, dumped into landfills, or spread on dirt roads. The suit also alleged that Texaco's negligence had resulted in the discharge of millions of gallons of raw crude oil. The plaintiffs argued that Texaco's practices not only contaminated the region's ecosystems but also damaged the health, culture, and livelihood of 30,000 indigenous people. In 1994 a

> *Policymakers have been reluctant to deal with the issue of municipal solid waste, which is often viewed as an annoyance rather than as a serious environmental problem.*
>
> NIALL BENVIE/CORBIS

similar lawsuit was filed on behalf of Peruvian plaintiffs, who argued they had been affected by Texaco's actions as well.

Texaco maintained that the plaintiff's attorneys never presented any credible, substantiated scientific evidence to support their claims, arguing that no reputable study has shown a cause-and-effect relationship between its oil operations and disease. The company noted that there are gaps in data and flaws in research, and that the primary cause of diseases in the Oriente are "poverty, poor sanitation, naturally occurring bacteria and parasites, a lack of access to clean water, and insufficient infrastructure." Two independent audits subsequently found that Texaco acted responsibility and that there was no lasting or significant environmental impact from the oil operations.[2]

After signing a remediation agreement with the government in 1995, Texaco began a $40 million cleanup program, surveying and cleaning up more than 250 wells, replanting cleared lands, and removing contaminated soil. The company also provided funding for social programs in the area, including the construction of roads, airports, schools, medical facilities, and water systems. When the remediation was completed in 1998, Ecuador's Minister of Energy and Mines reviewed and certified the project, and the parties signed a Final Release of Claims and Delivery of Equipment. Local municipalities signed a negotiated settlement with Texaco Petroleum that released the company from any future obligations or liabilities.[3]

The U.S. District Court ruled in favor of Texaco, not on the merits of the complaints against the company, but over the issue of venue—which court had legal jurisdiction over the dispute. The judge ruled that it was appropriate for the cases to be heard in Ecuador rather than in the United States. Upon plaintiffs' appeal of the judge's ruling, the U.S. Court of Appeals affirmed that the cases did not belong in the U.S. judicial system but that any eventual ruling could be enforced by a U.S. court. An American legal team subsequently filed a $1 billion lawsuit in Lago Agrio, Ecuador, on behalf of 88 plaintiffs in 2003. The suit alleged that from 1971 to 1992, Texaco Petroleum recklessly dumped oil waste containing heavy metals and carcinogens in more than 600 ponds over a 2,000-square-mile area. One toxics specialist estimated the cost of cleanup at $5 billion because "the damage is to the entire ecosystem."[4] In December 2004, lawyers for the Ecuadorean indigenous groups suing the company submitted documentary evidence to the court that they said showed Texaco never finished the cleanup of the contamination. The company responded that the documents had "no scientific value" and that Petroecuador had accepted the remedial work as complete in 1998, freeing Texaco of further responsibility or liability. A full ruling on the case is not expected for at least two years.[5]

The Ecuadorean case is being watched closely by advocates for indigenous peoples, environmental organizations, and American companies doing business abroad. Those who have studied transnational environmental cases note that legal wrangling can go on for years. Environmental activists usually prefer cases such as this one to be heard in the United States or another developed country, where courts are more independent, there are numerous public interest firms willing to take on the case, and class-action suits draw media and public attention that might cause a company to negotiate a settlement. Jurisdictional issues are compounded even when the plaintiff wins against a multinational corporation, due to the difficulty of collecting damages from the defendant.[6]

The job of cleaning up humanity's mess, whether it be household garbage or radioactive material produced from nuclear power plants, has become a more visible and acute problem on the environmental policy agenda. In years past, the issue has literally and figuratively been buried at the bottom of the pile of environmental problems facing policymakers. Historically, we have simply covered up the refuse of life with dirt or dumped it where it was out of sight (and out of mind). Now, old habits are coming back to haunt us as we produce more waste than ever before and run out of places to put it.

This chapter explores the management of waste and the strategies that are being developed to try to deal with this ongoing, highly politicized, and increasingly global problem. The discussion begins by identifying the various types of waste produced and the attempts that have been made to deal with it, including municipal solid waste. The main focus of the chapter is an analysis of the regulatory framework of waste management and the role of different levels of government that are grappling with a growing problem that has fewer resources for its solution. Two key statutes are analyzed: the Resource Conservation and Recovery Act (RCRA), and the Comprehensive Environmental Response, Compensation, and Liability Act (CERCLA), along with the Brownfields Prevention Initiative under RCRA. Separate sections deal with the policy issue of nuclear waste resulting from civilian use and from the military's attempt to dispose of nuclear weapons. The chapter concludes with an overview of the global toxics legacy and a discussion about the creation of international regimes to control hazardous waste trade.

THE NATURE OF WASTE:
GENERATION AND DISPOSAL

Historians who have studied human development note that there has not always been a refuse problem, at least not of the magnitude seen in modern times. Garbage is primarily an urban issue, exacerbated by limited space and dense populations. It must also be perceived as having a negative effect on human life, or else it is viewed as an annoyance rather than as a health or environmental problem.

Such a transition of perception occurred in the United States between 1880 and 1920, when the "garbage nuisance" was first recognized. City dwellers could no longer ignore the piles of garbage, and the manure from horse-drawn streetcars, that covered sidewalks and streets and polluted local waterways. A sense of community responsibility evolved as citizens developed an awareness of doing something about the problem. Garbage was seen not only as a health issue but also as an aesthetic one, because it detracted from the overall attractiveness of city living. Gradually, municipal governments developed street cleaning and disposal programs (controlled by health officials and representatives of civic organizations) to begin dealing with the massive wastes generated by a growing industrial society.[7]

Just before the turn of the century, the United States imported one of the most common European methods of waste disposal—the "destructor," or garbage furnace. The British, with insufficient cheap land or water as dumping areas, had turned to incineration, which was hailed as a waste panacea. Cities throughout the United States quickly installed incinerators, while researchers continued to experiment with other European technologies such as extracting oil and other by-products through the compression of city garbage. During the first quarter of the 20th century the emphasis was on waste elimination, with little thought given to controlling the generation of waste. After the 1970s, however, the growth of the American economy changed the refuse situation with a dramatic increase in the manufacture of packaging materials—plastics, paper, and synthetics—that became a part of the waste stream. This not only increased the amount of waste, but posed new collection and disposal problems for local governments. One researcher estimates that solid waste increased about five times as rapidly as population increased after World War I. The most dramatic change in the composition of waste was the massive increase in the proportion of paper, which by 1975 accounted for nearly half of all municipal refuse. This increase is attributed to rampant consumerism during the 1970s, which fostered a boom in the packaging industry.[8] An even more pervasive waste problem emerged after World Wars I and II with the tremendous increase in chemical products, which were being discharged into the air, water, and/or land.

THE UNIVERSE OF WASTES

Waste is a generic term used to describe material that has no obvious or significant economic or other benefit to humans. Waste includes five major categories of materials that differ in their physical properties and origins.

The largest component of the waste stream is industrial waste, which is nonhazardous and is generated by activities such as manufacturing, mining, coal combustion, and oil and gas production. It makes up nearly 94 percent of the waste universe. The second largest segment—about 5 percent—is hazardous waste, which is primarily generated by industry and meets a specific legal definition. It comes under federal regulations because it poses a serious threat to human health or the environment if not handled properly. Sometimes the terms *toxic waste* and *hazardous waste* are used interchangeably, but this is not technically correct. Toxicity refers to a substance's ability to cause harm, and thus all waste could conceivably come under that definition. Because some wastes present only a minimal amount of harm if stored or disposed of properly, they are not considered hazardous. To be considered hazardous, waste must meet four criteria: the potential to ignite or cause a fire; the potential to corrode; the potential to explode or generate poisonous gases; and the capacity to be sufficiently toxic to health. Federal regulations also classify as hazardous any other wastes mixed with hazardous waste, as well as by-products of the treatment of hazardous waste.

The problem of handling hazardous waste has become acute because waste-generating industries in the past were often unaware of or unconcerned about the potential toxic effects of hazardous waste. Dangerous chemicals may percolate from holding ponds into underlying groundwater or wash over the ground into surface water and wetlands. Some hazardous waste evaporates into the air or explodes, other types soak into the soil and contaminate the ground, and some forms bioaccumulate in plants and animals that might be consumed later by humans. Typical hazardous wastes include dioxin, petroleum, lead, and asbestos.

The third category of waste, composing about 1 percent, is municipal solid waste (MSW), the garbage and trash generated by households, offices, and similar facilities. Americans deserve their reputation for being a "throwaway society"; the amount of trash produced per person, per day in the United States has jumped from 2.68 pounds in 1960 to 4.45 pounds in 2003, the most recent year for which figures are available. By weight, most MSW consists of containers and packaging (31.7 percent), followed by nondurable goods such as paper, plastics, and textiles (26.3 percent), and durable goods such as tires, appliances, steel, and aluminum (16.7 percent).[9] A more specific breakdown of MSW generation shows that paper makes up more than a third of the waste stream, as seen in Figure 5.1. Overall, MSW generation grew from 88.1 million tons in 1960 to 121.1 million tons in 1970, 151.6 million tons in 1980, 205.2 million tons in 1990, 234 million tons in 2000, and 236.2 million tons in 2003.[10] The EPA had previously predicted that 216 million tons would be generated by 2000, and 250 million tons by 2010—figures that clearly underestimated Americans' ability to produce trash.

The last two components of the waste stream are medical and radioactive wastes, each of which makes up less than one tenth of 1 percent of the waste stream. Hospitals and other medical and dental facilities generate more than a half million tons per year of waste that must be specially managed.[11] This type of waste gained attention in the late 1980s, when miles of beaches in New Jersey and New York had to be closed because improperly handled syringes and vials of blood began washing ashore, raising fears about the spread of acquired immunodeficiency syndrome (AIDS).

Radioactive waste includes fuel used in nuclear reactors, spent fuel from weapons production, and mill tailings from the processing of uranium ore. This category also includes substances that have become contaminated by radiation, either directly or accidentally.

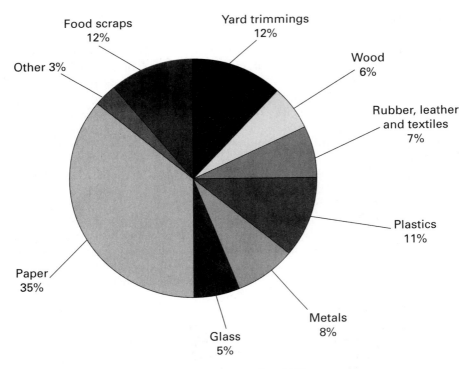

FIGURE 5.1 Municipal Solid Waste Generation, 2003

SOURCE: U.S. Environmental Protection Agency, *Executive Summary: Municipal Solid Waste Generation, Recycling, and Disposal in the United States: Facts and Figures for 2003 at www.epa.gov/msw/ accessed September 15, 2005.*

DISPOSING OF THE PROBLEM

Primitive cultures had an easy answer to disposal—they simply left what needed to be disposed where they had created it. Leftover or spoiled food and excrement were allowed to rot on the ground, where they naturally decomposed and returned to the earth as fertilizing compost, completing the naturally occurring ecological cycle. Aside from odors and foraging wildlife, waste did not pose much of a problem until it got in the way of other human activities. As the population grew, people began to burn their waste or bury it in the ground—practices that have remained unchanged throughout most of our history. The method of disposal now used depends largely on what type of waste is being managed, as the following overview indicates.

Burial and Landfills

Dumping and burial have been among the most common ways of disposing of municipal waste, although communities have developed sanitary landfills as a way of avoiding the environmental problems caused by burial. The number of landfills declined as the federal government began regulating waste disposal in the 1960s;

the number dropped further in 1979, when the EPA issued minimum criteria for landfill management. One of the biggest concerns about landfill operations has been pollution; because most landfills accept whatever household garbage is collected by waste haulers, there is often little screening of what gets dumped. As a result, landfills may contain a variety of substances, including paints, solvents, and toxic chemicals, that residents routinely put into their curbside trash. In older landfills, leachate (formed when water from rain or the waste itself percolates through the landfill) sometimes seeps into the ground, polluting the surrounding groundwater. Today's sanitary landfills, in contrast, are located on land where the risk of seepage is minimal, and most facilities are lined with layers of clay and plastic. A complex series of pipes and pumping equipment collects and distills the leachate and vents flammable methane gas, which is formed by the decomposition of waste. Many landfills now recover the gas and distribute it to customers or use it to generate electricity.

Historically, the key criterion for landfill operation was accessibility; but that gradually changed to a goal of minimizing health risks. In the 1930s, the United States switched from open dumping to using sanitary landfills, where waste is compacted and buried. Most cities established their landfills in the most inexpensive and accessible land available—typically a gravel pit or wetland—paying little attention to environmental considerations. With the advent of the environmental movement in the 1960s and 1970s, planners began to consider whether a proposed site was near a residential area, was susceptible to natural phenomena such as earthquakes or flooding, or was a potential threat to water quality; they also considered the hauling distance from where the refuse was collected.

In the 1980s, considerable attention was focused on the problem of landfill capacity. Projections warned that only 20 percent of the landfills in operation in 1986 would be open in the year 2008, despite increasing amounts of waste. Due to this shortage of landfill space, the cost of disposal rose astronomically. The shortage occurred because the criteria for what becomes an acceptable disposal site changed, making it difficult to increase both the number and capacity of burial facilities. Disposal costs today increase by as much as a dollar per ton for every mile the garbage is transported. Today's landfill operations are tightly regulated by federal restrictions that govern the location, design, operating and closure requirements, and cleanup standards for existing contamination. It is important to note that many of those restrictions were added only because of political pressure from environmental organizations. The number of MSW landfills has decreased substantially, from almost 8,000 in 1988 to 1,767 in 2002, as seen in Figure 5.2. Slightly more than 55 percent of MSW was disposed of in landfills in 2003, and the percentage of MSW going to landfills continues to decrease.

Incineration

Many European nations have been successful at instituting waste incineration programs to deal with municipal waste. Their modern facilities produce minimal levels of visible emissions and have the added advantage of generating energy

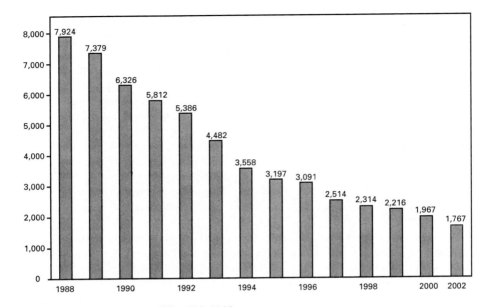

FIGURE 5.2 U.S. Landfills, 1988–2002

SOURCE: U.S. Environmental Protection Agency, *Executive Summary: Municipal Solid Waste Generation, Recycling, and Disposal in the United States: Facts and Figures for 2003* at www.epa.gov/msw/ accessed September 15, 2005.

while reducing the amount of waste by up to 90 percent in volume and 75 percent in weight.

In contrast, since the first garbage furnace was installed in 1885 on Governor's Island, New York, the United States has been unsuccessful in convincing both policy makers and citizens of the acceptability of incineration as a disposal method. In 1960, nearly 31 percent of MSW was disposed of through combustion; by 2003, only 14 percent was combusted in 95 facilities nationwide.[12]

Incineration was initially used as a disposal method because it was considered the most sanitary and economical method available. Modifications of the European technology proved ineffective, however, for U.S. needs. Sanitation engineers became critical of incineration facilities, which often produced gas and smoke emissions because the waste was not completely burned when furnace temperatures were lowered to save on fuel consumption. Beyond their design and operational problems, many incinerators were built by unscrupulous or inexperienced companies; by 1909, 102 of the 180 furnaces erected between 1885 and 1908 had been abandoned or dismantled. Later adaptations of English technology produced a second generation of incinerators, and the facilities flourished until the 1960s. At that point, concerns about air pollution surfaced, and cities such as Los Angeles began to legislate against incinerators, setting standards so high that they virtually outlawed the plants. Although the technology was available to increase efficiency and reduce polluting emissions, the cost of upgrading equipment was high in comparison to disposal in sanitary landfills.

There is still some support for incineration as a concept, especially among those who note the advantage of reducing the volume of waste or of using the incinerator's capacity as an energy generator. Critics argue that even with improved technology, many facilities have suffered from mechanical breakdowns and costly repairs. Attempts to transfer European incineration technology to the United States have often been unsuccessful because American trash contains considerably more plastic that, when burned, produces toxic gases and leads to corrosion of equipment. Even plants that run efficiently are being closely scrutinized for adverse health effects. Environmental groups have raised questions about the toxicity of both the gases and the ash produced by the combustion process.

Despite these objections and problems, officials are taking a second look at waste-to-energy plants for MSW. Most of the plants are called "mass burn" facilities because they use unsegregated waste as a fuel, producing electricity that can then be sold to customers. Refuse-derived fuel plants remove materials that can be recycled from the waste stream, such as plastics and glass, and shred the remaining components, which are then burned in boilers. They have several advantages over other municipal disposal options because they require no change in waste collection patterns, their management can be turned over to a private owner if desired, low-cost financing mechanisms are available, and the market for the electricity they produce is guaranteed under the 1978 Public Utilities Regulatory Policies Act.

Public opposition to incineration has proved to be the most formidable barrier to siting any new facilities, thus ending projects throughout the United States—from the LANCER facility in Los Angeles to the Brooklyn Navy Yard, where opponents promised to block a proposed incinerator with their bodies. New Jersey residents even rejected a referendum on the state's ballot over an incinerator that had been planned and approved for a decade. Political leaders have found the topic so volatile that it has created an acronym of its own—NIMTOO—for "not in my term of office." The phrase refers to the virtual paralysis over waste management decision making that keeps municipal officials from approving incineration projects in favor of more expensive disposal solutions. The situation is different from that in Europe, where incineration has been more widely accepted. The difference lies perhaps in the contrast of political systems. Nations like Denmark and Germany have a strong history of centralized decision making, which precludes the kinds of public participation and access to the legal system that allows citizens in the United States to have such an impact on decisions, including the siting of hazardous waste facilities.

Ocean Dumping

The dumping of wastes into the ocean is one of the few disposal methods that has received almost universal condemnation. Initial objections to the practice were not necessarily environmental—too much of the garbage dumped off the New York coast in the early 1900s floated back to shore. The practice was also considered too costly, because barges had to tow the garbage to deep water to keep it from floating back to the surface and washing up on local beaches. As downstream cities filed lawsuits against upstream cities, the legal ramifications of dumping municipal waste into waterways limited the practice as well. Burial of waste seemed much more attractive and inexpensive to early sanitation engineers by the 1920s. In 1933, New Jersey coastal cities went to court to force New York City to halt ocean dumping. The U.S. Supreme Court affirmed a ruling in 1934, when the practice of ocean dumping of MSW ceased as a major means of disposal.

The Supreme Court ruling applied only to municipal waste, and the ocean dumping of industrial and commercial waste continued unabated. Over the course of the 1960s, an estimated 50 million tons of waste were dumped into the ocean, most of it off the East Coast, where the rate doubled between 1959 and 1968. In the mid-1970s, nearly 120 ocean sites for waste disposal were supervised by the U.S. Coast Guard. Of particular concern has been the use of ocean dumping for toxic wastes. Not until passage of the Marine Protection, Research, and Sanctuaries Act in 1972 was there a federal effort to stop the practice. In 1988, the Ocean Dumping Ban Act restricted offshore dumping of sewage sludge and other wastes.

The ocean depths have also been considered as sites for the burial of radioactive waste; for more than a dozen years, the United States was part of an eight-nation, $100 million research effort that had considerable scientific support. But the issue was so politically sensitive that the research program was cut off as Congress turned its focus to geological storage.

Recycling

The terms *recycling* and *recovery* refer to the reuse of materials. A majority of waste management analysts believe recycling represents one of the most underused yet promising strategies for waste disposal. There are two aspects of recycling: primary recycling, in which the original material is made back into the same material and is also recyclable (such as newspapers back into newspapers); and secondary recycling, in which products are made into other products that may or may not be recyclable (such as cereal boxes made out of wastepaper). Recycling gained acceptance in the early 1970s as the public became more aware of the garbage crisis, the need to conserve natural resources, and the shortage of landfill space. About 7 percent of the MSW was recovered in the 1960s and 1970s; the amount then increased to nearly 10 percent in 1980, and 14 percent by 1990. In 2003, recycling and composting increased to almost 31 percent, diverting more than 72 million tons from disposal.[13]

Composting has grown as a method of disposing of certain segments of the MSW stream, such as food scraps, yard trimmings, and other organic materials from residential, commercial, and institutional sources. In 2003, nearly 3,500 community composting programs were operating, in addition to individual citizens doing backyard composting. Between 1960 and 1990, the amount of MSW recovered for composting was negligible; by 2003, nearly 17 million tons were being composted.[14]

Recycling is actually less an environmental issue than it is an extremely volatile economic supply-and-demand issue. A shortage of markets for recycled goods represents the biggest obstacle to this waste management approach. During the early 1970s, recycling gained acceptance not only in the public's mind but economically as well. Rising costs of land disposal and incineration made recycling a booming business. Junked autos, worthless a few years before, were bringing up to $50 each, and prices for copper scrap rose 100 percent. Lead batteries became profitable recycling targets when the price of battery lead rose fourfold. Under President Richard Nixon, the federal government considered providing tax credits and direct cash subsidies to encourage the sale of recycled materials; but a 1974 EPA report recommended that such incentives were unnecessary, because demand for recycling was high and prices were rising. Some states sought their own forms of monetary incentives—for example, Oregon, which pioneered a bottle-deposit law in 1972. The federal subsidy and incentive concepts never gained acceptance in Congress, however, and were not revived by President Gerald Ford when he assumed office after Nixon's resignation.

Unfortunately for the future of recycling, prices collapsed in 1974 as quickly as they had risen, with wastepaper prices dropping from $60 per ton in March 1974 to $5 by mid-1975. In the late 1980s and early 1990s, supplies of newspapers, cans, plastic, and glass began to pile up when communities and individuals believed they might be able to squeeze cash from trash, even when there were few markets for recycled goods. As demand for recycled goods increased, in some communities "recycling bandits" were taking newspapers out of curbside containers in the middle of the night or yanking it out of landfills. Ambitious recycling targets set by states in the 1990s are being missed, and even in model communities like Seattle, recycling has declined. In Connecticut, a projected reduction in waste of 40 percent by 2000 is only 25 percent in 2005.[15]

The EPA's 2003 recycling report found that the highest rate of recovery was in the category of containers and packaging (31.7 percent), followed by non-durable goods such as paper, plastics, rubber, leather and textiles (26.3 percent), and durable goods such as steel, glass, and wood at 16.7 percent. Among the most recovered products in 2003 were lead-acid batteries (93 percent), major steel appliances (90 percent), corrugated boxes (71 percent), newspapers (82 percent), steel cans (60 percent), and aluminum beverage cans (44 percent).[16]

Recycling can be made more attractive to both consumers and recyclers in several ways. The most obvious is to boost the demand to create an appetite for the swollen supply of materials, or apply sanctions against those who use virgin material. In 1992, for example, the federal government took the incentive route by directing its agencies to purchase environmentally sound supplies, including those made of recycled materials, and several states have enacted similar legislation. Other approaches have included providing tax incentives for new recycling operations, mandating commercial recycling, and recycling organic waste. Nearly every state requires newspaper publishers to use some recycled fiber in their paper. Others have invested money into facilities that turn old newspapers into usable pulp in a process called de-inking, so publishers have pushed their suppliers to increase demand.

Is recycling a viable waste disposal alternative in the United States? Recycling programs here have not been nearly as successful as programs in other parts of the world. Even though they do not produce nearly the amounts of waste that the United States does, other countries much more commonly use recycling.

Deposits on beverage containers are almost universally used, and more reverse vending machines (where returned containers are accepted) are common in Europe. In Ireland, consumers are charged a small fee (equivalent to about 5 cents U.S.) for each grocery bag the store must provide, and recycling bins are commonly placed at tourist attractions. Source separation programs are in place throughout Western Europe and Japan, and even in developing nations like Egypt and Thailand, institutionalized scavenging and recycling programs are fully operational.

Although more materials are being recycled, the number of curbside recycling programs has decreased to about 8,775 in 2002, down from 9,700 the previous year. EPA believes the decrease in programs may be due to some consolidation of programs, and it is likely that some waste may be taken to transfer stations, drop-off centers, buyback programs, and deposit systems.[17] To encourage more public-private partnerships, organizations such as the National Recycling Coalition help create programs to promote product stewardship, using a collaborative process rather than confrontational tactics. Current partnerships include the Reuse-A-Shoe program with Nike, the No Computer Should Go To Waste initiative with Dell, and similar alliances with the Glass Packaging Institute, Recycle Alliance America, TI Paper Company, and International Paper.[18] What all this means is that a number of obstacles remain to be overcome before recycling—despite its inherent attractiveness—can be considered more than a supplemental answer to the solid waste dilemma.

Source Reduction

The EPA first identified source reduction (or waste prevention) as its first preference in the integrated waste management hierarchy in 1989. This includes the reuse of products and on-site, or backyard, composting of yard trimmings as a way of keeping material out of the waste stream. Source reduction's benefits are twofold. It decreases the amount of waste that must be managed and preserves natural resources and reduces pollution generated during the manufacturing and packaging process. The Pollution Prevention Act of 1990 required the EPA to develop and implement a strategy to promote source reduction. Source reduction relies largely on behavioral changes, and some corporations have begun to reduce the amount of waste they generate as models for residential consumers. Simple changes like two-sided copying of paper and the reduction of transport packaging by industry have yielded substantial benefits. In 2005, eight of EPA's 10 regional pollution prevention offices funded programs for source reduction assistance, using outcome-based metrics as part of the funding process. Grant applicants are required to show how many pounds of pollution are reduced, how many BTUs of energy are conserved, how many gallons of water are saved, or how many dollars are saved through pollution prevention.[19] Because of activities such as these, the EPA has documented a dramatic increase in source reduction, from just over 0.5 million tons prevented from entering the waste stream in 1992, to over 55 million tons in 2000. Much of that increase comes from a reduction in the amount of yard trimmings disposed of each year, through either composting or the use of mulching lawn mowers.

RCRA AND SUPERFUND

Unlike some environmental protection issues for which the federal government has assumed primary responsibility, waste management regulations are usually locally enacted and implemented. The issue is complicated because neither policy makers nor the public initially considered waste—especially hazardous waste—to be a serious problem, making it difficult to push the issue onto the policy agenda. Some observers believe that the problem is not garbage per se, but improper management of hazardous waste, litter, and uncontrolled dumping.

Three major pieces of federal legislation underscore the government's hands-off policy toward waste; these laws have placed the problem in the hands of local government. Initially, the focus of regulation was on what was considered the most visible problem—solid waste. In 1965, Congress passed the Solid Waste Disposal Act (SWDA), designed to offer financial and technical assistance to local governments rather than for regulatory purposes. The federal Bureau of Solid Waste Management, housed in the Department of Health, Education and Welfare, had jurisdiction over solid waste but shared responsibility with the Bureau of Mines in the Department of the Interior. The agencies were underfunded and suffered from heavy personnel turnover; the Bureau of Solid Waste Management moved its headquarters three times in five years. Creation of the Environmental Protection Agency in 1970 led to a consolidation of agency responsibilities, coinciding with the passage of amendments to the SWDA—the Resource Recovery Act of 1970. The legislation authorized a 14-fold increase in funding, from $17 million to $239 million, for demonstration grants for recycling systems and for studies of methods to encourage resource recovery. The 1970 legislation also provided the foundation for the development of state waste management programs; and by 1975, forty-eight states had developed some form of program, with budgets ranging from zero to $1.2 million. Most of the state waste management programs were minimal, structuring themselves around the federal support programs rather than using federal assistance to help them develop a more comprehensive effort, and the statute remained essentially nonregulatory.[20]

With the passage of the Resource Conservation and Recovery Act (RCRA) in 1976, Congress intruded into what had been essentially local and state jurisdiction.[21] The act required states to develop solid waste management plans and mandated the closing of all open dumps. The only disposal methods allowed under the legislation were sanitary landfills or recycling, with little attention paid to other potentially effective options such as bottle deposit or waste recovery facilities. Another portion of the RCRA dealt with hazardous waste management, but gave the EPA the responsibility of determining what waste was solid and what part was hazardous—a task that is not as easy as it might have seemed to Congress at the time the legislation was enacted.

One of the problems faced by some local officials is that there simply is not enough landfill space available in their area to dispose of wastes properly, and despite the RCRA legislation, many states were slow to develop alternatives. Other states have a surplus of landfill capacity. As a result, communities turned to

exporting their waste to other states. In a 1978 case involving Philadelphia and
New Jersey, the U.S. Supreme Court ruled that attempts by the states to restrict
interstate transfers of waste violated the Commerce Clause of the Constitution.[22]
The Supreme Court reiterated that position in two cases in 1992 and two more in
1994; as a result, there was little that states with plenty of landfill space—such as
Indiana and New Mexico—could do to stop other states' dumping. Under the
Court's ruling, state and local governments cannot ban, impose restrictions on, or
place surcharges on solid waste simply on the basis of its origin. Publicly owned
facilities, however, can restrict the solid waste that they accept to waste generated
within the state.[23]

In the 1980s, Congress seemed to have difficulty developing hazardous waste
legislation that was acceptable to both the industries that produced the waste and
the environmental group supporters who believed the issue was not receiving
appropriate attention from federal and state regulators. The 1980 amendments to
the RCRA allowed for broad exemptions to what was considered hazardous
waste, and another set of amendments in 1984 still failed to remedy earlier
deficiencies in the law. The RCRA expired in 1988, with several states still
unable to complete the solid waste management plans required by the 1976 law.
Congress chose to rely upon the EPA to "regulate solutions" to hazardous waste,
while Congress itself seemed more interested in dealing with MSW problems.[24]

Congressional attempts to pass a sweeping reauthorization of RCRA have
been unsuccessful, as the continuing legislative gridlock over solid waste demonstrates. Congress has repeatedly rejected a national bottle deposit system, avoided
the issue of industrial wastes from manufacturing and mining, and rolled back
industry-wide recycling rates for paper and plastic. Both business and environmental groups have opposed most reauthorization efforts thus far because
proposed legislation neither promotes enough recycling nor creates markets for
recycled materials.

Policy making is often triggered when specific events capture the attention of
both the media and the public, and this is especially true of hazardous waste. As
discussed in Chapter 1, disclosure of massive contamination at Love Canal in
New York, and at a site near Louisville, Kentucky, was the catalyst for a change
in the regulatory focus. Citizens began contacting their representatives in Congress, demanding that some form of action be taken, and Congress turned to the
EPA for guidance on types of legislative remedies that might be available. Both
Congress and the EPA did an environmental policy about-face by shifting their
attention from solid to hazardous and toxic waste. Facing political pressures from
citizens' groups and public concerns for immediate action shortly after the passage
of RCRA in 1976, the EPA's Office of Solid Waste abruptly changed focus.
With the election of Ronald Reagan, the federal solid waste effort was completely eclipsed by hazardous waste concerns. The EPA's solid waste budget was
reduced from $29 million in 1979, to $16 million in 1981, to $320,000 in 1982;
meanwhile, staff was reduced from 128 to 74 in 1981, and 73 of those 74
positions were eliminated in 1982. The RCRA's hazardous waste provisions
require permits for companies storing, treating, or disposing of hazardous waste
and give EPA the authority to levy fines or hold individuals criminally liable for
improperly disposed waste. This created a cradle-to-grave program by which

EPA regulates hazardous wastes from the time they are generated to the time of disposal.

Abandoned waste sites became an extremely visible problem that forced Congress to revamp the regulatory provisions of the RCRA with the enactment in 1980 of the Comprehensive Environmental Response, Compensation, and Liability Act (CERCLA), more commonly known as Superfund. The CERCLA legislation initially included a $1.6 billion trust fund authorized over five years to clean up abandoned toxic and hazardous waste sites throughout the United States. But further research indicated that the number and magnitude of site cleanups was much larger than originally estimated.[25] Realizing the long-term nature of waste cleanup, Congress reauthorized the program for another five years under the 1986 Superfund Amendments and Reauthorization Act (SARA). Legislators were dissatisfied with the slow pace of cleanup (only six sites had been cleaned up since 1980), so SARA added $8.5 billion to the fund; in 1990, Congress voted to extend CERCLA to September 30, 1994, with another $5.1 billion authorization. Oil and chemical companies were also taxed to augment the congressional appropriation, but that provision of the law was allowed to expire at the end of 1995, further reducing the program's operating budget. Members of Congress were unable to decide the thorny issue of how to finance the program, with debate over how much of a site's cleanup costs should be paid for by government and how much should be paid for by private companies.

Under Superfund, the EPA established a National Priorities List (NPL) of targeted sites in September 1983. The NPL is a relatively small subset of a larger inventory of tens of thousands of potential hazardous waste sites. Cleanup projects vary considerably from site to site, ranging from an abandoned steel mill to small parcels of land where toxic waste was once stored and leaked into the ground. Most of the sites are landfills, industrial lagoons, and manufacturing sites. As of June 2005, 64 sites were proposed for the NPL list, 1,244 were on the NPL final list, and 296 had been deleted.[26] In fiscal year 2004, the Superfund program spent $507 million to perform construction and post-construction activities and to conduct and oversee emergency response actions. Over 52 percent of the Superfund obligations for long-term, ongoing cleanup work are committed to just nine sites.[27]

Most of the nation's hazardous waste is treated or disposed of on-site; only a small percentage is transported off-site for treatment, storage, or disposal. This avoids the problems associated with transporting waste and trying to find a place to take it once it has been removed. Congress also dealt with the cleanup problem under the corrective action program of the RCRA amendments. The legislation also requires companies that are permitted to operate a hazardous waste treatment, storage, or disposal facility to be responsible for the cleanup of that facility. Unlike Superfund, where the federal government must find the responsible party, RCRA permittees must themselves submit a cleanup plan.

Underground storage tanks (USTs) present an additional hazardous waste problem because they may leak and contaminate drinking-water supplies. The United States is estimated to have over 2 million underground tanks that store petroleum and other chemicals, and the EPA estimates that 20 percent of the regulated tanks are leaking or have the potential to leak. Many of the tanks were installed during the 1950s, and their average lifetime use is only 15–20 years. The EPA began regulating the tanks in 1984 under RCRA amendments, requiring owners and operators to meet strict requirements for design, construction, and installation, including repair or closure of systems that do not meet federal guidelines. When the deadline for repairs and replacement of USTs arrived in December 1998, some owners hurriedly tried to replace aging tanks. Thousands of gas stations and other facilities across the United States were forced to close down.

The nation's multiple hazardous waste programs have come under tremendous criticism from a variety of stakeholders, giving Congress ample reason to avoid or delay reauthorization and providing justification for not increasing the program's budget. In a December 2004 report, EPA projected that as many as 350,000 contaminated sites will require cleanup over the next 30 years under existing regulations, because nearly 10,000 new sites are discovered each year. About 43 percent of the sites involve USTs, and hazardous waste properties account for another 50 percent; but between the two, they account for only 22 percent of the costs. The remaining 7 percent of sites, including those on the NPL, tend to be larger, more complex, and more costly to remediate, according to EPA.[28]

Less than 1 percent of the projected average number of sites that would need to be decontaminated by 2033 is part of Superfund, but would require about 15 percent of the funding. Federal agencies other than the Department of Defense and Department of Energy have been spending about $200 million annually for site cleanups, but estimated $21 billion more cleanup work needs to be done over the next 30 years. The total cost for that period would be $180–$280 billion.[29]

Another criticism relates to who ought to be responsible for paying for the cleanup. Congress has been divided on the issue of whether to revise the "polluter pays" concept, which involves extensive research and often costly litigation to determine who originally created the waste. Industry has balked at one of the key components of the legislation, known as joint and several retroactive liability, which makes polluting companies responsible for the entire cost of cleaning up sites where wastes were dumped decades ago—even if they were responsible for only a portion of the contamination or before dumping was made illegal.

Compensation for individuals seeking to recover damage claims has also been very contentious. Congress continues to be heavily lobbied—a lobbying effort led by the Chemical Manufacturers' Association (CMA)—to make it difficult for an individual to bring legal action against a company believed to be responsible for the improper storage or handling of hazardous waste. Proving that a site caused health problems leads to a complex legal maze from which few plaintiffs successfully emerge. Several obstacles face those victims seeking compensation because of toxic waste problems, including that many chemical-caused illnesses have a long latency period (perhaps 20–30 years) that makes assessment of the effects of exposure difficult. Some state laws mandate that the statute of limitations begins with the first date of exposure, limiting claims by those exposed over a long period of time. In addition, hazardous waste injuries require potential claimants to submit to (and pay for) sophisticated and expensive medical and toxicological testing and to pay legal fees that may extend for years. Class-action suits are difficult to pursue because, even if a group of workers were exposed to a chemical hazard, the effects on one worker, a 40-year-old male, are likely to be considerably different from the effects on a 20-something female of childbearing age. Not surprisingly, potential industrial defendants have opposed attempts to legislate ways of easing the compensation process.

One of the most visible legal actions has been pursued against W. R. Grace Company for its actions at a vermiculite mine in Libby, Montana. In February 2005, federal prosecutors charged the company and seven high-ranking employees of releasing cancer-causing asbestos into the air and trying to hide the danger to workers and local residents. The indictment also accused the company and officials of trying to obstruct EPA efforts to investigate the extent of asbestos contamination in Libby, along with wire fraud and violations of the federal Clean Air Act.[30]

W. R. Grace purchased the mine in 1963 from the Zonolite Company for $9 million. Zonolite had operated the facility for decades, mining vermiculite—a mineral frequently used in insulating materials, for fireproofing, and for potting soil. Many homes built in Libby were insulated with Zonolite products, and Grace was considered by many long-time workers as providing "the Cadillac of jobs at the time" in the town.[31] The company is alleged to have covered up reports and health studies dating back to 1976 that showed a link between tremolite asbestos, contained in the ore processed at the mine, and lung diseases, including cancer. The death rate from asbestos in Libby and surrounding areas is 40 to 80 times higher than elsewhere in the state, and asbestos exposure has afflicted many people who never even worked in the mine. Dust from the operations settled all over the town, near the railroad tracks where material was carted away, adjacent to a Little League baseball field, and at a high school where mining scraps were used to pave a running track.[32]

The problem gained national attention in 1999 following a report about worker health that ran in a Seattle newspaper. EPA officials began their investigation, which the Montana U.S. Attorney has called a "human environmental tragedy" for which Grace and top officials must be held accountable.[33] Grace filed for bankruptcy protection in April 2001, after dozens of asbestos-related injury lawsuits had been filed. The area has been declared a Superfund site, and more than $55 million has been spent on cleanup so far.

BROWNFIELDS

The term *brownfield* refers to a slightly different type of waste site, defined by the EPA as abandoned, idled, or underused industrial and commercial facilities where expansion or redevelopment is complicated by real or perceived environmental contamination. As part of a partnership between the federal government and local communities, EPA manages these sites under the Brownfields Economic Redevelopment Initiative and the RCRA Brownfields Prevention Initiative, launched in 1998. The program has thus far spent $280 million at 2,600 sites across the United States. Funding is used to assess and test for contamination at a site and to arrange for voluntary cleanup with a goal of reuse and redevelopment.

Benefits of the program include preventing further contamination and associated potential health threats; revitalizing communities around abandoned sites; preserving valuable agricultural land and green space; and providing environmental job training for residents affected by brownfields. EPA estimates that an estimated 17,000 jobs have been created thus far.

An important element of brownfields management is community participation, and organizations associated with the Brownfields Non-Profits Network are working toward both small- and large-scale redevelopment efforts. For example, in 1996 a local nonprofit organization, WIRE-Net, began working on finding land for a new business and industrial park on the west side of Cleveland. Through the Non-Profits Network, the group selected a consultant to perform an assessment of a 15-acre site and obtained a $250,000 bridge loan to complete testing and cleanup work. The funds will be repaid from a special state grant awarded to WIRE-Net to get the site ready for new construction.

Equally important is the development of the environmental expertise needed to attempt to reclaim these sites, some of which are on tribal lands or closed military bases. Carnegie Mellon University has established training programs in conjunction with the University of Pittsburgh, and sponsored numerous conferences in conjunction with the EPA. Such efforts also have an international component, with several European universities developing technology and training on-site cleanup abroad.

NUCLEAR WASTE

Among the more politicized waste management problems to find their way onto the policy agenda are those involving the back end of the nuclear fuel cycle and the disposal of nuclear waste from military bases and nuclear weapons facilities. *Back-end waste* refers to solids, liquids, gases, and sludge, which must be treated to remove contaminants or diluted to reduce their toxicity and then stored. Radioactive waste decays at varying rates, so different types of disposal are needed for different types of waste. Although low-level radioactive waste can safely be stored in containers that are buried in shallow trenches, researchers have had to look at alternatives for disposing of high-level radioactive waste. Under the provisions of the 1982 Nuclear Waste Policy Act, the Department of Energy (DOE) was required to assume ownership of these wastes in 1998 and to store them. The initial plan was to store the waste in a temporary aboveground site, to be used only until a permanent site was ready.

After years of bitter congressional debate over where the repository would be located, in 1987 Congress directed that DOE focus on one site—Yucca Mountain, Nevada, located about 90 miles northeast of Las Vegas. State officials and the Nevada congressional delegation have protested the siting ever since, joined by environmental organizations and some scientists who believe the location is unsafe. In 1998, the Senate Energy and Natural Resources Committee refused to consider a bill that would have created an interim high-level nuclear waste facility next to the Yucca Mountain site. The Clinton administration and Nevada senators opposed the legislation, which was supported by the utility industry. Their lobbyists argued that almost 40,000 tons of nuclear wastes—consisting primarily of used reactor fuel rods—are piling up at power plants in 34 states while the government fails to provide the centralized storage promised under the 1982 law.

The issue also reached the bureaucratic agenda of the Nuclear Regulatory Commission through the Nuclear Waste Technical Review Board, which was established by Congress to review the DOE's work. The Yucca Mountain site came to exemplify what happens when scientists disagree and inconsistency occurs among studies. One 1997 DOE study found that rainwater, which could dissolve nuclear waste, has seeped from the top of the mountain, running down nearly 800 feet at a rate much faster than scientists had expected. This finding led Nevada officials to claim that the site should be disqualified as a suitable location. Hydrologists and officials of the Nuclear Energy Institute (a trade association for nuclear utilities) disagreed, however, noting that the water was not flowing like a household faucet running at 45 gallons per minute; instead, only minuscule amounts were dripping through the cracks in the rock strata.[34]

The EPA had originally been seeking a site that would be stable for 10,000 years. However, a 1998 study by the California Institute of Technology and the Harvard-Smithsonian Center for Astrophysics in Cambridge, Massachusetts, warned that the ground around the site could be considered stable only over the next 1,000 years. Using Department of Defense satellites, researchers found that the Yucca Mountain region was seismically active and therefore the geological foundation could stretch more than three feet in the 1,000-year period. The movement could crush any canisters of nuclear waste buried there, potentially exposing a wide area of the Southwest to radiation.

The DOE turned in late 1998 to another study, which found reasonable assurance that Yucca Mountain would meet long-term safety standards for many thousands of years. After years of research on the site's hydrology and geology, scientists reported that the performance of a geological repository over such long periods cannot be proven beyond all doubt; they added that uncertainties can be reduced but never completely eliminated. The 80,000 tons of used reactor fuel, which would be placed 1,000 feet below the surface, will remain deadly for an estimated 300,000 years.

While scientists argued over the reliability of various studies, politicians and interest groups continued the lengthy battle in Washington, D.C. Secretary of Energy Spencer Abraham noted that a permanent underground depository was far preferable to storing waste in temporary, aboveground facilities at 131 sites near cities and waterways. He also raised the issue of national security, which became especially salient after the terrorist attacks on the World Trade Center in 2001. "Scientists have studied the safety and suitability of Yucca Mountain for the past 24 years at a cost of more than $4 billion," he notes. "The science is sound, and the national interests served by a permanent repository are compelling."[35] Members of Nevada's congressional delegation introduced legislation to fund more studies of long-term solutions for storage, with one representative stating that "Yucca Mountain is a politician's solution to a problem that requires real science and will have consequences lasting hundreds of thousands of years. A problem of this magnitude deserves solutions founded on the recommendations of scientists, and not subject to the clumsy intrigues and estimations of short-sighted politicians."[36]

At the same time Yucca Mountain's fate was being debated, the federal government approved a plan to store 5 million cubic feet of transuranic waste (tools, rags, clothing, and other materials contaminated with uranium or pluto-nium isotopes during nuclear weapons production). The Waste Isolation Pilot Project (WIPP) complex near Carlsbad, New Mexico, took nearly 20 years to plan, develop, and build, at a cost of nearly $2 billion. The mile-square maze of tunnels in a geological salt formation a half mile underground was further delayed by legal challenges until 1998, when it was formally certified by the EPA. Environmental groups opposed the project because of concerns about the health risks of shipping nuclear waste by truck to the site and fears that the location was geologically unstable.

Nonetheless, on March 26, 1999, the first shipment, consisting of 600 pounds of nuclear debris from the Los Alamos National Laboratory, was trucked to the site, with only a handful of protestors as witnesses. Energy secretary Bill Richardson claimed that the WIPP's opening was part of the cleanup of the legacy of the Cold War and its waste. "The opening of this facility is a step to meeting this obligation," he said.[37]

President George W. Bush attempted to end the stalemate over Yucca Mountain on February 15, 2002, by approving the site. Under the 1982 statute, Nevada responded by vetoing the president's action. In his statement of reasons for disapproving the project, Nevada Governor Kenny Guinn told Congress:

> Nevada will not allow it to happen. Not simply because it is the wrong thing to do, at the wrong time, from the standpoint of environmental equity. Even when carrying the load of others, Nevadans will never tire of serving their country for a worthy cause. We will not permit Yucca Mountain to happen—and it will not happen—because the project is manifestly not a worthy cause. . . . I assure you, the only thing inevitable about Yucca Mountain is that it will plot the course of so many other doomed DOE mega-projects.[38]

Not unexpectedly, the U.S. House of Representatives voted to override the Nevada veto in May 2002; and two months later, the U.S. Senate followed. On July 23, 2002, President George W. Bush signed legislation that officially designated Yucca Mountain as the nation's nuclear waste dump, paving the way for DOE to seek a license for the project. Nevada Senator Harry Reid blamed the outcome on nuclear lobbyists and their "unending source of money" that per-petuated what he called "the big lie" that the facility was urgently needed. Nevada's other senator, John Ensign, raised the NIMBY—"not in my backyard"—issue, saying no one wanted to reopen the debate. Their arguments were countered by Alaska's Frank Murkowski, who said nuclear power itself would be threatened, the government could face lawsuits, and lawmakers would have to start looking all over again for a waste site.[39]

Murkowski was right on one point—a variety of lawsuits have been filed by the State of Nevada; and Reid moved to cut $153 million from the $489 million Bush had requested for Yucca Mountain in the following year's budget, citing more pressing priorities. Nevada also filed a petition with the Nuclear Regulatory Commission (NRC) seeking a change in rules that would require DOE to prove the site will be safe. Governor Guinn and other state officials continue to oppose Yucca Mountain despite the president's action, stating that they believed their best chance to defeat the project was in the federal courts, "where impartial judges will hear the factual and scientific arguments as to why Yucca Mountain is not a safe place to store this nation's high-level nuclear waste."[40] Environmental groups, still dissatisfied with the government's solution, renewed their focus on the handling and transport of the waste, calling the proposed shipments a "mobile Chernobyl." The debate over the project's safety, funding, and transportation of waste simmered, with the Nevada Commission on Nuclear Projects calling the repository project a "dead man walking."[41]

But a far more serious problem may have ended the Yucca Mountain saga. In March 2005, officials from the DOE and Interior departments revealed the existence of a series of e-mails sent by government scientists between 1998 and 2000 that suggest some project documents may have been falsified. The private exchanges, written by three U.S. Geological Survey hydrologists, suggest that workers were planning to fabricate their data and records to help the project move forward. The documents dealt with computer modeling of water infiltration into Yucca Mountain; one note said, "This is as good as it's going to get. If they need more proof, I will be happy to make up more stuff." Interior Department officials refused to make the scientists available to testify before a congressional panel investigating the facility.[42]

While Yucca Mountain has been the focus of attention on nuclear waste, another serious problem relates to the waste created from decades of uranium ore processing in southeastern Utah at a site administered by the Department of Energy. Unlike Yucca Mountain or sites adjacent to power plants, the Utah mill facility is located in a flood plain 750 feet from the Colorado River, the source of drinking water for an estimated 25 million people in three states. In addition to uranium, the ore contains potentially deadly chemicals such as radon and ammonia, which can cause leukemia and lung cancer. The substances leak into the shallow groundwater and into wetlands from a pile covering 130 acres and containing 12 million tons of dirt and waste, some of which is filled into an earthen berm. The waste is already killing fish, although some studies show the effects dissipate about a half mile downstream

What makes the issue politically vexing is that it falls under the jurisdiction of three federal agencies. The uranium tailings have sat at the Utah site for 56 years, long before the creation of the EPA and DOE. Other mills decommissioned under the NRC were transferred to DOE in 1978 by congressional order and then cleaned up; but at the time, the Utah mill was still producing small amounts of uranium, and the site was not transferred to DOE until 2001. The EPA has sought to have the waste pile transferred to one of three proposed sites at an estimated cost of $407 million to $543 million, depending upon how the waste is moved.[43]

In April 2005, the Department of Energy announced that it would relocate the radioactive waste to a site about 30 miles north near Crescent Junction, Utah. There, it will be buried in a hole lined with a protective layer to keep it from seeping into the groundwater and then covered with another layer of material. The move may take up to 10 years, although an exact timeline has not yet been established. Still, political leaders and environmental groups were ecstatic that a decision had finally been made. U.S. Rep. Jim Matheson (D–UT) said "I certainly hoped for this decision. Moving the pile has always been, in my opinion, the right thing to do."[44]

Another View, Another Voice

Nils J. Diaz
"We used to be a safety agency. Well, 9/11 changed that completely. We are now a safety, security and preparedness agency. We are no longer one-dimensional."

These words from Nils J. Diaz, Chairman of the U.S. Nuclear Regulatory Agency (NRC), exemplify the changes occurring in nuclear power and waste policy since the attacks on the World Trade Center in 2001. Established by the Energy Reorganization Act of 1974 to regulate civilian use of nuclear materials, the NRC has jurisdiction over nuclear reactors, materials, and waste. It is governed by a five-member commission whose members serve five-year terms; in July 1996, President Bill Clinton named Diaz a member of the commission. President George W. Bush renominated Diaz for a second five-year term in July 2001; and on April 1, 2003, President Bush designated Diaz as Chairman of the Commission, serving as the principal executive officer and the official spokesman for the NRC.

An established nuclear scientist, Dr. Diaz received his B.S. degree in Mechanical Engineering from the University of Villanova, Havana, and an M.S. and Ph.D. in Nuclear Engineering Sciences from the University of Florida. He has received formal training and practice in nuclear medicine and health physics and was licensed by the NRC as a senior reactor operator for 12 years. He was Professor of Nuclear Engineering Sciences at the University of Florida, director of the Innovative Nuclear Space Power Institute, and president and principal engineer of Florida Nuclear Associates, Inc. He also spent one year in Spain as principal advisor to that nation's Nuclear Regulatory Commission. From 1971 to 1996, he worked as a consultant on nuclear engineering for private industry, the U.S. government, and for several foreign governments.

His career in nuclear energy, Diaz says, comes from an early taste for science, and he strongly encourages more young people to enter the field: "Nuclear energy and radiation technologies are no longer 'rocket science' and thus, should not be intimidating to the young." He advocates introducing science, engineering, and technology into the grade-school-level curriculum, especially for Hispanics. In 2002, *Hispanic Business* named Diaz one of the country's Most Influential Hispanics.

His official NRC biography notes that Diaz has been

> a strong advocate of making sound regulatory decisions and of communicating such decisions in a clear manner to the American people. He has been a strong promoter of an increased and a transparent focus on safety-significant issues and of more timely decision making in such matters as power reactor license renewals, power uprates, adjudicatory proceedings and new reactor licensing.

But the 9/11 attack changed the agency's focus from production to safety, as Diaz has noted on several occasions, calling recent years a period of fundamental change. In prior years, nuclear power was equated with radiation and concerns for public health. Now, the emphasis on protecting facilities from terrorist attacks and finding safe ways to transport nuclear waste has driven the agency's mission. As chair, Diaz has actually been accused of being too safety conscious.

But when it comes to the by-products of nuclear power, such as spent fuel pools, Diaz admits he has taken a more proactive approach so that security efforts reach beyond the reactors themselves. The NRC has sought additional enhancements with plant-specific studies, and is working with the Department of Homeland Security to coordinate nuclear waste transport. Diaz also says that the license application process for the Yucca Mountain storage facility is taking longer than expected because of the massive adjudicatory process involved—an issue he inherited when he became chairman of the NRC. The issue of nuclear waste continues to be highly politicized, and due to the terrorist attacks in New York, Diaz must transform himself from a scientist and engineer to a safety and security expert. At the March 2005 NRC Regulatory Information Conference, he told conference attendees that the agency had taken down its website in the aftermath of 9/11, removing documents that could reasonably be expected to be useful to a terrorist, and public access was suspended again in October 2004. The NRC's principles of openness were, in one sense, compromised. Diaz noted, "We should not knowingly provide road maps and blueprints to terrorists or cookbooks for creating nuclear materials."

SOURCES:
"Nuclear Energy for the Future," *Hispanic Engineer,* May 13, 2003, at www.hispanicengineer.com, accessed March 15, 2005.
Nuclear Energy Institute, "Excerpts from Media Briefing at The Energy Daily, May 27, 2004," at www.nei.org, accessed March 15, 2005.
U.S. Nuclear Regulatory Commission, "Chairman Nils J. Diaz, Ph.D.," at www.nrc.gov, accessed March 15, 2005.
U.S. Nuclear Regulatory Commission, "Remarks of Chairman Nils J. Diaz to the NRC Regulatory Information Conference," at www.nrc.gov/reading-rm, accessed March 15, 2005.
U.S. Nuclear Regulatory Commission, "Who We Are," at www.nrc.gov/who-we-are, accessed March 15, 2005.

CLEANING UP MILITARY WASTE

Still unresolved, however, are the prospects for long-term environmental cleanup of military bases. For decades, the Department of Defense (DOD) held itself exempt from environmental legislation under the guise of national security. Environmental groups accused the agency of disposing of solvents, dead batteries, dirty oil, and unexploded shells and bombs by dumping them on-site, thereby contaminating the underlying water or soil. In the 1980s, the DOD was estimated to be generating 500,000 tons of toxic waste per year—more than the amount being generated by the top five U.S. chemical companies combined. One agency report identified nearly 20,000 sites at 1,800 military installations that showed varying levels of contamination, nearly a hundred of which warranted placement on the NPL.[45]

In 1984, the courts directed the DOE to accept responsibility for the cleanup resulting from decades of military weapons production at over 100 sites in 30 states around the country. Since 1989, DOE has spent over $20 billion on cleanup tasks, with the end nowhere in sight. Many researchers believe it will take decades before cleanups at all weapons sites are completed, at a total cost of almost $150 billion, while others believe the sites may be too contaminated ever to be cleaned up.[46]

To facilitate public oversight and monitoring, in 1998 a coalition of 39 environmental groups reached agreement over a 1989 lawsuit that requires the DOE to provide greater access to information about the cleanup process. Now the agency must create a publicly accessible database on contaminated facilities and provide $6.25 million to help citizen's groups and Indian tribes conduct technical and scientific reviews of cleanup activities.[47]

Two of the nation's most controversial military sites are the Atlantic Fleet Weapons Training Area, and the Naval Ammunitions Facility on Vieques Island, Puerto Rico. The U.S. Navy purchased about two-thirds of the land area in 1942, primarily from large sugar plantation owners, for live ordnance delivery and amphibious assault landings by the Marine Corps during World War II. Tons of live and spent munitions, including depleted uranium, have been found on Vieques, along with dozens of sites on the Navy's Camp Garcia where there is visible evidence that hazardous materials were released. The landfill at the 55-acre camp is filled with over 3,000 tons of construction debris, scrap metal, and general waste; there are industrial or manufacturing areas where gasoline, diesel, and waste oil were stored and soil may be contaminated; four lagoons used to treat domestic wastewater and two storage areas for waste batteries must also be cleaned up.[48]

In 1978 the governor of Puerto Rico filed suit to stop the Navy from using the portions of the land it owns, and adjacent waters, for training operations; but a request for injunction was denied. The problem reached the policy agenda in the late 1990s after a series of highly publicized demonstrations where protesters, including celebrities and political figures, sought an end to the use of an island as a bombing range. Over 9,000 people live on the island, and the Committee for the Rescue and Development of Vieques, an advocacy organization, claims that over 1,000 acres of the island still contain live ammunition. In February 2000, President Bill Clinton announced a compromise had been reached that would allow the Navy to resume inert bombing in exchange for $40 million in housing and infrastructure aid for Puerto Rico.

Vieques exemplifies the difficulties that arise when a military site is involved—jurisdictional disputes, which are fairly common in environmental politics. The EPA does not control or manage contaminated facilities; its role is regulation and enforcement. The intent of Congress was to make the agency independent so that compliance could be assured. At the same time, the DOD operates under its own political agenda and direction; thus, environmental remediation is not always its highest priority. While staffers talk of a partnership arrangement between the two agencies, in reality there has been more study and discussion than actual cleanup, and there are often overlapping statutory provisions and goals. Under RCRA, the EPA signed a Consent Order with the Navy to conduct an investigation of any environmental damage. This statute was applicable because at the time, the Navy was still conducting bombing on Vieques; Superfund applies only to sites that are no longer in use. The Navy had already conducted its own investigation, as had the Puerto Rican Environmental Quality Board.

As part of the Defense Authorization Bill for FY 2001, the Navy turned over 8,148 acres of land to the Municipality of Vieques, the U.S. Department of the Interior, and the Puerto Rico Conservation Trust. About half of the land was to be used to promote economic development and employment opportunities for the island's residents. Then, in 2003 the Navy announced that it would discontinue using Vieques as a bombing range. About 3,100 acres were to be transferred to the U.S. Fish and Wildlife Service as a wildlife refuge, and all temporary facilities and structures would be demolished. The Navy pledged a cleanup as the Principal Responsible Party, this time under Superfund standards, because the site was no longer active.[49]

The twist in the dispute is that the new designation—the Vieques and Culebra National Wildlife Refuges—while ostensibly designed to protect endangered plant and animal species—restricts public access to contaminated sites. Any Superfund designation that adds Vieques to the NPL may use different cleanup standards and prioritization of remediation because the goal is to protect wildlife, not human lives.

In 2005 the Navy began detonating unexploded bombs on the island, and groups protested what EPA called "open detonation" because military toxins were being dispersed on the island's residents as part of the cleanup process. In addition, by fencing off wilderness zones, protesters argue, the Navy says that there are no threats to humans due to contamination in the areas; and therefore, no clean up is necessary.[50] To satisfy residents' complaints about the pace of the cleanup, Rep. Jose E. Serrano (D-Puerto Rico) secured $1 million in the 2004 omnibus spending bill for assistance. Still another federal agency, the National Oceanic and Atmospheric Administration (NOAA) is now involved in providing assistance to the DOD, EPA, and Department of the Interior.[51] Vieques was eventually added to the NPL under CERCLA in April 2005.

The Vieques example illustrates how complex the issue of cleaning up waste at military facilities has become. A site cleanup can be politicized when political leaders sense a threat to their constituency and use contamination as a way of showing how they are working for those living in their area. There can be turf battles among competing agencies or competition for limited federal dollars. Human health appears to have become almost secondary, as has science, in determining where problems are placed on the waste policy agenda.

Thinking Globally

Until recently, most nations dealt with their waste problems independently of one another. Due to various developments in the way waste is managed, the issue has now become globalized, especially when developed countries attempt to ship their waste abroad. The issue gained international prominence in 1988 when 3,000 tons of a flaky black material was dumped on a Haitian beach. A barge carrying the substance had entered the port with a permit to unload "fertilizer," which later turned out to be ash laced with toxic residue from a Philadelphia municipal incinerator.

Hazardous waste trade is now one of the most important global environmental policy issues, for several reasons. There is a great amount of variation in what each nation defines as "hazardous" when it comes to waste. In industrialized countries, most substances that pose a potential risk (usually from manufacturing) are given hazardous status. In developing nations, the lack of technical expertise and testing facilities might mean that the list of substances considered hazardous is closer to guesswork than to science. The most common definition used internationally refers to wastes that, if improperly managed or disposed, could harm humans and/or the environment because they are toxic, corrosive, explosive, or combustible.[52] The complexity of waste types also requires specialized disposal techniques in order to reduce risk potential. Dumping large quantities of sometimes unknown substances in landfills is not the most desirable option, but it is comparatively inexpensive. One study found a tremendous disparity in hazardous waste disposal costs between developed and developing nations, ranging from $2,000 per ton in one European country to $40 per ton in an African nation. With fewer regulatory controls and enforcement mechanisms, the economic incentive for waste trade is understandable.

A study of waste trading among rich nations found that the major waste disposal firms often operate far outside their own country of origin, and mergers of large companies are a common phenomenon. One of the largest European disposal companies, Generale des Eaux of France, has operations in Chile, Australia, and New Zealand. Sometimes, the management of these firms may have an inadequate communication infrastructure with its partners and local authorities.[53]

Waste management has also gained a more global focus as the nations of the former Soviet Union have appealed to the industrialized world for assistance in dealing with the phenomenal amount of toxic waste and radioactive materials produced from decades of military activity and inattention to environmental contamination. For decades, billions of gallons of liquid radioactive waste were secretly pumped underground near major rivers in Russia, and scientists have little information about the potential risk the practice now poses. It is estimated that cleaning up nuclear power plants like Chernobyl will take as long as 100 years and will cost billions of dollars more in financial assistance. Although the area of the former Soviet Union continues to suffer from massive pollution of its water and air from manufacturing and other industrial processes, radioactive contamination is by far its most pressing, and most expensive, challenge. Existing international institutions are simply not prepared to deal with either the cost or the coordination of this legacy of the communist regime.[54]

The United States is now attempting to lend its expertise to dealing with spent nuclear fuel from decommissioned Russian submarines. The U.S.-funded Nunn-Lugar Program opened a facility in the Arctic port of Severodvinsk in 2002 that is expected to unload spent nuclear fuel from six submarines each year as part of U.S. efforts to help Russia secure and eliminate weapons of mass destruction. Still unanswered, however, is what to do with the nuclear waste from the submarine reactors, although Russian officials have previously said they would build a dump site on a remote Arctic archipelago.

It is the perceived inequity of how hazardous waste is handled that has also made it an increasingly global issue. Organizations like Greenpeace call efforts to ship waste abroad "toxic terrorism," and the group's members have helped publicize the lack of monitoring and regulations over what materials were being transported, often under the guise of recycling. Many poor countries are willing to accept hazardous wastes, even though they may lack the necessary facilities or processes to deal with them. But O'Neill notes, too, that many less developed countries—especially Africa—that are supported by international environmental organizations are now refusing to accept the waste from industrialized nations. Waste trade among the United States, Canada, and Mexico is lawful under the North American Free Trade Agreement (NAFTA), as are shipments within the United States to Native American tribal lands. There are also bilateral and regional agreements, such as one between France and Germany, the Waigani Convention of 1995, addressing the South Pacific, and the 1996 Barcelona Convention governing waste trade in the Mediterranean region.[55]

Hazardous waste trade remains high on the policy agenda despite more than 30 years of attempts at developing an acceptable international regime. At the 1972 UN Conference on the Human Environment, delegates made a commitment to regulate waste trading, although it was not until 1984–1985 that a UN Environment Programme committee developed the Cairo Guidelines to implement that pledge. The guidelines included notification procedures, prior consent by receiving nations, and verification that the receiving nation has requirements for disposal at least as stringent as those of the exporter. Despite those restrictions, a coalition of African nations argued that the agreement was tantamount to exploitation or "waste colonialism." In 1987, the United Nations attempted to devise an agreement that would satisfy the African nations (who sought an outright ban on exports) and exporters (still seeking inexpensive ways of disposing of their wastes). In 1989, two attempts were made to further restrict the international trade in wastes. A group of 68 less industrialized nations from Africa, the Caribbean, and the Pacific, collectively known as the ACP countries, joined with European Community (EC) officials in signing the Lome Convention, which banned all radioactive and hazardous waste shipments from the EC and African, Caribbean and Pacific (ACP) countries. A second agreement—the Basel Convention on the Control of Transboundary Movements of Hazardous Wastes and Their Disposal, which took effect in 1992—did not ban waste trade but allowed hazardous wastes to be exported as long as there is "informed consent" or full notification and acceptance of any shipments. Even though members of the EC and other nations had pledged not to export their hazardous wastes regardless of the Basel Convention, 12 African states subsequently signed the Bamako Convention in 1991, banning the import of hazardous wastes from any country—a move that further emphasized their determination not to become a dumping ground for other countries.

Led by Greenpeace, many environmental groups pointed out the deficiencies in the Basel Convention—especially the lack of a clear definition of hazardous waste. The prior notification procedures were attacked as being ineffective, the convention did not cover radioactive waste, and there were no incentives for source reduction and waste minimization. Exporters circumvented the various international agreements simply by relabeling waste as being destined for recycling rather than disposal.[56]

After a series of meetings among the parties to the convention, and despite opposition from hazardous waste producers—the United States, Canada, Australia, and Japan—the Basel Ban Amendment was adopted in September 1995. The amendment banned exports of hazardous waste destined for disposal, as well as waste designated for recycling purposes. Attempts were made to convince member nations that they should not ratify the amendment, focusing on Technical Working Group meetings that were less visible to press their arguments. A new nongovernmental organization, the Basel Action Network (BAN) formed to lobby governments and gain grassroots support. Jennifer Clapp points out that what made the Basel Convention and the subsequent Basel Ban Amendment so noteworthy was the increased activism and lobbying of the global recycling industry. In the late 1990s the industry employed some 1.5 million workers and was worth about $160 billion per year. Despite the industry's clout, however, countries began to ratify the ban amendment, in large part due to the continuing pressure of environmental organizations.[57]

Despite agreements among various countries to implement source reduction strategies, the total amount of hazardous waste generated among the Organization for Economic Cooperation and Development (OECD) countries has increased substantially since 1989. What is most important, however, is that countries differ substantially when it comes to imports and exports, generation of wastes and disposal. Middle Eastern countries produce over 1 million tons of hazardous waste per year, but only Saudi Arabia has even a minimal level of disposal facilities. In English-speaking Africa, 2.23 million tons are produced annually, and over half of that total comes from South Africa. But only South Africa, Namibia, and Mauritius have commercial waste facilities. Although the countries of the former Soviet Union have reported a gradual reduction in the amount of hazardous waste that is being produced, they face a disposal crisis, due largely to the stockpiles left over from the Cold War.[58]

It appears that waste trade regulation will consist of two types of strategies: voluntary, regionally based agreements like NAFTA, and unilateral actions taken by individual countries that attempt both waste minimization and the use of more advanced technologies to deal with their own waste. On the global level, there is a call for a commonly accepted definition and classification of hazardous waste, the creation of an international clearinghouse for data on management and toxicity, and increased monitoring.

There has been some success, however, in reaching international agreement on persistent organic pollutants, or POPs. In 1998, over 100 governments met in Montreal, Canada, for talks on an international agreement to minimize emissions and releases of 12 POPs, (or the "dirty dozen") such as dichlorodiphenyltrichloroethane (DDT) and polychlorinated biphenyls (PCBs), into the environment. The issue was returned to the UN Environment Programme agenda because of growing scientific evidence that exposure to even very low doses of certain pollutants can lead to a number of diseases like cancer, immune and reproductive system disorders, and interference with infant and child development. Over 170 types of POPs have been found in human tissue, and more types have been found in animals.

The globalized nature of the problem stems from two factors: (a) decaying and leaching chemicals from dump sites; and (b) toxic drums, first used from 1950 to 1980, that circulate through a process called the "grasshopper effect." Pollutants released in one part of the world can—through a repeated, and often seasonal, process of evaporation and deposit—be transported through the atmosphere to regions far away from the original source. Through bioaccumulation, the pollutants are also absorbed in the fatty tissue of living organisms, where concentrations can become magnified by up to 70,000 times background levels. The result is that persistent organic pollutants can be found in humans and other animals in regions thousands of miles away, such as the Arctic. Researchers believe that some POPs may last more than 100 years in the natural environment, creating a long-term policy problem.

As a follow-up to the 1979 Geneva Convention on Long-Range Transboundary Air Pollution, the meeting resulted in the Protocol on Persistent Organic Pollutants, which focuses specifically on 11 pesticides, two industrial chemicals, and three by-products/ contaminants. The agreement's objective is the elimination of any discharges or emissions of POPs; a ban on the production and use of some products, such as toxaphene and endrin; the scheduled elimination of other products like DDT and PCBs in the future; and a requirement that parties reduce emissions of other substances, such as dioxins, below 1990 levels.

This is an area of international environmental policy where issues overlap—waste management and transboundary pollution—and the need for collaboration and cooperation are essential. Depending upon how the POPs issue is framed, countries may view the problem as one that is largely the concern of individual States, or one that is profoundly global.

AMERICAN POLICY STALLED:
TOO LITTLE, TOO LATE

Various agencies and analysts are exploring a number of waste management strategies, ranging from technological solutions such as soil washing, chemical dechlorination, underground vacuum extraction, and bioremediation (the use of microbes to break down organic contaminants) to the use of price incentives and cost-based disposal fees. Despite these proposals, the waste management issue has been called an environmental policy paradox. Even though officials have been aware of the shortage of landfill space for decades and could have anticipated the need for alternatives, they have been unable to develop a viable long-term policy to deal with the problem. Observers point to the lack of a publicly perceived crisis, the incentives that have caused policy makers to choose short-term, low-cost options, and the incremental nature of the policy process. Regarding hazardous waste, officials at the federal level have failed to follow through on policy development with an appropriate level of resources to clean up the thousands of identified sites in the United States. In addition, the involvement of organized crime in the disposal industry has been connected to illegal disposal, or "midnight dumping" of hazardous wastes—a problem not yet solved by government officials at any level.

It is equally accurate to characterize America's waste management practices as the policy of deferral. The inability of policy makers to plan now for future disposal needs (whether the waste be solid, hazardous, or radioactive) simply means that they are putting off until tomorrow an inevitable, and growing, environmental protection problem. Future generations will be forced to deal with the mounting heaps of trash, barrels of toxic waste, and radioactive refuse that are already piling up in our cities, at chemical companies, and at utilities all around the country. Other analysts note that there is a lack of information about the full costs of various disposal alternatives. Without sufficient research into the "true" costs of waste management strategies, it is impossible for the most efficient systems to be developed.

Meanwhile, it appears as if the future of American waste management will involve a combination and integration of disposal methods, rather than any single strategy. Technological strategies and price incentives are of little value, however, until the legislative gridlock is broken and policy makers get serious about finding a solution, rather than just passing stopgap measures for short-term fixes. We know the problem is there, but no one seems willing to get down and dirty to tackle it.

NOTES

1. ChevronTexaco, "Ecuador Current Issues," at www.texaco.com/sitelets/ecuador/en, accessed January 2, 2005.

2. ChevronTexaco, "Background on Texaco Petroleum Company's Former Operations in Ecuador," at www.texaco.com/sitelets/ecuador/en/overview, accessed January 2, 2005.

3. Ibid.

4. Marc Lifsher, "Chevron Would Face $5 Billion Tab for Amazon Cleanup, Expert Says," *Wall Street Journal*, October 30, 2003, at www.texacorainforest.com/wallstreet, accessed January 2, 2005.

5. "Plaintiffs vs. ChevronTexaco in Ecuador Suit Submit Report," *Dow Jones Newswires*, December 1, 2004, at www.ecuador.org/, accessed January 2, 2005.

6. Brooke A. Masters, "Case in Ecuador Viewed as Key Pollution Fight," *Washington Post*, May 6, 2003, at www.texacorainforest.com, accessed January 2, 2005. See also Suzana Sawyer, *Crude Chronicles: Indigenous Politics, Multinational Oil, and Neoliberalism in Ecuador* (Durham, NC: Duke University Press, 2004).

7. Martin V. Melosi, *Garbage in the Cities: Refuse, Reform and the Environment, 1880–1980* (College Station: Texas A&M University Press, 1981), 3. For a contemporary view, see Martin V. Melosi, *Effluent America: Cities, Industry, Energy, and the Environment* (Pittsburgh, PA: University of Pittsburgh Press, 2001).

8. Ibid., 189–192. In fairness to industry, however, it should be noted that the development of packaging has many beneficial consequences. Packaging has extended the shelf life of many goods (especially produce and dairy products) that otherwise might rot or spoil. Packaging also allows products to be stored and shipped in bulk and often results in lower consumer prices.

9. U.S. Environmental Protection Agency. *Municipal Solid Waste Generation, Recycling, and Disposal in the United States: Facts and Figures for 2003* (Washington, DC: Author, May 17, 2005), 7.

10. Ibid.

11. Ibid., 3.

12. Ibid., 11.

13. Ibid., 2.

14. U.S. Environmental Protection Agency, *Municipal Solid Waste Generation*, 1–2.

15. Traci Watson, "Recycling Is Old News," *USA Today*, July 6, 2004. See also U.S. Environmental Protection Agency, *Measuring Recycling: A Guide for State and Local Governments* (Washington, DC: Environmental Protection Agency, 1997); and Richard A. Denison, ed., *Recycling and Incineration: Evaluating the Choices* (Washington, DC: Island Press, 1990).

16. U.S. Environmental Protection Agency, *Municipal Solid Waste Generation*.

17. U.S. Environmental Protection Agency, *Municipal Solid Waste: Basic Facts*, at www.epa.gov/msw, accessed May 25, 2005.

18. National Recycling Coalition, at www.nrc-recycle.org/partnerships, accessed May 25, 2005.

19. U.S. Environmental Protection Agency, "Pollution Prevention Program," at www.epa.gov, accessed May 26, 2005.

20. Louis Blumberg and Gottlieb, *War on Waste: Can America Win Its Battle With Garbage?* (Washington, DC: Island Press, 1989), 63.

21. See William L. Kovacs and John F. Klusik, "The New Federal Role in Solid Waste Management: The Resource Recovery and Conservation Act of 1976," *Columbia Journal of Environmental Law, 3* (March 1977): 205.

22. *City of Philadelphia v. New Jersey*, 437 U.S. 617 (1978).

23. See Rosemary O'Leary, "Trash Talk: The Supreme Court and the Interstate Transportation of Waste," *Public Administration Review, 57*, no. 4 (July–August 1997): 281–284.

24. See "Recent Developments, Federal Regulation of Solid Waste Reduction and Recycling," *Harvard Journal on Legislation, 29* (1992): 251–254. For a more comprehensive analysis of the policy process as it relates to both the RCRA and Superfund, see Charles E. Davis, *The Politics of Hazardous Waste* (Englewood Cliffs, NJ: Prentice-Hall, 1993).

25. For an estimate of Superfund costs and issues, see Katherine N. Probst and David M. Konisky, *Superfund's Future: What Will It Cost?* (Washington, DC: Resources for the Future Press, 2001).

26. U.S. Environmental Protection Agency, "Current NPL Updates: New Proposed and New Final NPL Sites," at www.epa.gov/superfund/sites/npl, accessed May 27, 2005.

27. U.S. Environmental Protection Agency, "Superfund National Accomplishments Summary Fiscal Year 2004," at www.epa.gov, accessed March 5, 2005.

28. U.S. Environmental Protection Agency, "New Report Projects Number, Cost, and Nature of Contaminated Site Cleanups in the U.S. Over Next 30 Years," News release, at www.epa.gov/superfund/news, accessed December 6, 2004.

29. John Heilprin, "EPA Sees Toxic Waste Sites, Costs Growing," *Newsday*, December 3, 2004, at www.newsday.com/news/politics/wire, accessed December 6, 2004

30. Bob Anez, "W. R. Grace Accused of Hiding Cancer Risk," at www.chej.org, accessed February 10, 2005.

31. Carrie Johnson and Dina ElBoghdady, "Prosperity Turned to Poison in Mining Town," *Washington Post,* February 8, 2005, at www.washingtonpost.com, accessed February 10, 2005.

32. Carrie Johnson and Dina ElBoghdady, "Md. Firm Accused of Asbestos Coverup," *Washington Post,* February 8, 2005, at www.washingtonpost.com, accessed February 10, 2005.

33. Anez, "W. R. Grace Accused of Hiding Cancer Risk."

34. Matthew J. Wald, "Study Aids Opponents of Nevada Burial," *Arizona Republic,* April 7, 2005, A3.

35. Spencer Abraham, "One Safe Site Is Best," *Washington Post,* March 26, 2002, A-19.

36. Shelley Berkley, "Yucca Mountain: A History of Nuclear Politics," March 13, 2002, at www.house.gov/berkley/2002, accessed April 18, 2002. Berkley is a member of the U.S. House of Representatives from Nevada.

37. See Tony Davis, "Nuclear Waste Dump Opens," *High Country News,* April 12, 1999, 5; and James Brooke, "Deep Desert Grave Awaits First Load of Nuclear Waste," *New York Times,* March 26, 1999, A-17.

38. Kenny C. Guinn, *Statement of Reasons Supporting the Governor of Nevada's Notice of Disapproval of the Proposed Yucca Mountain Project* (April 8, 2002). www.gov.state.nv.us

39. "Senate Approves Yucca Mountain Nuclear Waste Site," July 10, 2002, at www.cnn.com/2002, accessed July 21, 2002.

40. Doug Abrahams, "Bush Approves Yucca Site for Nation's Nuclear Waste," *Arizona Republic,* July 24, 2002, A-6.

41. "Nevada Panel Optimistic Yucca Mountain Project Can Be Killed," *Las Vegas Sun,* February 5, 2005, at www.lasvegassun.com, accessed February 7, 2005.

42. Doug Abrahams, "Fake Paper Sets Back Nuke-Waste Dump Plan," *Arizona Republic,* March 17, 2005, A-14; Erica Werner, "Yucca Mountain E-Mails Get Released," *Arizona Republic,* April 2, 2005, A-15; Erica Werner, "Interior Turns Down Request for Testimony from Yucca Mountain Scientists," *Las Vegas Sun,* April 8, 2005, at www.lasvegassun.com, accessed April 9, 2005; "Toxic E-Mails," *Washington Post,* April 9, 2005, at www.washingtonpost.com, accessed April 9, 2005.

43. Travis Reed, "Nuke-Waste Site Stirs Debate," *Arizona Republic,* March 27, 2005, A-13.

44. Travis Reed, "Nuclear Tailings Near River to Be Moved," *Arizona Republic,* April 7, 2005, A-4.

45. See Michael Renner, "Military Mop-Up," *WorldWatch,* 7, no. 5 (September–October 1994), 23–29; and Seth Shulman, *The Threat at Home: Confronting the Toxic Legacy of the U.S. Military* (Boston: Beacon, 1992).

46. Katherine N. Probst, "Long Term Stewardship and the Nuclear Weapons Complex," *Resources* (Spring 1998), 14–16.

47. Michael Cabanatuan, "Settlement to Ease Public Monitoring of Nuclear Weapons Cleanup Sites," *San Francisco Chronicle,* December 15, 1998, A-22.

48. Joanisabel Gonzalez-Velazquez "Navy in Advanced Stage to Begin Vieques Cleanup," *Puerto Rico Herald,* August 13, 2003, at www.puerto-herald.org/issues/2003, accessed May 27, 2005.

49. U.S. Fish and Wildlife Service, "Vieques and Culebra Proposed Superfund Listing," at www.fws.gov/southeast/vieques, accessed May 27, 2005.

50. "Protest in Vieques: The Navy Is 'Bombing' Again," *San Francisco Bay View,* May 18, 2005, at www.sfbayview.com, accessed May 27, 2005.

51. Cong. Jose E. Serrano, "Serrano Secures $1 Million for Vieques Cleanup," News release, December 3, 2004, at www.house.gov/serrano, accessed May 27, 2005.

52. This terminology is derived from both the U.S. Environmental Protection Agency language and that of the Organization for Economic Cooperation and Development (OECP).

53. Kate O'Neill. *Waste Trading Among Rich Nations: Building a New Theory of Environmental Regulation* (Cambridge, MA: MIT Press, 2000), 35.

54. See Ed Bellinger et al., eds., *Environmental Assessment in Countries in Transition* (New York: CEU Press, 2000).

55. O'Neill, *Waste Trading Among Rich Nations*, 37–41.

56. See Jennifer Clapp, *Toxic Exports: The Transfer of Hazardous Wastes from Rich to Poor Countries* (Ithaca, NY: Cornell University Press, 2001): 54–58.

57. Ibid., 82–83.

58. O'Neill, *Waste Trading Among Rich Nations*, 209–210.

FURTHER READING

Robert Allen. *The Dioxin War: Truth and Lies About a Perfect Poison.* Chicago: Pluto Press, 2005.

Michael R. Edelstein. *Contaminated Communities: Coping with Residential Toxic Exposure.* Boulder, CO: Westview Press, 2004.

Liz Harris. *Tilting at Mills: Green Dreams, Dirty Dealings, and the Corporate Squeeze.* Boston: Houghton Mifflin, 2003.

Christian Ludwig, Stefanie Hellweg, and Samuel Stucki. *Municipal Solid Waste Management: Strategies and Technologies for Sustainable Solutions.* New York: Springer, 2003.

Andy Meharg. *Venomous Earth: How Arsenic Is Causing the Worst Mass Poisoning Ever.* New York: Palgrave Macmillan, 2005.

Elizabeth Royte. *Garbage Land: On the Secret Trail of Trash.* Boston: Little, Brown, 2005.

Suzana Sawyer. *Crude Chronicles: Indigenous Politics, Multinational Oil, and Neoliberalism in Ecuador.* Durham, NC: Duke University Press, 2004.

John Timbrell. *The Poison Paradox.* Oxford, UK: Oxford University Press, 2005.

J. Samuel Walker. *Three Mile Island: A Nuclear Crisis in Historical Perspective.* Berkeley: University of California Press, 2004.

6

The Politics of Energy

Twenty-five years from now, people are going to look back and say
'I like my hydrogen-powered automobile.'
—PRESIDENT GEORGE W. BUSH, APRIL 27, 2005[1]

In spring 2005, President Bush crisscrossed the country in an effort to build support for his energy proposals, which had failed to gather sufficient congressional or public support during his first term in office. His Nuclear Power 2010 Initiative and Nuclear Hydrogen Initiative had been mired in what he called "regulatory uncertainty," and review of 32 proposed new projects to expand or build liquefied natural gas terminals had stalled. Gas prices were rapidly exceeding even the most pessimistic forecasts; in 2000, the Energy Information Administration (EIA) had predicted prices of $20 per barrel of crude oil by 2020, but in 2005, costs were already over $70 a barrel.

The theme of the Bush administration's plan was to end U.S. dependence upon foreign sources of energy at a time when domestic consumption was rising more rapidly than production. "Our dependence on foreign energy is like a foreign tax on the American people," the president noted. "It's a tax our citizens pay every day in higher gasoline prices and higher costs to heat and cool their homes. It's a tax on jobs and it's a tax that is increasing every year."[2]

Energy concerns are growing much faster than prices, however. Prior administrations' policies were based on resource scarcity, but by 2005, the growth in oil use in the transportation sector and the accompanying rising imports in Middle Eastern oil were underscored by the emphasis on energy security. A 2005 report by Resources for the Future predicts that oil production will become

Wind farms, such as the one shown here, were first built in the 1970s as a source of renewable energy, but much of the public considers the large structures as a visual blight.

JUDYTH PRATT, ECOSENSE/CORBIS

increasingly concentrated in the Persian Gulf region, where an estimated two thirds of global reserves are located. In comparison, estimated reserves in the United States are about 2 percent of the global total. "Intense concentration of supply in any one region would be cause for concern," the study notes, "but that concern is intensified by the history of political upheaval and violence in the Middle East."[3]

Although there is agreement about the potential economic crisis that would transpire if the nation's energy supplies were disrupted, "there are emerging concerns that deserve equal attention, namely the resilience of the domestic energy infrastructure—oil and gas terminals and pipelines, nuclear power plants, and the electricity grid—to terrorist attacks."[4]

This change in focus, which is part of the process of problem definition and the framing of energy policy, has pushed energy issues higher on the environmental agenda. Whereas the president told Congress, "I wish I could simply wave a magic wand and lower gas prices tomorrow,"[5] analysts note, "Like it or not, Americans must confront the reality that oil prices are set by worldwide markets that respond to many economic and political factors beyond the U.S. government's control."[6]

Energy has been called a "transparent" sector of society because no one buys or uses it as an end in itself. All demand for energy is indirect and derived only from the benefits it provides. People do not buy gasoline because they want gasoline, but because they need it for their cars to take them where they want to go. Similarly, a manufacturing plant needs electricity only to run the machines that make the products the company sells.

Our growing electricity needs make the debate both timely and controversial. Two thirds of American oil consumption is from the transportation sector—highways, air routes, and long-distance railroads—with no other fuel potentially viable for these uses.[7] Large developing countries such as China and India are also fueling the energy debate as the demand for automobiles increases. According to the *International Energy Outlook 2004,* worldwide energy demand is expected to expand by 54 percent between 2001 and 2025.[8]

This chapter examines the changing politics of energy, reviewing the various energy sources and looking at the political environment and regulatory aspects of energy policy, from the nuclear power debate to increasing consumer interest in fuel efficiency ratings and hybrid vehicles. The chapter concludes with an overview of global energy trends and projections for changes in energy use and conservation.

THE ENERGY PIE

Energy is needed to produce goods and services in four basic economic sectors: residential (heat for rooms and hot water, lighting, appliances), commercial (including air conditioners in commercial buildings), industrial (especially steel, paper, and chemicals), and transportation (of both people and goods). Historically, the crux of the energy policy debate has been to find efficient, environmentally safe, economical, and stable sources of supply to meet those needs. The United States has periodically experienced global energy transitions that mark changes in energy supplies and needs. In 1850, the United States derived nearly 90 percent of its energy needs from wood, which remained the dominant fuel into the late 19th century. In 1910, coal replaced wood as the dominant fuel, capturing 70 percent of all energy produced and consumed. Along with the transition from wood to coal came the migration from rural areas to the cities, the development of an industrial base, and the railroad era. Table 6.1 shows the changes that have occurred in energy production since 1950. In 1970, oil and gas reached the 70 percent level and became dominant fuels, and it was not until 1990 that geothermal, solar, and wind power sources became a statistically significant source of energy in the United States.

Edward Teller, the "father of the atomic bomb," once commented:

No single prescription exists for a solution to the energy problem. Energy conservation is not enough. Petroleum is not enough. Nuclear energy is not enough. Solar energy and geothermal energy are not enough. New ideas and developments will not be enough. Only the proper combination of all these will suffice.[9]

Teller suggests that the answer to our global energy needs is like a recipe for an "energy pie," which is essentially the situation in the United States today; it must be found in a blend of energy sources and strategies, rather than in a single fuel. This concept seems relatively reasonable were the costs and benefits of various forms of energy equal, but that is far from the case. Some forms of energy are relatively inexpensive to produce but are not in abundant supply. Other sources are expensive but less polluting. Still others are considered unsafe but could be made available to consumers around the world for pennies a day, improving the standard of living for millions of people in developing nations. Figure 6.1 illustrates the 2005 energy pie.

Fossil Fuels

For thousands of years, humanity's primary sources of power were draft animals, water, and wind. Industrialization and the introduction of fossil fuels for power followed the invention of machines that could harness natural power sources. Oil, coal, and natural gas became the elements of what has been called the fossil fuel revolution—the expansion of power sources and, subsequently, the rise of the United States as a superpower in the global economy. Although developing nations are still largely dependent upon biomass energy (primarily fuelwood), industrialized countries have expanded their fuel mix through petroleum exports and an increasing reliance upon nuclear power.

Initially, the United States depended on "Old King Coal" as its primary fuel source. Demand came from the transportation industry, as railroads moved

T A B L E 6.1 U.S. Energy Production (by Source) 1950–2003 (quadrillion Btu)

Year	Coal	Natural Gas Dry	Crude Oil	Natural Gas Liquid	Nuclear	Hydro	Biomass	Geothermal	Solar	Wind	Total
1950	14.06	6.233	11.447	0.823	0	1.415	1.562	0	n/a	n/a	36.54
1960	10.817	12.656	14.936	1.461	0.008	1.606	1.32	0.001	n/a	n/a	42.804
1970	14.607	21.666	20.401	2.512	0.239	2.634	1.431	0.11	n/a	n/a	63.501
1980	18.598	19.908	18.249	2.254	2.739	2.90	2.485	0.11	n/a	n/a	67.241
1990	22.456	18.326	15.571	2.175	6.104	3.046	2.662	0.336	0.060	0.029	70.835
2000	22.623	19.662	12.358	2.611	7.862	2.811	2.907	0.317	0.066	0.057	71.902
2003	22.311	19.641	12.145	2.343	7.973	2.779	2.884	0.314	0.063	0.108	70.474

SOURCE: U.S. Department of Energy. Energy Information Administration. Annual Energy Review, 2003 at www.eia.doe.gov/emev accessed June 21, 2005.

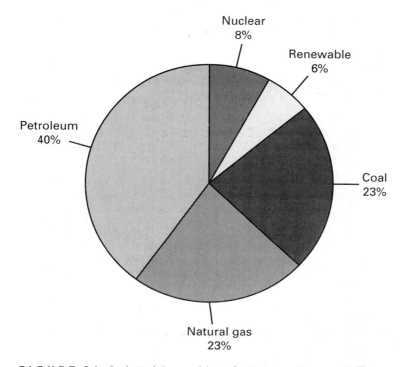

FIGURE 6.1 Projected Composition of U.S. Energy Demand, 2005

SOURCE: Energy Information Administration, U.S. Department of Energy, at www.eia.doe.gov, accessed January 15, 2005.

westward, and from metal industries (iron and steel) that forged the new tracks. Coal, found in 38 states, was a relatively inexpensive and reliable energy source, and by the end of World War I, it accounted for about 75 percent of total U.S. energy use. Between then and World War II, automobiles began to be mass-produced; moreover, trucks and diesel locomotives requiring petroleum reduced the country's dependence on coal while natural gas replaced coal in household furnaces and heaters. After World War II, new household appliances appeared—electric dishwashers, clothes dryers, and washing machines—that further expanded the demand for electricity.[10] Whereas coal still accounts for about one quarter of the energy pie, the average age of coal-burning plants is 25 years; consequently, facilities are quickly becoming outdated and closed down, partially in response to the air quality concerns outlined in Chapter 8. But Vice President Dick Cheney has called for building between 1,300 and 1,900 new power plants, more than doubling the current number.[11]

The United States has huge reserves of natural gas, which makes up another quarter of the energy pie; the country is estimated to have the sixth largest proven reserves of natural gas in the world. Initially heralded as a clean, virtually pollution-free source of energy, the expansion of natural gas production has been heavily criticized by environmental organizations. A proposal for a pipeline from Wyoming to California was derailed when researchers found that the planned route passed through habitats of the endangered desert tortoise. Other plans to open up the outer continental shelf—including areas off the East Coast from central New Jersey to southern Georgia, along the eastern part of the Gulf of Mexico, and the California coast near Santa Barbara—have been stalled due to intense opposition. In his 2005 energy proposal, President Bush sought support for new technologies that would assist in locating, producing, and transporting natural gas and make storage safer.

About 20 percent of the U.S. energy pie is made up of crude oil, most of it imported from the Persian Gulf. In October 1973, nations of the Organization of the Petroleum Exporting Countries (OPEC) sharply increased the price of a barrel of oil from an average cost of $4 a barrel to nearly $12, leading to a fuel crisis that, at least momentarily, focused the political agenda on energy. In late 1975, Congress passed the Energy Policy and Conservation Act, which called for a phased deregulation of oil. But as quickly as they had surfaced, concerns about the country's energy policies faded; even a second energy crisis in 1979–1981 that raised crude oil prices from $14 to $37 a barrel failed to ignite public interest. Americans assumed that there was an unlimited supply of fuel available—it was simply a matter of turning on the spigot. Upon assuming office in 1981, President Ronald Reagan accelerated the process for price decontrols, making energy policy more market oriented and reducing the federal government's role. The high cost of imported crude oil led to a reduction in U.S. petroleum consumption between 1978 and 1982; there was more fuel substitution, more efficient consumption of oil, a diversification of supply sources, and price-induced conservation. By the mid-1980s, OPEC nations sharply lowered the price for crude oil; in 1985–1986, the cost for imported oil fell from $27 a barrel to $14 a barrel.[12]

In August 1990 Iraq's leader, Saddam Hussein, ordered his troops into Kuwait, once again threatening the world's oil supplies. Few Americans showed much evidence of concern about whether their local gasoline pumps would go dry. The price of oil, which averaged $16 a barrel at the end of July 1990, exceeded $28 by late August and reached $36 a barrel in September. Realizing that the long-term demand for crude oil would be jeopardized by prolonged periods of high oil prices, OPEC nations boosted their oil production to make up for the supply lost during the Iraqi invasion. Prices quickly began to fall, and more importance was placed on energy conservation.

When President George H. W. Bush signed the Energy Policy Act of 1992—the first major legislative attempt to curb U.S. oil dependence in more than a decade—his action failed to generate more than a single day's media headlines. Even repeated bombings of Iraq by the United States and its allies in 1998, intense political unrest in the Middle East, a rise in oil prices that began in late spring 1999, and the terrorist attacks of September 11, 2001, did not seem to resonate with the American public as having a potential impact on petroleum supplies.

By 2005, when gasoline prices topped $3 per gallon in some parts of the country, consumers began paying more attention. Sales of hybrid vehicles such as the Toyota Prius and Honda Insight, and the natural-gas-powered Honda Civic GX grew at an annual growth rate of 89 percent. These cars still make up a small fraction of the new vehicle market, and consumers added their names to waiting lists and paid more than the suggested manufacturer prices just to get better mileage. But the president's Hydrogen Initiative, which calls for spending $1.2 billion over five years to develop vehicles with hydrogen fuel cells and infrastructure technologies, faces many obstacles. The high cost and technological barriers associated with the fuel's distribution, storage, and use are likely to place this option several decades away—not 15 years, as the president predicted.[13]

Congress, sensing an opening in the policy window, came back to the issue of drilling in the Arctic National Wildlife Refuge (ANWR) in April 2005. The House handed the president a victory by agreeing to provisions that would open up the coastal plain to oil drilling. The administration argued that environmentally responsible exploration and development could provide up to 1 million barrels of oil per day using less than 2,000 acres of the refuge's total land area.

Renewable Energy

Renewable energy sources, could conceivably serve as an alternative to our existing reliance on fossil fuels. These sources have been used extensively in other countries but, with the exception of hydropower, not in the United States. Currently, renewable energy sources make up about 6 percent of the energy pie—a number expected to grow to 10 percent by 2025, according to the Energy Information Administration.[14]

Supporters of renewable energy sources point out that they produce no waste to be disposed of and no greenhouse gases. They generally are safe for workers, and facilities can be constructed more quickly than can plants using fossil fuels or nuclear power. Their biggest drawbacks are unreliability as a fuel source and the higher cost of producing and distributing the electricity they generate. But the subject of renewable energy returns to the policy agenda from time to time due to focusing events like the massive electric power blackouts over most of the northeastern United States in 1965, the Arab oil embargo in 1973, and historic highs in the cost of crude oil in 2005.

The political process has greatly affected U.S. attention to alternative fuel sources and the federal government's support for renewable energy research can be tied to both electoral cycles and the cost of oil. The passage of the 1978 Public Utilities Regulatory Policies Act (PURPA), for example, requires utilities to purchase power from nonutilities at an "avoided cost" rate (the rate of expense the utility would have incurred had it generated the energy itself). PURPA became an incentive for alternative sources like cogenerators (large, industrial power users produce steam and electricity for their own needs and sell the excess to local utilities) and small hydroelectric plants that were guaranteed a market for the electricity they generated. Although hydroelectric power is among the cheapest sources of energy available, its use is becoming more limited as environmental groups have lobbied against the siting of new dams along waterways. A 1997 report to the Western Water Policy Review Advisory Commission noted that existing dams alter water temperature and the timing and magnitude of river flows; block fish migration and spawning; entrap nutrients and sediment, which harm the riparian habitat; and change the chemical makeup of downstream flows.[15]

Other forms of renewable energy—solar, wind, and geothermal power—were hailed as promising energy sources during the 1970s, when the newly created Energy Research and Development Administration funded proposals for "soft" energy. But by the mid-1980s, political support had faded and research dollars disappeared. Under the Reagan administration, budget cuts forced the Colorado-based Solar Energy Research Institute (SERI), headed by 1970's Earth Day organizer Denis Hayes, to halve its workforce, which went from 1,000 to 500 in only a few months.

The lack of tax incentives, government support, and higher production costs, coupled with a dying grassroots movement favoring alternative power, has suppressed or delayed the adoption of nonfossil fuel applications throughout the United States. Tax subsidies for renewable energy expired in December 2003 but were reinstated in September 2004, giving producers new hope that there would be a more favorable change in policy.

Another View, Another Voice

Western Governors' Association
Although it represents only 18 of the 50 states, the Western Governors' Association (WGA) has become a major stakeholder in the development of environmental policy, addressing issues and formulating policies that frequently become adopted as national policy. Established in 1984, the WGA took the lead in environmental management with Enlibra—a set of shared principles and a vision statement to guide development and decision making—adopted in 1999.

Policy direction is identified each year by the chair of the WGA and the board of directors, who review and approve a strategic agenda that focuses on specific issues of interest to the region. Topics have included threatened and endangered species, wildfires, drought preparedness, healthy forests and rangelands, and the environmental permit process. The group provides a forum for the exchange of ideas and experiences, the building of regional capacity, research and dissemination of findings, the formation of coalitions and partnerships to advance regional interests, and the building of public understanding for regional issues and policy positions.

An independent, nonprofit organization that includes three U.S.-flag islands in the Pacific, the WGA is one of the strongest voices in the development of U.S. energy policy, in part because of the region's natural resources and history of energy development. Following their April 2004 North American Energy Summit, the leaders unanimously adopted a resolution in June 2004 to explore opportunities to develop "a clean, secure and diversified energy system for the West and to capitalize on the region's immense energy resources." The initiative, spearheaded by New Mexico Governor Bill Richardson and California Governor Arnold Schwarzenegger, examines the feasibility and actions required to reach a goal of 30,000 megawatts of clean energy by 2015 and a 20 percent improvement in energy efficiency by 2020. The Clean and Diversified Energy Working Group, headed by Wyoming Governor Dave Freudenthal, is comprised of state, local, and Native American leaders, along with representatives of environmental organizations, air quality agencies, and leaders from the private sector and federal agencies, including those of Mexico and Canada.

The resolution recognizes the importance of traditional resources such as coal, natural gas, oil, and hydropower; but notes that solar, wind, geothermal, biomass, and advanced technologies for clean coal and natural gas "are relatively untapped but hugely promising. Together, the combination of these resources provides the foundation for a clean, diversified and secure energy future for the West." The resolution is specifically concerned with increasing the contribution of renewable energy, energy efficiency, and clean energy technologies.

The WGA's concerns about energy are not unlike those of citizens in other U.S. regions, but the organization is at the forefront of practical applications. Because of concerns about energy shortages and price spikes and the needs of its growing population, western governors are sensitive to issues raised by power plant emissions and air quality, energy efficiency in the U.S.-Mexico border region, and market-based incentives for facilities powered by renewable energy. Four member states have established Renewable Portfolio Standards, and nearly every state has adopted tax and other incentives to promote renewable energy development and to promote energy efficiency.

Due to the nature of its membership, the WGA is able to establish viable long-term goals. Although the electoral process results in changes in gubernatorial members nearly every year, there is continuity because of the organization's staff and the fact that many governors formerly served as state or congressional legislators.

Past members, such as former Oregon governor John Kitzhaber and Utah Governor Mike Leavitt, who served as administrator of the Environmental Protection Agency before becoming Secretary of Health and Human Services under President George W. Bush, have played key roles in promoting collaborative approaches to environmental problem solving.

The 2004 energy initiative places a special emphasis on long-term wind-energy potential in the western plains and mountain states, calling for a more aggressive effort to develop wind power. It also stresses cooperation with the California Energy Commission's Renewable Energy Program, established in 1998, and the Western Regional Air Partnership. By establishing specific targets for clean energy development, WGA seeks to meet the West's generation and transmission needs over the next 25 years.

SOURCES:
Western Governors' Association, "2005 Strategic Agenda," at www.westgov.org, accessed January 19, 2005.
Western Governors' Association, "North American Energy Summit Kicks off with Proposed Clean Energy Initiative, CBM Best Practices Handbook," News release, April 14, 2004, at www.westgov.org, accessed January 19, 2005.
Western Governors' Association, Policy Resolution 04–14, *Clean and Diversified Energy Initiative for the West*, June 22, 2004, at www.wga.org, accessed January 19, 2005.
Western Governors' Association, "Western Governors Launch Initiative to Spur Clean, Diversified Energy in the West," News release, at www.wga.org, June 22, 2004, accessed January 19, 2005.

Despite limited federal support for alternative energy, state governments moved forward with their own policies. Regulatory bodies can require utilities to develop a portfolio of energy sources, including power generated by renewable energy providers, to make the cost of environmentally friendly energy more acceptable to consumers. By 2005, eighteen states had adopted renewable energy portfolio standards requiring a certain percentage of the state's electricity to come from renewable sources (see Table 6.2). Arizona's Corporation Commission, for instance, requires that a minimum of 1.1 percent of the state's power from companies it regulates be generated from renewable resources by 2007. The commission's staff is recommending that the minimum be raised to 5 percent by 2015 and 15 percent by 2025. Most states do not favor one source of alternative energy over another; but the thresholds they establish do create stronger markets, especially for solar and wind power.[16]

Local governments have also attempted to increase the market for renewable energy, although on a considerably smaller scale. The San Francisco Public Utilities Commission, for instance, is requiring energy efficiency measures, including rooftop solar panels, on 1,600 housing units being developed.[17] In Los Angeles, the city's Department of Water and Power voted to reinstate its program for businesses and

T A B L E 6.2   **States with Renewable Energy Portfolio Standards, 2005**

Arizona	Maryland
California	Massachusetts
Colorado	Minnesota
Connecticut	Nevada
Florida	New Jersey
Hawaii	New Mexico
Illinois	Pennsylvania
Iowa	Tennessee
Maine	Wisconsin

SOURCE: Energy Information Administration, U.S. Department of Energy, at www.eia.doe.gov/cneaf, accessed March 20, 2005.

property owners who install solar electric systems through its Solar Incentive Program, which had been suspended in June 2003.[18]

The direction of renewable energy appeared to be changing in 2004. President Bush announced a new Solar Energy Development Policy, establishing a framework for land managers to use in processing right-of-way applications for commercial solar energy projects on public lands managed by the Bureau of Land Management (BLM). The scale is significant because the Department of Interior manages one in every five acres of land in the United States, and the BLM has jurisdiction over 261 million acres of the DOI land. In 2004 the solar energy program was a key part of the president's energy proposals, with a focus on public land in the Southwest, where solar energy production is thought to have the highest potential. Generators producing about 370 megawatts (MW) of solar power are already installed in the West, mostly in southern California. 370 MW would supply energy for 370,000 homes. A typical large electrical generating plant produces 1,000 megawatts.

Solar energy supporters also note that the cost of photovoltaics (PV) manufacturing has gone down more than 95 percent since 1978. Advances in the microchip and LED industries have spilled over to PV, resulting in the construction of more automated, large-scale factories. One of the most popular applications—solar water heating—has become cost competitive with conventional energy technologies. A reduction in energy consumption by 50 percent allows most owners to pay for the installed cost of their solar water heating systems within four to eight years.

But by 2005, when the president made another attempt to gain congressional support for his energy policies, solar energy was mentioned in the context of tax incentives and research and development, rather than new initiatives or funding for specific projects. Instead, solar power appeared to have lost out to hydrogen, ethanol, and biomass for transportation fuels and to nuclear power for electricity.

At least at the state and local levels, another promising renewable energy source now gaining governmental support is wind power, which dates back to around A.D. 50 in China, Afghanistan, and Persia. A Danish inventor, Poul La

Cor, built a practical four-blade windmill in 1891; the first utility-scale wind generator was built on the shores of the Caspian Sea in 1931.[19] An estimated 6 million small windmills operated in the United States between 1850 and 1970. They were owned primarily by farmers to provide electricity for their family's use and for tending to the farm animals. Wind-power companies were supported by the U.S. Federal Wind Energy Program after the energy crisis of the 1970s, with an estimated 17,000 machines installed between 1981 and 1990. Suppliers received a 15 percent federal energy tax credit, and in California, where large-scale wind farms were built, a 50 percent credit encouraged additional wind-power development. Operating difficulties and competition from Danish companies that invested in the U.S. market reduced output in the mid to late 1980s. By 2005, about 1 percent of American electricity was produced by wind power.[20]

But several new projects have gone from the wishful thinking stage to potential as the technology progressed and citizens became more accustomed to seeing wind turbines on the landscape. The American Wind Energy Institute (AWEI) reports there are now wind-energy facilities in almost every state west of the Mississippi, led by California with 2,043 MW and Texas with 1,293 MW. An estimated 3,000 MW of new capacity will be installed by 2009, the association says. With a favorable political climate, the United States could have 100,000 MW of installed wind power by 2013 and a full potential of 600,000 MW by that date. A steady supply of 60 megawatts of electricity can provide sufficient power for 60,000 homes.[21]

Wind is classified into power classes, based on wind speed. Class 1 is the lowest at about 13 miles per hour (mph), and Class 7 (27 mph) is the highest; large utility-scale turbines usually require Class 4 (17 mph) winds or higher. In addition to wind speed, companies considering land as potential wind farms must survey sites for their potential environmental sensitivity and distance from urban areas. Land-use conflicts may eliminate some areas, such as forests, farmlands, or rangeland. Although most policy makers support efforts to diversify energy sources, the projects can also be politically controversial. Alameda County, California, placed a moratorium on new wind farms because turbines had killed hundreds of birds of prey; and in Tucker County, West Virginia, hundreds of bats that had flown into the turbines were killed. In Cape Cod, Massachusetts, residents opposed a project that they felt would spoil their view. Environmental groups have raised questions about the potential impact of wind farms on fish populations and migratory birds.[22]

A California-based company is planning the world's largest wind farm in South Dakota; about one third of the state is considered suitable for future power development based on wind speed and land use. The Rolling Thunder project would be 10 times the size of the largest wind farm currently making electricity along the Washington-Oregon border. The largest concentration of wind turbines in the United States is on Buffalo Ridge in southwestern Minnesota, where more than 600 turbines capable of producing 500 MW of power operate on 25 individual wind farms.

South Dakota has relied upon plants run on fossil fuels and hydroelectric power from four Missouri River dams, and only about 1 percent of the state's energy is produced from wind. Studies have shown that the state has nearly unlimited potential for wind farms and perhaps could supply a double-digit percentage of the nation's needs. But the state lacks the transmission capacity to export power to big cities in other states. Other big projects have been proposed for the state's Pine Ridge Indian Reservation and for a site in eastern North Dakota.[23]

As a way of reducing public opposition to the visual impact of wind turbines, offshore sites are now being considered. The proposed Long Island Offshore Wind Initiative in New York would include up to 50 wind turbines built two to five miles offshore that would be "pollution-free, boundless and blow a gust of clean air into the future of energy production," according to a Natural Resources Defense Council spokesperson. But surfing and fishing enthusiasts applauded the efforts of New Jersey governor Richard Codey when he announced a moratorium on offshore wind farms in 2004.

Alternative-Fuel Vehicles

Alternative-fuel vehicles, once touted as the panacea for a country that loves to drive, have suffered from a lack of political support and public acceptance. That lack of political support is illustrated by a suit filed by the environmental law group, Earthjustice, against 18 federal agencies in 2002 for failing to comply with the 1992 Energy Policy Act. One provision of the statute, enacted during the Gulf War as a way of reducing dependence on foreign oil, required federal agencies to increase their purchase of alternative-fuel vehicles to 75 percent by 2000. The suit alleges that none of the agencies, including the Department of Energy, which is charged with enforcing the act, met the 75 percent standard; the Interior Department, for instance, reported 31 percent, and the Commerce Department reported 17 percent. "It is truly startling to find such wholesale noncompliance," said Earthjustice attorney Jay Tutchman, representing the Sierra Club, the Center for Biological Diversity, and the Bluewater Network in the suit. Tutchman also noted a loophole in the 1992 act: Although it requires agencies to buy vehicles capable of running on alternative fuels, there is no requirement that they actually run on an alternative fuel source.[24]

THE NUCLEAR POWER DEBATE

Support for nuclear power as an energy source began in the United States in 1960, when Southern California Edison announced plans to build a huge facility at San Onofre, California. Pacific Gas and Electric made a similar announcement of plans to build a privately funded plant at Bodega Bay, California, although the latter project was never built. The companies were encouraged by the Atomic Energy Commission (AEC), the federal agency charged with regulating the new facilities. The AEC announced its objective of making nuclear power economically competitive by 1968 in those parts of the country that were dependent upon high-cost fossil fuels. In 1962, as an incentive for utility companies to build large-capacity nuclear plants, the AEC offered to pay part of the design costs. The rush to build began; orders for new plants grew steadily between 1966 and 1974 and then dropped off sharply between 1975 and 1978. No orders for nuclear generating units have been placed by a utility or government agency since 1978, and no new facility has been issued a full-power operating license since 1996 (see Figure 6.2). About one eighth of the nation's energy comes from the 104 nuclear power plants currently operating in the United States.

What happened to undermine the promising beginnings of nuclear power? Many factors were at work:

 Silent spring

1. The growth of the environmental movement in the early 1970s, combined with zealous antiwar sentiment, led to a strong sense of public opposition to anything associated with nuclear weapons, including nuclear power as an energy source.

2. That same public pressure led to increased government sensitivity about the impacts of new projects, as seen in the history of legislation outlined in Chapter 1. In 1971, the U.S. Court of Appeals ruled that the AEC had failed to follow the provisions of the National Environmental Policy Act in licensing the Calvert Cliffs facility near Baltimore, Maryland; the court made a similar ruling on the Quad Cities nuclear power station on the Mississippi River in Illinois. Both decisions focused attention on the environmental impacts of nuclear facilities and led to increased scrutiny of license applications.

3. Media coverage of a malfunctioning cooling system at Three Mile Island in 1979 and the explosion of a nuclear reactor at Chernobyl in 1986 made utilities still considering nuclear power think twice about the effects of widespread public opposition to such projects. These attitudes are still prevalent today and account for the general reluctance of policy makers even to consider this power source as an option.

4. Economics played a key role in scuttling the building of new facilities. Government estimates on the growth in demand for electricity in the 1970s turned out to be overly optimistic. As the demand for energy decreased, the cost of building new plants rose, making them non–cost-effective. In 1971 the estimated cost of building a typical facility was $345 million, but by 1980 the figure had climbed to $3.2 billion. The federal government had spent nearly $18 billion in subsidizing the commercial development of nuclear power by 1980, and smaller utilities could not afford to build on their own.

5. In addition, construction and licensing of new plants were taking as long as 10 years, delaying the point at which utilities could begin passing the costs on to consumers and recouping their investments. Financial horror stories began to proliferate. Of the five nuclear reactors started in the 1970s by the Washington Public Power Supply System, only one has been completed, and the utility ultimately defaulted on $2.25 billion in bonds in 1983. When the Long Island Lighting Company began building its Shoreham plant in April 1973, the cost was estimated at $300 million. The project was delayed by protests from nearby residents and by federally mandated design changes, and the cost escalated to $5.5 billion by the time the plant was completed in December 1984.[25] Suddenly, plans for all types of power plants—not just nuclear—were being shelved as too costly.

With the Bush administration's support of nuclear power as a key source of energy, utility companies are now rethinking their options. The initial 40-year

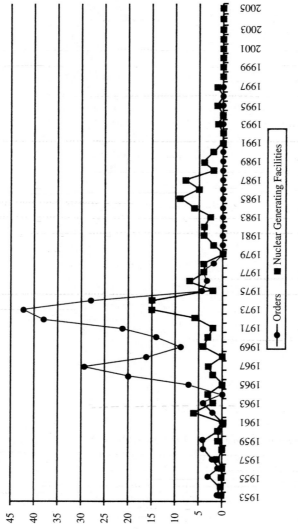

FIGURE 6.2 Construction of Nuclear Generating Facilities, 1953–2005

operating licenses of about 10 percent of current nuclear reactors in the United States are scheduled to expire by the end of 2010. The Electric Power Research Institute notes, however, that because the facilities have been well maintained and the Nuclear Regulatory Commission (NRC) has carefully scrutinized the safety and environmental records, the inherent operational limitations have been extended. In 2000, the NRC extended the license renewals for two nuclear plants for an additional 20 years; the industry expects to be revitalized, supplying some of the most competitive power generators available.[26]

The industry itself has continued moving forward, despite the lack of orders from the United States. Four large electric companies—Entergy, Exelon, Dominion, and Duke Power—have expressed interest in new reactors, and Duke officials have met with the NRC to prepare an application for a reactor license. Westinghouse is trying to sell its next-generation reactors to China, and European companies are pushing their technologies in the United States. Sen. Pete Dominici (R–NM) has suggested that nuclear power be classified with solar and wind generation as a renewable energy source in order to qualify for federal tax credits.[27]

Will nuclear power ever be reconsidered as a major source of energy? The answer to that question has little to do with science or technology and much to do with politics. Some industry officials believe such a change can take place only if Congress streamlines the regulatory framework for licensing facilities. Other analysts feel that utilities would be more likely to gain public acceptance for new nuclear facilities if they were sited or expanded near existing plants rather than in new areas. Public opposition to nuclear facilities, although still strong, appears to have leveled off. Attempts to close down facilities or ban nuclear power altogether have not been successful in some states, suggesting that Americans may not be so disenchanted with nuclear power as to close down the industry completely. But most observers believe that, unless Congress moves forward with a plan to store nuclear waste (see Chapter 5), the nuclear energy debate will remain at a standstill.

CAFE STANDARDS

Environmental groups have long sought to address the nation's energy problems through revisions to new car corporate average fuel economy (CAFE) standards. Depending upon which standard is used, the United States could save billions of gallons of gasoline by making cars more fuel efficient. The 1975 Energy Policy and Conservation Act raised standards beginning with model year 1978, requiring cars to meet a fleet average of 27.5 miles per gallon (mpg) by 1985. The National Highway Traffic Safety Administration required light-duty trucks (pickup trucks, minivans, and sports utility vehicles) to achieve a fleet average of at least 20.7 mpg. This was a substantial increase for cars, which averaged 16 mpg in 1977, and for new trucks, which averaged about 13 mpg.[28] Between 1978 and 1985 there were significant reductions in oil consumption, although studies were inconclusive regarding whether the change was due to reduced gasoline prices or to implementation of the new CAFE standards. Automakers had changed as well, producing smaller, more lightweight cars that were more fuel efficient. But the unintended consequence of the new policy was an increase in traffic fatalities that were attributed to the size and weight of the smaller cars. This raised the issue of whether safety was being sacrificed for fuel economy.

Congress subsequently forbade the expenditure of Department of Transportation funds to make any revisions in CAFE standards; automakers lobbied heavily to oppose any changes, citing a lack of sufficient technology to meet any fuel efficiency increase. In July 2001, the National Academy of Sciences' National Research Council released a report concluding that "significant" reductions in fuel consumption could be achieved within 15 years using existing technologies.

Spurred on by California regulations and new federal emissions standards, gas-electric hybrid cars and trucks have gradually found a niche with drivers seeking high-mileage, low-pollution vehicles. By early 2005, drivers could choose from 31 different gasoline-fueled cars that qualify as Partial Zero Emissions Vehicles (PZEV), ranging from the lower-end Hyundai to the BMW. But the cars are more expensive; and in many areas, availability is extremely limited, with waiting lists of two years or more.

The reality is that for the near term, 90 percent of drivers will choose from cars manufactured by the six largest automakers. In one 2004 study, the Union of Concerned Scientists found that Honda vehicles produced the least amount of pollutants on average, with General Motors characterized as "moving backwards" and "stuck in reverse."[29]

A similar study of cars and trucks sold in the United States was reported by the American Council for an Energy-Efficient Economy, which ranked 2004 model year cars and passenger trucks based on the amount of pollutants they emit. The study rated the natural-gas-powered Honda Civic GX as the "greenest" vehicle, followed by Honda's hybrid-electric Insight and the Toyota Prius. The Ford Focus wagon ranked first among compact wagons, the Chevrolet Impala was the top midsize car, and the Toyota Highlander was the best of the midsize sports utility vehicles. At the bottom: Volkswagen's diesel-powered Touareg sport utility vehicle.[30]

Organizations like Resources for the Future support higher gasoline prices instead of increases in CAFE standards. This would motivate new car buyers to demand better fuel economy from the manufacturers, and once that demand was established, automakers would be less reluctant to produce more fuel-efficient vehicles. Higher gas prices have the added benefit of forcing the public to drive less, to maintain their cars better, or to carpool—strategies that reduce the emissions of carbon dioxide.[31] Public response to having to pay more to drive bigger vehicles that get low gasoline mileage efficiency is not likely to be supportive.

THE HISTORY OF POLICY PARALYSIS

Historically, U.S. energy policy has been separated by type of fuel, with different institutional associations and interests for each type and few attempts at coalition building. Coal interests from the Northeast have dealt with the Bureau of Mines, while states with uranium were more likely to converse with the Atomic Energy committees in Congress and the Nuclear Regulatory Commission. Seldom did jurisdictional boundaries cross over from one fuel to another; as a result, terms like *disarray, turmoil,* and *inertia* are often used to describe U.S. energy policy. Those terms are in part applicable due to the maze of legislative and regulatory obstacles that have developed, along with a profusion of competing interests. The result is an energy policy that is highly segmented and neither comprehensive nor effective. Although many analysts have attempted to explain why U.S. energy policy has been so ineffective, the consensus appears to be that the government has intervened unnecessarily rather than allowing market forces to allocate scarce energy resources. How did such a policy develop?

Before 1900, the U.S. government had an ad hoc approach to what was perceived to be an unlimited supply of energy resources. A sense of abundance and virtual giveaways of public lands resulted in many valuable resources coming under private ownership. Although there were early rumblings of competition among interests representing the various fuels, it was not until after the turn of the century that the government began to intervene. To assure a stable and competitive oil market, the government relied upon the Sherman Anti-Trust Act in 1911 to break up the Standard Oil monopoly, and during World War I, President Woodrow Wilson established the Petroleum Advisory Committee to allocate American supplies. After the 1921 Teapot Dome scandal, in which officials were convicted of leasing federal lands to oil companies in exchange for bribes, the Federal Oil Conservation Board was created to oversee the oil industry. By the 1930s, the federal government's role had changed to one of consumer protection, expanding its jurisdiction with the Natural Gas Act of 1938 and the creation of the Tennessee Valley Authority. An attempt was never made to coordinate policy across fuel and use areas. Each area of energy supply—coal, gas, hydropower, oil, and nuclear power—was handled separately, as was each consumption sector—utilities, transportation, industrial, and residential. During the 1950s, as Congress approved a massive interstate highway system and transportation network, the Supreme Court ratified the Federal Power Commission's power to regulate natural gas prices, which held prices artificially low as gas consumption skyrocketed.[32]

As the environmental movement developed in the late 1960s and early 1970s, the process of developing energy policy became increasingly complex as more interests demanded to be included in the decision-making process. At the same time, the importance of energy as a political issue brought in congressional leaders who sought to respond to their constituents' demands that something be done about the long lines at the gas pumps and rising prices for fuels. Between 1969 and 1973, a confluence of negative factors and events changed the history of American energy policy forever. First, predictions by a few officials about a dependence on foreign oil came true. Although the United States first began importing oil as early as 1947, oil from Arab sources reached over a million barrels a day by 1973, more than double the amount imported 18 months earlier and 30 percent of total U.S. demand. Second, domestic oil production decreased because of price disparities over foreign oil and increasing costs for exploration and recovery. Third, new environmental legislation discouraged production of coal and nuclear power and brought a delay in completion of the trans-Alaska pipeline at the same time that Americans were driving more miles than ever before. Finally, the highly publicized Santa Barbara oil spill in 1969 had led to a five-year moratorium on offshore drilling, further restricting American oil production. The result was a nation made vulnerable to the vagaries of Middle Eastern politics.

The Nixon administration's approach to energy policy in the 1970s was marked by a series of failed attempts to do something about the impending crisis. Initially, the government imposed an Economic Stabilization Program, which not only froze prices on crude oil and petroleum products for 90 days but also froze wages and prices nationwide. In early 1973, Nixon restructured the country's mandatory oil import quota plan, which had limited foreign oil imports and allowed an unlimited purchase of home heating oil and diesel fuel for a four-month period. This action was followed by the creation of a handpicked Special Committee on Energy comprised of key Nixon advisers, who recommended that steps be taken to cope with price increase and fuel shortages. The strategy was to

increase energy supplies, with little concern for modifying demand or conserving energy. By midyear, the administration's mandatory fuel allocation program had led to the closure of hundreds of independent gasoline stations. Then the administration shifted its policies once again by proposing that $100 million be spent on research and development for new energy technology and creation of a Federal Energy Administration to coordinate policy.

In October 1973, OPEC members, resentful of U.S. aid to Israel, voted to cut their oil production and to end all petroleum exports to the United States, resulting in a sharp increase in world oil prices and forcing the Nixon administration to drastically revise its approach. Nixon responded with Project Independence to eliminate foreign oil imports by 1980, and Congress enacted the Emergency Petroleum Allocation Act to distribute fuel supplies evenly.

Analyses of the politics of energy during this period point out several lessons

learned from the 1973 crisis. For example, a "cry-wolf syndrome" arose when the first warnings appeared about dependence on foreign oil. One survey had even found that most Americans were unaware that the United States imported any oil and were unable to understand how the most technically advanced nation in the world was simply unable to produce enough oil to meet demand. As a result, the

concerns were often ignored or disbelieved. Decisions were often based on misleading or poor-quality information, and confused and often contradictory policies resulted. A turnover in leadership (four different people held the position of White House energy policy coordinator in 1973) exacerbated the problem. From 1971 to 1973, the role of "energy czar" passed through the hands of seven men, each of whom had a different concept of what U.S. energy policy should be. Some, such as Secretary of Agriculture Earl Butz, were given new titles and responsibilities; others, such as George Lincoln, were made heads of agencies that were then abruptly abolished (Office of Emergency Planning).[33] Last, by treating each fuel source separately and allowing the disparate interest groups to be so deeply involved in the decision-making process, the government never really took control of the crisis.

Public opinion about energy policy has changed over time in response to fuel supplies and the state of the economy. Support for more oil and coal production peaked at the height of the second energy crisis in 1980, according to one study.

When gasoline prices soared, support for off-shore drilling and strip-mined coal became popular. As the economy improves, however, the public takes a more pro-environmental stance. After the Three Mile Island incident, support for nuclear power dropped dramatically; although ironically, the same trend did not hold true for the 1986 accident at the Chernobyl nuclear facility.[34] Although Greenpeace has chronicled a substantive list of nuclear accidents and events at facilities around the world since World War II, only a handful have been widely publicized. As a result, most consumers in the United States believe that with minor exceptions, nuclear power production has been safe.

As a result of the 1973 oil crisis, a host of agencies took turns formulating energy policy. The Federal Energy Administration was created in May 1974, but the agency lacked both direction and a clear sense of mission. It was designed to bring together smaller agencies that had historically been in conflict with one another and was caught between the competing objectives of regulating prices and expediting domestic resource development. After Nixon's resignation, Congress attempted to pick up the pieces by enacting the Energy Policy and Conservation Act of 1975, which levied a windfall profits tax on oil to control imports and gave the president the power to ration gas in an emergency. Other provisions included appliance standards, improved fuel efficiency standards, and authorized petroleum stockpiling.

The politics of energy took a different turn during President Jimmy Carter's administration. The creation of a separate, cabinet-level Department of Energy in 1977 underscored the nation's crisis mentality and reflected Carter's campaign promise to reorganize government. The agency was charged with regulating fuel consumption, providing incentives for energy conservation, and conducting research and development into alternative energy sources. In 1977 an acute natural gas shortage led Carter to propose his National Energy Plan (NEP), and he characterized the energy situation as "the moral equivalent of war." The NEP differed from the Nixon administration's strategies because it called for greater fuel efficiency and conservation rather than increased production. In 1977 Congress also replaced the Federal Power Commission, which had been created in 1920, with the Federal Energy Regulatory Commission (FERC), giving the agency responsibility for oversight of the electric power and natural gas industries.

By the time Congress passed the National Energy Act in October 1978, Carter's NEP had been gutted. In retrospect, it has been argued that the Carter proposal was doomed from the beginning. Members of Congress found that their constituents were unwilling to make sacrifices (like reducing the number of miles they drove yearly) because they didn't think there really was an energy shortage. Voters made it clear that they believed the entire energy crisis was concocted by the big oil companies to force prices upward and generate bigger profits. In addition, the Carter administration was guilty of taking its case directly to the people, rather than developing a program in consultation with Congress.

The Reagan administration, in contrast, marks an eight-year period of amicable cooperation between the petroleum and coal industries and the administration and a dramatic shift in energy research and development.[35] Reagan's strategy, outlined in his 1981 National Energy Plan, was to limit governmental intervention as much as possible—especially with regard to regulatory agencies—while supporting nuclear power and cutting research funds for alternative energy sources. Renouncing the Carter administration's goal of meeting 20 percent of the nation's energy needs through solar power by the year 2000, Reagan even had his staff remove the solar panels Carter had installed at the White House. Reagan was unsuccessful in dissolving the Department of Energy, which he viewed as indicative of Carter's "big government" approach. Federal subsidies for alternative energy sources like wind power were eliminated by the mid-1980s, further reducing industry incentives. The Reagan presidency was marked by a return to the strategies of the 1960s—including reliance on the free market to control prices, dependence on fossil fuels, tax benefits for oil producers, and little support for conservation.

George H. W. Bush continued the policies initiated by his predecessor. His 1991 national energy strategy sought to achieve roughly equal measures of new energy production and conservation. A cornerstone of that policy was to open up 1.5 million acres of the 19-million-acre Arctic National Wildlife Refuge in northeast Alaska for oil and gas exploration. After the Persian Gulf War in 1991, Congress seemed more inclined to move forward on energy policy, finally enacting the comprehensive Energy Policy Act of 1992 just prior to the November election. The new law allowed restructuring of the electric utility industry to promote more competition, provide tax relief to independent oil and gas drillers, encourage energy conservation and efficiency, promote renewable energy and cars that run on alternative fuels, make it easier to build nuclear power plants, authorize billions of dollars for energy-related research and development, and create a climate protection office within the Energy Department. Critics point out that the bill did not address the issue of automobile fuel efficiency (one of the planks in Bill Clinton's environmental platform), and did not significantly reduce U.S. dependence on foreign oil, but rather capped existing levels of use. Still, it marked the first time in a decade that Congress was able to compromise on the most contentious provisions—those dealing with alternative fuels and energy-related tax provisions.[36]

Early in his presidency, Bill Clinton proposed a broad tax on all forms of energy in order to raise federal revenue to reduce the budget deficit. The proposed tax—called a BTU tax because it was based on the heating ability of different fuels as measured in British thermal units—would have raised the prices of gasoline, electricity, and other energy sources. Environmental groups supported the measure as a way to promote conservation and to begin moving away from fossil fuel consumption. The tax would have raised approximately $22 billion per year, only a tiny fraction of the $6 trillion U.S. economy, but opposition from Democratic and Republican senators representing energy-producing states killed the idea.[37] The administration was successful in raising gasoline taxes by 4.3 cents per gallon in 1993, however, as part of its deficit reduction plan. During the summer of the 1996 campaign, when gas prices jumped 17 percent, Republican candidate Bob Dole called for a repeal of the gas tax, and President Clinton called for an investigation of the oil companies and ordered the release of 12 million barrels of oil from the nation's Strategic Oil Reserve to soften the price increase.[38] Increasing energy taxes sufficiently for significant conservation or revenue purposes requires more political skill than recent presidents and their congressional allies have been able to muster.

Clinton's record on energy policy did improve in 1998 when he announced a 12-year extension of the federal ban on new oil and gas drilling off the East and West Coasts. The drilling moratorium had been imposed by President Bush in 1990 and was scheduled to expire in 2000. Although environmental organizations had hoped the president would make the federal ban permanent, the extension until 2012 was considered a reasonable compromise between environmental protection and the interests of oil and gas firms, which had argued that improved technology is making drilling safer.

The president extended the drilling moratorium (which is permanent in marine sanctuaries) by executive order in June 1998. Two months later, California Senator Barbara Boxer urged Interior Secretary Bruce Babbitt to ban drilling on 40 existing, yet undeveloped, leases off the coast of California.[39] The leases, owned by several different oil companies, were not made a part of Clinton's drilling moratorium and include portions of the Santa Maria Basin, termed "the Saudi Arabia of California." The area is a vast reservoir of more than 500 million barrels of petroleum and still undetermined billions of cubic feet of natural gas. To lease owners, the oil and gas resources could mean a reduction of the nation's dependence on imported oil. Any interference in their legal right to develop the leases would constitute an illegal taking, although some observers believe that some kind of plan could be arranged to compensate the oil companies for the billions of dollars already spent on buying up leases. To environmental groups like the League for Coastal Protection and the Environmental Defense Center in San Luis Obispo, California, a potential leak not only poses environmental hazards, it also threatens the region's economy, which is largely dependent on tourism. But as one representative of the Western States Petroleum Association (the region's main oil industry trade group) put it, "There are a lot of [oil] resources off this coast. When it comes down to it, it's hard for me to believe that the Congress and the secretary of the interior are willing to walk away from them."[40]

Those factors were of key importance to incoming President George W. Bush, who issued his plan for a national energy policy in May 2001, appointing Spencer Abraham as his secretary of energy. As part of his proposal, Bush sought to increase supplies of oil and gas by opening up drilling in the Arctic National Wildlife Refuge. The president has made reducing the United States' dependence upon foreign oil his top domestic priority, even though attempts to open up exploration within the refuge had been tried unsuccessfully for decades. Geologists believe the refuge has the largest untapped reserve of oil in the country. Environmental groups criticized the plan, and even as war with Iraq threatened oil supplies and prices at the pump rose significantly, Congress refused to approve the president's drilling proposal.

The Bush administration also looked to other domestic sources of fossil fuel—five basins along the Rocky Mountains, which the industry refers to as a "Persian Gulf of natural gas."[41] The U.S. Geological Survey estimated that 137 trillion cubic feet of natural gas and several billion barrels of oil could lie within the region, centered around Colorado, Montana, New Mexico, Utah, and Wyoming. Although the federal government owns some of the area and drilling rights beneath some private lands, the patchwork system of ownership and conflicting laws over land use have led to confusion and fragmentation, making a comprehensive drilling plan difficult. The administration established a task force in May 2001 to speed decisions on drilling permits because industry officials complained that red tape and rigid legal interpretations are strangling domestic energy production. "We're hoping," said the chair of the Independent Petroleum Association of America, "that the seemingly endless reviews come to a conclusion."[42]

Attempts to move the administration's energy proposals forward were thwarted in part to allegations surrounding vice president Dick Cheney and the National Energy Policy Development Group. Cheney convened the group, also called the energy task force, to develop an assessment of the nation's energy needs and to make recommendations to the president. The members, government officials with extensive experience within the energy industry, met for three months in closed-door sessions before releasing its report in May 2001. As one critic noted, "The report was an orgy of industry plunder, recommending the transfer of billions of dollars of public wealth to the oil, coal, and nuclear industries. Paying lip service to conservation and environmental concerns, the report focused almost exclusively on deregulation, giant subsidies, and tax breaks for every major corporate polluter in the energy field."[43]

The issue became supercharged when the task force refused to make its records public. The General Accounting Office unsuccessfully filed suit in federal district court; the U.S. Supreme Court ruled against the Sierra Club and the organization Judicial Watch in 2004. In a May 2005 unanimous decision, the U.S. Court of Appeals for the District of Columbia ruled against the two groups again, supporting the Bush administration's contention that Cheney was free to meet with energy industry lobbyists in 2001 when the national energy policy task force was meeting. The justices noted that the Open Meetings Act was not applicable to the case, because two White House officials had testified that industry members offered opinions only at advisory meetings and did not have a vote during the internal deliberations of the task force. The court noted that the smaller stakeholder meetings were forums to collect individual views, rather than to bring a collective judgment to bear. Another suit, filed under the Freedom of Information Act by the Natural Resources Defense Council, resulted in the organization eventually gaining access to about 20,000 documents; but no logs from the vice president's meetings were included.

Environmental organizations charged that the task force proposals were a form of payback for corporate leaders who had contributed to the president's reelection campaign. Others referred to "corporate cronyism" because the task force members had conflicts of interest with the decisions being made about companies they had represented or worked for. Senate democrats were able to block the task force's 105 proposals in legislative form; but the administration countered by moving them to the regulatory arena, where they did not require congressional approval. Several Clinton-era regulations were eliminated, and Clean Air Act provisions were substantially weakened. Although the incident may have been a minor public relations nightmare for the president, the end result was that most of the task force recommendations were implemented. The court rulings appear to have brought an end to litigation regarding Cheney's group.

In December 2004, Bush announced the appointment of Sam Bodman as his new secretary of energy to replace Spencer Abraham. Bodman, who had previously served in the administration as Deputy Secretary of Commerce and Deputy Secretary of the Treasury, has a background in chemical engineering and taught at the Massachusetts Institute of Technology prior to working with an investment company and as chair of a global industrial company. In accepting the president's nomination, Bodman said he would build on Abraham's record and carry forward Bush's "vision of sound energy policy to ensure a steady supply of affordable energy for America's homes and businesses, and to work toward the day when America achieves energy independence." Bush noted, "In academics, in business and in government Sam Bodman has been a problem solver who knows how to set goals and he knows how to reach them."[44]

President Bush's proposals in 2005 differed substantially from how the public viewed the energy debate. Polls showed that Americans preferred energy con-servation to increased production of domestic energy supplies, with 56 percent opposing the president's plans to open up exploration and drilling for oil in the Arctic National Wildlife Refuge. Despite their opposition to specific policies, however, three out of five Americans said they expected Bush to do a good job in improving the nation's energy policies.[45]

In March 2005, President Bush traveled to Columbus, Ohio, where he called upon Congress to pass an energy bill that would meet four major objectives: promote conservation and efficiency, increase domestic production, diversify the nation's energy supply, and modernize the energy infrastructure while upholding the responsibility to be good stewards of the environment.[46] The proposal was not new, but rather a reiteration of the president's call for a comprehensive energy bill that had been announced when he first came into office. Bush may have perceived that the policy window was opening during his second term in a way that it had not been in 2001. With larger partisan majorities in the House and the Senate resulting from the 2004 elections, uncertainty over oil supplies in the Middle East, and historic highs in the cost of crude oil, the political environment certainly was more promising than in previous years.

Just a few days after the president announced that passage of his energy package would be a top priority, the country came one step closer to approving drilling in ANWR when the Senate, which had traditionally been a dead end for ANWR bills, voted 51–49 to put an ANWR drilling proposal in the federal budget. The vote indicated sufficient support for the Bush administration to move its proposals forward; seven moderate Republicans joined the Democrats in voting against opening up ANWR to drilling; three Democratic senators voted with the majority. Rather than including ANWR as a separate piece of legislation, making it part of the federal budget reconciliation process was considered an "end run" by some senators. Others supported the vote as the only way they could avoid a filibuster in the Senate.[47] Sen. Pete Dominici, chairman of the Senate Energy and Natural Resources Committee, commented, "I think we will one day look back in bewilderment at the doomsday predictions and wonder why we had so little faith in ourselves for so long."[48] Sen. Maria Cantwell (D-WA), leader of the opposition to the inclusion of the provision in the budget, noted, "We won't see this oil for ten years. It will have minimal impact. It is foolish to say oil development and a wildlife refuge can co-exist."[49] The Senate vote did not mean that oil companies would scramble to set up drilling platforms, however. The House had not included the Arctic refuge measure in its budget, so the issue would have to be negotiated between the two bodies.

At the same time the ANWR debate was under way, the chair of the House Resources Committee, Rep. Richard Pombo (R-CA), was using what environmental activists called a "stealth strategy" to overturn a quarter century of bans against offshore oil and gas drilling. Draft legislation for the State Enhanced Authority for Coastal and Offshore Resources Act of 2005, or SEACOR, would eliminate the drilling moratoriums established by Congress in 1982. Although Pombo's staff called SEACOR "one of a number of policy concepts that originated in the House Resources Committee," that was "not ready for prime time," a marine conservation advocate with Environmental Defense feared it would be added onto an omnibus energy bill at the last minute without public scrutiny.[50]

Does the resurrection of ANWR and coastal oil drilling proposals indicate changes in policy direction under Bush, or some other driver? Some researchers believe that each episode of short supply and higher energy prices contributes to the perception that the nation lacks an energy policy, and that we have failed to learn from past lessons. One study notes, however, that in the three decades since the 1973 Arab oil embargo, the period has been one of general price and supply stability that is generally broken with shorter episodes when price became more volatile and supplies of fuel less certain.

It isn't that energy policy has failed to be responsive to crises; rather, it is hard in the face of lengthy periods of stability and declining prices for conventional fuels to sustain certain policy courses that shield the nation from the occasional episodes of instability.[51]

Thinking Globally

Energy is considered to be a global issue, for a number of reasons. It transcends the traditional boundaries of the nation-state and cannot be resolved by a single country. It is an issue that possesses a present imperative that forces nations to press for resolution. For example, oil is a finite commodity; thus, it is crucial that alternative energy sources be found. The resolution of energy scarcity requires policy action—it will not resolve itself. Finally, energy is a global issue because of its persistence on the policy agenda—there is no consensus on how to solve the problems of supply and demand that have been identified.

Energy consumption is closely tied to economic development. Throughout the 1990s, forecasters believed that as we entered the next century, in addition to increasing demand, there would be a changing profile of fuel use. But many factors determine the world's demand for energy, and expectations for economic growth and energy market performance in many areas of the world are changing dramatically.

Another factor that influences forecasts for global energy consumption is the signing of the Kyoto Protocol of the Framework Convention on Climate Change, described more fully in Chapter 10. Russia became the final signatory to bring the treaty into force in 2004, despite U.S. refusal to ratify the agreement. It is unclear how much Kyoto will alter energy production and consumption patterns, however, without U.S. support.

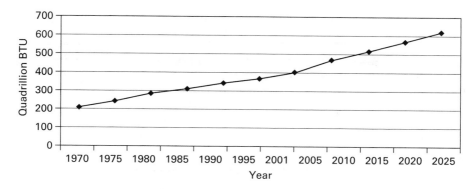

FIGURE 6.3 World Marketed Energy Consumption, 1970–2025

SOURCE: Energy Information Administration, U.S. Department of Energy, International Energy Outlook 2004, at www.eia.doe.gov/oiaf/ieo, accessed January 18, 2005.

In its long-term International Energy Outlook 2004, the U.S. Energy Information Administration (EIA) predicted that world energy consumption is projected to increase by 54 percent from 2001 to 2025, as seen in Figure 6.3.

The strongest growth in energy consumption is expected to be in the developing countries, especially in China and India where there has been strong economic growth. In the developing world as a whole, energy consumption is expected to grow at an annual rate of 2.7 percent; energy consumption in industrialized countries, in contrast, is expected to grow at a rate of 1.2 percent per year over the same period. The transitional economies of the former Soviet Union and in Eastern Europe are expected to create an increase in energy demand of 1.5 percent per year.[52]

The world energy pie is likely to continue reflecting the focus on oil as the dominant energy fuel, with its share remaining at 39 percent through 2025. Natural gas is projected to be the fastest growing primary energy source worldwide; average growth is currently 2.2 percent, and its share of the pie should increase from 18 percent in 2001 to 25 percent in 2025. Hydropower and other renewable energy sources are projected to grow by 1.9 percent annually while maintaining their market share at 8 percent.

Of particular concern to policy makers is the increasing use of coal in China and India, with small decreases in Western and Eastern Europe due to increased reliance upon natural gas. Coal emission increases may have substantial air quality impacts in Asia as the rest of the world moves to cleaner sources of power. World carbon dioxide emissions are forecast to grow by nearly 2 percent each year, for a projected 72 percent increase over 1990 levels by 2025. By then, carbon dioxide emissions in the developing world (including China and India) are expected to surpass those of industrialized countries, largely because of their reliance on coal, the most carbon-intensive of fossil fuels.[53]

Another energy issue that continues on the policy agenda is nuclear power. Although world nuclear power capacity is expected to rise by 4.1 percent per year, primarily in China, South Korea and India, industrialized countries are more likely to extend licenses for existing nuclear facilities rather than building new ones.[54]

Nuclear power remains an important segment of the energy pie in the countries of the former Soviet Union, as seen in Table 6.3, with Lithuania depending upon nuclear power plants for over 80 percent of its electricity supply. Older nuclear plants in the former Soviet republics pose unique energy production problems. With the collapse of the Soviet regime and the accessibility of formerly classified information, researchers are learning about flaws and previously unreported incidents at several nuclear facilities. Observers point to the lack of replacement parts for reactors, an aging infrastructure, insufficient security, and limited employee training as evidence that some states cannot operate existing facilities effectively.[55]

TABLE 6.3 World Nuclear Power Reactors and Production by Country, 2003

Country	No. of Units*	Electricity from Nuclear Power	Rank
Argentina	3	7.23	23
Armenia	1	40.54	9
Belgium	7	57.32	3
Brazil	2	3.99	26
Bulgaria	4	47.30	5
Canada	14	12.32	21
China	11	1.43	29
Czech Republic	6	24.54	17
DPR Korea	1	0	N/A
Finland	4	29.81	15
France	59	77.97	2
Germany	19	29.85	14
Hungary	4	36.14	12
India	21	3.68	27
Iran	2	0	N/A
Japan	57	34.47	13
Korea RP	20	38.62	11
Lithuania	2	80.12	1
Mexico	2	4.07	24
Netherlands	1	4.00	25
Pakistan	2	2.54	28
Romania	2	10.33	22
Russia	33	15.98	20
South Africa	2	5.87	24
Slovakia	8	54.73	4
Slovenia	1	40.74	8
Spain	9	25.76	16
Sweden	11	45.75	6
Switzerland	5	39.53	10
United Kingdom	31	22.42	18
Ukraine	17	45.66	7
United States	104	20.34	19

*Includes reactors in operation and under construction

SOURCE: Compiled with data from the International Atomic Energy Agency at www.iaea.org, accessed March 20, 2005.

Although developing countries appear to recognize the inevitable demand for more energy capacity as their economies and population grow (especially electricity for residential use), the source of new power remains controversial. Global opposition is growing for new energy production from hydropower, due to the impact of megaprojects like the huge dams being built in China and India. There are an estimated 45,000 large dams in the world, and most of them were constructed during the 1970s. Half of the world's dams are in China and India, many of them previously financed by the World Bank. Facing opposition from environmental groups and concerns about costs and benefits, the Bank did not provide funding for China's controversial $25 billion Three Gorges Dam, the largest hydroelectric project in history. When it is completed in 2009, the dam will span 1.3 miles of the Yangtze River, create a 400-mile-long reservoir, and generate about 10 percent of the country's energy. But in the process, the dam will also inundate 19 cities and 326 villages, forcing the relocation of nearly 2 million people.[56]

One final global strategy to meet the world's energy needs is the so-called conservation alternative—a dramatic change in consumption patterns worldwide. Proponents believe that we must all go on an "energy diet," and that rather than looking for new sources of power, we should be conserving what is available and getting more out of it. Thus far, however, whereas there has been support for conservation as a key element of future energy planning, international rhetoric has failed to result in any substantial changes—evidence of the kind of institutional immobilism characterizing the stage in the policy process when governments fail to see a "problem" that requires them to take action. In the case of energy, most Americans do not have a sense that anything is "wrong." As population growth in the industrialized world has slowed, the demand for energy is also slowly reducing, due in part to technological advances. Still, industrialized countries account for one half of all energy consumption in the industrial sector worldwide, with the United States using one half that amount.

Policy analysts note that this is the kind of situation in which policy makers seldom are willing to move forward. The conditions associated with energy use have not produced sufficient anxiety, discontent, or dissatisfaction that would cause the public to seek a remedy. In order for this to happen, people would have to have some criterion or standard by which the troubling condition is judged to be not only unreasonable or unacceptable but also appropriate for government to handle. The world's primary consumers of energy simply do not sense that a problem exists; they continue to purchase fuel-guzzling vehicles and increase their residential use of power at a rate that signals complacency and inattentiveness rather than awareness of a global environmental problem.

NOTES

1. The White House. "President Discusses Energy at National Small Business Conference," Transcript of speech, April 27, 2005, at www.whitehouse.gov/news/releases, accessed April 28, 2005.

2. Ibid.

3. Ian W.H. Parry and J.W. Anderson, "Petroleum: Energy Independence Is Unrealistic," *Resources, 156* (Winter 2005), 12.

4. William A. Pizer, "Setting Energy Policy in the Modern Era," *Resources, 156* (Winter 2005), 9.

5. Deb Riechmann, "Bush Urges Energy Bill Passage Before Break," *Arizona Republic,* April 21, 2005, A-8.

6. Parry and Anderson, "Petroleum," 12.

7. Ibid., 11.

8. Energy Information Agency, U.S. Department of Energy, *International Energy Outlook 2004,* at www.eia.doe.gov/oiaf/ieo, accessed January 18, 2005.

9. Edward Teller, *Energy from Heaven and Earth* (San Francisco: Freeman, 1979), 2.

10. There are numerous accounts of the development of American energy resources. See, for example, Robert J. Kalter and William A. Vogely, eds., *Energy Supply and Government Policy* (Ithaca, NY: Cornell University Press, 1976); Daniel Yergin, *The Prize: The Epic Quest for Oil, Money, and Power* (New York: Simon and Schuster, 1991); Richard Rudolph and Scott Ridley, *Power Struggle: The Hundred-Year War over Electricity* (New York: Harper and Row, 1986); and Walter Rosenbaum, *Energy Politics and Public Policy,* 2nd ed. (Washington, DC: Congressional Quarterly Press, 1987).

11. Laura Paskus, "The Winds of Change," *High Country News, 37,* no. 8 (May 2, 2005), 13.

12. Robert L. Bamberger, *Energy Policy: Setting the Stage for the Current Debate* (Washington, D.C.: Congressional Research Service, May 7, 2002), 3–4.

13. Richard G. Newall, "The Hydrogen Economy," *Resources, 156* (Winter 2005), 23.

14. Department of the Interior, Bureau of Land Management, "New Policy Encourages Solar Energy's Development on America's Public Lands," News, October 21, 2004, at www.blm.gov/nhp/news, accessed October 21, 2004.

15. Bruce C. Driver and Gregg Eisenberg, *Western Hydropower: Changing Values/New Visions* (Boulder, CO: Western Water Policy Review Advisory Commission, August 1997), 15.

16. Max Jarman, "'Other' Energy May Get Push," *Arizona Republic,* March 18, 2005, D-1.

17. Solar Electric Power Association, "San Francisco CA, USA: Solar Energy Systems Planned for 1,600 Housing Unit Development," September 6, 2004, at www.solarelectricpower.org, accessed January 18, 2005.

18. Solar Electric Power Association, "Los Angeles, CA, USA: Los Angeles Department of Water and Power to Reinstate Solar Program," September 9, 2004, at www.solarelectricpower.org, accessed January 18, 2005.

19. Jim Motavalli, "Catching the Wind," *E Magazine,* January–February 2005, at www. emagazine.com, accessed January 16, 2005.

20. Ibid.

21. Doug Abrahms, "Wind Power Set to Soar," *Arizona Republic,* January 5, 2005, D-1.

22. Ibid.

23. Joe Kafka. "Huge Wind Farm Planned for South Dakota," *Rapid City Journal,* October 10, 2004, at www.rapidcityjournal.com, accessed October 16, 2004. See also "South Dakota Wind Resources," accessed at www.eere.energy.gov, October 16, 2004.

24. "U.S. Agencies Sued on Alternative Fuel Rule," *San Francisco Chronicle,* January 3, 2002, A-3.

25. For perspectives on what happened at WPPSS and Shoreham, see Howard Gleckman, *WPSS: From Dream to Default* (New York: The Bond Buyer, 1983); and Karl Grossman, *Power Crazy* (New York: Grove Press, 1986).

26. Taylor Moore and John Carey, "License Renewal Revitalizes the Nuclear Industry," *EPRI Journal, 25,* no. 3 (Fall 2000), 8.

27. Matthew L. Wald, "Power Producers Seek Latest Models of Nuclear Reactors," *New York Times,* March 15, 2005, at www.nytimes.com, accessed March 15, 2005.

28. Paul R. Portnoy, "Penny-Wise and Pound Fuelish? New Car Mileage Standards in the United States," *Resources, 147* (Spring 2002), 11.

29. Bob Golfen, "Clean Cars Among the Gas-Fueled," *Arizona Republic,* December 11, 2004, B-3.

30. American Council for an Energy-Efficient Economy, "Green Light, Red Light: Model Year 2004's 'Greenest' and 'Meanest' Vehicles Announced," news release, February 10, 2004, at www.greenercars.com, accessed December 28, 2004.

31. Portnoy, "Penny-Wise and Pound Fuelish?" 15.

32. James Everett Katz, *Congress and National Energy Policy* (New Brunswick, NJ: Transaction Books, 1984), 5–7.

33. See John C. Whitaker, *Striking a Balance: Environmental and Natural Resources Policy in the Nixon-Ford Years* (Washington, DC: American Enterprise Institute, 1976), 66–68.

34. Eric R. A. N. Smith, *Energy, The Environment, and Public Opinion* (Lanham, MD: Rowman & Littlefield, 2002, 87–90.

35. See Claude E. Barfield, *Science Policy from Ford to Reagan: Change and Continuity* (Washington, DC: American Enterprise Institute, 1982); and Don E. Kash and Robert W. Rycroft, *U.S. Energy Policy: Crisis and Complacency* (Norman: University of Oklahoma Press, 1984).

36. Holly Idelson, "National Energy Strategy Provisions," *Congressional Quarterly,* November 28, 1992, 3722–3730.

37. Susan Dentzer, "RIP for the BTU Tax," *U.S. News and World Report,* June 21, 1993, 95.

38. Howard Gleckman, "Gas Pump Politics," *Business Week,* May 13, 1996, 40–41.

39. Marc Sandalow, "Boxer Calls for Total Ban on New Offshore Oil Drilling," *San Francisco Chronicle,* August 1, 1998, A-1.

40. "Offshore Oil Rigs: More in California's Future?" *San Francisco Chronicle,* August 9, 1998, A-1.

41. Mike Soraghan, "Battles Over Drilling Shifting to Rockies," *Denver Post,* at www.denverpost.com/cda, accessed April 23, 2002.

42. Dan Morgan and Ellen Nakashima, "Search for Oil Targets Rockies," *Washington Post,* April 18, 2002, A-1. See also Ray Ring, "Local Governments Tackle an In-Your-Face Rush on Coalbed Methane," *High Country News,* September 2, 2002, 1.

43. Robert F. Kennedy Jr., "Dick Cheney's Energy Crisis," *Sierra* (October–November 2004), 46.

44. H. Josef Herbert, " 'Problem Solver' Bodman Chosen as Energy Secretary," *Arizona Republic,* December 11, 2004; The White House. "President Nominates Sam Bodman as Secretary of Energy," News release, December 10, 2004, at www.whitehouse.gov/news, accessed December 11, 2004.

45. Lydia Saad, "Americans Mostly 'Green' in the Energy vs. Environment Debate," *Gallup Poll Monthly,* No. 426 (March 2001), 33–34.

46. White House, "Securing Our Nation's Energy Future," Fact sheet, March 9, 2005, at www.whitehouse.gov, accessed March 11, 2005.

47. H. Joseph Hebert, "Senate Backs Drilling in Alaskan Refuge," *Arizona Republic,* March 17, 2005, A-10.

48. Arctic Power, "ANWR: One Step Closer to Reality," March 16, 2005, at www.anwr.org, accessed March 17, 2005.

49. Herbert, "Senate Backs Drilling."

50. Jane Kay, "Quiet Talk of Drilling Offshore," *San Francisco Chronicle,* March 10, 2005, at www.sfgate.com, accessed March 10, 2005.

51. Bamberger, *Energy Policy,* 4.

52. Energy Information Administration, *International Energy Outlook 2004,* at www.eia.doe.gov/oiaf/ieo, accessed January 18, 2005.

53. Ibid.

54. Ibid.

55. See Judith Thornton and Charles E. Ziegler, eds., *Russia's Far East: A Region at Risk* (Seattle: University of Washington Press, 2002); Paul R. Josephson, *Red Atom: Russia's Nuclear Power Program from Stalin to Today* (New York: Freeman, 2000).

56. Ian Phillips, "World's Dams Damaging Environment, Report Says," *Arizona Republic,* November 17, 2000, A-4; "The Great Dam of China," *Mother Jones,* May–June 2002, 74.

FURTHER READING

Rick Bass. *Caribou Rising.* San Francisco: Sierra Club Books, 2004.

Julian Darley. *High Noon for Natural Gas: The New Energy Crisis.* White River Junction, VT: Chelsea Green, 2005.

Richard Heinberg. *Powerdown: Options and Actions for a Post-Carbon World.* Gabriola Island, BC: Consortium Press, 2005.

Karl Mallon. *Renewable Energy Policy and Politics: A Handbook for Decisionmakers.* London: Earthscan Publications, 2005.

Richard D. Morgenstern and Paul R. Portney, eds. *New Approaches on Energy and the Environment: Policy Advice for the President.* Washington, DC: Resources for the Future Press, 2005.

Robert W. Righter. *Hetch Hetchy: San Francisco, Yosemite, and the Politics of Water and Power.* New York: Oxford University Press, 2005.

Vaclav Smil. *Energy at the Crossroads: Global Perspectives and Uncertainties.* Cambridge, MA: MIT Press, 2004.

J. Samuel Walker. *Three Mile Island: A Nuclear Crisis in Historical Perspective.* Berkeley: University of California Press, 2004.

Matthew Yeomans. *Oil: Anatomy of an Industry.* New York: The New Press, 2004.

The Politics of Water

> We view water as the lifeblood of our communities because water
> brings us together as a community and water is essential to the
> continued survival of our way of life.
> —NEW MEXICO ACEQUIA ASSOCIATION[1]

From our earliest recorded history, humanity has congregated around sources of water—rivers, lakes, springs, and streams—and where those sources meet. The Romans were among the first to engineer a way of tapping into water and channeling it to where it was needed, building the Aqua Appia, or aqueduct, throughout the city. Similar systems, some of which were designed for agricultural use, were developed in Egypt and in Peru; many aqueducts date back thousands of years.

In the American Southwest, especially in the Rio Grande region, water control systems date back to the Anasazi culture, the ancestors of the Pueblo Indians; and to the Tewa, Tiwa, and Keresan tribes. When Spanish conquistadores arrived, they noted the resemblance of the ditches built for water diversion in what is now New Mexico to the canals used for irrigation in Spain, built by the Moors. Land-grant concessions used to encourage immigration to the Spanish colonies were accompanied by the construction of dams, reservoirs, and aqueducts, called *acequia* (from the Arabic word *as-saquiya*). The colonists were not allowed to build anywhere they wanted; local officials such as the governor and *alcalde mayor* (chief judge) made recommendations on the granting of water rights to the new *pobladores* (settlers). In a region that experienced less than 15 inches of annual rainfall, the building and maintenance of the acequias was essential to the survival of the entire community.[2]

> *Volunteers continue the tradition of cleaning out the* acequia, *part of the water distribution heritage of communities throughout New Mexico.*
>
> ANITA LAVADIE

Access to irrigation water is governed by laws with roots in Spanish legal principles—the fair and equitable delivery of irrigation water to the *parciantes* (stakeholders, or users). Most of the regulations and principles were not codified until the mid-19th century, and an entire acequia culture has developed as a result of conflicts over water rights jurisdiction and adjudication. There is a nearly universal rule of common property regimes that requires each property owner to contribute to the maintenance of the system in direct proportion to the benefits received. The ancient *alcaldes de aquas* (Spanish water managers) are now known locally in New Mexico as *mayordomos;* community acequia associations belong to a statewide organization and participate in a Congreso de las Acequias to draft recommendations on water policy.[3]

Today, the cleaning and care of the acequia *madre,* or mother ditch, is not only a tradition, but part of an intricate system defining water rights and laws. The annual spring cleaning of the acequias brings community members together, with the mayordomo assigning work teams who burn and cut weeds, repair the banks of the acequia, or open silted channels so that water will flow freely prior to planting. One researcher believes that the acequia associations, and the degree to which they maintain their solidarity, is at the heart of determining whether water is a public good that can be bought and sold in the market, or part of the collective rights of a community.[4]

The public good concept, similar to the metaphor of a commons as discussed in Chapter 10, is an excellent starting point for understanding how water policy flows from both local and global problems. Management of water resources involves two major issues: the availability of water and its quality. Water scarcity and water pollution are global issues that have become increasingly politicized worldwide. The basic issue is that while the world's population tripled in the 20th century, demand for water increased sixfold. About 0.025 percent of the world's water supply is easily and economically available for human use—the rest is "locked up" in oceans, polar ice caps, and surface collectors such as lakes and rivers; in clouds; or under the earth's surface, yet too deep to be drilled in wells.

Even when water is available, it is often contaminated and unfit for human use. The debate over how best to improve water quality focuses on two issues: first, the pollution of surface waters (rivers, streams, lakes, wetlands, and even drainage ditches), largely from discharges directly into waterways; and second, the pollution of groundwater, which flows beneath the earth's surface and serves as a primary source of drinking water.

This chapter examines water resource supply and management both in the United States and internationally. The first half of the chapter briefly reviews water use trends; the second half focuses on water pollution and an analysis of how politics have affected water quality, especially in preserving wetlands. The chapter concludes with a review of the political factors that have led to a water policy stalemate in both developing and industrialized nations.

Another View, Another Voice

The Kugeria Women's Water Project

In the Kirinyaga District, about 70 miles north of Nairobi, Kenya, women have traditionally walked three or four miles from their homes to collect water. Sometimes, when local supplies were scarce, they purchased what they could from water sellers at inflated prices. Because of drought and lack of a reliable source, agriculture was impossible. The local groundwater was a source of disease transmission, and the nearest surface water, the River Kiye, is 11 kilometers away. In 1986, a group of men from the area started the Teithia Self Help Project to bring water to the community, but it failed due to mismanagement. Women were excluded from the effort; most do not have access to education and play no role in community affairs.

Frustrated with the men's failures, the Kugeria Water Project, formed in July 1990, brought together 120 women whose primary purpose is to bring water to the 3,000 residents in the area. They formed a water users association (WUA), a democratic-style scheme to build capacity and address ownership issues. Kugeria means "to try" in the local Kikuyu language, and the women faced enormous obstacles, both technical and cultural. Initially, each member contributed the equivalent of about two cents each to cover registration, communication, and record-keeping costs. Later, they contributed another $1.20 to meet the costs of surveying the water intake point on the river to the distribution point 16 kilometers away.

In 1991, the women sought funding from the Africa 2000 Network (an initiative set up by the United Nations Development Programme) and technical assistance from Kenya's Ministry of Water Development. They visited other villages on exchange programs to see how other Kenyan women were developing their own water projects and to share experiences. The Network provided about $60,000 in supplies while the women provided unskilled labor, including digging about 11 kilometers of trenches from the river to Murinduko Village.

Today, the project is privately run, financially solvent, and serves 300 families. Water meters are connected to consumer lines to each member's home, and the costs are paid for based on consumption. The funds are used to maintain and expand the project. A visitor notes that one reason for the success of the project is that the women developed effective water usage regulations and rigorously maintain them. If someone breaks a regulation, all of which are known by the participants, there are swift consequences.

In addition to learning the skills necessary to run a water system, the Kugeria Women's Water Project has changed the lives of women in the area. Few women own property (in some countries in Africa they are prohibited from doing so), and in the past they had no power in the decisions made about natural resources. There is now a sufficient supply of water for irrigating a small agricultural operation. Sanitation has improved, and there has been a drastic reduction in waterborne diseases. Women who previously walked long distances to collect water now spend that time working on plots growing vegetables for family consumption in the spaces between managed cash crops. During times of drought, there is less dependence upon handouts.

Women have become community leaders, and they have sought additional services for the region, including the building of a medical clinic and family planning services through the assistance of the German Foundation for World Population. The project creates self-employment for local youth and has brought women together in other ways. In 2000, the women received about $7,700 from the Expanded Triple Up Program (ETUP), which allows them to graduate from a grant to a credit facility. Initially, about $2,300 was used to purchase three heifers, and each project member who receives one is required to pay back the cost to the project within a specified time. The funds will go into a revolving fund to ensure that all members will eventually receive a heifer.

SOURCES:
Federation of American Women's Clubs Overseas, "Kugeria," *FAWCO Forum,* Winter 2004, at www.fawco.org, accessed March 21, 2005.
Jacqueline N. Kabari, "Success Story," at www.ceasurf.org, accessed March 20, 2005.
W.A. Rodgers, *The Cross Borders Biodiversity Project,* May 2002, at www.xborderbiodiversity.org, accessed March 20, 2005.
United National Population Fund, "Population and the Environment," *State of the World Population 2004,* at www.unfpa.org, accessed March 20, 2005.
Women's Environment and Development Organization, "Breaking Down Barriers," at www.wedo.org, accessed March 20, 2005.

TRENDS IN WATER USE

How much water do we need, and how much do we have? That question is at the heart of the water management debate, which is complicated by inexact science and reporting methodologies that are inconsistent over time. The U.S. Geological Survey (USGS) has been compiling water use data since 1950 to analyze the source, use, and disposition of water resources at the local, state, and national levels. In the agency's reports, water use is divided into eight categories: public supply, domestic, irrigation, livestock, aquaculture (fish farms and hatcheries), industrial, mining, and thermoelectric power. All of these categories are subject to factors such as population growth and shifts, economic trends, legal decisions, and periodic droughts. In 2000, for instance, the most recent year for which statistics are available, water use was affected by climatic extremes. Much of the West experienced severe drought, and weather in the Midwest and Northeast was characterized by prolonged periods of cooler and wetter than normal conditions.[5]

Estimates show that total water usage in the United States increased steadily from 1950 to 1980, declined more than 9 percent from 1980 to 1985, and has varied less than 3 percent across the five-year intervals since 1985. Water use peaked in 1980 because of large industrial, irrigation, and thermoelectric power withdrawals; but the implementation of federal legislation has affected industrial use because of requirements that encourage conservation, greater efficiency, and technologies that decrease water use.[6]

Agricultural water use is also behind water policy decisions. Irrigation is the answer to growing crops in areas that receive insufficient natural rainfall. Piping systems and wells transfer water from natural sources (lakes, streams, or aquifers) to fields, basically altering the natural hydrological cycle.[7] There are also differences in the way agricultural water is used. It takes 500–1,500 tons of water to irrigate a ton of potatoes; 3,500–5,700 tons of water to produce a ton of chicken, and 15,000–70,000 tons of water to produce a ton of beef. Can future water needs be predicted without knowing if people will eat 2,300 calories per day (the minimum level of health set by the Food and Agriculture Organization), or will they eat 3,300 calories a day, as people in the wealthier nations do? What portion of those calories will come from meat? For livestock, it is over the time to produce marketable meat. For people, it is over that same period. It is estimated that all the grain fed to U.S. livestock is equivalent to the amount needed to feed 400 million people.[8]

Statistics like these represent policy trade-offs. Should water be prioritized to produce power and increase industrial capacity? Should the emphasis be placed on conserving water for personal use and for drinking, or for agriculture to feed hungry people? Should resources be directed toward developing more efficient practices and technology, or to expansion of the water supply infrastructure? The answers to these policy choices vary considerably from one region to another, as the following discussion illustrates.

WATER RESOURCE MANAGEMENT
IN THE UNITED STATES

American water policy is among the most politicized in the world. As this overview indicates, it is colored by political appointments and powerful industry lobbies. U.S. water policy has recently changed as political clout has shifted from the farm and agricultural lobby, which controlled policy at the turn of the century, to the urban interests now dominating Congress. Water management in the United States has primarily been the responsibility of two federal agencies, although that responsibility is shared with many public and private entities, ranging from local sewage companies and irrigation districts to state water boards. The Corps of Engineers, originally created in 1802 under the Department of the Army, became the main construction arm of the federal government. In 1824, Congress gave the corps authority over navigational operations, and the agency gained additional jurisdiction through the Flood Control Act of 1936. Just four years after Franklin Roosevelt began his New Deal, the corps embarked on a reservoir construction program that erected 10 large dams a year, on average, for 50 years. The authority was expanded further in 1972 with passage of the Clean Water Act, which broadened its jurisdiction to include wetlands permits.

The Reclamation Service (later renamed the Bureau of Reclamation) was authorized by Congress in 1902 with responsibility for aiding western settlement in a 17-state area.[9] The bureau was popular among western farmers because its charter included a limitation to serve only those landowners who held title to 160 acres or less; thus, the agency rapidly came to be influenced by local interests. During its early years, the bureau constructed massive water development projects, canals, and public works programs, such as Washington's Grand Coulee Dam (the largest single-purpose peacetime appropriation in U.S. history) and California's Central Valley Project. Between them, the two federal agencies quickly established a reputation as the home of the pork barrel—congressionally approved water projects that benefited a single district. Projects such as dams and flood control channels brought a visible product (and jobs) to the home base of a member of Congress, paid for by liberal cost-sharing formulas and substantial federal financing. In 1920, the Federal Water

Power Act created the Federal Power Commission, which was replaced in 1977 by the Federal Energy Regulatory Commission (FERC). The commission was initially responsible for regulating the nation's water resources, but its charter was eventually redirected to oversee the electric power and natural gas industries.

A close-knit relationship has always existed between the congressional oversight committees, the two agencies, and local water interest lobbies. Decisions on which projects to fund, and at what level, were frequently made by those leaders with the most political clout—or because of pressure from campaign contributors—rather than on the merits of good water management. Around 1900, for example, the National Rivers Congress, comprised of powerful business figures, contractors, and members of Congress (who were honorary members of the group), began monitoring Corps of Engineers projects. This group of lobbyists was extremely successful at convincing Congress to continue authorizing funds for projects that had long since been completed. The water lobby became so powerful that in its heyday in the early 1960s, the chair of the House Appropriations Committee would boast that "practically every Congressional district" was included in the omnibus public works bills, and that "there is something here for everybody."[10]

For the most part, America's growth spurt continued unabated after World War II, and few questioned the advisability of massive undertakings by the corps and the Bureau of Reclamation. New water technology, modern farming and cropping techniques, and widespread pesticide use made agricultural expansion a key element of the postwar boom, with cheap, government-subsidized water the key. Land irrigated with government-financed water grew from 2.7 million acres in 1930 to more than 4 million acres after the war and to nearly 7 million acres by 1960. But during the late 1950s and mid-1960s, water resource planning changed from an emphasis on economic development to municipal, industrial, and recreational purposes. The water lobby was forced to make some concessions to environmental groups, which were outraged when projects began to infringe upon scenic or preserved areas—such as a proposal to build Echo Park Dam in Dinosaur National Monument.[11] The Sierra Club mobilized its members upon learning about a plan to build a hydroelectric plant in the Grand Canyon; and in so doing, the group lost its federal tax-exempt status.

By the mid-1970s, environmental groups had turned their attention to water issues and were becoming a potent force in policy making. Groups such as the Sierra Club, the American Rivers Conservation Council, the National Wildlife Federation, and the Natural Resources Defense Council pressured Congress to follow the requirements of the National Environmental Policy Act (NEPA) and used litigation as a tool for forcing compliance with new legislative initiatives. Bolstered by environmental support during his campaign, President Jimmy Carter began his administration in 1977 by developing a "hit list" of 19 water projects that were to be deleted from the federal budget, including the Central Arizona Project. Carter underestimated the powerful water industry lobby, however, which was able to convince Congress to restore all 19 appropriations.

Water industry officials cheered the 1980 election of Ronald Reagan, believing his appointment of Robert Broadbent, a Nevada legislator, as head of the Bureau of Reclamation was a positive omen. It turned out to be a conflicting sign, however, as Reagan continued Carter's cost-sharing requirements on water projects (the portion of a water project to be borne by the federal government). As state and local governments began to realize that they might have to pay a larger share of the cost for many of the projects, they became less attractive, and in some cases, financially burdensome. Part of the shift in policy can be traced to the growing clout of urban political interests over those of agriculture, as city politicians began to question why farmers were getting all the cheap water.[12]

Equally important was the discovery of dead waterfowl at the Kesterson National Wildlife Refuge in California's San Joaquin Valley. Ducks and geese were dying of a mysterious sickness that not only killed them, but resulted in birth deformities in their chicks. The eventual cause was found to be selenium, a trace element that can be toxic in high concentrations. The selenium was carried by the San Luis Drain from the politically powerful Westlands Water District in Fresno and Tulare Counties. In 1985, Secretary of the Interior Donald Hodel called for a halt in the drainage by June 30, 1986; but by then the public had lost its patience with the Bureau of Reclamation's projects and its negligence.[13] By 1987, the policy change became clear when James Zigler, the Department of the Interior's assistant secretary for water and science, announced that the bureau was changing its mission from an agency based on federally supported construction to one based on resource management. The empire-building days of the corps and the bureau were over, replaced by an administration that was paying more attention to urban needs for a stable water supply than to agricultural interests seeking cheap water for their fields.

Like other natural resources, water is often assumed to be in endless supply, and many Americans just pay their monthly water bill (usually from a local or municipal water district) without complaint. Similar in structure to other types of public utilities, water costs may be limited and users are seldom penalized for overconsumption, even in arid regions of the West. However, pricing inequities continue to be at the heart of the battle over water management in the United States. The "real" cost of providing and distributing water is often impossible to determine, and historically, municipalities have been reluctant to try to pass those costs on to developers and commercial interests. City leaders often avoided charging a new business the true cost of water delivery for fear it would discourage economic growth. As a result, the rate structure has often allowed large users to benefit because of a system that charges the user less for using more water. Favored customers often receive preferential pricing, and some cities served by the same water district often unknowingly subsidize the water costs of other cities in their area through complex pricing arrangements. Residential users tend to subsidize industrial users throughout most of the United States today.

Another new wrinkle has been the development of "water markets"— transactions ranging from transfers of water rights to the sale and lease of either those rights or the land above the water source. Market transfers are dependent upon the concept of reallocating water supplies, rather than coming up with new sources of water. Part of the affection for the market concept was purely economic—new capital projects were becoming increasingly expensive and politically unpopular in much of the West. One group even began purchasing water rights in Colorado as an investment, with the expectation that as supplies diminished the rights could be sold for a tidy profit. Cities such as Phoenix and

Scottsdale also have been active in the water market, buying thousands of acres of farmland outside their city limits to have a water source as their population increases and water within city boundaries runs short. Reallocation is gradually being looked upon as an alternative to finding a new allocation as the primary mode of water development.[14]

Water management is also highly dependent upon weather patterns, which may vary in both the short and long term. Much of the attention on water supply is focused on the West because of extensive drought. The Midwest and Northeastern United States have been characterized by periods of cooler and wetter than normal conditions, with above-average precipitation. As a result, water management issues are lower on the regions' environmental policy agenda than they are in the Southwest.

A single season's change in weather patterns, especially amounts of precipitation, can lead to accelerated government policy making. The winter storms of 2004–2005, for instance, filled lakes and reservoirs throughout much of the Southwest and reduced overall water demand in many areas. In June 2005, Arizona officials projected that the state would not need to draw upon its full allocation from the Colorado River, and agreed to store some of the extra water in its underground "water banks" to benefit Nevada, which has dealt with years of drought and urban expansion. The deal requires Nevada to pay Arizona $330 million to store its water, and when the state needs to draw water supplies, will take it directly from the Colorado River drainage into Lake Mead. Arizona, in return, will take less water from the Colorado and will instead pump its allocation from the water banks using wells. The agreement provides additional revenue for Arizona while Nevada maintains a reliable source of water in Arizona's "bank."[15]

The American water wars have also touched our southern border with Mexico, where the Colorado River flows on its way to the Gulf of California. In 1922, Congress approved the Colorado River Compact, which divided up the river's resources, giving the three lower basin states (California, Arizona, and Nevada) and the four upper basin states (Wyoming, Colorado, New Mexico, and Utah) 7.5 million acre-feet for each region. (An acre-foot is the volume of water that covers 1 acre to a depth of 1 foot, or 325,851 gallons. This is about enough water to serve one or two households for one year.) It should be noted, however, that the actual flow of the river is closer to 14 rather than 15 million acre-feet. Congress also authorized the building of Hoover Dam in 1928, giving the United States total control over the Colorado River—a situation that understandably made our Mexican neighbors nervous. Seeking to keep Mexico as a wartime ally, the United States signed a treaty in 1944 that assigned 1.5 million acre-feet to Mexico and created the International Boundary Water Commission to administer the treaty. In the early 1960s, a combination of population growth, the drilling of wells on the U.S. side, saline runoff from drainage projects, and construction of the Glen Canyon Dam in Utah began affecting both the quantity and quality of Mexico's water allocation. It took nearly 10 years for the two sides to reach an agreement that, in 1973, guaranteed Mexico a fair share of the Colorado River in usable form. The responsibility for implementing the numerous treaties between the two countries that relate to water and resolving any differences belongs to the renamed International Boundary and Water Commission.

Today, the issue of maintaining an adequate supply for Mexico remains unresolved. Stakeholders have identified several problems that require U.S. and Mexican collaboration and cooperation. Among them are the need for an international collaborative plan for surface water and groundwater, the quantity of water flowing through the Rio Grande, competition between El Paso and Ciudad Juarez for the same water sources, and development of a sustainable water supply.[16]

The growing pressure to tap more and more of the earth's water resources is having some negative impacts. More urban communities are tapping into underground aquifers, drying them up as residential and agricultural demand increases. In cities such as Beijing, Mexico City, Houston, New Orleans, and Phoenix, water levels are dropping as a result of heavy pumping, leading to subsidence—literally, the sinking of the city. In addition to a reduction in the availability of a valuable commodity, it is unlikely that the water in the aquifers will ever be fully replaced. Water is being withdrawn from aquifers much faster than it can be recharged— replenished by rain and runoff.

The water scarcity and management problem has two basic solutions: conservation and technology. The first is relatively straightforward—convince users to use less. The second involves a wide range of options, from ancient to modern technological solutions. Water conservation is being implemented in many regions, ranging from urban communities to rural irrigation improvements, in an attempt to reduce residents' dependency upon existing sources. Some of the easiest conservation efforts have been accomplished by metropolitan water districts that have enacted consumption ordinances or made water-saving showerheads and low-flow toilets available. These efforts are not temporary responses to drought; studies indicate that by 2010, southern California will have enough water to fulfill only 70 percent of its needs, making demand management practices a more likely strategy for reducing consumption.[17]

WETLANDS PROTECTION

Although the water resource debate in the United States has focused primarily on the issue of supply, water quality is an equally enduring problem for policy makers. Historically, legislative efforts to reduce pollution at the source have been ineffective, as will be seen later in this chapter. Scientists are also looking at wetlands restoration as another strategy for improving water quality. Wetlands are sensitive ecological areas that serve as breeding grounds for migratory birds and as plant habitats. They also serve as natural flood and storm control systems, and some communities are experimenting with using wetlands as a way of treating wastewater. Wetlands have become an increasingly important topic on the environmental protection agenda as scientists monitor the numbers of acres of wetlands lost to development.

One difficulty encountered by policy makers is determining the scope of the problem of wetlands protection. In order to formulate policy, scientists and researchers within the government must be able to define what the term *wetlands* means and then inventory how many acres of land fall under that definition. The Clean Water Act of 1972 included provisions requiring anyone seeking to build or otherwise conduct business that would alter the landscape of wetlands to first obtain a permit from the Army Corps of Engineers. Of particular interest in the act is Section 404, which makes it unlawful to put dredged or fill material into navigable waters—the term *wetlands* was never mentioned in the legislation. But in 1975 a Washington, D.C., Court of Appeals decision held that the Clean Water Act applied not only to rivers but also to wetlands that drain into rivers; eventually, the statute was applied to isolated wetlands with no connection to rivers or waterways. Four agencies—the Department of Agriculture, the EPA, the Department of the Interior, and the Army Corps of Engineers—have developed regulations to implement the law and to designate which areas are defined as wetlands, among them an estimated 77 million acres of wetlands that are privately owned. Because each of the agencies has its own interpretation of the wetlands designation, the importance of wetlands preservation has collided with private property rights and become one of the most contentious water management issues in the United States.

The U.S. Fish and Wildlife Service (USFWS) has adopted this definition from a 1979 report:

Wetlands are lands transitional between terrestrial and aquatic systems where the water table usually at or near the surface of the land is covered by shallow water. For purposes of this classification wetlands must have one or more of the following three attributes: (1) at least periodically, the land supports predominantly hydrophytes; (2) the substrate is predominantly undrained hydric soil; and (3) the substrate is nonsoil and is saturated with water or covered by shallow water at some time during the growing season of the year.[18]

With regard to how many acres are considered wetlands, the Emergency Wetland Resources Act of 1986 directs the USFWS to inventory the nation's wetlands and provide reports to Congress every 10 years. Data from the most recent inventory conducted in 1997 indicate that an average of 101,000 acres of wetlands was lost from 1992 to 1997, with almost 69,000 acres gained, for an overall annual net loss of 32,600 acres per year.[19] Under the direction of the Bush administration, the USFWS is accelerating the completion of the next National Wetlands Inventory Status and Trends Report. Instead of the 2010 deadline, the agency will complete the report by the end of 2005.[20] But it may be several years before an accurate accounting of current wetlands statistics is available, even under the new schedule.

Despite the lack of vital information, wetlands policy has become highly politicized in the two decades since the court's interpretation of the Clean Water Act. At the height of his campaign for president in 1988, George H. W. Bush announced on the shores of Boston Harbor that there would be "no net loss" of the nation's remaining wetlands—a concept that was the brainchild of then Conservation Foundation president William K. Reilly (later Bush's nominee to become administrator of the EPA). During the 1992 presidential campaign, the phrase came back to haunt Bush as one of the major failures of his administration, eliciting criticism from both environmental groups and property owners.[21]

Farmers have been among the most vocal critics of federal wetlands policies. Their concerns were brought to the president's attention by a group called the National Wetlands Coalition—led by farming, oil and gas, and housing industry representatives—which had formed in 1989 to oppose sections of the wetlands program implementation. The organization asked the White House Council on Competitiveness, chaired by Vice President Dan Quayle, to develop a less restrictive wetlands definition. The result was the release of the *Federal Manual for Identifying and Delineating Jurisdictional Wetlands* in August 1991. Under the new directive, the definition of *wetlands* was expanded, and an additional 50 million acres of land came under federal protection.[22]

More than 80,000 formal comments, most of them highly critical of the proposed manual, were sent to the EPA. Critics of the proposed rules change argued that millions of acres of previously protected land would be open to development, and environmental groups called upon Congress to study the problem further.[23] In contrast to the president's policy, a December 1991 report by the National Research Council recommended that the United States embark upon a policy of wetlands restoration, with a goal of a net gain of 10 million acres of wetlands by 2010—a program that went far beyond the Bush administration's policy of "no net loss." Failure to implement such a policy, the report warned, would lead to permanent ecological damage that would reduce the quality of American life.[24]

While Congress held hearings over the wetlands designations, each agency charged with implementing the Clean Water Act interpreted President Bush's proposals in different ways. The Army Corps of Engineers used a 1987 version of a wetlands manual, the Environmental Protection Agency (EPA) and Fish and Wildlife Service used another developed in 1989, the Soil Conservation Service had its own slightly different criteria, and some federal agencies adopted the 1991 manual's proposed rules.[25]

In February 1991, the president announced his Coastal America initiative, coordinated by the Council on Environmental Quality (CEQ), to establish a partnership among federal agencies responsible for the management, regulation, and stewardship of coastal living resources. Wetlands protection came under the proposal, focusing on regional activities that provide direct local and watershed action as well as national projects.[26] Although the initiative continued to operate when President Clinton took office in 1993, the new administration reexamined federal wetlands policies almost immediately, in large part due to court rulings that questioned whether the government had the authority to place sanctions on those who failed to meet wetlands permit criteria.

In 1995, the debate resumed as the Republican-controlled Congress sought to rewrite a Clean Water Act that would have established another new classification scheme for wetlands. Under the proposal, the least valuable lands would no longer be protected by the federal government, and less protection would be given to the remaining wetlands. The measure also would have required government agencies to compensate landowners for any loss in property values of 20 percent or more resulting from wetlands regulations, but the proposals failed to obtain sufficient bipartisan support. Clinton was unable to make significant progress with a new wetlands policy due to congressional leaders working at cross purposes, stalling any major programs. In addition, just as Clinton was leaving office in January 2001, the U.S. Supreme Court issued a decision concerning what the court termed "isolated" waters used as habitat for migratory birds, further confusing the definition of wetlands.

In a further setback for environmental groups supporting the strengthening the Clean Water Act, the EPA and Army Corps of Engineers published an Advance Notice of Proposed Rulemaking (ANPRM) in January 2003. Under the proposed rule, developers would be given more latitude in filling creeks, ponds, ephemeral streams, and wetlands without federal permits; and industries would be allowed to dump pollutants into unprotected waters. Eighteen months later, a coalition of opponents to the proposed rule released a report citing 15 case studies where the Bush administration had directed federal regulators "to withhold protection from tens of millions of acres of wetlands, streams, and other waters, unless they first get permissions from their national headquarters in Washington, D.C."[27]

President Bush moved forward in his water policy changes, announcing a new wetlands initiative on Earth Day 2004 that called for restoring at least 1 million acres of additional wetlands, improving the condition of at least 1 million acres of existing degraded wetlands, and extending protection to at least 1 million acres of imperiled wetlands by 2009. Overall, the Bush policy would move beyond his father's "no net loss" of wetlands through expanded incentive and partnership measures, such as the Department of Agriculture's Wetland Reserve Program, and through grants under the Department of Interior's North American Wetlands Conservation Act, also signed by George H. W. Bush.[28]

A year later, the CEQ released a report noting that on the first anniversary of the president's wetlands initiative, 328,000 acres had been restored or created, 154,000 acres had been improved, and 350,000 acres had been protected. CEQ chairman James Connaughton emphasized once again the administration's preference for incentives to encourage private stewardship and conservation partnerships rather than government enforcement: "Working collaboratively with private landowners and local officials has proven remarkably effective in improving and sustaining America's wetlands."[29]

With the change of administration from one political party to another, federal agencies have bounced back and forth regarding wetlands policies. Unlike executive branch or congressional staff, agency personnel tend to remain in their positions regardless of who occupies the White House. With attention to wetlands protection somewhat low on the president's environmental agenda, much of the implementation and enforcement of policy lies with career employees, who may or not share the chief executive's policy priorities.

EVERGLADES RESTORATION

The Florida Everglades encompasses an ecosystem that once stretched from the Kissimmee chain of lakes to Florida Bay. The Everglades, a subtropical wetlands in the southern region of the state, provides habitat for diverse plant and animal species and a landscape of cypress swamps, coastal lagoons, sawgrass sloughs, and coral reefs. In 1947, Marjory Stoneman Douglas referred to the Everglades as a river of grass—a unique region of the earth, remote, never wholly known.[30] In its natural state, the area also serves as a complex freshwater filtration and distribution system. However, that system has been altered by human decisions and policies. In the late 1800s, primitive canals began being built to drain the region, and by the end of the 20th century, an estimated 1,700 miles of canals and levees had been built. More than half of the area was lost to development; the Central & Southern Florida Project (CSFP), designed to provide flood protection and water management, led to unintended adverse effects on the ecosystem.[31]

It was not until 1992 and the Water Resources Development Act (amended in 1996) that the Army Corps of Engineers, responsible for much of the building of the canals and levees, was directed to reevaluate the performance and impacts of the CSFP. The agency mission changed from stemming the flow of freshwater to capturing, storing, and redistributing water and regulating the quality, quantity, timing, and distribution of water flows.[32] The Water Resources Development Act of 2000 represents the results of the reevaluation—60 elements that will take 20 to 30 years to construct, at an estimated cost of between $7.5 and $8.7 billion, making it the world's largest ecosystem restoration project. The Comprehensive Everglades Restoration Plan (CERP) is a framework and guide that covers 16 counties over an 18,000 acre area, including surface water storage reservoirs, management of Lake Okeechobee, underground water storage, reuse of wastewater, improved water conservation, treatment of wetlands and improved water delivery to estuaries, removal of barriers, and storage of water in existing quarries.[33]

In March 2003, the Corps and the South Florida Water Management District, partners in the implementation of CERP, developed a vision statement and a set of guiding principles to accomplish the project's goals. The vision is to restore, preserve, and protect the South Florida ecosystem while providing for other water-related needs of the region, including water supply and flood protection. The statement notes:

> Although the future Everglades ecosystem will be a "new" Everglades because it will be smaller than the pre-drainage system, restoration will have been successful if the new system responds to the recovery of these defining characteristics by functionally behaving as a wild Everglades system rather than as a set of managed, disconnected wetlands.[34]

CERP's guiding principles include implementation in an open, collaborative process, incorporating interdisciplinary and interagency teams and comprehensive programs of public outreach and public involvement; the proper balance of meeting plan budgets, schedules, and overall plan goals and objectives; application of a system-wide science strategy and adaptive management program; operational flexibility; and evaluation and assessment based on an open-ended learning and planning process.[35]

The state of Florida is an active stakeholder in the restoration of the Everglades, and Governor Jeb Bush has committed his administration to maintaining water quality. He has signed legislation reauthorizing the Everglades Forever Act and to meeting the EPA's water quality standard by December 31, 2006. Funding provided by the state legislature provides the South Florida Water Quality District with an estimated $650 million over 13 years to implement advanced water treatment tools, including algae-based technology that will reduce the amount of phosphorus entering the ecosystem.[36]

Not unexpectedly, implementation of a policy of this magnitude has not been without pitfalls, both political and practical. Some of the CERP funding comes from property taxes levied on owners in the 16-county region covered by the project. It is the only taxing district in the region whose leaders are appointed by the governor, rather than elected by voters, thus increasing the politicization of the process.[37] Funding estimates have increased regularly as new challenges to the cleanup process arise. In June 2005, a federal judge ruled that both the State of Florida and the federal government had violated a court settlement agreement reached in 1992 by allowing repeated excessive discharges of phosphorus into the Loxahatchee National Wildlife Refuge. Farms, dairies, and residential runoff have been blamed for upsetting the chemical balance of the Everglades by adding too much phosphorus to the wetlands. The governments had also failed to meet an October 1, 2003, deadline to construct a 16,000-acre treatment area on time, according to a lawsuit brought by the Miccosukee tribe and a coalition of environmental groups.[38]

The CERP is an exceptionally ambitious project that is attempting to restore the harm done by more than a century's worth of human influence and damage. Florida's Department of Environmental Protection notes that progress has already been made in reducing phosphorus levels from 170 parts per billion a decade ago to 12 parts per billion now. Environmental organizations feel that only legal intervention will force government agencies to comply with federal and state laws and standards. The CERP vision statement reinforces the magnitude of the task: the integration of natural and human system objectives into a single design, recoupling an array of public interests into a common strategy for the future of south Florida.[39]

THE NATURE AND CAUSES OF WATER POLLUTION

In 1965, when he signed the Water Quality Act, President Lyndon B. Johnson (LBJ) predicted that Washington's Potomac River would be reopened for swimming by 1975.[40] Yet the Potomac's tidal basin, with its Japanese cherry trees, has been called "the best decorated sewer in the world," making LBJ's prediction premature and unrealistic, as is the case with most of the legislative attempts to improve the quality of America's water supply. Several factors have contributed to make the nation's waterways and drinking water as polluted now as they were in the 1960s. The debate over how best to improve water quality focuses on two issues: first, pollution of surface waters (rivers, streams, lakes, wetlands, and even drainage ditches), largely from discharges directly into waterways; and second, the pollution of groundwater, which flows beneath the earth's surface and is the source of nearly half of the nation's drinking water.

Sources of groundwater contamination include landfills, biocide applications on farmland and urban lawns, underground storage tanks, leakage of hazardous waste, and waste disposal wells.

The current level of water pollution is due largely to massive industrialization and inadequate waste disposal strategies that took place in the United States during the mid to late 19th century. At that time, local officials were generally reluctant to antagonize industry by trying to stop the widespread practice of simply dumping industrial wastes into the closest waterway. Most of the early government concerns dealt with navigational hazards rather than health. In 1886, Congress prohibited the dumping of waste into New York harbor; this was followed by the 1899 Refuse Act, which prohibited the dumping of solid waste into commercial waterways. Not until the U.S. Public Health Service was formed in 1912 was serious consideration given to monitoring pollution levels. Today, much of what is known about trends in surface water quality comes from the U.S. Geological Survey, which monitors waterways through its National Ambient Stream Quality Accounting Network (NASQUAN), which began collecting information in 1974. Groundwater quality, in contrast, must be monitored either from wells or at the tap.

Basically, water contaminants can be divided into the following categories:

1. *Organisms:* Biological contaminants including bacteria, parasites, and viruses are included in this category. These occur in most water sources, although there are usually fewer in groundwater than in surface water. Human and animal wastes carry fecal coliform and fecal streptococcus bacteria, which may enter the water source from improper sewage treatment, cattle feedlots, or through failing, leaching septic tanks.

2. *Suspended and totally dissolved solids:* Soil particles, inorganic salts, and other substances may make water brown or turbid (cloudy) and may carry bacteria and other harmful substances that pollute water. The problem is particularly acute in areas with significant erosion, including logged watersheds, construction sites, and abused rangelands. Agricultural practices are thought to be the largest single source of unregulated water pollution.

3. *Nutrients:* Some contaminants, such as phosphorus, iron, and boron, can be harmful when ingested in excess quantities. Nitrates, which are not harmful in limited concentrations, occur naturally in some vegetables, such as beets and cabbage, and are used in the meat-curing process.

4. *Metals and toxics:* A wide spectrum of heavy metals is commonly found in drinking water; among the most dangerous of these metals is lead. In 1991, the EPA issued new regulations requiring municipal water suppliers to monitor lead levels, focusing on households at high risk (those with lead service pipes), and at the location where lead content is likely to be the highest—at the consumer's faucet. In areas where water quality standards are not met, suppliers must add bicarbonate and lime to lower the water's acidity chemically. Other contaminants include radioactive minerals and gases. Toxic concentrations usually come from sources such as pesticides and chemical solvents used in a variety of manufacturing processes.

5. *Municipal wastewater discharges:* Domestic sewage accounts for a large percentage of the materials handled by municipal wastewater treatment plants, but other substances also routinely enter the wastewater stream, including hazardous chemicals dumped down drains and sewers by individuals, industries, and businesses.

Americans have reason to be concerned about water quality. An EPA report based on the 2000 National Water Quality Inventory (required under the Clean Water Act) found that about 40 percent of the nation's streams, 45 percent of lakes, and 50 percent of estuaries that were assessed were not clean enough to support uses such as fishing and swimming. States, tribes, territories, and interstate commissions assessed approximately 700,000 miles of rivers and 17.34 million acres of lakes in the 2000 survey, or about one third of the U.S. waters. The water quality standards used in the assessment consist of three elements: the designated uses assigned to waters (such as drinking, swimming, or fishing); criteria to protect those uses (such as chemical-specific thresholds that should not be exceeded); and policies intended to keep waters that do meet standards from deteriorating from their current condition.

THE POLITICS OF WATER QUALITY

Like many environmental issues, the politics of water quality is not linked to a single act of legislation. One factor that makes water policy somewhat difficult to understand is that Congress has given regulatory responsibility for water quality to EPA and other agencies under several legislative mandates, as seen in Table 7.1.

Some of the authority comes not from water pollution legislation, but from related laws. The Resource Conservation and Recovery Act (RCRA), for example, gives the EPA the authority to regulate the treatment, transport, and storage of both hazardous and nonhazardous waste. The Comprehensive Environmental Response, Compensation, and Liability Act (CERCLA), more commonly known as Superfund, gives the EPA responsibility when groundwater is contaminated by inactive waste sites or accidental chemical releases. The Toxic Substances Control Act (TSCA) gives the EPA regulatory authority over the manufacture, use, and disposal of toxic chemicals; and the Federal Insecticide, Fungicide, and Rodenticide Act (FIFRA) regulates certain pesticides, which can also enter groundwater. Despite the overlap of these regulatory mandates, Congress has also enacted legislation specifically targeting surface and groundwater pollution.

Surface Water

The process of placing surface water on the political agenda has been a long one. Before World War II, only a few environmental organizations seemed interested in the deteriorating condition of America's lakes, rivers, and streams. The Izaak Walton League was among the first to draw attention to the contamination

T A B L E 7.1   Major Water Quality Legislation, 1948–2005

Year	Law	Provisions
1948	Federal Water Pollution Control Act	Authorized Surgeon General of the Public Health Service to prepare comprehensive programs for eliminating or reducing the pollution of interstate waters; gave the Federal Works administrator responsibility to assist state and local governments in constructing sewage treatment plants
1961	Amendments of 1961	Stipulated that federal agencies consider water quality as part of the planning process for reservoirs; gave authority to the Secretary of Health, Education and Welfare to assess water quality in the Great Lakes region
1966	Clean Water Restoration Act	Authorized the Secretary of the Interior to conduct a comprehensive study of the effects of water pollution in the U.S. estuaries; prohibited discharge of oil into navigable waters
1970	Reorganization Plan #3	Abolished the Federal Water Quality Administration from Department of Interior, and transferred all functions to the EPA
1970	Water Quality Improvement Act	Amended prohibitions on discharges of oil; authorized a National Contingency Plan to minimize damage from oil discharges; authorized demonstration projects to control mine water pollution and water pollution within the Great Lakes watersheds; provided direction for water quality agencies on compliance with applicable standards.
1972	Federal Water Pollution Control Act Amendments	Stipulated broad national objectives to restore the nation's waters; expanded provisions related to pollutant discharges; defined liability for discharges of oil and hazardous substances; established National Pollutant Discharge Elimination System (NPDES) authorizing EPA to issue permits for discharges; authorized Army Corps of Engineers to issue permits for discharges of dredged or fill material into navigable waters

(Continued)

TABLE 7.1 Major Water Quality Legislation, 1948–2005 *(Continued)*

Year	Law	Provisions
1977	Clean Water Act	Developed "best management practices"; authorized funds to complete the National Wetlands Inventory; authorized corps to issue permits for activities that cause only minimal environmental effects; transferred some regulatory responsibilities to states
1987	Water Quality Act	Established Chesapeake Bay Program, Great Lakes Program; required states to develop strategies for toxics cleanups in waters; increased penalties for violations of permits; enhanced state reporting of harmful effects of high acidity on lakes; funded state nonpoint source management programs under EPA authority; required EPA to study and monitor water quality effects attributable to dams; authorized program for nomination of estuaries of national significance

problem, noting in a report published in the late 1920s that 85 percent of the nation's waterways were polluted and that only 30 percent of all municipalities treated their wastes, many of them inadequately. Industrial interests like the American Petroleum Institute, the American Iron and Steel Institute, and the Manufacturing Chemists Association insisted that "streams were nature's sewers," and convinced key legislators that industrial dumping posed no environmental threat.[41]

The initial attempts to regulate surface water pollution were weak and ineffective. In 1948, Congress passed the first Water Pollution Control Act, which established the federal government's limited role in regulating interstate water pollution. The law also provided for studies, research, and limited funding for sewage treatment. It also authorized the surgeon general to prepare or adopt programs for eliminating or reducing pollution in cooperation with other agencies and the industries involved. The emphasis on a cooperative approach, coupled with provisions that were both cumbersome and often unworkable, gave the law little impact. In 1952, a report to Congress indicated not a single enforcement action had been taken, and Congress began to hold hearings on a revision to the legislation. The 1956 amendments to the act eliminated many of the difficulties of the 1948 law, but they still limited Congress's role to interstate waters and allowed Congress to delegate much of its authority to implement the law to the states. The amendments did, however, condition federal funding of sewage treatment facilities on the submission of adequate water pollution plans by the states. This provided an incentive for states to write water quality standards to meet state goals for surface water pollution. Still, only one enforcement action was filed under this authority over the next 15 years.

During the 1960s Congress, led by Senator Edmund Muskie of Maine, became restless over the slow pace of water pollution control, because it was obvious that states were doing an inadequate job. In 1965, passage of the Water Quality Act established a June 1967 deadline for a water quality standard for interstate waters, and streamlined federal enforcement efforts. A year later, the Clean Water Restoration Act provided $3.5 billion in federal grants for the construction of sewage treatment plants and for research on advanced waste treatment. These early attempts at water quality legislation were weak and ineffective. They allowed the states to classify waterways within their jurisdiction, so a state could decide that a particular stream was best used for industrial use rather than for swimming. The use designation of the Cuyahoga River in Ohio, for example, was waste disposal—a fact that did not seem to bother most residents until the river caught fire in 1969. From an enforcement standpoint, the initial pollution laws were meaningless. In the two decades before 1972, only one case of alleged violation of federal water pollution control law reached the courts; and in that case, over four years elapsed between the initial enforcement conference and the final consent decree.

President Richard Nixon's February 1970 message to Congress on the environment called for a new water pollution bill, which eventually became the 1972 Federal Water Pollution Control Act. The main emphasis of the legislation was on technological capability. In addition to establishing a regulatory framework for water quality, the bill gave the EPA six specific deadlines by which it was to grant permits to water pollution sources, issue effluent (wastewater) guidelines, require sources to install water pollution control technology, and eliminate discharges into the nation's waterways to make them safe for fishing and swimming. A key component of the legislation was the establishment of the National Pollution Discharge Elimination System (NPDES), which made it illegal to discharge anything at all unless the source had a federal permit to do so. The NPDES had a historical basis in the 1899 Refuse Act, which had previously been thought to apply only to discharges that obstructed navigation. But the U.S. Supreme Court broadened the interpretation of the act in two cases that made it applicable to any industrial waste.[42]

Water quality continued to capture media interest when consumer advocate Ralph Nader publicized contamination along a 150-mile stretch of the Mississippi River, between Baton Rouge and New Orleans, known as the "petrochemical corridor." Public outcry after a February 1977 spill of carbon tetrachloride (a potential carcinogen) into the Ohio River, which contaminated Cincinnati's water supply, further fueled the legislative fires, although Congress took no action to strengthen the 1972 law. The act was amended in 1977, but it was not until the mid-1980s that policy makers and environmental groups generally agreed that the 1972 legislation had been overly optimistic in setting target dates for the standards to be met. Little progress had been made in improving the overall quality of the nation's waterways, although given the pace of the country's population growth and economic expansion, the argument could be made that at least the situation did not get much worse, or worse as fast. In 1987, Congress enacted a new legislative mandate—the Water Quality Act—over two vetoes by President Ronald Reagan. The new legislation expanded congressional authority to regulate water pollution from point sources—a confined conveyance, such as a pipe, tunnel, well, or floating vessel (such as a ship) that discharges pollutants—as well as from nonpoint sources, which is basically anything else. The Water Quality Act also required every state and territory to establish safe levels of toxic pollutants in freshwater by 1990.

Groundwater and Drinking Water

The main groundwater source of drinking water is aquifers—layers of rock and earth that contain water, or could contain water. For most of the 20th century, groundwater was thought to be a virtually unlimited natural resource, constantly filtered and replenished and available for human use and consumption. Currently, about half of all drinking water is supplied through groundwater.[43]

As a policy issue, water quality has often suffered from differences of opinion over where the regulatory responsibility ought to lie, with regulatory authority divided between drinking water and groundwater. Federal authority to establish primary drinking water standards (those applying to materials that are human health standards) originated with the Interstate Quarantine Act of 1893, which allowed the surgeon general to make regulations covering only bacteriological contamination. But the first U.S. primary drinking water standard was not set until 1914 by the U.S. Public Health Service, whose main concern was the prevention of waterborne diseases. The federal standards were applicable only to systems that provided water to an interstate common carrier. From 1914 to 1974, the standards were revised four times—in 1925, 1942, 1946, and 1962—and were gradually extended to cover all U.S. water supplies.

Groundwater regulatory authority was treated somewhat differently from the way drinking water regulatory authority was treated. There were those who felt that the federal government should not be responsible for regulating and cleaning up groundwater. President Dwight Eisenhower, for example, believed water pollution was a "uniquely local blight" and felt that the primary obligation for providing a safe drinking water supply ought to rest with state and local officials, not with the federal government.[44] But with the creation of the EPA in 1970, the federal government reaffirmed its policy-making authority for water quality. With passage of the 1974 Safe Drinking Water Act, the EPA was authorized to identify which substances were contaminating the nation's water supply and set maximum contaminant levels, promulgated as the National Primary Drinking Water Regulations. The act was amended in 1986 to accelerate the EPA's regulation of toxic contaminants, and included a ban on lead pipe and lead solder in public water systems. It mandated greater protection of groundwater sources and set a three-year timetable for regulation of 83 specific chemical contaminants that may have an adverse health effect known or anticipated to occur in public water systems.

During the summer of 1996, Congress and the Clinton administration, anxious to provide some evidence to voters that they were able to address pressing national issues, enacted amendments to the Safe Drinking Water Act.

The amendments gave more discretion to states and local governments to determine what contaminants pose a threat to human health. The new law emphasized controlling the greatest risks for the most benefit at the least cost. It required local water agencies to issue annual reports disclosing the chemicals and bacteria in tap water. The reports must be written in simple, accessible language and sent to residents enclosed with their utility bills. Agencies must notify the public when water contaminants pose a serious threat. The law also authorized a $7.6 billion revolving fund to loan money to local water agencies for construction of new facilities. Small water systems can get waivers from compliance with the federal regulations. The measure was criticized by some Democrats for including water-related projects in states where Republicans were in tight reelection campaigns, and by environmental groups for weakening national water quality standards.[45]

Public policies designed to address the risks associated with drinking water contamination are not always founded on science and frequently are the result of political maneuvering. For example, just three days before he left office in 2001, President Bill Clinton proposed new regulations that would limit the amount of arsenic in drinking water from 50 parts per billion to 10 parts per billion—a standard that had been in place since 1942. The administration was responding to studies showing that even minute amounts of arsenic could be linked to an increased incidence of lung and bladder cancer. Environmental groups had sought an even lower standard—three parts per billion. Shortly after taking office, however, President G. W. Bush suspended implementation of the new standard, arguing that there was insufficient proof that it was needed. Officials in many rural communities, which depended upon wells as a drinking water source, had complained to the new administration that they could not afford to comply with the federal regulation.

EPA administrator Christine Whitman solicited new studies, including one from the National Academy of Sciences and others dealing with benefits and cost-effectiveness. Meanwhile, environmental groups attacked the president's action, running controversial advertisements that, some felt, suggested that Bush's decision would actually increase arsenic levels. Conservatives argued whether the government should be in the business of setting contaminant standards at all, noting that there will be substantial costs and minimal benefits for some communities. "Rather than wade into a debate over how much arsenic is acceptable in drinking water, the Bush administration should have reframed the issue as a debate over who is to make decisions for local communities: local citizens or the Feds," one columnist commented.[46]

Whether succumbing to public pressure, convinced by studies it had commissioned, or influenced by a combination of factors, the EPA changed direction on October 31, 2002, by announcing that the Clinton administration's standard would be implemented. A critic wrote:

> With its decision on arsenic, the EPA has reverted to the "Washington-knows best" mindset that has dominated environmental policy for far too long. Whitman can claim she's protecting Americans from arsenic in their water, but users of small water systems will be left holding the bill.[47]

TOXIC CONTAMINATION

Until the early 1960s and the publication of Rachel Carson's *Silent Spring,* Americans paid little attention to the millions of gallons of toxic chemicals that were routinely being poured into waterways, dumped onto remote sites, or even stored on private property. The dangers posed by the storage and handling of toxic chemicals were either unknown or ignored. Unless there is a focusing event, there is little incentive to move toxic contamination onto the political agenda as a water quality issue.

Groundwater can be contaminated from a variety of human sources—from dumping to runoff from agriculture use. Homeowners, for example, may unknowingly pour products down their kitchen drains or toilets that contaminate the sewage stream. Some toxic contamination has been deliberate; in other cases the groundwater was accidentally polluted long before researchers and officials even knew contamination was possible, or the extent to which it could be cleaned up.

A complication in the problem of toxic water contamination is that policies related to water quality have often conflicted with other environmental rules and regulations—what policy analysts refer to as spillover. The 1990 Clean Air Act Amendments, for instance, required some cities and states with the worst air quality to sell gasoline that was reformulated with oxygenates to improve combustion and reduce air pollutants. Manufacturers responded to the federal mandate to produce reformulated gasoline by adding methyl tertiary-butyl ether, or MTBE, in 1992. Some concerns were initially raised that MTBE exhaust created adverse health effects; but a more serious problem developed when the chemical, classified as a possible human carcinogen, began showing up in drinking water tests in the early and mid-1990s in California.[48] In 1999, California governor Gray Davis issued an executive order calling for the prohibition of MTBE in gasoline on grounds that it polluted underground drinking water when gasoline leaked from underground storage tanks. MTBE producers subsequently sued, arguing before the U.S. Court of Appeals that the state's action conflicted with the federal Clean Air Act, but the court upheld the ban in a June 2003 decision. By 2005, California's Department of Health Services had detected nearly 13,000 sources of MTBE in water in more than half the state's counties—the majority in Los Angeles County. The assistant city attorney for Santa Monica, California estimated it could take decades to clean up the contamination.[49]

While California quickly moved forward with its ban and monitoring program, federal policy became mired in election-year politics. Under the Clinton administration, the Clean Air Act Advisory Committee created the MTBE Blue Ribbon Panel, which held meetings and published a September 1999 report. The final recommendations included a substantial nationwide reduction in the use of MTBE, accelerating research on MTBE and its substitutes, and over 20 specific actions to improve the nation's water protection programs.[50]

In March 2000, EPA Administrator Carol Browner announced the beginning of regulatory action under the Toxic Substances Control Act to reduce or eliminate use of MTBE in gasoline. A draft regulation that said, "The use of MTBE as an additive in gasoline presents an unreasonable risk to the environment" was sent by EPA to the White House in January 2001, just as Clinton was leaving office.[51]

Under the Bush administration, EPA did not move forward with the proposal, despite dozens of studies and background papers on the environmental impacts of the additive's use. Instead, the new Congress considered proposals that would shield industry from lawsuits related to the additive. Environmental groups accused the president of favoring companies that contributed over $1 million to Republican candidates. "This is a classic case of the Bush administration helping its campaign contributor friends at the expense of public health," said the director of the Clean Air Trust.[52] Nearly 20 states have now banned MTBE on their own.

Some forms of toxic contamination are legal and permitted by officials. The nation's pulp and paper mills have been targeted by environmental groups as among the biggest polluters of U.S. waterways, with bleaching plants the source of millions of pounds of chlorinated compounds annually. Among the compounds identified in bleach effluent are dioxins (a generic term applied to a group of suspected carcinogens that are the by-products of other substances or processes), which have been shown to cause reproductive disorders in animals and immune system suppression and impaired liver function in humans.

The pace at which toxic contamination has been regulated and enforced, both at the federal and state levels, has been uneven and decidedly sluggish. The Clean Water Act of 1972 required the EPA to impose the best available pollution control technology standards on industries that discharge toxic waste into rivers, lakes, and estuaries, or sewage treatment facilities. The agency did not take action to implement the law until 1976, when a lawsuit forced it to agree to regulate 24 of more than 50 industrial categories, including organic chemicals, pharmaceuticals, and pulp and paper industries. In 1987, Congress amended the legislation and ordered the EPA to update the old standards and to begin regulating additional categories by February 1991. When the congressional deadline passed, the Natural Resources Defense Council (NRDC) filed suit in U.S. District Court to force the agency to comply with the 1987 law. In its suit, the NRDC noted that the EPA had not developed rules for four of five industrial plants that dump toxic substances directly into surface waters. In 1992, the EPA agreed to settle the lawsuit and extend federal standards to 16 additional industry categories between 1996 and 2002, including industrial laundries, pesticide manufacturers, and hazardous waste facilities and incinerators.

Similarly, the states have failed to comply with the 1987 Water Quality Act provisions, which required them to impose limits on toxic pollution in their waters by 1990. In 1991, the EPA announced that it would impose federal rules on the 22 states and territories that had not set their own standards to reduce levels of toxic compounds, including pesticides, solvents, and heavy metals.

Why has water pollution taken so long to gain policy makers' attention, and why has the EPA been so reluctant to move forward on the legislative mandates? There are several possible explanations for the current status of water pollution control:

1. EPA officials cite staff and budgetary constraints that virtually crippled the agency during the 1980s, especially under President Reagan, that put many water quality initiatives on hold.

2. The federal government had delegated much of its responsibility to the states, which are required to issue permits to industries that discharge pollution onto

surface water. The permit limits vary from state to state and have generally been much more lenient than federal controls.

3. Water quality issues have tended to take a back seat to air quality issues when it comes to the political arena. Congressional committees have focused on the more politically visible issues of smog and auto emissions rather than water quality. Although the 1972 law eliminated the gross pollution that causes rivers and lakes to look or smell bad, the more invisible but nevertheless hazardous toxic pollutants have been largely ignored until recently.

4. The overlapping of jurisdictions and responsibilities between the federal and state governments has led to a competition among agencies.

5. Both environmental groups and public officials reluctantly admit that the compliance deadlines of the 1972 legislation were extremely unrealistic, forcing the EPA to scramble to come up with new rules that even the agency leadership knew were not attainable.

6. Despite attempts at innovative conservation strategies and protection of existing sources, one of the compelling factors in water quality policy today is cost. Many of the new federal requirements place a severe burden on small communities that cannot afford expensive water treatment plants on budgets that are already stretched thin. Small communities may not be able to take advantage of some treatment technologies, for example, and may not have access to alternative water supplies. Thus many of the proposed solutions may benefit large urban areas, leaving smaller, rural communities with few alternatives.

Thinking Globally

As one of the world's most industrialized countries, the United States has the advantage of technology and monetary resources to support attempts to preserve water resources and to ensure a safe supply of drinking water. To most Americans, water quality is as much a matter of aesthetics as of health—a view shared among developed countries. But from a global perspective, the concerns and attention paid to the issue of managing water resources are quite different. Table 7.2 shows the differences in annual water use in various countries around the world.

What differences are there between water management in the United States as compared to other nations?

1. In most developing countries, water policy has been almost totally health based; little attention is paid to the recreational or scenic value of waterways—values considered luxuries in economies struggling to fund any type of environmental program at all. Although all nations respond to the problem of water scarcity through the strategies outlined earlier in this chapter, what minimal environmental resources developing countries have must be spread thinly between air and water pollution, with groundwater contamination receiving the bulk of funds. Many countries have only marginal enforcement operations to handle water pollution, and legislation to control and punish polluters is weak where it exists at all. There is a shortage of lawyers with expertise in environmental law and even fewer judges who are informed or sympathetic.

2. Water management policies in many developing countries have led to soil erosion and desertification, which threaten nearly a third of the Earth's surface.

TABLE 7.2 Annual Water Use in Different Countries

Country	Annual Use per Capita (gallons)	Residential Use (%)	Industry/Agricultural Use (%)
United States	525,000	10	90
Canada	310,000	13	87
Belgium	221,000	6	94
India	132,000	3	97
China	122,000	6	94
Poland	112,000	14	86
Nicaragua	72,000	18	82
Malta	16,000	100	0

SOURCE: U.S. Environmental Protection Agency, *Water on Tap: A Consumer's Guide to the Nation's Drinking Water*, at www.epa.gov/safewater/wot, accessed October 13, 2002.

Desertification refers to the process by which the land gradually becomes less capable of supporting life, and nonproductive. Desertification has four primary causes: overgrazing on rangelands, overcultivation of croplands, waterlogging and salting of irrigated lands, and deforestation. An additional 100 million acres, mostly in India and Pakistan, are estimated by the UN Environment Programme to suffer from salinization, which occurs in dry regions when evaporation near the soil surface leaves behind a thin salt residue. Salinity also affects water quality in Peru and Mexico, where the annual loss of output as a result of salinization is estimated at 1 million tons of food grains, or enough to provide basic rations to 5 million people.

3. Enduring drought has led to not only a water shortage but also declining water quality. In China, for instance, more than half of the nation's 700 cities suffer chronic water shortages, causing $15 billion in lost industrial output every year. An estimated 23 million people are short of drinking water, and more than 73 million acres of farmland have been damaged. The problem stems from the fact that China has about as much water as Canada but 40 times more people. As the cities grow, the demand increases, wetlands dry up as water is diverted, and species of fish are disappearing.[53]

4. Most countries responding to water problems do so on a place-specific basis, using scientific, engineering, and institutional knowledge that has limited transferability, according to the organization Resources for the Future. Some simply cannot afford the technologies and strategies that have been internationally accepted to face individual environmental challenges, whether on a municipal or corporate level. Foreign investors come into an area using pollution control measures that correspond to their own capabilities and profit-making agendas, with little regard for local culture and values. As a result, "it is difficult to develop commonly understood and generally applicable management policies, practices, and interventions at regional or global scale."[54]

5. The potential for conflict over transboundary water pollution and shared watercourses is much greater on other continents than it is in North America. Almost 40 percent of the world's population lives in international river basins; nearly 50 countries on four continents have more than three quarters of their total land in the 214 multinational river basins, including 57 in Africa and 48 in Europe. Thirteen of the river basins are shared by five or more countries; in Europe, four river basins are shared by four or more countries and regulated by more than 175 treaties.

In developing countries, in contrast, there are significantly fewer agreements on shared water resources. Africa has a complex system of river basins, but less than 40 treaties regulate their use. In Asia, only 30 treaties have been drawn up to regulate the five basins shared by four or more countries.[55]

International cooperation on water issues can be traced back to the 16th century when water was viewed as an economic commodity; control over water focused on navigation of watercourses and the shared use of water for agriculture, fishing, and later, industry. Over time, pollution of watercourses among neighboring nations, along with concerns about downstream users, led to hundreds of regional agreements over water use. The 1997 United Nations Convention on the Law of the Non-Navigational Uses of International Watercourses sought to codify what historically was customary law. The lack of support for the agreement is due in part to new definitions of watercourses, which originally were considered parts of rivers or lakes that straddled or crossed borders. Now, that perspective is seen as too narrow as countries address problems like riparian areas, the relationship between surface water and groundwater, and the role of state sovereignty.[56]

Finally, environmental organizations in the United States have a longer history and have been much more successful than have their counterparts in other countries in raising the public's awareness about water quality. For instance, Clean Water Action, known initially as the Fisherman's Clean Water Action Group, was formed in 1971 and subsequently focused on implementation of the Clean Water Act of 1972. Over time, it has become a clearinghouse for a national coalition of state and local advocacy organizations that focus on clean and affordable drinking water.[57] In many developing nations, polluted waters have always been a way of life, and there is little knowledge regarding the care and advantages of clean water. As a result, there have been fewer grassroots efforts to demand stronger enforcement and less media attention to gross violations and health risks.

Although efforts are being made to transfer American technology to both developed and developing nations to improve water quality, most observers believe the best that can be done for now is to buy time. Early efforts at providing assistance in the former Soviet Union were often poorly thought out or were abandoned before fulfillment, leading some governments to rethink their aid plans. As one researcher notes:

> What the West needs at this point is not a detailed blueprint for future action, but a new intellectual framework for approaching the problem: patience is necessary. More importantly, policymakers must think in terms of multiyear time frames, collective action, mechanisms for developing joint strategies, and coordination.[58]

NOTES

1. New Mexico Acequia Association, "Our Mission," at www.acequiaweb.org, accessed May 20, 2005. The author is indebted to Anita Lavadie of Taos, New Mexico, for introducing her to the history and custom of acequia culture.

2. See Jose A. Rivera, *Acequia Culture: Water Land, and Community in the Southwest* (Albuquerque: University of New Mexico Press, 1998). See also La Mesilla Acequia, "History of Acequias,"at www.lmacequia.org, accessed May 20, 2005; Charles L. Briggs and John R. Van Ness, *Land, Water, and Culture: New Perspectives on Hispanic Land Grants* (Albuquerque: University of New Mexico Press, 1987); and Michael C. Meyer, *Water in the Hispanic Southwest: A Social and Legal History, 1550–1850* (Tucson: University of Arizona Press, 1984).

3. Stanley G. Crawford, *Mayordomo: Chronicle of an Acequia in Northern New Mexico* (Albuquerque: University of New Mexico Press, 1988).

4. Jose Rivera, "Acequias de Comun and Sustainable Development: Reflections from the Upper Rio Grande Watershed," Paper presented at the Congreso Nacional, October 5, 2000, at www.lamcequia.org, accessed May 20, 2005.

5. U.S. Geological Survey, *Estimated Use of Water in the United States in 2000,* U.S.G.S. Circular 1268 (2004), at www.usgs.gov, accessed May 22, 2005.

6. Ibid.

7. Jacques Leslie, "Running Dry: What Happens When the World No Longer Has Enough Freshwater?" *Harper's, 301,* no. 1802 (July 2000): 37–52.

8. Ibid., 49–50.

9. See George Wharton James, *Reclaiming the Arid West: The Story of the United States Reclamation Service* (New York: Dodd, Mead, 1917).

10. Robert Gottlieb, *A Life of Its Own: The Politics and Power of Water* (New York: Harcourt Brace Jovanovich, 1988), 48.

11. See Wallace Stegner, *This Is Dinosaur* (New York: Knopf, 1955). At that time, the Bureau of Reclamation also had the proposed Glen Canyon Dam near the Arizona-Utah border on the drawing boards; the project was eventually built after the Echo Park controversy. Even though the Glen Canyon project provides hydroelectric power to 400,000 people in seven states, its original purpose was to store water in Lake Powell, which holds 26.7 million acre-feet of water when full. Environmentalists are now seeking to see Lake Powell drained to restore Glen Canyon to its original beauty.

12. See Constance Elizabeth Hunt, *Down by the River* (Washington, DC: Island Press, 1988), 11–14.

13. See Tom Harris, *Death in the Marsh* (Washington, DC: Island Press, 1991).

14. Gottlieb, A *Life of Its Own,* 270–271.

15. Shaun McKinnon, "State's Draw of River Water Declines," *Arizona Republic,* June 24, 2005, B-1.

16. The issues were discussed as part of a series of border roundtable discussions in 2000 and 2001 in preparation of the Draft Border XXI Plan.

17. See Benedykt Dziegielewski and Duane D. Baumann, "Tapping Alternatives: The Benefits of Managing Urban Water Demands," *Environment, 34,* no. 9 (November 1992): 6–11.

18. U.S. Fish and Wildlife Service, *Classification of Wetlands and Deepwater Habitats of the United States* (Washington, DC: Author, December 1979), at http://wetlands.fws.gov, accessed June 25, 2005.

19. U.S. Fish and Wildlife Service, *National Wetlands Inventory,* at www.nwi.fws.gov, accessed July 28, 2002.

20. Coastal America, "President Bush's Wetlands Initiative on Track," News release, April 21, 2005, at www.coastalamerica.gov, accessed June 25, 2005.

21. See Frank Graham Jr., "Of Broccoli and Marshes," *Audubon, 7,* (July 1990): 102.

22. Federal Interagency Committee for Wetland Delineation, *Federal Manual for Identifying and Delineating Jurisdictional Wetlands* (Washington, D.C.: U.S. GPO, January, 1989.

23. Warren E. Leary, "In Wetlands Debate, Acres and Dollars Hinge on Definitions," *New York Times,* October 15, 1991, C-4.

24. William K. Stevens, "Panel Urges Big Wetlands Restoration Project," *New York Times,* December 12, 1991, A-16.

25. Jon Kusler, "Wetlands Delineation: An Issue of Science or Politics?" *Environment, 34,* no. 2 (March 1992): 7–11, 29–37.

26. Coastal America, *1992 Memorandum of Understanding,* at www.coastalamerica.gov, accessed June 25, 2005.

27. Earthjustice, "America's Waters Vulnerable to Development, Pollution," News release, August 12, 2004, at www.earthjustice.org/news, accessed June 25, 2005.

28. White House, "President Announces Wetlands Initiative on Earth Day," News release, April 22, 2004, at www.whitehouse.gov/news, accessed June 25, 2005.

29. Coastal America, "President Bush's Wetlands Initiative on Track."

30. Marjory Stoneman Douglas, *The Everglades: River of Grass* (Sarasota, FL: Pineapple Press, 1997). Douglas writes about the Everglades in another genre in *A River in Flood, and Other Florida Stories* (Gainesville: University Press of Florida, 1998).

31. See Steven M. Davis and John C. Ogden, eds., *Everglades: The Ecosystem and Its Restoration* (Delray Beach, FL: St. Lucie Press, 1994); Thomas E. Lodge, *The Everglades Handbook: Understanding the Ecosystem* (Delray Beach, FL: St. Lucie Press, 1994); David McCally, *The Everglades: An Environmental History* (Gainesville: University Press of Florida, 1999); Ted Levin, *Liquid Land: A Journey Through the Florida Everglades* (Athens: University of Georgia Press, 2003).

32. Comprehensive Everglades Restoration Plan, "About Everglades Restoration," at www.evergladesplan.org, accessed June 11, 2005.

33. Ibid.

34. Comprehensive Everglades Restoration Plan, "CERP Vision Statement," at www.evergladesplan.org, accessed June 11, 2005.

35. Ibid.

36. Florida Department of Environmental Protection, "Everglades Forever Act," at www.dep.state.fl.us/evergladesforever, accessed June 11, 2005.

37. Pamela Smith Hayford, "Everglades Restoration to Top $600 million," *News-Press,* June 9, 2005, at www.news-press.com, accessed June 11, 2005.

38. "Judge Finds Violations of Everglades Cleanup Deal," *Sun-Sentinel,* at www.sun-sentinel.com/news, accessed June 11, 2005.

39. Comprehensive Everglades Restoration Plan, "CERP Vision Statement."

40. "Remarks at the Signing of the Water Quality Act of 1965, October 2, 1965," *Public Papers of the President: Lyndon B. Johnson* (Washington, DC: U.S. Government Printing Office, 1966), 1035.

41. Gottlieb, *A Life of Its Own,* 163.

42. The Court's interpretation is outlined in *United States v. Republic Steel Corporation,* 362 U.S. 482 (1960); *United States v. Standard Oil Company,* 384 U.S. 224 (1966).

43. Stormwater runoff is becoming an increasingly important issue in urban water policy. See Tom Arrandale, "Pollution in the Gutter," *Governing,* December 1998, 51–60.

44. James Ridgeway, *The Politics of Ecology* (New York: Dutton, 1970), 51.

45. David Hosansky, "Drinking Water Bill Clears, Clinton Expected to Sign," *Congressional Quarterly Weekly Report,* August 3, 1996, 2179.

46. Jonathan H. Adler, "Wrong Way On Water," *National Review Online,* November 13, 2001, at www.nationalreview.com, accessed July 27, 2002.

47. Ibid.

48. Pete Yost, "Money, Politics and Pollution: How Policy Is Changed," *Detroit News,* February 16, 2004, at www.detnews.com/2004, accessed January 1, 2005.

49. California Department of Health Services, "MTBE Regulations," at www.dhs.ca.gov/ps/ddwem/chemicals/MTBE, accessed January 1, 2005.

50. Environmental Protection Agency, *Achieving Clean Air and Clean Water: The Report of the Blue Ribbon Panel on Oxygenates in Gasoline,* EPA420-R-99-021 (September 15, 1999), at www.epa.gov, accessed January 1, 2005.

51. Yost, "Money, Politics and Pollution."

52. Ibid.

53. Philip P. Pan, "The Wetlands Are Running Dry," *Washington Post National Weekly Edition,* July 9–15, 2001, 17.

54. Baruch Boxer, "Global Water Management Dilemmas," *Resources* (Winter 2001), 5–9.

55. Robin Clarke, *Water: The International Crisis* (Cambridge, MA: MIT Press, 1993), 91–92.

56. David Hunter, James Salzman, and Durwood Zaelke, *International Environmental Law and Policy,* 2nd ed. (New York: Foundation Press, 2002), 794–796.

57. Christopher J. Bosso, *Environment, Inc.: From Grassroots to Beltway* (Lawrence: University Press of Kansas, 2005), 64.

58. Murray Feshbach, *Ecological Disaster: Cleaning Up the Hidden Legacy of the Soviet Regime* (New York: Twentieth Century Press, 1995), 106.

FURTHER READING

Robin Kundis Craig. *The Clean Water Act and the Constitution.* Washington, DC: Environmental Law Institute, 2005.

Caroline Figueres, John Rockstrom, and Cecilia Tortajada. *Rethinking Water Management.* London: Earthscan Publications, 2003.

Robert Jerome Glennon. *Water Follies: Groundwater Pumping and the Fate of America.* Covelo, CA: Island Press, 2004.

Constance Elizabeth Hunt. *Thirsty Planet: Strategies for Sustainable Water Management.* New York: Palgrave Macmillan, 2004.

William R. Lowry. *Dam Politics: Restoring America's Rivers.* Washington, DC: Georgetown University Press, 2003.

Fred Pearce. *Keepers of the Spring: Reclaiming Our Water in an Age of Globalization.* Covelo, CA: Island Press, 2005.

Anita Roddick and Brooke S. Biggs. *Troubled Water: Saints, Sinners, Truth and Lies About the Global Water Crisis.* White River Junction, VT: Chelsea Green, 2005.

Jeffrey Rothfeder. *Every Drop for Sale: Our Desperate Battle Over Water in a World About to Run Out.* New York: Penguin, 2004.

Paul A. Sabatier et al., eds. *Swimming Upstream: Collaborative Approaches to Watershed Management.* Cambridge, MA: MIT Press, 2005.

Sharon Spray and Karen McGlothlin, eds. *Wetlands.* Lanham, MD: Rowman & Littlefield, 2004.

Julie Trotter and Paul Slack. *Managing Water Resources, Past and Present.* New York: Oxford University Press, 2005.

Kenneth M. Vigil. *Clean Water: An Introduction to Water Quality and Water Pollution Control.* Corvallis: Oregon State University Press, 2003.

8

Air Quality:
Pollution and Solutions

We can't afford to wait until all the evidence is in.
The stakes could not be higher.
—DR. ALAN LLOYD, CHAIR, CALIFORNIA AIR RESOURCES BOARD[1]

California has always been the vanguard state when it comes to air quality policy, primarily because many of its cities rank in the top tier of metropolitan areas that regularly exceed federal pollution control standards. Los Angeles, for example, is the only U.S. city rated "extreme" for pollution by the Environmental Protection Agency (EPA).

In September 2004, California's Air Resources Board (CARB), which governs mobile sources of air pollution like cars and trucks, adopted landmark regulations to reduce tailpipe carbon dioxide emissions that increase global warming. Under the new rules, automobile manufacturers were given until the 2009 model year to start producing vehicles that will eventually reduce greenhouse gas emissions from new cars by an estimated 34 percent, phased in over a seven-year period. CARB staff estimated compliance would add about $1,000 to the cost of the cleaner-burning car, a figure disputed by automakers, who testified at a hearing that the cost would be closer to $3,000. The overall cost to the industry was estimated at $6 billion.[2]

> *Particulate matter produced from wildfires in the West creates serious health problems for sensitive persons, obscures visibility, and reduces regional air quality.*
>
> ANITA LAVADIE

The policy change is critical for several reasons. In California, transportation sources produce nearly 60 percent of the state's carbon dioxide emissions that contribute to smog; 98 percent of the state's total carbon dioxide emissions come from burning fossil fuels. The number of vehicles per person has doubled in California since 1940, increasing the magnitude of the problem. In setting the new standards, California forces automakers to build vehicles for an even larger market; and seven other eastern states, including New York and Massachusetts, promised they would adopt similar regulations. Under the 1970 Clean Air Act, California can set air pollution limits that are stricter than existing federal standards. Canada is also considering adopting the California standards.[3] Examples like this point to one of the few policy problems—air quality—in which state governments have clearly taken the lead while the federal government makes minimal progress. The State and Territorial Air Pollution Program Administrators (STAPPA), for instance, was an active participant in Senate hearings on the administration's 2002 proposals to change regulations on New Source Review, described later in this chapter.[4]

At times, public officials have been overly optimistic about how much improvement could be attained. On August 14, 1943, Los Angeles Mayor Fletcher E. Bowron announced at a press conference that the city's smog would be entirely eliminated within four months.[5] The city's air quality at the time was perceived as a product of the region's burgeoning industry—a relatively recent urban development. But air pollution was a problem long before the mayor of Los Angeles made his prediction. There are references to the fumes produced at the asphalt mining town of Hit, about 100 miles west of Babylon, in the writings of King Tukulti in around B.C. 900, and in B.C. 61, the philosopher Seneca reported on the "heavy air of Rome" and its "pestilential vapors and soot." Marco Polo refused to use coal as a fuel because of its smoky odors. Foreigners traveling to Elizabethan England were astonished and revolted at the filthy smoke produced by domestic fires and workshops.[6]

The history of cleaning up urban air pollution is marked by small successes on what has proven to be a much longer road than most early municipal officials ever anticipated. Three characteristics can be used to describe global attempts to improve air quality: (a) In the United States, local government historically has been given most of the responsibility for pollution control; (b) policy efforts have been split between those who desire improvement because of impaired visibility and aesthetic reasons and those who recognize the health effects of pollution, especially particulate matter and ozone; and (c) in most other parts of the world, national governments, rather than municipalities, have taken the initiative for improving air quality, with varying degrees of success. This chapter reviews these characteristics and the challenge of developing policies to control air pollution both in the United States and in other countries. It also explores the ways in which the problem has been expanded to other concerns such as toxic air pollution, visibility, and transboundary air pollution.

THE COMPONENTS OF AIR POLLUTION

Until well into the 20th century, the components of pollution were thought to be primarily smoke and soot (suspended particulate matter) and sulfur dioxide— waste products from home heating, industrial facilities, and utility power plants. With industrialization and the advent of the automobile, that list has expanded to include a broad range of emissions, including some considered toxic. These pollutants are found in the atmosphere; and although most are human-made, some, like particulate matter, include the fine particles of dust and vegetation that are natural in origin and small enough to penetrate the most sensitive regions of the respiratory tract.

As Table 8.1 indicates, today the term *air pollution* is usually applied internationally to the six conventional (or criteria) pollutants identified and measured by the EPA: carbon monoxide, lead, nitrous oxides, ozone, particulate matter, and sulfur oxides. The EPA's Office of Air Quality Planning and Standards reviews the status of the six pollutants, which are measured in parts per million (ppm) by volume, milligrams per cubic meter of air, and micrograms per cubic meter of air. The EPA periodically makes changes in the national standards for air quality, usually lowering the levels of pollutants that are considered to be exceeding allowable exposure. Based on federal legislation, the EPA sets target dates by which regions throughout the United States are required to meet the standards; and if they are not met, various sanctions are imposed. These range from fines for noncompliance to actually shutting down polluting facilities.

TABLE 8.1 **Components and Health Effects of Air Pollution**

Criteria Pollutant	Sources	Health Effects
Carbon monoxide (CO)	Motor vehicles	Interferes with ability of the blood to absorb oxygen
Lead (Pb)	Motor vehicles, lead smelters	Affects kidneys, reproductive and nervous systems; accumulates in bones; may cause hyperactivity in children
Nitrous oxides (NO_x)	Electric utility boilers, motor vehicles	Causes increased susceptibility to viral infections, lung irritation
Ozone	Formed by a chemical reaction of NO_2 and hydrocarbons	Irritates respiratory system; impairs lung function; aggravates asthma
Particulate matter	Combustion from industry, forest fires, windblown dust, vehicles	Organic carcinogenic (PM_{10}) compounds can migrate into lungs, increasing respiratory distress
Sulfur oxides (SO_2)	Utility plant boilers, oil and chemical refineries	Aggravates symptoms of heart and lung disease; increases respiratory illnesses and colds

There are three primary categories of sources for conventional pollutants: stationary or point sources, such as factories and power plants; mobile sources, including cars, trucks, and aircraft; and domestic sources, such as home heating or consumer products.

Current air quality law establishes two types of standards for conventional pollutants. Primary standards set limits to protect public health, including the health of "sensitive" populations such as asthmatics, children, and the elderly. Secondary standards set limits to protect public welfare, including protection against decreased visibility and against damage to animals, crops, vegetation, and buildings.

AIR QUALITY AND HEALTH

The most serious air quality impact that concerns policy makers now is health. It is difficult to pinpoint exactly when concerns about health effects of air pollution made their way to the policy agenda. One factor that made it difficult for policy makers to reach consensus on what to do about air pollution was the lack of a consensus about its sources. Smoky chimneys and smokestacks were considered part of the price urban dwellers paid for living in an industrialized society, and most people were probably unaware of any damage to their health.

The emphasis on the health effects of pollution was due largely to the role of the U.S. Public Health Service, which was given responsibility for air pollution legislation from 1959 until the passage of the Clean Air Act in 1963. Although little policy initiation occurred before 1963, the surgeon general did convene the First National Conference on Air Pollution in 1958.

More than 100 published studies have identified the health effects of urban ozone pollution. People breathing ozone, even at concentrations below the current national standards, appear to be susceptible to increased respiratory hospital admissions, frequent and severe asthma attacks, inflammation of the upper airways, coughing and breathing pains, reaction to irritants, sensitivity to allergens, and decreased lung function much like that smokers experience. Epidemiological studies show a strong correlation between increased mortality and ozone pollution.

Dozens of studies have focused on the impact of pollution on children, who are most at risk. One of the most recently reported studies, the Children's Health Study conducted by the University of Southern California over an eight-year period, found that children from ages 10 to 18 suffered clinically significant reductions in lung function as they reached adulthood. Fine particulate matter, rather than ozone, appeared to have the greatest effect on lung capacity, which was particularly important because researchers monitored older children and over a longer period than previous researchers had done.[7]

Reports by environmental and consumer groups have given the public more information than ever before on the status of the air quality not only in their own state, but throughout the nation. The reports have received considerable attention from the media, and they have served as a way of keeping air quality on the political agenda. Usually published in nontechnical formats, the reports have become a way of keeping score on how much progress the EPA and its state

TABLE 8.2   U.S. Asthma Capitals, 2005

1.	Knoxville, TN	11.	Indianapolis, IN
2.	Memphis, TN	12.	Columbus, OH
3.	Louisville, KY	13.	Pittsburgh, PA
4.	Toledo, OH	14.	Phoenix-Mesa, AZ
5.	Washington, DC	15.	Birmingham, AL
6.	St. Louis, MO	16.	Chattanooga, TN
7.	Allentown, PA	17.	Detroit, MI
8.	Springfield, MA	18.	Atlanta, GA
9.	Grand Rapids, MI	19.	Lancaster, PA
10.	Scranton, PA	20.	Fresno, CA

SOURCE: "2005 Ranking: The U.S. Asthma Capitals," at www.asthmacapitals.com, accessed February 16, 2005.

counterparts have made per year. In addition, more information is available than ever before on the health impacts of air pollution—much of it distributed on the Internet.

Researchers from the Asthma and Allergy Foundation of America, in conjunction with the Research Triangle Institute, for instance, created an interactive map for consumers on the country's asthma capitals. Their 2005 ranking of U.S. metropolitan areas is based on analysis of data regarding 12 individual factors, including reported and predicted prevalence of asthma, annual pollen levels, public smoking laws, and the reported number of quick-relief rescue medications prescribed per patient. All but two of the top 20 worst cities for those with asthma were east of the Mississippi River (see Table 8.2).

This ranking is in stark contrast to indices for air quality based on criteria pollutants. The American Lung Association (ALA) issues an annual public report assessing U.S. air quality on a national basis. Metropolitan areas and counties are ranked according to short-term and year-round particle pollution and for ozone pollution, a major component of smog. Over time, the rankings of various areas have changed somewhat, although California's South Coast Air Basin (which includes Los Angeles, Orange, Riverside, and San Bernardino counties) is perennially identified with the nation's worst air quality, as seen in Table 8.3. But several other cities that had previously escaped the list were designated among the worst ozone areas in 2005, including Hanford-Corcoran, California, and the Pittsburgh, Pennsylvania, area. In contrast, some metropolitan regions that had been on the list for years—such as San Diego, California, and Phoenix-Mesa, Arizona—had sufficiently better air quality to have dropped off the top 20 listing.

At the opposite end of the pollution spectrum are the nation's cleanest cities for ozone air pollution (see Table 8.4). What makes the information intriguing is that many of these areas, such as Colorado Springs, Colorado, and Spokane, Washington, have a population of about a half million persons, and Honolulu,

TABLE 8.3 Top 20 Metropolitan Areas With the Worst Ozone Air Pollution, 2000--2005

2000 Rank	2005 Rank	Metropolitan Area*
1	1	Los Angeles–Long Beach–Riverside, CA
2	2	Bakersfield, CA
3	3	Fresno-Madera, CA
4	4	Visalia-Porterville, CA
10	5	Merced, CA
5	6	Houston-Baytown-Huntsville, TX
11	7	Sacramento-Arden-Arcade-Truckee, CA-NV
14	8	Dallas–Ft.Worth, TX
16	9	New York-Newark-Bridgeport, NY-NJ-CT-PA
13	10	Philadelphia-Camden-Vineland, PA-NJ-DE-MD
7	11	Washington–Baltimore–Northern Virginia, DC-MD-VA-WV
8	12	Charlotte-Gastonia-Salisbury, NC-SC
**	13	Hanford-Corcoran, CA
**	13	Cleveland-Akron-Elyria, OH
12	15	Knoxville-Sevierville, La Follette, TN
**	15	Modesto, CA
**	17	Pittsburgh, New Castle, PA
**	18	Youngstown–Warren–East Liverpool, OH-PA
**	19	Columbus-Marion-Chillicothe, OH
**	20	Detroit-Warren-Flint, MI
**	20	Buffalo-Niagara-Cattaraugus, NY

*The U.S. Census Bureau revised definitions for metropolitan statistical areas in 2003, making some comparisons with previous reports difficult.

**These metropolitan areas were not listed among the top 20 in the 2000 report.

SOURCE: American Lung Association, *State of the Air 2005*, at www.lungusa.org, accessed April 29, 2005.

Hawaii, is nearing 1 million. This shows that even in urban areas, pollution is influenced by factors other than population, such as weather and topography.

PUBLIC POLICY RESPONSES

For most of the 20th century, air pollution was considered a local problem in the United States. As a result, most of the efforts to do something about it have been accomplished by municipal governments. By 1912, industrial smoke, the hallmark of urban growth after the turn of the century, was regulated in 28 U.S. cities with populations of 200,000 or more. Smoke was the prime target of most

TABLE 8.4 Cities With the Least Ozone Air Pollution, in Alphabetical Order, 2005

Ames-Boone, IA

Bellingham, WA

Brownsville-Harlingen-Raymondville, TX

Cedar Rapids, IA

Colorado Springs, CO

Deltona–Daytona Beach–Palm Coast, FL

Des Moines-Newton-Pella, IA

Duluth, MN-WI

Eugene-Springfield, OR

Fargo-Wahpeton, ND-MN

Farmington, NM

Flagstaff, AZ

Fort Polk South–De Ridder, LA

Honolulu, HI

Jacksonville, FL

Laredo, TX

Lincoln, NE

Logan, UT-ID

Medford, OR

Mt. Vernon–Anacortes, WA

Salem, OR

Salinas, CA

Sioux Falls, SD

Spokane, WA

Wausau-Merrill, WI

SOURCE: American Lung Association, *State of the Air 2005,* at www.lungusa.org, accessed April 29, 2005.

ordinances because it was visible, but little attention was paid to controlling the problem.[8]

Until the passage of the Clean Air Act in 1963, the federal government took only minimal interest in the problem. In 1912, the Bureau of Mines conducted research on smoke control, which at the time was considered to be the only form of pollution. In 1925, the Public Health Service began to study carbon monoxide in automotive exhaust; but for the most part, the federal role was minor. In 1948, a six-day smog siege in Donora, Pennsylvania, killed 20 persons and sickened 6,000 residents, focusing national attention on a problem that until then had been considered unique to Los Angeles. The Donora incident was followed in December 1952 by a similar sulfurous smog episode in London, and in 1953 by another incident in New York, resulting in 200 deaths.[9] All three events lent some urgency to the problem. As city officials began to realize the irrelevance of political boundaries to pollution control, they began to coordinate their regulatory efforts.

The discovery in 1949 that automobiles were a prime source of pollution forestalled statewide controls on industrial sources, and local government stepped in to fill the void left by federal inaction. In 1955, Los Angeles officials began to coordinate their efforts with the nation's top automakers, and Congress appropriated $5 million for research into motor vehicle emissions—the beginning of federal intervention in urban air pollution regulation. Research in the early 1960s debunked the idea that pollution was a problem only in the area immediately adjacent to the source or in urban areas. Studies began to show that pollution was being transported over long distances, causing environmental damage in regions far removed from the actual source. Long-range transport of sulfur and nitrogen compounds across international boundaries—a phenomenon known as acid rain—made air pollution a global problem. These findings made air quality much more than a simple local question and focused problem solving on Congress.

During the 1960s, four members of Congress did attempt to bring the federal government back into the air pollution policy debate: Edmund Muskie, senator from Maine; Abraham Rubicoff, former secretary of the Department of Health, Education, and Welfare (HEW); Kennedy Roberts, member of Congress from Alabama; and Paul Schenck, member of Congress from Ohio. Their efforts were largely responsible for passage of the pioneering 1963 Clean Air Act, which expanded research and technical assistance programs, gave the federal government investigative and abatement authority, and encouraged the automobile and petroleum industries to develop exhaust control devices. In November 1967, President Lyndon Johnson signed a second air quality bill, which left the primary responsibility for air pollution control with the state and local governments, suggesting that the federal agencies study, but not establish, national automobile emission standards.

Meanwhile, environmental groups were pressuring Muskie to produce a new federal bill. The senator, an early contender for the 1972 Democratic presidential nomination, felt the sting of their criticism. A 1970 report by consumer activist Ralph Nader referred to "the collapse of the federal air pollution effort" and laid the blame squarely on Muskie's shoulders.[10] Muskie and the members of his Public Works Committee staff, relying on estimates provided by the National Air Pollution Control Administration (a part of HEW), proposed tough new federal standards for air quality and a timetable by which the standards had to be met through the filing of state implementation plans (SIPs). Some groups had called the states' response to the 1967 law "disappointing" because so little progress had been made in its implementation.

The 1970 Clean Air Act required the newly created Environmental Protection Agency to (1) develop federal air quality standards, the National Ambient Air Quality Standards, or NAAQS; (2) establish emission standards for motor vehicles, effective with fiscal 1975; and (3) develop emission standards and hazardous emission levels for new stationary sources. The legislation went further than ever before by giving the EPA responsibility for regulating fuels and fuel additives, for certifying and subsidizing on-the-road inspections and assembly-line testing of auto emission control systems.[11] States faced a formidable task when the 1970 act gave them responsibility for preparing emission reduction plans that would achieve the new federal standards within three years. If the states did not comply, the legislation authorized the EPA to step in and promulgate a federal plan. In addition to facing tight deadlines for plan preparation, neither the states nor the newly created EPA knew very much about translating federal standards into emission limits on sources. Therefore, relatively crude rules—like requiring all sources to diminish emissions by some specified percentage—were often employed.[12]

Critics charge that the 1970 law had several major faults. First, there was some ambiguity over the intent of the act with regard to the setting of auto emission levels. The legislation gave automakers a one-year extension if they made a good-faith effort to comply but found that technology was not available to meet the new standards. Second, Congress appropriated only minimal amounts for research into the development of control devices that were in some cases required but did not yet exist. Third, stationary sources such as steel mills and utility power plants faced serious problems because control devices were either prohibitively expensive or technologically unfeasible.[13]

Five major automakers (Chrysler, Ford, General Motors, International Harvester, and Volvo) responded in early 1972 by filing for an extension of the requirement that they meet emission standards by 1975, arguing that they needed additional time to comply with the law. EPA administrator William Ruckelshaus denied their request for an extension, so the automakers appealed to the federal court, which ordered Ruckelshaus to review his original denial.[14] The automobile manufacturers argued that the necessary catalyst technology would not be available in time to meet the federal deadline, and Chrysler and American Motors testified that, even if the vehicles could be mass-produced in time, they would break down.[15] Ruckelshaus again denied the request for an extension, then reconsidered and granted the automakers what they were seeking, setting interim standards that the automobile companies did not appeal.

Implementation of the 1970 law was further hampered by what one observer has called "the enduring reluctance of the public to make significant sacrifices for the sake of healthy air."[16] The nation was locked into a pattern of rapid inflation and high unemployment, which was coupled with the imposition of an oil embargo by the Organization of the Petroleum Exporting Countries (OPEC) in October 1973. With rising concern over energy supplies, in March 1974, President Nixon proposed a package of 13 amendments to the 1970 Clean Air Act, thereby freezing the interim 1975 auto emission standards for two more years. In 1975, the automakers applied for another one-year extension, which was granted by new EPA administrator Russell Train, largely as a result of claims that the catalysts produced a sulfuric acid mist.[17]

By 1975, the deadline for states to attain the pollution standards expired, and many areas were still not in compliance. The NAAQS for ozone, which had been set at 0.08 parts per million (ppm), was routinely being violated. Industry pressure to relax the emission standards on automobiles resulted in the passage of new Clean Air Act amendments in 1977. The legislation suspended the deadlines for automakers and extended the deadlines by which states were to have attained federal standards to 1982. If a state's implementation plan made all reasonable attempts to meet the standards but was unable to do so, the state had to submit a second plan that would bring the area into compliance no later than December 1987. This issue primarily affected California. A key element of the 1977 law was a provision, shepherded through Congress by the Sierra Club, that states be required to show that any new sources of pollution would not worsen existing pollution conditions. This complex concept, known as prevention of significant deterioration (PSD), required businesses to install the best available control technology (BACT) to ensure that any potential pollution was minimized.

The concept had first been outlined in a 1972 Sierra Club suit against EPA administrator William Ruckelshaus[18] in which the organization argued that EPA guidelines under the 1970 Clean Air Act would permit significant deterioration of the nation's clean air, violating congressional intent. The federal district court agreed, ruling that the EPA could not approve state implementation plans that degraded existing air quality even if the region still met national air quality standards. The EPA appealed, but the U.S. Supreme Court's 4–4 ruling in 1973 upheld the district court. The EPA proposed new regulations to implement the Court's ruling in 1974.

The 1977 amendments required more aggressive antipollution programs and gave the EPA authority to designate those regions that did not meet federal standards as "nonattainment" areas. The amendments included a new provision requiring the EPA to reevaluate the NAAQS and to revise them as necessary, at least once every five years. Researchers from Johns Hopkins University recommended, for example, that the ozone standard be lowered from 0.08 to 0.06 ppm to protect public health. Despite concerns about the health risks of ozone, the EPA actually weakened the NAAQS in 1979 when it raised the one-hour standard to 0.12 ppm. Even with the revised ozone levels, by 1982, numerous areas were still out of compliance. Even though the 1977 amendments required the EPA to review the NAAQS every five years, the agency missed the 1985 deadline, giving itself a two-year extension. In 1990, the EPA missed another five-year deadline.

The EPA showed more flexibility toward industry with the introduction in 1979 of a "bubble" policy, which allowed businesses to find the least expensive method of reducing pollution from an entire plant or series of plants rather than from an individual source (as if the entire facility were under a regulatory bubble). The policy allowed companies to choose how to reduce emissions and to use more innovative strategies than were previously required.

The Clean Air Act was scheduled for reauthorization in 1981, but a change in policy direction came with the Reagan administration. As a result, the 1970 legislation remained virtually unchanged until 1990.[19] Chief among the congressional barriers to a new law were Representative John Dingell, a Democrat from Michigan (and chairman of the House Energy and Commerce Committee), who stalled efforts to enact legislation that would impose new standards on automakers; and Senate Majority Leader Robert Byrd, a Democrat from West Virginia, who protected the interests and jobs of the coal miners in his region affected by acid rain proposals.

Clean air legislation regained its place on the policy agenda in the late 1980s, partly because of changes taking place in Congress. Restless Democrats in the House were openly expressing their hostility to Dingell and Henry Waxman of California, members of the House Energy and Commerce Committee, whose personal battles were perceived as holding up the reauthorization. The result was the formation of the Group of Nine—moderate Democrats hoping to break the legislative logjam over urban smog. In the Senate, Byrd was replaced as majority leader by George Mitchell of Maine, who promised an end to the deadlock. Both houses had the opportunity to end the deadlock when the Bush administration unveiled its own clean air proposal, forcing the key players to resolve their differences.[20]

The resulting legislation, signed by President Bush in 1990, contained several proposals that went far beyond those in the 1970 and 1977 acts. The bill established five categories of nonattainment (marginal, moderate, serious, severe, or extreme) and set new deadlines by which areas in those categories must meet federal ozone standards. Only one area, the Los Angeles/South Coast Air Basin, was classified as extreme by the EPA and was given 20 years to meet federal standards. In contrast, severe nonattainment areas were given 15 years from November 1990 (the enactment date of the amendments) to comply; serious areas, nine years; moderate areas, six years; and marginal areas, three years. Plants emitting any of 189 toxic air pollutants were required to cut emissions, and they would be forced to shut down by 2003 if these emissions subjected nearby residents to a cancer risk of more than 1 in10,000. Chemicals that harm earth's protective ozone layer were to be phased out more rapidly than required under the Montreal Protocol, to which the United States is a signatory (see Chapter 10). One of the bill's most contentious portions dealt with acid rain, requiring an annual reduction of sulfur dioxide emissions by 10 million tons by the year 2000, and annual nitrogen dioxide emission reductions of 2.7 million tons by that same date. The cost of the legislation, ranging from $25 to $35 billion dollars, was hotly debated.[21]

President Bush called passage of the 1990 Clean Air Act "the cornerstone of our environmental agenda." But the battle was far from over. Implementation of the 1990 act has been just as controversial as its development. Congressman Waxman charged, "We'll never see clean air in large parts of the country."[22]

Several factors hindered implementation of the 1990 air quality amendment. Among the hurdles faced by the EPA was the regulatory time frame of the 700-page legislation. The implementing regulations are among the most complex the agency has ever issued. Although the issue of nitrous oxide emissions (one of the two chemicals that cause acid rain) took only two pages of the 1990 act, the regulations crafted by the EPA took hundreds of pages. Due to the large volume and complexity of the rules, the EPA has been forced to rely upon outside consultants for many of its rulemakings and on its advisory committees for assistance in deciding which rules to tackle first. Many of those advisory groups, such as the Acid Rain Advisory Committee, with 44 members, were packed with industry members and few representatives of environmental groups.[23] The most complex provisions of the law are those dealing with air toxics, an area in which EPA staff members are notoriously short on expertise.

Within a year after the 1990 law was passed, Congress began stepping back from the thrust of the 1990 amendments. One portion of the legislation, for example, was designed to require state and local planners to adhere to air quality goals when formulating transportation projects. Theoretically, the intent was to force municipalities to look for alternatives to increased use of single-occupancy vehicles. But in 1991 President George H. W. Bush proposed, and Congress accepted, plans for a 185,000-mile national highway system that would increase auto use—at odds with the intent of the air quality act—by giving the most funds under the program to those states with the highest gasoline use.[24]

President Bush's 1992 State of the Union message stalled the implementation process when the president announced a 90-day freeze on all federal regulations and then extended it another 120 days after that. The freeze affected several clean air regulations, including the Pollution Prevention Act, which required polluters to report on the amount of toxic chemicals they generate in order to be authorized to release them. Later that year, the president overruled an EPA regulation requiring industries to obtain permits that include limits on the pollution emitted by each plant. Industry had originally sought the right to exceed the limits after making minor changes in plant operations, without going through the costly and time-consuming process of obtaining a new permit. Citizen groups considered the permit process an important opportunity for public participation; and the EPA, which drafted the regulation, agreed. Bush Sr. then overturned the regulation as a part of his emphasis on deregulation.

In November 1993, the Senate Environment and Public Works Committee issued a "report card" on implementation of the Pollution Prevention Act. The EPA received A's for its acid rain and stratospheric ozone programs, a B for its small business assistance program, a C for its management of the state implementation plan process, and D's for development of air toxic standards and for the implementation of the California Low Emission Vehicle Program.[25] The Senate study trumpeted the success of the acid rain program in devising a market-based approach to environmental regulation and emphasized the importance of environmental quality-based performance standards that create incentives for the development of new technologies.

Since the mid-1990s, most of the revisions in air quality policy have been regulatory, rather than legislative. Congress has attempted no major changes to the 1990 statute, relying instead upon the regulatory agencies to fine-tune the implementation of the law, focusing on ozone and particulate matter—two of the pollution sources with the greatest impact on health.

Ozone

Ozone, a photochemical oxidant that is a major component of smog and a major health and environmental concern, has been the most controversial of the criteria pollutants in the implementation of the 1990 Clean Air Act. In November 1991, most U.S. regions were designated as being either nonattainment or attainment areas, based on whether an area meets the NAAQS for the pollutant. Complicated formulas are used to determine attainment status, and each area was given a deadline by which it was required to comply. Those areas designated as nonattainment were also classified as extreme, severe, serious, moderate, marginal, or submarginal, using the NAAQS in place in 1979.

The American Lung Association (ALA) took the EPA to court in 1991 to force the EPA to revise the 1979 ozone standard of 0.12 ppm, which was supposed to have been reviewed in 1985 and in 1990. The agency missed both review deadlines, and the ALA contended that the EPA disregarded new scientific studies on the health effects of ozone. In 1994, responding to another ALA challenge, the EPA agreed to conduct a review of the studies.

These shortcomings were serious, but seemed manageable, until the dynamics of implementation underwent a fundamental change in November 1994 with the election of Republicans to statehouses and Republicans as the new majority party in Congress. During the first years of implementation, regulations focused on industrial polluters. But when the focus shifted to people's driving habits, opposition to clean air action skyrocketed. Disgruntled citizens generated considerable opposition to state implementation plans, joined by industry groups who saw a political opening to gain some regulatory relief. Governors, in response, began challenging the EPA. As long as Congress was there to back up the EPA, and reopening the act to weaken its provisions was not an option, the EPA could hold firm. Once the new Congress took office in 1995, however, amending the act was a real possibility; the EPA had to scramble to accommodate state demands.

Much of the criticism of the Clean Air Act in the states focused on the enhanced inspection and maintenance system, developed to replace the traditional tailpipe test required under the Clean Air Act. The system was to be implemented through centralized locations to ensure quality control and to separate clearly the testing and repairing of motor vehicles. The EPA required that states with ozone nonattainment areas include the enhanced program as part of their effort to reduce pollution; but in the fall of 1994, several states balked. Groups that represented not only service station owners who could perform the original testing but also motorists began criticizing the enhanced inspection and maintenance program; California was the first state to be permitted to develop an alternative system of testing at both centralized locations and traditional service stations. Additional states then began pressing the EPA for exemptions.[26] Other programs aimed at reducing vehicle emissions have been just as controversial. Illinois officials complained in early 1995 that the EPA had failed to provide guidance on how states were to require car pooling in companies with more than 100 employees. Pennsylvania officials excused employers in the Philadelphia area from complying with the car pool requirement.

Air quality policy has been affected in other ways. A 1995 budget bill that cut fiscal year 1995 spending prohibited the EPA from spending any money to force states to comply with vehicle inspection and maintenance and commuter vehicle trip-reduction programs. In November 1995, Congress passed a highway bill that included some clean air provisions: It ordered the EPA to give states full credit in determining their compliance with the law for noncentralized inspection and maintenance programs; and it abolished federal regulation of speed limits, a policy that the EPA estimated would increase nitrous oxide emissions by about 5 percent per year as vehicles traveled faster and burned more fuel. The following month,

Congress passed a bill making the commuter vehicle trip-reduction program optional, so that states with highly polluted areas would not be forced to require employers to mandate employee car pooling. Throughout the budget process in 1995, Congress included additional riders to appropriations and balanced budget bills that would have restricted EPA's implementation of the Clean Air and other acts; but President Clinton's vetoes blocked those measures, and Congress abandoned them in 1996. That same year, the EPA issued a three-volume document analyzing hundreds of new scientific studies that found evidence of adverse health effects from ozone levels allowed by the 1979 NAAQS.[27]

In July 1997, after public hearings and a formal comment period, the EPA issued a new eight-hour ozone standard of 0.08 ppm; in 1998, Congress set a July 2000 deadline for the next round of attainment designations. These actions prompted lawsuits from three states and several industry interests that believed there was no possibility of complying with the stricter ozone standard. Proponents of the new standard, such as Earthjustice, praised the EPA for taking "a major step forward in public health protection from ozone."[28] The various challenges to the 1997 standard were heard by the U.S. Court of Appeals; in a 1999 decision, the court ruled that the EPA had violated a little-known constitutional theory—the nondelegation doctrine. But the court reaffirmed that the EPA was to make the designations using the NAAQS.[29] When the statutory deadline for the agency to make new designations expired, the EPA still had not complied with the congressional mandate.

In 2001 and 2002, the courts reversed the earlier rulings, rejecting industry arguments and upholding the EPA's authority to set the ozone standard at 0.08 ppm. Even after the court rulings, the EPA failed to make the attainment designation deadline. Environmental groups accused the EPA of "dragging its feet" in implementing tougher air quality standards; and in May 2002, Earthjustice, a public interest law group representing several other organizations, filed notice to take EPA to court to once again.[30] In November 2002, the EPA entered into a consent decree with the environmental groups and agreed to set new ozone designations, using the 0.08 ppm standard, no later than April 2004. The agency complied; the 2004 ozone designations classified 126 areas, representing 474 counties and 31 states, as nonattainment areas. The South Coast Air Basin in southern California was the only area rated severe for ozone; three other California areas were ranked as serious. Most of the designations placed areas in the categories of moderate or marginal.[31]

The implementation process for the new ozone rules was contained in a 279-page document that immediately came under fire by groups that turned to the administrative rulemaking process to air their grievances. A coalition of environmental organizations filed petitions to seek reconsideration of new Bush administration rules on new source review, future designations of nonattainment areas, and clean fuel blends. Two industry coalitions filed petitions asking the EPA to extend deadlines for compliance with the ozone standard for large metropolitan areas because existing and potentially new pollution programs would not enable them to comply in time. Other legal actions were being pursued by the South Coast Air Quality Management District and six northeastern and mid-Atlantic states. Complicating the issue was the fact that rural areas may be penalized in the classification system because their air is polluted by upwind pollution sources transported from other areas.[32]

It is both the ozone standards and the way monitoring results are interpreted that are at the heart of the policy controversy. Those who focus on the health effects of ozone believe that the standards need to be refined even more to protect the public. Critics counter that the current standards are already so stringent that any changes would result in only imperceptible improvement. The ALA study has come under fire because its methodology "fudges the numbers." One analyst notes that 99 percent of residents in San Diego live in areas that are compliant with the EPA's ozone standard; only one rural area is in violation. The ALA *State of the Air Report* counts all 3 million residents as breathing air that violates ozone standards, thus exaggerating the number of people breathing polluted air.[33]

What is clear is that the debate over ozone is far from ending. Challenges to administrative rules and litigation are likely to tie up regulatory action for several years, and advocacy groups such as the Clean Air Task Force, Conservation Law Foundation, and Environmental Justice have joined forces to litigate new rules as quickly as they are promulgated. Coalitions of industry groups, such as the National Petrochemical and Refiners Association, the American Chemistry Council, and the National Association of Manufacturers, are demanding flexibility in meeting the ozone standards, hoping that Bush administration policies and a new EPA administrator will support their interests. But it is important to note that whereas the ozone standard has been the most publicized of the air quality criteria, similar battles are brewing over other pollutants.

Particulate Matter

The reduction of fine particulate matter (PM) has been approached through the regulatory arena rather than through legislation. As with ozone, research published in the 1990s focused attention on the health effects of particulate pollution, and many scientists became convinced that fine particles were the most serious public health threat from air pollution. The health effects of particulate matter at levels below the national air quality standards (as well as when air quality exceeds the standards) include increased respiratory hospital admissions, increased frequency and severity of asthma attacks, increased school absences, increased respiratory symptoms such as wheezing and coughing, increased hospitalization for cardiovascular problems, and increased mortality. In two major studies of particulate pollution, the risk of early death was estimated to be from 17 to 26 percent higher in areas with high levels of PM_{10}. A study by the Natural Resources Defense Council estimated that 64,000 people may die prematurely from cardiopulmonary causes linked to particulate air pollution. The research focused on the health effects of fine particles, released during combustion, that were not easily expelled by the respiratory system's normal safeguards when breathed by humans.[34]

The goal of air quality standards, as Congress provided in the Clean Air Act, was to "protect the public health" with an "adequate margin of safety." In the face of compelling research in peer-reviewed scientific publications concerning the health effects of particulates in November 1996, the EPA proposed a new $PM_{2.5}$ standard to regulate fine particles. The agency noted that the new particulate standards would result in 60,000 fewer bronchitis cases, 9,000 fewer hospitalizations for respiratory problems, fewer visits to doctors, less use of medication, less suffering by those with respiratory disease, improved visibility in national parks and wilderness areas, and prevention of as many as 20,000 premature deaths a year. The EPA also argued that every dollar spent on emissions reductions from 1970 to 1990 resulted in $15 to $20 worth of reduced health-care cost. Critics like the U.S. Conference of Mayors and the Air Quality Standards Coalition, comprised of industry executives, testified in congressional hearings that the proposed standards were too expensive and urged the EPA to do more research before finalizing the regulations.

It was not until 2004 that the EPA issued the country's first rules and designations for particulate matter—eight years after they were first proposed. The agency set standards for small particles, which aggravate those with lung and heart diseases, at $PM_{2.5}$—approximately 1/30th the size of an average human hair. In announcing the Clean Air Fine Particle Rules, the EPA reported that certain areas in 20 states as well as all or part of 224 counties nationwide (and the District of Columbia) had not attained national standards. These states have three years to submit plans to the EPA (similar to those for ozone pollution) that show how they will meet the $PM_{2.5}$ standards. The plans must show how standards will be attained by 2010, with a five-year extension possible for those with severe PM problems.[35]

The PM rules were part of a suite of actions issued by the EPA called the Clean Air Rules of 2004. They included the Interstate Air Rule, which provides states with a cap-and-trade system to deal with power plant emissions that cross state lines; a Clean Air Mercury Rule to regulate power plant mercury emissions for the first time; the Clean Air Nonroad Diesel Rule that requires changes to remove emissions from diesel fuel to remove sulfur; and the Clean Air Ozone Rules to designate areas where health-based standards (8-hour ground-level ozone pollution) are not being met.

THE CLEAR SKIES INITIATIVE

President George W. Bush's Clear Skies Initiative, announced on February 14, 2002, set mandatory emissions caps for three harmful air pollutants: sulfur dioxide, nitrogen oxides, and mercury. American power plants would be required to reduce air pollutants by an average of 70 percent, which the EPA predicted would allow most areas of the country to meet federal air quality standards. The cost was staggering, however—an estimated $6.5 billion annually by 2020, which officials said would be offset by benefits to human health and visibility.[36]

One element of the Bush administration's air quality policy dealt with new source review regulations, originally established in 1977 and revised under the Clinton administration, that require power plants, factories, and oil refineries to upgrade their pollution control equipment when a facility built before 1977 is expanded or improved. The Clinton-era rules were expected to reduce emissions from the nation's dirtiest plants by up to 95 percent.

The president announced his proposal to relax the Clinton regulations, which industry officials had called "overly burdensome" in June 2002. The Clear Skies legislation considered by Congress in 2002 and 2003 would have established a national "cap and trade" program that would set a ceiling on polluting emissions. Companies that reduced more than their share of emissions under the cap would be able to trade and sell emissions credits to companies that exceeded their emission permits. The changes were said to save companies billions of dollars that would have been spent on repairing aging facilities, an expense that executives said would ruin the industry.[37] Another provision would weaken the rights of states to sue neighboring states for cross-border pollution, as North Carolina has done, and to create state regulations that are tougher than federal ones, as is the case in California; California Governor Arnold Schwartzenegger sent senators a letter calling for the preservation of states' rights.[38]

One bright spot on the administration's air pollution agenda came in December 2003, when the EPA's Clean Air Mercury rule went into effect. The rule permanently caps mercury emissions from coal-fired power plants using two mechanisms: by requiring facilities to install new control technology and through a market-based cap and trade rule that would give companies flexibility in cutting emissions in two phases. Mercury was considered an important element of the Bush plan because it is a toxic, persistent pollutant that accumulates in the food chain and is usually absorbed by humans when eating fish.

The rest of the Clear Skies measures failed to get sufficient support in Congress; Democrats attempted to stall any legislative progress by commissioning a study by an 18-member panel of researchers and academicians from the National Academy of Sciences. The interim report, issued in January 2005, stated that Bush's proposed new source review regulations would not reduce pollution as much as existing Clean Air Act regulations would—a finding that immediately led to criticism by the administration and industry lobbyists. National Academy of Science officials announced the panel's study was subject to further review and revision, with a final report due in December 2005.[39]

The chairman of the White House Council on Environmental Quality, James Connaughton, criticized the panel for not taking into account the overall emission reductions that would come from capping pollution at more than 1,000 power plants. "That will far exceed the emission reductions that would come from the far fewer numbers that are subject to new source review."[40] Industry officials also criticized the report, with the director of the Electric Reliability Coordinating Council arguing that the president's proposal would result in more pollution reductions than under current rules, which may appear tougher, but in practice often lead to long legal battles. "There aren't the resources or time or patience to sue every power plant in America. By contrast, the Clear Skies program is implemented in one fell swoop across the country."[41]

Another version of the Clear Skies Act was introduced to the Senate in late January 2005 and followed by hearings before the Senate Environment and Public Works Committee. Among those testifying was John A. Paul, an Ohio pollution control official speaking on behalf of the State and Territorial Air

Pollution Program Administrators and the Association of Local Air Pollution Control Officials. Paul had called the new source review regulatory changes "serious detriments to public health and environmental protection" in his 2004 testimony before another Senate committee.[42] Paul had also gained prominence in 2004 when he told reporters that an EPA advisory committee he cochaired had been abruptly shelved after it requested comparative data on a Bush administration proposal to control mercury emissions.[43]

A few days after Paul testified against the 2005 proposal, the chair of the committee, Sen. James Inhofe (R-OK), sent a letter to Paul requesting financial statements, membership lists, and tax returns for the past six years for both groups. Longtime air quality activist Rep. Henry Waxman (D-CA) said, "There is not even any subtlety about this. This is a blatant attempt at intimidation and bullying so that experts will be afraid to speak out about a bill that rolls back air pollution protections for all Americans." A committee staff member said the request for the financial information had nothing to do with Clear Skies. "If we wanted to intimidate them, we would have done it before they testified, not after."[44]

Members of Congress further politicized what might have been an intensive scientific review process rather than a political battle. Sen. Jim Jeffords (I-VT), the ranking minority member on the Environment and Public Works Committee, accused the Bush administration of "recklessly tinkering with the Clean Air Act. They want to replace existing programs, like New Source Review, that have documented benefits, with a proposal that is weaker and slower when it comes to reducing emissions and protecting health and the environment."[45]

On March 9, 2005, Jeffords and Senator Lincoln Chafee (R-RI) joined seven Democrats on the committee to reject the bill in a 9–9 vote, effectively killing the Clear Skies Initiative's legislative provisions. The Sierra Club lauded the bipartisan effort to weaken air quality protections, calling for strong enforcement of the current legislation. "We should continue to move forward with an existing program that has a track record of success rather than open the door to a high risk scheme."[46]

Another View, Another Voice

Lincoln Chafee

Rhode Island senator John Chafee, who died in 1999, was part of a family political legacy. His great-grandfather had been the state's governor, as had one of his great-uncles. Another great-uncle had been a U.S. senator, serving for 23 years as part of the Republican leadership on environmental legislation. The legacy continues, however, through John's son, Lincoln Davenport Chafee, who was appointed by the governor of Rhode Island to fill the unexpired term of his father and is continuing the family's efforts to protect the environment

A native son of Rhode Island, Lincoln was born in Providence on March 26, 1953. He attended public schools and the prestigious Phillips Andover Academy. Lincoln stayed in Rhode Island to attend Brown University, where he received a degree in classics in 1975. He received the Francis M. Driscoll award for leadership, scholarship, and athletics at Brown, where he also participated on the school's wrestling team.

In most political families in the East, the son would have been expected to go on to law school and then, perhaps, into public service. Lincoln, however, followed the adage of "Go west, young man, go west" and enrolled in the horseshoeing program at Montana State University in Bozeman. He worked as a blacksmith at racetracks throughout the United States and Canada for seven years before returning to Rhode Island in 1983. He worked as a manager in a manufacturing plant at Quonset Point and as a planner.

In 1985, Chafee was elected as a delegate to the Rhode Island Constitutional Convention; and in 1986, he was elected to the first of two terms as a member of the Warwick City Council. He ran for mayor of Warwick in November 1992, becoming the city's first Republican elected mayor with a margin of 335 votes. He was reelected in 1994, 1996, and 1998; by this point, he had the support of 58 percent of the voters and every ward in the city. It was as mayor that he established his reputation for environmental protection and open space acquisition.

The jump from mayor to the U.S. Senate came with his father's unexpected death. After serving for one year by virtue of the gubernatorial appointment, Chafee ran successfully on his own in November 2000. He was appointed to the senate's committees on Environment and Public Works, Foreign Relations, and the Committee on Homeland Security and Governmental Affairs.

As chairman of the Subcommittee on Fish, Wildlife, and Water, he worked closely with former EPA Administrator Christine Todd Whitman, praising her for her vigilance as a guardian of the environment. Through the EPA, Rhode Island had been awarded $800,000 via a watershed initiative to improve the water quality and enhance restoration opportunities for Narragansett Bay. Chafee noted that he had received the announcement of Whitman's May 2003 resignation from the Bush administration "with sadness and regret. Governor Whitman was a strong, moderating voice in a very difficult job," he commented.

Chafee has been ranked as one of the "greenest" Republicans in the Senate, receiving a 100 percent rating from the National Parks Conservation Association from the 2003–2004 session, and a 72 percent rating from the League of Conservation Voters. In contrast, the conservative property rights group, American Lands Alliance, gave him a rating of only 11 percent.

Project Vote Smart, a nonpartisan, nonprofit organization that analyzes members of Congress and other political leaders on various key issues, notes that Chafee stands on the side of environmental groups on virtually every major issue. He supports the strengthening of the regulation and enforcement of the Clean Water Act and the Clean Air Act and seeks revisions in the 1872 General Mining Law to increase the fees charged to mining companies using federal lands. He encourages the further development and use of alternative fuels to reduce pollution and promotes the strengthening of emission controls on vehicles. He has also supported the use of pollution credits, which could be sold between nations to encourage industries to decrease their pollution levels.

Chafee has not been afraid to align himself with environmental interests in his first full term in the senate. In April 2004, he addressed the issue of mercury pollution from power plants in a letter to the new EPA Administrator, Mike Leavitt, accusing the agency of falling short on protecting children's health and the environment. He joined 44 other senators from both parties in calling upon the EPA to revamp a proposal that would allow increased levels of toxic mercury contamination. The Natural Resources Defense Council referred to him as an environmental watchdog who holds the swing vote on the Committee on Environment and Public Works. He was the lone Republican on the Senate Environment and Public Works Committee to vote against the Bush administration's Clear Skies Initiative in March 2005—an action that killed the measure. Chafee objected to the bill because of its failure to deal with carbon dioxide emissions, noting, "It's a shame that the U.S. Congress is the last bastion of denial on climate change." Sen. George Voinovich (R-Ohio) was frustrated by his colleague's defection. "Chafee thinks [global warming] is the biggest problem facing the world, and the chairman [Sen. James Inhofe] has a sign in his office saying this is a hoax."

SOURCES:
"Michael Kilian, "Committee Kills Bush Bid to Ease Pollution Rules," *Chicago Tribune*, March 10, 2005, at www.chicagotribune.com, accessed March 10, 2005.
League of Conservation Voters, "LCV Applauds Senate Environment and Public Works Committee Members for Defeating Bush Air Pollution Plan," News release, March 9, 2005, at www.lcv.org/News, accessed March 10, 2005.
Natural Resources Defense Council, "Bill Weakening Clean Air Act Dies in Senate Committee," News release, March 9, 2005, at www.nrdc.org/media, accessed March 10, 2005.
Natural Resources Defense Council, "Top Dogs," *Onearth* (Spring 2003), at www.nrdc.org, accessed March 11, 2005.
Project Vote Smart, "Senator Chafee, Issue Positions," at www.vote-smart.org, accessed March 11, 2005.
Project Vote Smart, "Lincoln Chafee, Public Statements," at www.vote-smart.org_detail, accessed March 11, 2005.
U.S. Senate, "Lincoln Chafee Biography," at www.chafee.senate.gov, accessed March 11, 2005.
Shankar Vedantam, "Pollution Law Revamp Hits Skids," *Arizona Republic,* March 10, 2005.

Because the legislative route to change appeared to have ended, the Bush administration again relied upon the regulatory process for change. On March 10, 2005, the day following the Senate vote, the EPA issued the Clean Air Interstate Rule (CAIR), which acting EPA Administrator Steve Johnson said "will result in the largest pollution reductions and health benefits of any air rule in more than a decade."[47] The final rule permanently caps emissions of sulfur dioxide and nitrogen oxides in 28 states in the eastern United States and the District of Columbia. The agency estimated the rule would result in $85 to $100 billion in health benefits and $2 billion in visibility benefits per year by 2015, annually preventing 17,000 premature deaths and reducing the number of lakes and streams considered acidic.[48]

Not surprisingly, the reaction to CAIR and the defeat of Clear Skies was mixed. The president of the industry group, Americans for Balanced Energy Choices, said that coal-based electricity generators would have to invest about $52 billion in new technology to comply with the new rule, preferring the legislative approach rather than regulation.[49] But Environmental Defense, an organization often at odds with the EPA on environmental protection, called the new rule a "big win for clean air." The group's comments echoed the language in the EPA's news releases on CAIR while saying that the Clear Skies proposals would clear the way for polluters to pollute more and were full of loopholes.[50]

As had been the case with the Healthy Forests Initiative described in Chapter 4, the Bush administration used a two-pronged approach, shepherding its proposals through the legislative and regulatory arenas simultaneously. Although the impact on air quality policy of CAIR and the mercury rules will not be as significant as that of the parallel timber/wildfire efforts on national forests, the strategy is proving to be a successful one for making policy change.

TOXIC AIR POLLUTANTS

Little is known about the health risk posed by the tens of thousands of synthetic chemicals available today. Although research is ongoing, many of the effects of toxic contamination, such as cancer, are not apparent until decades after exposure. Many of these substances are produced by factories and industrial processes, such as pulp and paper processors; but smaller sites, such as municipal waste dumps, dry cleaners, and print shops are also responsible for toxic emission releases. Pesticides and herbicides used in agricultural application also are released into the atmosphere.

Five metals found in air—beryllium, cadmium, lead, mercury, and nickel— are known to pose various hazards to human health. Except for lead, most of these substances pose a risk primarily to those living adjacent to the source, such as a waste dump or factory. Lead, however, is much more widely dispersed as a component of vehicle fuels and paints. Lead poisoning is characterized by anemia and may lead to brain dysfunction and neurological damage, especially in children. Elimination of lead from automobile fuels in the United States, Japan, and Canada has reduced emissions significantly, but few developing countries have attempted to phase out lead in gasoline. The problem is compounded by a lack of emission controls on lead smelters, battery manufacturing plants, and paint production facilities.

As is often the case in policy development, government regulation of toxics has typically come on the heels of crisis. In this case, the events occurred outside the United States. In July 1976, an explosion at an herbicide manufacturing facility in Sevesco, Italy, released a toxic cloud of dioxin and other chemicals that spread downwind. *Dioxin* is a generic term applied to a group of suspected cancer-causing substances that are known to cause severe reproductive disorders as well as immune system problems and impaired liver function. Although no deaths were directly attributed to the incident, within two weeks plants and animals were dying, and residents with skin lesions were being admitted to local hospitals. More than 700 people living near the plant were evacuated, and 5,000 others in the surrounding areas were told not to garden or let their children play outside. It took two weeks for local authorities to discover that a toxic chemical had been involved and to implement effective safeguards. The incident resulted in the Sevesco Directive in 1984—an agreement by members of the European Community that plants using hazardous chemicals must inform residents of the nature and quantity of the tonics they use and the risks they pose. Later that year, the accidental release of 40 tons of isocyanate at a Union Carbide facility in Bhopal, India, refocused attention on the need to require safeguards in developing nations as well. The incident resulted in death or injury to hundreds of thousands of residents near the plant.

Two landmark pieces of U.S. legislation—the Federal Insecticide, Fungicide, and Rodenticide Act (FIFRA) of 1972 and the 1976 Toxic Substances Control Act (TSCA), which regulates how toxic chemicals are to be used—were a result of such incidents. The laws allow the EPA to regulate chemicals that pose an unacceptable health risk—for example, polychlorinated biphenyls (PCBs), which were first regulated in 1978. In addition, the Emergency Planning and Community Right-to-Know Act of 1986 now gives communities access to information about toxic chemicals in their region. The law calls for extensive data collection and for the creation of state emergency response commissions to plan for chemical release emergencies. The federal government also coordinates the Toxics Release Inventory (TRI), an annual inventory of toxic releases and transfers of over 640 toxic chemicals from facilities nationwide. As information about the health effects of each substance is gathered, chemicals of little or no toxic concern are removed from the list while others are added. Before a new pesticide may be marketed or used in the United States, it must first be registered with the EPA after a series of health, economic, and cost-benefit studies. If the studies indicate that the risks outweigh the benefits, the EPA can refuse to register the product or regulate the frequency or level of application.

The EPA, state, local, and tribal air programs share the responsibility for controlling air toxics. The federal agency sets the standards for emissions, which state and local programs are responsible for implementing. Some state and local programs have also set their own rules for toxic emissions. EPA uses computer models to estimate ambient air toxics concentrations and population exposures nationwide, a process that introduces significant uncertainties, the agency admits.[51]

Yet some observers believe that U.S. progress toward controlling toxic air pollutants has been glacially slow. Before passage of the 1990 Clean Air Act, the EPA had completed regulations for only seven toxic chemicals, and no information was available on the toxic effects of nearly 80 percent of the chemicals used in commerce. In addition to publishing a list of source categories that emit certain levels of these pollutants, the EPA developed standards for pollution control equipment to reduce the risk from the contaminants.

In 2002, the EPA took another step in the campaign to understand the health effects of air pollution with publication of the National-Scale Air Toxics Assessment (NATA). The study, which used 1996 emissions data, analyzed 32 air tonics and diesel particulate matter (as a surrogate for diesel exhaust) to prioritize pollutants of particular concern, determine their sources, identify the need for additional data collection and research, and establish a baseline for future tracking efforts. The pollutants were selected from 188 toxic air pollutants for which EPA must develop emissions standards.

By developing an inventory of air toxics, the government hoped to characterize potential public health risks in the largest number of urban areas. The study did not identify specific geographic areas with significantly higher risks, nor did it identify the risks associated with each pollutant. The data used were from 1996 because they were the most complete and up-to-date available, although more recent information is still being gathered. These limitations, coupled with the fact that the EPA lacks the scientific information necessary to perform a full assessment of the other 156 air toxics, reduce the potential impact of the study for further regulatory efforts.

VISIBILITY

Although contemporary air quality concerns have focused primarily on the health effects of pollutants, it is important to remember that one reason public officials in Los Angeles first considered air pollution a problem in the context of visibility.

Complaints from the public about the haze over the city and the inability to see the mountains that ring the South Coast Air Basin drew attention to the problem long before health issues were studied and their impacts exposed. Visibility began decreasing in the 1940s as the West became more populated. But public interest did not coalesce until 1975, when the National Parks Conservation Association alerted its members to the growing clouds of sulfur dioxide, nitrous oxide, and fine particulates that had begun to build up in the atmosphere, often obscuring the vistas in the Grand Canyon and in Utah's Bryce Canyon. Primary sources of the brownish haze were believed to be fossil-fuel-fired power plants, copper smelters, industrial boilers, chemicals production, and mobile sources like cars and trucks. The pollutants, which can originate hundreds of miles away in urban areas, are transported to other areas on the desert winds.

By 1977, the problem was widespread enough to warrant a special section in the Clean Air Act Amendments; visibility regulations were promulgated in 1980. It is at this point that the National Park Service (NPS) took on the role of leader in visibility research. One controversial 1985 study found that visible plumes from stationary sources were not the most important source of visibility impairment. Rather, regional haze, including soil-related materials, seemed to be the cause. Through the remainder of the decade, disputes focused on whether human-caused sources were responsible for the visibility problems, with the 1987 Winter Haze Intensive Tracer Experiment (WHITEX) tests and other studies determining that emissions from the coal-fired Navajo Generating Plant at Page, Arizona, as the largest contributor. Interior Secretary Manuel Lucan Jr. promptly called for a new study, no doubt influenced by the fact that the federal government owned a quarter of the Navajo plant.

From a political standpoint, the NPS studies filled a void left by the EPA. The EPA had moved on to other air quality issues and focused its regulatory efforts on ozone. The NPS, however, was faced with the daily barrage of questions from park visitors, who wondered why such a national treasure in this part of the largely uninhabited West could become despoiled by urban centers and consumer needs for electric power.

In 1996 the congressionally created Visibility Transport Commission, made up of eight governors, four tribal leaders, and other advisors, made sweeping and unprecedented recommendations designed to gradually improve visibility in 16 national parks and wilderness areas in the Colorado Plateau. This time, the blame for the veil of haze was shared by fires and dust, along with the everyday actions of residents driving cars and of industries operating refineries. Chimney emissions in 11 states and northwest Mexico were also factors. The commission's recommendations, including a slow, voluntary reduction in emissions that would reduce pollution by 70 percent by 2040, were widely criticized because they failed to address the visibility problem in a timely manner and did not comprehensively identify what some felt was a single source.

Subsequently, the visibility issue was picked up by other environmental organizations. In 1998, the Sierra Club and the Grand Canyon Trust filed lawsuits against the owners of the last coal-fired plant without standard pollution control devices in the West—the Mojave Generating Station near Laughlin, Nevada, just 75 miles from the Grand Canyon. The suit charged that the plant's operators were guilty of years of violating Clean Air Act emissions standards—regulations unenforced by the EPA. Mojave releases 40,000 tons of sulfur dioxide and 10,000 tons of particulates into the air annually.

But the controversy over Mojave was much more than a battle between environmental groups and a corporation (Southern California Edison is the majority owner and operator of the plant). Caught in the middle were the Hopi and Navajo employees who had come to depend on the plant for jobs. A threatened closure of the plant would have significant economic impacts throughout the region; Native American leaders called on the company to install the necessary technology rather than shut down the plant.

In October 1999, following a court settlement, Southern California Edison agreed to spend $300 million on filters and scrubbers to reduce sulfur dioxide emissions by 85 percent and particulates by 99 percent by 2006. In addition to avoiding years of potential litigation, the agreement improves the utility's competitive position in a deregulated market, accelerating the installation of pollution control equipment the company said it had already planned to purchase. But environmental organizers disagreed, arguing that the cleanup plan was announced only after the two groups had filed the lawsuit.

The Mojave plant had been a "problem" for years, but environmental groups had never been able to move it from the systemic agenda to the institutional agenda. Even after passage of the Clean Air Act Amendments in 1990, the plant continued to operate in violation of the law's provisions. The heavy competition for a place on the policy agenda kept Mojave out of the majority of the public's attention, except for members of organizations like the Grand Canyon Trust. Rather than attempting to put pressure on federal legislators (many of whom were more sympathetic to the utility's interests), the groups chose to utilize the judicial arena as the best venue for pleading their case.

Similarly, groups like the Clean Air Trust (CAT) voiced their opposition to EPA plans announced in February 2004 to adopt new methods of measuring pollution in North Dakota, which wants to permit more energy development and pollution near Theodore Roosevelt National Park. The agency had opposed additional development in the area since 1999 because existing coal-burning electric power plants are pumping at least 100,000 tons of sulfur dioxide into the state's air. To improve air quality at the national park, the EPA estimates about 60,000 tons of pollutants would have to be eliminated. The measurement methods purportedly would show no problem from existing pollution, even though agency officials had previously called the state's methods "fundamentally flawed." The executive director of the CAT said the action "underscores a cornerstone of the Clean Air Act designed to keep national parks and other treasured lands from being shrouded by smog and soot. This could drastically weaken clean air protections at national parks and wilderness areas all across the nation."[52]

THINKING GLOBALLY: TRANSBOUNDARY AIR POLLUTION

Air pollutants do not recognize international boundaries or political jurisdictions. Pollution can be carried on air currents across nations, continents, and oceans. When the sources are so distant that the individual contributors to emissions cannot be determined, the problem is referred to as transboundary air pollution. In the 1970s, researchers began to develop a new understanding of the forces that lead to long-range transboundary air pollution and acid deposition; at the same time, environmental crises focused attention on transnational water pollution, as discussed in the previous chapter. These issues are of interest to most Americans when they involve the nations along the U.S. borders—Canada and Mexico. All three countries have a common interest in combining their technological resources to solve problems that literally "drift" into their boundaries. Although the problems are global in scope and importance, they are also somewhat regionalized.

For the United States and Canada, the major border issue is acid rain—or acid deposition, as it is also known. For many years, it had gone undetected because in its early stages there was little evidence of its impact. Today, no country on earth receives as high a proportion of acidic deposition from another nation as Canada receives from the United States. Approximately one half the total amount of acid deposition that falls on Canada comes from the United States, in comparison to the 20 percent Canadian sources deposit on the United States.[53]

There are three primary components of acid rain: sulfur dioxide, nitrous oxides, and volatile organic compounds (VOCs). The most common of the pollutants, sulfur dioxide, comes primarily from the combustion of coal, which reacts with oxygen in the air. The sulfur content of coal varies considerably with the geographic region in which it is mined, so not all areas experience acid deposition to the same degree. Coal from the western portion of the United States, for example, typically has a sulfur content of about 0.5 percent, which is considered to be very low. In contrast, coal mined in the northern region of Appalachia and some midwestern states has a sulfur concentration of 2 to 3 percent. Scientists measure acid deposition as wet (rain, snow, fog) and dry (particles and gases). Acidity is measured on a pH scale from 1 to 14, with lemon juice measured at 1, vinegar at 3, and distilled water at 7. Although there is no single threshold value below which precipitation is considered to be "acid rain," readings below 4.5 are generally considered highly acidic. The most widely accepted standard for unpolluted precipitation is 5.6, which is 25 times the acidity of pure water.[54]

Acid rain causes several types of environmental damage, and because its effects are not merely localized, it can cause increased acidity levels in bodies of water that are fed by rainfall. The impact can damage entire ecosystems and may show up along the entire food chain. Researchers have found reduced yields of crops attributable to acid rain, and studies show it also contributes to health problems. Soil nutrients are declining in Canada, and the long-term impact also includes damage to our cultural heritage: There is evidence that acid rain has damaged some of the world's most beautiful historical artifacts.

Canada and the United States have a long history of disputes as well as cooperative agreements related to transboundary pollution, the most famous of which is the Trail Smelter Arbitration of 1941. The case involved sulfur emissions from a smelter built in Canada in 1896 just a few miles north of the United States border. Originally the claims against the smelter dealt with plumes of sulfur that traveled across the border and damaged the property of apple growers in Washington State, but the case later formed the basis for questions of jurisdiction in international environmental law that would be reflected in subsequent treaties.[55]

Negotiations on transboundary air pollution issues between the United States and Canada were driven by Title IV of the 1990 Clean Air Act Amendments and subsequently enacted in the 1991 U.S.-Canada Bilateral Air Quality Agreement. The United

States agreed to reduce its sulfur dioxide (SO_2) emissions by 10 million tons below 1980 levels by the year 2000; achieve a permanent national emissions cap of 8.95 million tons of SO_2 per year for electric utilities by 2010; and develop additional standards if it is determined that annual emissions will be exceeded. Canada agreed to reduce its SO_2 emissions; reduce its nitrous oxide (NO_x) emissions by 100,000 tons annually by 2000; and to meet technology-based standards for reducing NO_x from mobile sources. The reductions were expected to come from a tightening of restrictions placed on fossil-fuel-fired power plants, along with the promotion of pollution prevention and energy-efficient strategies and technologies. The International Joint Commission (IJC), a permanent bilateral commission of three members from each country that originally dealt with water quality issues stemming from the 1909 Boundary Waters Treaty, provides the institutional structure for dealing with transboundary air pollution issues.

Since the treaty went into force, significant progress has been made; Canada surpassed both of its commitments to reduce emissions of SO_2. The U.S. EPA's Acid Rain Program and controls on motor vehicles reduced emissions of SO_2 well below the 1999 limits, with projections that the pattern would continue through 2010. The two countries have now agreed to address the issues of ground-level ozone and particulate matter emissions.

Some U.S. officials consider the U.S.-Canadian response to acid rain as a model for tackling emerging environmental issues. The agreements made by these countries have incorporated input from stakeholders such as utilities, coal and gas companies, emissions control equipment vendors, labor leaders, academicians, and state and provincial pollution control agencies, along with environmental organizations. The use of continuous monitoring and reporting systems, excessive emissions penalties, and market-based incentives are said to create a program that will achieve cost-effective emission reductions.

In contrast, the transboundary air pollution issues between the United States and Mexico are perceived as being more complex and more difficult to solve than are those with Canada. The severity of environmental problems is increasing dramatically, due largely to the growth of industry and population along the Mexican side of the border. In cities like San Antonio, Texas, transboundary water pollution has been more of an issue than air quality due to the area's history of flooding from the San Antonio River. As a way of dealing with an issue that affects several states, the Western Governors' Association (WGA) is addressing the problem of border congestion and the resulting air pollution problem. In 1998, the organization began doing research at four of the most heavily traveled border crossings: San Ysidro–Otay Mesa–Tijuana, El Paso–Ciudad Juarez, Nogales-Nogales, and Laredo–Nuevo Laredo. The research findings, along with the development of consensus solutions to the problems faced by border communities, are a small step toward finding a way of addressing transboundary pollution that can be replicated in other parts of the world.

The United and Mexico have signed several bilateral air quality agreements as part of the Agreement on Cooperation for the Protection and Improvement of the Environment in the Border Area. One agreement deals with transboundary air pollution from major stationary sources like factories and studies of potential control measures; another relates to emission limits on copper smelters. Negotiations with Mexico are complicated by state laws that both authorize and limit the scope of authority of local governments, agencies, and authorities, as well as of the state government itself. Texas, for example, established a Texas-Mexico authority "to study all Texas-Mexico issues and problems, including health and environment." It allows the state to "explore, develop, and negotiate interstate compacts relating to trade, infrastructure, and other matters with the appropriate officials of the united Mexican states or any of its political subdivisions or any other foreign trading partners."[56]

Other countries have responded to transboundary air pollution through the multilateral Geneva Convention on Long-Range Transboundary Pollution, which entered into force in 1983. Most European countries, as well as the United States and Canada, are party to the convention, which was originally designed as a response to the problem of acid deposition. The convention calls for scientific cooperation and the sharing of information, and a monitoring program that evaluates European pollutants. Parties agree to exchange data on emissions, and in the protocols agreed upon subsequent to the convention, will share technological and market-based alternatives to reduce certain pollutants to targeted levels.[57] Subsequent protocols have been developed on heavy metals, persistent organic pollutants, and ground-level ozone.

Nations cooperate in addressing problems of transboundary air pollution for several reasons. It may be in their own self-interest to support cooperative pollution reduction agreements in order to protect the quality of life within their own boundaries. It is to their advantage to help establish dispute resolution mechanisms so they can pressure their neighbors to comply with environmental accords. Nations may recognize that collective benefits such as a stable climate and healthy oceans are in everyone's interest and compel some sacrifice of the freedom to engage in polluting activities. International organizations, norms, and laws play an important role in reflecting that self-interest. Cooperative efforts are bolstered through scientific research that clearly and compellingly identifies collective threats and offers feasible solutions. As scientific consensus develops over an environmental problem, nations are encouraged to participate in solutions. Some countries seek to be leaders in the global community, while others simply wish to avoid the criticisms of others. Domestic politics plays a critical role, and environmental activists demand that their own governments comply with their global commitments and contribute to collective solutions. Political leaders may see global environmental leadership as central to their own political prospects or part of their personal policy agenda. Industries that must comply with domestic environmental regulations have a strong incentive to urge their governments to pressure other countries to enforce similar standards on their industries. In some cases, economic powerhouses like the United States can compel compliance by other nations that want to continue trade with them or otherwise benefit through cooperative relations.

From an international perspective, there is mixed success in controlling transboundary air pollution. Industrialized nations in Western Europe come close to matching the U.S. record in curbing pollutants, whereas the problems facing Eastern Europe are still being identified. In developing nations, attempts to control emissions that travel from one region to another are often thwarted by policies that encourage economic growth at the expense of the environment. As with many other environmental protection policies, there is no "one size fits all" solution for this problem, and there are only very limited resources to use for policy implementation.

NOTES

1. Carl T. Hall, "Air Board's Tough Smog Rules Defy Auto Industry," *San Francisco Chronicle,* September 25, 2004, at www.sfgate.com, accessed October 20, 2004.

2. Jeff Plungis, "Auto Industry Claims It Would Spend $6B to Meet California Mandates to Reduce Gas Emissions," *The Detroit News,* September 23, 2004, at www.aiada.org, accessed October 20, 2004.

3. California Air Resources Board, "ARB Approves Greenhouse Gas Rule," News release, September 24, 2004, at www.arb.ca.gov, accessed October 20, 2004.

4. Statement of John A. Paul to U.S. Senate Democratic Policy Committee Hearing on New Source Review, February 6, 2004, at www.cleanairtrust.org/testimony.paul, accessed February 23, 2005.

5. Ed Ainsworth, "Fight to Banish Smog, Bring Sun Back to City Pressed," *Los Angeles Times,* October 13, 1946, 7.

6. For a chronology of the early air pollution efforts, see James E. Krier and Edmund Ursin, *Pollution and Policy* (Berkeley: University of California Press, 1977), 46–47. The history of discovery of atmospheric chemicals, urban air pollution, and impacts are covered in Mark Z. Jacobson, *Atmospheric Pollution: History, Science, and Regulation* (Cambridge, UK: Cambridge University Press, 2002).

7. W. James Gauderman et al., "The Effect of Air Pollution on Lung Development from 10 to 18 Years of Age," *New England Journal of Medicine, 315,* no. 11 (September 9, 2004): 1057–1067.

8. Krier and Ursin, *Pollution and Policy,* 47.

9. For a description of the London episode, see Peter Brimblecombe, *The Big Smoke* (London: Methuren, 1987) and Fred Pearce, "Back to the Days of Deadly Smogs," *New Scientist,* December 5, 1992, 25–28.

10. John C. Esposito, *Vanishing Air: The Ralph Nader Study Group Report on Air Pollution* (New York: Grossman, 1970), vii.

11. John C. Whitaker, *Striking a Balance: Environment and Natural Resources Policy in the Nixon-Ford Years* (Washington, DC: American Enterprise Institute, 1976), 94.

12. See Marc K. Landy, Marc J. Roberts, and Stephen R. Thomas, *The EPA: Asking the Wrong Questions: From Nixon to Clinton,* expanded ed. (New York: Oxford University Press, 1994).

13. See Alfred Marcus, "EPA," in *The Politics of Regulation,* James Q. Wilson, ed. (New York: Basic Books, 1980), 267–303.

14. *International Harvester v. Ruckelshaus,* District of Columbia Court of Appeals, 155 U.S. App. DC 411 (February 10, 1973).

15. Whitaker, *Striking a Balance,* 104.

16. Alfred A. Marcus, *Promise and Performance: Choosing and Implementing an Environmental Policy* (Westport, CT: Greenwood Press, 1980), 123.

17. Whitaker, *Striking a Balance,* 104.

18. *Sierra Club v. Ruckelshaus,* 344 F.Supp. 256 (1972). For an analysis of the case, see Thomas M. Disselhorst, "Sierra Club v. Ruckelshaus: On a Clear Day . . . ," *Ecology Law Quarterly, 4* (1975): 739–780.

19. See Arnold W. Reitze Jr., "A Century of Air Pollution Law: What's Worked, What's Failed, What Might Work," *Environmental Law, 21,* no. 4:2 (1991): 1549–1646.

20. For a detailed chronology of these events, see Richard E. Cohen, *Washington at Work: Back Rooms and Clean Air* (New York: Macmillan, 1992).

21. See Norman W. Fichthorn, "Command and Control vs. the Market: The Potential Effects of Other Clean Air Act Requirements on Acid Rain Compliance," *International Law, 21,* no. 4:2 (1991): 2069–2084; and Alyson Pytte, "A Decade's Acrimony Lifted in the Glow of Clean Air," *Congressional Quarterly Weekly Report,* October 27, 1990, 3587–3592.

22. Michael Weisskopf, "Writing Laws Is One Thing—Writing Rules Is Something Else," *Washington Post National Weekly Edition,* September 30-October 6, 1991, 31; see also Henry Waxman, "An Overview of the Clean Air Act Amendments of 1990," *Environmental Law, 21,* no. 4:2 (1991): 1721–1816.

23. Henry V. Nickel, "Now, the Rush to Regulate," *Environmental Forum, 8,* no. 1 (January–February 1991): 19.

24. Mark Mardon, "Last Gasp Next 185,000 Miles?" *Sierra, 76,* no. 5 (September–October 1991): 38–42.

25. See U.S. Senate Committee on Environment and Public Works, "Three Years Later: Report Card on the 1990 Clean Air Act Amendments," November 1993.

26. Alex Daniels, "Tempest in a Tailpipe," *Governing,* February 1995, 37–38.

27. Environmental Protection Agency, *Air Quality Criteria for Ozone and Related Photochemical Oxidants* (Washington, DC: EPA), July 1996.

28. Earthjustice, *The Campaign to Protect Public Health From Ground Level Ozone: A Third of a Century and Counting,* May 30, 2002. www.environmentaldefense.org, accessed September 15, 2005.

29. *American Trucking Association v. USEPA,* 175 F.3d 1027 (D.C. Cir. 1999).

30. H. Josef Hebert, "EPA Threatened with Ozone Suit," *Arizona Republic,* May 31, 2002, A6.

31. U.S. Environmental Protection Agency, "8-Hour Ozone Area Summary," April 11, 2005, at www.epa.gov/oar/oaqps/greenbook, accessed May 11, 2005.

32. Darren Samuelsohn, "EPA Agrees to Reassess Ozone Cleanup for Rural Areas," *Greenwire,* January 21, 2005, at www.eenews.net/Greenwire, accessed May 11, 2005.

33. Joel Schwartz, "State of the Scare," at www.techcentralstation.com, accessed May 11, 2005.

34. See *Breath-Taking: Premature Mortality Due to Particulate Air Pollution in 239 American Cities* (New York: Natural Resources Defense Council, May 1996). See also Douglas W. Docker et al., "An Association between Air Pollution and Mortality in Six U.S. Cities," *New England Journal of Medicine, 329,* no. 24 (December 9, 1993): 1753–1759; and C. Arden Pope III et al., "Particulate Air Pollution as a Predictor of Mortality in a Prospective Study of U.S. Adults," *American Journal of Respiratory Care Medicine, 151* (1995): 669–674.

35. Environmental Protection Agency, "EPA Announces Final Designations for First Fine Particle Standard," News release, December 17, 2004, at www.epa.gov, accessed January 2, 2005.

36. U.S. Environmental Protection Agency, "New EPA Data Shows Dramatic Air Quality Improvements from Clear Skies Initiative," News release, July 1, 2002, at www.epa.gov.epahome, accessed July 21, 2002.

37. Max Barman, "Bush's Utility Rule Proposal Fuels Debate Over Dirty Air," *Arizona Republic,* June 14, 2002, A-1.

38. Matthew Swivel, "A Cloudy Forecast for Clear Skies," *Forbes,* February 16, 2005, at www.forbes.com/business/2005, accessed February 23, 2005.

39. National Academy of Sciences, *Interim Report of the Committee on Changes in New Source Review Programs for Stationary Sources of Air Pollution* (Washington, DC: National Academies Press, 2005).

40. John Heilprin, "Academy Report Sees Benefits of Existing Clean Air Program," *San Francisco Chronicle,* January 13, 2005, at www.sfgate.com, accessed January 15, 2005.

41. Miguel Bustillo, "Bush's 'Clear Skies' Plan Is a Step Back, Report Says," *Los Angeles Times,* January 14, 2005, at www.latimes.com/news, accessed January 15, 2005.

42. Paul, Senate Democratic Policy Committee.

43. Alan C. Miller and Tom Hamburger, "Opponents of 'Clear Skies' Bill Examined," *Los Angeles Times,* February 19, 2005, at www.latimes.com/news, accessed February 23, 2005.

44. Ibid.

45. Julie Eilperin, "Panel Questions Bush Clean Air Plan," *Arizona Republic,* January 14, 2005, A-5.

46. Statement by Nat Mund, Sierra Club, "Senate Committee Upholds Clean Air Act Provisions," News release, March 9, 2005, at www.sierraclub.org/pressroom/releases, accessed March 11, 2005.

47. U.S. Environmental Protection Agency, "Clean Air Interstate Rule," at www.epa/gov/interstateairquality, accessed March 11, 2005.

48. U.S. Environmental Protection Agency, "Basic Information," at www.epa.gov/interstateairquality/basic.html, accessed March 11, 2005.

49. Americans for Balanced Energy Choices, "EPA Issues New Air Quality Rules," News release, March 10, 2005, at www.releases.usnewswire.com, accessed March 11, 2005.

50. Environmental Defense, "Big Win for Clean Air," at www.environmentaldefense.org, accessed March 11, 2005.

51. U.S. Environmental Protection Agency, Technology Transfer Network, National Air Toxics Assessment, "Frequently Asked Questions," at www.epa.gov/ttn/atw/nata, accessed May 15, 2005.

52. Clean Air Trust, "Clean Air Trust Assails Bush Administration for Weakening Clean Air Protections for National Parks," News release, February 13, 2004, at www.cleanairtrust.org, accessed February 23, 2005.

53. David Hunter, James Salzman, and Durwood Zaelke, *International Environmental Law and Policy*, 2nd ed. (New York: Foundation Press, 2002), 516.

54. Marvin S. Soroos, *The Endangered Atmosphere: Preserving the Global Commons* (Columbia: University of South Carolina Press, 1997), 31.

55. The Trail Smelter case can be found as *United States v. Canada*, Arbitral Tribunal, 1941, 3 UN Rep.Int'l. Arb. Awards. It later became the genesis for Principle 21 of the Stockholm Declaration.

56. Tex. Govt. Code Section 481.0075(a) (1995).

57. For more on the European response to the transboundary convention, see United Nations Economic Commission for Europe, *Strategy for EMEP 2000–2009* (Geneva: United Nations, 2001).

FURTHER READING

Committee on Air Quality Management in the United States, National Research Council. *Air Quality Management in the United States*. Washington, DC: National Academies Press, 2004.

Jack Doyle. *Trespass Against Us: Dow Chemical and the Toxic Century*. Monroe, ME: Common Courage Press, 2004.

George A. Gonzalez. *The Politics of Air Pollution: Urban Growth, Ecological Modernization, and Symbolic Inclusion*. Albany: State University of New York Press, 2005.

Robert J. Martineau and David P. Novello. *The Clean Air Act Handbook*, Second Ed. Washington, DC: American Bar Association, 2005.

Noga Morag-Levine. *Chasing the Wind: Regulating Air Pollution in the Common Law State*. Princeton: Princeton University Press, 2003.

National Academies of Science. *Interim Report of the Committee on Changes in New Source Review Programs for Stationary Sources of Air Pollution*. Washington, DC: National Academies Press, 2005.

Stefan Reis. *Costs of Air Pollution Control*. Berlin: Springer-Verlag, 2006.

Joe Sherman. *Gasp: The Book of Air*. Washington, DC: Shoemaker & Hoard, 2004.

Gerald T. Westbrook. *Acid Rains on Liberal Propaganda: Ultra Liberals, Far Lefters and Global Warmers Beware*. Lincoln, NE: Iuniverse, Inc, 2005.

9

Endangered Species
and Biodiversity

We are spending nature's capital faster than it can regenerate.
—DR. CLAUDE MARTIN, DIRECTOR GENERAL, WORLD WILDLIFE FUND[1]

In its *Living Planet Report 2004,* the World Wildlife Fund (WWF) warned that we no longer live within the sustainable limits of the planet. "We are running up an ecological debt which we won't be able to pay off unless governments restore the balance between our consumption of natural resources and the Earth's ability to renew them."[2]

The report uses a Living Planet Index (LPI) as an indicator of the state of the world's biodiversity, measuring trends in populations of 555 terrestrial species (mammals, birds, and reptiles), 323 freshwater species (vertebrates found in rivers, lakes, and wetland ecosystems), and 267 species living in marine ecosystems (mammals, birds, reptiles, and fish living in the world's oceans and coastal areas). Between 1970 and 2000, the terrestrial and marine indices declined about 30 percent, and the freshwater index by almost 50 percent.[3] In addition, the report shows that humans currently consume 20 percent more natural resources than the earth can produce as a result of increasing human demand for food, fiber, energy and water.[4]

◁
> *The Galapagos Islands of Ecuador are home to thousands of unusual species, like this great frigate bird, making this one of the most diverse bioregions on Earth.*
>
> WILLIAM R. MILLER

While the LPI provides a context for identifying species loss, it does not include coverage of the efforts being made to preserve biodiversity. From the early British societies established to study flora and fauna to more complex international regimes, humans have understood the importance of species, large and small, to the ecological food chain. Scientists have long argued that what might be considered an "insignificant" extinction has long-term ramifications for the global ecosystem. As a result, some societies have guarded the location of rare plants used for medicinal purposes and as elements of traditional cultural practices. Contemporary pharmaceutical companies are researching the potential of previously undiscovered plants for integration into modern medicine. Animal rights activists have protested and engaged in direct action to save the lives of farmed animals and against inhumane treatment of those used in experimentation and research. Some animals have been protected for symbolic reasons; others captured in media images have captured the public's interest, and eventually, that of policy makers. This chapter links the issues of endangered species and biodiversity, explaining how sometimes U.S. and international policy efforts have been parallel, and at other times, at cross purposes with one another. The chapter also examines how organized interests have framed biodiversity as a problem and explores the successes and failures of those efforts.

ENDANGERED SPECIES

Initially, international discussions about endangered species tended to focus on megafauna like elephants and whales; but as knowledge of factors influencing biodiversity has grown, so, too, has the debate over issues that are just now beginning to emerge in the global environmental arena.

For instance, when the parties to the Convention on International Trade in Endangered Species of Wild Fauna and Flora (CITES) met in Bangkok, Thailand, in October 2004, they considered issues ranging from a regional action plan to combat poachers and illegal traders in Caspian Sea caviar, to the illegal harvesting of 20 species of agarwood, a high-demand, fragrant wood used in traditional medicines and perfume. The new era of endangered species protection takes a much broader view of ecosystems and habitat protection.

We have only begun to understand the diversity and numbers of life-forms on this planet. As many as 30 million species, primarily insects and marine invertebrates, may currently exist; only about 5 percent of them have been named and identified. That number is thought to be only a tiny percentage of the species that have inhabited earth during its millions of years of history—perhaps less than 1 percent of as many as 4 billion. Some species have disappeared because of cataclysmic events, such as changes in sea levels or massive ice movements; the disappearance of others can be attributed to the appearance (and often, the intervention) of humans. In rare cases, a species believed to have gone extinct is spotted and biologists rush to confirm the sighting. The ivory-billed woodpecker, the third largest in the world, was last seen in northeastern Louisiana in 1944.

The bird's primary habitat is large trees, and scientists believed it had been pushed into extinction by massive logging in the Southeast. Although there had been some reports of sightings over the past 60 years, none were verified.

In February 2004, an amateur birdwatcher kayaking along the Cache River in south eastern Arkansas saw what he thought was an adult male ivory-billed woodpecker, and he reported his find to a local newsletter, which found its way to the internet. Other birders followed; the birds have been spotted within a two-mile area of the original sighting. Additional confirmation has come through the recordings of the bird's calls.

Estimates of the current rate of species extinction vary considerably and largely depend upon the period of time covered. From 1600 to 1980, for example, nearly 200 vertebrate extinctions were documented, over half of them birds. But since 1980, habitat destruction, hunting, pesticide use, pollution, and other human-made causes have led to the extinction of as many as 1,000 species per year, primarily in tropical regions. The Global 2000 Report to the President projected that between 0.5 million and 2 million species extinctions would occur by the turn of the century. Most of those losses were attributed to the clearing or degradation of tropical forests, although marine species are threatened by damming, siltation, and pollution.[5]

Increasingly, biodiversity is threatened by invasive species of both plants and animals. The globalization of trade, travel, and communication has meant that flora and fauna are being transported, sometimes unknowingly, from one bioregion to another. Sometimes those species are unable to survive in their new environment, but often, they thrive and lead to the extinction of plants and animals. The World Conservation Union notes that this process leads to the alteration of habitat and disruption of natural ecosystems, and these events are often catastrophic for native species.[6]

This chapter focuses on the politics and history of legislation and agreements, both in the United States and internationally, to protect wildlife, plants, and their habitats. It also explores the wildlife bureaucracy in the United States, the role of nongovernmental organizations (NGOs) in biodiversity protection, and international biodiversity policy.

PROTECTIVE LEGISLATION

The development of laws protecting wildlife can be traced back to earliest legal history, but those laws have often differed as to what has been protected and why. Under Roman law, wild animals, or *ferae naturae,* were given the same status as the oceans and air—they belonged to no one. As Anglo-Saxon law developed, however, an exception was made: Private landowners had the right to wildlife on their property. As land was parceled out to the nobility as "royal forests" around 450 C.E., hunting restrictions began to be imposed, and only the king was given sole right to pursue fish or game anywhere he claimed as his realm. As the English political system developed, very few changes were made to the earlier system, perpetuating a situation in which only the wealthy or nobles were qualified to take game. Those same restrictions found their way to American shores and flourished until the mid-19th century, when a major policy shift occurred as the U.S. Supreme Court established the basis for state ownership of wildlife. The federal government's role in defining the legal status of wildlife was limited to an 1868 statute prohibiting the hunting of furbearing animals in Alaska and in 1894, a prohibition on hunting in Yellowstone National Park. The states began to regulate fishing within their waters just after the Civil War, and the Court upheld that policy, citing the commerce clause of Article 1, Section 8, of the Constitution. What is important about the decisions of this period, however, is that the states' regulatory authority was based on a fundamental 19th-century conception of the purpose of wildlife law—the preservation of a food supply.[7]

Contemporary U.S. legislation protecting plants and animals can be divided into four categories: migratory and game birds, wild horses and burros, marine mammals, and endangered species. What is unique about U.S. legislative provisions is that, in addition to offering protection for reasons of aesthetics or biological diversity, Congress has also sought to regulate the commerce and trade in these species. As public opinion shifts and the political environment responds, protective legislation for species also changes, although incrementally in comparison to the rate of extinction.

In December 2004, for instance, Sen. Conrad Burns (R–MT) quietly attached a rider to the federal budget signed by President Bush; the rider lifted the ban on slaughtering wild horses from the Wild Horse and Burro Protection Act of 1971. The law was initially enacted in response to the concerns of animal protection activists who had protested the government's hunting and shooting of animals across the West and then sending most of them to slaughter. The 1971 legislation gave the Bureau of Land Management (BLM) the authority to conduct periodic roundups of horses and burros to reduce the wild population, and allowed the animals to be "adopted" by individuals and advocacy groups.

The 1971 act represented the momentum of the environmental activism movement of the time, when species protection was high on the environmental policy agenda. Whether the species was a whale, rare plant, or indicator bird, groups formed to protect it and its habitat. Horses and burros came under the protective watch of groups such as Wild Horse Spirit, the Society for Animal Protective Legislation, and the Humane Society.

By the early 21st century, however, powerful ranching interests found support in more conservative members of Congress, arguing that the animals were overgrazing land that was needed by cattle for forage. By 2005, an estimated 35,000 wild horses and burros were roaming across 10 western states, with another 8,400 of these animals in captivity. The majority—about 19,000—are in Nevada, which has a pilot program to inject wild mares with long-term contraceptives. The BLM believes that only 28,000 wild horses and burros can survive without interfering with livestock grazing and other land uses. The lifting of the ban allowed the BLM to round up and sell "without limitation" every captured horse age 10 or older, as well as those that proved unadoptable after having been offered three times.[8]

The issues at stake go beyond just environmental ones. The problem of degraded land is due to damage from too many animals (cattle, sheep, horses, and others) in areas that cannot sustain them on natural food supplies. From an economic and cultural perspective, there is a substantial market for the meat from the approximately 50,000 domestic horses killed for food each year at one of the country's three authorized slaughterhouses. Some Indian tribes hold a contrasting view; they consider the wild horses as wildlife that should not be touched. The issues have not really changed since the 1971 law was enacted, but the balance of political power has.

Shortly after media attention about Sen. Burns's amendment surfaced, and animal activists found out what had happened, public opinion awakened again. When phrases like "wild horse slaughter" became associated with photographs of herds "awaiting their fates," horse advocates contacted members of Congress, urging them to restore the ban. In 2005, Reps. Nick Rahall (D-WV) and Ed Whitfield (D-KY) introduced a House amendment that would repeal the language inserted into the budget bill by Burns. Rahall noted, "When Americans picture the West, I doubt they envision wild horses being rounded up and sent to slaughterhouses to be processed into cuisine for foreign gourmets."[9]

Public outrage flared again in April 2005 after 41 horses sold by the BLM ended up in an Illinois meatpacking plant. Six were sold to an Oklahoma man who claimed he wanted them for a youth camp, and 35 were sold to a South Dakota Indian tribe that traded them to a third party, who also sold them to the slaughterhouse. The BLM attempted to adopt safeguards for the program almost immediately afterward by requiring buyers to sign a statement saying they have no intention of reselling the animals for slaughter—an action the Humane Society of the United States called "very weak, surprisingly weak."[10] The Ford Motor Company, which has sold its Mustang automobile since 1964, immediately pledged about $20,000 to buy 52 horses from the BLM, citing the mustang as a "great symbol for our country."[11]

As mentioned previously in the Introduction, this illustrates Downs' issue-attention cycle and the pendulum swings of public opinion. Iconic species, especially animals, evoke the support of Americans whose images of "wild life" may be based more on wishful thinking than on reality.

As an indicator of how recently American concern for endangered species has reached the political agenda, three separate legislative efforts have been enacted—all within the last 40 years. The first, the Endangered Species Preservation Act of 1966, mandated the secretary of the interior to develop a program to conserve, protect, restore, and propagate selected species of native fish and wildlife. Its provisions were primarily designed, however, to protect habitats through land acquisition—and little else. The species protected under the law were those "threatened with extinction" based on a finding by the secretary in consultation with interested persons, but the procedures for doing that went no further. It did not limit the taking of these species, or commerce in them, but it was an important first step in the development of the law.

The Endangered Species Conservation Act of 1969 attempted to remedy those limitations by further defining the types of protected wildlife; and more important, by including wildlife threatened with worldwide extinction and prohibiting their importation into the United States—an international aspect not included in the earlier legislation. Instead of using the broad term *fish and wildlife* (which was interpreted as only vertebrates), the 1969 law included any wild mammal, fish, wild bird, amphibian, reptile, mollusk, or crustacean. The list of species was to be developed using the best scientific and commercial data available, with procedures for designation pursuant to the rulemaking in the Administrative Procedure Act. This formalized a process that had been haphazard and highly discretionary under the 1966 act.

President Richard Nixon warned that the two laws did not provide sufficient management tools needed to act early enough to save a vanishing species. He urged Congress to enact a more comprehensive law, which became the Endangered Species Act (ESA) of 1973. The law has several notable features that distinguish it from previous efforts.

1. It required all federal agencies, not just the two departments identified in the 1966 and 1969 acts, to seek to conserve endangered species, broadening the base of protective efforts.

2. It expanded conservation measures that could be undertaken under the act to include all methods and procedures necessary to protect the species rather than emphasizing habitat protection only.

3. It broadened the definition of wildlife to include any member of the animal kingdom.

4. It created two classes of species: those "endangered" (in danger of extinction throughout all or a significant portion of its range) and those "threatened" (any species likely to become an endangered species within the foreseeable future).

Table 9.1 identifies the number of species in the United States listed as threatened or endangered as of June 8, 2005.

From an administrative standpoint, the 1973 law was considerably more complex than were previous legislative efforts. It included a circuitous route by which a species was to be listed by the secretary of the interior, delisted when the species' population stabilized, and changed from threatened to endangered and vice versa. The secretaries of commerce and the interior have virtually unlimited discretion in deciding when to consider the status of a species, because the law established no priorities or time limitations. Generally, a species is considered for listing upon petition of an interested group that has developed scientific evidence regarding the species' population. Reports are then considered by the secretary of the interior, although the time frame for consideration is totally discretionary. Some species have become extinct while waiting to be listed.

Listing, however, is but the first phase in a very lengthy process. Once a species is added to the list (which is made official by publishing a notice in the *Federal Register*), the federal government must decide how much of its habitat needs to be protected. The 1973 law is somewhat vague in indicating how "critical" habitat is to be determined and when that determination must be made. The law then requires the government to develop a recovery plan for the species. The law defines *recovery* as the process by which the decline of an endangered or

TABLE 9.1 Summary of Threatened and Endangered Species (As of December 26, 2005)

Group	Endangered U.S	Endangered Foreign	Threatened U.S	Threatened Foreign	Total species	U.S. Species with Recovery Plans
Mammals	68	251	11	20	350	55
Birds	77	175	13	6	271	78
Reptiles	14	64	22	16	116	33
Amphibians	12	8	9	1	30	16
Fishes	71	11	43	1	126	96
Clams	62	2	8	0	72	69
Snails	24	1	11	0	36	23
Insects	35	4	9	0	48	32
Arachnids	12	0	0	0	12	5
Crustaceans	19	0	3	0	22	13
Animal Sub Total	394	517	129	44	1083	420
Flowering Plants	571	1	143	0	715	584
Conifers and Cycads	2	0	1	2	5	3
Ferns and Allies	24	0	2	0	26	26
Lichens	2	0	0	0	2	2
Plant Sub Total	599	1	146	2	748	615
Grand Total	993	517	275	46	1831	1035

SOURCE: U.S. Fish and Wildlife Service at www.ecos.fws.gov accessed October 15, 2005.

threatened species is arrested or reversed and threats to its survival are neutralized to ensure its long-term survival in the wild. The plan delineates, justifies, and schedules the research and management actions necessary to support the recovery of a species, including those that, if successful, will permit reclassification or delisting. Typical recovery plans involve extensive public participation and include the cost of each strategy.

One of the most controversial aspects of the planning process is the assignment of individual species recovery priorities, which signifies the imminence of extinction and the designation of those species to which a known threat or conflict exists (usually from development projects). About one quarter of the listed species are in conflict with other activities and receive the designation. The law was amended in 1988, to make more specific the requirement that the secretaries of the interior and commerce develop and implement recovery plans and to require a status report every two years on the efforts to develop recovery plans for all listed species and on the status of all species for which recovery plans have been developed.

The ESA also protects plants; in 1977, it listed the first four plant species (all found on San Clemente Island, off the California coast). Before the 1988 amendments were instituted, it was illegal only to "remove and reduce to possession" listed plants—and then only those on lands under federal jurisdiction. Under the amended provisions, there is a prohibition against maliciously damaging or destroying plants on federal lands; it is now illegal to remove, destroy, or damage any listed plant on state or private land in knowing violation of state law. In 1994, the secretary of the interior expanded the law's reach even further by prohibiting "significant habitat modification or degradation where it actually kills or injures wildlife." The regulation would set the stage for a series of legal challenges over the secretary's authority under the ESA.[12]

THE MAKING OF WILDLIFE POLICY

Federal authority for the regulation and protection of wildlife is a case study in the growth of the American bureaucracy. It is characterized not only by name changes and power struggles within the agencies, but by external political pressure. Power is shared by several agencies, most of which have their counterparts at the state level. Until 1939, the Bureau of Biological Survey in the Department of Agriculture held regulatory authority for all wildlife—with the exception of marine fisheries, which were under the jurisdiction of the Bureau of Fisheries in the Department of Commerce. Both agencies were absorbed by the Department of the Interior and then consolidated into the U.S. Fish and Wildlife Service in 1940; but in 1956, the Fish and Wildlife Act divided authority into a Bureau of Sports Fisheries and Wildlife and a Bureau of Commercial Fisheries, leaving the organization much the same as it had been prior to 1939. President Richard Nixon's federal reorganization of 1970 transferred the Bureau of Commercial Fisheries to the National Oceanic and Atmospheric Administration, and the agency became the National Marine Fisheries Service, once again under the Department of Commerce. The Bureau of Sports Fisheries and Wildlife went back to its previous designation as the Fish and Wildlife Service in 1974, remaining in the Department of the Interior.

The structure of congressional committees also contributes to the fragmentation of policy making, because various committees and subcommittees have jurisdiction over different types of animals and their habitats. Political change can add to the confusion over which committee handles which species, as was the case in 1995 when the members of the 104th Congress entirely eliminated the Merchant Marine and Fisheries Committee, which had been in existence for 107 years. Its duties and staff were then parceled out to other committees, making the protection of the oceans and sealife more complex.

Congress, in the 1988 amendments to the ESA, directed federal agencies to more closely monitor those species facing substantial declines of their populations and to carry out emergency listing when necessary. Generally speaking, the longer a species has been listed, the better the chances for its population to stabilize or improve. For the most part, those species listed for less than three years do not yet have final approved recovery plans, although they may have plans in some stage of development. Recovery outlines are developed within 60 days of publication of the final rule listing a species. The outlines are submitted to the director of the Fish and Wildlife Service to be used as a guide for activities until recovery plans are developed and approved.

In response to criticism from various interests about how the ESA was being implemented, President Clinton established the National Biological Service within the Department of the Interior as a way of improving the existing bank of information on species and their habitat. The agency was given responsibility for developing an inventory of plant and animal populations, but some members of Congress viewed it as a base for advocates seeking to expand the scope of the ESA. Clinton's advisors believed that the new bureau was absolutely essential if the federal government hoped to speed up the process of listing and recovery, which had fallen far behind in the review process.

But the 1995 change from a Democrat-controlled Congress, which supported the ESA in principle, to a Republican one, which sought major reforms, marked a major turnaround for the nation's wildlife policies. The Endangered Species Act officially expired on October 1, 1992, but Congress still appropriates funds and can continue do so unless the act is totally repealed. As one of its initial actions, the Republican leadership declared a moratorium on the listing of any new species under the ESA, using the argument that there was uncertainty about how best to implement its provisions. The moratorium lasted until May 1996, creating an additional backlog of casework for agencies already besieged by budget cuts and an overall lack of resources. Republicans also targeted the National Biological Service, whose budget was included under the Department of the Interior. In a conference agreement, legislators agreed to eliminate the agency and shift most of its functions to the U.S. Geological Survey, whose budget was slashed along with its ability to implement much of its chartered responsibilities. President Clinton vetoed the interior appropriations bill, objecting to provisions that included a 10 percent spending reduction for the department, along with a laundry list of issues relating to grazing on federal lands, offshore oil drilling, and mining patents.[13]

Amending the ESA was a top priority of congressional Republicans in the 104th and 105th Congresses, aiming at a major ESA reform proposal. Several bills sought to eliminate species recovery as the primary goal of the act; they also provided more opportunities for states and landowners to be more involved in decisions related to endangered species, created biodiversity reserves, gave more leeway to landowners, and would reimburse private property owners for loss in land value resulting from endangered species regulation. Conservatives and property rights activists kept the pressure on the leadership to pass reform legislation, but failed.

Both the Clinton administration and Congress agreed that the ESA was flawed, but a major disagreement between the two branches was whether the law ought to be repealed so that policy makers could begin with a clean slate. Or whether piecemeal, incremental changes could be made that would satisfy all the parties involved. Some reforms were made through the regulatory process, circumventing the legislature and therefore not requiring actual amendments to the law. President Clinton's efforts to defeat Republican plans to gut the ESA were successful, and by the 106th Congress, it appeared that most representatives were prepared to move on to other issues. On Earth Day 1998, President Clinton and

Vice President Al Gore called on Congress to support, not thwart, their efforts.[14] Meanwhile, federal agencies and nongovernmental organizations were pressuring the administration to deal with the backlog of listings resulting from the 1995–1996 moratorium.

In 1998, the U.S. Fish and Wildlife Service (USFWS) adopted a new policy called Listing Priority Guidelines, which was designed to delist and reclassify 29 birds, mammals, fish, and plants that have achieved, or are moving toward, recovery. The two-year project amounted to the most extensive delisting and reclassification since adoption of the ESA in 1973, because 16 species had been restored in more than 25 years. By removing recovered species from the list, the agency could redirect its resources to species with greater needs. Still, the overall numbers were small. By June 2005, forty species, some of which had been listed as early as 1967, had been delisted. Sixteen of the 33 were classified as recovered, nine had become extinct, and the remaining species either had gone through a taxonomic revision or had been delisted erroneously based on new or inaccurate data.[15]

Political struggles and partisanship characterize the progress that is being made in the listing process. In 1980, for example, 281 species (primarily birds and plants) were added to the list; 10 years later, 596 (mostly plants) were added. Prior to the 1996 moratorium on listings, 1,053 species were added; a year later, only 79 more were included. Federal officials have added an average of 9.5 species a year under the administration of George W. Bush, compared with 65 a year under the Clinton administration and 59 a year under President George H.W. Bush.[16] Recent efforts to seek changes in the ESA have been led by Rep. Richard Pombo (R-CA), chairman of the House Resources Committee. The act "has been a failure in terms of what its initial goals were, in terms of identifying and recovering species."[17]

Species recovery plans are a second controversial element of species protection. Prior to the 1990s, the USFWS relied upon this strategy to save endangered species, a process that often took years and resulted in limited success. In 1985, for example, the USFWS decided to remove the last six California condors from the wild as a way of protecting the species. After a monumental tracking and trapping effort, and amidst considerable public opposition and an injunction by the National Audubon Society, staff from the San Diego Wild Animal Park captured the last of the known wild birds in 1987. The government allowed several nonprofit groups to begin captive breeding programs, and eventually they began to release young condors back into their natural habitat in southern California and northern Arizona and to track their activities. Critics believed the efforts were counterproductive because many of the re-released birds later died. Supporters of the program grew even more pessimistic when researchers discovered that the first three chicks born in the wild in 18 years had died within three weeks of each other in 2002. One of the chicks had died from ingesting shards of plastic and glass, along with a dozen bottle caps.[18]

Another species management tool, the designation of critical habitat, is designed to provide protection for specific areas deemed essential to the survival of a species once it is listed. A survey by the National Wildlife Federation (NWF) found that the government was using questionable economic analyses in making habitat designations. As a result, between 2001 and 2003, only 41 million of the 83 million acres of critical habitat initially proposed by federal biologists were approved. In a case involving 15 vernal pool species in California, the USFWS decided not to designate nearly 1 million acres that biologists had recommended as critical habitat. The NWF charged that the decision was based on an analysis that inflated the cost of the designation. Federal officials counter that the action reflects a policy shift that Interior Secretary Gale Norton calls the "New Environmentalism." According to one official, "It's a different way of looking at how to administer the act. We are putting our efforts on the up-front end of conservation, as opposed to the emergency listing end."[19]

Another policy shift involves transferring responsibility for wildlife management from the federal government to the states. Critics of this concept believe it only passes the responsibility for wildlife control on to the states—it is an unfunded mandate that requires additional staff but no money. Environmental groups, which have traditionally opposed blanket national wildlife management plans, have sometimes given their approval to localized efforts to deal with specific problem colonies. Officials from the Fish and Wildlife Service believe the proposal gives states a voice in plans affecting species within its borders. But what does "management" mean, and how should each state respond?

Nowhere is the issue more contentious than in Yellowstone National Park, where preservation of the park's American buffalo herd exemplifies the political considerations state officials are currently facing. Prior to European settlement, an estimated 30 to 75 million buffalo (also known as bison) roamed the West; by 1890, the animals had almost been wiped out because of target shooting and hunting, including organized hunts conducted from train cars. Reintroduction and intensive wildlife management throughout the Greater Yellowstone Ecosystem has led to the protection of about 3,000–3,500 free-roaming animals today.[20]

A major policy shift occurred in 1969 when park managers decided to turn from intensive management to natural regulation, allowing buffalo to extend their range and to migrate beyond the national park boundaries. Researchers have determined that the herds carry the brucellosis virus, which causes cows to abort, although there have been no reported cases of transmission of the organism to domestic cattle that graze on the public lands intersecting the buffalo range and migration routes. The pivotal issue is how buffalo should be "managed" when they cross an administrative park boundary; in the past, animals have been herded with snowmobiles, yelled at and hazed by activists trying to force them back across park borders, and trapped. In winter 1988, near the park's northern boundary, 569 animals were shot; and in 1990, game wardens escorted hunters to a designated shooting area after animal rights protesters had confronted the hunters. The hunt, which one activist compared to "shooting a car," brought negative publicity to the state and numerous protests, and sport hunting was discontinued. Nearly 1,100 buffalo were slaughtered by the agency as a preventative measure to keep the area "brucellosis-free" in 1996. The most controversial action was a March 2003 decision to capture about 110 buffalo, many of which were still within the park when they were herded up. Environmental organizations like the Bear Creek Council and Fund for Animals protested the capture and killing of the buffalo and accused the

National Park Service of abusing its discretion. One activist commented, "Sending Yellowstone buffalo to slaughter, the Department of Interior's Park Service has sacrificed treasured wildlife and its own integrity for politics, pure and simple."[21]

Another option, organized sport hunting, was revived in a vote by the state legislature in 2003 and in December 2004 when the Montana Fish, Wildlife and Parks Commission approved a limited one-month hunting season in an area where buffalo are known to migrate in winter. Montana Department of Livestock officials had recommended the issuance of five licenses; commissioners sought 25, and eventually settled on 10 permits. The licenses, issued through a public lottery, would allow a more conventional hunt rather than the escorted, prearranged excursions into the park. A three-month hunt scheduled for November 2005 was also approved by the commission.[22]

The commission's decision led to a strong public outcry against the hunt. Members of one activist group, the Buffalo Field Campaign, announced that they would apply for permits and said they would buy licenses but not participate in the hunt if their names were selected. The clothing company, Patagonia, announced that it would reimburse the cost of the permits ($75 for residents and $750 for nonresidents) for anyone who decided not to take part. More than 8,300 people paid $3 each to apply for the hunting permits. An Idaho newspaper noted, "If it's the thrill of the hunt that people seek, surely they won't find it here. And if it's the meat that they want, let them go to the supermarket."[23]

But on January 6, on a 4—1 vote, the quasi-judicial commission agreed to reconsider its position. The reason? Just a few hours before the meeting, three new commission members had been appointed by the state's new governor, Brian Schweitzer, who said he was not opposed to bison hunting but was concerned about the circumstances. "There will be a significant hunt. There's going to be a hunt next year. I just don't want a black-eye hunt. I don't think we should have the equivalent of shooting refrigerators."[24]

On January 10, just five days before the hunt was scheduled to begin, the commission voted to postpone the hunting season for bison in southwestern Montana. But the vote did not end the controversy for long. The following day, the commission voted 3—2 to enter the names of those who had already applied for hunting permits into a lottery for 10 bison licenses that could be used for a three-month hunting season beginning in November 2005 over a larger area. The commissioners released an announcement confirming their support for the hunt, which is not expected to be used as a way to regulate the bison populations. Instead, the legislature's intent, they said, "is to allow Montana hunters to harvest wild, free-roaming bison under fair chase conditions and to reduce damage to private property by altering bison behavior and distribution."

The news releases also noted that public bison hunts are already established in several western states, including Alaska, Arizona, South Dakota, Utah, and Wyoming.[25] In September 2005, the commission agreed to establish a 90-day hunt of 25 bison between November 15, 2005 and January 15, 2006. Another 25 licenses were authorized for use between January 16, 2006 and February 15, 2006. The licenses allow hunting over more than 460,000 acres of wildlife habitat in southwestern Montana. Members of the Buffalo Field Campaign planned to videotape and photograph the hunt, and to bring the media to the area on field tours.

Sixteen of the licenses were allotted to Montana's Native American tribes, in accordance with a new state law, and ten more were awarded to hunters who had their licenses drawn in 2004 before the 2005 hunt was postponed.

Another View, Another Voice

Brian Schweitzer

In November 2004, Montana voters ended two decades of Republican rule with the election of Brian Schweitzer as governor. President George W. Bush won reelection in the "red" state by more than 20 percentage points, and its three-member congressional delegation is said to hover between conservative and ultraconservative. So how did a Democrat like Schweitzer beat a Republican secretary of state who had been active for more than two decades in the state?

Some observers believe Schweitzer's victory was due to his appeal to hunters and outdoors enthusiasts; Montana has the highest percentage of hunters of any state in the nation. The grandson of homesteaders, Schweitzer is proud of being a hunter; his platform included a plan to protect hunting and fishing access rights on public and private lands. He won the endorsement of groups like the Headwaters Fish and Game Association and pro-gun organizations that traditionally favored Republican candidates.

The fourth of six children, Schweitzer was born in Havre, Montana, in 1955 and raised on his parents' cattle ranch. He attended Colorado State University, where he earned a degree in International Agronomy and later, a master's degree in soil science from Montana State University. He married his Montana-born wife in 1981, and they have three teenage children.

His nonpolitical experience is as varied as his personal interests are. Schweitzer has worked in agricultural irrigation development, including a seven-year stint in Saudi Arabia, and he has operated farms and ranches in Montana. He learned to fly his own plane, and has worked with Native American tribal organizations.

His life experiences led to an appointment to the Montana State U.S. Department of Agriculture Farm Service Agency committee in 1993, and to a seat on the Montana Rural Development Partnership Board in 1996. He gained national exposure with an appointment to the National Drought Task Force in 1999.

In 2000, Schweitzer mounted an unsuccessful campaign for the Senate against Conrad Burns. The difference between that race and the one in 2004 was part strategy, part timing. In 2000 Schweitzer barnstormed the state, running as an old-school economic populist, aligning himself with small business and against out-of-state corporate interests that supported Burns. When Governor Judy Martz's popularity hit bottom in 1993, she decided not to run for reelection, opening the political window of opportunity for Schweitzer. In the gubernatorial race, Schweitzer was portrayed as a gun-owning outdoorsman whose conservative views fit the state's voters and their interests, including those of environmentalists. His views resonated with the 85 percent of the state's residents who own or are employed by small businesses, and with those who believed it was time for a change in the state house.

Since 1972, Montana law has required that the governor and lieutenant governor run as a team, and Schweitzer took the unusual route of naming a Billings, Montana, small business owner—a Republican state senator—as his running mate. It was the first bipartisan ticket in the state's history, and it provided a balance that was attractive to voters; Schweitzer beat his Republican challenger by four percentage points.

After being inaugurated in the capitol rotunda in Helena on January 3, 2005, Schweitzer and his running mate joined an Indian drumming circle. The new lieutenant governor told the participants, "I want you to know my heart will be beating at the same rate as those drums and that your governor down this hall will hear those drums for the next four years."

Schweitzer has been credited with some phrases that exemplify his western upbringing. In commenting on the nomination of former Utah governor Mike Leavitt (who also served as administrator of the EPA) as secretary of Health and Human Services under George W. Bush, he referenced Leavitt's loyalty to the Bush administration: "Once they come in and work for the ranch, they toe the company line," and added that Leavitt "seems to be riding for the president's brand." As the first Democrat elected governor of Montana in 24 years, Schweitzer brings a new perspective not only to the bison hunt, but to state politics as well.

SOURCES:
Sarah Cooke, "Brian Schweitzer Inaugurated," *Helena Independent Record,* January 3, 2005, at www.helenair.com, accessed January 15, 2005.
Betsy Marston, "Heard Around the West," *High Country News,* March 21, 2005, 24.
George Ochenski, "Horns of a Dilemma," *Missoula Independent,* January 13, 2005, at www.everyweek.com/News, accessed January 14, 2005.
David Sirota, "Top Billings," *Washington Monthly,* December 2004, at www.washingtonmonthly.com, accessed January 15, 2005.
State of Montana, "Biography: Governor Brian Schweitzer," at www.governor.mt.gov, accessed January 15, 2005.

The Montana commission's action, although controversial and highly visible, is restricted to state efforts to manage wildlife; its impact is therefore somewhat limited. A much more controversial element of species recovery policy is the habitat conservation plan (HCP). The process of developing these plans stems from two sections in the ESA that provide the means for federal agencies to authorize, fund, or carry out development projects while ensuring that such projects do not jeopardize the existence of the species. However, because private and nonfederal developers were not covered by the statute, problems would be created should a project result in the killing, harming, or harassment of a threatened or endangered species. In 1982, Congress amended the ESA by allowing the creation of HCPs, which allow development to continue even if there is a threat to a species, as long as some form of conservation mitigation takes place. A landowner can be issued a permit to legally proceed with an activity that would otherwise be illegal and harmful to a species by enhancing or restoring a degraded or former habitat, creating new habitats, or establishing a buffer area around existing habitats. The compromise concept was designed to allow developers, environmental groups, and government agencies to come up with "creative partnerships" without halting development altogether or placing a burden on private property owners. Realizing that plans alone were insufficient, the USFWS developed Habitat Acquisition Projects to provide up to 75 percent of the cost for purchasing land deemed essential to the development of a comprehensive conservation plan.

The ESA is more likely to be the subject of debate in the judicial arena rather than in Congress, where amendments and repeal attempts have made little progress. Many of the disputes involve private property owners who have sued for compensation for economic losses, to which they believe they are entitled under the Constitution when the government "takes" their land by declaring it part of an endangered or threatened species' habitat. In 1975, the USFWS had expanded its definition of *harm* to a species by including any action that caused the destruction of critical habitat, even if the species itself was not harmed. In a 6—3 decision in 1995, the U.S. Supreme Court upheld the federal government's definition of what constitutes *harm* under a policy that allowed logging in areas that had been declared critical habitat for the threatened Northern Spotted Owl.

In *Babbitt v. Sweet Home Chapter of Communities for a Greater Oregon,*[26] the latter a timber-industry-sponsored group, the Court ruled that the common meaning of the term *harm* is broad and in the context of the ESA would encompass habitat modification that injures or kills members of an endangered species. The decision upheld the secretary of the interior's 1994 regulation, as the majority of the Court also noted that the statute had been reasonably interpreted. Dissenters on the Court argued that the definition was so broad that it had the effect of penalizing actions regardless of whether they were intended or foreseeable.[27]

Environmental organizations hailed the *Sweet Home* decision as precedent for protecting entire ecosystems rather than individual species. These groups believe that the decision gives government agencies such as the Fish and Wildlife Service more discretion in implementing the law. But groups within the environmental opposition called upon Congress to take action to alter the ESA. One critic called the Court's ruling "one more step down the road to agency control" and said it gave administrative agencies much more power than the Constitution intended.[28]

Groups like Defenders of Wildlife have accused the Bush administration of working "systematically to undermine the Endangered Species Act, employing a wide variety of tactics to circumvent the clear language of the law and to skew its function in favor of corporate special interests."[29] In a study of 120 federal court decisions resolving ESA issues between January 21, 2001, and October 31, 2003, in which Bush administration officials exerted influence over legal strategy and outcome, the administration presented arguments hostile to the ESA in 63 percent of cases, defined as contradicting established legal interpretations of the act. In 89 percent of the "ESA-hostile" cases, courts found that the administration had acted illegally and ruled against them.[30] The study identified several legalistic strategies and tactics that the Bush administration "is now using in its systematic effort to sabotage the ESA, including ignoring court orders, slanting science, creating an artificial budget crisis, and helping friends in industry."[31]

In one 2003 court case brought by the Center for Biological Diversity against Interior Secretary Gale Norton, the judge noted, "Defendant and [Fish and Wildlife Service] have been told by no fewer than three federal courts, including the Ninth Circuit, that its position is untenable and in contravention of the ESA. This argument has failed three times. It fails yet again here."[32]

There is a growing wave of opinion that the debate over the future of endangered species (and biodiversity in general) is becoming more political and less scientific in nature. Some observers of the process believe that the most important decisions about species survival are being made by political appointees who make policy only in response to the groups who provide financial support for their benefactors. This produces, the observers argue, a system in which there is a natural tension between politicians and scientists; and as the issue of conserving biodiversity becomes more important, it inevitably becomes more political. For political leaders, species recovery efforts often become media events, as was the case in 1998 when Interior Secretary Bruce Babbitt announced that the Peregrine Falcon's numbers had increased sufficiently to be removed from the federal list of endangered species. In 1970, when the bird was initially listed, pesticide poisoning had reduced the bird's numbers to only 39 pairs in the continental United States. By the time of Babbitt's announcement, an estimated 1,600 breeding pairs were thought to exist in North America. Babbitt used the occasion in Stone Mountain, Georgia, to release a small falcon from its cage, commenting, "The Endangered Species Act is working. It's a part of our American spirit and heritage."[33] Although the peregrine's delisting was highly publicized and applauded, it also could be seen as a policy that favors high-profile species over those that are less attractive or well known. Thousands of species face similar extinction struggles, and only a few animals, such as the prairie dog and desert bighorn sheep, are the beneficiaries of public support and media attention.

Environmental group leaders note three factors that make it difficult to keep biodiversity on the public agenda: a lack of an easily identifiable opponent, a lack of any immediate impact on human lifestyles, and a lack of cohesiveness by large groups around the widespread preservation of species. It is difficult, they say, to generate support or motivate groups to mobilize to action even though species are becoming extinct; one reason is that people's daily lives do not appear to be affected. The most difficult task seems to be convincing people, despite their concerns for endangered species, that there is a relationship between their own activities and the causes of endangerment. Consequently, public attention begins to dissipate as policy makers realize the full costs of implementing protection measures.

A paradox faced by the ESA is that a species is not protected until its population becomes so low that it is likely to become extinct. When that happens, recovery becomes both inefficient and costly. Recovery then begins to compromise the activities of other agencies (international, federal, state, and local), which must change their policies to accommodate the situation, thus increasing the probability of conflict. What this tells us about the future of endangered species and their habitats is that their protection requires the building of a much broader political constituency than the one currently in existence. The actions of isolated organizations dedicated to the preservation of an individual species are unlikely to convince policy makers that there is a need for change. Instead, public policy is more likely to be politicized by groups whose economic prospects are influenced by what happens to their future.

THE ROLE OF ORGANIZED INTERESTS

Government agencies are responsible for implementing the legislative aspects of wildlife protection, but environmental organizations, industry trade associations, and grassroots opposition groups have clashed over how the laws ought to be interpreted. Wildlife protection groups began to flourish in the late 19th century, and many of them survived to become the mainstays of the contemporary environmental movement, such as the National Audubon Society, founded in 1905. Others, such as the Wilderness Society (1935) and the National Wildlife Federation (1936), were products of the surge of interest instigated by President Theodore Roosevelt. The vast majority of wildlife organizations, however, have a more recent origin, partly due to a spate of legislative activity just after Earth Day 1970. The National Wildlife Federation, which monitors environmental organizations, reported that of the 108 national wildlife and humane organizations identified in its study, 14 percent had been founded before 1940 and 68 percent since 1966. The decade surrounding Earth Day (1965–1975) accounted for the founding of 38 percent of all groups with a species orientation.[34]

The tactics used by groups to influence the implementation of wildlife policy range from the traditional to the radical. Some organizations see their role within the context of legislation, such as the Wilderness Society's efforts at lobbying Congress to increase appropriations for habitat protection. Other groups focus on advocating for species by lobbying the implementing agency directly.

Several organizations have taken independent steps to preserve species, bypassing the federal bureaucracy. The Nature Conservancy (founded in 1951), for instance, buys up endangered habitats to save the species living on them from extinction. The organization has purchased or negotiated donations of more than 5 million acres worldwide, making the group the custodian of the largest private nature sanctuary in the world. Another notable accomplishment of the group is its Biological and Conservation Data System, a biogeographic database of more than 400,000 entries that can be used to assess species diversity on a region-by-region basis. The system allows the group to establish protection priorities and is also used by public agencies and resource planners in preparing environmental impact studies.

Conflicts over goals—and species—also bring organizations into the policy process. In New Mexico, the mountain lion is a protected species. It preys on the endangered desert bighorn sheep, which has been declining in population for decades. According to the New Mexico Department of Game and Fish, only about 130 bighorn remain in the state; mountain lions caused 30 of the last 40 recorded deaths of these sheep. To relieve predation pressures on the endangered animals, the state decided to allow hunters to kill more mountain lions in designated bighorn habitats.

The policy is opposed by several organizations, including the group called Animal Protection of New Mexico. The organization is concerned that the increase in hunting quotas will reduce the mountain lion population by as much as a third, instead of the 10 percent estimated by the state agency. Some researchers also oppose the plan, believing that it represents an antiquated view of predator species and that there is insufficient evidence to support the expanded hunt. Because mountain lions are extremely elusive, no one really knows how many there are in New Mexico; and the state's kill allowance is based on mathematical models. The two species are on a collision course that pits wildlife managers, hunters, and species' organizations against one another.[35]

Other organizations have taken a collaborative approach to species protection. In August 2002, the USFWS removed the Robbins' cinquefoil, a rare member of the rose family, from the federal List of Endangered and Threatened Plants. The plant is found only in the alpine zone of the White Mountain National Forest in New Hampshire, and it was on the brink of extinction due to disturbances by hikers on the Appalachian Trail and by plant collectors. The 93,000-member Appalachian Mountain Club rerouted the trail away from the primary habitat and worked with national forest officials to erect an enclosure around the primary population of the plant. The New England Wild Flower Society became involved by propagating the endangered plant over several decades, establishing two new populations of the species and reducing the threat of extinction.[36]

Somewhat ironically, sport hunting organizations such as Ducks Unlimited and the Boone and Crockett Club (which Teddy Roosevelt founded in 1887) have also been active in species preservation. Many of the national hunting organizations have dedicated their efforts to preserving wildlife habitat and supporting the enforcement of game laws. They have been instrumental in advocating management policies for species such as the North American deer, wild turkey, pronghorn antelope, and migratory waterfowl. Equally active have been recreational fishing enthusiasts, who have joined environmental organizations in seeking a ban on gill and entangled nets. The American Sportfishing Association and fishing equipment manufacturers contributed funds toward a successful ban on netting in Florida waters, with most of the donations coming from rank-and-file anglers.

The ESA has also been the focus of some of the environmental opposition groups discussed earlier in Chapter 2. Typical is the organization called Grassroots ESA Coalition, an umbrella group headquartered in Battle Ground, Washington. It claims to represent more than 350 other organizations seeking to "reform the ESA in a way that benefits both wildlife and people, something the old law has failed to do."[37] Unlike industry groups with the financial resources to make campaign contributions, the Grassroots ESA Coalition has urged its members to contact members of Congress through telephone calls and letter-writing campaigns in support of reform legislation. Other organizations have called for an outright repeal of the ESA rather than for incremental reforms.

INTERNATIONAL BIODIVERSITY AGREEMENTS AND POLICIES

Most of the international regimes that have been established to protect diversity are considered "soft law," meaning that participating nations may have the right to reject decisions or regulations that they impose. Enforcement is often negligible, with the only real pressure to comply coming from public opinion or diplomatic channels. The range of agreements, however, covers species protection, habitat conservation, species management, and scientific research, as seen in Table 9.2.

Three of these biological diversity agreements are of particular importance due to the scope of their coverage, the number of nations participating, and the legal and structural mechanisms that have been developed to implement them. They are described in the following sections.

Convention on Trade in Endangered Species of Wild Fauna and Flora

The development of an international regime to protect endangered species has come largely from the leadership of the United States. The 1969 Endangered Species Conservation Act included a provision directing the secretaries of the interior and commerce to convene an international meeting before June 30,

TABLE 9.2 **Major International Biological Diversity Agreements**

Agreement	Date
Convention Relative to the Preservation of Fauna and Flora in the Nature State	1933
World Heritage Convention	1972
Convention for the Protection of the World Cultural and Natural Heritage	1972
Convention on International Trade in Endangered Species of Wild Fauna and Flora	1973
Convention on the Conservation of Migratory Species of Animals	1979
Convention on the Conservation of European Wildlife and Natural Habitats	1979
World Charter for Nature	1982
Agreement on the Conservation of Seals in the Wadden Sea	1990
Agreement on the Conservation of Small Cetaceans of the Baltic and North Seas	1991
Agreement on the Conservation of Populations of European Bats	1991
Convention on Biological Diversity	1992
Convention for the Conservation of the Biodiversity and Protection of Wilderness Areas in Central America	1992
Memorandum of Understanding Concerning Conservation Measures for the Slender-billed Curlew	1994
Agreement on the Conservation of African-Eurasian Migratory Waterbirds	1995
Agreement on the Conservation of Cetaceans of the Black Sea, Mediterranean Sea, and Contiguous Atlantic Area	1996
Memorandum of Understanding Concerning Conservation Measures for the Siberian Crane	1998
Memorandum of Understanding for the Conservation of African Sea Turtles	1999
Cartegena Protocol on Biosafety	2000
Memorandum of Understanding on the Conservation and Management of Marine Turtles and Their Habitats of the Indian Ocean and Southeast Asia	2000
International Undertaking on Plant Genetic Resources	2001

1971, to develop an international agreement on the conservation of endangered species. Although it was a year and a half late, that meeting produced the Convention on Trade in Endangered Species of Wild Fauna and Flora, or CITES as it is better known. The United States was the first nation to ratify the convention in January 1974, and it became effective July 1, 1975. There are now 160 parties to the convention.

It is important to note, however, that CITES is not strictly a conservation agreement; it focuses on matters of international trade rather than on preservation per se. A key aspect of the CITES treaty is that it creates three levels of species vulnerability: Appendix I (all species threatened with extinction that are or may be affected by trade), Appendix II (all species that are not now threatened with extinction but that may become so unless trade in specimens is strictly regulated), and Appendix III (species subject to regulation for the purpose of preventing exploitation). About 5,000 species of animals and 25,000 species of plants are now protected by CITES.[38] Within 90 days of the date when a species is added to an appendix, and upon a showing of an overriding economic interest, party nations may make a "reservation" to the convention. The reservation means that they do not accept the listing of a species in a particular appendix and, therefore, are not subject to the trade prohibitions.

CITES establishes an elaborate series of trade permits within each category and between importing and exporting authorities. Exempt from the trade restrictions are specimens acquired before the convention applied to that species, specimens that are personal or household effects, and specimens used in scientific research. The CITES agreement is supported by a secretariat, provided through the UN Environment Programme, and a Conference of the Parties (COP), which meets every two years for the purpose of regulating trade in each species.

When the CITES agreement was first ratified, it was supported by most of the nations that are active in wildlife trading because it helps them to protect their resources from illegal traders and poachers. Several countries that are deeply involved in wildlife trading as importers and exporters of products chose not to sign the CITES agreement. The result is an active animal-smuggling industry, much of it centered in Southeast Asia. Japan, the world's biggest importer of illegally traded goods, initially made 12 reservations to the convention, including two species of endangered sea turtles, although it agreed to phase out its trade in those species. The sea turtle shells, primarily those of the hawksbill and olive ridley species, are made into eyeglass frames, cigarette lighters, combs, handbags, belts, and shoes.

Perhaps the most publicized and controversial listing under CITES is the African elephant. The elephant had already been listed by the United States as a threatened species in 1978, but in 1988 the World Wildlife Fund and Conservation International sponsored a scientific study of the African elephant population and recommended that it be listed under CITES Appendix I: threatened with extinction. The listing was supported by the United States and several other nations (including Kenya and Tanzania) at the October 1989 COP, along with a proposed ban on trade in ivory products—a position opposed by Botswana, Malawi, Mozambique, South Africa, Zambia, and Zimbabwe. Their opposition was due to several of the nations having managed to increase their elephant herds through nationally supported economic incentives. They felt there was no need for their countries to suffer the loss of the lucrative ivory trade because herds in other African states were being diminished through poor wildlife management practices.

In the end, the United States-led position won, and the elephant achieved Appendix I status. Prices in African raw ivory dropped by as much as 90 percent, reducing any real incentives for poaching and smuggling, and it appeared that the problem was resolved. But the issue continued to be raised at the 1992 and 1994 COPs, as African representatives sought relief from CITES to sell ivory from culled elephants, arguing that they had managed their herds effectively to stabilize the population. They felt as if they were being penalized for their efforts, and they denounced attempts by countries without elephants to dominate the discussion. Environmental organizations, who were actively monitoring the CITES meetings, pointed out that the elephant population still had declined, convincing members to keep the ivory trade ban in effect.[39]

In 1997, however, there was an abrupt shift of policy when environmental ministers representing 138 nations met in Zimbabwe. After years of rancorous debate, Botswana, Namibia, and Zimbabwe were given permission to sell previously stockpiled ivory tusks to Japan under an experimental program that included an international monitoring system and increased enforcement of antipoaching laws.[40] At the November 2002 COP in Santiago, Chile, Botswana, Namibia, South Africa, Zambia, and Zimbabwe sought approval to sell a total of 96 tons of ivory in a one-time sale to help them clear out stockpiles from elephants that had died naturally, with proceeds going to elephant management and conservation programs. The five southern African nations argued that they have healthy elephant populations in their countries, and in some cases, huge herds are causing environmental damage. Botswana's elephant population was about 54,000 in 1990, and a decade later, it had more than doubled to about 120,000—too many animals for the country's arid plains.

A flaw in the CITES provisions is that CITES has little real power over the actions of individual nations and whether they choose to comply with the treaty. For example, the parties established a panel comprised of affected states and nongovernmental organization representatives to monitor elephant populations and determine whether the species should be downlisted on a case-by-case basis. But the panel's recommendations are only advisory, and no mechanism exists within the secretariat to prosecute noncompliance with the convention. Thus, any real efforts at species protection are voluntary and reliant upon the parties' recognition of the value of preserving biodiversity.

International Convention on the Regulation of Whaling

The protection of whales is covered under the second of the three major international environmental agreements, the 1946 International Convention on the Regulation of Whaling (ICRW). Humanity's fascination with the huge mammals dates back to the biblical story of Jonah and the publication of Herman Melville's novel, *Moby Dick,* in 1851. The story of the sperm whale was both fanciful and fearful, focusing attention on the animal's power and beauty. Researchers are in agreement about two things: (a) the mammals are intelligent and have a complex communication system, and (b) hunting has diminished their numbers to the point where most species are now endangered. The whaling industry of the 18th and 19th centuries hunted the animals for food, whale oil, and hides, and sometimes for sport.

The threat of extinction led to the ICRW, which applies to all waters where whales are found, including their migration routes. The purpose of the convention, however, seems contradictory; it calls for both the conservation of whale stocks and the orderly development of the whale industry. The International Whaling Commission (IWC), which serves as a data-gathering body and monitors whaling activities, has no enforcement capabilities and no provisions for the settling of disputes; any infractions must be taken to the country under which the vessel's flag is being flown. As a result, many vessels register with governments displaying lax enforcement or disinterest in the ICRW, recognizing that they are unlikely to face any type of sanction.

At the 1972 Stockholm Conference on the Human Environment, delegates called for a 10-year moratorium on commercial whaling; but the policy did not go into force until 1986. At that time, the IWC approved a cessation of all commercial whaling while a survey of whale stocks and potential catch limits was conducted. Norway, Japan, the Soviet Union, and Peru lodged formal objections to the moratorium (Peru later withdrew). Iceland officially withdrew as a party to the IWC in 1992, and Japan and Norway threatened to withdraw as well. Although Norway had participated in meetings to resolve whaling controversies as early as 1988, its leaders subsequently announced that it would resume commercial whaling in 1993 because Norway had formally objected to the moratorium from the beginning. Once it resumed the hunt for minke whales, Norway began to increase its catch every year in violation of the moratorium. Norwegian hunting boats are allowed by the government to harpoon 797 minke whales in 2005; in 2004, the quota was 670.[41]

Nongovernmental organizations like Greenpeace, EarthTrust, and the Sea Shepherd Society have been at the forefront of efforts to focus attention on whaling practices and the potential for extinction, but their efforts to ban whaling altogether are thwarted by sections of the agreement that contain exceptions to the moratorium. For instance, there is an aboriginal exception to allow whale hunting by certain coastal communities that depend upon subsistence whaling. The IWC has never defined what constitutes an aboriginal group, but Japan has argued that the exception should apply to its coastal villages where whale meat is used for local consumption. The United States has faced a somewhat different circumstance because the federal government signed agreements with tribal groups to allow whaling for cultural or subsistence reasons. Tribes in Alaska and in Washington State have defied the IWC moratorium in controversial hunts that have been an embarrassment to the United States, which has been supportive of antiwhaling policies. In 2002, the IWC's Scientific Committee agreed to create new categories of whale stocks that are subject to aboriginal subsistence whaling, from 2003 to 2006–2007, including Eastern North Pacific gray whales (traditional subsistence needs), West Greenland fin whales (Greenlanders), West Greenland minke whales (Greenlanders), East Greenland minke whales (Greenlanders), and humpback whales. These whales would be used exclusively for local consumption and monitored by the governments of St. Vincent and The Grenadines.[42]

Article VIII allows nations to obtain a permit "to kill, take, and treat whales for purposes of scientific research," thus exempting those parties from the Convention. During the 1990s, the Japanese government interpreted the scientific research clause very liberally, allowing vessels to harvest minke whales, remove tissue and organ samples, and then freeze and later sell the whale meat to consumers. The convention calls for the processing of the carcasses "so far as practicable," with the proceeds dealt with by the government. Japan considered its practice of selling the remaining whale parts as part of its compliance with the convention's instructions. Proceeds from the sale of whale meat, along with smaller amounts of skin and blubber, added up to about $52 million in 2003.

Environmental groups argued that Japan's "scientific research" was simply an excuse for continuing whale hunting, and switched their goals from the sustainable use of whales to species conservation, despite the IWC's Revised Management Procedure that set zero catch limits while the moratorium remains in place. Angered by the IWC's whale protection policies, representatives from the Faroe Islands, Greenland, Iceland, and Norway signed an agreement in 1992 to establish a regional organization of their own, the North Atlantic Marine Mammal Commission (NAMMCO). Observers believe the new group not only serves as a challenge to the legitimacy and integrity of the IWC but also provides an option for countries that choose to leave the IWC or object to its procedures.[43]

Several nations have attempted to broker agreements that would bring the parties back into the IWC to find ways of addressing their opposition. In 1994, France proposed a Southern Ocean Whaling Sanctuary; Ireland and Australia proposed a global whale sanctuary in 1997; and a 1998 plan would have allowed countries to hunt whales in their own coastal waters up to 200 miles offshore. At the IWC 2002 meeting in Japan, several proposals for sanctuaries in the South Pacific were defeated. Similarly, the threat of any form of penalty has been ineffective. The United States has the authority to impose trade sanctions on any country that violates the ICRW. Other legislation, such as the Marine Mammal Protection Act and the Fishermen's Protective Act's Pelly Amendment, provides species protection.

Strong and organized opposition to Japan's whale hunts erupted again in June 2005 at the IWC meeting in South Korea. The Japanese delegation submitted plans to the scientific committee of the IWC that would expand the hunting of whales for scientific purposes in the Southern Ocean. Specifically, Japan sought to increase its annual intake of minke whales from 440 to 935 and expand its hunt to include 10 fin whales a year in 2005–2006 and 2006–2007, with an increase to 40 in 2007–2008. The most publicly contentious proposal was to include 50 humpback whales in 2007–2008—the public has embraced this species since the contemporary whale wars began. Japan also announced that it would leave the IWC if the organization failed to approve a contentious set of rules that would allow limited commercial whaling.[44]

Australia's delegation took the lead in opposing Japan, using its diplomatic missions around the world to put pressure on the country's leaders and to line up the necessary votes to defeat the Japanese proposals. Joined by Britain, France, and Germany, along with Ireland, Italy, Sweden, Mexico, Brazil, Argentina, New Zealand, Austria, Finland, The Netherlands, and Portugal, Australia's foreign minister told Parliament that the nation remains steadfast against any forms of commercial or scientific whaling. The Australian prime minister also warned his Japanese counterpart that the country would face a worldwide backlash over its expansion plans.[45]

The level of public outrage is best illustrated by "a modest proposal" from the Australian press.

> Knowledge-hungry Australian scientists would be able to hunt and kill several hundred Japanese whale scientists per year to obtain important information such as how old they are, where they live and how their loins taste when marinated, barbecued and served with a feisty shiraz. It will be a controversial move, but killing Japanese pro-whalers and dissecting them into tasty bite-sized pieces is the only way to help solve enduring mysteries about this enigmatic species.[46]

✒ Convention on Biological Diversity

A third major international species protection agreement is the Convention on Biological Diversity (CBD), which was negotiated both before and during the Earth Summit in Rio de Janeiro in June 1992. Unlike the dissension that marked the initial reservations to CITES, the biodiversity convention gained the support of virtually every member of the United Nations except the United States. President George Bush, who had threatened to boycott the conference, refused to sign the biodiversity treaty in an action that embarrassed the U.S. delegation in a highly publicized dispute. Under the terms of the agreement, the parties agree that a state has sovereignty over the genetic resources within its borders, including any valuable drugs and medicines that may be developed from endangered animals and plants. The convention is an important extension of CITES because it commits countries to draw up national strategies to conserve not only the plants and animals within their borders but also the habitats in which they live. Other provisions require countries to pass laws to protect endangered species, expand protected areas, restore damaged ones, and promote public awareness of the need for conservation and sustainable use of biological resources. When President Clinton assumed office, he signed the treaty; but because the Republican-controlled Congress refused to ratify it with a two-thirds vote, the United States was allowed only an observer role when the first COP was held in 1994.[47] Under President George W. Bush, the convention remains unratified.

Before the Earth Summit, habitat protection found international support largely through organizations such as the International Union for Conservation of Nature and Natural Resources (IUCN) and by regimes such as the International Convention Concerning the Protection of World Cultural and Natural Heritage, which entered into force in 1972. The World Heritage List is established by an international committee of the United Nations to designate sites of "outstanding universal value." At its June 2002 session in Budapest, Hungary, nine new sites were added, bringing the total to 730 sites in 125 countries. Whereas some sites are primarily historically or archaeologically valuable, such as the Mahabodhi Temple Complex at Bodh Gaya, India, others, like the marine zone around Cocos Island National Park in Costa Rica, are themselves important ecosystems.[48]

A challenge facing global efforts to preserve wildlife habitats is basically one of economics: In times of declining budgets, many governments are finding it difficult to support parks and reserves over human needs. Countries such as New Zealand, for example, are reorganizing their parks to earn more revenue from them, and several African nations are using tourism as a way of financing wildlife refuges. But there are less obvious problems as well. Most national parks are outlined by some type of physical barrier, such as a fence or moat, but animals within do not always respect those limitations. Large mammals and birds of prey, for example, demand a large ecosystem for their habitat, which may cross national borders. This makes it unlikely that, even when strictly protected, national parks by themselves will be able to conserve all, or even most, species.

PROTECTING THE WORLD'S FORESTS

The protection of endangered species has been the center of the biodiversity controversy during the last three decades, but an even longer- running debate has continued over the world's forests, which cover almost one third of the Earth's surface land. The issue is complicated because the planet is home to a variety of forest ecosystems, from the ancient forests of the United States, to the boreal forests of northern Canada and Russia, to the tropical forests circling the equator between the Tropic of Cancer and the Tropic of Capricorn. Forest resources are spread throughout the planet; they comprise 0.1 percent of the landmass of Egypt and Quatar, in comparison to nearly 96 percent of the Cook Islands.

The management of forest resources has become an interest of global concern because in many instances, the conflicts that have erupted represent a duel between the "haves" and the "have-nots." The issue has pitted environmental activists from urban areas against rural landowners, and representatives of industrialized nations against developing nations that have accused developed countries of "economic imperialism" in their attempts to control the fate of other countries' natural resources. The physical and biological diversity of forests, the large number of forest owners with often-conflicting objectives, and increasing demands for wood for fuel, paper, shelter, and artistic uses have made forest management— especially challenging for policy makers.

Deforestation is an extremely volatile global environmental issue. The boreal forests of the far north comprise nearly one third of the world's timberland, serving as a major carbon sink as well as home to plants and animals and to a million indigenous people who have lived in the forests for centuries. Russia, for example, contains about one fifth of the world's forests; an estimated 19 percent are currently under threat from logging and mining, according to the World Resources Institute.[49] Massive logging in Canada has disrupted ecosystems, displaced native peoples, polluted rivers with toxic chemicals used in the bleaching of pulp, and subsidized major multinational corporations.[50] An estimated 90 percent of boreal logging is clear-cutting; and 25 percent of these areas do not regenerate as topsoil erodes away during and after logging, which also destroys permafrost, the layer below the topsoil that acts as a heat reservoir in the winter. As the permafrost retreats, risks to the forests from fires, pests, and species composition grows; the downward spiral contributes to the threat of global climate change as the carbon sink is lost, and carbon from dead trees is increasingly released into the atmosphere.[51]

Logging of similar forests in Russia is occurring even faster in an effort to generate much-needed foreign currency. Clear-cutting, combined with emissions from smelters and radioactive pollution, poses a serious threat to forests throughout the former Soviet Union. Scandinavian forests, largely in private hands, are facing similar problems. Private landowners log old-growth forests next to lands where trees are protected. Although reforestation is standard practice, and a few companies have switched to chlorine-free production of paper, biodiversity has suffered. There are major challenges to boreal forests throughout the world: below-cost timber subsidies that waste resources, minimal environmental review of proposed logging efforts, disposal of timberlands that are home to indigenous peoples, and large-scale clear-cutting that threatens the sustainability of forest production.[52]

Because almost all boreal forest policy is governed by sovereign nations rather than by international accord, individual countries have approached timber management in their own way. British Columbia, for example, has developed an ambitious program to replant forest lands that were heavily harvested in the 19th and early 20th centuries. Little value had been assigned to forests, which were continuously cut so the land could be used for agriculture. By the 1940s, officials realized that the provincial forests were not limitless, and timber companies began replanting areas that had been clear-cut. The Forest Act of 1947 recognized the forests as economic resources and established the goal of ensuring a perpetual supply of timber under the principle of sustained-yield forestry. By the early 1970s, provincial officials began to realize that logging rates were not sustainable, as timber cuts continued to climb as the promise of immediate jobs and profits overwhelmed a projected loss of sustainability. Modernization of logging technology resulted in job losses as timber harvests leveled off and increasing international competition impinged on profits. Preservationists lobbied successfully for the creation of parks that also reduced the potential supply of timber.[53] In 1993 the government, prompted by projections that forest harvests were likely to decline by 15—30 percent over the next 50 years, established a Forest Sector Strategy Committee to find ways to balance the competing values of forests and review policies that protect watersheds, wildlife, and the rights and concerns of indigenous peoples.[54]

British Columbia is an important case study in forest management because of its biological, cultural, and geographical diversity. Nearly two-thirds of the Canadian province is forested, providing over 60 percent of the province's export revenues (estimated at over $17 billion a year). Unlike the United States, where the federal government retains control of lands with public domain forests, in British Columbia, 94 percent of the land is publicly owned but managed by the provincial government. The provincial leaders make decisions as to whether the lands are best used for recreation, mining, or logging, or set aside as preserves and parks.

Timber policy in the province has been shaped by rapid population growth and accompanying development, along with the increasing clout of environmental organizations like the Forest Alliance of British Columbia and the Western Canada Wilderness Committee. Along with the Sierra Club and Greenpeace, these groups focused attention on the large temperate rain forest on the west coast of Vancouver Island near the Clayoquot Sound. The area is nearly pristine, with huge tracts of ecologically sensitive habitat and one of the largest protected old-growth forests in North America. As environmental groups sought to ban logging and to establish the area as a protected park, timber interests sought to log the area, supported by the indigenous Nuu-chah-nulth people, whose interests in the forest were primarily economic.

Although the Clayoquot controversy is far from over, the provincial government has established an extremely elaborate forest management program to protect the area in its present natural state. What makes this forest policy particularly noteworthy is that it was framed by environmental and timber groups based on scientific studies rather than simply rhetoric. Both sides brought in their own foresters and biologists, attempting to convince policy makers of the scientific validity of their claims. The result, as one observer notes, has been a debate imbued with scientific uncertainty crafted by knowledge brokers who continue to attempt to frame forest management policy in their own terms.[55]

Similar problems plague the world's tropical rain forests, four-fifths of which are concentrated in nine countries: Bolivia, Brazil (with one third of the worldwide total), Columbia, Gabon, Indonesia (with another one third), Malaysia, Peru, Venezuela, and the Democratic Republic of Congo. Two major issues are currently being addressed by global policy makers.

1. Although there is a lack of precise information about the rate of loss, there is consensus among scientists that tropical forests are disappearing at an alarming and ever-increasing rate.

2. There is also agreement that failure to effectively manage tropical forests can result in some negative impacts, including the loss of wood products for fuel and other uses, soil erosion, global warming, shrinking populations of plants in the wild, destruction of fish-breeding areas, and loss of biological diversity and wildlife habitat.

Deforestation in tropical areas occurs primarily on lands not held by private citizens, especially in developing areas, where over four-fifths of closed forest areas is public land. In some countries, nearly 100 percent of all natural forest is government owned, so that officials have total authority over the use and preservation of the land. Thus the rates of deforestation vary considerably from one region of the world to another.

The logging of tropical forests and their products has been occurring for nearly 500 years, beginning with the collection of rare and valuable spices such as pepper and cinnamon by Southeast Asian traders. However, early merchants tended to collect only what they wanted and did not destroy the forests in their search for spices. During most of the 19th century, Europeans sought African hardwood for furniture but left the rest of the forest intact. Latin American forests, in contrast, were often burned to the ground as Spanish settlers established colonial outposts and set up plantation agriculture. The export of agricultural commodities quickly proved to be a lucrative enterprise for several nations. The United States entered the picture in the 1880s when U.S. investors edged out their Spanish competitors and built huge sugar-processing facilities dependent upon crops in Cuba and in the Pacific islands of Hawaii and the Philippines. The sugar barons' quest for increased profits led to more and more forest acreage being cleared; sugar cane became the primary vegetation in many areas, pushing out tropical woods. The logging of native forests for sugar cane was followed by devoting massive acreage to growing tropical fruits, such as bananas in Costa Rica and Nicaragua.

In the 1920s and 1930s, international journals of forestry documented the rapid destruction of tropical forests. However, little political attention was paid to the problem at that time, as was the case between World War II and the advent of the international environmental movement in the early 1970s. The more highly publicized issues of pollution crowded the top of the environmental protection agenda, especially in industrialized nations. It was not until the early 1980s that international organizations—such as the UN's Food and Agriculture Organization (FAO), the UN Development Programme, and the World Bank—began to systematically review scientific literature on deforestation.[56]

Some forest protection issues are of relatively recent origin. In southern Chile, for example, widespread logging did not begin until the 1980s, when native trees were cut and ground into small chips that are shipped to Japan to be processed into paper. Although 30 million acres of Chilean forest are protected in reserves, the 19 million acres estimated to be in private hands are often destructively cut by landowners seeking quick profits. The forestry industry has grown into one of Chile's main export earners. Attempts by groups such as the California-based Ancient Forests International and Chile's National Committee for the Defense of the Flora and Fauna have been largely unsuccessful in convincing the Chilean government to enforce existing regulations that limit cutting and provide for restoration. Few violators are prosecuted and even fewer are convicted by Chilean courts.[57]

Now, as tropical forest resources are being depleted in some countries, international attention is focusing on regions where commercial logging was previously limited or inaccessible. Because the demand for tropical woods has not slowed, logging cartels are looking at areas of New Guinea, China, and New Caledonia; all are considered hot-spot regions of destruction. This means that more nations, by necessity, will become stakeholders and involved in the debate over forest diversity. China, for example, has come under international criticism due to its huge imports of timber from countries where illegal logging is rampant. After it discovered a smuggling route (controlled by crime syndicates) that sends 20 shiploads a month of exotic hardwood logs from Indonesia to China, the British group, Environmental Investigation Agency, called China "the largest buyer of stolen timber in the world." Chinese officials respond that it is the responsibility of timber-exporting countries to monitor shipments, not their own customs officials—who they insist check all incoming timber to make certain it is legal.[58]

Efforts to protect tropical forests are much better funded and organized than attempts to preserve the earth's ancient and boreal forest regions. Environmental organizations throughout the world have rallied against tropical deforestation, agreeing for the most part on the urgency of the problem. But the groups differ significantly in their approaches to what should be done.

Globally, there is a division between the more radical groups seeking to ban trade in timber from virgin rain forests (such as the World Rainforest Movement), and more traditional groups, primarily in the United States, that believe the solution is to "green" the development process. Mainstream organizations such as the World Resources Institute and Friends of the Earth have supported the World Bank's efforts to improve economic conditions in developing countries. Other groups, such as Greenpeace, have established tropical forest units within their organization and lobbied government officials to add more land to existing forest reserves, such as Costa Rica's Monteverde Cloud Forest. Indigenous peoples' groups, such as India's Chipko Andalan movement, have attempted to resist state encroachment upon their homelands. The groups are seeking to control not only forest practices but also mining, the siting of dams, and other projects affecting natural resources and land management.

To slow the world demand for exotic woods, the more radical groups have proposed a ban on the sale of tropical timber. They want the International Tropical Timber Organization (ITTO) to severely restrict timber harvests and trade. Developing nations have been critical of the United States and environmental groups for failing to recognize their people's desire to overcome widespread poverty in areas dependent upon forest products and their allied jobs, including shipping and processing industries. ITTO administers the 1984 and 1994 International Tropical Timber Agreement, but critics argue that the group has the somewhat contradictory role of both protecting forests and regulating the timber trade upon which many of its member nations depend. Some attempts have been made to reduce trade in tropical wood under CITES, which covers both fauna and flora. The 1994 agreement contains 13 specific objectives, but no overarching directives—an issue that has become problematic for the group.

In February 2005, at the United Nations Conference for the Negotiation of a Successor Agreement to the International Tropical Timber Agreement (held in Geneva, Switzerland), efforts to focus future efforts were unsuccessful. Representatives of over 180 governments and organizations agreed to continue policies such as encouraging members to recognize the role of forest-dependent indigenous peoples and to improve the marketing and distribution of tropical timber exports from sustainably managed and legally harvested sources. But administrative problems (the distribution of votes and voluntary funding for projects) remained unresolved, as was the obligation of members to submit timber statistics. ITTO reported that many delegates preferred to play a waiting game on the core issues of finance, scope, and organizational matters, although some "imaginative and radical proposals" were made. "Considerable time was spent on 'ventilating' these proposals but the overall response was cautious, exploratory, and noncommittal."[59]

Because it has been very difficult to reach multilateral regimes using ITTO as a platform, many countries are now making individual agreements with member states. In 1997, the United States worked out a compromise with Brazil to allow the United Nations to monitor trade in mahogany, although environmental groups had sought to have mahogany products included on a list that would have allowed only controlled trade. The United States imported an estimated $37.5 million worth of Brazilian mahogany in 2001, primarily for use in furniture and caskets. Concerned about rampant logging, the Brazilian government outlawed the mahogany trade in October 2001. But in May 2002, U.S. Department of Agriculture officials and Customs agents stopped 15 shipments of the rare wood during inspections at U.S. ports. Initially, it appeared that the mahogany, worth about $10 million, had been harvested legally, based on documents accompanying the shipments. But at the urging of Greenpeace, which has been documenting mahogany logging in Brazil for several years, the documents were inspected further, and Brazil questioned the validity of the export permits accompanying the shipments.[60]

Other than an outright ban on timber, other solutions to tropical deforestation vary in their practicality and level of international support. The World Wildlife Fund and Friends of the Earth, for example, believe that the equipment and the types of forest management being used in these regions needs to be modernized. Current harvesting practices, they argue, are inefficient and waste much of the forest's resources. They have called for an end to existing logging practices and feel that technological advances could bring about extraction that is more compatible with sustainable management. Other observers believe that a complete restructuring of timber taxing and sales practices is needed, because governments in these areas receive only a fraction of the rents from logging. Virtually all tropical countries also provide generous tax incentives for timber processing and logging, with the benefits accruing to the wealthiest strata of the population. The most commonly voiced solution is the creation of forest reserves, which many researchers argue is the only way to save tropical forests at this point. They believe that destruction is proceeding too fast for restoration to be effective, because a damaged tropical forest does not regenerate quickly. The idea is costly, even when coupled with the concept of debt-for-nature swaps that allow developing countries to repay outstanding loans to industrialized nations and lending institutions by establishing forest reserves as a way of paying off their foreign debt. But even the most optimistic estimates show that tropical deforestation is outpacing any current attempts to slow the rate of loss.

NOTES

1. World Wildlife Fund, "WWF Update on Alarming State of the World," October 21, 2004, at www.panda.org/news, accessed November 6, 2004.

2. Ibid.

3. World Wildlife Fund, *Living Planet Report 2004* (Gland, Switzerland: World Wildlife Fund International, 2), at www.worldwildlife.org, accessed November 1, 2004.

4. World Wildlife Fund, "WWF Update."

5. U.S. Executive Office of the President, Council on Environmental Quality, *The Global 2000 Report to the President,* vol. 1 (Washington, DC: U.S. Government Printing Office, 1980), 37.

6. World Conservation Union, "Invasive Species Specialist Group," at www.issg.org, accessed June 16, 2002. See also Yvonne Baskin, *A Plague of Rats and Rubbervines: The Growing Threat of Species Invasion* (Washington, DC: Island Press, 2002); and Sally Deneen, "Going, Going: Exotic Species Are Decimating America's Native Wildlife," May–June 2002, at www.emagazine.com, accessed June 16, 2002.

7. U.S. Executive Office of the President, U.S. Council on Environmental Quality, *The Evolution of National Wildlife Law* (Washington, DC: Government Printing Office, 1977), 17. A critical decision of this period, *Geer v. Connecticut,* 161 U.S. 519 (1896), upheld a state law regulating the transportation of game birds outside Connecticut. Despite the narrow legal issue raised in the case, it is considered to be the bulwark of the state ownership doctrine even today.

8. Scott Sonner, "Debate Over Wild Horses a Turf Battle," *Newsday,* June 7, 2005, at www.newsday.com/news, accessed June 8, 2005; Scott Sonner, "Mustangs Now Suitable for Slaughter," *Arizona Republic,* February 25, 2005, A-14; and Andrew Murr, "A New Range War," *Newsweek,* February 7, 2005, 51.

9. Murr, "A New Range War."

10. Scott Sonner, "Critics Say New BLM Rules Won't Save Wild Horses from Slaughter," *Las Vegas Sun,* May 24, 2005, at www.lasvegassun.com, accessed June 8, 2005.

11. "Ford to Finance Effort to House Wild Horses," *Chicago Tribune,* June 1, 2005, at www.chicagotribune.com/news, accessed June 8, 2005.

12. See Brian Czech and Paul R. Krausman. *The Endangered Species Act: History, Conservation Biology, and Public Policy* (Baltimore: Johns Hopkins University Press, 2001).

13. Bob Benenson, "Conferees' Interior Initiatives May Get Clinton's Veto," *Congressional Quarterly Weekly Report,* September 23, 1995, 2883–2884.

14. The White House. "President Clinton: Saving America's Natural Treasures," News release, April 22, 1998, at www.whitehouse.gov, accessed April 23, 1998.

15. U.S. Fish and Wildlife Service, *Delisted Species Report,* June 8, 2005, at www.ecos.fws.gov, accessed June 8, 2005.

16. U.S. Fish and Wildlife Service, *Number of U.S. Listed Species Per Calendar Year,* at www.ecos.fws.gov, accessed June 8, 2005; Juliet Eilperin, "Endangered Species Act's Protections Are Trimmed," *Washington Post,* July 4, 2004, at www.washingtonpost.com, accessed April 9, 2005.

17. Ibid.

18. James A. Tober, *Wildlife and the Public Interest: Nonprofit Organizations and Federal Wildlife Policy* (New York: Praeger, 1989), 59–83; Mark Crawford, "The Last Days of the Wild Condor?" *Science, 229* (August 30, 1985): 845; David Phillips and Hugh Nash, *The Condor Question: Captive or Forever Free?* (San Francisco: Friends of the Earth, 1981); William W. Johnson, "California Condor: Embroiled in a Flap Not of Its Own Making," *Smithsonian,* December 1985, 73–80; "Condor Chick Deaths Alarm Biologists," CNN.com, October 24, 2002, at www.cnn.com, accessed October 25, 2002; "Condor Death Frustrates Biologists," October 23, 2002, at www.abcnews.go.com/wire, accessed October 25, 2002.

19. Juliet Eilperin, "Endangered Species Acts Protections Are Trimmed."

20. Greater Yellowstone Coalition, "Wildlife: Buffalo in Greater Yellowstone," at www.greateryellowstone.org, accessed January 9, 2005.

21. Greater Yellowstone Coalition, "National Park Service Slaughtering Yellowstone Buffalo," News release, March 5, 2003, at www.greateryellowstone.org, accessed January 9, 2005.

22. "Panel Oks Resumption of Buffalo Hunt in Montana," *Billings Gazette,* December 17, 2004, at www.billingsgazette.com, accessed January 9, 2005.

23. "Montana Should Not Call Bison Slaughter a Hunt," *Idaho State Journal,* January 7, 2005, at www.journalnet.com, accessed January 9, 2005.

24. "Montana Wildlife Commission May Cancel Bison Hunt," *Arizona Daily Sun,* January 7, 2005, A-4.

25. Montana Fish, Wildlife and Parks Commission, "FWP Commission Agrees to Hold Drawing for 10 Bison Hunting Licenses," News release, January 11, 2005, at www.fwp.state.mt.us, accessed January 14, 2005.

26. 115 S. Ct. 2407 1995.

27. See John H. Cushman Jr., "Environmentalists Win Victory, But Action by Congress May Interrupt the Celebration," *New York Times,* June 30, 1995; and "Regulating Habitat Modification," *Congressional Digest,* March 1996, 72.

28. "Sweet Home v. Babbitt," Update (Stewards of the Range, Boise, ID, August 1995), 3.

29. Defenders of Wildlife, *Sabotaging the Endangered Species Act: How the Bush Administration Uses the Judicial System to Undermine Wildlife Protections,* Executive Summary, I, at www.defenders.org, accessed April 8, 2005.

30. Ibid.

31. Ibid.

32. *Center for Biological Diversity v. Norton,* 240 F.Supp.2d 1090 (D. Ariz. 2003).

33. Pam Easton, "Peregrines Make a Comeback," August 25, 1998, at www.abcnews.com, accessed August 25, 1998.

34. Tober, *Wildlife and the Public Interest,* 24.

35. Krista West, "Lion Versus Lamb: In New Mexico, a Battle Brews Between Two Rare Species," *Scientific American, 286,* no. 5 (May 2002): 20–21.

36. United States Fish and Wildlife Service, "Rare White Mountains Plant Recovers: Endangered Species Success Story," News release, August 28, 2002, at www.news.fws.gov, accessed October 11, 2002.

37. Grassroots ESA Coalition Mission Statement (ESA Coalition: Battle Ground, WA, 1995).

38. www.cites.org, accessed October 25, 2002.

39. See "Elephant Skin and Bones," *The Economist,* February 29, 1992, 48; Peter Aldhouse, "Critics Urge Reform of CITES Endangered List," *Nature, 355* (February 27, 1992): 758–759; Peter Aldhouse, "African Rift in Kyoto," *Nature, 354* (November 21, 1991): 175; Steven R. Weisman, "Bluefin Tuna and African Elephants Win Some Help at a Global Meeting," *New York Times,* March 11, 1992, A-8.

40. See Robin Sharpe, "The African Elephant: Conservation and CITES," *Oryx,* April 1997; Susan L. Crowley, "Saving Africa's Elephants: No Easy Answers," *African Wildlife News,* May–June 1997; John Tuxill, "Losing Strands in the Web of Life: Vertebrate Declines and the Conservation of Biological Diversity," *WorldWatch Paper, 141,* May 1998, 61–62.

41. Eric Talmadge, "Japan Prepares Defense for Whaling Resumption," *Arizona Republic,* May 21, 2005, A-30.

42. International Whaling Commission, "Final Press Release," at www.iwcoffice.org, accessed October 23, 2002.

43. David D. Caron, "The International Whaling Commission and the North Atlantic Marine Mammal Commission: The Institutional Risks of Coercion in Consensual Structures," *American Journal of International Law, 89* (1995): 154. See also Patricia Birnie, "International Legal Issues in the Management and Protection of the Whale: A Review of Four Decades of Experience," *Natural Resources Journal* (1989): 903.

44. "Australia to Lead Protest Against Japan's Whaling," Reuters, June 2, 2005, at www.reuters.com, accessed June 8, 2005.

45. Ibid.

46. Emma Tom, "A Modest Proposal: Let's Eat Japanese Scientists," *Courier-Mail,* June 8, 2005 at www.thecouriermail.news.com.au, accessed June 8, 2005.

47. David E. Pitt, "A Biological Treaty to Save Species Becomes Law," *New York Times,* January 2, 1994, 1:4; Kal Raustiala and David G. Victor, "The Future of the Convention on Biological Diversity," *Environment, 38,* no. 4 (May 1996): 17–20, 37–45.

48. "World Heritage Committee Inscribes 9 New Sites on the World Heritage List," at whc.unesco.org/nwhc, accessed October 11, 2002.

49. "Temperate and Boreal Forests," World Resources Institute, at www.wri.org/wri/biodiv/temperate, accessed October 11, 2002.

50. See Chris Tollefson, ed., *The Wealth of Forests: Markets, Regulation and Sustainable Forestry* (Vancouver: University of British Columbia Press, 1999).

51. Anjali Acharya, "Plundering the Boreal Forests," *WorldWatch* (May–June 1995): 21–29.

52. Ibid.

53. Western Canada Wilderness Committee, "How to Save Jobs in the B.C. Woods," *Educational Report, 12,* no. 8 (Winter 1993–1994).

54. See B. Willems-Braun, "Buried Epistemologies: The Politics of Nature in (Post) Colonial British Columbia," *Annals of the Association of American Geographers, 87* (1997): 3–31; Government of British Columbia, *British Columbia's Forest Renewal Plan* (Victoria: Queen's Printer, 1994): 1–5.

55. For a general background on the Clayoquot Sound dispute, see Ronald MacIssac, Anne Champagne, and Ron MacIssac, eds., *Clayoquot Mass Trials: Defending the Rainforest* (Philadelphia, PA, and Gabriola Island, BC: New Society Publishers, 1994); Tzeporah Berman, *Clayoquot and Dissent* (Vancouver: Ronsdale Press, 1994). The evolution of British Columbia's forest management policies is outlined by Sheldon Kamieniecki in "Testing Alternative Theories of Agenda Setting: Forest Policy Change in British Columbia, Canada," paper presented at the annual meeting of the American Political Science Association, Boston, 1998.

56. Solon L. Barraclough and Krishna B. Ghimire, *Agricultural Expansion and Tropical Deforestation: Poverty, International Trade and Land Use* (London: Earthscan, 2000).

57. See Kari Keipi, ed., *Forest Resource Policy in Latin America* (Baltimore: Johns Hopkins University Press, 1999). Greenpeace reports on the mahogany trade in "Lust for 'Green Gold' Drives Amazon Destruction," October 17, 2002, at www.greenpeace.org, accessed October 25, 2002.

58. Tim Johnson, "China Protects Its Timber But Imports Rare Woods," *Arizona Republic,* March 6, 2005, A-28.

59. "More Negotiations in June," *ITTO Tropical Forest Update,* at www.itto.org, accessed June 9, 2005.

60. John Heilprin, "Brazilian Wood Held at US Ports," *Arizona Republic,* May 5, 2002, A-10.

FURTHER READING

Nina Fascione, Aimee Delach, and Martin E. Smith, eds. *People and Predators: From Conflict to Coexistence.* Covelo, CA: Island Press, 2005.

John Leland. *Aliens in the Backyard: Plant and Animal Imports into America.* Columbia, SC: University of South Carolina Press, 2005.

Martin Nie. *Beyond Wolves.* Minneapolis, MN: University of Minnesota Press, 2003.

Marie-Claude Smouts. *Tropical Forests, International Jungle: The Underside of Global Ecopolitics.* New York: Palgrave Macmillan, 2003.

Sharon L. Spray and Karen L. McGlothlin, eds. *Loss of Biodiversity.* Lanham, MD: Rowman & Littlefield, 2004.

Craig W. Thomas. *Bureaucratic Landscapes: Interagency Cooperation and the Preservation of Diversity.* Cambridge, MA: MIT Press, 2003.

10

The Global Commons

Today is a day of celebration and also a day to renew our resolve.
—HIROSHI OHKI, JAPANESE ENVIRONMENTAL MINISTER ON THE KYOTO
PROTOCOL'S ENTRY INTO FORCE[1]

On February 16, 2005, the Kyoto Protocol went into force after seven years of negotiations to limit carbon dioxide and other gases considered to be the cause of global warming. Japanese officials celebrated the enactment at the convention hall where the agreement had been reached in December 1997. For some the celebration was bittersweet, because the world's biggest emitter of greenhouse gases refused to ratify the agreement, saying that it would harm the U.S. economy while developing nations like China and India would not face any restrictions. The only other country joining the United States was Australia, whose Environment Minister noted the nation would not participate until the major polluters also ratified the regime.

Many believe that the global community's failure to persuade the U.S. to ratify the Kyoto agreement is critical. Some European nations made behind-the-scenes threats to punish the United States economically by imposing tariffs on imported goods. Others feared that under President George W. Bush, the nation would suffer diplomatic consequences for virtually leaving the negotiations table. A global climate change report issued by the Pew Center in 2004 was more optimistic, stating that "developments in Congress, at the state level, and in the business community suggest growing support for stronger efforts to reduce U.S. emissions. New steps are being taken, and a genuine debate over U.S. climate policy has begun."[2]

Pollution from utility plants worldwide contributes to greenhouse gases and the impact of global warming, believed to be accelerating more quickly than predicted.

RICK MOORE/GRAND CANYON TRUST

Global climate change is no longer considered part of an environmental scare campaign or the product of doomsayers predicting that the end is near. Instead, it is an environmental problem that has been accepted as valid by virtually the entire scientific community—and, begrudgingly, by most of the world's political leaders. It is also an example of a situation that affects the entirety of the global commons.

The terms *commons* and *common pool resources* were popularized by American biologist Garrett Hardin in his 1968 essay, "The Tragedy of the Commons."[3] Using as an analogy the medieval practice of grazing cattle on an open pasture, Hardin theorized that each livestock herder would graze as many cattle on the pasture (the commons) as possible if acting purely from economic self-interest. The result, of course, would be overgrazing of the commons to the point where all the herds would starve.

Implicit in Hardin's metaphor is the idea of common-property resources, which share two characteristics. The first is that the physical nature of the resource is such that controlled access by potential users is costly, and in some cases, virtually impossible. The second characteristic is that each user is capable of subtracting from the welfare of other users.[4] This concept is especially applicable to the two topics covered in this chapter: the atmosphere and the oceans. It also exemplifies how environmental politics has been globalized and transnationalized. A global approach requires policy makers to consider how human activities affect the entire planet, rather than looking only at what is happening in their own backyards.

Issues related to common pool resources are not new; they have been debated since scientists first began recognizing the impact of human behavior on the environment. But the expansion of technology, new findings on health effects of pollutants, concerns about national security, and dwindling resources have brought these issues back to the diplomatic table. This chapter explores the new developments in problem identification as well as in policy adoption with an explanation of both U.S. and international perspectives.

THE ATMOSPHERE

Ever since the 1860s, when British scientist John Tyndall first described a phenomena we now call the greenhouse effect, society has learned how human activities affect the atmosphere and climate. For decades, researchers were unable to agree on whether our future was tied to an impending ice age that would result in continental glaciation or to a warming trend that would melt the glaciers and send coastal cities into the sea. The debate flourished around the turn of the century when Nobel Prize–winning Swedish scientist Svante Arrhenius calculated that a doubling of the carbon dioxide in the atmosphere would raise the earth's average surface temperature. His calculations were confirmed by American geologists Thomas Chamberlain and C. F. Tolman, who studied the role that the oceans play as a major reservoir of carbon dioxide. In the 1930s, after three decades of warming temperatures and the development of a massive dust bowl in the central United States, other scientists warned of the dangers of rising temperatures, which had already been tied to increasing levels of carbon dioxide in the atmosphere. But between the 1940s and 1970s, global temperatures fell, and many reputable scientists prophesied a new ice age rather than a warming trend.[5] The global warming forecast was resurrected again in June 1988 when Dr. James Hansen, director of the National Aeronautics and Space Administration (NASA) Institute for Space Studies told a Senate Committee, "The greenhouse effect is here."

Humans' ability to cause changes in the atmosphere is a relatively recent phenomenon; primitive peoples did not have the technology to alter the environment as we do today. With the Industrial Revolution came technological devices—the steam engine, electric generator, and internal combustion engine—that have forever altered the planet, the water we drink, and the air we breathe. That ability to alter the environment is threatening to some, but others consider it a natural part of the evolutionary process. Some believe that earth exists as a living organism in which internal control mechanisms maintain the stability of life—a theory called the Gaia hypothesis.[6] According to this theory, environmental problems such as ozone depletion will be brought under control naturally by the environment itself, which will make the necessary adjustments to sustain life. Critics of the theory, however, refer to policies built on such optimism as "environmental brinksmanship" and warn that we cannot rely upon untried regulatory mechanisms to protect the planet from large-scale human interference.

One factor that distinguishes the atmosphere from other environmental issues is that it is not a distinct category in international law. Although scientists recognize "airsheds" from a spatial dimension based on fluctuating masses of air, the idea that the atmosphere is common property that ignores political jurisdictions is still not universally accepted. Developing nations point to industrialized states as the source of the problem, and hold them responsible for coming up with solutions that do not penalize nations seeking to become more developed.

This section of the chapter looks at two issues with obvious global dimensions: climate change and stratospheric ozone depletion. It provides an overview of the scientific controversies and identifies the ways in which the two issues differ politically.

GLOBAL CLIMATE CHANGE

Although global climate change is ostensibly a subject for scientific debate, it reached the political agenda at full force between 1997 and 1999. *Global warming* refers to the process by which solar radiation passes through the earth's atmosphere and is absorbed by the surface or reradiated back into the atmosphere. The phenomenon is also called the greenhouse effect because some heat is trapped in

TABLE 10.1 Major Greenhouse Gases

Gas	Where It Comes From
Carbon dioxide	Fossil-fuel sources including utility power plants, refineries, automobiles
Chlorofluorocarbons (CFCs)	Solvents, foam insulation, fire extinguishers, air conditioners
Halons	Compounds used in fire extinguishers
Methane	Natural sources such as decaying vegetation, cattle, rice paddies, landfills, oil-field operations
Nitrous oxides	Fertilizers, bacteria

the atmosphere, warming the earth like the panels of a greenhouse, but keeping some of the heat from going back out.

About 20 so-called greenhouse gases (GHG) make up the earth's atmosphere; the five major sources are identified in Table 10.1. Changes in the volume of these gases affect the rate at which energy is absorbed, which then affects the earth's temperature. Greenhouse gases are emitted or absorbed by virtually every form of human activity (anthropogenic sources), as well as by oceans, terrestrial plants, and animals, all of which contribute to the carbon dioxide cycle. Scientists are primarily concerned about increases in levels of carbon dioxide, because it is difficult to quantify the exact cause and effect of other greenhouse gases. The more carbon dioxide builds up, the more heat is trapped near the earth.

Although researchers began studying the effect of carbon dioxide on climate in the early part of this century, the implications of such changes were not seriously considered until the early 1970s. A World Climate Conference in Geneva in 1979, convened by the World Meteorological Organization (WMO) was one of the first efforts at organizing international research, followed by a series of studies and conferences over the next 10 years. One of the most respected reports was published in 1987 by the World Commission on Environment and Development, which recommended a global approach to a broad spectrum of environmental problems, including greenhouse warming.[7]

There is little controversy over the scientific evidence that the levels of carbon dioxide have increased by about 50 percent since the late 1700s, 25 percent over the past century, and are now increasing at the rate of 0.5 percent each year. Most of the studies agree that continued emissions of greenhouse gases will lead to a warming of the earth's temperature between 1.5 and 4.5 degrees Celsius (or 2.7 to 8.1 degrees Fahrenheit). So far this century, global average temperatures have risen between 0.5 and 1 degree Fahrenheit.

Why should we be concerned about what seems like relatively small changes in temperature? Several possible scenarios are attributed to global climate change. One of the most respected scientists to have studied the issue, Dr. Stephen H. Schneider of the National Center for Atmospheric Research, believes that the temperature increases will lead to a rise in sea levels through the heating of the oceans, and possibly through the melting of polar ice. Drought and prolonged heat would be expected to lead to more severe air pollution and air stagnation, and to increased energy use, leading to a need for more power production. Some of the changes forecast might not be as negative. Climate change might lengthen the growing season for grain in Siberia, allowing some nations to increase their food production. The flip side of the equation, however, would be a loss to U.S. farmers, who are currently the world's leading grain exporters, along with an accompanying impact on our economy.

Recently, researchers have challenged traditional views about forest management practices, theorizing that there is also a linkage between global warming and what appears to be an unnatural and unprecedented increase in wildfires. The severity of fires in the United States, Indonesia, and Australia has historically been blamed on forest policies that have suppressed natural fire regimes, promoting dense, overcrowded forests. Some studies using soil deposits as old as 8,000 years now suggest that climate change has resulted in thousands of years of large, intense fires dating back to a cooler, wetter period known as the Little Ice Age. Researchers interpret this information to mean that there is a longer record of climate change that has been continuously changing.[8]

Are the models and predictions correct? Despite human advances and technological breakthroughs, the atmosphere remains an element of the environment that is imperfectly understood and uncontrolled by humankind. The uncertainty over global climate change comes from three sources: predicting future climate, predicting future impacts, and assessing costs and benefits of policy responses.[9] Polarization among the members of the scientific community has spilled over to the political arena, where policy makers are trying to decide which view is the most reliable. The debate is joined by industry representatives (primarily electric utilities) who argue that it is foolhardy to make costly changes in technology or lifestyle changes until all the evidence is available. They seek support and funding for further study and analysis until a general scientific consensus can be reached.

Nonetheless, a growing body of scientific evidence indicates that, given the various scenarios, it is imperative that steps be taken immediately to avoid the devastating effects of climatic change being forecast. Using the Precautionary Principle as a basis for decision making, there is general agreement of a need for a major reduction in carbon dioxide emissions. Such a strategy would require substantive (and costly) changes in the way we live, and not only in the United States. Although the burden of cost is likely to fall disproportionately on the industrialized nations of the Northern Hemisphere, developing countries in the Southern Hemisphere will be asked to make drastic changes in their current patterns of energy use. This raises a host of policy questions. Will industrialized nations share their technology and expertise with the less developed countries? If so, will they also give their financial support to those nations to help them reduce their dependence upon fossil fuels? Could developing countries, already facing massive foreign debt, afford to switch to alternative fuels without aid from the Northern Hemisphere? Is the United States willing to set an example with its policies and rely more on energy conservation and nonfossil fuel sources?

Despite these uncertainties, one compelling argument is for an "insurance policy" approach. Such a strategy calls for reductions in energy consumption and enhanced conservation—policies that would benefit the United States by reducing the nation's dependence upon foreign oil. The energy savings would have spillover effects as well, such as reducing the need to drill for oil in environmentally sensitive areas and reducing the emissions that contribute to acid rain. Such policies would not solve global climate change, advocates say, but would buy more time for additional research and the opportunity to find better solutions. Even though most scientists admit that additional research is needed to predict the timing and magnitude of potential effects, there is a growing consensus that some initial steps such as those to reduce carbon dioxide emissions can be taken now without a major economic disruption.

Dealing with atmospheric change became an even more complex issue toward the end of the 20th century, when scientific debate and political pressures escalated.[10] New studies made scientific consensus more difficult as research funds decreased, especially in the United States. To complicate matters, in 1998 the EPA reported that the catalytic converter, developed by automakers to reduce nitrous oxide emissions that are a component of smog, is actually contributing to global warming. The EPA found that nitrous oxide emissions are increasing rapidly, due to more vehicles on the road and an increase in the number of miles traveled by cars that have catalytic converters. Still another study reported that some satellite data that showed a cooling of the earth's atmosphere was flawed because of "quirkiness" in the satellite orbits. The finding, reported in 1998, seemed to reinforce data showing a gradual global warming, although other scientists downplayed the study.[11]

Other groups began to mobilize to force the issue back onto the political agenda. In 1999, the American Geophysical Union issued a statement claiming that while there has been a "substantial increase" in atmospheric concentrations of carbon dioxide and other greenhouse gases, and that current levels were expected to increase, there was still considerable uncertainty about the effects on earth. The group also noted that potential changes might be rapid and geographically unevenly distributed, causing more disruption. Still, the AGU recommended that "the present level of scientific uncertainty does not justify inaction in the mitigation of human-induced climate change and/or the adaptation to it."[12] The Global Coral Reef Alliance and the World Conservation Union also blamed the killing of the world's marine life and coral reefs on global warming and the subsequent increase in sea-surface temperatures.[13] A similar debate erupted on the economic front, focusing on the costs of global warming. A 1998 study by the President's Council of Economic Advisers predicted that American households would pay only $70 to $110 a year more for energy. The study, which relied on an optimistic model that required only small emission reductions from U.S. companies, was heavily criticized by environmental organizations.[14]

While researchers argued among themselves, U.S. policy makers appeared hesitant to make decisions on how to proceed, perhaps due to lukewarm and sometimes conflicting responses by their constituents. A 1997 Gallup Poll found that most Americans believed automobile exhaust was a major cause of global warming but did not want policy makers to take steps that would incur high economic costs, such as great increases in energy rates or unemployment. The study also found most respondents were opposed to any global treaty that would hold the United States to stricter energy standards than those for other large nations.[15] Another 1997 poll, by the Survey Research Unit at Ohio State University, noted that substantial proportions of Americans said that they believed in the existence of global warming, and 61 percent believed the results would be bad. Over three quarters of the respondents said they would be willing to pay higher utility bills in order to reduce the amount of air pollution resulting from some electricity generation. They also advocated significant effort by the government and businesses to combat global warming, while voicing pessimism about how much was actually being done.[16]

Progress toward achieving political consensus (among both scientists and policy makers) was slow until the late 1980s and mid-1990s.[17] The creation of the Intergovernmental Panel on Climate Change (IPCC) in 1988 marked the beginning of contemporary efforts to bring science and policy together, followed by a series of conferences including governments that had previously been working independently on the issue. In 1990, the Second World Climate Conference recommended the development of a Framework Convention on Climate Change (FCCC). Prior to the 1992 Earth Summit in Rio de Janeiro, delegates to the International Negotiating Committee agreed to develop the framework convention; 154 governments signed the document, after which they attended a series of Conferences of the Parties (COPs). In March 1995, the first COP adopted the Berlin Mandate, putting all FCCC parties on a schedule to negotiate and develop a legal instrument at the next COP. A second COP, held in Berlin in July 1996, placed an emphasis on emission reductions from industrialized countries. The first two COPs formulated the protocol and worked toward ratification of the agreement—a difficult task because the agreement requires that it be ratified by 55 percent of the signatories, contributing 55 percent of developed countries' greenhouse gas emissions, before it can go into effect. Because the United States produces 36 percent of those emissions, its participation became essential for the protocol to succeed.

The parties meeting in Kyoto for COP 3 in December 1997 had an ominous task: to gain the political support of the United States, which historically had refused to agree with the goal of reducing emissions to 1990 levels by the year 2000. The Clinton administration entered the debate in 1993, and policy changed abruptly when the president announced his support for the FCCC but said that the United States wanted the emissions deadline extended to between 2008 and 2012. His position was heavily criticized by members of Congress, who were unconvinced that the purported threat of climate change was serious enough to force Americans to pay more for energy. When Vice President Al Gore addressed the Kyoto COP, he stressed that the U.S. position was that some developing countries should also be willing to reduce their emissions levels, as the industrialized countries had agreed to do. He then chided Congress, saying, "Congress' approach to climate change is: know nothing, do nothing, say nothing."[18] His criticisms were not unfounded. Members agreed to cut $200 million from appropriations for energy efficiency and research into renewable resources; and further, they attempted to eliminate funding for any program that even talked about climate change, whether in public forums or administration planning sessions. The result, some officials believed, would be to bar EPA and White

House advisors from doing anything, even simply talking about it, to advance the climate change debate.[19]

The resulting agreement, the Kyoto Protocol to the 1992 Climate Change Treaty, was designed to reduce emissions from six greenhouse gases to 1990 levels between 2008 and 2012—the target date sought by the U.S. delegation. Countries unable to meet their own emissions targets could purchase emissions credits from other nations that met their targets.[20] Developing countries such as China and India set voluntary reduction targets. This was one of the more controversial issues at Kyoto, because these two nations are major emitters of greenhouse gases. The agreement, however, marked only the beginning of what became a long process of negotiations and conferences, as evidenced by the numerous COPs that subsequently were convened.

At the November 1998 COP 4 in Buenos Aires, participants developed financial mechanisms to assist the developing world in responding to the challenges related to climate change, producing the Buenos Aires Plan of Action. At COP 5 in Bonn, Germany, work continued on strengthening implementation plans for the FCCC. A year later, at COP 6 (held in November 2000 in The Hague), The Netherlands, Russia, Japan, Germany, Canada, and Australia became key signatories; but the deadline for implementation decisions was not met, and the conference was suspended. Although President Bill Clinton signed the protocol, he did not submit it to the U.S. Senate for ratification, where it was unlikely he could gather the necessary votes for passage.

The 2000 presidential election results brought an abrupt turnaround in U.S. policies with the election of George W. Bush. In February 2001, the president announced that the United States would not honor its previous commitment to support the Kyoto Protocol. As negotiations continued at the second session of the Bonn COP in July 2001, the parties outlined basic principles; but enforcement was still an issue. Three months later, delegates from 165 countries meeting in Marrakesh, Morocco, for COP 7 adopted complex legal text requiring industrialized nations to cut or limit greenhouse gas by an average 5.2 percent from 1990 levels by 2012. The requirements could be offset by managing forest and agricultural areas, known as carbon sinks, by providing assistance to developing countries; or through emissions trading that allows countries to buy and sell the right to pollute.[21] At the November 2002 COP in New Delhi, India, environment ministers from 169 nations approved the Delhi Ministerial Declaration just as the talks were poised to collapse. The declaration did not include demands from industrialized countries that developing countries initiate dialogue to make further commitments after the enforcement of the Kyoto agreement, which had been ratified by 96 countries as the conference concluded.

The United States faced a barrage of international criticism for the Bush administration's position on the Kyoto agreement; Greenpeace claimed that the United States was "isolated in the world in its rejection of the protocol." At an April 2001 meeting in New York, Japan's Environment Minister said, "[the Japanese] believe the participation of the United States is crucial. All countries expressed concern and urged the United States to make an open, cabinet-level review." The head of international negotiations, Dutch Environment Minister Jan Pronk, said that despite the United States' rejection of the protocol, it was alive, and although "not completely healthy, it is recovering."[22] Bush countered with a proposal of his own in February and in June 2001, announcing that the United States would conduct additional research to address scientific uncertainties and encourage technological innovation and calling the Kyoto agreement "unrealistic." Critics argued that the administration was doing the bidding of energy industry lobbyists and auto manufacturers seeking to change the protocol's cuts in greenhouse gas.[23]

The Bush proposal was followed by a slight policy shift two months later, when the administration issued its third formal national communication under the FCCC. The report outlined the president's commitment to reduce greenhouse gas intensity in the United States by 18 percent over the next decade through voluntary, incentive-based, and existing mandatory measures. It also called for a global partnership, stating that "the United States intends to continue to be a constructive and active Party to the Framework Convention."[24]

The move was heavily criticized for both scientific and political reasons. "The U.S. stands out in the cold," said Princeton University professor Michael Oppenheimer. "This is one of the biggest problems the world is going to face, and the U.S. doesn't have a policy." Other experts warned that European nations required to pay for pollution controls to reduce emissions might try to punish American companies, which do not have to comply, by placing tariffs on U.S. goods.[25]

After languishing at the diplomatic table for years, the Kyoto Protocol was ratified on November 5, 2004, as President Vladimir V. Putin's signature made Russia the 126th country to agree to the global warming agreement. With the refusal of the United States and Australia to sign the treaty, Russia was left as the only country producing sufficient emissions to reach the 55 percent threshold.

The Russian Federation's decision to join the treaty came after prolonged internal, and surprisingly public, debate. Opponents argued that the treaty would do grave economic harm to the country and would limit industrial growth at a time when the government had promised to double Russia's gross domestic product. The decision to ratify was based less on global environmental concerns than on Putin's ability to bargain with European political leaders to endorse Russia's bid to become a member of the World Trade Organization. In addition, Putin had little to lose because Russia's industrial output had collapsed since 1990—the benchmark year for emissions calculation—so no additional regulations, taxes, or pollution controls would be needed for the country to comply. Ninety days after Russia presented its ratification documents to the United Nations, the treaty's provisions became binding.[26]

The structure of future implementation of the agreement changed to incorporate new stakeholders and principles. Canada served as host of the first Meeting of the Parties to the Kyoto Protocol in Montreal, in December 2005. Although the meeting was held in conjunction with the 11th session of the COP to the Climate Change Convention, it was the initial session involving all the nations that had become signatories to Kyoto.

The Bush administration continues to counter criticism of the government's decision not to move toward ratification with point-by-point lists of how the president's programs have been successful. In meeting a commitment to a comprehensive strategy to reduce the greenhouse gas intensity of the American economy by 18 percent by 2012, the president has focused on several objectives, including:

- Creating an interagency, cabinet-level committee to coordinate and prioritize federal research on global climate science and advanced energy technologies
- Increasing the budget for climate change activities by 14 percent from FY 2004 to FY 2005
- Proposing energy tax incentives that promote greenhouse gas emission reductions to spur the use of cleaner, renewable energy and more energy-efficient technologies
- Continuing strong support for the Climate Change Technology Program to accelerate the development and deployment of key technologies that can achieve substantial greenhouse gas emissions reductions, including a Hydrogen Fuel Initiative, the "FutureGen" coal-fired, zero-emissions electricity generation power plant, and an internationally supported fusion energy project
- Funding the Climate Change Research Initiative and a 10-year Federal Strategic Research Plan
- Hosting the first ever Earth Observation Summit to generate strong, international support to link technological assets into a coordinated, sustained, and comprehensive global earth observation system
- Developing a Climate VISION Partnership of 12 industrial sectors to voluntarily reduce greenhouse gas emissions over the next decade
- Creating the Climate Leaders program, under the auspices of the EPA, to encourage individual companies to develop long-term, comprehensive climate change strategies
- Proposing recommendations for the Department of Energy's greenhouse gas emissions reduction registry
- Creating targeted incentives for greenhouse gas sequestration to encourage wider use of land management practices that remove carbon from the atmosphere or reduce greenhouse gas emissions
- Finalizing regulations requiring an increase in the fuel economy of light trucks
- Developing the SmartWay Transport Partnership to establish incentives for fuel efficiency improvements in various freight industry sectors
- Engaging in multilateral negotiations to create or revitalize international climate change initiatives, including the Renewable Energy and Energy Efficiency Partnership, the International Partnership for a Hydrogen Economy, and the President's Initiative Against Illegal Logging[27]

Efforts by members of Congress to push global warming policy forward had met with opposition from the Bush administration in many prior sessions. Post-Kyoto, Sens. John McCain (R-AZ) and Joe Lieberman (D-CT) tried to negotiate a bipartisan strategy to require that U.S. emissions of greenhouse gases be no more in 2010 than they were in 2000, a measure that had been defeated in October 2003. Under the senators' Climate Stewardship Act of 2005, the U.S. obligation to reduce emissions would be easier to meet than under the Kyoto Protocol. "The need is more urgent, the case is more clear than ever, and as we begin this battle today, we know there are special interests who will try to stop it, but we are beginning with a sense of commitment and optimism," Lieberman said. "This is one of the toughest tests for political leadership."[28]

The politics of climate change negotiations are best characterized by the various divisions among countries, some of which are more likely to experience projected negative impacts than others. As has been the case with many global environmental issues, there is a major split between the industrialized countries of the Northern Hemisphere and the developing countries of the Southern Hemisphere. Though developed countries have been dealing with the issues for over a decade and are aware of the ramifications of the problem, developing nations are less likely to perceive global warming as a potential risk. They are less represented on various international study boards and have devoted fewer resources to research on the potential impact of global climate change. As a result, some are understandably less concerned and less anxious about finding a solution.

The Organization of the Petroleum Exporting Countries (OPEC) has tended to support proposals that guarantee there would be no reduction in the use of oil, as well as a compensation fund that would reimburse their members if emissions reductions reduced both demand and prices. Most members of the European Community made commitments to reduce carbon dioxide (CO_2) emissions, as did Japan.

The 30 nations that make up the Alliance of Small Island States (AOSIS) are likely to be the most affected by climate change and are thus extremely active in negotiations. Projected sea-level increases and storm surges pose a severe risk for low-lying countries as well as nations with coastal ecosystems. Islands like the Maldives and the Cook Islands could be submerged, and there could be widespread damage to coral reefs, saltwater intrusion into freshwater systems, and disruption of tourism. Members of AOSIS have proposed a 20 percent decrease in greenhouse gas emissions from 1990 levels for all industrialized countries by 2005.

Along with these political divisions, two factors have been identified that make the establishment of an effective climate change agreement problematic. Powerful interests, especially within the United States, appear to be opposed—at least in principle—to any measure to mitigate climate change; and many still do not recognize the scientific legitimacy of the problem. The decision of the United States not to ratify the Kyoto Protocol allows developing countries like China to delay consideration of prevention strategies. The second factor lies within the protocol itself. Many provisions are still vague and unsettled, including agreement on compliance and control procedures. Questions related to the high level of uncertainty in the current protocol must be answered, they argue, "because otherwise ratification by the United States and some other crucial players is unthinkable."[29]

STRATOSPHERIC OZONE DEPLETION

Ozone is an element of the earth's atmosphere caused by a photochemical reaction of hydrocarbons (produced mainly from the burning of fossil fuels) and sunlight. Ozone can be both "bad" and "good." At the earth's surface, ozone is a major component of smog; but higher up in the stratosphere (6–30 miles above earth's surface), the ozone layer provides a filtering layer of protection against the harmful effects of ultraviolet (UV) radiation. Without such protection against UV radiation, medical experts believe there would be a substantial increase in skin cancers and genetic changes in some types of plants and animals.

In the early 1970s, scientists warned that the exhaust gases from high-flying supersonic transport planes could damage the ozone layer. In studying components of the high-altitude atmosphere, the researchers discovered that chlorofluorocarbons (CFCs), which are synthetic, reacted with UV light when released into the atmosphere, forming chlorine. Chlorine is known to attack ozone molecules, and the researchers warned that unless steps were taken to reduce CFC production, from 7 to 13 percent of the earth's protective ozone layer would be destroyed. CFCs are found in thousands of synthetic products and are used primarily in air conditioning and refrigeration, foam packaging, and insulation. They are also used in cleaning the sides of the space shuttles, in sterilizing whole blood, and as a solvent in cleaning computers.

Congress responded in 1977 by including provisions in the Clean Air Act Amendments, which authorized the EPA administrator to regulate substances affecting the stratosphere. In 1978, the EPA banned the use of CFCs in most aerosols. At the time, scientists were unable to measure the damage to the ozone layer; but on the strength of theoretical evidence alone, Congress responded.[30] With the election of Ronald Reagan in 1980, research into CFCs came to a standstill and the search for substitute compounds subsided. Even though the United States had banned CFCs in aerosols, the nonaerosol use of CFCs grew to record levels—and the United States was producing about one third of the world total.

The issue gained new prominence in 1985, when a group of British scientists (who had been monitoring ozone levels for 30 years) found a "hole" in the ozone layer above Antarctica. The hole, approximately the size of North America, lasted nearly three months each year.[31] Later that year, the National Science Foundation sent its own team of researchers to Antarctica; although they could not agree on an exact cause, they concluded that chlorine chemistry was somehow involved, and that the hole was getting larger. In 1992, one study by the European Ozone Secretariat and another by NASA concluded that the ozone shield had also thinned markedly over the Northern Hemisphere. Although researchers were unable to discover an ozone hole over North America similar to the one over the Antarctic, they warned that the increased levels of ozone-destroying chemicals were cause for alarm. As the scientific evidence of stratospheric ozone depletion mounted, the environmental protection wheels began to turn in the political arena.

Even though the evidence that CFCs are responsible for ozone depletion is not irrefutable, the government and industry response to **CFCs** differed from **the response to** global climate change in four major ways.

Issue Complexity

The issue of stratospheric ozone depletion was perceived as a more "manageable" problem than that of global climate change, which is a much more complex and multifaceted problem than is developing substitutes for CFCs. Whereas industry officials called for more research into greenhouse gases before they were willing to accede to costly changes in production and technology, CFC manufacturers almost immediately agreed that CFC production should be reduced, even without proof that CFCs were damaging the ozone layer.

In 1988 the DuPont Company, inventor and world's largest user of CFCs, announced that it was phasing out production of two types of CFCs altogether. Other manufacturers and users of CFCs followed suit, and competition began to find replacement products and processes. The significance of the CFC strategy, from a political standpoint at least, is that the United States and its industry leaders were willing to take action even before all of the scientific evidence was in. This "preventive action on a global scale" was a unique approach to environmental protection. Rather than bucking the trend and refusing to cooperate, companies such as DuPont immediately began researching alternatives and substitutes for CFCs. And rather than stalling for time, the U.S. government took a leadership role and sought the strongest action possible—a complete ban on CFCs. The cost of finding replacements for the estimated 3,500 applications in which CFCs are used could reach $36 billion between now and 2075, according to the EPA.[32] As a result, what might initially be seen as an unreasonable cost of compliance is now being viewed as a new marketplace by many in the chemical industry. Forced to find substitutes for products and processes, some companies anticipate higher profits; others fear that substitute substances will have their own complications. For example, hydrochlorofluorocarbons (HCFCs) were originally considered as a replacement for CFCs and halons because they are less harmful to the ozone layer. Hydrofluorocarbons (HFCs), another potential replacement for CFCs, were also considered because researchers were certain that HFCs do not damage the ozone layer. However, because HFCs are a type of greenhouse gas, this choice only complicated the debate by substituting one hazard for another.

Acceptability

The U.S. government accepted the premise that a unilateral phaseout of CFCs was not acceptable for solving such a global problem. The United States initiated an international agreement to phase out CFC production within 10 years, a move that led to the signing in September 1987 of the Montreal Protocol on Substances that Deplete the Ozone Layer. The document set a strict timetable of step-by-step reductions in CFCs and other ozone-depleting substances, leading to a complete production ban by 2000. Developing nations were given a 10-year grace period before full compliance is required, but many refused to sign the treaty because of the expense involved in switching to new technology.

After scientists warned that the 50 percent reduction was not adequate to reduce the destruction of the ozone layer, the United States enacted even more stringent domestic legislation via Title VI of the Clean Air Act Amendments of 1990. The legislation required an accelerated phaseout of the compounds that pose the greatest threat to the ozone layer: CFCs, halons, carbon tetrachloride, and methyl chloroform. The act also contained a requirement for the elimination of these compounds as soon as possible, and no later than 2002. Under the terms of the amendments, the EPA now requires the mandatory nationwide recycling of CFCs in motor vehicle air conditioners, the biggest user of CFCs in the United States. The American efforts were not designed to replace a stronger version of the Montreal Protocol, but instead were expected to serve as a model for future international agreements. Subsequent Conferences of the Parties in London in 1990, in Copenhagen in 1992, Vienna in 1994, and in Montreal in 1997 led to an acceleration of the CFC phaseout, leading to a complete ban by 2010. The conferences also established a global phaseout of methyl bromide (used to fumigate soils and crops), which may be responsible for 10 percent of the ozone lost so far, as a "controlled substance," meaning that emissions would be frozen at 1991 levels. The 1997 amendments set deadlines for the phaseout at 2005 in developed countries and 2015 in developing countries. Several nations did not concede to the methyl bromide agreement; China opened a new facility and expanded the country's production capacity of the substance to a point that now exceeds the output of methyl bromide by all other developing countries. The 1999 Beijing Amendments set new trade rules for HCFCs and expanded the number of controlled compounds. However, no phaseout schedules have been agreed upon for HFCs or perfluorocarbon (PFC), another potential substitute that is also a greenhouse gas.

Ozone-depleting substances (ODS) are largely a problem emanating from the Northern Hemisphere, but the efforts to raise living standards in the Southern Hemisphere could have a tremendous impact on emissions levels. Participation by developing countries is critical, because increased use of CFCs in China and India could largely negate reductions in emissions throughout the rest of the world. The Montreal Protocol gave developing countries an additional 10 years to comply with the production bans and included promises from the Northern Hemisphere to help fund the transition in the Southern Hemisphere to ODS alternatives. A crucial element of the ozone protection agreements was the creation of a multilateral fund to help developing countries finance their implementation of the international commitments. The budget during the fund's three-year pilot phase (from 1991 to 1994) was $1.3 billion. Twenty-five countries contributed $860 million to the core fund, and $420 million came from individual countries for parallel funding or co-funding of specific projects. Thirty-four countries contributed to the replenishment of the fund in 1994, including 13 recipient countries. In exchange for the new round of financial support, the 80 countries participating in the fund agreed on a restructuring of the governing process. Actions by the 32-member governing council now require support from 60 percent of the members; these members must also have contributed at least 60 percent of the funds.

Only a few countries have implemented laws and regulations to ensure reduction in the manufacturing or use of CFCs. Despite the consensus concerning the threat of ozone depletion, the relatively small number of CFC producers, and other factors that should have led to rapid effective international action, the protocol was still slow in coming (the agreement was signed 13 years after publication of the first article that suggested the ozone layer was threatened) and slow in being implemented.

Media Coverage

Media coverage of the ozone-depletion issue kept attention focused on U.S. efforts to develop an international agreement and prevented the administration negotiators from weakening the proposed CFC controls. For example, on May 29, 1987, the media published reports that Secretary of the Interior Donald Hodel was attempting to revoke the authority of the U.S. delegation to negotiate significant reductions in ozone-destroying compounds. After newspaper headlines reading, "Advice on Ozone May Be: 'Wear Hats and Stand in Shade,'" and "Administration Ozone Policy May Favor Sunglasses, Hats; Support for Chemical Cutbacks Reconsidered," the public outcry over the apparent change in the U.S. position created a backlash that virtually guaranteed the imposition of stringent controls.[33]

Over 200 media correspondents covered the Montreal meeting, and consumers became more aware of the potential impact of continued CFC use. Media coverage of global climate change, in contrast, has been colored by the lack of scientific consensus on the rate of onset and the potential magnitude of the problem. The attention given to greenhouse gases has not been as focused, if only because the potential impacts are more uncertain, less tangible, and less immediate than are those of ozone depletion. Global climate change lacks an equivalent to the ozone hole upon which the media and public can focus their attention.[34]

It is this lack of scientific consensus that is perhaps the most important difference in how the policy debate has developed. At least initially, concerns about greenhouse gases were dominated by scientists who debated the consequences of human interference in the environment. There were many more attempts to measure the nature of global climate change before taking action than had been the case with CFCs. Increased production of carbon dioxide and rising atmospheric turbidity were recognized as two important factors capable of causing climate change, but there was uncertainty whether the result would be a warming or a cooling of the atmosphere. There have been dozens of scientific congresses and meetings, but the task of building consensus among scientists has been formidable.

Political Support

The climate change issue lacks the support of major actors in the political arena, especially the United States. For an international agreement to be effective, it must also be supported by the developing countries, which are becoming dependent upon fossil fuels. This was not the case with CFCs and the Montreal Protocol. In that instance, sufficient concessions could be made outside the fish-bowl of media publicity to allow room for negotiation and compromise. Climate change does not have a similarly low profile; therefore, the process of reconciling differences among developing and industrialized nations to produce a binding agreement will be much more politicized and thus much more difficult.

Still, Richard E. Benedick, who served as one of the U.S. negotiators on the Montreal agreement, believes the impact of the protocol goes beyond science alone:

> In the realm of international relations, there will always be resistance to change, and there will always be uncertainties—political, economic, scientific, psychological. The ozone protocol's greatest significance, in fact, may be as much in the domain of ethics as environment: its success may help to change attitudes among critical segments of society in the face of uncertain but potentially grave threats that require coordinated action by sovereign states. The treaty showed that even in the real world of ambiguity and imperfect knowledge, the international community is capable of undertaking difficult cooperative actions for the benefit of future generations.[35]

U.S. OCEANS POLICY

Nothing exemplifies the concept of a global commons more than the earth's oceans and seas. They are the source of all living things, a factor in our weather and climate, a source of food, a transportation network, and the home of valuable marine resources. Yet for most of human history, the oceans have also been a dumping ground, assimilating (to some degree) our wastes and receiving little attention from policy makers until the last 40 years. Most of the focus has been on international agreements, and the United States has only recently reentered the policy debate on the use of marine resources.

Initially, the U.S. response to dealing with oceans as a part of the total geophysical environment was driven by technology. From the first workable scuba experiments in 1825, to the commercial recovery of bromine from sea-water in 1933, to the first offshore oil well built beyond sight of land in 1948, government efforts have been driven by "new and expanded ocean industries [that] offer some of the Nation's most inviting opportunities for economic growth."[36]

The first legislation to define a national oceans policy was the Marine Resources and Engineering Development Act of 1966, P.L. 89-454. The act created the 15-member Commission on Marine Science, Engineering and Resources, commonly referred to as the Stratton Commission after its chair, Dr. Julius Stratton. The commission was charged with examining the development, utilization, and preservation of the marine environment. Its report, *Our Nation and the Sea*, recognized the importance of oceans for security, the increasing demands for food and raw materials, the position and influence of the United

States in the world community, the importance of oceans for recreational use, and the quality of the environment. The report also noted the sea's potential as a source of food, drugs, and minerals, as well as depicting the sea as "the last frontier" to be conquered by man. Consideration of humans' impact on the ocean, although mentioned, was secondary to recommendations related to "the full realization of the potential of the sea."[37]

A major recommendation of the commission in 1970 was to create an independent National Oceanic and Atmospheric Administration (NOAA) to ensure "the full and wise use of the marine environment"—language remarkably similar to the terms used by Gifford Pinchot in references to other natural resources. At the time, the Nixon administration was examining a broad executive branch reorganization plan, with one proposal that would replace the Department of Interior with a new Department of Natural Resources. The new department would include NOAA and some elements of the Environmental Science Services Administration (ESSA) of the Department of Commerce. Due to political tensions between the White House and the Secretary of Interior, turf battles led to the inclusion of NOAA within Commerce under Reorganization Plan #4 of 1970.[38]

The reorganization did not include all of the Stratton Commission's recommendations (including one that would have included the Coast Guard under NOAA), but it did extend the Department of Commerce's jurisdiction in programs ranging from the Marine Minerals Technology Center (from the Department of the Interior) and the National Data Buoy Project (from the Department of Transportation) to the National Oceanographic Data Center, previously managed by the U.S. Navy. Nixon's executive order to create NOAA resulted in a merger of some of the nation's oldest agencies, including the United States Coast and Geodetic Survey, created in 1807, the Weather Bureau (formed in 1870), and the Bureau of Commercial Fisheries (1871).[39]

Following the 1970 reorganization, the primary policy instrument is the Oceans Act of 2000, which directs the president to consult with state and local governments and other nonfederal interests on the most pressing issues facing the nation regarding the use and stewardship of ocean and coastal resources. Implementation of the act is under the jurisdiction of the little-publicized U.S. Commission on Ocean Policy, a 16-member group appointed by the president, which first met in September 2001. In preparing its initial 2004 report, the commission members held nine regional meetings and had 18 site visits around the country, gathering technical and scientific information and accepting testimony from 37 governors, five tribal leaders, one regional governors' association, and more than 800 interested stakeholders.[40]

The final report identified various needed changes, based on three fundamental themes:

- Creating a new ocean policy framework to improve decision making
- Strengthening science and generating high-quality, accessible information to inform decision makers
- Enhancing ocean education to instill future leaders and informed citizens with a stewardship ethic

In the words of the 2004 report:

A new national ocean policy framework must be established to improve federal leadership and coordination to enable agencies to address the ocean, land and air as one inter-connected system. This framework also enhances opportunities for state, territorial, tribal, and local entities to develop common regional goals and priorities.[41]

While the commission was developing its suite of recommendations, including the establishment of a National Ocean Council in the Executive Office of the President, and a doubling of the U.S. investment in ocean research, a private 18-member commission was established by the Pew Charitable Trust. The group's purpose was to focus on "improving ocean stewardship through recommendations to sustain marine life." For more than two years, the Pew Oceans Commission conducted a national dialogue on ocean issues, with 15 regional meetings, public hearings and workshops, along with 12 focus groups with fishers. The May 2003 report noted that America's oceans are in crisis, and the government is not making the best use of information already at hand. "The root of this crisis is a failure of both perspective and governance," the report notes. "We have failed to conceive of the oceans as our largest public domain, to be managed holistically for the greater public good in perpetuity."[42]

In comparison to the study by the U.S. Oceans Commission, the Pew group's report focused attention on the dimensions of coastal development and associated sprawl, degradation of coastal rivers and bays, and invasive species that have established themselves in coastal waters. Both commissions recognized overfishing and destructive fishing practices. But the Pew report traced the problem to the Stratton Commission and its reflection of the values of an earlier effort characterizing U.S. ocean governance as being in disarray. "We have continued to approach our oceans with a frontier mentality. The result is a hodgepodge of ocean laws and programs that do not provide unified, clearly stated goals and measurable objectives. Authority over marine resources is fragmented geographically and institutionally."[43]

The Pew report calls for a more substantial investment in understanding and managing oceans resulting from changes in perspectives on ocean resources over the last 30 years. "National ocean policy and governance must be realigned to reflect and apply principles of ecosystem health and integrity, sustainability, and precaution. Decisions should be founded upon the best available science and flow from processes that are equitable, transparent, and collaborative."[44]

Stakeholder reaction to the two panels' reports was supportive, but not widely publicized. Acknowledging the unexpected attention to ocean and marine policy after a gap of three decades, some organizations were cautiously optimistic, noting that the recommendations would require a test of political willpower.[45] The National Coalition for Marine Conservation, the oldest U.S. public advocacy group dedicated exclusively to conserving the world's ocean fish, questions whether the two groups' recommendations are valuable if the funding necessary to implement existing programs is unavailable. In early 2005, for instance, NOAA announced that its budget did not include money for the Pacific Fishery

Management Council's participation in a Fishery Management Plan (FMP) for tunas, marlin, sharks, and swordfish. Funding was eventually restored, but concerns were raised by other organizations about marine resource priorities.[46]

Some groups, noting the impact of the December 2004 tsunami disaster in southeast Asia, tracked legislative responses that authorized additional funding for ocean research and education, along with improved coastal observation data systems.[47] But the tsunami came more than 18 months after the Pew study was released, and 8 months after the U.S. Commission on Ocean Policy's preliminary report was released. A more likely policy driver is national security and, as the U.S. Department of State notes, "the ability to freely navigate and overfly the oceans as essential preconditions for projecting military power."[48]

Statements like this one are important because they indicate that current U.S. ocean policy, while giving lip service to ecological and scientific issues, is at its core an effort to balance interests among competing objectives. "The alternative is increased competition, and conflict over control of the oceans and marine resources to the potential detriment of the United States' interests and the marine environmental generally."[49]

Another View, Another Voice

Women Exploring the Ocean
When considering the topic of oceanographic exploration, the first scientist that people usually think of is Jacques Cousteau, the French oceanographer. Women in careers associated with oceans are rarely mentioned—a problem identified by a group of scientists and workers at the Woods Hole Oceanographic Institution (WHOI) in Massachusetts. They have created a website, *Women Exploring the Oceans,* to engage the public and students in the day-to-day work of women marine scientists. The site, funded by the National Science Foundation through the Program Awards to Facilitate Geoscience Education and WHOI, is designed "to encourage young women to pursue careers in science and to remove the mystery that surrounds being a scientist."

The site features one woman's career, giving a complete profile of her work as well as an interview, photo gallery, and related links. In a section called "More Remarkable Careers," the site profiles the careers of 13 other women representing many of the subdisciplines within marine science—chemistry, biology, physics, engineering, mathematics, geology, and geophysics. Some of the women interviewed are researchers; others are teaching at universities, serving as program administrators, or working in the private sector. Not all have doctoral degrees; some have gone from college to work as programmers, laboratory technicians, and data analysts.

Ashanti Pyrtle is one of a handful of female African American oceanographers, and she admits to "being a Jacques Cousteau nut." She did a project on dolphins in the third grade, and from then on, always picked some aspect of the ocean as a topic for her projects. In the summer between fifth and sixth grade, she met a family friend in Alabama who was a graduate student in marine biology. "She was really cool. She even had a dog. And she spent a day with a little fifth grader, rowing in a boat and talking about oceanography. By the time I came back to school in sixth grade, [she] was my role model, my idol. I wanted to be like her."

Pyrtle became a marine science major at Texas A&M University at Galveston; during the summer, she interned as an organic chemist. After completing her doctoral degree, she became a program coordinator at the University of South Florida, where she is now assisting minority graduate students for academic faculty positions while continuing her aquatic research. As a chemical oceanographer, she studies radioactive contamination in lakes, rivers, and oceans. Her first project involved the examination of sediment cores collected from a frigid lake in northern Siberia to show how radioactive fallout from nuclear weapons tests contaminates chunks of ice, which melt as they float out to sea.

Another woman profiled on the website is Kathryn Kelly, an affiliate professor at the Applied Physics Laboratory at the School of Oceanography at the University of Washington. In sharp contrast to the stereotype of a woman diving off an ocean platform, Kelley's work focuses on analyzing computer images to determine how the ocean influences climate. She is attempting to determine the most important factors influencing sea-surface temperatures, working from eight years of records ranging from ocean currents and winds to the upwelling of water from beneath the surface.

Kelley came from a science-oriented family and says she became more interested in the subject after taking an 8th-grade class. She was also influenced by Maria Goeppert-Myer, who became the second woman to be awarded the Nobel Prize in physics. She attended the University of California, Berkeley, during the tumultuous years when the campus was in turmoil over the Vietnam War. She became disillusioned with her choice of a career and left school to learn auto mechanics. After being out of school for five years, she returned to Berkeley in the engineering program and later took a position as a postdoctoral scholar at Woods Hole. After 13 years, Kelley and her husband moved to Seattle to work at the University of Washington's School of Oceanography—although she does all her work on land, not at sea. In her website interview, she admits that she has faced unfairness in her career choice, but believes that she may have made the path a little easier for the next woman to go through.

Why is the website important? "As the new millennium begins we believe it appropriate to step back and assess what women scientists across the country andacross the world are accomplishing today, and how they are no longer considered 'unique' but instead are an accepted and integral part of the scientific community."

SOURCE:
The website is at www.womenoceanographers.org

GLOBAL OCEANS POLICY

U.S. ocean policy focuses on the reconciliation of science and socioeconomic issues that are often based on political will. In contrast, on the global level, the two major ocean-related environmental policy issues are (a) protection of the world's marine resources, and (b) control of marine pollution. Both issues are multifaceted, and few international regimes have successfully attempted to deal with oceanic policy. One reason for the lack of effective agreements is that we know very little about the oceans; as a result, policy makers are perceived as hesitant and less inclined to sign treaties that might negatively affect their nation in the future. In addition, the oceans affect virtually every country—even landlocked ones—and a rogue state or major international stakeholder can thwart policy making simply by refusing to adhere to or sign a regime. These problems frame the issue of ocean politics, beginning with the protection of marine resources.

Overfishing

Overfishing is perhaps one of the most critical issues. Fish are an important renewable resource, serving as both a food source and as income for much of the developing world. Once thought of as an inexhaustible bounty of food, marine resources are quickly being depleted because of technological advances and the world's increasing appetite for fish. Awareness of the problem began in 1936 after the publication of John Steinbeck's novel, *Cannery Row*, which chronicled the Pacific sardine fishery and the abundance of the sea. Less than 30 years later the fishery collapsed, and small sardine fishing enterprises are only now beginning to open. A similar event occurred in Peru from the 1950s to the 1970s, when anchovy fishing made up about one fifth of the world's entire fish take. In what has been called "the most spectacular collapse in the history of fisheries exploitation," annual landings plunged from 10 million metric tons to less than 1 million metric tons within the next 10 years.[50] The United Nations Food and Agriculture Organization (FAO) estimates that 52 percent of the world's marine fishery resources are fully exploited, and another 24 percent are overexploited. In some areas, catches of commercially valuable fish species may be three times greater than permitted levels due to illegal, unreported, and unregulated (IUU) fishing activities. Production levels in 12 of the FAO's 16 world fishing regions have fallen to historically low levels.[51]

Global fisheries governance is a patchwork of programs and regimes that reveal a lack of international consensus on global overfishing. The United Nations serves as a forum for many current agreements, such as the 1995 United Nations Agreement on Straddling and Highly Migratory Fish Stocks, also known as the UN Fish Agreement, or UNFA. The UNFA is a framework convention for the management of fish stocks in high seas. Regional fisheries management organizations (RFMOs) exist to deal with issues specific to particular areas (such as the Northwest Atlantic Fisheries Organization), with groups that focus on specific species (Save the Stripers, Menhaden Matter), with legal advocates (Natural Resources Defense Council, Conservation Law Foundation), or with industrial fisheries. Other stakeholders include processing companies, fishing-boat owners, fisher associations, and indigenous culture organizations.

Driftnets

Among the more controversial overfishing issues is the use of driftnets. These nets hang vertically like curtains in the open ocean and stretch for 20 to 40 miles, sweeping over an area of the ocean the size of Ohio. The nearly invisible nets, invented in Japan, are suspended by floats at the ocean's surface and catch fish by their gills as they attempt to swim through. In addition to being extremely efficient at catching fish, the driftnets capture marine mammals, birds, and nontarget fish (called bycatch). The Sierra Club estimated that 7 million dolphins were killed between the 1960s and 1980s, when driftnets were commonly used. Driftnets were also blamed for a 1988 crash in the Alaska pink salmon industry, when Alaskan trawlers took only 12 million fish, rather than an expected 40 million.[52] The use of driftnets virtually ended in 1990 when American environmental organizations urged a boycott of any tuna that was caught in drift nets because of the damage done to the dolphin population. The action led to the labeling of cans as "dolphin safe" when several companies began to comply. In 1995, the United States and 10 other fishing nations agreed that there would be a move towards dolphin-safe fishing practices so that their catch would be allowed into the U.S. market.

A year later, the Clinton administration proposed reversing the ban that allowed only dolphin-safe tuna into the U.S. market and allowed the use of the nets. In an unusual division among environmental organizations, groups such as Greenpeace, the World Wildlife Federation, the National Wildlife Federation, and the Environmental Defense Fund agreed with Vice President Al Gore's proposal to reinstate driftnet use. Their position was that the fishing industry had improved the methods by which tuna are caught. But the proposal was strongly opposed by the Sierra Club and the Earth Island Institute, which called Gore's plan "the dolphin death act."[53]

Driftnet policy stems from the Wellington Convention, also known as the Convention for the Prohibition of Fishing with Long Driftnets in the South Pacific, which entered into force in 1992; but the convention applies only to fishing vessels engaged in driftnet fishing within the convention area. The European Union (EU) also began prohibiting most driftnet use in 1992, and it adopted a more comprehensive ban in 2002. Driftnets continue to be used in the Mediterranean, especially by non-EU countries fishing for bluefin tuna and swordfish. Another loophole in the convention is that it does not apply to the Baltic Sea, although the EU has proposed to phase out their use completely by 2007.

Marine Pollution

Land-based marine pollution (LBMP) contributes over 70 percent of the oceans' toxic contaminants, creating an overload of nutrients, dredged materials, and synthetic organic compounds that pose a threat when they are taken up through the food chain. They become a human health hazard when they accumulate in food fish, affecting coastal residents who depend upon fish as a primary food source. Floating debris, like bottles and other nonbiodegradable items, and pollution from oil tankers keep this problem in the arena of public interest. Small discharges from ships are more commonplace and sometimes more harmful than tanker spills. The chemical composition of oil varies, as does their environmental impact. Spills in the open ocean, for example, can be more easily dispersed by wind and wave action than can pollution resulting from a spill in a smaller setting.

Marine pollution poses some serious environmental policy issues that are complicated by the nature of the oceans themselves. First, there is much uncertainty about the short- and long-term effects of ocean pollution. Scientists are still not sure of the potential impact on human health or of the ability of the oceans to adapt to change. Evidence suggests that the marine food chain is easily disrupted and that any major changes could affect the chemical balance between marine organisms and seawater.

Second, marine pollution concerns not only what is dumped into the oceans but also its effect on coastal zones and beaches and the world's 35 major seas, some coastal and some enclosed by land. Demographic changes are also leading to an increase in land-based marine pollution. Over half the world's population lives within a 120-mile coastal strip representing only 10 percent of the earth's entire land surface. The residue of coastal life runs into the ocean, where it contaminates ecosystems and can lead to atmospheric deposition. Millions of dollars of tourist business are estimated to be lost every time beaches are closed because of pollution when debris washes ashore. Six of these great bodies of water—the Baltic, Mediterranean, Black, Caspian, Yellow, and South China seas—are suffering from ecosystem disasters to the point where they are on the verge of collapse.

The political system has approached the protection of the oceans and its resources in several ways, beginning in 1926 with an agreement by seven nations to control oil pollution. In 1954, for example, in response to the growing transport industry, 32 nations met to draft the International Convention for the Prevention of Pollution of the Sea by Oil (OILPOL). Representing 95 percent of the world's shipping tonnage, the parties prohibited discharges of oil within 50 miles of the coast, with fines extended to ports that were unable to accommodate waste oil. The act was amended and strengthened in 1962 and 1969, when provisions were attached regulating any type of ship discharges.[54]

Recognizing the limitations of existing oil pollution regulations, several more agreements were signed over the next 10 years: the London Dumping Convention (1972), which limited the disposal of many pollutants at sea, including high-level radioactive waste, and the MARPOL Convention (1973), also known as the Convention of the Prevention of Pollution by Ships. In 1974, the UN Environment Programme prioritized oceans through the creation of the Regional Seas Programme. The program, which covers 10 regions and involves more than 120 coastal states, is one of the few regional approaches to solving common pool problems. The International Convention on Oil Pollution Preparedness, Response and Cooperation, adopted in 1990, requires parties to establish measures for dealing with pollution incidents, either nationally or in cooperation with other countries. Ships are required to develop and carry an oil pollution emergency plan, and to report incidents to coastal authorities. Parties to the convention, which entered into force in 1995, are required to assist others in the event of a pollution emergency; and provision is made for the reimbursement of any assistance provided.[55]

UN CONVENTION ON THE LAW OF THE SEA

Since the 17th century, the oceans have been subject to the freedom of the seas doctrine—a principle that essentially limits national rights and jurisdiction over the oceans to a narrow belt of sea surrounding a nation's coastline. The remainder of the seas was proclaimed to be free and belonging to no one—a part of the global commons shared by all. But by the mid-20th century, a combination of technology, competing claims to offshore resources, the threat of pollution, and overfishing led to international conflict and instability.

The United States was at the forefront of the challenges to the doctrine; in 1945 President Harry S. Truman unilaterally extended U.S. jurisdiction over all natural resources on the nation's continental shelf; this move was followed with similar actions by Argentina (1946), Chile and Peru (1947) and in 1950, Ecuador, which asserted its rights over a 200-mile zone. After World War II, Egypt, Ethiopia, Saudi Arabia, Libya, Venezuela, and some Eastern European countries claimed a 12-mile territorial sea, and several southeast Asian countries claimed rights over the waters separating their island nations.[56]

Although calls for an international regime for the oceans had been made in the late 1950s and 1960s, the Third United Nations Convention on the Law of the Sea (UNCLOS) was not convened until 1973, ending nine years later with the 1982 adoption of the UN Convention on the Law of the Sea, considered by some to be one of the 20th century's most notable achievements in international diplomacy. The convention was adopted as a package deal, to be accepted as a whole in all its parts without reservation on any aspect. What makes this agreement so important is its comprehensiveness; it establishes more equitable relationships among the member states and distinct zones of sovereignty and jurisdiction for coastal nations. Its 320 articles and nine annexes include rules for the high seas and the rights and duties of members with respect to navigation, protection of the marine environment, and research. It lays down rules for drawing sea boundaries, transit passage for international navigation, and the establishment of a 200-nautical-mile exclusive economic zone (EEZ) over which coastal states have sovereign rights with respect to natural resources and economic activities.

The UNCLOS agreement provides the legal framework to govern the oceans and their resources, recognizing for the first time that the resources of the deep seabed are part of the world's common heritage. The convention did not enter into force until 1994, a year after it obtained the necessary 60 ratifications. A key feature of the convention is an elaborate system of dispute settlement mechanisms, including compulsory procedures entailing binding decisions by the International Tribunal for the Law of the Sea and the Commission on the Limits of the Continental Shelf. Landlocked and geographically disadvantaged nations have the opportunity, under the agreement, to participate in exploiting part of the zones' fisheries on an equitable basis, with special protection given to highly migratory species of fish and mammals.[57]

The United States initially refused to ratify the convention, and in 1994 Secretary of State Warren Christopher announced that the United States would accept changes that made the agreement more acceptable to business interests. One of the more controversial issues dealt with the mining rights to the seabed floor, a proposal that President Ronald Reagan had rejected in 1982, saying it clashed with free-enterprise principles by requiring mining companies to pay substantial royalties and to share sophisticated technology with developing countries.[58] American negotiators eventually developed an acceptable provision that allows the United States and other industrial countries to have an effective veto over the convention's administrative body, the International Seabed Authority.

Despite a 2004 recommendation from the U.S. Commission on Ocean Policy that the United States accede to the convention, the U.S. Senate still refuses to ratify the agreement.

The treaty is typical of the kinds of disputes that are becoming increasingly common between rich and poor countries in dealing with common pool resources. Wealthy nations such as the United States resent being asked (or forced) to share their more advanced technology with newly developing or poorer countries. There is additional antagonism when poorer countries demand some form of redistribution of wealth in the belief that the oceans and their resources should be more equitably shared. Although the Law of the Sea is now in force, there will undoubtedly be continuing ethical and economic disputes as the convention is fully implemented.

Various theoretical explanations have been put forth as to why some countries seem to have taken a more aggressive approach than others have to resolving common pool resource problems like those regarding the oceans.

> Leaders commonly possess a more advanced domestic environmental policy apparatus, and often are subject to more intense domestic political pressure than other countries. Leaders are most often motivated by being the first to suffer environmental damage; being the first often means being most severely affected as well.[59]

Laggard states, in contrast, may have only a minimal interest in environmental protection or may lack the resources to do so. At times, laggard states may oppose a policy because of economic interests that outweigh environmental ones, or they may be pressured by domestic interests to take a more conservative approach.

This model appears applicable to virtually all of the issues and agreements outlined in this chapter. What the model does not do, however, is provide a sense of how environmental concerns might be made more salient to nations that face daunting economic challenges, or to those leaders who prioritize short-term economic visions over long-term environmental concerns that affect the entire planet.

NOTES

1. Joseph Coleman, "Kyoto Pact to Stem Greenhouse Gases Goes into Effect," *Arizona Republic,* February 17, 2005, A-20.

2. Pew Charitable Trust, "Global Climate Change, What's Being Done," at www.pewclimate.org, accessed February 18, 2005.

3. Garrett Hardin, "The Tragedy of the Commons," *Science, 162* (December 13, 1968): 1243–1248.

4. See Lynda M. Warren, "Protecting the Global Commons," *Forum for Applied Research and Public Policy, 16,* no. 3 (Fall 2001): 6–13; John A. Baden and Douglas S. Noonan, *Managing the Commons,* 2nd eds. (Bloomington: Indiana University Press, 1998); Susan J. Buck, *The Global Commons: An Introduction* (Covelo, CA: Island Press, 1998); and David Feeny et al., "The

Tragedy of the Commons: Twenty-Two Years Later," in *Green Planet Blues,* ed. Ken Conca, Michael Alberty, and Geoffrey D. Dabelko (Boulder, CO: Westview Press, 1995), 54.

5. See, for example, J. D. Hays, John Imbrie, and N. J. Shackleton, "Variations in the Earth's Orbit: Pacemakers of the Ice Ages," *Science, 194* (December 10, 1976): 1121–1131. The authors conclude, "A model of future climate change based on the observed orbital–climate relationships, but ignoring anthropogenic effects, predicts that the long-term trend over the next several thousand years is towards extensive Northern Hemisphere glaciation" (p. 1131).

6. See James E. Lovelock, *Gaia* (Oxford: Oxford University Press, 1979).

7. World Commission on Environment and Development, *Our Common Future* (Oxford, UK: Oxford University Press, 1987).

8. Bettina Boxall, "Wildfires Linked to Global Warming," *Arizona Republic,* November 7, 2004, A-12.

9. See, for example, James F. Kasting, "The Carbon Cycle, Climate, and the Long-Term Effects of Fossil Fuel Burning," *Consequences, 4,* no. 1 (1998): 15–27; Jonathan Patz, Paul R. Epstein, and Thomas A. Burke, "Global Climate Change and Emerging Infection Diseases," *Journal of the American Medical Association,* January 17, 1996; and John P. Holden et al., "Scientists' Statement on Global Climatic Disruption (1997)," at www.ozone.org, accessed July 18, 1998.

10. See Clark A. Miller, "Challenges in the Application of Science to Global Affairs: Contingency, Trust, and Moral Order," in *Changing the Atmosphere: Expert Knowledge and Environmental Governance,* eds. Clark A. Miller and Paul N. Edwards (Cambridge, MA: MIT Press, 2001): 247–285.

11. Dian J. Gaffen, "Falling Satellites, Rising Temperatures?" *Nature, 394* (August 13, 1998): 615–616.

12. American Geophysical Union, Statement, January 29, 1999, at www.agu.org/sci_soc, accessed February 1, 1999.

13. "Coral Reefs Hurt by Warming," Reuters New Service, November 13, 1998.

14. H. Josef Hebert, "Global Warming Costs Analyzed by White House," *San Francisco Chronicle,* August 1, 1998, A-8.

15. Alec Gallup and Lydia Sand, "Public Concerned, Not Alarmed About Global Warming," Gallup Poll, December 2, 1997, at www.gallup.com, accessed January 5, 1998.

16. John A. Krosnick, Penny S. Visser, and Allyson L. Holbrook, "American Opinion on Global Warming," *Resources, 133* (Fall 1998): 5–9.

17. See Daniel Bodansky, "The History of the Global Climate Change Regime," in *International Relations and Global Climate Change,* eds. Urs Luterbacher and Detlef F. Sprinz (Cambridge, MA: MIT Press, 2001): 23–40.

18. "Vice President Gore Announces New Data Showing Warmest June on Record," News release, July 14, 1998, at www.whitehouse.gov/ceq, accessed July 15, 1998.

19. Allan Freedman, "Clinton's Global Warming Plans Take Heat from Congress," *Congressional Quarterly Weekly Report* (October 25, 1997): 2598. Other criticisms came from American business interests. See "Big U.S. Industries Launch Attack on Warming Treaty," *Wall Street Journal,* December 12, 1997, A-3.

20. See David G. Victor, *The Collapse of the Kyoto Protocol and the Struggle to Slow Global Warming* (Princeton, NJ: Princeton University Press, 2001).

21. Quirin Schiermeier, "Accord in Morocco Breathes Fresh Life into Kyoto Protocol," *Nature, 414,* no. 6861 (November 15, 2001): 238.

22. "Environment Ministers to Bush: Kyoto Still Alive," April 22, 2001, at www.enn.com, accessed July 31, 2002.

23. "Bush Offers Alternative Environment Plan," June 11, 2001, at www.cnn.com, accessed July 31, 2002; Andrew C. Revkin, "Dispute Arises Over a Push to Change Climate Change Panel," *New York Times,* April 2, 2002, at www.nytimes.com, accessed April 2, 2002. See also Bette Hileman, "Bush's Plan to Cut CO_2 Emissions," *Chemical and Engineering News, 80,* no. 7 (February 18, 2002): 10.

24. "Introduction and Overview," *U.S. Climate Action Report 2002.*

25. Seth Borenstein, "Global-Warming Treaty Is Approved by Russians," *Arizona Republic,* October 1, 2004, A-22.

26. "Kyoto Ratification," *Washington Post,* November 6, 2004, at www.washingtonpost.com, accessed November 6, 2004; Steven Lee Myers, "Putin Ratifies Kyoto Protocol on Emissions," *New York Times,* November 6, 2004, at www.nytimes.com, accessed November 6, 2004.

27. White House. Office of the Press Secretary. "The Bush Administration's Actions on Global Climate Change," Fact sheet, November 19, 2004, at www.state.gov, accessed June 5, 2005.

28. Richard Maurer, "Senators Reintroduce Bill on Gas Emissions," *Arizona Republic,* February 11, 2005, A-4.

29. Urs Luterbacher and Detlef F. Sprinz, "Conclusions," in *International Relations and Global Climate Change,* 297–307.

30. For a narrative description of the rise of the ozone depletion issue to the top of the environmental protection agenda, see John J. Nance, *What Goes Up: The Global Assault on Our Atmosphere* (New York: Morrow, 1991).

31. See Susan Solomon et al., "On Depletion of Antarctic Ozone," *Nature, 321* (June 19, 1986): 755–758.

32. Martha M. Hamilton, "The Challenge to Make Industry Ozone-Friendly," *Washington Post National Weekly Edition,* October 7–13, 1991, 21.

33. Steven J. Shimburg, "Stratospheric Ozone and Climate Protection: Domestic Legislation and the International Process," *Environmental Law, 21,* no. 2175 (1991): 2188.

34. Peter M. Morrisette, "The Montreal Protocol: Lessons for Formulating Policies for Global Warming," *Policy Studies Journal, 19,* no. 2 (Spring 1991): 152–161. Many researchers believe it is essential that joint implementation be used as a strategy to gain compliance with international environmental agreements. See, for example, Farhana Yamin, "The Use of Joint Implementation to Increase Compliance with the Climate Change Convention," in *Improving Compliance with International Environmental Law,* eds. James Cameron, Jacob Werksman, and Peter Roderick (London: Earthscan, 1996), 229–242; and Axel Michaelowa, "Joint Implementation—The Baseline Issue," *Global Environmental Change, 18,* no. 1 (April 1998): 81–92.

35. Richard E. Benedick, *Ozone Diplomacy: New Directions in Safeguarding the Planet,* enlarged ed. (Cambridge, MA: Harvard University Press, 1998), 331–332.

36. The Stratton Commission, *Our Nation and the Sea* (Washington, DC: 1969), at www.lib.noaa.gov/edocs/stratton, accessed June 5, 2005.

37. Ibid.

38. National Oceanic and Atmospheric Agency, "A History of NOAA," at www.history.noaa.gov, accessed June 5, 2005.

39. American Geological Institute, "Oceans Policy," at www.agiweb.org/gap, accessed June 5, 2005.

40. Oceans Act of 2000 (P.L. 106-256). See also U.S. Commission of Ocean Policy, at www.oceancommission.gov, accessed September 6, 2004.

41. U.S. Commission on Ocean Policy, "A Blueprint for U.S. National Ocean Policy for the 21st Century: U.S. Commission on Ocean Policy Releases Preliminary Report," News release, April 20, 2004, at www.oceancommission.gov/newsnotices, accessed September 6, 2004.

42. Pew Charitable Trust, Pew Oceans Commission, *America's Living Oceans: Charting a Course for Sea Change* (May 2003), vii, at www.pewtrusts.org, accessed September 18, 2005.

43. Ibid., viii.

44. Ibid., x.

45. Adrienne Froelich, "Washington Watch: A Sea Change for U.S. Ocean Policy?" American Institute of Biological Sciences, at www.aibs.org/washington-watch, accessed June 5, 2005.

46. National Coalition for Marine Conservation, "NOAA Restores Funding for Pacific Highly Migratory Species," March 14, 2005, at www.savethefish.org, accessed June 6, 2005.

47. American Geological Institute, "Oceans Policy."

48. U.S. Department of State. Bureau of Oceans and International Environmental and Scientific Affairs. "Oceans, Fisheries, and Marine Conservation," at www.state.gov, accessed June 5, 2005.

49. Ibid.

50. Merry Camhi, "Overfishing Threatens Sea's Bounty," *Forum for Applied Research and Public Policy* (Summer 1996).

51. Government of Canada. Overfishing and International Fisheries Governance. "State of the Global Fishery," at www.dfo-mpo.gc.ca, accessed June 6, 2005.

52. Brian J. Rothchild, "How Beautiful Are Ocean Fisheries?" *Consequences 2* (1996): 15.

53. Gary Lee, "Tuna Fishing Bill Divides Environmental Activists," *Washington Post,* July 8, 1996, A-7; Tim Eichenberg, "End Sea Mammal Massacre," *Los Angeles Times*, August 19, 2002.

54. David Hunter, James Salzman, and Durwood Zaelke, *International Environmental Law and Policy,* 2nd ed. (New York: Foundation Press, 2002), 710.

55. Ibid, 731.

56. United Nations, Division for Ocean Affairs and Law of the Sea, "A Historical Perspective," at www.un.org/Depts/los, accessed June 5, 2005.

57. "Sea Law Convention Enters into Force," *UN Chronicle, 32* (March 1995): 8–12.

58. Steven Greenhouse, "U.S., Having Won Changes, Is Set to Sign the Law of the Sea," *New York Times,* July 1, 1994, A-1.

59. Robert O. Keohane, Peter M. Haas, and Marc A. Levy, "The Effectiveness of International Environmental Institutions," in *Institutions for the Earth: Sources of Effective International Environmental Protection,* eds. Peter M. Haas, Robert O. Keohane, and Marc A. Levy (Cambridge: MIT Press, 1993), 3–24.

FURTHER READING

Stephen O. Andersen. *Protecting the Ozone Layer: The United Nations History.* London: Earthscan Publications, 2005.

Andrew E. Dessler and Edward A. Parson. *The Science and Politics of Global Climate Change: A Guide to the Debate.* Cambridge, UK: Cambridge University Press, 2005.

Nives Dolsak and Elinor Ostrom, eds. *The Commons in the New Millennium: Challenges and Adaptation.* Cambridge, MA: MIT Press, 2003.

Richard Ellis. *The Empty Ocean.* Covelo, CA: Island Press, 2003.

Linda K. Glover and Sylvia A. Earle, eds. *Defying Ocean's End: An Agenda for Action.* Covelo, CA: Island Press, 2005.

Norichika Kanie and Peter M. Haas. *Emerging Forces in Environmental Governance.* New York: United Nations University Press, 2005.

Mark Lacy. *Security and Climate Change.* Philadelphia: Taylor & Francis, 2005.

David L. Levy and Peter J. Newell, eds. *The Business of Global Environmental Governance.* Cambridge, MA: MIT Press, 2005.

David Michel. *Climate Policy for the 21st Century: Meeting the Long-Term Challenge of Global Warming.* Baltimore: Johns Hopkins Center for Transatlantic Relations, 2005.

Jim Motavalli, ed. *Feeling the Heat.* Philadelphia: Routledge, 2004.

Frahana Yamin and Joanna Depledge. *The International Climate Change Regime: A Guide to Rules, Institutions and Procedures.* Cambridge, UK: Cambridge University Press, 2005.

11

Population and Sustainability

> A letter to the editor or to my congressman won't be enough.
> So I'll get 34 million friends to donate a dollar.
> —JANE ROBERTS, REDLANDS, CA, FOUNDER OF 34 MILLION
> FRIENDS OF UNPFA[1]

In 2002, Jane Roberts was outraged when she heard the Bush administration's decision to withhold $34 million in congressionally appropriated funds for the United Nations Population Fund (UNPFA) for contraception and gynecological services, teen-pregnancy prevention, and HIV/AIDS prevention in 142 countries. The money represents 13 percent of the agency's funds; the United States is the only country ever to deny funding to the program for nonbudgetary reasons. Hundreds of miles away, Lois Abraham of Taos, New Mexico, had the same idea: to develop a grassroots movement of individuals around the world who would support their commitment to improving the health and well-being of individuals and communities around the world. Roberts and Abraham formed an organization, 34 Million Friends of UNPFA, to try to recoup some of the monies denied the agency by the administration's decision. Together, their efforts have brought together more than 100,000 individuals who have contributed more than $2 million, some for a dollar or two, some for much larger amounts.[2]

> Issues related to population migration and refugees have shifted the focus of population management from numbers to problems like AIDS prevention, gender equity, and poverty.
>
> JOSEPH SOHM, CHROMOSOHM

Issues related to population and sustainability can often seem overwhelming. The sheer number of people living on the planet who are in need of food, shelter, health care, and education is mind boggling. How can an individual, or a $1 contribution, begin to make a difference in improving the quality of life for an estimated 6.4 billion people, a population growing at the rate of 225,000 per day?

The scale and breadth of the issue has changed dramatically since 1994, when 179 countries met in Cairo for the International Conference on Population and Development. The conference goal was to develop a global Programme of Action that would link the alleviation of poverty to women's rights and universal access to reproductive health. The "Cairo Consensus" gave priority to investing in people and broadening opportunities, rather than reducing population growth. Ten years later, the United Nations Population Fund's *State of World Population 2004* found that inadequate resources, gender bias, and gaps in serving the poor and adolescents are undermining further progress while challenges mount, as outlined in Table 11.1.

The politicization of population management is part of a gradual eroding of American support since the program began in 1969. Supporters of the Fund, such as the Sierra Club, believe it insures that women have access to voluntary family planning, economic opportunities, and education that contribute to increased opportunities for women to choose the size and spacing of their families. This empowers women and girls and helps to slow population growth, ultimately securing a more sustainable future.[3]

Critics counter that the United Nations agency funds coercive abortion and involuntary sterilization practices in China as part of the country's one-child policy. Congress has passed legislation refusing to fund any program that assists China's policy. Conservative leaders alleged that just by working in China, the UN was giving tacit approval to the one-child policy. Officials at the United Nations, including Secretary General Kofi Annan, denied that the agency would ever condone or support coercive activities of any kind, anywhere.

> UNFPA has been and remains steadfast as a leading voice for human rights and for the principles enshrined in the United Nations Charter and the Universal Declaration of Human Rights as well as the Programme of Action agreed at the International Conference on Population and Development in Cairo in 1994, all of which condemn coercion in all forms.[4]

Population growth and the increased consumption and pollution accompanying it pose a profound challenge to the idea of ecological sustainability. This chapter explores the struggle to manage human population growth from an environmental perspective. It begins by presenting a summary of the U.S. role in the family planning debate, the scale of the global population boom, and the factors that have caused the problems to be more acute in some areas than in

TABLE 11.1 World Population Trends, by the Numbers

- The world's population is expected to increase from 6.4 billion today to 8.9 billion by 2050.
- The 50 poorest countries will triple in size, to 1.7 billion people.
- Overall population growth has declined from 2 percent to 1.3 percent since 1970.
- In 2000, young adults aged 15–29 comprised more than 40 percent of all adults in 100 nations.
- In most African countries, over half the population is under the age of 15.
- There are 1.2 billion people between the ages of 10 and 19 on earth now.
- Sixty-one percent of married couples are using modern contraception in developing world countries today, compared with 10–15 percent in 1960.
- About 350 million women still lack access to a full range of contraceptive methods.
- Between 2000 and 2015, the number of reproductive age couples is expected to grow by 23 percent.
- The number of children born each day is roughly 225,000.
- The number of women in Africa who will have an unsafe abortion each day is 10,000.
- The lifetime risk of a woman dying in pregnancy or childbirth in West Africa is 1 in 12; in developed regions, the comparable risk is 1 in 4,000.
- The average number of children born per woman, worldwide, in the 1960s was 6.
- The average number of children born per woman today is just under 3.
- Half of the human population lives on or near the world's coasts.
- The number of urban dwellers will rise from 3 billion (48 percent of the total population) in 2003 to 5 billion (60 percent) by 2030.
- Today there are 20 cities of more than 10 million people, and 15 of those cities are in developing countries. By 2015, there will be 22 megacities, 16 of them in developing countries.
- Half a billion people live in countries defined as water-stressed or water-scarce; and by 2025, that figure is expected to be between 2.4 billion and 3.4 billion people.
- Some 2.8 billion people still struggle to survive on less than $2 a day.
- Five million new HIV infections occurred during 2003.
- Young people aged 15–24 account for half of all new HIV infections—one every 14 seconds.
- One in every 35 persons is an international migrant.

SOURCE: Compiled from United Nations Population Fund, *State of the World Population 2004*, at www.unpfa.org, accessed June 6, 2005.

others, identifying trends and projections. It reviews the evidence for the assumption that not enough natural resources are available, even with enhanced technology, to provide for the growing number of individuals born each year if present demographic trends continue into the new millennium. The chapter then outlines the nature of the policy shifts that now go beyond reproductive health to an emphasis on a global effort to end poverty and work toward sustainability.

THE ROLE OF THE UNITED STATES

Domestically, population management efforts within the United States are autho-rized under Title X of the Public Health Service Act, created in 1970. The only federal program devoted exclusively to family planning and reproductive health, it is administered through the Office of Population Affairs under the budget of the Health Resources and Services Administration, a part of the cabinet-level Department of Health and Human Services. Title X funding ($280 million for fiscal year 2004) supports a nationwide network of about 4,600 community-based clinics serving 5 million persons per year. Clinics provide family planning services to low-income and uninsured individuals regardless of their ability to pay.[5]

The U.S. Department of State's Bureau of Population, Refugees, and Migration (PRM) holds primary responsibility for developing and implementing the administration's policies on population, refugees, and migration; it also administers refugee assistance and admissions programs. Along with the U.S. Agency for International Development (AID), which administers U.S. interna-tional population programs, PRM coordinates U.S. international population policy through bilateral and multilateral agreements.[6]

The U.S. role in global family planning efforts has been somewhat contra-dictory over time. It is a role that has resulted from changes in political leadership rather than from scientific investigation or research. AID began promoting large-scale national family planning programs funded through international aid in the early 1960s, providing health-care workers in many developing countries. Congress first earmarked foreign assistance appropriations in 1968, with nearly $4 billion in assistance allocated through AID over the next two decades. Initially, the United States also supported UN programs for education and family planning. But during the administration of President Ronald Reagan, the United States made an abrupt change in policy direction and adopted what came to be known as the Mexico City Policy. The United States cut off its support of the UNPFA and the International Planned Parenthood Federation, the largest multilateral agency and the largest private voluntary organization providing family planning services in developing countries.

The sudden policy about-face became tied to the issue of abortion, even though U.S. law (the 1973 Helms Amendment of the foreign assistance act) explicitly prohibits government funding for abortion programs overseas), and even though legal abortions are permitted in only a few countries. In 1985, the Kemp-Kasten Amendment to the foreign assistance act banned any U.S. contribution to "any organization or program that supports or partici-pates in the management of a program of coercive abortion or involuntary sterilization." The passage of the legislation effectively cut off U.S. support to China's family planning program, which was alleged to force women to have abortions, despite denials by the Chinese government. Congressional attempts to restore the UN funding by stipulating that the money not be spent in China were vetoed by President George Bush in November 1989.[7] The Bush administration's position puzzled those who pointed out that, by cutting back its aid to the UN program, the United States was actually encouraging the demand for abortion in those nations where there are no other alternatives.

The United States stood virtually alone in its refusal to contribute to the UN program, having previously been the primary donor. But after the U.S. policy change, Germany, Canada, the United Kingdom, Japan, and the Scandinavian countries increased their donations, with Japan becoming the major donor and exceeding what the United States had previously contributed.[8] After years of congressional debate, the result was that from 1986 to 1992 the United States eliminated all contributions to the UN program, with only a few bilateral assistance programs remaining intact.

In 1993, the Clinton administration reversed prior policies and began restoring U.S. aid to the UN program, with $430 million earmarked for international population assistance—the most ever contributed in the history of the program. In 1996, Congress agreed to appropriate $385 million for international family planning assistance and defeated a proposal by House Republicans to limit assistance to any international program that spent its own funds on any kind of abortion-related services (everyone agreed that U.S. funds could not be used to provide these services). The law required another vote by Congress before the funds could be released, and one of the few pieces of legislation enacted during the first few months of the new Congress in 1997 released the funds.[9]

However, as the UNPFA marked its 30th anniversary in 1999, it was clear that the reduced participation of the United States had taken its toll on the organization's efforts to build integrative reproductive health programs. A four-year decline in donor contributions resulted in a $72 million shortfall in 1999; available resources covered only two thirds of the fund's commitments to country programs. The result, UN officials said, would be an additional 1.4 million unwanted pregnancies, 570,000 induced abortions, and over 670,000 unwanted births.

Responding to an urgent appeal for funds, the government of The Netherlands pledged an additional 10 million Dutch guilders (about $4.7 million) to the fund for 1999, and another $4 million was awarded by the United Nations Foundation, created by media mogul Ted Turner. His group's contribution allocated $2.3 million to improve adolescent reproductive health in the Pacific region; about $1.1 million to promote Jordanian adolescent girls' health and well-being; and $707,726 to enhance the reproductive health of adolescents in the Russian Federation.

In July 1999, the U.S. Congress voted to restore funding to the UNPFA in fiscal year 2000, due to increasing criticism of the U.S. role. The action was tied to another brokered agreement under which the United States would pay about $1 billion in back dues to the United Nations to retain its voting rights, with a restriction that the funds not be used for any international family planning groups that support abortion. Women's groups and organizations like Planned Parenthood described the action as a compromise that made the women of the world the bargaining chip.

A new president brought a new agenda, and another shift in policy under George W. Bush. The president had sent a three-member fact-finding committee to China in 2002 to determine whether allegations of forced abortions were true.

The committee returned to the United States and wrote in a State Department report that the United Nations program did not knowingly support coercive abortions. In fact, the report concluded that UN programs improved women's lives by helping them prevent unwanted pregnancies through education and birth control, reducing the need for abortions.

The president ignored the report, signing into law the Foreign Operations, Export Financing, and Related Programs Appropriations Act of 2002. In signing the legislation, aimed primarily at the country's war on terrorism, the president included a statement that said the bill does not interfere with U.S. policies regarding bilateral international family planning assistance, ensuring "that U.S. funds are not made available to organizations supporting or participating in the management of a program of coercive abortion or involuntary sterilization." The act also gave the president additional discretion to determine the appropriate level of funding for UNPFA; he subsequently directed that the appropriated funds be transferred to the Child Survival and Health Programs Fund administered by the U.S. Agency for International Development.[10] In September, 2005, for the fourth consecutive year, the Bush administration withheld $34 million from UNPFA, saying the agency contributes to China's abortion program. Although Congress had agreed to appropriate the funds for UNPFA, legislation also gave President Bush the authority to decline to spend the money. The fund's executive director, as well as other family planning groups, said they were disheartened by the President's action, since one goal of the UNPFA is to encourage women to use voluntary family planning to avoid abortion.

SUSTAINABLE DEVELOPMENT

In 1968, when Paul Ehrlich's book, *The Population Bomb,* first appeared, most Americans were shocked. Ehrlich predicted a population explosion accompanied by massive famine and starvation—a prophecy that nevertheless did not come to pass. The reason? In the mid-1970s there was a slight decline in the global population growth rate, and it looked as though the population might stabilize at about 10.2 billion toward the end of the next century. Many demographers called Ehrlich an alarmist, while others argued that population growth was actually a positive force because it accelerated progress and development, forcing humanity to use more ingenuity and resourcefulness. Regardless of the timeliness of the prediction, Ehrlich was correct in pointing out that the earth is a closed system, with limited resources. How can policy makers deal with population growth, no matter what the actual rate of increase might be, and insufficient resources for that population?

A key phrase often used to answer that question, and one that has appeared often in this book, is *sustainable development.* The term is used to describe policies that balance the needs of people today against the resources that will be needed in the future. It takes into consideration policies related to agriculture production, energy efficiency, health, reduction of poverty, and reduction in consumption.

Individuals practice this concept when they recycle cans, bottles, newspapers, and plastics; carpool to work or bicycle instead of commuting alone in automobiles; turn their thermostats down to use less electricity; or install solar heating systems in their home. Each of these actions is recognition that the earth's resources are not unlimited and that we must restrict our consumption of those resources.

The possibility of sustainable development is built on the idea of carrying capacity. The carrying capacity of an ecosystem is the limit of resource consumption and pollution production that it can maintain without undergoing a significant transformation. If the carrying capacity is exceeded, then life cannot continue unless it adapts to a new level of consumption or receives external resources. Carrying capacity is affected by three main factors: the size of the human population, the per capita consumption of resources, and the pollution and environmental degradation resulting from consumption of each unit of resources. The task of residents of any ecosystem is to determine the level of resource consumption and pollution production that is sustainable. That level may not be obvious until it is too late; but there are some intermediate indicators, such as the buildup of pollution and an increase in the resultant harms or a decline in a resource as it is depleted faster than it is replenished. According to the WorldWatch Institute, some question exists whether the earth can even carry today's population at a "moderately comfortable" standard for the long term, let alone with 3 billion more people.[11]

Population growth and consumption in the wealthy countries are the primary sources of global environmental threats. Although population growth rates have stabilized in these nations, consumption of resources and generation of pollution and wastes continue to grow. But population growth in the developing world increases the pressure on the biosphere. The problems of environmental degradation and poverty are intricately intertwined. Many of the most pressing environmental problems are the by-products of modern, industrialized life. As one writer put it, "poverty can drive ecological deterioration when desperate people overexploit their resource base, sacrificing the future to salvage the present." Environmental decline "perpetuates poverty, as degraded ecosystems offer diminishing yields to their poor inhabitants. A self-feeding downward spiral of economic deprivation and ecological degradation takes hold."[12] People in the developing world depend immediately and directly on natural resources for their survival. In their struggle for survival, the poor of the world are likely to harm their environment and make their survival even more tenuous. Further, as resources are stretched for survival, poorer countries will be even less able to mediate the effects of climate change and other problems—unlike residents of the developed world, who will have the resources to protect themselves against at least some environmental threats.

The idea of sustainable development as used by the World Bank, United Nations, industry groups, and others is a very optimistic concept assuming that economic growth will produce the wealth to pay for technological innovations that reduce environmental impacts. Free trade, neoliberal restructuring of national economies and policies, and economic growth and consumption are all compatible with environmental sustainability. But this view of sustainability clashes with the ideas of carrying capacity and scarcity.[13] Studies by ecologists point to an inevitable crisis as exponential growth clashes with the finite resources of earth. Developed by the Club of Rome, the Limits to Growth computer model—one of the earliest projections of the future of natural resources, technology, and pollution—concluded that by the year 2100 most nonrenewable resources would be exhausted, food supplies would dwindle, and massive famine and pollution would cause widespread deaths.[14] Many have criticized that study, but few challenge the idea of limits; disagreements focus on when they will occur and how the variables interact.

Some optimists believe that pollution in the Western world "will end within our lifetime." They argue that the "most feared environmental catastrophes, such as runaway global warming," are unlikely. Environmentalism, "which binds nations to a common concern, will be the best thing that's ever happened to international relations."[15] Nearly all technical trends are toward new devices and modes of production that are more efficient, use fewer resources, produce less waste, and cause less ecological disruption than technology of the past. Others find that "just about every important measure of human welfare shows improvement over the decades and centuries"—life expectancy, price of raw materials, price of food, cleanliness of the environment, population growth, extinction of species, and the quality of farmland.[16] Some economists argue that we will never deplete resources—earth's air, water, and crust will serve earth dwellers for millions of years to come. The problem is not the existence of these resources, "but whether we are willing to pay the price to extract and use those resources."[17]

The optimists may be right in claiming that human ingenuity can respond to these problems and reverse these troubling trends. But the inexorable pressure from exponential growth threatens to overwhelm even the most optimistic projections. "We may be smart enough to devise environmentally friendly solutions to scarcity," one scholar has written, but we must emphasize "early detection and prevention of scarcity, not adaptation to it." But if we are not as smart and as proactive as optimists claim we are, "we will have burned our bridges: the soils, waters, and forests will be irreversibly damaged, and our societies, especially the poorest ones, will be so riven with discord that even heroic efforts at social renovation will fail."[18]

TRENDS IN POPULATION AND PROJECTIONS

In 1798, Thomas Robert Malthus published "An Essay on the Principle of Population," in which he first argued that the "power of population" is indefinitely greater than the power of earth to produce subsistence for humanity.[19] One idea that has subsequently dominated the study of demography—the science of population—is demographic transition theory, a term used to describe a three-phase ecologic transition that leads to global overpopulation. In the first phase, human demands remain within limits that can be sustained by the environment, so there is enough food, water, and other resources for the needs of the population. In the second phase, human demands begin to exceed a sustainable limit

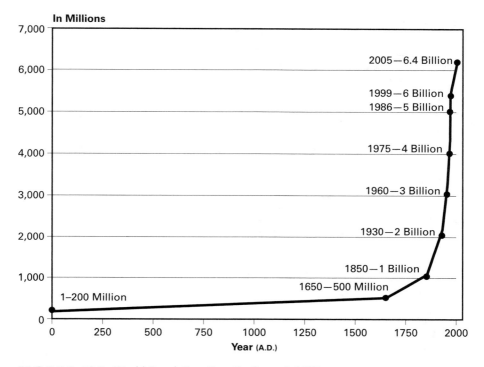

FIGURE 11.1 World Population Growth, through 2005

SOURCE: U.S. Census Bureau, "World Population Information," at www.census.gov/ipc, accessed June 23, 2005

and continue to grow. In the third phase, the ecosystem is unable to sustain the population, because there is little control over birth and death rates, and the system collapses.[20]

Although the demographic transition theory has been criticized,[21] many demographers believe that the earth has already reached that third stage. The numbers of people already on the planet are staggering, and the projections for the future are considered even more alarming by some observers. The magnitude of growth in world population is disturbing, especially if we look closely at the last 150 years. Figure 11.1 provides a look at the milestone dates in world population growth from the year 1 through 2005.

As the growth curve in this figure indicates, it took 200 years (from 1650 to 1850) for the global population to double from 500 million to 1 billion, but it took only 45 years (from 1930 to 1975) for it to double from 2 billion to 4 billion, and the trend continues. The UN projections through the year 2025 show an even greater increase, as seen in Figure 11.2. The world's total population is expected to grow to a projected 8.2 billion by 2025 and to 8.9 billion by 2050.

Demographers have identified several factors to which population increases in some regions can be attributed. Some of those changes began to occur long ago, and others are more recent in origin. First, there have been dramatic changes

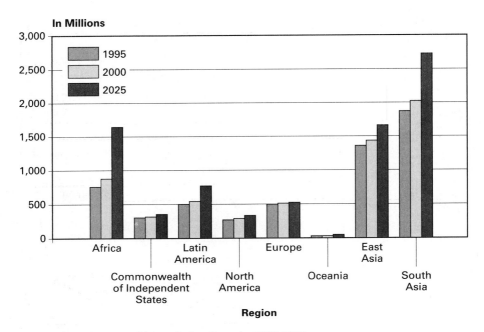

FIGURE 11.2 World Population Growth, 1995–2025

SOURCE: United Nations Population Fund, at www.unfpa.org, accessed June 25, 2005

in our way of life and ability to survive. Humans' transition from hunting and gathering to the agricultural revolution about 8,000 years ago removed much of the risk of dying from starvation, raising the world's overall standard of living, and high death rates kept the number of people in the world from growing rapidly until the mid-18th century. Second, in the category of more contemporary change, the rapid acceleration in growth after 1750 was almost entirely due to the declines in death rates, which occurred with the Industrial Revolution. Rapid advances in science lowered the death rate by finding cures for common diseases that had previously wiped out large segments of the population. Introduction of the pesticide DDT, for example, dramatically reduced deaths from malaria, which is transmitted by mosquitoes, and similar victories reduced deaths resulting from yellow fever, smallpox, cholera, and other infectious disease. Similarly, acknowledgment of the theory that germs were responsible for disease caused a gradual acceptance of basic sanitary practices such as washing hands and bathing, which further reduced the spread of disease. The impact of DDT and other health and technological advances can be seen clearly in Figure 11.1, where the growth curve begins its steep incline. Advances in medicine have also reduced infant mortality rates to the point where the birth rate continues to exceed the death rate—the bottom line in population growth. The result is that many fewer people die than are born each year.

A primary difficulty in making decisions about population policy is that, in the past, demographic data were often insufficient or contradictory, especially in developing nations. Since the 1970s, however, nearly every nation in the world has conducted some type of census or national population register. Studies of world population by various agencies and organizations have identified several critical trends that go far beyond previous concerns about the growth in population numbers.

1. There are differences in the ages of populations in the industrialized and developing worlds. At the beginning of the 21st century, 4 out of 10 adults living in developing countries were aged 15–29—what the WorldWatch Institute calls a "youth bulge." According to their report, "These youth-laden places were roughly two-and-a-half times as likely to experience outbreaks of civil conflict in the 1990s as other nations. To avoid violence and unrest, governments need to address poverty and the lack of economic opportunity in the short term and high fertility rates in the long term."[22]

2. The population is becoming more urbanized, and due to rural-to-urban migration, the number of persons living in cities is growing twice as fast as total population growth. By 2007, most of the world's people will be living in cities, which will require more social services and resources.

3. Two out of five people struggle to survive on less than $2 per day. "Poverty perpetuates and is exacerbated by poor health, gender inequality, and rapid population growth," the UNPFA reports. "Policy makers have been slow to address the inequitable distribution of health information and services that helps keep people poor. Poor women give birth at earlier ages and have more children throughout their lives than wealthier women."[23]

4. In the past 20 years, the AIDS pandemic has killed more than 20 million people and infected nearly twice that number. In some areas of sub-Saharan Africa, 25 percent of the workforce is HIV positive. Studies show, the UN reports, that if 15 percent of a country's population is HIV positive, its gross domestic product will decline by 1 percent a year, contributing to the cycle of poverty.

5. There were an estimated 175 million international migrants in the world in 2000, an increase from 79 million in 1960. The policy ramifications of migration are widespread, ranging from the tightening of borders to denying financial and social assistance to those entering a country illegally. World Bank economist Herman Daly observes that if globalization leads to uncontrolled migration of cheap labor all over the world, "the strains—on local communities and national economies, both sending and receiving— could be catastrophic." Daly notes, "Immigration is a policy, not a person."[24]

6. As economic reforms have opened up the economies of some nations, food production has increased. But much of the arable land in the less developed countries is dedicated to the production of cash crops that are used to generate foreign capital to service debt or finance economic development. Consequently, food production for domestic use suffers. Commodity prices are unstable; when they are high, exporting nations benefit, as revenues exceed those that would result from growing food. However, as world commodity prices have fallen, less revenue is available for debt service and development, and countries have to import food to make up for the shortfall

in food grown for local people. Trade agreements prohibit exporting countries from processing food, thereby increasing their profits; shippers, brokers, processors, and wholesalers all live in developed countries and capture the bulk of the profits from food sales. Foreign debt, assistance programs that promote cash crop production, pressures to generate foreign capital to pay for industrialization, inexorable pressure from population growth, and the increasing use of marginal lands for food production have combined to produce the food crisis in Africa and parts of Asia and Latin America. The problem is not one of scarcity as much as it is of the economic system by which food is distributed. Foreign aid is also a problem: Sending large shipments of food for distribution to poor nations sometimes disrupts domestic food production, drives down prices, and harms local farmers.

GLOBAL POPULATION AND SUSTAINABILITY EFFORTS

The UN has now become the primary agent of worldwide family planning programs and has made a number of efforts to address the population-sustainability issue. The UN Fund for Population Activities was established as a trust fund in 1967, financed by voluntary contributions from members. During its first 15 years, the fund allocated over $1 billion in family planning assistance to member states. Following the 1968 UN Conference on Human Rights, the Tehran Proclamation identified the ability to control one's fertility and therefore access to birth control as a basic human right. The UN organization, renamed the UN Population Fund, has held five world conferences: in Rome (1954), Belgrade (1965), Bucharest (1974), Mexico City (1984), and Cairo (1994). At the Bucharest conference, the UN's World Population Plan of Action was established, led by the United States and other industrialized nations that urged developing countries to set targets for lowering their fertility rates. Many developing nations and Eastern bloc nations rebelled, accusing the UN of supporting efforts by former colonial masters to suppress emerging nations and limit the strength of their armies. Ten years later, at the Mexico City conference, those misconceptions vanished as leaders from 150 nations committed themselves to a voluntary reduction in population growth and a strong national family planning program. Although there was continuing concern about the continuation of high population growth rates in developing nations, fertility rates had declined modestly since the Bucharest meeting.

In the years intervening between the population conferences, the UN's Conference on Environment and Development, held in 1992 in Rio de Janeiro, indicated how hesitant delegates were to tackle the population issue head on. For example, the phrase "appropriate demographic policies" was substituted in conference documents for the more traditional phrase "family planning," and many representatives of NGOs were critical of industrialized countries, which they perceived as failing to take responsibility for their own overconsumption of resources. But the meeting did produce, as part of its Agenda 21, a chapter on demographic dynamics and sustainability. Delegates agreed that women's role should be strengthened and their rights fully recognized. They also noted that governments should ensure that women and men have the same right to decide freely and responsibly on the number and spacing of their children. But representatives of the Vatican and the Philippines were successful in weakening the exact language on family planning and in removing any remarks on contraceptives.[25]

At the 1994 Cairo conference, the issue of abortion overshadowed nearly every other agenda item. Delegates reached an uneasy compromise after what one observer termed "a Vatican-led handful of countries held the meeting hostage."[26] The final document provided that abortions "should be safe" where they are legal and that they should "in no case . . . be promoted as a method of family planning."[27] Vatican officials argued that economic reform should be the major focus of global leaders: "Demographic growth is the child of poverty . . . Rather than reduce the numbers at the world's table, you need to increase the courses and distribute them better."[28] Other religious groups and foundations launched campaigns aimed at drawing attention to overconsumption in the United States and other wealthy nations, paralleling arguments of economists that the United States needs to save and invest more and consume less.

The "Program of Action," a 113-page document approved in April 1994 by the UN committee responsible for the Cairo meeting, provides the basic outline for a 20-year plan to promote women's rights and reduce population growth to 7.27 billion by 2015. A central theme embraced by nearly every one of the 150 delegates was the empowerment of women. Although few participants were completely happy with the results of the report, as one observer put it, "conferences and documents like these never get out ahead of where the people who agree to them are comfortable. What these conferences do is take an aerial snapshot of where we're at."[29]

One of the most promising products of the conference was the creation of "Partners in Population and Development: A South-South Initiative," announced by 10 developing countries that came together to share their successes in reducing population growth. These successful strategies include offering a wide range of choices for family planning and careful integration with local cultural and political conditions. The Women's Environment and Development Organization, formed in 1989, played a major role in shaping the agenda of the Cairo meeting, and promised to maintain the pressure on governments and international bodies to include gender equality and empowerment of women in family planning and reproductive health efforts.

Many challenges remain, however, in determining how to finance and deliver family planning and related services in ways that are consistent with local religious, cultural, social, and economic conditions. In many less developed countries, family planning services are still widely seen as a First World idea. Much of the focus will have to be on those countries that have the greatest population growth rates and the fewest resources to help empower women.

Most nations have not adopted explicit policies to manage their population, but there is implicit agreement that the key to balancing resources to people is by reducing fertility, especially in those countries where resources are scarce. Family planning efforts vary considerably in various parts of the world, and thus some countries have made more progress in reducing birth rates than have others. Information about birth control and access to contraception are known to be major causes of declining fertility. According to the 2004 UNFPA study, gaps in reproductive and sexual health care account for one fifth of the worldwide burden of illness and premature death, and one third of the illness and death among women of reproductive age.[30] In 2004, the 57th World Assembly recognized the Cairo consensus and adopted the World Health Organization's first reproductive health strategy to accelerate progress toward the UN's Millennium Goals. Still, complications of pregnancy and childbirth remain a leading cause of death and illness among women—they result in 529,000 deaths each year, mostly from preventable causes.[31]

Globally, most of the countries that initially adopted family planning programs were Asian and included both large and small nations. India became the first country to adopt an official policy in 1951 to slow population growth; but no other nations followed suit until nearly a decade later, when Pakistan, the Republic of Korea, China, and Fiji adopted similar policies. In the early 1960s, when oral contraceptives and intrauterine devices were first becoming available, about 60 million women, or 18 percent of the women of childbearing age in the developing world, were practicing family planning. By the mid-1990s, about 55 percent of couples in developing countries were using contraception to control their fertility, with about 75 percent in the industrialized nations of the world. In 2004, more than 350 million couples still lack access to a full range of family planning services.

There are a number of economic, social, and religious reasons that countries have shunned family planning as a way of bringing the birth rate down, especially in centrally planned countries such as China and Cuba. In many of these cultures, families simply want more children, even though more babies means more mouths to feed. Having more children may also mean more hands at work in the field or more help in caring for aging parents. Population limitation is in direct opposition to the teachings of the Catholic Church, which has encouraged procreation and discouraged birth control and abortion, as is the case in most Islamic nations. When Pope John Paul II assumed office in 1978, the Vatican took a more active role than previously in opposing abortion and contraception. In 1984, the Pope sent a statement to the head of the UNPFA in which he noted that contraception "increased sexual permissiveness and promoted irresponsible conduct," a view that continues to represent the Vatican's perspective with the naming of Pope Benedict. Many couples refuse to use birth control devices because of rumors and myths about their effectiveness. In India, women refused to use a loop-shaped intrauterine device when word spread that it would swim through the bloodstream and reach the brain or give the man a shock during intercourse. Vasectomy has been only marginally successful because of fears by men that it would reduce their virility. As a result, the use of contraception varies considerably from one nation to another.

Contraception use is generally highest in the nations of Europe and lowest in Africa—a trend mirrored in population growth rates. Some countries that have recognized the problem have taken steps to make contraception more available and acceptable, while others have made only nominal efforts. Government-sponsored family planning programs have been the primary mechanism for population control in most developing countries. About a dozen nations have established a cabinet-level ministry for population, generally in developing countries where the issue is considered serious enough to require an official program. The commitment is often not very firm, however, in countries with an Islamic or Roman Catholic religious tradition. The more successful efforts have been in countries where indigenous NGOs have been the most active. Working at the grassroots level, NGOs appear to develop a greater sense of trust with people than with programs offered by the government or foreign donors. They are also more adaptable to local circumstance and have more flexibility in their operations than do more structured programs.[32]

Generally speaking, economic inequality is the best predictor of fertility rates. Residents of poorer nations want more babies because they are a source of labor, while those in midrange economies choose goods over babies. Citizens of rich nations (such as the United States) can usually afford to have both—babies and goods. For many people in wealthy countries, even though wealth is not evenly distributed, family planning is less of a priority and there is little incentive to limit family size.

In response to a national population crisis in the 1950s and 1960s, China implemented its "later, longer, fewer" program in 1971 to reduce the number of individuals having children at an early age, imposing a limit of two children per family. The policy had little impact on the overall population, and in 1979, the government tightened the policy by mandating that families could have no more than one child. The policy met with internal resistance and external criticism, based primarily on allegations of coerced abortions. China has gradually begun to loosen its one-child policy, although it is too early to estimate the impact on the nation's population. In 2002, China's parliament, the National People's Congress, enacted a national provision that allows provinces to make their own laws to fit special circumstances. Shortly thereafter, the Provincial People's Congress in the rural province of Anhui passed a local birth control law tailored to its local needs. The law identifies 13 categories of couples that permit the family to have a second child, such as divorcees where both partners have only one child from previous marriages, farm couples whose first child is a girl, and coal miners—a risky occupation in China.[33]

Concerns about population and sustainability are rarely reflected in legal instruments. Nations retain sovereignty over family planning policies, and international law is considered "soft" because it typically takes the form of a nonbinding resolution or statement. The 1948 Universal Declaration of Human Rights, for instance, states that men and women have the right to marry and found a family. "The family is the natural and fundamental group unit of society and is entitled to protection by society and the State."[34] Although the declaration is considered to be customary law, resolutions like the Final Act of the UN International Conference on Human Rights (1988) and the Declaration on Social Progress and Development (1970), which recognize the right to determine the number and spacing of children, are not generally recognized.

IMPLICATIONS FOR POLICY MAKERS

Population management and sustainability are inextricably linked to other types of public policy; social, cultural, and religious beliefs; economics; and political forces that are constantly changing. Population and sustainability have thus become the most critical, yet unresolved, issues facing policy makers today. The consequences of population growth, regardless of the exact magnitude and timing, have considerable repercussions for the resources of both developed and developing nations. The problem is exacerbated by substantial disagreement among scientists as to the seriousness of the problem, making it difficult for policy makers to decide what kind of action, if any, to take. There are also opposing views on whether the population issue ought to be addressed by individual nations, allowing them to develop policies to control their own fertility rates and resource use, or whether the problem should be dealt with on a global scale by organizations such as the United Nations.

For a number of reasons, population management has slipped from the top of the political agenda, both in the United States and globally. Biologist and "population buff" Garrett Hardin, who was at the forefront of the ethical debate over population management, argued that among other factors, a change in public attitude is to blame. He noted that population is a chronic problem rather than a critical one, with the media preferring the latter to the former. As a result, the media is much more interested in covering "crises" such as the continuing conflict in the Middle East than in reporting that a quarter of a million people were born on the day that Iraq invaded Kuwait. Hardin also pointed out that many people fail to make the connection between population size and problems like air pollution from too many automobiles. Finally, he held that population questions raise issues that might be perceived as being selfish, bigoted, provincial, or even racist—criticisms that he himself had to bear.[35]

In the United States, members of Congress have not made population a high priority, because they have little political incentive to do so. Few interest groups support a particular policy, and the nation lacks a strong constituency for policy change in a system where institutional fragmentation is the norm. Most environmental organizations have only tangentially addressed population growth management, preferring instead to focus on more specific resource issues.

But the most important policy implication relates to whether there will be sufficient natural resources to sustain the growth in population, wherever it may occur. A key indicator is the adequacy of the food supply, which has thus far kept pace with population growth in all regions of the world except Africa. But most studies of world population projections note that world food production potential is dependent upon increasing the amount of land under cultivation and increasing inputs of capital and fertilizers. Developing countries seeking to modernize their agricultural practices risk causing additional harm to the environment, whether by cutting timber in order to grow crops or by adding more chemicals to the soil and water supply. Another important consideration is whether there will be sufficient energy resources for the growing population. Developing countries seeking to modernize and grow will place additional demands on natural resources to produce the power needed for everything from household appliances to factories.

Last, the developing nations still suspect that countries such as the United States are more interested in curbing population growth in poorer countries as a way of protecting the environment rather than concentrating on reducing excess consumption in wealthier nations. This view has been expressed at numerous international conferences and exemplifies the continuing divisiveness between the industrialized nations of the world that already have the benefits of development and those countries that are still seeking to attain them. Some in the South also contend that the real population growth problem is in the North, because the environmental and natural resource impact of each person in the wealthy world is many times that of residents of the developing world. The UNPFA notes that a child born today in an industrialized country will add more to consumption and pollution over his or her lifetime than will 30 to 50 children born in developing countries. "The ecological 'footprint' of the more affluent is far deeper than that of the poor, and in many cases, exceeds the regenerative capacity of the earth."[36] If population growth is to be curtailed in the South to reduce pollution and resource use, it must be combined with restraint on the consumptive patterns of the North.

Another View, Another Voice

Samuel C. Johnson

The phrase "corporate environmental philanthropy" may seem like an oxymoron; but to Samuel C. Johnson, who died in 2004, it defined a business mission centered on the concept of sustainable development.

Sam, as he was known, might have been considered an unlikely environmentalist. He was born in Racine, Wisconsin, in 1928 and received his bachelor's degree from Cornell University and a master's degree in business from Harvard. From 1952 to 1954, he served as an intelligence officer with the Air Force, and then joined the family business as an assistant to the president—his father. The business was S.C. Johnson & Son, Inc. (previously known as Johnson Wax)—a wax company started by Sam's great-grandfather. After Sam became chairman in 1967, the privately owned company grew from $171 million to four businesses with more than $6 billion in total annual sales today.

Johnson's philosophy was based on what he called the "inside out" theory: Take care of your own backyard and good things will spread out from there. Unlike most firms, which keep company giving below 2 percent, Johnson's maintained a commitment of corporate philanthropy at 5 percent for local, national, and global causes. He provided grants, scholarships, and funding for projects in his hometown of Racine, and served from 1990 to 2000 as a member of the board of governors for The Nature Conservancy. He became known internationally for his support as a founding member of the World Business Council for Sustainable Development and as a director of the World Resources Institute.

Throughout his life, Johnson received numerous environmental awards for his work, including a Lifetime Environmental Stewardship Award from the UN Environment Programme and the Rene Dubos Environmental Award for his leadership and commitment to improving both the natural and cultural environments. One business magazine called him corporate America's leading environmentalist, but Johnson noted that he had never been interested in being a celebrity. After giving $1 million to The Nature Conservancy in 1994, he donated 18,000 acres for a preserve in Caatinga, Brazil. At a Nature Conservancy event in 2001, he said, "To be an environmentalist, you don't have to be some herbal-inhaling, Birkenstock-wearing, twig-and-berry-eating tree-hugger. You don't have to drive a moped. You don't have to live like a rabbit. And you don't have to believe that the only way to save the Earth is to get rid of the people."

Johnson called the idea of sustainable development "eco efficiency"— ecological efficiency coupled with economic efficiency. He voluntarily banned use of chloro-fluorocarbon propellants in aerosol products worldwide in 1975, three years before the U.S. government decided to ban the ozone-depleting substances. He set aggressive goals for the company to reduce packaging, increased the use of recycled materials, and reduced point-source pollution in his manufacturing facilities. His efforts were part of the Johnson family's "This We Believe" statement of values and principles that guided the business.

In a February 2004 interview with the World Business Council for Sustainable Development, Johnson noted, "People will always need good jobs, and a safe healthy environment. They cannot have one without the other. Short-term decisions that fail to consider this fact shortchange the future, and threaten our planet's very existence." He credited sustainable development for helping his company's business to realize hundreds of millions of dollars in cost savings from environmental efforts. "A sustainable enterprise is dependent upon a sustainable environment," he said. "Management decisions that fail to reflect this put a company at grave, future risk.

SOURCES:
"A Sustainable Enterprise Is Dependent on a Sustainable Environment," at www.wbcsd.org, accessed October 13, 2004.
"Samuel C. Johnson," Press information from S.C. Johnson, at www.scjohnson.com/family, accessed October 13, 2004.
Amy Rabideau Silvers. "Concern for Business, Earth," *Milwaukee Journal Sentinel,* May 22, 2004, at www.jsonline.com/news, accessed October 13, 2004.

NOTES

1. United Nations Population Fund, "34 Million Friends of UNFPA," at www.unpfa.org, accessed June 10, 2005.

2. Ibid.

3. Sierra Club, "United Nations Population Fund," at www.sierraclub.org/population, accessed July 22, 2002.

4. "UNFPA Expresses Regret at U.S. Decision Not to Grant It Funding," News release, July 22, 2002, at www.unpfa.org, accessed July 22, 2002.

5. Office of Population Affairs, "Office of Family Planning," at http://opa.osophs.dhhs.gov, accessed October 19, 2004.

6. U.S. Department of State, "Bureau of Population, Refugees, and Migration," at www.state.gov/g/prm, accessed January 1, 2005.

7. Phillip Davis, "The Big O: Zero Population Growth," *Buzzworm* (November–December 1992), 54.

8. Peter J. Donaldson and Amy Ong Tsui, "International Family Planning Movement," *Population Bulletin, 45,* no. 3 (November 1990): 14.

9. P.L. 104–208.

10. The president's actions are outlined in his January 10, 2002, statement, "President Signs Foreign Operations Appropriations Act," at www.whitehouse.gov/news, accessed October 6,

2002, and in Presidential Determination No. 2002-32, at www.whitehouse.gov/news, accessed October 6, 2002.

11. "Population Beyond the Numbers," *WorldWatch Magazine,* September–October 2004, at www.worldwatch.org, accessed June 6, 2005.

12. Alan B. Durning, *Poverty and the Environment: Reversing the Downward Spiral,* WorldWatch Paper 92 (Washington, DC: WorldWatch Institute, 1989): 40–41.

13. For further discussion of these issues, see World Commission on Environment and Development, *Our Common Future* (New York: Oxford University Press, 1987); Robert Repetto, "Agenda for Action," in *The Global Possible: Resources, Development, and the New Century,* ed. Robert Repetto (New Haven, CT: Yale University Press, 1985): 496–519.

14. Donella H. Meadows et al., *The Limits to Growth* (New York: Universe Books, 1972).

15. Gregg Easterbrook, *A Moment on the Earth: The Coming Age of Environmental Optimism* (New York: Viking Penguin, 1995), xvi.

16. Julian Simon, "Pre-Debate Statement," in *Scarcity or Abundance? A Debate on the Environment,* ed. Norman Myer and Julian L. Simon (New York: Norton, 1994), 5–22.

17. Tom Tietenberg, *Environmental and Natural Resource Economics,* 3rd ed. (New York: HarperCollins, 1992), 356–357.

18. Thomas F. Homer-Dixon, quoted in William K. Stevens, "Feeding a Booming Population without Destroying the Planet," *New York Times,* April 5, 1994.

19. See Philip Appleman, ed., *Thomas Robert Malthus: An Essay on the Principle of Population* (New York: Norton, 1976). For biographical material on Malthus and his theories, see Jane S. Nickerson, *Homage to Malthus* (Port Washington, NY: Kennikat Press, 1975); David V. Glass, *Introduction to Malthus* (New York: Wiley, 1953); William Petersen, *Malthus* (Cambridge, MA: Harvard University Press, 1979); Donald Winch, *Malthus* (New York: Oxford University Press, 1987).

20. For a historical perspective on demographic transition theory, see the work of Kingsley Davis, "The World Demographic Transition," *Annals of the American Academy of Political and Social Science, 237* (January 1945): 1–11; George Stolntiz, "The Demographic Transition: From High to Low Birth Rates and Death Rates," in *Population: The Vital Revolution,* ed. Ronald Freedman (Garden City, NY: Anchor Books, 1964).

21. See, for example, Ansley Coale, "The History of the Human Population," *Scientific American, 231* (1974): 40–51; Kingsley Davis, "The Theory of Change and Response in Modern Demographic History," *Population Index, 29,* no. 4 (1963): 345–366.

22. "Population Beyond the Numbers,"*WorldWatch Magazine,* September–October 2004.

23. United Nations Population Fund, *State of the World Population 2004,* Press summary, at www.unfpa.org/swp/2004, accessed October 8, 2004.

24. "Population Beyond the Numbers,"*WorldWatch Magazine,* September–October 2004.

25. See Michael Grubb et al., *The Earth Summit Agreements: A Guide and Assessment* (London: Earthscan, 1993), 106–108.

26. Emily MacFarquhar, "Unfinished Business," *U.S. News and World Report,* September 19, 1994, 57.

27. United Nations Conference on Population, "Plan of Action," September 1994, Paragraph 8.25 at www.iisd.ca, accessed September 20, 2005.

28. Alan Cowell, "Is This Abortion?" *New York Times,* August 11, 1994.

29. Barbara Crossette, "U.N. Meeting Facing Angry Debate on Population," *New York Times,* September 4, 1994.

30. *State of the World Population 2004.*

31. Ibid.

32. See Julie Fisher, "Third World NGOs: A Missing Piece in the Population Puzzle," *Environment, 36,* no. 7 (September 1994): 6–11.

33. "China Region Allows More 2-Kid Clans," *Arizona Republic,* August 25, 2002, A-24.

34. Universal Declaration of Human Rights, Article 16 (1948).

35. Garrett Hardin, "Sheer Numbers," *E Magazine, 1,* no. 6 (November–December 1990): 40–47.

36. *State of the World Population 2004.*

FURTHER READING

Marco Keiner, Martina Koll-Schretzenmayr and Willy A. Schmid, eds. *Managing Urban Futures: Sustainability and Urban Growth in Developing Countries.* Hampshire, UK: Ashgate Publishing, 2006.

Jorg Kohn. *The Political Economy of Sustainability.* Williston, VT: Elgar, 2006.

Jeffrey M. McKee. *Sparing Nature: The Conflict Between Human Population Growth and Earth's Biodiversity.* Piscataway, NJ: Rutgers University Press, 2003.

Daniela Meadows, Jorgnen Randers, and Dennis Meadows. *Limits to Growth: The 30-Year Update.* White River Junction, VT: Chelsea Green, 2004.

Bryan G. Norton. *Sustainability: A Philosophy of Adaptive Ecosystem Management.* Chicago: University of Chicago Press, 2006.

Giok Ling Ooi. *Sustainability and Cities: Concept and Assessment.* Hackensack, NJ: World Scientific Publishing, 2006.

Romina Picolotti and Jorge Daniel Taillant, eds. *Linking Human Rights and the Environment.* Tucson: University of Arizona Press, 2003.

United Nations. *State of World Population: The Cairo Consensus at Ten.* New York: United Nations Publications, 2005.

Mary Warnock. *Making Babies: Is There a Right to Have Children?* New York: Oxford University Press, 2003.

12

Emerging Issues
in Environmental Policy

Today we are faced with a challenge that calls for a shift in our thinking,
so that humanity stops threatening its life-support system.
—WANGARI MUTA MAATHAI, NOBEL PEACE PRIZE RECIPIENT[1]

In 2004, "Kenya's Green Militant," Wangari Muta Maathai, became the first
African woman to be awarded the Nobel Peace Prize. Maathai's award is
especially notable because for the first time, the Norwegian Nobel Committee
linked an environmental issue—sustainability—with democracy and peace. The
award announcement notes, "Peace on earth depends on our ability to secure our
living environment. Maathai stands at the front of the fight to promote ecologically
viable social, economic and cultural development in Kenya and Africa."[2]

Many observers were surprised at the committee's choice, because Maathai is
not well known outside the global environmental community. She has been
called a "firebrand," "a threat to the order and security of Kenya," a "busybody,"
and "a mad woman" because of her efforts to plant millions of trees, her struggles
to enrich the lives of women, and her fight against an autocratic government in
her home country.

> *Policymakers face two types of environmental problems: enduring ones such as the protection of pristine wilderness areas, and emerging ones that are only beginning to appear on the policy agenda.*
>
> TOM TILL

Born into a family of farmers in
Nyeri, Kenya, in 1940, Maathai won a
scholarship to study in the United
States at Mount St. Scholastica College.
She received her master's degree from
the University of Pittsburgh, and was
the first woman in East Africa to earn a

Ph.D. for her work in biology (1971). She was the first female professor at the University of Nairobi.

Maathai's environmental activism began in 1966, when she returned to Kenya from the United States and witnessed the effects of degradation of forests and farmland due to deforestation. Fertilizers and heavy rains had ruined valuable agricultural land, and silt clogged the rivers. She introduced the idea of involving village women's groups in planting trees—and called the organization the Green Belt Movement under the auspices of the National Council of Women of Kenya. Over three decades, more than 30 million trees were planted—providing jobs for 10,000 women, who plant and sell seedlings.

The Green Belt Movement was also significant because it allowed women to stay closer to their homes and families, earning an income from their harvests rather than traveling farther afield to gather firewood. In addition to increasing productivity, the movement gives women a way to fight deforestation and become more self-sufficient.[3]

Maathai also became a potent political leader through protests against Kenya's president, Daniel arap Moi, who ruled for two decades until he lost a presidential election in 2002. Moi proposed building the tallest skyscraper in Africa, along with a six-story statue of himself, in the only public green space in Nairobi. Maathai publicly criticized Moi for his plan, stating, "We can provide parks for rhino and elephants. Why can't we provide open spaces for the people? Why are we creating environmental havoc in urban areas?" She later filed a $200 million lawsuit against the project, and although she lost in court, she managed to scare away potential investors and the plan collapsed. In 1992, she gathered with a group of women who stripped naked in Nairobi to protest police abuses—an act considered culturally taboo for sons to see their mothers naked. Several years later, she was whipped and arrested in an effort to disperse protesters rallying against the building of a luxury housing development in the Karura Forest outside Nairobi. She insisted upon signing her police report in blood from the head injury she had received.[4]

Maathai was elected to Kenya's Parliament in January 2003, and became the Assistant Secretary for Environment, Wildlife, and Natural Resources. When told she was being honored with the Nobel Peace Prize, she celebrated in her home of Nyeri at the foothills of Mount Kenya, and removed her jewelry to kneel in the dirt to plant the seeds of a tree.

At least for a flicker in time, the attention that focused on Maathai's award also placed a spotlight on the environment, and the acknowledgment of issues like sustainability that continue to plague the planet. But as Anthony Downs noted in his model of the issue-attention cycle described in the Introduction, that interest waxes and wanes as other issues crowd the policy agenda, replacing some and pushing others to the top. Although this chapter does not intend to serve as a prognostication of future events, it does highlight some of the policy problems that are now emerging for decision makers to address.

BUSHMEAT

At first glance, human consumption of wild animals may not seem like a critical environmental issue. Bushmeat—usually monkeys, great apes like gorillas and chimpanzees, rats, porcupines, and small antelope—has been a traditional source of food in Africa, and in some areas, it carries spiritual significance. But consumption is becoming more important due to the expanding trade in endangered species and the spread of diseases such as anthrax and ebola from uninspected animal carcasses. As logging operations have spread into forests in Western and Central Africa, trade in bushmeat has expanded out of both cultural tradition and economic necessity. Logging companies often fail to provide food for their workers, who have become dependent on bushmeat traders who arrive with the animals on the back of logging trucks.

The problem is not limited only to policies in Africa. Animal protection advocates estimate about a million tons of meat leave equatorial Africa each year, putting unsustainable pressure on endangered species.[5]

A documentary film made by the Television Trust for the Environment and shown on British television estimated that as many as 10 tons of African bushmeat may be reaching London every day. The film, *No Hiding Place,* shows that hunting for subsistence has been replaced by a flourishing urban market where organized couriers distribute the meat to many European capitals, where it arrives with no customs or health checks.[6]

According to one nongovernmental organization (NGO), the Born Free Foundation, customers and butchers often assume that the meat they are buying comes from beef or goat. But a survey conducted by the group found that 25 percent of the products surveyed from Nairobi butchers was bushmeat, and 19 percent was a mixture of game and meat from domesticated animals.[7]

In the West African capital city of Malabo, Equatorial Guinea, tables in the central market feature several endangered species of monkey, including the drill—a baboon-like species that can weigh up to 50 pounds. Monkey meat sells for more than $6 a pound, making it a prime target for commercial hunters, who sell the food to restaurants and wealthy clients. One Malabo vendor expressed no remorse, saying "There are plenty of animals in the forest. Our people have been eating them for a long time. It is part of our culture."[8]

But officials from the nonprofit Bioko Biodiversity Protection Program note that the number of drills being sold as bushmeat is at an unsustainable level. The program, an academic partnership between Arcadia University in Glenside, Pennsylvania, and the National University of Equatorial Guinea in Malabo, conducts an ongoing survey of large forest mammals and the Malabo bushmeat market. A local resident working for the project visits the central market almost every day, recording the animal sales, how they were killed, their sex, and where they originated. An estimated 50,000 animal carcasses have been recorded in nine years.[9]

Swiss photojournalist Karl Ammann says he first recognized the scale of the bushmeat trade in Zaire in 1988, when dugout canoes carried the carcasses of primates up and down the river. Now, he serves as an advocate for primates as an advisor to the World Society for the Protection of Animals. He believes that current policies are not sufficient to deal with the problem, which has been called the biggest conservation issue facing Africa since elephant ivory. Although some organizations have set up rescue nurseries and sanctuaries for primates orphaned by hunters, Ammann believes they deal only with the by-products of the bushmeat trade. Instead, he has recommended that inspection checkpoints be set up at major road junctions used by logging trucks, and that the hunters observe a closed season to limit hunting during certain times of the year. He also feels that the spread of guns and sale of ammunition has increased hunting, and that licensing permit procedures need to be toughened. Conservation targets, set on a country-by-country basis, would also serve as an incentive to limiting hunting, because few bushmeat traders are ever arrested and prosecuted.[10]

Another factor affecting bushmeat trade is cultural sensitivity. Critics of Ammann and other endangered species advocates believe it is inappropriate for those outside Africa to denounce indigenous peoples' practices and that on some occasions, compromises must be made. Others point out that the bushmeat trade cannot be a priority in countries whose economic and political plight is so severe. A hunter can sell a large gorilla carcass for $60, while a dead chimpanzee is worth as much as $35. Attempts to evoke empathy for apes and other primates to keep people from eating them are misguided, they say, and force Western values on a population where bushmeat is considered wholesome, and starvation is sometimes the only alternative.

One California-based NGO, the Bushmeat Project, has as its mission "the attempt to convert poachers to protectors." The group has established a small protected area where a former gorilla hunter and a small team of conservationists are helping two communities manage a forest with the intention of developing gorilla research and tourism as an alternative to hunting and logging. The project's Conservation Values Education Program has been used in rural villages and schools in Cameroon to teach hunters and elders how to incorporate legends into a curriculum that stresses conservation.

Political responses have been minimal, many conservation organizations believe. In Cameroon, for instance, bushmeat trading is illegal, as is hunting in the six-month off-season. Despite the policy, an estimated 90 tons of bushmeat arrives in Yaounde markets each month. Of that total, about 5 percent are protected species like elephant and gorilla, which sell for twice the price of pork or beef. Bushmeat is served at state functions—an indication of the government's indifference toward the issue. The United Nations declared Cameroon's Dja reserve as a UNESCO World Heritage Site and World Biosphere reserve, but more than 100 hunting camps are located there. Guards, paid for by the European Union (EU) to prevent poaching, have had limited impact.[11]

The International Fund for Animal Welfare and the European Association of Zoos and Aquaria attempted to persuade the European Parliament (EP) to take action in January 2002 by submitting a petition with 2 million signatures pro-testing bushmeat trade. Two years later, the EP voted overwhelmingly for a resolution to develop an EU Bushmeat Strategy plan to conserve biodiversity and protect the endangered species that are part of the bushmeat trade. The resolution also demands a ban on the import of products of companies that act illegally and aggravate the bushmeat problem by allowing their workers to hunt for bushmeat or use company transportation facilities for poached animals.[12]

But the head of the United Kingdom's Natural Environment Research Council believes that EU policies are actually contributing to bushmeat trade, because international fishing fleets are depleting native stocks and turning the 40 percent of Africa's people who live in coastal areas from the sea to forests to find sources of protein. "The European Union has exported its excess fishing capacity to West Africa, and indirectly it's fueling the bushmeat trade, which is devastating the forests—together with South Korea and Japan," according to professor John Lawton.[13]

A study reported by the nonprofit American Association for the Advance-ment of Science (AAAS) in November 2004 corroborated claims that over-fishing by regional and fishing fleets can lead to increases in wildlife hunting, trade, and consumption—"among the most immediate threats to tropical wildlife." The 30-year study in Ghana found that declining fish stocks suggest marine resources are nearing collapse, along with sharp declines in wildlife abundance, emphasizing the need for ecologically sound, inexpensive protein alternatives to wild animals. From 1976 to 1992, the study found the number of reported bushmeat hunters in five wildlife reserves increased when regional fish supplies dropped, as did bushmeat sales in 12 rural markets.[14] The findings suggest that people substitute wildlife for fish in years of fish scarcity.

The United States has had a limited political role in dealing with the bushmeat issue in comparison with NGOs. In November 2000, President Bill Clinton signed the Great Ape Conservation Act into law; but the measure provided only $5 million in funding for grants to wildlife management organi-zations in Africa and Asia. The legislation had been supported by the Humane Society of the United States, The Fund for Animals, and the Doris Day Animal League. The Bushmeat Crisis Task Force (BCTF), a consortium of more than 30 groups formed in 1999, has encouraged the establishment of a U.S. Interagency Bushmeat Task Force that could have the legal authority to address the illegal importation of bushmeat into the country. The organization notes that there is a lack of information coordination and understanding among agencies regarding incoming bushmeat shipments despite considerable risks to human, wildlife, and livestock health.[15]

It is likely, however, that political action will be tedious and ineffective in comparison to what other groups are advocating—an appeal directly to con-sumers. Conservation International has undertaken an educational campaign in Ghana to change behaviors by talking about bushmeat as a loss of cultural heritage—an approach that resonates in Africa, where there is a deep cultural link with wildlife. Until these changes become widespread, though, sections of the Congo Basin continue to be identified as suffering from "empty forest syndrome"—filled with trees, but devoid of large animals. As the director of the

Bushmeat Crisis Task Force notes, "It's a really odd feeling to walk through a forest that's literally silent."[16]

CLIMATE JUSTICE

For the past two decades, much of the world's focus on global climate change has centered on the potential environmental impacts that are forecast to occur. The Intergovernmental Panel on Climate Change (IPCC) has issued reports on how increasing concentrations of greenhouse gases are likely to result in drier conditions and reduced water supplies in some areas, and heavier rainfall and potential polar melting that could raise sea levels, as explained earlier in Chapter 10. Attempts to deal with the human impacts of climate change have been at the problem identification stage; potential solutions to the more technical aspects of global warming include the 1992 United Nations Framework Convention on Climate Change (UNFCCC) and the Kyoto Protocol. Many of the institutional responses related to humans have focused on health impacts.[17]

Although many stakeholders applauded when the Kyoto agreement went into force in 2005, marking a new phase in climate change policy, a significant level of criticism has been leveled at international responses to impacts on indigenous peoples. The phrase "climate justice" has become part of the debate, with supporters seeking "to put a human face" on climate change. Critics of existing policy believe that negotiations to find solutions have been mired in the technical arena, derailed by special interest groups representing the fossil fuel industry. "The biggest injustice of climate change," according to the group CorpWatch, "is that the hardest hit are the least responsible for contributing to the problem."[18]

Concerns about the impact of climate change on indigenous populations have risen as scientific evidence mounts and groups become more cohesive. However, any evidence of policy change has been limited and incremental, consisting primarily of position statements. In the United States, for instance, a series of workshops were held beginning in 1997 to assess the potential consequences of climate variability as part of the U.S. Global Change Research Program. One of the sessions—the Native Peoples/Native Homelands workshop, took place in Albuquerque, New Mexico, in October 1998. Participants in the Circles of Wisdom meetings, including Native American tribal representatives, requested a study of the impact of climate imbalance on indigenous peoples and a subsequent call to action—the Albuquerque Declaration.[19]

At the International Workshop on International Policies on Climate and Indigenous Peoples in Geneva in 1999, participants again asked that indigenous groups be involved in both meetings and Conferences of the Parties (COP) associated with major international agreements. That sentiment was formalized in the May 2000 Quito Declaration requesting that the UN guarantee the adequate participation of indigenous peoples in activities related to the UNFCCC. Another document, the September 2000 Declaration of the First International Forum of Indigenous Peoples on Climate Change (held in Lyon, France), also called for full participation in the UNFCCC. The Lyon Declaration criticized Western scientists for dismissing indigenous peoples "as sentimental and superstitious and accused us of being an obstacle to development. Paradoxically, those that previously turned deaf ears to our warnings, now are dismayed because their own model of 'development' endangers our Mother Earth."[20] Similar declarations were issued at the second international forum in The Hague and at the third forum in Bonn, Germany, in July 2001.

The problem was reframed entirely in September 2001, when U.S. delegates to the World Conference Against Racism (WCAR) condemned the Bush administration's stance on the Kyoto Protocol and the WCAR as "similar acts of environmental racism and climate injustice."[21] Groups associated with the environmental justice movement contended that "people of color, indigenous peoples, and workers bear a disproportionate health, social, and economic burden of a society addicted to a fossil fuel economy."[22] By adding native peoples to their constituency and issuing a "solidarity statement," organizations targeting environmental racism piggybacked their issue on another with global ramifications.

A few months later, the Indigenous Peoples and Local Communities Caucus called upon the COP 7 representatives meeting in Marrakech, Morocco, to "recognize the particularity and specificity of Indigenous Peoples in relation to climate change and grant Indigenous Peoples Special Status." They claimed that the Kyoto Protocol and UNFCCC "do not take into account the sacred nature of the Earth nor do they include the particular and specific rights of Indigenous Peoples."[23]

Seeking formal recognition and participation at the Earth Summit in Johannesburg in 2002, a coalition of groups issued the Bali Principles of Climate Justice. The term *climate justice* was used to describe the goals of broadening the constituency, providing leadership on climate change, and building an international movement.[24]

Later that year, the Indigenous Peoples Caucus held a Climate Justice Summit in New Delhi in sessions that paralleled the COP8 meetings on the Kyoto Protocol. Once again, participants demanded an adequate opportunity to participate fully, seeking accreditation with special status and the inclusion of indigenous peoples and climate change as a regular agenda item at future COPs.[25]

Efforts to gain recognition continued with the March 2004 written intervention submitted by the International Indian Treaty Council and its affiliate, the Indigenous Environmental Network to the United Nations Economic and Social Council. The statement, circulated by the U.N. Secretary-General, presented the groups' view that continued fossil fuel extraction activities and deforestation are a direct threat to indigenous peoples' self-determination, cultural rights, food security, issues of religious tolerance, and human rights.[26]

One of the few indigenous populations to gain attention from U.S. environmental organizations consists of the members of the Inuit Circumpolar Conference, which represents 150,000 people throughout the Arctic. Groups like the Center for International Environmental Law and Earthjustice are providing assistance to the Inuit, who have already faced declines in their ability to hunt and travel during hostile weather. According to the 2004 Arctic Climate Impact Assessment, climate change is warming the Arctic at nearly twice the rate of the rest of the planet. The legal organizations have submitted a petition to the Inter-American Commission on Human Rights, arguing that the United States is threatening the continued existence of the Inuit and their culture. Similar concerns are being raised about the fate of the Sammi people of northwestern Europe.[27]

But climate justice is still only an emerging issue on the environmental policy agenda, as stakeholders attempt to build sufficient public and political interest. Even in those countries where global warming is likely to have a significant impact on indigenous peoples, political support has been difficult to muster. Australia, which has refused to ratify the Kyoto Protocol because it provides "no environmental gain," generates the most greenhouse emissions per capita in the world. The country is home to a large aboriginal population, many of whom live in coastal communities across the northern part of Australia, where cataclysmic weather events are likely to occur. Despite the potentially devastating effect on the country's indigenous population, Australia and the United States are the only major industrialized countries that have refused to ratify the international climate change agreement. As one member of the Australian Green Party commented at the commencement of the Kyoto Protocol, "This is a great occasion for the planet but a terrible moment for Australia."[28]

ENVIRONMENTAL DISASTERS

The earth has experienced, and humanity has survived, thousands of natural disasters since early recorded history. A volcanic eruption decimated Pompeii in 79 AD; tens of thousands were killed in an earthquake and tsunami near what is now Beirut, Lebanon in 551 AD; in 1556, an estimated 800,000 thousand were killed in an earthquake in Shensi, China; a volcanic eruption from Mt. Tambora in Indonesia killed 90,000 in 1815; sea flooding in Bangladesh in 1970 led to the deaths of between 200-500,000 people. In the U.S., the city of Galveston, Texas took a direct hit from a hurricane in 1900, killing 7,000; the San Francisco earthquake (and the resulting fire) of 1906 left 3,000 dead; 739 people died in a 1995 heatwave in Chicago.[29]

Human-caused or non-weather related disasters are also woven into history: one-third of the European population is estimated to have died between 1346 and 1352 from bubonic plague—and 25 million were killed worldwide; famine caused 10 million deaths in India in 1769; a breach in a hydroelectric project dam in Shimantan led to 85,000 deaths in 1975; in 1984, nearly 4,000 people were killed in a chemical explosion in Bhopal, India. Although the oil fires in Kuwait during the Gulf War were a result of deliberate sabotage by Iraq rather than an act of nature, the effects were just as catastrophic. An estimated 6 million barrels of oil were spilled, covering about 600 square miles of water and blackening about 300 miles of shoreline.[30]

So many of these events have occurred recently that the United Nations designated the 1990s as the International Decade for Natural Disaster Reduction, with over 100 countries, including the U.S., developing programs to reduce the harm caused by extreme natural events. The federal government has gone through a series of political responses, from the Mississippi Flood Control Act of 1928 that resulted from flooding in 1927, the Federal Disaster Relief Act of 1950, which marked the beginning of a half-century of laws, programs, and policies to soften the impact of natural disasters on people and their communities, and the creation of the Federal Emergency Management Agency in 1979.[31]

Historically, the damage caused by these events has been measured in the number of lives lost, structures damaged or destroyed, acres burned, jobs and customers lost, persons displaced, property losses, and costs to insurers. Rarely has attention been given to the environmental damage caused by these events, such as damage to wetlands from hurricanes, soil erosion and habitat destruction from wildfires, chemical leaks from structures damaged and destroyed, fish kills from flooding, and dying coastal reefs resulting from tsunamis. The Oakland (CA) Hills Fire in 1991 burned only 1,600 acres, but 3,349 structures were burned and 25 people were killed in the 9-hour fire, with the damage estimated at $1.5 billion. The native oaks and grassland had been transformed by non-native plants and trees that were highly flammable, and residents failed to clear debris, such as eucalyptus leaves, from their property. The narrow, steep canyons were prone to landslides and erosion, and almost immediately, the City of Oakland spent $5 million on aerial reseeding and placing hundreds of straw bale check dams in gullies.[32]

But the emphasis of a regional task force, a hazard mitigation team, the governor's office, university researchers, local utility districts and national fire organizations, was on evaluating emergency preparedness, improving communications, increasing the quality of the infrastructure, and developing new zoning and design standards. The experts' environmental focus was not on the ecological damage that had taken place, but on developing future landscape standards to reduce the potential for future fires as homes were rebuilt on the same land.

Three naturally occurring events within a ten-month period changed the policy agenda to place more attention on the environmental impact of disasters: a tsunami caused by an earthquake off the coast of Indonesia on December 26, 2004, and three catastrophic hurricanes, Katrina, Rita, and Wilma off the Gulf Coast in September 2005. Even preliminary estimates of the environmental impact of the tsunami are complicated because the initial response has been on rescue efforts and rebuilding, and because so many countries experienced differing levels of damage.

Officials from Walhi, one of Indonesia's leading environmental groups, report the environmental damage in Banda Aceh province "has been huge, from the obvious and visible damage along the coastal areas to the possibility of extinction for certain species." The group itself was unable to carry out an assessment because so many of its members were killed in the flooding. The Indonesian chapter of The Nature Conservancy said that "Initial reports indicate that natural ecological systems such as coral reefs, mangroves and wetlands have suffered extensive impacts. Important research facilities for studying and monitoring these environments are reportedly also damaged."[33]

Preliminary research shows that the region's environment was damaged in many ways, from groundwater that became polluted when septic tanks were damaged, to rice fields ruined by salt in the seawater, to species of coral, algae and other marine invertebrates that could not withstand the wave energy generated by the tsunami. It could take several decades for the ecosystem to recover from the sedimentation caused by extreme runoff and the churning up of coastal silt. In Sri Lanka, another area that experienced tsunami damage, The Nature

Conservancy reported that scientists were finding an increase in invasive species, and marine areas were clogged with debris that could cause long term damage to coral reefs.[34]

Thousands of miles away from the Indian Ocean, the hurricane-ravaged Gulf Coast faced similar problems, even though the region is much more industrialized and hazard mitigation plans had been developed. Pollution from oil refineries and chemical plants, and the waste from flooded cars and buildings spilled into Lake Ponchartrain, local canals and waterways, and into the warm waters of the Gulf. Animal and human carcasses increased concerns about public health problems, as did the threat of illness from mosquitoes and water-borne diseases. Officials turned to incineration as a way of dealing with the damage done to residential and commercial buildings, since local landfills were insufficient to handle the debris. Smoke from the incineration piles mingled with smoke from the burning buildings in New Orleans, increasing air quality concerns. Long term ecological damage to the region will take months, if not years, of assessment, including water quality studies, surveys of wildlife and marine habitats, changes in vegetation and tree regeneration, and effects on marine ecosystems.

A related impact of these disasters is the designation of "environmental refugees"—a term used to describe people who are forced from their homelands because of floods, earthquakes, tsunamis, drought, or other naturally-occurring events. While the phrase originally was applied to those experiencing natural disasters, it is also used to refer to situations that are often provoked or amplified by human activities such as building hydroelectric plants and dams that displace entire communities, clearing forests, and overgrazing. In the 1970s, millions of people living in five countries in the Sahel region of Africa left because of catastrophic drought. The International Federation of Red Cross and Red Crescent Societies estimates that in 1998, an estimated 25 million people were forced to leave their homes because of environmental disaster, a figure larger than the number displaced because of war. An estimated 96 percent of environmental refugees come from developing countries.[35]

Central America, for example, was devastated by Hurricane Mitch in October 1998; an estimated 15,000 people were killed, most of them in Honduras. The country was once almost entirely forested, but has lost about a quarter million acres per year to human activities such as logging, burning, and the clearing of rainforests. The sloping hillsides are prone to mudslides and flooding, and some 2 million persons were left homeless or jobless. While emergency relief efforts helped initially, months and years later, people begin to realize that their homes cannot be rebuilt, or the jobs they once held are no longer there.[36] That is when the migration usually begins.

When Hurricane Katrina hit the coast of Louisiana and Mississippi, hundreds of thousands of residents were evacuated and others left voluntarily to stay with friends and family in other parts of the U.S. Those sent to Texas had to be re-evacuated just weeks later when Hurricane Rita moved toward Houston and the Gulf Coast was again devastated. In both disasters, people often ended up far from home in shelters, convention centers, county fairgrounds, and in temporary tent cities. Many affected by the two hurricanes had the same realization as those living in Honduras—there was nothing to move back to. Casino jobs along the Mississippi River that sustained many families were washed out with the storm surge. The tourist industry would take years to rebuild as the infrastructure was repaired. What little housing remained was reserved for those involved in the reconstruction process, or bulldozed because of flood damage and mold.

But will the extent of these three natural disasters be sufficient to move this problem higher on the political agenda? Does the sudden incidence of these events over such a time period make the issue more salient to the public and to policymakers? One commonly shared belief is that the larger debate will be economic rather than environmental. Who should assume the responsibility for the human costs? What action will be taken, property rights advocates ask, to restrict the rights of private land owners without compensation? Will local officials concerned about property values and tax revenues offer incentives for rebuilding in areas likely to experience natural disasters in the future? How much will the debate be framed by political partisanship rather than science? It will take considerably longer to assess and repair environmental damage than to make decisions about rebuilding and who to blame.

E-WASTE

When the first computers became available in the 1960s, their average use "life" was about 10 years before requiring replacement. Today that period is estimated at about four years, and for the most innovative products, less than two years. As the world becomes saturated with electronic devices, from cell phones and computers to video game consoles and fax and copy machines, environmental policy makers are facing a new problem: What happens when these products and equipment are no longer operational or are unwanted and must be discarded?

For years, consumers just tossed their electronic waste, or e-waste as it is often called, into their trash. Much of it, especially bulky items like computer and television monitors, was deemed to be of little value and usually ended up in landfills. Although there is some awareness about the recycling of the computer paper used in the electronic age, hardly anyone seemed to care about the recycling of computer keyboards and other peripherals that created that paper. But gradually, officials began to recognize the tremendous amount of electronic solid waste that was being generated. According to the International Association of Electronics Recyclers, Americans dispose of 2 million tons of electronic products a year, including 50 million computers and 130 million cell phones; by 2010, the nation will be discarding 400 million units annually.[37] Other estimates of computer use indicate that between 2000 and 2007, about 500 million personal computers will become obsolete and enter the municipal solid waste (MSW) stream.[38]

The numbers alone do not tell the story. Electronic waste comprises anywhere from 1 to 4 percent of the MSW stream. The Environmental Protection Agency (EPA), which is coordinating federal efforts to gather more accurate information, notes that e-waste is growing two to three times faster than any other element of the waste stream, such as paper and yard waste. The EU estimates that electronic waste is growing three times faster than MSW in its member countries.[39]

T A B L E 12.1 Hazardous Contaminants in Electronic Waste

Contaminant	Source	Hazard
Cadmium	Chip resistors, infrared detectors, semiconductors	Can accumulate in kidneys through exposure. Cadmium is persistent, bioaccumulative, and toxic.
Lead	Glass panels in computer monitors, lead soldering of printed circuit boards	Can damage central and peripheral nervous systems, blood systems, and kidneys. Can have negative effects on children's brains; can accumulate in environment.
Mercury	Thermostats, position sensors, relays and switches on printed circuit boards, discharge lamps, batteries, medical equipment, data transmission, cell phones	Transformed into methylated mercury when found in waterways. Accumulates in living organisms and becomes part of food chain. Can cause brain damage.
Chromium VI	Galvanized steel plates	Can damage DNA; linked to asthmatic bronchitis.
Flame retardants	Printed circuit boards, plastic covers and cables	May act as an endocrine disrupter; may increase cancer risk.
Plastic	Screws, inserts, coatings, paints, foams, labels	Exposure may increase various health risks.

SOURCE: U.S. Environmental Protection Agency, "Frequent Questions," at www.epa.gov, accessed February 7, 2005.

It is not just the bulkiness of e-waste that is leading to the formulation and adoption of new policies; it is what is inside the devices themselves. Table 12.1 shows that the types and hazards of the contaminants of e-waste are as much a part of the problem as are recycling and landfill concerns. This "electronic baggage"— or waste electrical and electronic equipment (WEEE), as it is termed in a recent EU memorandum, exceeds by far the environmental burden due to the protection of materials constituting the other substreams of the MSW.[40]

The policy response to e-waste varies considerably. At the international level, the focus has been on regulation of hazardous waste through recyclers, who commonly ship materials to Asia, where contaminants often leach into waterways and make their way into the food chain. For many years, electronic components were sent to China, where they were dismantled and sold as scrap. But the country's landfills and storage capabilities were overwhelmed, and it became more and more difficult for industrialized countries to find suitable depositories. The 1992 Basel Convention controls the export of hazardous waste, and has been somewhat effective in regulating shipments, although the United States is the only developed country that has failed to ratify the treaty.

In the EU, where more than 90 percent of WEEE goes to landfills or is incinerated or recovered without any pretreatment, individual member nations are in various phases of drafting and considering legislation. But unilateral approaches fail to deal with cross-border movements of e-waste, especially to countries where less expensive waste-dumping sites are plentiful. A lack of harmonized European regulations, and divergent national requirements on the phasing out of specific substances, are also affecting trade among EU members. Two separate EU directives dealt with the need for producers to take responsibility for certain aspects of waste management for their products—a concept that is just beginning to be adopted in the United States. To prevent the generation of hazardous wastes, the directives require the substitution of various toxic materials in new electrical and electronic equipment sold beginning July 1, 2006.[41]

The U.S. approach has been directed toward federal studies, state-level statutes, and public-private partnerships. In addition to efforts to survey the amount of e-waste that is being both produced and discarded, in January 2003 the EPA mounted a consumer electronics campaign called "Plug-In To eCycling." The program, part of the nationwide Resource Conservation Challenge, focuses on three major areas: providing public information about electronics recycling, facilitating partnerships to promote shared responsibility for safe electronics recycling, and establishing pilot projects to test innovative approaches.[42]

States have taken a leading role in pushing forward their own regulations and programs, rather than relying upon federal directives. One study found that as of 2005, nearly 24 states had active or pending legislation that would require electronic manufacturers to charge consumers a fee for disposing of their product.[43] California, the first state to implement comprehensive legislation, enacted its Electronic Waste Recycling Act in 2003. The statute calls for the reduction of hazardous substances used in certain electronic products sold in California, the collection of an e-waste recycling fee (which ranges from $6 to $10) at the point of sale that started January 1, 2005; the distribution of recovery and recycling payments to entities to cover the cost of e-waste collection and recycling; and a directive to establish environmentally preferred purchasing criteria for state agencies.[44] A similar law was signed in April 2004 in Maine: an Act to Protect Public Health and the Environment by Providing for a System of Shared Responsibility for the Safe Collection and Recycling of Electronic Waste. The state had already enacted legislation prohibiting the disposal of mercury-added products and cathode ray tubes (CRTs). Beginning January 1, 2006, manufacturers were required to pay a portion of the handling and recycling costs for television and computer monitors.[45] In April 2000, Massachusetts passed a resolution prohibiting the disposal of discarded CRTs.

On the local government level, both the number and reach of e-waste programs have increased dramatically. In July 2001, the Northeast Recycling Council's nationwide survey of government-operated electronics recycling programs identified 486 programs in 29 states and the District of Columbia. By January 2003, more than 1,000 programs were under way in at least 35 states. A significant number of the programs, most of them newly launched, are now in operation in cities with populations in excess of a million. A growing trend, the survey found, was that the e-waste programs are expanding to cover both residential and small business users, who are charged more in end-of-life fees as a potential way of financially supporting the overall program.[46]

Environmental organizations such as the Silicon Valley Toxics Coalition, GrassRoots Recycling Network, Californians Against Waste, and the Texas Campaign for the Environment have sought to focus more attention on end-of-life programs that require electronics manufacturers to take back their products. Some seek to create partnerships with companies; Dell, Hewlett Packard, IBM, and Sony have established voluntary programs. Critics argue that consumers are reluctant to pay a fee to discard a computer or monitor and are likely to dump the product. Instead, point-of-purchase charges appear to be making headway. This form of consumer-funded front-end financing system, which uses advance recovery fees (ARFs) that are transmitted by retailers to governments, does little to encourage clean production, according to one group. Instead, there are calls for incentives as a way of encouraging better design to reduce the volume and toxicity of electronic waste.[47]

Other partnerships have been created with office-product retailers like Staples, which recycled about 210,000 pounds of electronic trash in 2004. In cooperation with the EPA, other companies—like Office Depot—have agreed to recycle electronics for no charge several times per year.

Whatever the approach taken, policy makers' biggest challenge may be in keeping the pace of regulations and legislation abreast with the amount of e-waste that is being created worldwide. The federal government disposes of 10,000 computers per week, as EPA officials note, "This complex waste stream poses challenging management issues and potential liability concerns for federal facilities."[48]

OUTDOOR ACCESSIBILITY

Not far from Killarney National Park in Ireland, the Pairc Naisiunt a Chill Airne Cloghereen Nature Trail lies deep in shadows and damp woods. A path of wood chippings leads the occasional visitor along a wide swath through rhododendrons and grasses that add their heady scents to the moist air. What makes this trail unique is that it is designed for use by persons with disabilities—and it is one of a small number of such facilities outside the United States that incorporates special features allowing those, who might otherwise not have the opportunity, to experience nature up-close, and to do so in a protected setting.

The Cloghereen Nature Trail was established as a project of the Killarney Soroptimists club for the 1987 European Year of the Environment. The trail, which was built with local contributions and a grant from Ireland's Environment Awareness Bureau, opened on September 22, 1988. It is not elaborate; visitors wishing to visit find there is only a small car park and no designated parking spots for people with disabilities. It is easy to drive past the site without seeing it, because the park's signage blends into the surrounding bushes and real estate signs for nearby properties. But just past the blockade that keeps motorized vehicles out of the area, visitors find a rope trail with a flat surface that makes this park accessible to those who are physically impaired or blind. There is no admission fee, no interpretive center, and only a single Braille plaque at the entryway; but it is a start.

Ireland, like many European nations, has intermittently shown progress in making outdoor areas accessible to persons with disabilities (PWD). Some national parks now have accessible restrooms and ramps leading to historic sites. Other areas, especially those farther from urban areas, seldom have designated parking spots for vehicles with disabled placards. Interpretive programs for persons who are blind or deaf are rare. But as the number of individuals around the world with disabilities grows due to changing population demographics, outdoor accessibility is emerging as an issue that political leaders are only beginning to understand.

There is no official accounting of the number of Americans with disabilities; however, estimates place the figure at over 50 million, ranging from those with mobility impairments who use wheelchairs, walkers, or braces to persons who are deaf, blind, or have "invisible" disabilities such as chronic illnesses. Others have disabilities—due to military injuries, sports, or automobile accidents—that limit their daily activities.[49] When President H. W. Bush signed the Americans with Disabilities Act of 1990 (ADA), it is doubtful that either he or most members of Congress had considered the issues that would arise through implementation of the statute. Even advocates for PWD had focused their attention on gaining physical access to public facilities and private accommodations such as courthouses, city hall buildings, movie theaters, hotels, and restaurants. The emphasis was clearly on physical structures like buildings, and minimal attention was paid to the outdoors.

Two of the leading advocates for PWD in the Senate hearings, Sen. Orrin Hatch (R–UT), and Sen. Ted Kennedy (D–MA), sought an end to discrimination based on disability in federal wilderness areas. Kennedy noted:

> The opportunity of spending time in an area where human influence does not impede the free play of natural forces or interfere with the natural processes in the ecosystem is an unforgettable and very uplifting experience. This opportunity is very seldom available to persons with disabilities. I am concerned that our wilderness designations may discriminate against the handicapped by denying them access to our most pristine environments.[50]

The hearings produced an amendment to the proposed legislation, Section 507(a) of the ADA, requiring the National Council on Disability, an independent federal agency, to conduct a study on how wilderness designations and practices affect the ability of PWD to use the National Wilderness Preservation System. Subsequently, that study led to similar ones conducted by other agencies, from the National Park Service (NPS), USDA Forest Service (USFS), and Bureau of Reclamation to others on playgrounds, historic sites, and beaches.[51]

The NPS was one of the first agencies to recognize the need for making outdoor areas accessible, establishing a Special Programs and Populations Branch in 1980 to oversee use of NPS lands and facilities by PWD. Over time, the agency has instituted policies for three types of outdoor areas: those that are developed; undeveloped areas outside the immediate influence of buildings, roads and cars; and threshold areas. The agency treats PWDs who use wheelchairs as pedestrians, not as operators of motor vehicles; and motorized equipment cannot be used in wilderness areas. It is also NPS policy "to provide the highest level of accessibility in all visitor and management buildings and facilities as is possible and feasible, consistent with the nature of the area and facility. The degree of accessibility provided will be proportionately related to the degree of man-made modifications made to the area or facility and to the significance of the facility."[52]

In summer 2005, the federal U.S. Access Board proposed new guidelines for outdoor developed areas including trails, beach access routes, and picnic and camping sites; the guidelines focused on those areas owned or managed by the federal government, such as national parks. Simultaneously, the USFS began implementing a directive for new or reconstructed outdoor recreation facilities and trails managed by the agency.[53]

More controversial have been issues related to whether federal regulations require agencies to modify or alter wilderness areas for the sole purpose of making them accessible. Environmental organizations have expressed concerns about how the ADA might apply to remote trails or campsites, or to unspoiled sections of beaches or deserts that are under federal jurisdiction. The USFS policy, for instance, states that wilderness values must dominate over all other considerations in wilderness resource management. However, local managers have some latitude for decisions on access as determined on a case-by-case basis, depending upon environmental conditions, and they may issue special permits to authorize otherwise prohibited activities.

Even though it is feasible to make most outdoor areas accessible, some government entities have balked, usually because of the cost involved. In California, a class-action suit was filed in Federal District Court against the state's Department of Parks and Recreation for failing to make its facilities accessible, in violation of the ADA. Despite numerous complaints that picnic areas, trails, and campgrounds were inaccessible, the state failed to meet the ADA requirements.[54]

The issue of accessibility is not as simple as it might seem. Whereas few people would accept discrimination against PWD in urban settings, wilderness and outdoor areas are a totally different matter to some. Questions are often raised about how areas can be maintained as pristine if PWDs demand that they be allowed to take a motorized wheelchair into areas where other vehicles are prohibited. Trekkers express concern about encountering PWDs who overestimate their ability and need emergency assistance far from rescue facilities or medical care providers. Some users cannot yet accept that PWDs enjoy rock climbing, horseback riding, or backpacking as much as those without disabilities do. Stereotypes are difficult to erase.

Recommendations on how to make outdoor areas more accessible include:

- Installing a telephone device for the deaf (TDD) at ranger stations and interpretive centers
- Producing Braille or large-print brochures for those with low vision or those who are blind

- Providing signage for accessible entrances and specific information on levels of accessibility and trail difficulty ratings
- Creating additional parking areas for vans or vehicles used by PWDs at trailheads, portage areas, and fishing piers
- Allowing individualized motorized access to certain areas
- Widening existing trails and paths

It is clear, though, that changes in government policies must be made to ensure that all people, regardless of their ability level, have access to outdoor areas. As one user states, "My disability does not prevent me from enjoying wilderness areas, it just adds a logistical element as to how to get into these areas."[55]

POLLUTED BEACHES

Local, state, and federal governments are attempting to protect the nation's groundwater supplies, rivers, and lakes from pollution, but they are paying less attention to the skyrocketing jump in the number of "no swimming" days at ocean and Great Lakes beaches. According to an October 2004 report from the Natural Resources Defense Council (NRDC), there were more than 18,000 days of beach closings and advisories because of contamination in 2003—an increase of more than 51 percent from 2002—and the trend is expected to continue.[56] The 2004 NRDC report listed four municipal governments as "beach buddies" that follow adequate monitoring and notification policies, and four others as "beach bums" because they fail to regularly monitor swimmer safety and have no program to notify the public when health standards are exceeded. The Beach Buddies were Newport Beach, California; Willard Beach in South Portland, Maine; Ocean City, Maryland; and Warren Town Beach, Rhode Island. Beach Bums were Bar Harbor, Maine; Kennebunkport, Maine; St. Lawrence County, New York; and Frenchman's Bar, Vancouver, Washington.[57]

Coastal water quality comes under the jurisdiction of the U.S. Environmental Protection Agency (EPA), which sets standards for water pollution. Responsibility for monitoring beaches is left to the states, whose primary task is controlling sources of beachwater contamination such as runoff from roads and agricultural areas, sewage discharges, boating waste, and stormwater from new development. State and local governments have failed to identify and control sources of bacteria and other pollution-tainted water near beaches, the NRDC report notes, despite requirements of the federal Beaches Environmental Assessment and Coastal Health (BEACH) Act of 2000. The BEACH Act represents amendments to the Federal Water Pollution Control Act (33 U.S.C. 1313) by adding several new sections related to water quality criteria, monitoring, and notification. States with coastal recreation areas are required to adopt the EPA's 1986 recommended health standards for pathogens, or ones equally protective of public health, by April 2004. States are also encouraged, but not required, to monitor beachwater contamination and to notify the public when health risks are present.[58]

When the compliance deadline arrived, only 11 of the 35 affected states and territories had adopted criteria for pathogens; the Bush administration subsequently announced a proposed rule that would establish standards for the states that had failed to do so. Jim Connaughton, chair of the Council on Environmental Quality (CEQ), noted the administration's support for full compliance. "While we generally prefer for states to implement their own standards," he said, "we support EPA's commitment to fulfilling its oversight responsibility."[59] EPA released a Proposed Rule on July 9, 2004, for noncompliant states, setting new water quality standards for coastal recreation waters to protect human health. The Clean Beaches Plan also included increased pathogen monitoring and nine epidemiological studies to develop better pathogen indicators of illnesses at beaches. In October 2004, state beach program leaders attended the National Beach Conference, sponsored by EPA's Office of Water; and in December 2004, the agency gave Congress a statute-mandated report on the progress of BEACH Act implementation.[60]

The EPA's plan to implement the BEACH Act was more symbolic than substantive, even though President Bush had declared 2004 as the Year of Clean Water. As initially enacted, the statute included a $30 million appropriation in grants to help develop, improve, and implement beach monitoring programs to be administered through the EPA's budget and distributed on an annual basis for each of fiscal years 2001 through 2005. In 2004, however, the Bush administration's budget included only $2 million for beachwater monitoring grants—less than 7 percent of the amount Congress approved when the program was created in October 2000.

Typical of many environmental issues, polluted beaches are ignored until there is a focusing event, such as when medical waste washed up on eastern U.S. shores where children were playing. With minimal funding from Congress, minimal interest by the Bush administration, and minimal concern by the public, this problem may not fully emerge as part of the environmental agenda until crisis forces it onto the decision-making agenda.

NOTES

1. Wangari Muta Maathai, "The Nobel Lecture," December 10, 2004, at www.nobel.no/eng_lect_2004b, accessed December 11, 2004.

2. The Norwegian Nobel Committee, "The Nobel Peace Prize," News release, at www.nobelprize.org/peace, accessed October 20, 2004.

3. Wangari Maathai, *The Green Belt Movement: Sharing the Approach and the Experience* (New York: Lantern Books, 2005).

4. Emily Wax, "Kenya's 'Green Militant' Wins Nobel Peace Prize," *Washington Post,* October 9, 2004, A-1.

5. Alex Kirby, "EU Fishing 'Drives Bushmeat Trade,'" *BBC News Online,* at www.eurocbc.org, accessed January 16, 2005.

6. Alex Kirby, "The Cost of Bushmeat," at http://news.bbc.co.uk, accessed November 8, 2004.

7. "Bushmeat Trade Flourishing in 'Hot Spots,' " Reuters Foundation AlertNet, at www.alertnet.org, accessed October 13, 2004.

8. Information on the Bioko program is available at www.bioko.org.

9. The Bushmeat Project, "Death in the Forest: Logging Business Means Death for Thousands of Gorillas and Chimpanzees," at www.bushmeat.net, accessed November 8, 2004.

10. Ibid.

11. "Africa's Vanishing Apes," *The Economist,* January 10, 2002, at www.economist.com/world/africa, accessed January 16, 2005.

12. Animal News Center, "European Parliament Votes to Tackle 'Bushmeat' Crisis," January 24, 2004, at www.buzzle.com, accessed January 16, 2005.

13. Kirby, "The Cost of Bushmeat."

14. American Association for the Advancement of Science, "Declining Fish Supply Increases West African Bushmeat Consumption," News release, November 11, 2004, at www.aaas.org, accessed January 16, 2005.

15. Bushmeat Crisis Task Force, "U.S. Government Interagency Bushmeat Task Force," at www.bushmeat.org, accessed January 16, 2005.

16. Paul Clarke, "Bushmeat on the Menu," *E Magazine* (March—April 2003), at www.emagazine.com/view, accessed January 16, 2005.

17. See, for example, World Health Organization, *Climate Change and Human Health: Risks and Responses* (Geneva, Switzerland: World Health Organization, 2003).

18. CorpWatch, "Bali Principles of Climate Justice," August 28, 2002, at www.corpwatch.org, accessed March 7, 2005.

19. U.S. Global Change Research Program, "Native Peoples/Native Homelands," at www.usgcrp.gov, accessed March 7, 2005. The text of the Albuquerque Declaration can be found at www.earthsummit2002.org.

20. "Declaration of the First International Forum of Indigenous Peoples on Climate Change," September 8, 2000, at www.wrm.org.uy, accessed March 7, 2005.

21. Redefining Progress, "First Kyoto, Now Durban," News release, September 4, 2001, at www.ejcc.org/media_archive, accessed September 20, 2005.

22. Ibid.

23. Indigenous Peoples and Local Communities Caucus, "Marrakech Statement on Climate Change," November 5, 2001, at www.tebtebba.org, accessed March 7, 2005.

24. "Bali Principles of Climate Justice," August 29, 2002, at www.corpwatch.org/article, accessed March 7, 2005.

25. Indigenous Peoples Caucus, "Indigenous Peoples Statement," October 24, 2002, at www.tebtebba.org accessed September 20, 2005.

26. United Nations Economic and Social Council, "Promotion and Protection of Human Rights: Information and Education," statement submitted by the International Indian Treaty Council, March 3, 2004, at www.unhchr.org, accessed March 7, 2005.

27. Earthjustice, "The Inuit Struggle for Survival," *In Brief* (Spring 2005): 1–3; and Arctic Council, "Climate Change," at www.arcticpeoples.org, accessed March 7, 2005.

28. Ilana Eldridge, "Indigenous Australians, Big Losers with Global Warming," *Inter Press Service,* February 2005, at www.ipsnews.net, accessed March 7, 2005.

29. Even before the Indian Ocean tsunami and Hurricanes Katrina, Rita, and Wilma there was a vast amount of scholarly research on natural disasters. See, for example David Alexander, *Natural Disasters in the Modern World* (London: Terra Publishing, 1999); William Bronson, *The Earth Shook, The Sky Burned* (San Francisco: Chronicle Books, 1989); Stanley A. Changnon,

ed., *The Great Flood of 1993: Causes, Impacts and Responses* (Boulder, CO: Westview, 1996); Graham A. Tobin and Burrell E. Montz, *Natural Hazards: Explanation and Integration* (New York: Guilford, 1997).

30. The events in Kuwait have been termed ecological terrorism in some reports. See Roy Popkin, "Responding to Eco-Terrorism," *EPA Journal* (July–August 1991) at www.epa.gov/history accessed September 22, 2005.

31. For coverage of the political response to natural disasters, see Rutherford H. Platt, *Disasters and Democracy: The Politics of Extreme Natural Events* (Washington, DC: Island Press, 1999).

32. Ibid.

33. "Tsunami Environmental Damage Widespread, Experts Say," (January 19, 2005) at www.planetark.com accessed September 22, 2005; National Oceanic and Atmospheric Administration, "Potential Ecological Impacts of Indian Ocean Tsunami on Nearshore Marine Ecosystems," (January 6, 2005) at www.noaaews.noaa.gov accessed September 22, 2005.

34. The Nature Conservancy, "First Environmental Survey of Tsunami Damage Shows Sri Lankan Coasts and Forests Hurt But Rebounding," (February 24, 2005) at www.nature.org accessed September 22, 2005.

35. Mary Jo McConahay, "No Place to Call Home," *Sierra* (November 2001) at www.sierraclub.org/sierra accessed September 22, 2005.

36. Ibid.

37. Juliet Eilperin, "Dead Electronics Going to Waste," *Washington Post,* January 21, 2005, at www.washingtonpost.com, accessed February 7, 2005.

38. U.S. Environmental Protection Agency, "Electronic Waste and eCycling," at www.epa.gov, accessed February 7, 2005.

39. U.S. Environmental Protection Agency, "Frequent Questions," at www.epa.gov, accessed February 7, 2005.

40. European Union, *Explanatory Memorandum: Waste Electrical and Electronic Equipment,* at www.europa.eu.int/comm/environment/waste, accessed February 7, 2005.

41. Ibid.

42. U.S. Environmental Protection Agency, "Plug-In To eCycling," at www.epa.gov, accessed February 7, 2005.

43. Computer TakeBack Campaign, "E Waste Legislation in the US," at www.computertakeback.com, accessed February 7, 2005.

44. State of California, Electronic Waste Recycling Act of 2003 (SB 20; Chapter 526, Statutes of 2003, and SB 50, Chapter 863, Statutes of 2004).

45. State of Maine, Department of Environmental Protection, "Maine's E-Waste Law," at www.maine.gov/dep/rwm, accessed February 7, 2005. See also, Natural Resources Council of Maine, "Legislature Adopts 'Electronic-Waste Bill,'" at www.maineenvironment.org/toxics, accessed February 7, 2005.

46. Northeast Recycling Council, "National Electronics Recycling Program Updated," at www.nerc.org, accessed February 7, 2005.

47. Computer TakeBack Campaign, "Legislation and Policy," at www.computertakeback.com, accessed February 7, 2005.

48. Eilperin, "Dead Electronics Going to Waste."

49. See Jacqueline Vaughn Switzer, *Disabled Rights:American Disability Policy and the Fight for Equality* (Washington, DC: Georgetown University Press, 2003).

50. Testimony of Sen. Edward Kennedy, U.S. Congress, Senate, Hearing on the Americans with Disabilities Act, *Congressional Record* (September 7, 1989):19833. For another perspective, see

Edward H. Stone, "There's a Wheelchair in the Woods," *Parks and Recreation,* December 1971, 19–22, 45; and Terry Brown and Rachel Kaplan, "Beyond Accessibility: Nature Areas and Well-Being," National Center on Accessibility, at www.indiana.edu/~nca/research, accessed January 18, 1998.

51. National Council on Disability, *Wilderness Accessibility for People with Disabilities: A Report to the President and the Congress of the United States on Section 507(a) of the Americans with Disabilities Act* (Washington, DC: National Council on Disability, December 1, 1992). See also Robert C. Lucas, *Wilderness Management: A Literature Review* (Missoula, MT: U.S. Forest Service [undated]); Duncan S. Ballantyne, *Accommodation of Disabled Visitors at Historic Sites in the National Park System* (Waltham, MA: Howard Russell Associates, 1983).

52. Ballantyne, *Accomodations of Disabled Visitors.*

53. United States Access Board, "Board to Proposed Guidelines for Outdoor Developed Areas," *Access Currents, 11,* no. 1 (January–February 2005): 2.

54. Disability Rights Advocates, "State Parks Say to Disabled 'Take A Hike . . . Somewhere Else,'" News release, January 29, 1999.

55. National Council on Disability, 37.

56. Natural Resources Defense Council, "Pollution-Related Beach Closings and Advisories Skyrocket in 2003," at www.nrdc.org/water/oceans, accessed October 20, 2004.

57. Natural Resources Defense Council, "Testing the Waters: A Guide to Water Quality at Vacation Beaches," at www.nrdc.org/water/oceans, accessed October 20, 2004.

58. U.S. Environmental Protection Agency, "Beach Standards, Monitoring and Notification," at www.epa.gov/waterscience, accessed September 20, 2005.

59. U.S. Environmental Protection Agency, "Bush Administration Makes Strong Commitment to Clean Beaches," News release, August 4, 2004, at www.epa.gov/newsroom, accessed September 20, 2005.

60. U.S. Environmental Protection Agency, "Clean Beaches Plan."

FURTHER READING

C. Emdad Haque, ed. *Mitigation of Natural Hazards and Disasters: International Perspectives.* New York: Springer, 2006.

Climate for Change: Non-State Actors and the Global Politics of the Greenhouse. Cambridge, UK: Cambridge University Press, 2006.

Matthew J. Hoffman. *Ozone Depletion and Climate Change: Constructing A Global Response.* Albany: SUNY Press, 2006.

W. Scott Ingram. *The Chernobyl Nuclear Disaster.* New York: Facts on File, 2005.

Wangari Maathai. *The Green Belt Movement: Sharing the Approach and the Experience* (New York: Lantern Books, 2005).

Jacqueline Vaughn Switzer. *Disabled Rights: American Disability Policy and the Fight for Equality* (Washington, DC: Georgetown University Press, 2003).

United Nations Environment Programme. *After the Tsunami: Rapid Environmental Assessment.* New York: United Nations Environment Programme, 2005.

APPENDIX A: MAJOR U.S. ENVIRONMENTAL LEGISLATION, 1947–2005

Year	Air Quality	Water Quality	Pesticides, Toxics	Solid Waste	Land	Other
1947 Truman			Federal Insecticide, Fungicide, and Rodenticide Act			
1956 Eisenhower		Water Pollution Control Act				
1963 Kennedy	Clean Air Act					
1964 Johnson					Land and Water Conservation Fund Act	
1965 Johnson		Water Quality Act				Highway Beautification Act
1966 Johnson						Endangered Species Preservation Act
1967 Johnson	Air Quality Act					
1968 Johnson					National Wild and Scenic Rivers Act/ National Trails System Act	
1969 Nixon						National Environmental Policy Act/Endangered Species Act Amendments
1970 Nixon	Clean Air Act Amendments	Water Quality Improvement Act		Resource Recovery Act		Environment Education Act

Year / President						
1971 Nixon					Alaska Native Claims Settlement Act	
1972 Nixon		Federal Water Pollution Control Act	Federal Environmental Pesticides Control Act	Coastal Zone Management Act		Marine Protection Research and Sanctuaries Act/Noise Control Act
1973 Nixon						Endangered Species Act
1974 Nixon		Safe Drinking Water Act				
1976 Ford			Toxic Substances Control Act	Resource Conservation and Recovery Act	Federal Land Policy and Management Act/National Forest Management Act	
1977 Carter	Clean Air Act Amendments	Clean Water Act Amendments			Surface Mining Control and Reclamation Act/Soil and Water Conservation Act	
1978 Carter						Public Utility Regulatory Policies Act/National Energy Act
1980 Carter			Comprehensive Environmental Response, Compensation, and Liability Act (Superfund)		Alaska National Interest Lands Conservation Act	Fish and Wildlife Conservation Act
1982 Reagan						Nuclear Waste Policy Act
1984 Reagan				Resource Conservation and Recovery Act Amendments		

(Continued)

(Continued)

Year	Air Quality	Water Quality	Pesticides, Toxics	Solid Waste	Land	Other
1985 Reagan						Food Security Act
1986 Reagan		Safe Drinking Water Act	Superfund Amendments and Reauthorization Act			
1987 Reagan		Clean Water Act Amendments				Nuclear Waste Policy Act Amendments/Global Climate Protection Act
1988 Reagan				Federal Insecticide, Fungicide, and Rodenticide Act Amendments		Ocean Dumping Act
1990 Bush	Clean Air Act Amendments					
1992 Bush						Energy Policy Act
1994 Clinton					California Desert Protection Act	
1996 Clinton		Safe Drinking Water Act Amendments				Food Quality Protection Act
2002 G. W. Bush			Small Business Liability Relief and Brownfields Revitalization Act			
2003 G. W. Bush					Healthy Forests Restoration Act	
2005 G. W. Bush						Energy Policy Act

APPENDIX B: MAJOR INTERNATIONAL ENVIRONMENTAL AGREEMENTS, 1900–2005*

Year	Environmental Agreement
1906	Convention Concerning the Equitable Distribution of the Waters of the Rio Grande for Irrigation
1916	Convention for the Protection of Migratory Birds
1933	Convention on the Preservation of Fauna and Flora in Their Natural State
1946	International Convention for the Regulation of Whaling
1947	General Agreement on Tariffs and Trade
1951	International Plant Protection Convention
1954	International Convention for the Protection of the Seas by Oil
1958	Convention on the Continental Shelf
1958	Convention on the Territorial Sea and Contiguous Zone
1958	Convention on the High Seas
1958	Geneva Convention on Fishing and Conservation of the Living Resources of the High Seas
1959	Antarctic Treaty
1960	Paris Convention on Third Party Liability in the Field of Nuclear Energy
1963	Berne Convention on the International Commission for the Protection of the Rhine Against Pollution
1963	Vienna Convention on Civil Liability for Nuclear Damage
1964	Convention for the International Council for the Exploration of the Sea
1966	International Convention for the Conservation of Atlantic Tunas
1968	African Convention on the Conservation of Nature and Natural Resources
1970	Declaration of Principles Governing the Seabed and the Ocean Floor, and the Subsoil Thereof, Beyond the Limits of National Jurisdiction
1971	Ramsar Convention on Wetlands of International Importance Especially as Waterfowl Habitat
1972	Convention for the Protection of the World Cultural and Natural Heritage
1972	Convention on the Prevention of Marine Pollution by Dumping of Wastes and Other Matter
1972	Stockholm Declaration of the United Nations Conference on the Human Environment
1973	Convention on International Trade in Endangered Species of Wild Fauna and Flora
1973	International Convention for the Prevention of Pollution from Ships
1979	International Convention on Long-Range Transboundary Air Pollution
1980	Convention on the Conservation of Antarctic Marine Living Resources
1982	United Nations Convention on the Law of the Sea
1982	World Charter on Nature
1983	Cartagena Agreement
1985	Vienna Convention for the Protection of the Ozone Layer
1985	International Tropical Timber Agreement
1987	Montreal Protocol on Substances That Deplete the Ozone Layer

(Continued)

*These agreements are in various stages of implementation, based upon the status and participation of the parties involved. Stages include adoption, ratification, acceptance or approval, acts of formal confirmation, entry into force, and accession.

(Continued)

Year	Environmental Agreement
1989	Basel Convention on the Control of Transboundary Movements of Hazardous Wastes and Their Disposal
1990	Wellington Convention for the Prohibition of Fishing with Long Driftnets in the South Pacific
1990	London Adjustments and Amendments to the Montreal Protocol
1991	Bamako Convention on the Ban of Import Into Africa and the Control of Trans-boundary Movement and Management of Hazardous Wastes Within Africa
1991	Protocol on Environmental Protection to the Antarctic Treaty
1991	Declaration on the Protection of the Arctic Environment
1992	Framework Convention on Climate Change
1992	Convention on Biological Diversity
1992	North American Free Trade Agreement
1992	Copenhagen Amendments and Adjustments to the Montreal Protocol
1992	Rio Declaration on Environment and Development
1994	Amendments to the International Tropical Timber Agreement
1994	United Nations Convention to Combat Desertification in Those Countries Experiencing Serious Drought and/or Desertification, Particularly in Africa
1994	Vienna Adjustments to the Montreal Protocol
1994	Convention on Nuclear Safety
1995	Global Program of Action for the Protection of the Marine Environment from Land-Based Activities
1995	Washington Declaration on Protection of Marine Resources from Land-Based Activities
1995	Straddling Stocks Convention
1996	Protocol to the Convention on the Prevention of Marine Pollution by Dumping of Wastes and Other Matter
1997	Kyoto Protocol to the United Nations Framework Convention on Climate Change
1997	Montreal Amendments and Adjustments to the Montreal Protocol
1997	Convention on the Law of the Non-Navigational Uses of International Watercourses
1997	Protocol to Amend the 1963 Vienna Convention on Civil Liability for Nuclear Damage
1997	Convention on Supplementary Compensation for Nuclear Damage
1998	Convention on Access to Information, Public Participation in Decision Making and Access to Justice in Environmental Matters
1998	Rotterdam Convention on Prior Informed Consent Procedure for Certain Hazardous Chemicals and Pesticides in International Trade
1998	Protocol on Persistent Organic Pollutants
1998	Protocol on Heavy Metals
1999	Protocol to the Cartagena Agreement
1999	Protocol to Abate Acidification, Eutrophication and Ground-Level Ozone
1999	Protocol on Liability
1999	Beijing Amendments and Adjustments to the Montreal Protocol
2000	Cartagena Protocol on Biosafety to the Convention on Biological Diversity
2001	Stockholm Convention on Persistent Organic Pollutants
2002	Delhi Ministerial Declaration
2002	Convention for Cooperation in the Protection and Sustainable Marine and Coastal Environment of the North-East Pacific (Antigua Convention)

APPENDIX C: ENVIRONMENTAL FILM
RESOURCES, 1995–2005

Alaska: The Last Frontier? (1996) 27 minutes
Shows the difficulties of balancing the needs of indigenous peoples and the wilderness with economic development and modern life in Alaska. Annenberg/CPB Collection (South Burlington, VT)

Aliens from Planet Earth (2002) 25 minutes
Documents the effect on global diversity caused by humans introducing nonnative species into new areas; also looks at the politics and economics of species invasions. Films for the Humanities and Sciences (New York)

American Values, American Wilderness (2005) 57 minutes
Presents the diverse values of a broad spectrum of Americans about wilderness as a place of sanctuary for animals and plants, as the sources of clean air and water, as a place for spiritual renewal, and as a legacy for future generations. High Plains Films (Missoula, MT)

An American Nile (1997) 55 minutes
Charts the dramatic transformation of the Colorado River from a wild desert waterway, including the construction of Hoover Dam and environmental battles over potential damming of the Grand Canyon. Home Vision Cinema: Public Media Incorporated (Chicago)

Ansel Adams (2002) 100 minutes
Portrays the American artist and photographer whose work was inextricably linked with the environmental movement. PBS Home Video (Alexandria, VA)

The Ash Barge Odyssey (2001) 57 minutes
Explains the 1986 story of a barge loaded with 14,000 tons of incinerated trash that sailed from Philadelphia and around the world in search of a landfill. Most of the ash was eventually dumped at sea; 3,000 tons was left on a beach in Haiti before being returned to the U.S. Michael Thomas Productions (Montgomeryville, PA)

Baked Alaska (2003) 26 minutes
Documents how rising global temperatures and the battle over the Arctic National Wildlife Refuge are impacting life in Alaska. Bullfrog Films (Oley, PA)

Black Sea: Voyage of Healing (1999) 54 minutes
Chronicles a symposium held onboard a cruise ship as it circumnavigates six countries, while participants seek to find solutions to the environmental crisis facing the region. Bullfrog Films (Oley, PA)

Borderline Cases: Environmental Matters at the U.S.–Mexico Border (1997) 65 minutes
Describes problems caused when some factories along the U.S.–Mexico border were not required to comply with environmental regulations. Bullfrog Films (Oley, PA)

The Boyhood of John Muir (1997) 78 minutes
Tells the story of John Muir as he grows up in 19th-century Wisconsin, detailing the events and people who guided him toward a new life as a leader of the preservationist movement. Bullfrog Films (Oley, PA)

The Bratsk Sea (2001) 50 minutes
Shows how human health and living conditions in the city of Bratsk, Siberia, have been degraded because of the huge chemical and power plants in the area. Artistic License (Sacramento, CA)

Broken Limbs: Apples, Agriculture, and the New American Farmer (2004) 57 minutes
Explores how small farmers in the Apple Capital of the World in Wenatchee, Washington, are forced to fight to make a living against corporate farms in an age of sustainable agriculture. Bullfrog Films (Oley, PA)

The Buffalo War (2001) 57 minutes
Story of the battle over the yearly slaughter of America's last wild bison that stray from Yellowstone National Park in winter, and the activism of groups trying to save the animals. **Bullfrog Films** (Oley, PA)

Cadillac Desert (1997) 55 minutes
Traces the fierce political and environmental battles that raged around the transformation of California's Central Valley and the recent trend of diverting water away from agriculture and toward cities and wildlife. Home Vision Cinema: Public Media Incorporated (Chicago)

Crapshoot: The Gamble with Our Wastes (2004) 52 minutes
Takes viewers on a global tour of sewage practices as activists challenge our fundamental attitudes toward waste. Bullfrog Films (Oley, PA)

Cull of the Wild: The Truth Behind Trapping (2002) 27 minutes
Examines the history and legacy of the trapping industry in the United States, explaining the dangers to nontarget animals and household pets. Bullfrog Films (Oley, PA)

David Brower (1997) 56 minutes
Retrospective of the late environmental leader who was a pioneer in the Sierra Club and Friends of the Earth; portrays his battle for environmental restoration. Bullfrog Films (Oley, PA)

Downwind/Downstream (1998) 59 minutes
Documents the serious threat to water quality, sub-alpine ecosystems, and public health in the Colorado Rockies from mining operations, acid rain, and urbanization. Bullfrog Films (Oley, PA)

Drowned Out: We Can't Wish Them Away (2003) 75 minutes
Tells how villagers in Jalsindhi, India, have engaged in hunger strikes, rallies, police brutality, and a six-year long court case to protest the Narmada Dam that will drown their village. Bullfrog Films (Oley, PA)

Drumbeat for Mother Earth (2000) 54 minutes
Explores how many scientists and tribal people consider persistent toxic chemicals to be the greatest threat to the long-term survival of indigenous peoples. Bullfrog Films (Oley, PA)

Eagle Odyssey (2004) 50 minutes
Chronicles efforts to save the white-tailed sea eagle and considers its relationship to humans in the Scottish heartland. Mike Percival Films (UK)

Ecofeminism Now! (1996) 37 minutes
Offers an introduction to the theory and practice of ecofeminism. Medusa Productions (Minnesota)

El Caballo (2001) 57 minutes
Presents the controversy over wild horses, protected by the 1971 Free-Roaming Wild Horse and Burro Act, and examines how their numbers are dwindling. High Plains Films (Missoula, MT)

Empty Oceans, Empty Nets (2003) 55 minutes
Explains how the world's single largest source of protein, our oceans, are at risk in many areas as part of the global fisheries crisis. Bullfrog Films (Oley, PA)

End of the Road (2000) 18 minutes
Short documentary regarding the half-million miles of roads already constructed in the National Forests and summarizing the controversy over the nation's roadless rules. High Plains Films (Missoula, MT)

The Environmental Impact of War (1999) 28 minutes
Explores the environmental damage created from wars; also considers the adverse effects on human health, local economies, and ecosystems. Center for Defense Information (Washington, DC)

Farming the Seas (2004) 56 minutes
Examines the problems facing the world's oceans, including the farming of commercially valuable fish and shellfish, the transmission of disease, overfishing, and the threat of genetically engineered fish entering wild populations. Bullfrog Films (Oley, PA)

Field of Genes (1998) 44 minutes
Looks at the evolution of transgenic food, the role of multinational chemical companies, and the bio-technology industry; also criticizes the use of genetically altered food. Bullfrog Films (Oley, PA)

Fires of the Amazon (2002) 44 minutes
Documents the destruction of the Amazon rain forest, explaining the rapid rate of logging and burning and the growing political clout of local residents. Bullfrog Films (Oley, PA)

Fisheries: Beyond the Crisis (1998) 46 minutes
Two-part illustration of the problem of managing fisheries in a sustainable manner, with examples from Canada's Bay of Fundy and from South India. Bullfrog Films (Oley, PA)

Fishing in the Sea of Greed (1998) 45 minutes
Documents the response of one fishing community in India to the industries that have begun to dominate the peoples' livelihood and decimate their environment. First Run/Icarus Films (Brooklyn, NY)

Fooling with Nature (1998) 60 minutes
Examines new evidence in the controversy over the danger of chemicals to human health and the environment. PBS Video (Alexandria, VA)

The Four Corners: A National Sacrifice Area? (1996) minutes
Explores the environmental degradation of the Southwest, reclamation of mining sites, air quality problems, and the role of native peoples. Bullfrog Films (Oley, PA)

Fury for the Sound: The Women at Clayoquot (1997) 86 minutes
Reveals the important role of women in establishing grassroots social movements to protest logging in Clayoquot Sound in British Columbia. TellTale Productions (Vancouver, BC)

The Future of Food (2004) 89 minutes
Investigates unlabeled genetically modified foods that have become increasingly prevalent in grocery stores; examines the market and political forces that are changing what we eat. Lily Films (Mill Valley, CA)

Global Warming and the Greenhouse Effect (2004) 20 minutes
Describes the effects of industrialization on the emissions of greenhouse gases; attempts to deal with the problem of global warming. Educational Video Network (Huntsville, TX)

The God Squad and the Case of the Northern Spotted Owl (2001) 57 minutes
Chronicles the controversial actions of the Endangered Species Committee and proposed timber sales in southwest Oregon that mirror the debate over old-growth forests. Bullfrog Films (Oley, PA)

The Golf War (2000) 39 minutes
Explores the dramatic conflict between peasants in a seaside community in the Philippines as they resist economic development and confront golf enthusiasts (including Tiger Woods) who want to build a tourist resort on ancestral farmland. Bullfrog Films (Oley, PA)

Good Wood (1999) 45 minutes
Asks whether it is possible to stop deforestation while also sustaining communities that depend on the forest for their livelihood; includes coverage of communities in Honduras, British Columbia, and Mexico. Bullfrog Films (Oley, PA)

Grand Canyon (2002) 95 minutes
Documents the human history of the Grand Canyon, including its discovery and exploration, environmental conditions, recreational use, and history. Firstlight Pictures (Maplewood, NJ)

The Greatest Good (2005) 120 minutes
U.S. Forest Service centennial film traces the agency's history throughout the 20th century, examining conflicts over timber, grazing, fire, wilderness, and recreation. USDA Forest Service (Washington, DC)

The Great Forest (2003) 104 minutes
Identifies the conflict between conservationists and the wood products industry in three short documentaries examining the loss of virgin forests in the East. High Plains Films (Missoula, MT)

The Great Warming (2003) 138 minutes
Three-part documentary on global warming, including the science and consequences of climate change; also presents people and communities who are trying to combat the problem. Filmwest Distributors (Kelowna, BC)

Healing the Earth (1995) 28 minutes
Shows how we can help heal the earth through cooperation between communities and the government on Superfund projects and the use of bioremediation. National Geographic Society (Washington, DC)

Heavy Metal (2004) 56 minutes
Explores the controversy behind a century of mining in Idaho's panhandle and details the efforts of activists caught in the middle as they try to protect human health and wildlife. Green Planet Films (Corte Madera, CA)

High Stakes at the Salton Sea (2002) 57 minutes
Explains how the increasing salinization of California's Salton Sea has forced state policy makers into difficult decisions about water use and species protection. Water Education Foundation (Sacramento, CA)

Hoover Dam (1999) 60 minutes
Describes the making of a national monument and the environmental conflicts involved, using archival footage and photographs. PBS Video (Alexandria, VA)

How Serious Is Global Warming? (1996) 31 minutes
Presents commentaries by a series of researchers in energy policy and climate on the nature and implications of global warming. Hawkhill Video (Madison, WI)

Human Faces Behind the Rain Forest (2001) 30 minutes
Documents the dramatic events surrounding the harvest of the opium poppy crop in the Columbian rain forest through the experiences of the indigenous peoples involved. First Run/Icarus Films (Brooklyn, NY)

In the Light of Reverence (2001)
Chronicles the issues of land-based religion and sacred places for Native Americas; profiles the Hopi's fight to preserve their land and water from strip mining and climbers, examines the Lakota struggle to protect Devil's Tower, and looks at disputes over sacred land near Mt. Shasta, California. Bullfrog Films (Oley, PA)

Keepers of the Coast (1996) 31 minutes
Shows the work of local surfers through the Surfrider Foundation to educate the public and protest the pollution of coastlines. Bullfrog Films (Oley, PA)

Killing Coyote (2000) 83 minutes
Documents the trapping, hunting, and killing of an estimated 400,000 coyotes in the United States each year; shows the effects of pitting ranchers, hunters, political officials and environmental groups against one another. High Plains Films (Missoula, MT)

Laid to Waste (1996) 52 minutes
Shows how the residents of Chester, Pennsylvania, fight the location of another waste treatment plant in their city through community action. University of California (Berkeley, CA)

Last Oasis (1997) 55 minutes
The story of how America's large dams became examples for water projects in developing countries. Home Vision Cinema: Public Media Incorporated (Chicago)

The Last Stand: Ancient Redwoods and the Bottom Line (2002) 57 minutes
Examines the destruction of the ancient redwoods in Northern California, with testimony from economists, scientists, forest activists, and local residents. University of California Extension Center for Media (Berkeley, CA)

The Last Stand: The Struggle for the Ballona Wetlands (2000) 57 minutes
Covers the struggle over the Ballona Wetlands ecosystem as local citizen groups challenge Playa Vista, the largest development in the United States. The Video Project (San Francisco)

Libby, Montana (2004) 124 minutes
Presents emotional coverage of the blue-collar working community of Libby during its mining heyday and the controversy over asbestos used in the Kootenai Valley. High Plains Films (Missoula, MT)

Logs, Lies, and Videotape (1996) 12 minutes
Looks at the impact of a logging measure passed by Congress that directs the Forest Service and Bureau

of Land Management to accelerate salvage logging. Green Fire Productions (Eugene, OR)

Monumental (2004) 74 minutes
Follows the growth of the Sierra Club and its leader, David Brower, including profiles of key controversies over dam-building projects in the West. Bullfrog Films (Oley, PA)

Motor (1999) 38 minutes
Shows how recreational use by off-highway vehicles, personal watercraft, and other motorized vehicles are affecting wilderness areas and the nation's lakes, deserts, and forests. High Plains Films (Missoula, MT)

Mulholland's Dream (1997) 85 minutes
Tells of William Mulholland's search for water for the people of Los Angeles and the building of the aqueduct 250 miles from the Owens Valley to southern California. Home Vision Cinema: Public Media Incorporated (Chicago)

The Naturalist (2001) 32 minutes
Profiles Kent Bonar, the "John Muir of the Ozarks," who lives without up-to-date amenities as a modern-day woodsman dedicated to preserving the world around him. High Plains Films (Missoula, MT)

Net Loss: The Storm Over Salmon Fishing (2003) 52 minutes
Assesses the risks and benefits of salmon farming through interviews with government and industry officials, native people, and scientists. Bullfrog Films (Oley, PA)

Oil on Ice (2004) 90 minutes
Investigates the possible environmental and cultural effects of proposed drilling in Alaska's Arctic National Wildlife Refuge. The film emphasizes the impact on the native Gwich'in people, caribou herds, and global climate. Sierra Club Productions (San Francisco)

Powder River Country (2005) 34 minutes
Shows the transformation of Wyoming's Bighorn Mountains area, which is a potential new source of natural gas during a time of energy debates. High Plains Films (Missoula, MT)

Radioactive America (2000) 29 minutes
Documents the issue of nuclear waste disposal in the United States, focusing on the Oak Ridge National Laboratory in Tennessee and the Hanford site in Washington State. Center for Defense Information (Washington, DC)

Razing Appalachia (2003) 54 minutes
Portrays the struggle of the people of Blair, West Virginia, against a mining company whose jobs in local coal mines are a major source of employment for the region. Bullfrog Films (Oley, PA)

Regopstaan's Dream (2000) 52 minutes
Last surviving South African Bushmen tell their stories about their fight to claim ancestral land in the Kalahari Gemsbok National Park. First Run/Icarus Films (Brooklyn, NY)

Restoring the Everglades (1998) 15 minutes
Reviews issues of wetland conservation, agricultural pollution, and efforts to restore the National Park. National Parks and Conservation Association (Washington, DC)

Save the Sungmi Mountain (2003) 36 minutes
Documents the efforts of the municipal government in Seoul, Korea, to build a reservoir on top of a mountain; examines the struggle between politicians and villagers who oppose the project. Diffusion Films (Korea)

Silent Sentinels (1999) 57 minutes
Examines the world's coral reefs and shows how damaging climatic conditions and pollution cause coral bleaching and loss of diversity. Bullfrog Films (Oley, PA)

Subdivide and Conquer (1999) 57 minutes
Looks at the issue of urban and suburban sprawl in the United States, exploring its effects on the sense of community and the environment. Bullfrog Films (Oley, PA)

Since the Company Came (2000) 52 minutes
Story of a remote village in the Solomon Islands that invites a Malaysian company to log the tribal land and then faces disputes over logging royalties, preservation of forests, and native traditions. First Run/Icarus Films (Brooklyn, NY)

Suzuki Speaks (2004) 45 minutes
Profiles environmentalist and scientist David Suzuki, giving his perspective on what it means to be a human in our interconnected universe. Avanti Pictures (Canada)

Tales of the San Joaquin (2004) 27 minutes
Explores this California river's history and the issues of water rights that developed after the building of the Friant Dam in the 1940s. Christopher Beaver Films (Sausalito, CA)

Tampering with Nature (2001) 43 minutes
Looks at the potential results of genetic engineering, pollution, food contamination, and human cloning; outlines the environmental policies being developed. ABC News (New York)

Thirst (2004) 62 minutes
Without narrative, shows how the debate over water rights between communities and corporations can serve as the catalyst for resistance to globalization. Bullfrog Films (Oley, PA)

Toxic Waters (2000) 58 minutes
Documents what happens when ordinary citizens in Delaware County, Pennsylvania, discover toxic waste in the neighborhood. Michael Thomas Productions (Montgomeryville, PA)

Trade Secrets (2001) 120 minutes
Looks at the 40-year history of the American chemical industry and the dissemination of information regarding potential threats to human health. Films for the Humanities and Sciences (Princeton, NJ)

Trinkets and Beads (1996) 53 minutes
Documents the lives of the Huaorani, a small tribe of Ecuadorian Indians, who after pressure from foreign oil companies agreed to allow oil drilling on their land. First Run/Icarus Films (Brooklyn, NY)

Troubled Waters: The Dilemmas of Dams (2003) 53 minutes
Using personal interviews and archival footage, looks at the controversies over dams from the perspectives of environmental, cultural, economic, and spiritual issues. The Video Project (San Francisco)

Up Close and Toxic (2003) 45 minutes
Reveals how indoor air pollution is more serious than ambient (outdoor) pollution, even though most people believe they are safer inside their homes. Bullfrog Films (Oley, PA)

The Urban Explosion (1999) 56 minutes
Explores four megacities (Mexico City, Istanbul, Shanghai, and New York) to investigate the challenge of sustaining the urban population without destroying the environment. Screenscope (Washington, DC)

Varmints (1998) 91 minutes
Discusses the ethics of hunting prairie dogs in the West and examines the conflicts that develop over wildlife management and endangered species. High Plains Films (Missoula, MT)

The Venus Project (2004) 52 minutes
Documents what might happen if a catastrophic climate change took place; considers the impact of the greenhouse effect on a global basis. The Video Project (San Francisco)

Voices from the Frontlines (1997) 38 minutes
Profiles the Los Angeles-based Labor/Community Strategy Center, a grassroots, nonprofit political organization involved in environmental issues. Cinema Guild (New York)

Water for the Fields (2003) 27 minutes
Explores the issue of agricultural irrigation throughout the world, showing innovative ideas and the destruction caused by deforestation. DW-TV (Germany)

Water, Land, People and Conflict (1998) 29 minutes
Argues that the idea of a healthy environment is just as vital to national security as military strength. Center for Defense Information (Washington, DC)

Water-Willies in the Global Village (2000) 30 minutes
Demonstrates the clashes of tradition, land-use disputes, and ecological crises that exist in Tejalpa, Mexico. Gringoyo Productions.

A Whale of a Tale (2004) 90 minutes
Views whales from various perspectives throughout history and explains humans' conflicted history with the mammal. National Film Board (Canada)

Whose Home on the Range? (1999) 55 minutes
Covers the opposition to federal land management policies in Catron County, New Mexico; examines conflicts among ranchers, loggers, environmental groups, and the U.S. Forest Service. Bullfrog Films (Oley, PA)

Wildland (2000) 35 minutes
Expresses the importance of retaining untouched wilderness; features the nation's most prominent natural spaces. High Plains Films (Missoula, MT)

Wildlife for Sale: Dead or Alive (1998) 47 minutes
Presents documentary coverage of the multi-billion-dollar market in wildlife worldwide, examining both the legal and illegal aspects of this trade. Bullfrog Films (Oley, PA)

Wind Over Water: The Debate Over Wind Power (2004) 32 minutes
Using Cape Cod, Massachusetts, as an example of the debate over wind power, examines the impact of the $5 billion industry in the United States. The Video Project (San Francisco)

Wind River (1999) 34 minutes
Describes how water rights are awarded to Wyoming farmers on a seniority basis, examining core community values and concerns over fairness. High Plains Films (Missoula, MT)

Wolf: An Ancient Spirit Returns (2004) 45 minutes
Identifies the issues surrounding the reintroduction of wolves to Yellowstone National Park and their role in the ecosystem. Bullfrog Films (Oley, PA)

Index